CONCISE SECOND EDITION

Worlds Together, Worlds Apart

Volume 2

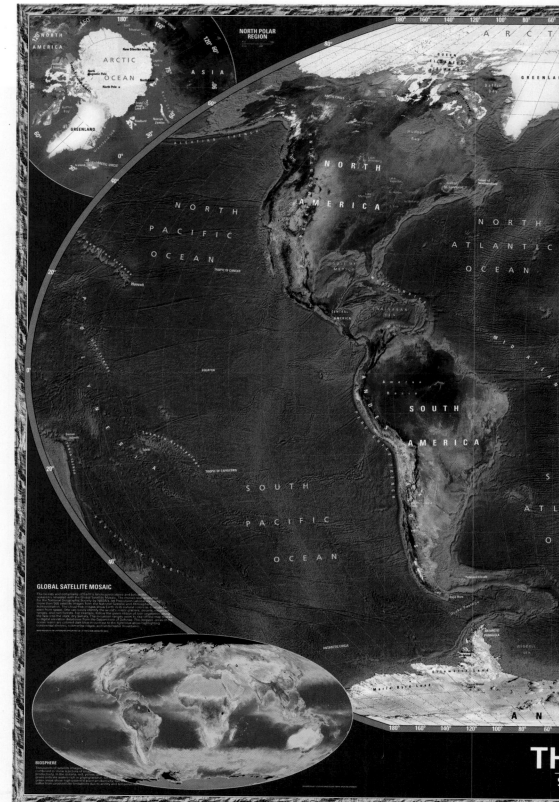

NORTH POLAR REGION

NORTH AMERICA

ARCTIC OCEAN

ASIA

GREENLAND

ARCTIC

GREENLAND

NORTH AMERICA

ALEUTIAN TRENCH

NORTH PACIFIC OCEAN

NORTH ATLANTIC OCEAN

Hawaii

TROPIC OF CANCER

GULF OF MEXICO

CENTRAL AMERICA

CARIBBEAN SEA

MID ATLANTIC

EQUATOR

Amazon Basin

SOUTH AMERICA

ANDES

Samoa Islands

Tonga

Tahiti

TROPIC OF CAPRICORN

SOUTH PACIFIC OCEAN

SOUTH ATLANTIC OCEAN

Falkland Islands

Cape Horn

Drake Passage

ANTARCTIC PENINSULA

WEDDELL SEA

ELLSWORTH LAND

Marie Byrd Land

ANTARCTICA

GLOBAL SATELLITE MOSAIC

The beauty and complexity of Earth's landscapes from above and the oceansbelow revealed with the Global Satellite Mosaic. The mosaic was produced for the National Geographic Society by NASA's Jet Propulsion Laboratory from more than 500 satellite images from the National Oceanic and Atmospheric Administration. The cloud-free images show Earth in its natural colors as it would be seen from space. One can easily identify the world's major glaciers, deserts, mountain ranges, and rain forests. For example, follow the green ribbon of lush vegetation from the Nile into the stark, dry Sahara. The mountain ranges seem to rise off the map thanks to digital elevation data from the Department of Defense. The deepest areas of the ocean realm are colored dark blue in contrast to the light blue areas highlighting continental shelves, submarine ridges, and underwater mountains.

BIOSPHERE

Thousands of satellite images of plant life both on land and in the ocean were combined to show a picture of productivity. In the oceans, red, yellow, and green indicate waters rich in phytoplankton. On land, green areas show high potential plant productivity; tan and yellow areas suffer from productivity limitations due to aridity and temperature.

TH

SOUTH POLAR REGION

ANTARCTICA

WEST ANTARCTICA

EAST ANTARCTICA

Weddell Sea

Queen Maud Land

Antarctic Peninsula

South Pole

Ross Ice Shelf

Ross Sea

Wilkes Land

South Magnetic Pole

NORTH PACIFIC OCEAN

ASIA

SIBERIA

EUROPE

Aral Sea

Black Sea

Plateau of Tibet

INDIA

ARABIAN SEA

BAY OF BENGAL

PHILIPPINE SEA

SOUTH CHINA SEA

MICRONESIA

INDONESIA

NEW GUINEA

AUSTRALIA

INDIAN OCEAN

MADAGASCAR

SOUTHWEST INDIAN RIDGE

SOUTHEAST INDIAN RIDGE

KERGUELEN PLATEAU

TROPIC OF CANCER

EQUATOR

TROPIC OF CAPRICORN

SOUTH PACIFIC OCEAN

New Caledonia

TASMAN SEA

NEW ZEALAND

North Island

South Island

THE NEED FOR SATELLITES

The Global Satellite Mosaic along with the biosphere image (lower left) and the temperature image (lower right) provides an integrated view of our world.

SCALE 1:38,681,000

ICA

SURFACE TEMPERATURE

Reddish colors vividly show average high temperatures on the two largest continents, Africa and Asia.

LD
P

CONCISE SECOND EDITION

Worlds Together, Worlds Apart

VOLUME 2
From 1000 CE to the Present

Elizabeth Pollard, Clifford Rosenberg, Robert Tignor

with Jeremy Adelman, Stephen Aron, Peter Brown,
Benjamin Elman, Stephen Kotkin, Xinru Liu, Suzanne Marchand,
Holly Pittman, Gyan Prakash, Brent Shaw, Michael Tsin

W. W. NORTON & COMPANY · NEW YORK · LONDON

To my parents, John and Catherine, who encouraged me to see the world; and to my husband Brad and children Amelia and Jake, with whom I now share that adventure. —EAP

To my students. —CR

W. W. Norton & Company has been independent since its founding in 1923, when William Warder Norton and Mary D. Herter Norton first published lectures delivered at the People's Institute, the adult education division of New York City's Cooper Union. The firm soon expanded its program beyond the Institute, publishing books by celebrated academics from America and abroad. By midcentury, the two major pillars of Norton's publishing program—trade books and college texts—were firmly established. In the 1950s, the Norton family transferred control of the company to its employees, and today—with a staff of four hundred and a comparable number of trade, college, and professional titles published each year—W. W. Norton & Company stands as the largest and oldest publishing house owned wholly by its employees.

Editor: Jon Durbin
Project Editor: Jennifer Barnhardt
Editorial Assistant: Lily Gellman
Managing Editor, College: Marian Johnson
Managing Editor, College Digital Media: Kim Yi
Production Manager: Ashley Horna
Media Editor: Carson Russell
Associate Media Editor: Sarah Rose Aquilina
Media Project Editor: Rachel Mayer
Media Editorial Assistant: Alexandra Malakhoff
Ebook Production: Michael Hicks
Marketing Manager, History: Sarah England Bartley
Design Director: Rubina Yeh
Designer: Lissi Sigillo
Director of College Permissions: Megan Schindel
Permissions Associate: Elizabeth Trammell
Photo Editor: Agnieszka Czapski
Composition: Cenveo Publishing Services
Illustrations: Mapping Specialists, Ltd.
Manufacturing: LSC Communications–Crawfordsville

Permission to use copyrighted material is included in the credits section of this book, which begins on page C-1.

The Library of Congress has cataloged the Full Edition as follows:

Names: Tignor, Robert L., author.
Title: Worlds together, worlds apart : a history of the world from the
    beginnings of humankind to the present / Robert Tignor ... [and eleven
    others].
Description: Fifth edition. | New York : W. W. Norton & Company, [2018] |
    Includes bibliographical references and index.
Identifiers: LCCN 2017032085 | ISBN 9780393624786 (hardcover)
Subjects: LCSH: World history—Textbooks. | World
    history—Examinations—Study guides. | Advanced placement programs
    (Education)—Examinations—Study guides.
Classification: LCC D21 .T53 2018 | DDC 909—dc23 LC record available at https://lccn.loc.gov/2017032085

ISBN this edition: 978-0-393-66846-9 (softcover)

W. W. Norton & Company, Inc., 500 Fifth Avenue, New York, N.Y. 10110

www.wwnorton.com
W. W. Norton & Company Ltd., 15 Carlisle Street, London W1D 3BS

1 2 3 4 5 6 7 8 9 0

BRIEF CONTENTS

CONTENTS

10

Becoming "The World,"

1000–1300 CE   443

11

Crisis and Recovery in Afro-Eurasia, 1300–1500   **497**

12

Contact, Commerce, and Colonization, 1450–1600   545

13

Worlds Entangled, 1600–1750   591

14

Cultures of Splendor and
Power, 1500–1780   645

15

Reordering the World, 1750–1850   693

16

Alternative Visions of the
Nineteenth Century   739

17

Nations and Empires, 1850–1914 — 787

18

An Unsettled World,
1890–1914   835

19

Of Masses and Visions of the Modern, 1910–1939   883

20

The Three-World Order, 1940–1975   933

21

CURRENT TRENDS IN WORLD HISTORY

GLOBAL THEMES AND SOURCES

MAPS

PREFACE

Worlds Together, Worlds Apart sets the standard for instructors who want to teach a globally integrated world history survey course. Building on the success of the First Concise Edition, co-authors Elizabeth Pollard (San Diego State University) and Clifford Rosenberg (City University of New York) and general editor Robert Tignor (Princeton University) have created this dynamic and highly accessible new Concise Second Edition of *Worlds Together, Worlds Apart*. A full third shorter than its parent text, written with clear, accessible prose and explanations, and with substantially more pedagogy support than any other text in the marketplace to guide students' reading and develop their historical thinking skills, the Concise Second Edition continues to offer a coherent, cutting-edge survey of the field built around world historical stories of significance. This concise, globally integrated, chronological approach not only makes it easy for students to see connections and comparisons across time and place, but also makes the teaching of the course more manageable for instructors compared with more civilizational and regional approaches. Some of the major stories dealt with in the chapters of the Concise Second Edition are the spread of humans across the planet, the first global agricultural revolution, the creation of empires, the building of the Silk Roads, the spread of the Black Death across Afro-Eurasia, the impact of New World silver on global trade, alternative ways of organizing societies during the rise of nineteenth-century capitalism, and the rise of the nation-state.

The New Concise Second Edition

In response to substantive feedback from highly experienced frontline world history instructors, the new Concise Second Edition has been streamlined and simplified. With its new handy compact format, engaging design, sharpened guided-reading pedagogy, and newly revamped end-of-chapter readings—each highlighting a target historical thinking skill—this edition improves accessibility while strengthening history skills development. Expanded coverage of environmental history, new online **History Skills Tutorials**, a new **Interactive Instructor's Guide**, and **InQuizitive**, Norton's award-winning adaptive learning tool, support a state-of-the-art learning experience.

HIGHLIGHTS of the Concise Second Edition

- **A more accessible global framework** No introductory text does a better job of helping students make comparisons and connections across time and place. Co-authors Beth Pollard and Cliff Rosenberg are experienced teachers who have successfully introduced students to world history in this global way. This edition is more accessible than ever with sharpened guided reading pedagogy and a heavily revised and simplified map program.
    - **Sharpened guided-reading pedagogy** in each chapter helps students make global connections and comparisons as they read:
        - A redesigned chapter-opening spread provides a conceptual road map for the presentation that follows. Revised **Chapter Outlines** and **Core Objectives** identify important global concepts and developments before students start reading. A **(NEW) Global Storylines** feature addresses major chapter themes region by region. And a **(NEW) Big Picture** feature poses a question that highlights the chapter's most important global core objective.
        - Throughout the chapter, **(NEW) Key Term marginal definitions** expand on boldfaced key terms in the text to make the narrative more accessible. And the renamed **Core Objective flags** reference the Core Objectives throughout the chapter so that students know when to focus in on the most relevant material.
        - End-of-chapter features include **Tracing the Global Storylines** summaries that remind students of the overarching global stories introduced at the start of each chapter and show their impact on each region, visual **Chronologies** that compare—region by region—the dates of key events covered in the chapter, and simplified **Thinking about Global Connections** questions.
- **A strengthened focus on global history skills with (NEW) primary sources** In the text and accompanying digital resources, a wealth of features engage students in making connections across time and space. These features promote analysis and interpretation of primary source documents, images, and maps, helping students develop the skills promoted by the American Historical Association, the College Board, and various state guidelines.
    - Chapter-ending **Global Themes and Sources** sections provide an in-text reader:
        - These sections, each containing a handful of primary source documents on a single topic, focus on one of the four major historical thinking skills promoted by the AHA and the College Board (context, causation, comparison, and continuity and change). They replace the shorter "Competing Perspectives" primary sources from the First Concise Edition.

- ◦ **(NEW)** pre-reading **Historical Thinking Skills Questions** guide students in the targeted critical thinking skill and in interpretation of the primary sources.
  - ◦ **(NEW)** headnotes specific to each source, as well as source-specific questions.
- • **Interpreting Visual Evidence** sections engage students in analyzing historical images.
- • Updated **Current Trends in World History** features highlight cutting-edge research that is relevant to global issues today.
- • A **redesigned visual program** facilitates visual analysis and interpretation while highlighting global comparisons and connections.
  - ◦ Enlarged **images** (roughly 10% **NEW** to the Concise Second Edition) are easier to analyze.
  - ◦ **A heavily revised and simplified map program**, including **(NEW) The Global View**, a two-page map spread that illustrates the overarching story featured in a chapter. Like all of the revised maps, these spreads focus on just one or two developments to simplify interpretation.
- • **(NEW) scholarship on environmental history** With an author team made up of experts on each global region, *Worlds Together, Worlds Apart* has always reflected exceptionally balanced scholarship. The Concise Second Edition offers new coverage of numerous topics, but it places special emphasis on one overarching issue that is of particular interest to students and instructors: the environment's role in world history.

Some examples in Volume One:
- ◦ **Chapter 1: (NEW)** material on climate change and hominid evolution, and a **(NEW)** section on the environmental impact of the agricultural revolution and herding.
- ◦ **Chapter 4: (NEW)** section on environmental crisis, economic decline, and migration, with a fascinating discussion on climate change in India and how it influenced the development of Vedic-Brahmanic culture and the rice economy.
- ◦ **Chapter 10: (NEW)** section on environmental challenges and fragmentation discusses the impact of severe climate conditions on eastern Mediterranean and Islamic lands between the eleventh and twelfth centuries, including the fragmentation of Islamic political institutions.

Some examples in Volume Two:
- ◦ **Chapter 13: (NEW)** section on global commerce and climate change that addresses mercantilism and chartered companies, and a fascinating **(NEW)** discussion on the Little Ice Age.
- ◦ **Chapter 14: (NEW)** section on formation of American identities that details the environmental impacts of scientific studies that promoted colonization and entrepreneurial activity in the Americas.

- Chapter 18: (NEW) section on protecting the environment discusses Teddy Roosevelt's promotion of conservation of nature, as well as parallel movements in Europe. (NEW) Current Trends in World History feature, Adapting to the Environment: Russian Peasants Take On the Steppe, reveals growing awareness of the need for sustainable agricultural methods.

- New support for teaching global history A team of highly experienced instructors, led by Lead Media Author Alan Karras (University of California, Berkeley), has developed accompanying resources that reflect and complement the Concise Second Edition's distinctive pedagogy while supporting nationally recognized outcomes for the World History survey. Engaging activities and questions move students beyond comprehension to analysis and concept application. These new resources also make it easier than ever for instructors to design and teach a course with a global framework.

  - (NEW) History Skills Tutorials combine author videos and interactive assessments in an innovative digital setting to teach students how to analyze the maps, images, and documents in the book and beyond. Instructors can assign these tutorials at the beginning of the semester to prepare students for primary source analysis assignments or incorporate them throughout the semester as a tool for reinforcing skills in working with written and visual sources as well as with maps.

  - InQuizitive, W. W. Norton's award-winning adaptive learning tool, features new coverage in every chapter to reflect the new concepts and sources introduced in the book.

  - (NEW) Interactive Instructor's Guide (IIG) supports the teaching of global history by providing a searchable, sortable online way to prepare for lectures. The IIG contains resources drawn from the revamped Instructor's Manual. For selected chapters, the authors have created new videos providing best practices for teaching the transregional and comparative connections in the book.

  - Primary Source Exercises introduce primary sources from outside the book that build on the key historical developments and global storylines in each chapter. A brief quiz including multiple-choice and short-response questions provides opportunities for assessment.

As you can see, we have worked hard to make the Concise Second Edition of *Worlds Together, Worlds Apart* a powerful learning and teaching tool for students and instructors who want to take a more global approach to world history.

Our Major Themes

The primary organizing framework of *Worlds Together, Worlds Apart*—one that runs through the chapters and connects the different parts of the book—is the theme of **interconnection and divergence**. While describing movements that facilitated global connectedness, this book also shows how different regions developed their own ways of incorporating or resisting connections and change.

Themes that stand out in *Worlds Together, Worlds Apart* highlight the importance of trade and cultural exchange through the recurring efforts of people **crossing borders—religious, political, and cultural—that brought the world together**. Merchants and educated men and women traded goods and ideas. Whole communities, in addition to select groups, moved to safer or more promising environments. This transregional exchange of ideas, goods, and peoples produced **transformations and conflicts**—a second important theme. The movements of ideas, peoples, products, and germs over long distances upset the balance of power across the world and within individual societies. Such movements changed the relationships of population groups with other peoples and areas of the world and led over time to dramatic shifts in the ascendancy of regions. **Changes in power arrangements** within and between regions explain which parts of the world and regional groups benefited from integration and which resisted it. Finally, we highlight **the important roles that gendered roles and identities as well as environmental forces play in shaping the evolution of societies**. These themes (trade and cultural exchange, transformation and conflict, alterations in the balance of power, gender, and the environment) are woven into every chapter of this work. While we highlight these major themes throughout, we tell the stories of the people caught in these currents of exchange, conflict, changing power relations, gendered expectations and environmental developments.

Overview of Volume One

Volume One of *Worlds Together, Worlds Apart* deals with the period from the beginnings of human history through the Mongol invasions of the thirteenth century and the spread of the Black Death across Afro-Eurasia. It is divided into eleven chapters, each of which marks a distinct historical period. Hence, each chapter has an overarching theme or small set of themes that holds otherwise highly diverse material together.

Chapter 1, "Becoming Human," presents cultural and biological perspectives on the way that early hominids became truly human. We believe that this chapter is important in establishing the global context of world history. We believe, too, that our chapter is unique in its focus on a range of creation narratives that explain how humans became humans. We discuss how early humans became bipedal and how they developed complex cognitive processes such as language and artistic abilities. Recent research indicates that *Homo sapiens* originated in Africa, as long as 300,000 years ago. These early men and women migrated out of the African landmass as early as 180,000 years ago, gradually populating all regions of the world. We note, as we update this chapter with some of the newest archaeological discoveries, that the narrative of human evolution and our spread across the planet is a rapidly changing story thanks to new hominid finds and new ways to analyze them. Also in this chapter, we describe the domestication of plants and animals and the founding of the first village settlements around the globe. With our strengthened coverage of environmental history, we include new material on the role of climate in human evolution and in the domestication of plants and animals and ultimately settled village life. Finally, we have updated the **Current Trends in World History** feature in this chapter to discuss "Big History" and how it has affected our thinking and research on the origins of the cosmos and early human development.

Chapter 2, "Rivers, Cities, and First States, 3500–2000 BCE," covers the period during which five of the world's great river basins experienced extraordinary breakthroughs in human activity. On the floodplains of the Tigris and Euphrates in Mesopotamia, the Nile in Egypt, the Indus in modern-day northern India and Pakistan, and the Yellow and Yangzi in China, men and women mastered the annual floods and became expert in seeding and cultivating foodstuffs. In these areas, populations became dense and the world's earliest cities formed. All of these river-basin cultures had much in common. They had highly developed hierarchical political, social, and cultural systems, priestly and bureaucratic classes, and organized religious and cultural systems. The development of these major complex societies is a turning point in world history, ushering in the beginnings of profound distinctions between urban and rural communities as well as between the wealthy and poor. New material in Chapter 2 includes discussions on the role of the Ghaggar-Hakra River in Harappan civilization, the amazing "oldest papyri ever" and the new insights they yielded into Egyptian pyramid construction, and added material on exciting finds at Dhaskalio (off the coast of Keros) in the Aegean Sea.

Extensive climate and technological changes serve as major turning points for **Chapter 3, "Nomads, Territorial States, and Microsocieties, 2000–1200 BCE."** Drought, environmental degradation, and political instability brought the first river-basin societies to an abrupt end around 2000 BCE. When aridity forced tribal and nomadic peoples living on the fringes of the settled populations to move closer to settled areas, they brought with them an insurmountable military advantage. They had become adept at yoking horses to war chariots, and hence they were in a position to subjugate or intermarry with the peoples in the settled societies in the river basins. Around 2000 BCE, these peoples established new territorial kingdoms in Mesopotamia, Egypt, the Indus Valley, and China, which gave way a millennium later (1000 BCE) to even larger, militarily and politically more powerful states. In the Americas, the Mediterranean, sub-Saharan Africa, and the Pacific, microsocieties arose as an alternative form of political organization in which peoples lived in much smaller-scale societies that showcased their own unique and compelling features. New material includes a revised and updated **Current Trends in World History** feature, "Climate Change and the Collapse of River-Basin Societies," updated treatment of Hatshepsut and

Thutmosis III, the Hittites, Lady Fu Hao, and a new discussion on the *Ashva-medha* to give more texture to the Vedic treatment.

Chapter 4, "First Empires and Common Cultures in Afro-Eurasia, 1250–325 BCE," describes the different ways in which larger-scale societies grew and became unified. In the case of the world's first empires, the Neo-Assyrian and Persian, political power was the main unifying element. These two states established different models that future empires would emulate. The Neo-Assyrians used brutal force to intimidate and subjugate different groups within their societies and in neighboring states. The Persians followed a pattern that relied less on coercion and more on tributary relationships while permitting cultural diversity. The Zhou state in China offered a third way of maintaining political unity, basing its rule on the doctrine of the mandate of heaven, which legitimated its rulers' succession as long as they were able to maintain stability and order. Vedic society in South Asia offered a dramatically different model, in which religion and culture were the main unifying forces. Religion moves to the forefront of the narrative in other ways in this chapter. The birth of monotheism occurred in the Zoroastrian and Hebrew faiths. Both religions endure today. A major overhaul of the **Global Themes and Sources** section facilitates a comparison of imperial control in the four major regions, from harshest to least central, making use of two new sources: Sargon II's Lamassu inscription at Dur-Sharrukin, and a text on karma and reincarnation from *The Upanishads*.

The last millennium before the Common Era witnessed some of the most monumental developments in human history. In the six and a half centuries discussed in **Chapter 5, "Worlds Turned Inside Out, 1000–350 BCE,"** teachers and thinkers came to the fore. Confucius, the Buddha, Plato, and Aristotle, to name only the best known of this brilliant group, offered new insights into the natural world and provided new guidelines for governing justly and living ethically. In this era, small-scale societies, benefiting from more intimate relationships, took the place of the first great empires, now in decline. These highly individualistic cultures developed new strategies for political organization, even experimenting with a democratic polity. In Africa, the Bantu peoples spread across sub-Saharan Africa, and the Sudanic peoples of Meroe created a society that blended Egyptian and sub-Saharan influences. These were all dynamic hybrid societies building on existing knowledge. Equally dramatic transformations occurred in the Americas, where the Olmec and Chavín peoples were creating hierarchical societies of a type never before seen in their part of the world. New material includes a substantially revised and updated **Current Trends in World History** feature on Axial Age thinkers and their ideas.

Chapter 6, "Shrinking the Afro-Eurasian World, 350–100 BCE," describes two major forces that simultaneously integrated large segments of the Afro-Eurasian landmass culturally and economically. The first was Hellenism, whose leading figure, Alexander the Great, paved the way in North Africa, Southwest Asia, and central Asia for the first transregional cultural system in world history. Second, a trading network known as the Silk Roads, stretching from Palmyra in the west to central Asia in the east, came into being. Buddhism was the first religion to seize on the Silk Roads' more formal existence as its followers moved quickly, with the support of the Mauryan Empire, to spread their ideas into central Asia. New material includes a substantially revised **Global Themes and Sources** section on the causes and effects of the spread of Hellenism and Buddhism, and new discussions on the Magadha Empire to better lay the groundwork for the Mauryan Empire.

Chapter 7, "Han Dynasty China and Imperial Rome, 300 BCE–300 CE," compares Han China and the Roman Empire, the two political, economic, and cultural systems that dominated much of the Afro-Eurasian landmass from 200 BCE to 200 CE. Both the Han Dynasty and the Roman Empire ruled effectively in their own ways, providing an instructive comparative case study. Both left their imprint on Afro-Eurasia, and rulers for centuries afterward tried to revive these glorious empires and use them as models of greatness. This chapter also discusses the effect of state sponsorship on religion as Christianity came into existence in the context of the late Roman Empire and Buddhism was introduced to China during the decline of the Han. New material has been added on the nature of the connection between the Han Dynasty and the Roman Empire in the **Current Trends in World History** feature.

New political systems and the newly spreading religions that emerged in the aftermath of a crumbling Roman Empire and post-Han Dynasty are the primary emphases of **Chapter 8, "The Rise of Universalizing Religions, 300–600 CE."** In the west, the Byzantine Empire, claiming to be the successor state to the Roman Empire, embraced Christianity as its state religion. In the east, Tang rulers patronized Buddhism to such a degree that Confucian statesmen feared it had become the state religion. Both Buddhism and Christianity enjoyed spectacular success in the politically fragmented post-Han era in China and in the feudal world of western Europe. These dynamic religions represent a decisive transformation in world history. Christianity enjoyed its eventual successes through state sponsorship via the Roman and Byzantine empires and by providing spiritual comfort and hope during the chaotic years of Rome's decline. Buddhism grew through imperial sponsorship and through significant changes to its fundamental beliefs when adherents to the faith deified the Buddha and created notions of an afterlife. In Africa, a wide range of significant developments occurred, and a myriad of cultural practices existed; yet large common cultures also arose. The Bantu peoples that spread throughout the southern half of the landmass spoke closely related languages and developed similar political institutions based on the prestige of individuals of high achievement. In the Americas, the Olmecs established their own form of the city-state, while the Maya owed their success to a decentralized common culture built around a strong religious belief system and a series of spiritual centers. New material comparing the "fall" of the Roman empire and the Han dynasty has been added to the **Current Trends in World History** feature. The Maya coverage has been updated to account for the new LIDAR imaging that challenges the traditional narrative, and the **Global Themes and Sources** section on pilgrimages has been expanded with longer excerpts and new travelers with a focus on continuity and change over time.

In a relatively remote corner of the Arabian Peninsula, another world religion, Islam, exploded with world-changing consequences, as **Chapter 9, "New Empires and Common Cultures, 600–1000 CE,"** describes. The rise of Islam provides a contrast to the ways in which other universalizing religions and political empires interacted. Islam and its empire arose in a fashion quite different from Christianity and the Roman Empire. Christianity took over an already existing empire—the Roman—after suffering persecution at its hands for several centuries. In contrast, Islam created an empire almost at the moment of its emergence. By the time the Abbasid Empire came into being in the middle of the eighth century, Islamic armies, political leaders, and clerics exercised power over much of the Afro-Eurasian landmass, from southern Spain across North Africa all the way to central Asia. The Tang Empire in China, however, served as a counterweight to Islam's power, both politically and intellectually. Confucianism enjoyed a spectacular recovery in this period. With the support of the Tang rulers, Confucianism slowed the spread of Buddhism and further reinforced China's development along different, more secular pathways. Japan and Korea enter our narrative of world history at this time, as tributary states to Tang China and as hybrid cultures that mixed Chinese customs and practices with their own. The Christian world split in this period between western Roman Catholicism and eastern Greek Orthodoxy. Both branches of Christianity played a role in unifying societies, especially in western Europe, which lacked strong political rule. New material includes expanded in-text coverage of the "Green Revolutions" in Islam and Tang China, an updated **Current Trends in World History** feature with the latest research on the origins of Islam, and a completely revised and expanded **Global Themes and Sources** exploration of women and empire.

In the three centuries from 1000 to 1300 CE (**Chapter 10, "Becoming 'The World,' 1000–1300 CE"**), Afro-Eurasia experienced an unprecedented rise in prosperity and population that spread into West Africa and eastern Africa. Just as important, the world in this period divided into regional zones that are recognizable today. At the same time, trade grew rapidly. A view of the major trading cities of this time demonstrates how commerce transformed cultures. Sub-Saharan Africa also underwent intense regional integration via the spread of the Mande-speaking peoples and the Mali Empire. The Americas witnessed their first empire in the form of the Chimú Empire in the Andes. This chapter ends with the Mongol conquests of the twelfth and thirteenth centuries, which brought massive destruction but also significant connectedness to Afro-Eurasia. The Mongol Empire, once in place, promoted long-distance commerce, scholarly exchange, and travel on an unprecedented scale. The Mongol story, highlighted in the new **Current Trends in World History** feature on "A Most Unusual Nomad State," underscores the important role that nomads played throughout the history of the early world. The **Global Themes and Sources** feature picks up on the theme of travelers from Chapter 8 and includes new and expanded sources for analyzing the continuities and changes over time in "world" travel.

The Black Death brought Afro-Eurasia's prosperity and population growth to a catastrophic end, as discussed in **Chapter 11, "Crisis and Recovery in Afro-Eurasia, 1300–1500."** The bubonic plague wiped out as much as two-thirds of the population in many of the densely settled locations of Afro-Eurasia, whose societies had already been brought to their knees by the Mongols' depredations. The destruction and dying of the fourteenth century saw traditional institutions give way and forced peoples to rebuild their cultures. The political systems that came into being at this time and the intense religious experimentation that took place effected a sharp break with the past. In the face of one of humanity's grimmest periods, peoples and societies demonstrated tremendous resilience as they looked for new ways to rebuild their communities, some turning inward and others seeking inspiration, conquests, and riches elsewhere. New material recasts the Renaissance, offers sources for comparing different communities' understandings of the causes and effects of the Black Death, and a new **Current Trends in World History** feature considers Ming fashion. Volume One concludes on the eve of the "Columbian Exchange," the moment when "old" worlds discovered "new" ones and a vast series of global interconnections and divergences commenced

Please note that the primary source readings (Global Themes and Sources) have been heavily revised throughout Volume One—with selections both expanded from the first edition and entirely new selections—to address the four major historical thinking skills as described by the AHA and the College Board. Critical thinking about what sources can reveal of their historical context is emphasized in each chapter.

Overview of Volume Two

The organizational structure for Volume Two reaffirms the authors' commitment to write a decentered, global history of the world. Christopher Columbus is not the starting point, as he is in so many modern world histories. Rather, we begin in the eleventh and twelfth centuries with two major developments in world history: the Mongol conquests and the Black Death. **Chapter 10, "Becoming 'The World,' 1000–1300 CE,"** describes an unprecedented rise in prosperity and population that Afro-Eurasia experienced, which spread into West Africa and eastern Africa. Just as important, the world in this period divided into regional zones that are recognizable today. At the same time, trade grew rapidly. A view of the major trading cities of this time demonstrates how commerce transformed cultures. Sub-Saharan Africa also underwent intense regional integration via the spread of the Mande-speaking peoples and the Mali Empire. The Americas witnessed their first empire in the form of the Chimú Empire in the Andes. This chapter ends with the Mongol conquests of the twelfth and thirteenth centuries, which brought massive destruction but also significant connectedness to Afro-Eurasia. The Mongol Empire, once in place, promoted long-distance commerce, scholarly exchange, and travel on an unprecedented scale. The Mongol story, highlighted in the new **Current Trends in World History** feature on "A Most Unusual Nomad State," underscores the important role that nomads played throughout the history of the early world. The **Global Themes and Sources** feature picks up on the theme of travelers from Chapter 8 and includes new and expanded sources for analyzing the continuities and changes over time in "world" travel.

The Black Death brought Afro-Eurasia's prosperity and population growth to a catastrophic end, as discussed in **Chapter 11, "Crisis and Recovery in Afro-Eurasia, 1300–1500."** The bubonic plague wiped out as much as two-thirds of the population in many of the densely settled locations of Afro-Eurasia, whose societies had already been brought to their knees by the Mongols' depredations. The destruction and dying of the fourteenth century saw traditional institutions give way and forced peoples to rebuild their cultures. The political systems that came into being at this time and the intense religious experimentation that took place effected a sharp break with the past. In the face of one of humanity's grimmest periods, peoples and societies demonstrated tremendous resilience as they looked for new ways to rebuild their communities, some turning inward and others seeking inspiration, conquests, and riches elsewhere. New material recasts the Renaissance, offers sources for comparing different communities' understandings of the causes and effects of the Black Death, and a new **Current Trends in World History** feature considers Ming fashion.

Chapter 12, "Contact, Commerce, and Colonization, 1450–1600," examines commerce and exploration after the collapse of the Mongol Empire. Disease and increasing trade linkages were vital factors. New material includes expanded coverage of the Ottoman Empire—in particular, its centrality to networks of trade and exploration. The chapter provides more specifics about the major sultans; the importance of the conquest of Syria and Egypt (1516–1517), and the resistance of Mamluk rulers; the Ottoman admiral and cartographer Piri Reis and his masterwork *The Book of the Sea*; the Ottomans' earliest military failures against the Safavid Empire; the trade routes that made Ottoman expansion possible and Ottoman expansion's interconnectedness with European expansion overseas; and the multiethnic legacy of centuries of Ottoman rule.

Europeans sailed across the Atlantic Ocean to find a more direct, less encumbered route to Asia and came upon lands, peoples, and products that they had not expected. One item, however, that they had sought in every part of the world, and that they found in abundance in the Americas, was precious metal. **Chapter 13, "Worlds Entangled, 1600–1750,"** discusses how New World silver from Mexico and Peru became the major currency of global commerce, facilitating the long-distance trading networks that had been revived after the Black Death. The effect of New World silver on the world economy was so great that it, even more than the Iberian explorations of the New World, brought the hemispheres together and transformed the terms on which peoples around the world interacted with one another. Sugar also linked the economies and polities of western Europe, Africa, and the Americas and was a powerful force in a triangular trade centered on the Atlantic Ocean. This trade involved the shipment of vast numbers of African captives to the Americas, where they toiled as slaves on sugar, tobacco, cotton, and rice plantations. New material includes new content on leading Ottoman intellectual Mustafa Ali and his magnum opus *The Essence of History* (1591); on the Little Ice Age (the sharp drop in global temperature from 1620 to 1680) and its contribution to a wave of political upheaval across Afro-Eurasia; on the impact of the Thirty Years' War; on the contribution of imported New World silver to the destabilization of the economy; on the Celali Revolt; and on the rising Manchu population's breach of China's Great Wall.

Chapter 14, "Cultures of Splendor and Power, 1500–1780," investigates the Ottoman scientists, Safavid and Mughal artists, and Chinese literati, as well as European thinkers, whose notable achievements were rooted in their own cultures but tempered by awareness of the intellectual activities of others. This chapter looks closely at the creation of culture as a historical process and describes how the massive increase in wealth during this period, growing out of global trade, led to one of the great periods of cultural flourishing in world history. Around 1800, transformations reverberated outward from the Atlantic world and altered economic and political relationships in the rest of the world. New content explores the religion, politics, and consequences of the Enlightenment, including, in particular, a new **Global Themes and Sources** section on commerce, civilization, and the Enlightenment.

Chapter 15, "Reordering the World, 1750–1850," discusses political revolutions in the Americas and Europe, focusing on new ideas about trade and labor. It contends that a powerful rhetoric of freedom and universal rights underlay the beginning of a "great divide" between peoples of European descent and others. The forces of laissez-faire capitalism, industrialization, the nation-state, and republicanism emanating from the Atlantic world not only attracted diverse groups around the world, but also threatened groups that put forth alternative visions. New ideas of freedom, as manifested in trading relations, labor, and political activities, clashed with older notions of inherited rights and statuses and further challenged the way men and women had lived in earlier times. These political, intellectual, and economic reorderings changed the way people around the world saw themselves and thus represent something quite novel in world history.

These new ways of envisioning the world did not go unchallenged, as **Chapter 16, "Alternative Visions of the Nineteenth Century,"** makes clear. Intense resistance to evolving modernity reflected the diversity of peoples around the world and their hopes for the future. Wahhabism in Islam, the "big men" of

Africa, Indian resistance in the United States and Mexico, socialism and communism in Europe, the Taiping Rebellion in China, and the Indian Mutiny in South Asia catapulted to historical prominence prophets and leaders whose visions often drew on earlier traditions and led these individuals to resist rapid change. New material includes a dramatically expanded and refocused **Global Themes and Sources** section on alternatives to nineteenth-century capitalism.

Chapter 17, "Nations and Empires, 1850–1914," deals with the political, economic, military, and ideological power that thrust Europe and North America to the fore of global events and led to an era of nationalism and modern imperialism, new forces in world history. Yet this period of seeming European supremacy was to prove short-lived. New content focuses on the Irish potato famine and its impact, Britain's imperial regime in India and the Caribbean and its application in Africa, and a new **Global Themes and Sources** section on the scramble for empire.

As **Chapter 18, "An Unsettled World, 1890–1914,"** demonstrates, even before World War I shattered Europe's moral certitude, many groups, both at home (feminists, Marxists, and unfulfilled nationalists) and abroad (anticolonial nationalists), had raised a chorus of complaints about European and North American dominance. Like Chapter 14, this chapter looks at the processes by which specific cultural movements arose and how they reflected the concerns of individual societies. Yet here, too, syncretic movements emerged in many cultures that reflected the sway of global imperialism, which by then had become a dominant force. New content includes a new **Current Trends in World History** feature, "Adapting to the Environment: Russian Peasants Take On the Steppe," and a new focus on the 1902 passage of the U.S. National Reclamation Act.

Chapter 19, "Of Masses and Visions of the Modern, 1910–1939," briefly covers World War I, then discusses how, from the end of that war until World War II, different visions of being modern competed around the world. The development of modernism and its effects on multiple cultures is the theme that integrates the diverse developments discussed in this chapter. In the decades between the world wars, proponents of liberal democracy struggled to defend their views and often to impose their will on authoritarian rulers and anticolonial nationalists. New content includes material on the impact of World War I in East Africa; Britain's affiliation with Russia and France in the Triple Entente in 1907; conflict in the Balkans and the chain reaction set off by the assassination of Austrian Archduke Franz-Ferdinand; a new focus on British and French conscription of their colonial subjects; the Ottoman alliance with the Central Powers; hastily drawn postwar borders in the Middle East and their later consequences in the twenty-first century; and an (all-new) **Global Themes and Sources** section, "Comparing and Contextualizing Totalitarianism."

Chapter 20, "The Three-World Order, 1940–1975," presents the effects of World War II as new adversaries arose after the war. A three-world order came into being—the First World, led by the United States and extolling capitalism, the nation-state, and democratic government; the Second World, led by the Soviet Union and favoring authoritarian polities and economies; and the Third World, made up of former colonies seeking an independent status and alternative routes to modernity for themselves in world affairs. The rise of this three-world order, which dominated the second half of the twentieth century, constitutes another major theme of world history. New content includes a revised **Global Themes and Sources** section on independence and nation building.

Chapter 21, "Globalization, 1970–2000," which begins with the end of the Cold War, shows that the modern world, while clearly more unified than before, still had profound cultural differences and political divisions. At the beginning of the twenty-first century, capital, commodities, peoples, and ideas moved rapidly over long distances. But cultural tensions and political impasses continued to exist. The rise of this form of globalism represented a vital new element as humankind headed into a new century and millennium. New content includes a revised **Global Themes and Sources** section with new primary sources on the power of grassroots democracy.

The **Epilogue, 2001–The Present,** tracks developments since the turn of the millennium. These last few years have brought profound changes to the world order, yet we hope that readers of *Worlds Together, Worlds Apart* will see more clearly how this most recent history is, in fact, entwined with the trends of much longer duration that are the chief focus of this book. New material includes a discussion of populist election victories; two new **Current Trends in World History** features, "Global Capitalism and the Great Contraction of 2008" and "Has *Homo sapiens* Entered a New Epoch—the Anthropocene?"; coverage of devastating hurricanes; new coverage of Donald Trump's election as U.S. president in 2016 as well as his policies, particularly regarding the U.S.-Mexico border, and his nativist attacks on immigrants and refugees; new content on ISIS and Syria; the U.S. summit with North Korea; and the U.S. withdrawal from the Joint Comprehensive Plan of Action (Iranian nuclear deal).

Please note that the primary source readings (Global Themes and Sources) have been heavily revised throughout Volume Two—with selections both expanded from the first edition and entirely new selections—to address the four major historical thinking skills as described by the AHA and the College Board. Critical thinking about what sources can reveal of their historical context is emphasized in each chapter.

Media Ancillaries

Lead media author Alan Karras (University of California, Berkeley) helped gather a team of innovative world history instructors, including Shane Carter, Sharon Cohen, Ryba Epstein, Derek O'Leary, Andrew Hardy, and others. Together, this team has ensured that the Concise Second Edition of *Worlds Together, Worlds Apart* is supported by an array of digital media with tools faculty need to meet course goals—in the classroom and online—and activities that will help students to develop core skills in reading comprehension, writing, and analysis and to better understand the geography and contexts in world history survey courses.

For Students

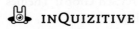 **INQUIZITIVE**

Quizzing to Learn (Shane Carter, Alan Karras)

InQuizitive, Norton's groundbreaking formative, adaptive quizzing platform, uses interactive questions and guided feedback to motivate students to read and understand the text. Varied question types—featuring images, maps, and primary sources—prompt critical and analytical thinking about each of the chapter's Core Objectives. Robust grading functionality helps instructors track their students' progress on learning outcomes.

(NEW) History Skills Tutorials

Accessible through the digital landing page with the code that is included in each new copy of the book, the History Skills Tutorials featuring author Elizabeth Pollard consist of three online modules that provide a framework for analyzing primary source documents, images, and maps. Each tutorial opens with author videos modeling the analysis process. Subsequent interactive activities challenge students to apply what they have learned.

Student Site

This free site offers students access to additional primary source documents and images, an expansive collection of author videos, and iMaps. It is ideal for instructors interested in granting students access to additional material without creating or administering online assignments.

Norton Ebooks

Norton Ebooks give students and instructors an enhanced reading experience at a fraction of the cost of a printed textbook. Students are able to have an active reading experience and can take notes, bookmark, search, highlight, and even read offline. As an instructor, you can add your own notes for students to see as they read the text. Norton ebooks can be viewed on—and synced between—all computers and mobile devices. The ebook for the Concise Second Edition includes embedded author videos, pop-up key term definitions, and enlargeable images and maps.

For Instructors

Resources for instructors are available at wwnorton.com/instructors.

Norton LMS Resources (Jacob Pomerantz, Alan Karras)

Free Norton Coursepacks (downloadable in learning management systems such as Blackboard, WebCT, D2L, and Moodle; additional formats can be provided upon request) include:

- **Primary Source Exercises:** One exercise per chapter provides 3–5 multiple-choice questions and two short-response questions (with sample answers). Each exercise contains 1–2 primary sources.
- **Online Reader:** Approximately 100 additional primary source documents and images that supplement the ones in the text. Also available grouped as Research Topics.
- **iMaps:** Interactive versions of each map from the text are provided on the Student Site and in the Coursepack, enabling students to explore different layers of information. Each iMap is supported by a Map Worksheet.
- **Chapter Quizzes:** These quizzes include answer references to each chapter's Core Objectives.
- **Office Hours Videos:** Authors Beth Pollard and Cliff Rosenberg as well as media author Alan Karras explain difficult concepts.
- **Flashcards:** Online cards for each chapter align key terms and events with brief descriptions and definitions. The cards can be "flipped," printed, or downloaded.
- **Chapter Outlines**
- **Chronologies**
- **Forum Prompts:** Discussion questions that can be used in face-to-face or online discussion boards to engage students in active discussions about the major themes and concepts in each chapter.
- **Questions from the Text:** The questions from Core Objectives, Global Storylines, Global Themes and Sources, and Thinking about Global Connections from the text are available for online assignments and grading.
- **Analyzing Global Developments:** Previously included in the text of the Concise First Edition, these features have been updated and transferred to the Coursepack for use as assigned activities.
- **StoryMaps:** Available in the Coursepack in PDF format for reference.
- **AHA Student Learning Outcomes:** The student learning outcomes based on the AHA's "Benchmarks for Professional Development" now include suggestions for using *Worlds Together, Worlds Apart,* Second Concise Edition to help students achieve these learning outcomes.

(NEW) Interactive Instructor's Guide (Sharon Cohen, Alan Karras)

The new IIG supports the teaching of global history by providing a searchable, sortable online way to prepare for lectures. For selected chapters, the authors have created videos providing best practices for teaching the transregional connections in the book as well as **NEW** suggested image and syllabus activities.

Classroom Presentation Tools (Derek O'Leary, Andrew Hardy, Alan Karras)

- **Lecture PowerPoints and Art PowerPoints** feature photographs and maps from the book, retouched for in-class presentation.
- *StoryMaps* break complex maps into a sequence of five annotated screens that focus on the story behind the geography. The ten StoryMaps include such topics as The Silk Roads, The Spread of the Black Death, and Population Growth and the Economy.

Instructor's Manual (Sharon Cohen, Alan Karras)

The Instructor's Manual for the Concise Second Edition of *Worlds Together, Worlds Apart* has everything instructors need to prepare lectures and classroom activities, including lecture outlines, lecture ideas, and suggested classroom activities. Our Popular Fallacy section provides an exercise that helps to dispel common misconceptions students may have about each chapter. The revamped Instructor's Manual features two **NEW** sections, one on the teaching of the primary sources in each chapter, and one on effectively incorporating all of Norton's media resources into a syllabus.

Test Bank (Ryba Epstein, Derek O'Leary, Alan Karras)

The Test Bank features more than 1,050 questions—including multiple-choice, true/false, matching, and essay questions—each aligned to a Global Storyline and Core Objective from the book. Classified according to level of difficulty and Bloom's Taxonomy (remembering, understanding, applying, analyzing, evaluating, and creating), they provide multiple avenues for comprehension and skill assessment. The Test Bank features 25% **NEW** questions. These questions are also available in ExamView Test Generator, where you can more easily create tests and manage test question selection.

Acknowledgments

The quality and range of reviews of this project were truly exceptional. The final version of the manuscript was greatly influenced by the thoughts and ideas of numerous instructors.

First Concise Edition Reviewers

Andreas Agocs, University of the Pacific
Anthony Barbieri-Low, University of California, Santa Barbara
Brett Berliner, Morgan State University

Carolyn Noelle Biltoft, Georgia State University
Gayle Brunelle, California State University, Fullerton
Grace Chee, West Los Angeles College
Stephen Colston, San Diego State University
Paula Devos, San Diego State University
Alan Karras, University of California, Berkeley
Elaine MacKinnon, University of West Georgia
Harold Marcuse, University of California, Santa Barbara
Eva Moe, Modesto Junior College
Alice Pate, Kennesaw State University
Chandrika Paul, Shippensburg University
Jared Poley, Georgia State University
Dana Rabin, University of Illinois
Masako Racel, Kennesaw State University
Charles Reed, Elizabeth City State University
Alice Roberti, Santa Rosa Junior College
Steven Rowe, Chicago State University
Lynn Sargeant, California State University, Fullerton
Robert Saunders, Farmingdale State College
Sharlene Sayegh-Canada, California State University, Long Beach
Jeffrey Shumway, Brigham Young University
Greg Smay, University of California, Berkeley
Lisa Tran, California State University, Fullerton
Michael Vann, California State University, Sacramento
Theodore Weeks, Southern Illinois University
Krzysztof Ziarek, University at Buffalo

Concise Second Edition Reviewers

Christian Davis, James Madison University
Robert Dietle, Western Kentucky University
Holly Hulburt, Southern Illinois University
Senya Lubisich, Citrus College
Anthony Makowski, Delaware County Community College
Anthonette McDaniel, Pellissippi State Community College
Charles Reed, Elizabeth City State University
Jason Sharples, Florida Atlantic University
Kristin Stapleton, University at Buffalo
Pamela Stewart, Arizona State University

For the Concise Second Edition, we have some familiar and new friends at
W. W. Norton to thank. Chief among them is Jon Durbin, who once again played
a major role in bringing this edition to publication. Sarah England Bartley has
put together a creative marketing plan for the book. Lissi Sigillo is responsible

for the book's beautiful and effective new design. Lily Gellman has been invaluable with her work on manuscript preparation. Carson Russell, Laura Wilk, Sarah Rose Aquilina, and Alexandra Malakhoff have done a masterful job of strengthening the media support materials to meet the ever more complex classroom and assessment needs of instructors. Agnieszka Czapski and Donna Ranieri have done a great job researching and securing the permissions for the new photos. Mapping Specialists have done a beautiful job transforming and revitalizing the map program. Emily Pace and Leah Gregory have done fantastic work hunting down hard-to-find copies of sources. Jennifer Barnhardt, our project editor, and Ashley Horna, our production manager, have accomplished a genuinely herculean task in getting the book published on time with a very tight schedule, and we are particularly thankful to them. Jennifer Greenstein and Norma Sims Roche each did an assiduous job with the copyediting, turning the chapters around quickly to meet our schedule. A special shout-out goes to Debra Morton-Hoyt and her team of cover designers. *Worlds Together, Worlds Apart* has always had incredibly creative and distinctive covers, and the Concise Second Edition covers are even more eye-catching and memorable than those of the first edition. We also want to thank the authors of the full edition for their participation in this Concise Second Edition while allowing the new authors considerable leeway to have their own input. Bravo!

ABOUT THE AUTHORS

Elizabeth Pollard (*Ph.D. University of Pennsylvania*) is associate professor of history at San Diego State University. Her research investigates women accused of witchcraft in the Roman world and explores the exchange of goods and ideas between the Mediterranean and the Indian Ocean in the early centuries of the Common Era. Her pedagogical interests include Digital Humanities approaches to Roman history and witchcraft studies as well as the impact of global perspectives on teaching, learning, and writing about the ancient Mediterranean.

Clifford Rosenberg (*Ph.D. Princeton University*) is associate professor of European history at City College and the Graduate Center, CUNY. He specializes in the history of modern France and its empire and is the author of *Policing Paris: The Origins of Modern Immigration Control between the Wars*. He is working now on a book about the spread of tuberculosis between France and Algeria since the mid-nineteenth century.

Robert Tignor (*Ph.D. Yale University*) is professor emeritus and the Rosengarten Professor of Modern and Contemporary History at Princeton University and the three-time chair of the history department. With Gyan Prakash, he introduced Princeton's first course in world history thirty years ago. Professor Tignor has taught graduate and undergraduate courses in African history and world history and has written extensively on the history of twentieth-century Egypt, Nigeria, and Kenya. Besides his many research trips to Africa, Professor Tignor has taught at the University of Ibadan in Nigeria and the University of Nairobi in Kenya.

Alan Karras (*Ph.D. University of Pennsylvania*) is the associate director of International & Area Studies at the University of California, Berkeley, and has previously served as chair of the College Board's test development committee for world history and as co-chair of the College Board's commission on AP history course revisions. The author and editor of several books, he has written about the eighteenth-century Atlantic world and, more broadly, global interactions that focus on illicit activities like smuggling and corruption. An advocate of linking the past to the present, he is now working on a history of corruption in empires, focusing on the East India Company.

Jeremy Adelman (*D.Phil. Oxford University*) has lived and worked in seven countries and on four continents. A graduate of the University of Toronto, he earned a master's degree in economic history at the London School of Economics (1985) and a doctorate in modern history at Oxford University (1989). He is the author or editor of ten books, including *Sovereignty and Revolution in the Iberian Atlantic* (2006) and *Worldly Philosopher: The Odyssey of Albert O. Hirschman* (2013), a chronicle of one of the twentieth century's most original thinkers. He has been awarded fellowships by the British Council, the Social Science and Humanities Research Council of Canada, the Guggenheim Memorial Foundation, and the American Council of Learned Societies (the Frederick Burkhardt Fellowship). He is currently the Henry Charles Lea Professor of History and the director of the Global History Lab at Princeton University. His next book is called *Earth Hunger: Markets, Resources, and the Need for Strangers*.

Stephen Aron (*Ph.D. University of California, Berkeley*) is professor of history at the University of California, Los Angeles, and executive director of the Institute for the Study of the American West, Autry National Center. A specialist in frontier and Western American history, Aron is the author of *How the West Was Lost: The Transformation of Kentucky from Daniel Boone to Henry Clay* and *American Confluence: The Missouri Frontier from Borderland to Border State*. He is currently editing the multivolume *Autry History of the American West* and writing a book with the tentative title *Can We All Just Get Along: An Alternative History of the American West*.

Peter Brown (*Ph.D. Oxford University*) is the Rollins Professor of History emeritus at Princeton University. He previously taught at London University and the University of California, Berkeley. He has written on the rise of Christianity and the end of the Roman Empire. His works include *Augustine of Hippo*; *The World of Late Antiquity*; *The Cult of the Saints*; *Body and Society*; *The Rise of Western Christendom*; and *Poverty and Leadership in the Later Roman Empire*. His most recent book is *Treasure in Heaven*.

Benjamin Elman (*Ph.D. University of Pennsylvania*) is professor of East Asian studies and history at Princeton University. He has served as the chair of the Princeton East Asian Studies Department and as director of the East Asian Studies Program. He taught at the University of California, Los Angeles, for over fifteen years, 1986–2002. His teaching and research fields include Chinese intellectual and cultural history, 1000–1900 CE; the history of science in China, 1600–1930; the history of education in late imperial China; and Sino-Japanese cultural history, 1600–1850. He is the author of seven books, four of them translated into Chinese, Korean, or Japanese: *From Philosophy to Philology: Intellectual and Social Aspects of Change in Late Imperial China*; *Classicism, Politics, and Kinship: The Ch'angchou School of New Text Confucianism in Late Imperial China*; *A Cultural History of Civil Examinations in Late Imperial China*; *On Their Own Terms: Science in China, 1550–1900*; *A Cultural History of Modern Science in China*; *Civil Examinations and Meritocracy in Late Imperial China, 1400–1900*; and *Science in China, 1600–1900: Essays by Benjamin A. Elman*. He is the creator of Classical Historiography for Chinese History at http://libguides.princeton.edu/chinese-historiography, a bibliography and teaching Web site published since 1996.

Stephen Kotkin (*Ph.D. University of California, Berkeley*) is professor of European and Asian history as well as international affairs at Princeton University. He formerly directed Princeton's program in Russian and Eurasian studies (1996–2009). He is the author of *Magnetic Mountain: Stalinism as a Civilization*; *Uncivil Society: 1989 and the Implosion of the Communist Establishment*; and *Armageddon Averted: The Soviet Collapse, 1970–2000*. He is a co-editor of *Mongolia in the Twentieth Century: Landlocked Cosmopolitan*. Professor Kotkin has twice been a visiting professor in Japan.

Xinru Liu (*Ph.D. University of Pennsylvania*) is associate professor of early Indian history and world history at the College of New Jersey. She is associated with the Institute of World History and the Chinese Academy of Social Sciences. She is the author of *Ancient India and Ancient China: Trade and Religious Exchanges, AD 1–600*; *Silk and Religion: An Exploration of Material Life and the Thought of People, AD 600–1200*; *Connections across Eurasia: Transportation, Communication, and Cultural Exchange on the Silk Roads*, coauthored with Lynda Norene Shaffer; and *A Social History of Ancient India* (in Chinese). Professor Liu promotes South Asian studies and world history studies in both the United States and the People's Republic of China.

Suzanne Marchand (*Ph.D. University of Chicago*) is professor of European and intellectual history at Louisiana State University, Baton Rouge. Professor Marchand also spent a number of years teaching at Princeton University. She is the author of *Down from Olympus: Archaeology and Philhellenism in Germany, 1750–1970* and *German Orientalism in the Age of Empire: Religion, Race, and Scholarship*.

Holly Pittman (*Ph.D. Columbia University*) is professor of art history at the University of Pennsylvania, where she teaches art and archaeology of Mesopotamia and the Iranian plateau. She also serves as curator in the Near East Section of the University of Pennsylvania Museum of Archaeology and Anthropology. Previously she served as a curator in the Ancient Near Eastern Art Department of the Metropolitan Museum of Art. She has written extensively on the art and culture of the Bronze Age in Southwest Asia and has participated in excavations in Cyprus, Turkey, Syria, and Iraq as well as in Iran, where she currently works. Her research investigates works of art as media through which patterns of thought, cultural development, and historical interactions of ancient cultures of Southwest Asia can be reconstructed.

Gyan Prakash (*Ph.D. University of Pennsylvania*) is professor of modern Indian history at Princeton University and a member of the Subaltern Studies Editorial Collective. He is the author of *Bonded Histories: Genealogies of Labor Servitude in Colonial India*; *Another Reason: Science and the Imagination of Modern India*; and *Mumbai Fables*. Professor Prakash edited *After Colonialism: Imperial Histories and Postcolonial Displacements* and *Noir Urbanisms*, co-edited *The Space of the Modern City* and *Utopia/Dystopia*, and has written a number of articles on colonialism and history writing. He is currently working on a history of the city of Bombay. With Robert Tignor, he introduced the modern world history course at Princeton University.

Brent Shaw (*Ph.D. Cambridge University*) is the Andrew Fleming West Professor of Classics at Princeton University, where he is director of the Program in the Ancient World. He was previously at the University of Pennsylvania, where he chaired the Graduate Group in Ancient History. His principal areas of specialization as a Roman historian are Roman family history and demography, sectarian violence and conflict in late antiquity, and the regional history of Africa as part of the Roman Empire. He has published *Spartacus and the Slave Wars: A Brief History with Documents*; edited the papers of Sir Moses Finley, *Economy and Society in Ancient Greece*; and published in a variety of books and journals, including the *Journal of Roman Studies*, the *American Historical Review*, the *Journal of Early Christian Studies*, and *Past & Present*.

Michael Tsin (*Ph.D. Princeton*) is associate professor of history and international studies at the University of North Carolina at Chapel Hill. He previously taught at the University of Illinois at Chicago, Princeton University, Columbia University, and the University of Florida. Professor Tsin's primary interests include the histories of modern China and colonialism. He is the author of *Nation, Governance, and Modernity in China: Canton, 1900–1927*. He is currently writing a social history of the reconfiguration of Chinese identity in the twentieth century.

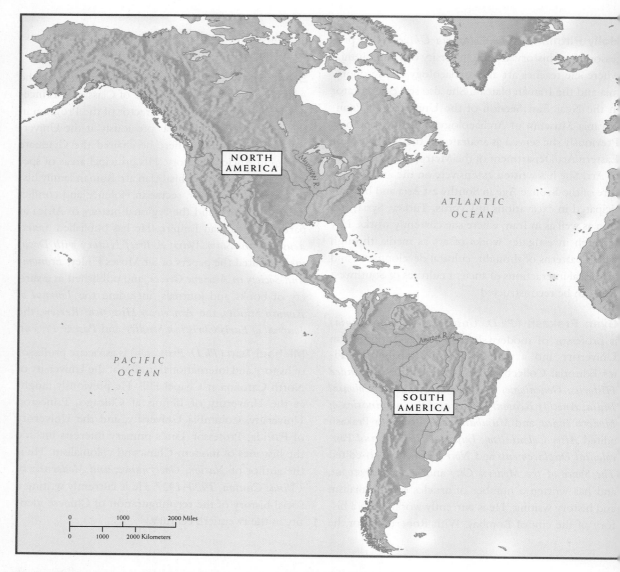

NORTH
AMERICA

Mississippi R.

ATLANTIC
OCEAN

PACIFIC
OCEAN

Amazon R.

SOUTH
AMERICA

| 0 | | 1000 | | 2000 Miles |
| 0 | 1000 | | 2000 Kilometers | |

The Geography of the Ancient and Modern Worlds

Today, geographers usually identify six inhabited continents: Africa, North America, South America, Europe, Asia, and Australia. Inside these continents they locate a vast number of subcontinental units, such as East Asia, South Asia, Southeast Asia, the Middle East, North Africa, and sub-Saharan Africa. Yet this geographic understanding would have been alien to premodern people, who did not think of themselves as inhabiting continents bounded by large bodies

of water. Lacking a firm command of the seas, they saw themselves as living on contiguous landmasses. Hence, in this textbook, we have chosen to use a set of geographic terms that more accurately reflect the world of the premoderns.

The most interconnected and populous landmass of premodern times was Afro-Eurasia. The term *Eurasia* is widely used in general histories, but we find it inadequate. The preferred term, from our perspective,

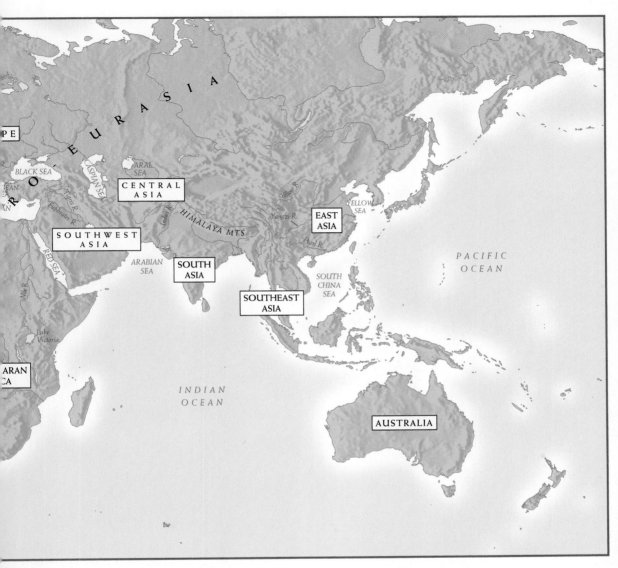

must be Afro-Eurasia, for the interconnected landmass of premodern—and, indeed, much of modern—times included large parts of Europe and Asia and significant regions in Africa—particularly Egypt, North Africa, and even parts of sub-Saharan Africa.

It was only in the period from 1000 to 1300 CE that the divisions of the world that we take for granted today began to take shape. The peoples of the northwestern part of Afro-Eurasia did not see themselves as European Christians, and hence as a distinct cultural entity, until the end of the Middle Ages. Islam did not arise and extend its influence throughout the middle zone of Afro-Eurasia until the eighth and ninth centuries. Nor did the peoples living in what we today term the Indian subcontinent feel a strong sense of their own cultural and political unity until the Delhi Sultanate and the Mughal Empire brought political unity to that vast region. As a result, we use the terms South Asia, Vedic society, and India in place of *Indian subcontinent* for the premodern part of our narrative, and we use Southwest Asia and North Africa to refer to what today is designated as the Middle East.

CONCISE SECOND EDITION

Worlds Together, Worlds Apart

Volume 2

10

Becoming "The World"

1000–1300 CE

In the late 1270s two Christian monks, Bar Sāwmā and Markōs, voyaged from what is now Beijing into the heart of the Islamic world. They were not Europeans. They were Uighurs, a Turkish people of central Asia, many of whom had converted to Christianity centuries earlier. The monks hoped to make a pilgrimage to Jerusalem in order to visit the tombs of the martyrs.

On their journey westward, Bar Sāwmā and Markōs traveled a world bound together by economic and cultural exchange. The two monks lingered at the magnificent trading hub of Kashgar in what is now western China, where caravan routes converged in a market for jade, exotic spices, and precious silks. Unable to continue on to Jerusalem due to the route's dangers (including murderous robbers), the monks parted ways at Baghdad. Bar Sāwmā was appointed an ambassador by the Buddhist Mongol il-Khan of Persia to drum up support among European leaders for an attack on Jerusalem to wrest it from Muslim control. He visited Constantinople (where the Byzantine emperor gave him gold and silver), Rome (where he met with the pope at the shrine of Saint Peter), and Paris (where he saw that city's vibrant university). In the end, neither monk ever reached Jerusalem or returned to China. Bar Sāwmā ended his days in Baghdad, and Markōs became patriarch of the Nestorian branch of Christianity, centered in modern-day Iran. Yet their voyages exemplified

Core Objectives

- **IDENTIFY** technological advances of this period, especially in ship design and navigation, and **EXPLAIN** how they facilitated the expansion of Afro-Eurasian trade.

- **DESCRIBE** the varied social and political forces that shaped the Islamic world, India, China, and Europe, and **EVALUATE** the degree to which these forces integrated cultures and geographic areas.

- **COMPARE** the internal integration and external interactions of sub-Saharan Africa with those of the Americas.

- **ASSESS** the impacts that the Mongol Empire had on Afro-Eurasian peoples and places.

the crisscrossing of people, money, goods, and ideas along the trade routes and sea-lanes that connected the world's regions.

Three related themes dominate the period from 1000 to 1300 CE. First, trade along sea-based routes increased and coastal trading cities began to expand dramatically. Second, greater trade and religious integration generated the world's four major cultural "spheres," whose inhabitants were linked by shared institutions and beliefs: the Islamic world, India, China, and Europe. Sub-Saharan Africa and the Americas also thrived during this period; however, they remained more fragmented, experiencing more limited political and economic integration. Third, the Mongol Empire, stretching from China to Persia and as far as eastern Europe, ruled over huge swaths of land in many of the world's major cultural spheres. Each of these three themes contributes to an understanding of how Afro-Eurasia became a "world" unified through trade, migration, and even religious conflict.

Global Storylines

- Advances in maritime technology lead to increased sea trade, transforming coastal cities into global trading hubs and elevating Afro-Eurasian trade to unprecedented levels.

- Intensified trade and religious integration shape four major cultural "spheres": the Islamic world, India, China, and Europe.

- Sub-Saharan Africa is drawn into Eurasian exchange, resulting in a true Afro-Eurasia–wide network, while the Americas experience more limited political, economic, and cultural integration.

- The Mongol Empire integrates many of the world's major cultural spheres.

Development of Maritime Trade

By the tenth century CE, sea routes were becoming more important than land networks for long-distance trade. Improved navigational aids, better map-making, refinements in shipbuilding, and new political support for shipping made seaborne trade easier and slashed its cost. These developments also fostered the growth of maritime commercial hubs (called anchorages), which further facilitated the expansion of maritime trade.

A new navigational instrument spurred this boom: the magnetic needle compass. This Chinese invention initially identified promising locations for houses and tombs, but eleventh-century sailors from Guangzhou (Canton) used it to find their way on the high seas. The use of this device eventually spread among navigators. The compass not only allowed sailing under cloudy skies, but it also improved mapmaking.

An array of new ship types—dhows, junks, and cogs—allowed for more impressive mastery of the seas. Dhows, ships with triangular sails called lateens, maximized the power of the monsoon trade winds on the Arabian Sea and the wider Indian Ocean. Sailing the South China seas were junks, large, flat-bottomed ships with internal sealed bulkheads, stern-mounted rudders, as many as four decks, six masts with a dozen sails, and the space to carry as many as 500 men. And, in the Atlantic, cogs, with their single mast and square sail, linked Genoa to locations as distant as the Azores and Iceland. The numbers testify to the power of the maritime revolution: while a porter could carry about 10 pounds over long distances, and animal-drawn wagons could move 100 pounds of goods over small distances, the Arab dhows could transport up to 5 tons of cargo, Atlantic cogs as much as 200 tons, and Chinese junks more than 500 tons.

Maritime traders enjoyed the protection of political authorities such as the Song rulers in China, who maintained a standing navy that protected traders and lighthouses that guided trading fleets in and out of harbors. The Fatimid caliphate in Egypt profited from maritime trade and defended merchant fleets from pirates, using armed convoys of ships to escort commercial fleets and regulate the ocean traffic. This system of protection soon spread to North Africa and southern Spain.

Long-distance trade spawned the growth of commercial cities. These cosmopolitan **entrepôts** served as transshipment centers, located on land between borders or in ports where ships could drop anchor. In these cities, traders exchanged commodities and replenished supplies. Beginning in the late tenth century CE, several regional centers became major anchorages of the maritime trade: in the west, the Egyptian port city of Alexandria on the Mediterranean (and Cairo, just up the Nile); near the tip of the Indian sub-continent, the port of Quilon (now Kollam); in the Malaysian Archipelago,

THE BIG PICTURE

How did the major cultural spheres of the Afro-Eurasian world from 1000 to 1300 CE develop their unique identities while becoming unified through trade, migration, and religion?

Core Objectives

IDENTIFY technological advances of this period, especially in ship design and navigation, and **EXPLAIN** how they facilitated the expansion of Afro-Eurasian trade.

Antique Chinese Compass
Chinese sailors from Guangzhou (Canton) started to use magnetic needle compasses in the eleventh century. By the thirteenth century, magnetic needle compasses were widely used on ships in the Indian Ocean and were starting to appear in the Mediterranean.

entrepôts
Multiethnic trading stations, often supported and protected by regional leaders, where traders exchanged commodities and replenished supplies in order to facilitate long-distance trade.

the city of Melaka; and in the east, the Chinese city of Quanzhou. (See Map 10.1.) These hubs thrived under the political stability of powerful rulers who recognized that trade would generate wealth for their regimes.

Cairo and Alexandria were the Mediterranean's main maritime commercial centers. Cairo was home to numerous Muslim and Jewish trading firms, and Alexandria was their lookout post on the Mediterranean. The Islamic legal system prevalent in Egypt promoted a favorable business environment. Through Alexandria, Europeans acquired silks from China, especially the coveted *zaytuni* (satin) fabric from Quanzhou. But many more goods passed through the Egyptian anchorage: from the Mediterranean, olive oil, glassware, flax, corals, and metals; from India, gemstones and aromatic perfumes; and from elsewhere, minerals and chemicals for dyeing or tanning, and raw materials such as timber and bamboo. Paper and books (including hand-copied Bibles, Talmuds, and Qurans) traveled along this network as well.

In South India during the tenth century CE, the Chola dynasty supported the port of Quilon, which was the nerve center of maritime trade between China and the Red Sea and the Mediterranean. Trade through Quilon continued to flourish long after the Chola golden age passed away. Personal relationships were key to trade at this anchorage, as elsewhere; for instance, when striking a deal with a local merchant, a Chinese trader might mention his Indian neighbor in Quanzhou and that family's residence in Quilon. Dhows arrived in Quilon laden not only with goods from the Red Sea and Africa, but also with traders, sojourners, and fugitives. Chinese junks unloaded silks and porcelain, and picked up passengers and commodities for East Asian markets. Muslims, the largest foreign community in Quilon, lived in their own neighborhoods and shipped horses from Arab countries to India and the southeast islands, where kings viewed them as symbols of royalty. There was even trade through Quilon in elephants and cattle from tropical countries, though the most common goods were spices, perfumes, and textiles.

East of Quilon, across the Bay of Bengal, Melaka became a key cosmopolitan entrepôt because of its strategic location and proximity to Malayan tropical produce. Indian, Javanese, and Chinese merchants and sailors spent months in such ports selling their goods, purchasing return cargo, and waiting for the winds to change direction so they could reach their next destination.

Dhow This modern dhow in the harbor of Zanzibar displays the characteristic triangular sail. The sail can make good use of the monsoon winds and thus has guided dhows on the Arabian Sea since ancient times.

During peak season, Southeast Asian ports were crowded with colorfully dressed foreign sailors, local Javanese artisans who produced finely textured batik handicrafts, and traders eager for profit. The traders converged from all over Asia to flood the markets with their merchandise and to search for pungent herbs, aromatic spices, and agrarian staples such as quick-ripening strains of rice to ship out.

In China, the Song government set up offices of seafaring affairs in its three major ports: Quanzhou, Guangzhou (Canton), and a third near present-day Shanghai. In return for a portion of the taxes on the goods passing through these entrepôts, these offices registered cargoes, sailors, and traders, while guards kept a keen eye on the traffic. All foreign traders in Song China were guests of the governor, who doubled as the chief of seafaring affairs. Every year, the governor conducted a wind-calling ritual. Traders of every origin—Arabs, Persians, Jews, Indians, and Chinese—witnessed the ceremony, then joined together for a sumptuous banquet. Although most foreign merchants did not reside apart from the rest of the city, they did maintain buildings for religious worship according to their faiths. A mosque from this period still stands on a busy street in Quanzhou. Hindu traders living in Quanzhou worshipped in a Buddhist shrine where statues of Hindu deities stood alongside those of Buddhist gods. Each of these bustling ports teemed with a cosmopolitan mix of peoples, goods, and ideas that flowed through growing maritime networks thanks to improved ships and better navigational tools.

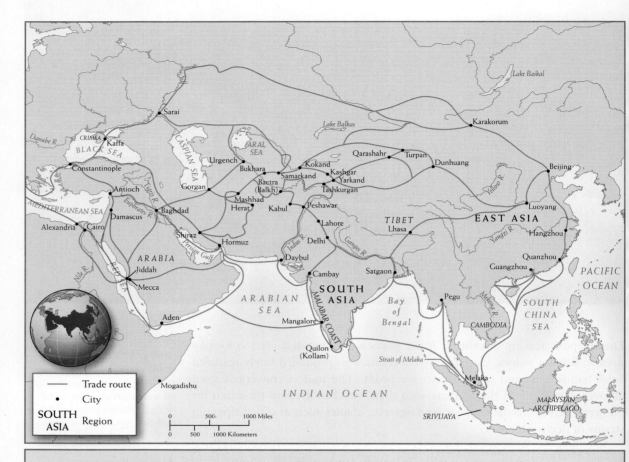

Map 10.1 Afro-Eurasian Trade, 1000–1300 CE

During the early second millennium, Afro-Eurasian merchants increasingly turned to the Indian Ocean to transport their goods. Locate the global hubs of Quilon, Alexandria, Cairo, Melaka, and Quanzhou on this map.

- What regions do each of these global hubs represent?
- Based on the map, why would sea travel have been preferable to overland travel?
- According to the text, what revolutions in maritime travel facilitated this development?

The Islamic World in a Time of Political Fragmentation

While the number of Muslim traders began to increase in commercial hubs from the Mediterranean to the South China Sea, it was not until the ninth and tenth centuries CE that Muslims became a majority within their own

Abbasid Empire (see Chapter 9), and even then rulers struggled to unite the diverse Islamic world. From the outset, Muslim rulers and clerics dealt with large non-Muslim populations, even as these groups were converting to Islam. Rulers accorded non-Muslims religious toleration as long as the non-Muslims accepted Islam's political dominion. Jewish, Christian, and Zoroastrian communities within Muslim lands were free to choose their own religious leaders and to settle internal disputes in their own religious courts. They did, however, have to pay a special tax, the *jizya*, and defer to their Muslim rulers. While tolerant, Islam was an expansionist, universalizing faith. Intense proselytizing—especially by Sufi missionaries (whose ideas are discussed later in this chapter)—carried the sacred word to new frontiers and, in the process, reinforced the spread of Islamic institutions that supported commercial exchange.

ENVIRONMENTAL CHALLENGES AND POLITICAL DIVISIONS

Severe climate conditions—freezing temperatures and lack of rainfall—afflicted the Eastern Mediterranean and the Islamic lands of Mesopotamia, the Iranian plateau, and the steppe region of central Asia in the late eleventh and early twelfth centuries. The Nile's low water levels devastated Egypt, the breadbasket for much of the area. At least one-quarter of the summer floods that normally brought sediment-enriching deposits to Egypt's soils and guaranteed abundant harvests failed in this period. Driven in part by drought, Turkish nomadic pastoralists poured out of the steppe lands of central Asia in search of better lands, wreaking political and economic havoc everywhere they invaded.

At the same time these climate-driven Turkish pastoralists were migrating and the Islamic faith was increasing its reach across Afro-Eurasia, the political institutions of Islam were fragmenting. (See Map 10.2.) From 950 to 1050 CE, it appeared that Shiism would be the vehicle for uniting the Islamic world. The Fatimid Shiites had established their authority over Egypt and much of North Africa (see Chapter 9), and the Abbasid state in Baghdad was controlled by a Shiite family, the Buyids. Each group created universities, in Cairo and Baghdad respectively, ensuring that leading centers of higher

jizya
Special tax that non-Muslims were forced to pay to their Islamic rulers in return for which they were given security and property and granted cultural autonomy.

learning were Shiite. But divisions also sapped Shiism, and Sunni Muslims began to challenge Shiite power and establish their own strongholds. In Baghdad, the Shiite Buyid family surrendered to the invading Seljuk Turks, a Sunni group, in 1055. A century later, the last of the Shiite Fatimid rulers gave way to a new Sunni regime in Egypt.

The Seljuk Turks who took Baghdad had been migrating into the Islamic heartland from the Asian steppes as early as the eighth century CE, bringing superior military skills and an intense devotion to Sunni Islam. When they flooded into the Iranian plateau in 1029, they contributed to the end of the magnificent cultural flourishing of the early eleventh century. When Seljuk warriors ultimately took Baghdad in 1055, they established a nomadic state in Mesopotamia over a once powerful Abbasid state that now lacked the resources to defend its lands and its peoples, weakened by famines and pestilence. The Seljuk invaders destroyed institutions of learning and public libraries and looted the region's antiquities. Once established in Baghdad, they founded outposts in Syria and Palestine, then moved into Anatolia after defeating Byzantine forces in 1071.

By the thirteenth century the Islamic heartland had fractured into three regions. In the east (central Asia, Iran, and eastern Iraq), the remnants of the old Abbasid state persevered, with a succession of caliphs claiming to speak for all of Islam yet deferring to their Turkish military commanders. In the core of the Islamic world—Egypt, Syria, and the Arabian Peninsula—where Arabic was the primary language, military men of non-Arab origin held the reins of power. Farther west in North Africa, Arab rulers prevailed, but the influence of Berbers, some from the northern Sahara, was extensive. Islam was a vibrant faith, but its polities were splintered.

THE SPREAD OF SUFISM

Even in the face of this political splintering, Islam's spread was facilitated by a popular, highly mystical and communal form of the religion, called **Sufism**. The term *Sufi* comes from the Arabic word for wool (*suf*), which many of the early mystics wrapped themselves in to mark their penitence. Seeking closer union with God, Sufis performed ecstatic rituals such as repeating over and over again the name of God. In time, groups of devotees gathered to read aloud the Quran and other religious tracts. Sufi mystics' desire to experience God's love found ready expression in poetry. Most admired of Islam's mystical love poets was Jalal al-Din Rumi (1207–1273), spiritual founder of the Mevlevi Sufi order, which became famous for the ceremonial dancing of its whirling devotees, known as dervishes.

Sufism
Emotional and mystical form of Islam that appealed to the common people.

Although many *ulama* (scholars) despised the Sufis and loathed their seeming lack of theological rigor, the movement spread with astonishing speed and offered a unifying force within Islam. Sufism's emotional content

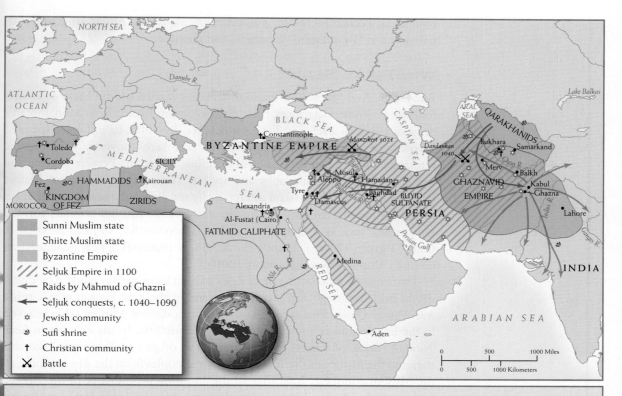

Map 10.2 The Islamic World, 900–1200 CE

The Islamic world experienced political disintegration in the first centuries of the second millennium.

- According to the map key, what were the two major types of Islamic states in this period? What were some of the major political entities?
- What were the sources of instability in this period according to the map?
- What do you note about the locations of Jewish and Christian communities, as well as Sufi shrines, across the Islamic world?

and strong social bonds, sustained in Sufi religious orders, or brotherhoods, added to its appeal for many. Sufi missionaries from these brotherhoods carried the universalizing faith to India, to Southeast Asia, across the Sahara Desert, and to many other distant locations. It was through these brotherhoods that Islam became truly a religion for the people. As trade increased and more converts appeared in the Islamic lands, urban and peasant populations came to understand the faith practiced by the political, commercial, and scholarly upper classes even while they remained attached to their Sufi brotherhood ways. Over time, Islam became even more accommodating, embracing Persian literature, Turkish ruling skills, and Arabic-language contributions in law, religion, literature, and science.

WHAT WAS ISLAM?

Buoyed by Arab dhows on the high seas and carried on the backs of camels following commercial routes, Islam had been transformed from Muhammad's original vision of a religion for Arab peoples. By 1300, its influence spanned Afro-Eurasia and reached multitudes of non-Arab converts. While Arabic remained the primary language of religious devotion, Persian became the language of Islamic philosophy and art and Turkish the language of Islamic law and administration. Islam attracted city dwellers and rural peasants alike, as well as its original audience of desert nomads. Muslim scholars formed universities, such as al-Qarawiyyin in Fez, Morocco (859 CE) and al-Azhar in Cairo, Egypt (970 CE). Islam's extraordinary universal appeal generated an intense cultural flowering around 1000 CE.

That cultural blossoming in all fields of high learning was marked by diversity in both language and ideas. Representing the new Persian ethnic pride was Abu al-Qasim Firdawsi (920–1020 CE), a devout Muslim who believed in the importance of pre-Islamic Sasanian traditions. In the epic poem *Shah Namah* (Book of Kings), he celebrated the origins of Persian culture and narrated the history of the Iranian highland peoples from the dawn of time to the Muslim conquest. Indicative of the enduring prominence of the Islamic faith and the Arabic language in thought was the legendary Ibn Rushd (1126–1198), known as Averroës in the western world. Steeped in the writings of Aristotle, Ibn Rushd's belief that faith and reason were compatible even influenced the thinking of the Christian world's leading philosopher and theologian, Thomas Aquinas (1225–1274).

During this period, the Islamic world became one of the four cultural spheres that would play a major role in world history, laying the foundation for what would become known as the Middle East up through the middle of the twentieth century. Islam became the majority religion of most of the inhabitants of Southwest Asia and North Africa, Arabic language use became widespread, and the Turks began to establish themselves as a dominant force, ultimately creating the Ottoman Empire, which would last into the twentieth century. The Islamic world became integral in transregional trade and in the creation and transmission of knowledge.

India as a Cultural Mosaic

With its pivotal location along land- and sea-based trade routes, India became an intersection for the trade, migration, and culture of Afro-Eurasian peoples. With 80 million inhabitants in 1000 CE, it had the second-largest population

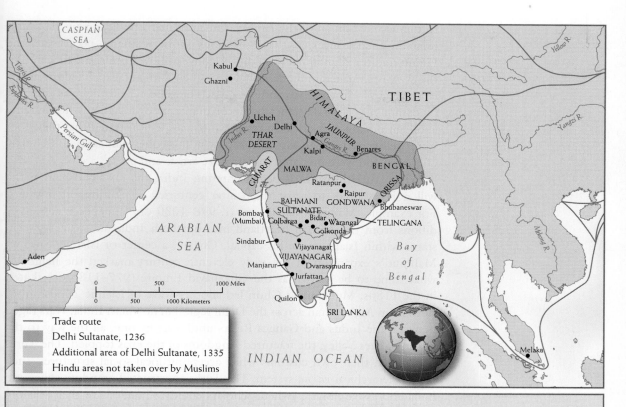

Trade route
Delhi Sultanate, 1236
Additional area of Delhi Sultanate, 1335
Hindu areas not taken over by Muslims

Map 10.3 South Asia in 1300

As the fourteenth century began, India was a blend of many cultures. Politically, the Turkish Muslim regime of the Delhi Sultanate dominated the region.

- What region was controlled by the Delhi Sultanate in 1236? How did the area controlled by the Delhi Sultanate change in just 100 years?
- How does the map suggest that trade routes helped to spread the Muslims' influence in India?
- Where on the map do Hindu areas resist Muslim political control? Based on your reading, what factors may have accounted for Hinduism's continued appeal despite the Muslims' political power?

in the region, not far behind China's 120 million. Turks ultimately spilled into India as they had into the Islamic heartlands, bringing their newfound Islamic beliefs. But the Turkish newcomers encountered an ethnic and religious mix of which they were just one part. (See Map 10.3.)

SHIFTING POLITICAL STRUCTURES

Before the Turks arrived, India was splintered among rival chiefs called *rajas*. These leaders gained support from Brahmans by doling out land grants to them. Since much of the land was uncultivated, the Brahmans first built temples, then converted the indigenous hunter-gatherer peoples to the Hindu traditions, and finally taught the converts how to cultivate the land. In this way, Brahmans simultaneously spread their faith and expanded the agrarian tax base for themselves and the rajas. They also repaid the rajas' support by compiling elaborate genealogies for them, endowing them with lengthy and legitimizing ancestries. In return, the rajas demonstrated that they, too, were well versed in Sanskrit culture, including equestrian skills and courtly etiquette, and were prepared to patronize artists and poets.

When Turkish warlords began entering India, the rajas had neither the will nor resources to resist them after centuries of fighting off invaders. For example, Mahmud of Ghazna (r. 998–1030 CE) launched many expeditions from the Afghan heartland into northern India and, eager to win status within Islam, made his capital, Ghazni, a center of Islamic learning. Mahmud's expansion in the early eleventh century marked the height of what came to be known as the Ghaznavid Empire (977–1186 CE). Later, in the 1180s, Muhammad Ghuri led another wave of Islamic Turkish invasions from Afghanistan across the Delhi region in northern India. Wars raged between the Indus and Ganges Rivers until, one by one, all the way to the lower Ganges Valley, the fractured kingdoms of the rajas toppled. The Turks introduced their own customs while accepting local social structures, such as the hierarchical *varna* system. The Turks constructed grand mosques and built impressive libraries where scholars could toil and share their wisdom with the court.

While the Ghaznavids were impressive, the most powerful and enduring of the Turkish Muslim regimes of northern India was the **Delhi Sultanate** (1206–1526), whose rulers brought political integration but also strengthened the cultural diversity and tolerance that were already a hallmark of the Indian social order. Sultans recruited local artisans for numerous building projects, and palaces and mosques became displays of Indian architectural tastes adopted by Turkish newcomers. But Islam never fully dominated South Asia because the sultans did not force their subjects to convert. Nor did they display much interest in the flourishing commercial life along the Indian coast. The sultans permitted these areas to develop on their own: Persian Zoroastrian traders settled on the coast around modern-day Mumbai while farther south, Arab traders controlled the Malabar coast. The Delhi Sultanate was a rich and powerful regime that brought political integration but did not enforce cultural homogeneity.

WHAT WAS INDIA?

During the eleventh, twelfth, and thirteenth centuries India became the most diverse and, in some respects, the most tolerant region in Afro-Eurasia. India

Delhi Sultanate (1206–1526)

A Turkish Muslim regime in northern India that, through its tolerance for cultural diversity, brought political integration without enforcing cultural homogeneity.

Hindu Temple When Buddhism started to decline in India, Hinduism was on the rise. Numerous Hindu temples were built, many of them adorned with ornate carvings like this small tenth-century temple in Bhubaneshwar, east India.

in this era arose as an impressive but fragile mosaic of cultures, religions, and ethnicities. When the Turks arrived, the local Hindu population, having had much experience with foreign invaders and immigrants, assimilated these intruders as they had done earlier peoples. Before long, the newcomers thought of themselves as Indians who, however, retained their Islamic beliefs and steppe ways. They continued to wear their distinctive trousers and robes and flaunted their horse-riding skills. At the same time, the local population embraced some of their conquerors' ways, donning the tunics and trousers that characterized central Asian peoples.

Diversity and cultural mixing became most visible in the multiple languages that flourished in India. Although the sultans spoke Turkish languages, they regarded Persian literature as a high cultural achievement and made Persian their courtly and administrative language. Meanwhile, most of their Hindu subjects spoke local languages, adhered to the regulations of the *varna* system of hierarchies, and practiced diverse forms of Hindu worship. The rulers in India did what Muslim rulers in Southwest Asia and the Mediterranean did with Christian and Jewish communities living in their midst: they collected the *jizya* tax and permitted communities to worship as they saw fit and to administer their own communal law. Ultimately, Islam proved in India that it did not have to be an intolerant conquering religion to prosper.

Although Buddhism had been in decline in India for centuries, it, too, became part of the cultural intermixing of this period. As Vedic Brahmanism evolved into Hinduism (see Chapter 8), it had absorbed many Buddhist doctrines and practices, such as nonviolence (*ahimsa*) and vegetarianism. The two religions became so similar in India that Hindus simply considered the Buddha to be one of their deities—an incarnation of the great god Vishnu. Many Buddhist moral teachings mixed with and became Hindu stories. Artistic motifs reflected a similar process of adoption and adaptation. Goddesses, some beautiful and others fierce, appeared alongside Buddhas, Vishnus, and Shivas as their consorts. The Turkish invaders' destruction of major monasteries in the thirteenth century deprived Buddhism of local spiritual leaders. Lacking dynastic support, Buddhists in India were more easily assimilated into the Hindu population or converted to Islam.

Once the initial disruptive effects of the Turkish invasions were absorbed, India remained a highly diverse and tolerant region during this period. Most important, India also emerged as one of the four major cultural spheres, enjoying a tremendous level of integration as Turkish-Muslim rulers and their traditions and practices were successfully intermixed with the native Hindu society, leading to a more integrated and peaceful India.

Song China: Insiders versus Outsiders

Core Objectives

DESCRIBE the varied social and political forces that shaped the Islamic world, China, and Europe, and **EVALUATE** the degree to which these forces integrated cultures and geographic areas.

The preeminent world power in 1000 CE was still China, despite its recent turmoil. In 907 CE the Tang dynasty splintered into regional kingdoms, mostly led by military generals. In 960 CE one of these generals, Zhao Kuangyin, ended the fragmentation, reunified China, and assumed the mandate of heaven for the Song dynasty (960–1279 CE). The following three centuries witnessed many economic and political successes, but northern nomadic tribes kept the Song dynasty from completely securing its reign. (See Map 10.4 and Map 10.5.) Ultimately, one of those nomadic groups, the Mongols, would bring the Song dynasty to an end, but not before Song influence had fanned out into Southeast Asia, helping to create new identities in the polities that developed there.

ECONOMIC AND POLITICAL DEVELOPMENTS

Chinese merchants, like those from India and the Islamic world, participated in Afro-Eurasia's powerful long-distance trade. Yet China's commercial successes could not have occurred without the country's strong agrarian base—especially its vast wheat, millet, and rice fields, which fed a population that reached 120 million. Crop cultivation benefited from breakthroughs in metalworking that produced stronger iron plows, which Song farmers harnessed to sturdy water buffalo to extend the agricultural frontier.

Map 10.4 East Asia in 1000 CE

Several states emerged in East Asia between 1000 and 1300 CE, but none were as strong as the Song dynasty in China. Using the key to the map, try to identify the factors that contributed to the Song state's economic dynamism.

- What do you note about the location of the major trading centers?
- What do you note about the distribution of the other trading centers?
- According to the map, what external factors kept the Song dynasty from completely securing its reign?

Manufacturing also flourished. With the use of piston-driven bellows to force air into furnaces, Song iron production in the eleventh century equaled that of Europe in the early eighteenth century. In the early tenth century, Chinese alchemists mixed saltpeter with sulfur and charcoal to produce a product that would burn and could be deployed on the battlefield: gunpowder. Song entrepreneurs were soon inventing a remarkable array of incendiary

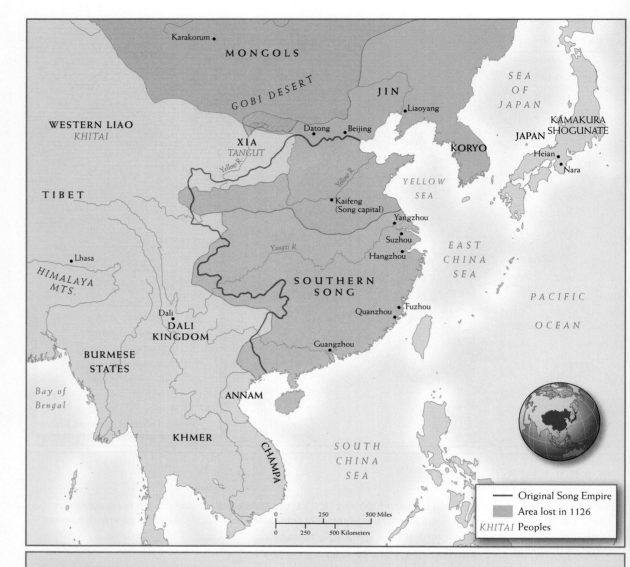

Map 10.5 East Asia in 1200

....

The Song dynasty regularly dealt with "barbarian" neighbors with a balance of military response and outright bribery.

- What were the major "barbarian" tribes on the borders of Song China during this period?
- Approximately what percentage of Song China was lost to the Jin in 1126?
- Apart from so-called barbarians, what other polities existed on the borders of Song China?

devices that flowed from their mastery of techniques for controlling explosions and high heat. At the same time, artisans were producing increasingly light, durable, and exquisitely beautiful porcelains. Before long, their porcelain was the envy of all Afro-Eurasia (hence the modern term "china" for fine dishes). Also flowing from the artisans' skillful hands were vast amounts of clothing and handicrafts, made from the fibers grown by Song farmers. In effect, the Song Chinese oversaw the world's first manufacturing revolution, producing finished goods on a large scale for consumption far and wide.

Expanding commerce transformed the role of money and its wide circulation. By now the Song government was annually minting nearly 2 million strings of currency, each containing 1,000 copper coins. As the economy grew, the supply of metal currency could not match the demand, which fueled East Asia's desire for gold from East Africa. At the same time, merchant guilds in northwestern Shanxi developed the first letters of exchange, or paper money, which they called **flying cash**. These letters linked northern traders with their colleagues in the south. Before long, printed money became more common than minted coins for trading purposes. Eventually, the Song dynasty began to issue more notes to pay its bills—a practice that ultimately contributed to runaway inflation.

Song emperors built on Tang political institutions by expanding a central bureaucracy of scholar-officials chosen even more extensively through competitive civil service examinations. Zhao Kuangyin, or Emperor Taizu (r. 960–976 CE), himself administered the final test for all who had passed the highest-level palace examination. In subsequent dynasties, the emperor was the nation's premier examiner, symbolically demanding oaths of allegiance from successful candidates. By 1100 these ranks of learned men had accumulated sufficient power to become China's new ruling elite. This expansion of the civil service examination system was crucial to a shift in power from the still significant hereditary aristocracy to a less wealthy but more highly schooled class of scholar-officials.

CHINA'S NEIGHBORS: NOMADS, JAPAN, AND SOUTHEAST ASIA

China's prosperity influenced its neighbors and its interactions with them. As Song China flourished, nomads on the outskirts eyed the Chinese successes closely. To the north, nomadic societies formed their own dynasties and adopted Chinese institutions. These non-Chinese nomads sought both to conquer and to copy China proper. Despite its sophisticated weapons, the Song army could not match its enemies on the steppe when the nomads united against them. Steel tips improved the arrows that Song soldiers shot from their crossbows, and flamethrowers and "crouching tiger" catapults sent incendiary bombs streaking into their enemies' ranks. But none of these

flying cash
Letters of exchange—early predecessors of paper money—first developed by guilds in the northern Song province Shanxi that eclipsed coins by the thirteenth century.

Core Objectives

DESCRIBE the social and political forces that shaped Song China, and **EVALUATE** the degree to which they integrated the cultures of East Asia.

Chinese and Barbarian After losing the north, the Chinese grew resentful of outsiders. They drew a dividing line between their own agrarian society and the nomadic warriors, calling them "barbarians." Such identities were not fixed, however. Chinese and so-called barbarians were mutually dependent.

breakthroughs was secret. Warrior neighbor on the steppe mastered the new arts of wa more fully than did the Song military. Con sequently, China drew on its economic suc cess (and the innovation of paper money) to "buy off" the borderlanders. This short-term solution, however, led to economic instability (particularly inflation) and military weakness especially as the Song forces were cut off, via the steppe nomads, from their supply of horses for warfare purposes.

Feeling the pull of China's economic and political gravity, cultures around China con solidated their own internal political authority and defined their own identities in order to keep from being swallowed up by China. At the same time, they increased their commercial transactions with China. In Japan, for instance, leaders distanced themselves from Chinese influences, but they also developed a strong sense of their islands' distinctive identity. Even so, the long-standing dominance of Chinese ways remained apparent at virtually every level of Japanese society, and was most pronounced at the imperial court in the capital city of Heian (present-day Kyoto), which was modeled after the Chinese capital city of Chang'an. Outside Kyoto, however, a less China-centered way of life existed and began to impose itself on the center. Here, local notables, mainly military leaders and large landowners, began to challenge the imperial court for dominance. This challenge was accompanied by the arrival of an important new social group in Japanese society—samurai warriors. By the beginning of the fourteenth century, Japan had multiple sources of political and cultural power: an imperial family with prestige but little authority; an endangered and declining aristocracy; power-ful landowning notables based in the provinces; and a rising and increasingly ambitious class of samurai.

During the Song period, Southeast Asia became a crossroads of Afro-Eurasian influences. The Malay Peninsula became home to many entrepôts for traders shuttling between India and China, because it connected the Bay of Bengal and the Indian Ocean with the South China Sea. (See Map 10.6.) Consequently, Southeast Asia was characterized by a fusion of religions and cultural influences: Vedic Brahmanism in Bali and other islands, Islam in Java and Sumatra, and Mahayana Buddhism in Vietnam and other parts of main-land Southeast Asia. Important Vedic and Buddhist kingdoms emerged in Southeast Asia. The most powerful and wealthy of these kingdoms was the Khmer Empire (889–1431 CE), with its capital at Angkor, in present-day Cambodia. Public works and magnificent temples dedicated to the revived

Angkor Wat Mistaken by later European explorers for a remnant of Alexander the Great's conquests, the enormous temple complexes built by the Khmer people in Angkor borrowed their intricate layout and stupa (a moundlike structure containing religious relics) architecture from the Brahmanic Indian temples of the time. As their capital, Angkor was a microcosm of the world for the Khmer, who aspired to represent the macrocosm of the universe in the magnificence of Angkor's buildings and their geometric layout.

Vedic gods from India went hand in hand with the earlier influence of Indian Buddhism. One of the greatest temple complexes in Angkor—Angkor Wat—exemplified the Khmers' heavy borrowing from Vedic Indian architecture and the revival of the Hindu pantheon within the Khmer royal state. Kingdoms like the Khmer Empire functioned as political buffers between the strong states of China and India and brought stability and further commercial prosperity to the region.

WHAT WAS CHINA?

Paradoxically, the increasing exchange between outsiders and insiders within China hardened the lines that divided them and gave residents of China's interior a highly developed sense of themselves as a distinct people possessing a superior culture. Exchanges with outsiders nurtured a "Chinese" identity among those who considered themselves true insiders and referred to themselves as "Han." Song Chinese grew increasingly suspicious and resentful toward the outsiders living in their midst. They called these outsiders "barbarians" and treated them accordingly.

Print culture crystallized the distinct Chinese identity. Of all Afro-Eurasian societies in 1300, the Chinese were the most advanced in their use of printing, book publishing, and circulation, in part due to the invention of a movable type printing press by the artisan Bi Sheng around 1040. Song dynasty printed books established classical Chinese as the common language of educated classes in East Asia. The Song government used its plentiful

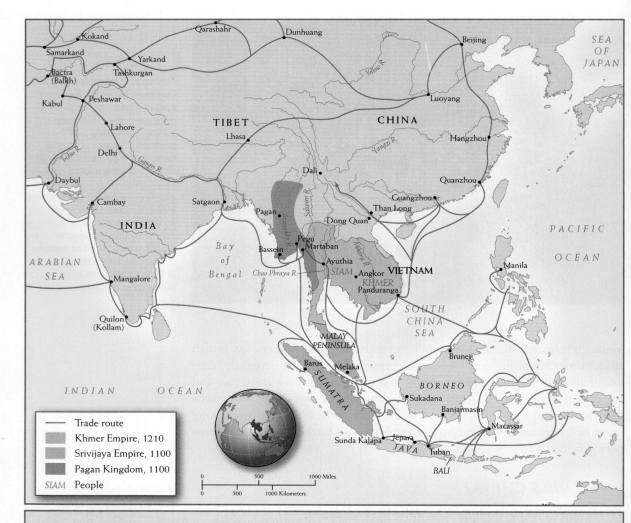

Map 10.6 Southeast Asia, 1000–1300 CE

....

Cross-cultural influences affected Southeast Asian societies during this period.

- What geographic features (rivers, mountains, islands, straits, etc.) shape Southeast Asia?
- What makes Southeast Asia unique geographically compared to other regions of the world?
- Based on the map, why were the kingdoms of Southeast Asia exposed to so many cross-cultural influences?

supply of paper to print books, especially medical texts, and to distribute calendars. The private publishing industry expanded, and printing houses throughout the country produced Confucian classics, works on history, philosophical treatises, and literature—all of which figured in the civil service examinations. Buddhist publications, too, were available everywhere.

China's huge population base, coupled with a strong agrarian base and manufacturing innovations, made it the wealthiest of the four major cultural spheres, and its common language and Confucian civil service system, which enabled a transfer of power from hereditary aristocrats to Confucian scholars, made it the most unified. China's influence on the surrounding region was tremendous.

Christian Europe

Europe, from 1000 to 1300 CE, was a region of strong contrasts. Intensely localized power was balanced by a shared sense of Europe's place in the world, especially with respect to Christian identity. Some inhabitants even began to believe in the existence of something called "Europe" and increasingly referred to themselves as "Europeans," especially in contrast to the world of Islam to the east and south. (See Map 10.7.)

LOCALIZATION OF POWER

From the agriculture-based manors of western Europe to the cities of Russia, power structures in Europe were localized. For example, in western Europe of the eleventh and twelfth centuries, the Franks became the unchallenged rulers after the collapse of Charlemagne's empire, yet they oversaw a somewhat fragmented manor-based economy and social structure. The peasantry's subjugation to this knightly class was at the heart of a system scholars have called feudalism (emphasizing the power of the local lords over the peasantry); but a more accurate term for the system is **manorialism**, which emphasizes instead the manor's role as the basic unit of economic power. The manor comprised the lord's fortified home (or castle), the surrounding fields controlled by the lord but worked by peasants (as free tenants or as serfs tied to the land), and the village in which those peasants lived. Although manorialism was driven by agriculture, limited manufacturing and trade augmented the manor economy. This system harnessed agrarian energy and helped western Europe shed its identity as a somewhat "barbarian" appendage of the Mediterranean.

Between 1100 and 1200, as many as 200,000 pioneering peasants emigrated from present-day Belgium, Holland, and northern Germany to the frontiers of Europe (now Poland, the Czech Republic, Hungary, and the

Core Objectives

COMPARE the role that religions and migration played in forging unified identities in Europe, India, and the Islamic worlds.

manorialism
System in which the manor (a lord's home, its associated industry, and surrounding fields) served as the basic unit of economic power; an alternative to the concept of feudalism (the hierarchical relationships of king, lords, and peasantry) for thinking about the nature of power in western Europe from 1000 to 1300 CE.

Map 10.7 Western Christendom in 1300

Catholic Europe expanded geographically and integrated culturally during this era.

- According to this map, into what areas did western Christendom successfully expand?
- What were the different means by which western Christianity expanded?
- Which are the earliest universities on the map? What might account for the flourishing of universities where they were located?

Baltic states). Despite its harsh climate and landscape, the area offered the promise of freedom from feudal lords' arbitrary justice and the imposition of forced labor that the peasants had experienced in western Europe. In a fragile balance between the native elites and liberty-seeking newcomers, castles and villages echoing the landscape of manorial France now replaced local economies that had been based on gathering honey, hunting, and the slave trade. For a thousand miles along the Baltic Sea, forest clearings dotted with new farmsteads and small towns edged inward from the coast up the river valleys.

Russian lands modeled themselves after Byzantium, not Rome or western Europe. Set in a giant borderland between the steppes of Inner Eurasia and the booming centers of Europe, Russia's cities lay at the crossroads of overland trade and migration. These cities were not agrarian centers, but hubs of expanding long-distance trade. Kiev became one of the region's greatest urban centers, a small-scale Constantinople with its own miniature Hagia Sophia. Russian Christians looked not to the Roman Catholic faith associated with the popes in Rome, but rather to Byzantium's Hagia Sophia and the Orthodoxy of the east as the source of religious authority. Russian Christianity remained that of a borderland—vivid oases of high culture set against the backdrop of vast forests and widely scattered settlements. Like the agricultural manors of western Europe, these Russian cities demonstrate the highly localized nature of power in Europe in this period.

WHAT WAS CHRISTIAN EUROPE?

Christianity in this era—primarily the Roman Catholicism of the west, but also the Orthodoxy of the east—became a universalizing faith that transformed the region becoming known as "Europe." The Christianity of post-Roman Europe had been a religion of monks, and its most dynamic centers were great monasteries. Members of the laity were expected to revere and support their monks, nuns, and clergy, but not to imitate them. By 1200, all this had changed. The internal colonization of western Europe—the clearing of woods and founding of villages—ensured that parish churches arose in all but the wildest landscapes. Now the clergy reached more deeply into the private lives of the laity. Marriage and divorce, previously considered family matters, became the domain of the church.

New understandings of religious devotion and innovative institutions for learning developed in the west. For instance, the followers of Francis of Assisi (1182–1226) emerged as an order of preachers who brought a message of repentance. Franciscans encouraged the laity—from the poorest to the elite—to feel remorse for their wrongdoings, to confess their sins to local priests, and to strive to be better Christians. At nearly the same time, intellectuals were beginning to gather in Paris to form one of the first European universities, a sort of trade guild of scholars. These professional thinkers

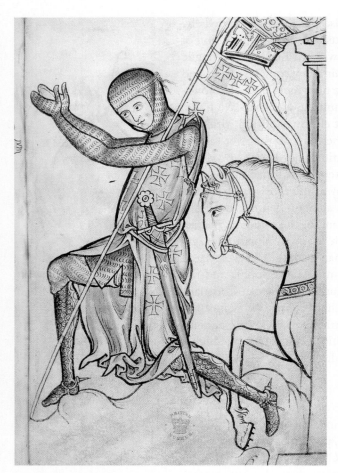

Crusader Kneeling, this Crusader promises to serve God (as he would serve a feudal lord) by going to fight on a Crusade (as he would fight for any lord to whom he had sworn loyalty). The two kinds of loyalty—to God and to one's lord—were deliberately confused in Crusader ideas. Both were about war, but fighting for God was unambiguously good, while fighting for a lord was not always so clear-cut.

endeavored to prove that Christianity was the only religion that fully addressed the concerns of all rational human beings. Such was the message of Thomas Aquinas, who wrote *Summa contra Gentiles* (Summary of Christian Belief against Non-Christians) in 1264. The growing number of churches, new religious orders, and universities began to change what it meant to live in a "Christian Europe."

RELATIONS WITH THE ISLAMIC WORLD

In the late eleventh century, western Europeans launched the Crusades, a wave of attacks against the Muslim world. The First Crusade began in 1095, when Pope Urban II appealed to the warrior nobility of France to put their violence to good use: they should combine their role as pilgrims to Jerusalem with that of soldiers in order to free the Christian "holy land" from Muslim rule. Such a just war, the clergy proposed, was a means for absolution, not a source of sin.

Starting in 1097, an armed host of around 60,000 men set out from northwestern Europe to seize Jerusalem. The crusading forces included knights in heavy armor as well as people drawn from Europe's impoverished masses, who joined the movement to help besiege cities and construct a network of castles as the Christian knights drove their frontier forward. The fleets of Venice, Genoa, and Pisa helped transport later Crusaders and supplied the kingdoms they created as they moved eastward. Later Crusaders, especially those from the upper class, brought their wives, who found a degree of autonomy away from their homeland. There are even accounts of a children's crusade (1212), inspired by the visions of a boy. Over time, the Crusades drew together a range of peoples from varied walks of life in common purpose.

No fewer than nine Crusades were fought over the two centuries that followed Urban II's call; but none of the coalitions, in the end, created lasting Christian kingdoms in the lands they "reconquered." Most knights returned home, their epic pilgrimages completed. The remaining fragile network of Crusader lordships barely threatened the Islamic heartland. The real prosperity and the capital cities of Muslim kingdoms lay inland, away from the coast—at Cairo, Damascus, and Baghdad. The assaults' long-term effect was to harden Muslim feelings against the Franks and the millions of nonwestern Christians who had previously lived peacefully in Egypt and Syria.

Even so, a range of sources offer Muslim and Christian perspectives that show tolerance of, and curiosity about, each other. For example, Usāmah ibn Munqidh (1095–1188), a learned Syrian leader, describes his shock at the Frankish Crusaders' backward medical practices and the freedom they offered their wives, in addition to well-meaning exchanges such as a particular Frank's confusion about the direction in which Muslims pray. Similarly, Jean de Joinville (1224/1225–1317), a French chronicler of Louis X of France who led the Seventh Crusade, marveled at the order within the sultan's camp and the role of musicians in calling the Muslim forces to hear the sultan's orders.

Other campaigns of Christian expansion, like the Iberian efforts to drive out the Muslims, were more successful. Beginning with the capture of Toledo in 1061, the Christian kings of northern Spain slowly pushed back the Muslims. Eventually they reached the heart of Andalusia in southern Iberia and conquered Seville, adding more than 100,000 square miles of territory to Christian Europe. Another force, from northern France, crossed Italy to conquer Muslim-held Sicily, ensuring Christian rule in that strategically located mid-Mediterranean island. Unlike the Crusaders' fragile foothold at the edge of the Middle East, these two conquests were a turning point in relations between Christian and Muslim power in the Mediterranean. Christianity—and in particular the rise of the Roman Catholic Church, the spread of universities, and the fight against the Muslims in their native and spiritual homelands—was a force that helped create a cultural sphere known as Europe, whose peoples would become known as European, at the western end of the Afro-Eurasian landmass during this period.

Worlds Coming Together: Sub-Saharan Africa and the Americas

From 1000 to 1300 CE, sub-Saharan Africa and the Americas became far more internally integrated—culturally, economically, and politically—than before. Islam's spread and the growing trade in gold, slaves, and other commodities brought sub-Saharan Africa more fully into the exchange networks of the Eastern Hemisphere, but the Americas remained isolated from Afro-Eurasian networks for several more centuries.

Core Objectives

COMPARE the internal integration and external interactions of sub-Saharan Africa with those of the Americas.

SUB-SAHARAN AFRICA COMES TOGETHER

During this period, sub-Saharan Africa's relationship to the rest of the world changed dramatically. While sub-Saharan Africa had never been a world entirely apart before 1000 CE, its integration with Eurasia now became much stronger. Increasingly, its hinterlands found themselves touched by the commercial and migratory impulses emanating from the Indian Ocean and Arabian Sea transformations. (See Map 10.8.)

West Africa and the Mande-Speaking Peoples Once trade routes bridged the Sahara Desert (see Chapter 9), the flow of commodities and ideas linked sub-Saharan Africa to North Africa and Southwest Asia. As the savanna region became increasingly connected to developments in Eurasia, Mande-speaking peoples became the primary agents for integration within and beyond West Africa. Exploiting their expertise in commerce and political organization, the Mande edged out rivals. The Mande homeland was a vast area, 1,000 miles wide between the bend in the Senegal River to the west and the bend of the Niger River to the east, and stretching more than 2,000 miles from the Senegal River in the north to the Bandama River in the south.

By the eleventh century, Mande-speaking peoples were spreading their cultural, commercial, and political hegemony from the savanna grasslands southward into the woodlands and tropical rain forests stretching to the Atlantic Ocean. Those dwelling in the rain forests organized small-scale societies led by local councils, while those in the savanna lands developed centralized forms of government under sacred kingships. Mande speakers believed that their kings had descended from the gods and that they enjoyed the gods' blessing.

As the Mande extended their territory to the Atlantic coast, they gained access to tradable items that residents of Africa's interior were eager to have—notably kola nuts and malaguetta peppers, for which the Mande exchanged iron products and manufactured textiles. Mande-speaking peoples, with their far-flung commercial networks and highly dispersed populations, dominated trans-Saharan trade in salt from the northern Sahel, gold from the Mande homeland, and slaves. By 1300, Mande-speaking merchants had followed the Senegal River to its outlet on the Atlantic coast and then pushed their commercial frontiers farther inland and down the coast. Thus, even before European explorers and traders arrived in the mid-fifteenth century, West African peoples had created dynamic networks linking the hinterlands with coastal trading hubs.

Mali Empire
West African empire, founded by the legendary king Sundiata in the early thirteenth century. It facilitated thriving commerce along routes linking the Atlantic Ocean, the Sahara, and beyond.

The Mali Empire In the early thirteenth century, the **Mali Empire** became the Mande successor state to the kingdom of Ghana (see Chapter 9). The origins of the Mali Empire and its legendary founder are enshrined in *The Epic of Sundiata*. Sundiata's triumph, which occurred in the first half of the thirteenth century, marked the victory of new cavalry forces over traditional foot soldiers. Horses now became prestige objects for the savanna peoples, symbols of state power.

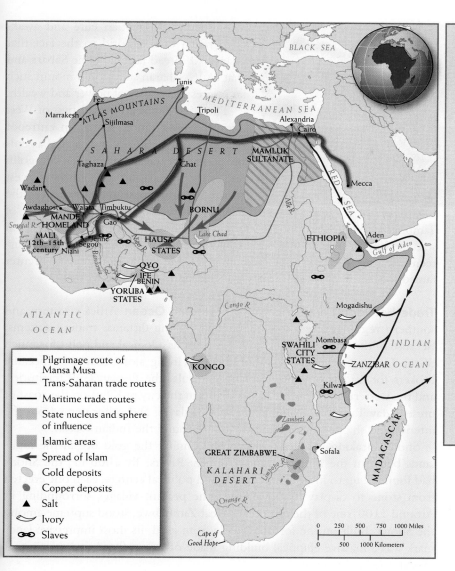

Map 10.8 Sub-Saharan Africa, 1300

Increased commercial contacts influenced the religious and political dimensions of sub-Saharan Africa at this time. Compare this map with Map 9.3.

- Where had strong Islamic communities emerged by 1300? By what routes might Islam have spread to those areas?

- According to this map, what types of activity were taking place in sub-Saharan West Africa?

- What goods were traded in sub-Saharan Africa, and along what routes did those exchanges take place?

Map legend:
- Pilgrimage route of Mansa Musa
- Trans-Saharan trade routes
- Maritime trade routes
- State nucleus and sphere of influence
- Islamic areas
- Spread of Islam
- Gold deposits
- Copper deposits
- Salt
- Ivory
- Slaves

Under the Mali Empire, commerce was in full swing. With Mande trade routes extending to the Atlantic Ocean and spanning the Sahara Desert, West Africa was no longer an isolated periphery of the central Muslim lands. The Mali king Mansa Musa (r. 1312–1332) made a celebrated hajj, or pilgrimage to Mecca, in 1324–1325, traveling through Cairo and impressing crowds with the size of his retinue—including soldiers, wives, consorts, and as many as 12,000 slaves—and his displays of wealth, especially many dazzling items made of gold. Mansa Musa's stopover in Cairo, one of Islam's primary cities,

West African Asante Gold This picture from the 1375 Catalan Atlas shows Mansa Musa, the king of Mali, on his throne, surrounded by images of gold. When Mansa Musa traveled on pilgrimage to Mecca (1324–1325), his entourage included soldiers, wives, consorts, and as many as 12,000 slaves, many wearing rich brocades woven of Persian silk. His caravan brought immense quantities of gold—nearly 100 camels each bearing 300-pound sacks of gold—and Mansa Musa distributed it lavishly. Preceding his retinue as it crossed the desert were 500 slaves, each carrying a golden staff.

astonished the Egyptian elite and awakened much of the world to the fact that Islam had spread far below the Sahara and that a sub-Saharan state could mount such an impressive display of power and wealth.

The Mali Empire boasted two of West Africa's largest cities. Jenne, an entrepôt dating back to 200 BCE, was a vital assembly point for caravans laden with salt, gold, and slaves preparing for journeys west to the Atlantic coast and north over the Sahara. More spectacular was the city of Timbuktu; founded around 1100 as a seasonal camp for nomads, it grew in size and importance under the patronage of various Mali kings. By the fourteenth century it was a thriving commercial, intellectual, and religious center famed for its three large mosques, which are still standing.

Trade between East Africa and the Indian Ocean Africa's eastern and southern regions were also integrated into long-distance trading systems. Because of the monsoon winds, East Africa was a logical end point for much of the Indian Ocean trade. Swahili peoples living along that coast became brokers for trade from the Arabian Peninsula, the Persian Gulf territories, and the western coast of India. Merchants in the city of Kilwa on the coast of present-day Tanzania brought ivory, gold, slaves, and other items from the interior and shipped them to destinations around the Indian Ocean.

Shona-speaking peoples grew rich by mining the gold ore in the highlands between the Limpopo and Zambezi Rivers. By 1000 CE, the Shona had founded up to fifty small religious and political centers, each one erected from stone to display its power over the peasant villages surrounding it. Around 1100, one of these centers, Great Zimbabwe, stood supreme among the Shona. Built on the fortunes made from gold, its most impressive landmark was a massive elliptical building made of stones fitted so expertly that they needed no grouting.

African slaves were as valuable as African gold in shipments to Indian Ocean as well as Mediterranean markets. Although the Quran mitigated the severity of slavery, requiring Muslim slave owners to treat their slaves kindly and praising those who freed their slaves, the African slave trade flourished under Islam. Africans became slaves either taken as prisoners of war or as criminals sold into slavery as punishment. Slaves might work as soldiers, seafarers on dhows, domestic servants, or plantation workers. Conditions for plantation laborers on the agricultural estates of lower Iraq were so oppressive that they led, in the ninth century CE, to one of the largest slave wars documented in world history (the Zanj rebellion). Yet in this era, plantation slave labor, like that which later became prominent in the Americas in the nineteenth century, was the exception, not the rule.

THE AMERICAS

During this period, the Americas were untouched by the connections reverberating across Afro-Eurasia. Apart from limited Viking contacts in North America (see Chapter 9), navigators still did not cross the large oceans that separated the Americas from other lands. Yet, here, too, commercial and expansionist impulses fostered closer contact among peoples who lived there.

Andean States of South America Growth and prosperity in the Andean region gave rise to South America's first empire. The **Chimú Empire** developed early in the second millennium in the fertile Moche Valley bordering the Pacific Ocean. (See Map 10.9.) Ultimately the Moche people expanded their influence across numerous valleys and ecological zones, from pastoral highlands to rich valley floodplains to the fecund fishing grounds of the Pacific coast. As their geographic reach grew, so did their wealth.

The Chimú economy was successful because it was highly commercialized. Agriculture was its base, and complex irrigation systems turned the arid coast into a string of fertile oases capable of feeding an increasingly dispersed population. Cotton became a lucrative export to distant markets along the Andes. Parades of llamas and porters lugged these commodities up and down the steep mountain chains that form the spine of South America. A well-trained bureaucracy oversaw the construction and maintenance of canals, and a hierarchy of provincial administrators watched over commercial hinterlands.

The Chimú Empire's biggest city, Chan Chan, held a core population of 30,000 inhabitants. A sprawling walled metropolis covering nearly 10 square miles, with extensive roads circulating through its neighborhoods, Chan Chan boasted ten huge palaces at its center. Protected by thick walls 30 feet high, these opulent residence halls symbolized the rulers' power. Within the compound, emperors erected burial complexes for storing their accumulated riches: fine cloth, gold and silver objects, splendid *Spondylus* shells, and other luxury goods. Around the compound spread neighborhoods for nobles and artisans; farther out stood rows of commoners' houses. The Chimú regime, centered at Chan Chan, lasted until Incan armies invaded in the 1460s and incorporated the Pacific state into their own immense empire.

Toltecs in Mesoamerica Additional hubs of regional trade developed farther north. By 1000 CE, Mesoamerica had seen the rise and fall of several complex societies, including Teotihuacán and the Maya (see Chapter 8). Caravans of porters bound the region together, working the intricate roads that connected the coast of the Gulf of Mexico to the Pacific and the southern lowlands of

Chimú Empire
South America's first empire, centered at Chan Chan, in the Moche Valley on the Pacific coast from 1000 through 1470 CE, whose development was fueled by agriculture and commercial exchange.

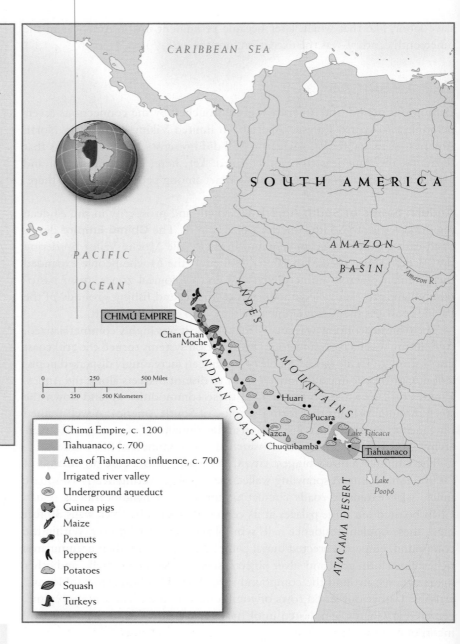

Map 10.9 Andean States, c. 700–1400 CE

Although the Andes region of South America was isolated from Afro-Eurasian developments before 1500, it was not stagnant. Indeed, political and cultural integration brought the peoples of this region closer together.

- Where are the areas of Chimú Empire and Tiahuanaco influence on the map?

- What was the ecology and geography of each region, and how might that have shaped each region's development?

- What crops and animals did the Chimú and Tiahuanaco benefit from?

CARIBBEAN SEA

SOUTH AMERICA

PACIFIC OCEAN

AMAZON BASIN

Amazon R.

ANDES

CHIMÚ EMPIRE

Chan Chan
Moche

ANDEAN COAST

MOUNTAINS

Huari

Pucara

Nazca
Chuquibamba

Lake Titicaca

Tiahuanaco

Lake Poopó

ATACAMA DESERT

0   250   500 Miles
0   250   500 Kilometers

Chimú Empire, c. 1200
Tiahuanaco, c. 700
Area of Tiahuanaco influence, c. 700
Irrigated river valley
Underground aqueduct
Guinea pigs
Maize
Peanuts
Peppers
Potatoes
Squash
Turkeys

Toltecs
Mesoamerican peoples who filled the political vacuum left by Teotihuacán's decline; established a temple-filled capital and commercial hub at Tula.

Central America to the arid regions of modern Texas. (See Map 10.10.) The **Toltecs** filled the political vacuum left by the decline of Teotihuacán and tapped into the commercial network radiating from the rich valley of central Mexico.

The Toltecs were a combination of migrant groups, farmers from the north and refugees from the south fleeing the strife that followed Teotihuacán's

Chan Chan The image shows some of the remains of Chan Chan. The city covered 15 square miles and was divided into neighborhoods for nobles, artisans, and commoners, with the elites living closest to the hub of governmental and spiritual power.

demise. These migrants settled northwest of Teotihuacán as the city waned, making their capital at Tula. They relied on a maize-based economy supplemented by beans, squash, and dog, deer, and rabbit meat. Their rulers made sure that enterprising merchants provided them with status goods such as ornamental pottery, rare shells and stones, and precious skins and feathers.

Tula was a commercial hub, a political capital, and a ceremonial center. While its layout differed from Teotihuacán's, many features revealed borrowings from other Mesoamerican peoples. Temples consisted of giant pyramids topped by colossal stone soldiers, and ball courts where subjects and conquered peoples alike played their ritual sport were found everywhere. The architecture and monumental art reflected the mixed and migratory origins of the Toltecs in a combination of Maya and Teotihuacáno influences. At its height, the Toltec capital teemed with 60,000 people, a huge metropolis by contemporary European standards (if small by Song Chinese and Abbasid standards).

Cahokians in North America As in South America and Mesoamerica, cities took shape at the hubs of trading networks across North America. The largest was **Cahokia**, along the Mississippi River near modern-day East St. Louis. A city of about 15,000, it approximated the size of London at the time. Farmers and hunters had settled in the region around 600 CE, attracted by its rich soil, its woodlands that provided fuel and game, and its access to trade via the Mississippi. Eventually, fields of maize and other crops fanned out toward the horizon. The hoe replaced the trusty digging stick, and satellite towns erected granaries to hold the growing harvests.

Cahokia
Commercial city on the Mississippi for regional and long-distance trade of commodities such as salt, shells, and skins and of manufactured goods such as pottery, textiles, and jewelry; marked by massive artificial hills, akin to earthen pyramids, used to honor spiritual forces.

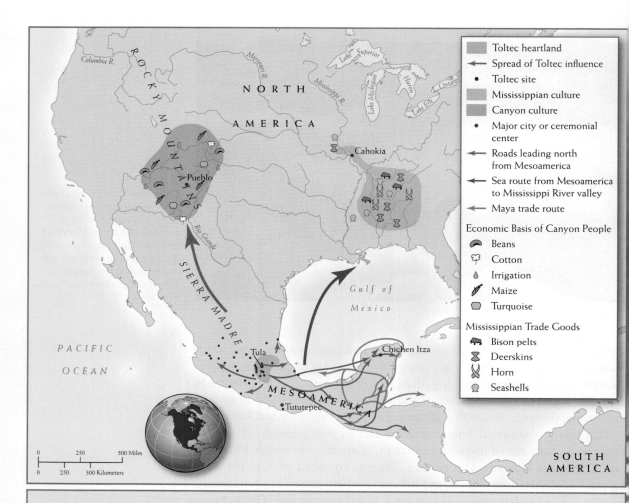

Map 10.10 Commercial Hubs in Mesoamerica and North America, 1000 CE

Both Cahokia and Tula were commercial hubs of vibrant regional trade networks.

- What routes linked Tula and the Toltecs with other regions?
- What goods circulated in the regions of Pueblo and Cahokia?
- Based on the map, what appear to be some of the differences between Canyon culture, Mississippian culture, and the Toltecs?

Cahokia became a commercial center for regional and long-distance trade. The hinterlands produced staples for Cahokia's urban consumers, and in return its crafts rode inland on the backs of porters and to distant markets in canoes. Woven fabrics and ceramics from Cahokia were exchanged for mica from the Appalachian Mountains, seashells and sharks' teeth from the Gulf of Mexico, and copper from the upper Great Lakes. Cahokia became more than an importer and exporter: it was the exchange hub for an entire regional network trading in salt, tools, pottery, woven stuffs, jewelry, and ceremonial goods.

Dominating Cahokia's urban landscape were enormous earthen mounds of sand and clay (thus the Cahokians' nickname of "mound people"). It was from these artificial hills that the people honored spiritual forces. Building these types of structures without draft animals, hydraulic tools, or even wheels was labor-intensive, so the Cahokians recruited neighboring people to help. A palisade around the city protected the metropolis from marauders.

Toltec Temple Tula, the capital of the Toltec Empire, carried on the Mesoamerican tradition of locating ceremonial architecture at the center of the city. The Pyramid of the Morning Star cast its shadow over all other buildings. And above them stood columns of the Atlantes, carved Toltec god-warriors, the figurative pillars of the empire itself. The walls of this pyramid were likely embellished with images of snakes and skulls. The north face of the pyramid has the image of a snake devouring a human.

Ultimately Cahokia's success bred its downfall. As woodlands fell to the axe and the soil lost its nutrients, timber and food became scarce. In contrast to the sturdy dhows of the Arabian Sea and the bulky junks of the China Sea, Cahokia's river canoes could carry only limited cargoes. Cahokia's commercial networks met their limits. When the creeks that fed its water system could not keep up with demand, engineers changed their course, but to no avail. By 1350 the city was practically empty. But Cahokia represented the growing networks of trade and migration in North America and the ability of North Americans to organize vibrant commercial societies.

Two forces contributed to greater integration in sub-Saharan Africa and the Americas from 1000 to 1300 CE: commercial exchange (of salt, gold, ivory, and slaves in sub-Saharan Africa and shells, pottery, textiles, and metals in the Americas) and urbanization (at Jenne, Timbuktu, and Great Zimbabwe in sub-Saharan Africa and at Chan Chan, Tula, and Cahokia in the Americas). By 1300, trans-Saharan and Indian Ocean exchange had brought Africa into full-fledged Afro-Eurasian networks of exchange and, as we will see in Chapter 12, transatlantic exchange would soon bring the Americas into a global network.

The Mongol Transformation of Afro-Eurasia

Commercial networks were clearly one way to integrate the world. But just as long-distance trade could connect people, so could conquerors. The Inner Eurasian steppes had already unleashed horse-riding warriors such as the Kushans and Xiongnu (see Chapters 6 and 7). Now, the Mongols created an empire that straddled east and west, expanding their reach not only through brutal conquest but also through intensified trade and cultural exchange. (See Map 10.11.)

Core Objectives

ASSESS the impacts that the Mongol Empire had on Afro-Eurasian peoples and places.

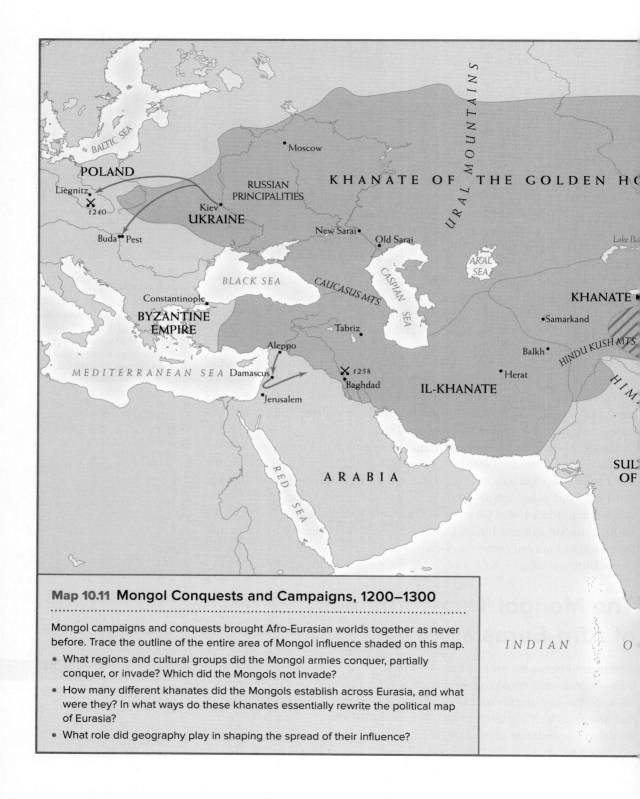

Map 10.11 Mongol Conquests and Campaigns, 1200–1300

Mongol campaigns and conquests brought Afro-Eurasian worlds together as never before. Trace the outline of the entire area of Mongol influence shaded on this map.

- What regions and cultural groups did the Mongol armies conquer, partially conquer, or invade? Which did the Mongols not invade?
- How many different khanates did the Mongols establish across Eurasia, and what were they? In what ways do these khanates essentially rewrite the political map of Eurasia?
- What role did geography play in shaping the spread of their influence?

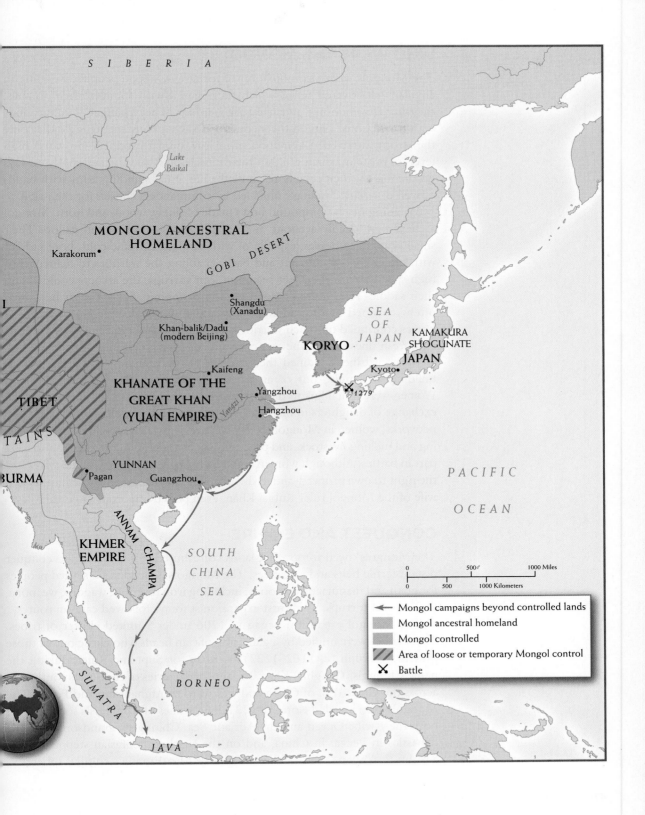

WHO WERE THE MONGOLS?

The Mongols were a combination of forest and steppe peoples. Residing in circular, felt-covered tents, which they shared with some of their animals, they lived by hunting and livestock herding. They changed campgrounds with the seasons. Life on the steppes was such a constant struggle that only the strong survived. Their food, primarily animal products, provided high levels of protein, which built up their muscle mass and their strength. Always on the march, their society resembled a perpetual standing army with bands of well-disciplined military units led by commanders chosen for their skill.

Wielding heavy compound bows made of sinew, wood, and horn, Mongol archers were deadly accurate at over 200 yards—even at full gallop. Their small but sturdy horses, capable of withstanding extreme cold, bore saddles with high supports in front and back, enabling the warriors to maneuver at high speeds. With their feet secure in iron stirrups, the archers could rise in their saddles to aim their arrows without stopping. These expert horsemen often remained in the saddle all day and night, even sleeping while their horses continued on. Each warrior kept many horses, replacing tired mounts with fresh ones so that the armies could cover up to 70 miles per day.

Mongol tribes solidified their conquests by extending kinship networks, building an empire out of an expanding confederation of familial tribes. Women were a vital link in those networks. Households sealed alliances by the exchange of daughters in marriage. In addition to their role in linking kinship networks, women in Mongol society were responsible for child-rearing, shearing and milking livestock, and processing pelts for clothing. But they also took part in battles. Although women could be bought and sold, Mongol wives had the right to own property and to divorce. Elite women, such as the mother and wife of the Mongol ruler Kublai Khan, even played important political roles.

CONQUEST AND EMPIRE

The Mongols' need for grazing lands contributed to their desire to conquer distant fertile belts and rich cities. The Mongols depended on settled peoples for grain and manufactured goods, including iron for tools, wagons, weapons, bridles, and stirrups. Their first expansionist forays followed caravan routes.

The Mongol expansion began in 1206 under a united cluster of tribes. These tribes were unified by a gathering of clan heads who chose one of those present, Temüjin (c. 1162–1227), as Khan, or Supreme Ruler. Taking the name Chinggis (Genghis) Khan, he launched a series of conquests southward across the Great Wall of China and westward to Afghanistan and Persia. The Mongols even invaded Korea in 1231. The armies of Chinggis's sons reached both the Pacific Ocean and the Adriatic Sea. Chinggis's grandsons founded dynasties in Persia, in China, and on the southern Eurasian steppes. Thus, a realm took shape that touched all four of Afro-Eurasia's cultural spheres.

Mongols in Abbasid Baghdad In the thirteenth century, Mongol tribes were streaming out of the steppes, crossing the whole of Asia and entering the eastern parts of Europe. Mongke Khan, a grandson of Chinggis, made clear the Mongol aspiration to world domination: he commanded his brother, Hulagu, to conquer Iran, Syria, Egypt, Byzantium, and Armenia, and he appointed another brother, Kublai, to rule over China, Tibet, and the northern parts of India.

When Hulagu reached Abbasid Baghdad in 1258, he encountered a feeble foe and a city that was a shadow of its former glorious self. Merely 10,000 horsemen faced his army of 200,000 soldiers, who were eager to acquire the booty of a wealthy city. Even before the battle had taken place, Baghdadi poets were composing elegies for their dead and mourning the defeat of Islam. The slaughter was vast. Hulagu himself boasted of taking the lives of at least 200,000 people. The Mongols hunted their adversaries in wells, latrines, and sewers and followed them into the upper floors of buildings, killing them on rooftops until, as an Iraqi Arab historian observed, "blood poured from the gutters into the streets. . . . The same happened in the mosques." In a few weeks of sheer terror, the Abbasid caliphate was demolished. Hulagu's forces showed no mercy to the caliph himself, who was rolled up in a carpet and trampled to death by horses. With Baghdad crushed, the Mongol armies pushed on to Syria, slaughtering Muslims along the way.

Mongols in China In the east, Mongol forces under Chinggis Khan had entered northern China at the beginning of the thirteenth century, defeating the Khitai army, which was no match for the Mongols' superior cavalry on the North China plain. Despite some serious setbacks due to the climate (including malaria for the men and the deaths of horses from the heat), Chinggis's grandson Kublai Khan (1215–1294) seized southern China from the Song dynasty beginning in the 1260s. The Song army fell before Mongol warriors brandishing the latest gunpowder-based weapons, technology the Mongols had borrowed from Chinese inventors and now used against them.

Hangzhou, the last Song capital, fell in 1276. Kublai Khan's most able commander, Bayan, led his crack Mongol forces in seizing town after town, moving ever closer to the capital, while the Dowager Empress tried to buy them off, proposing substantial tribute payments, but Bayan was uncompromising. Once conquered, the Dowager Empress and Hangzhou were treated well by the Mongols. In fact, Hangzhou was still one of the greatest cities in the world when it was visited by the Venetian traveler Marco Polo in the 1280s and by the Muslim traveler Ibn Battuta in the 1340s. Both men agreed that neither Europe nor the Islamic world had anything like it.

Kublai Khan founded his Yuan dynasty with a capital at Khan-balik (also called Dadu, which became present-day Beijing). The Mongol conquest of both north and south changed China's political and social landscape. But Mongol rule did

A Most Unusual Nomad State

Although nomadic pastoralists and sedentary agriculturalists depended on each other to flourish, their deep commitments to their institutions and ways of life made cooperation difficult. Pastoralists endeavored to be as self-sufficient as possible. They scorned peoples who dug in the soil. On the other hand, as we noted in Chapter 3, sedentary peoples, most notably their literate members, regarded herders as uncivilized barbarians. The Chinese, for instance, saw the steppe peoples who lived to the north of them, and who often invaded their state, as occupying the "inhospitable land of the barbarian" and its people as "avaricious and violent marauders."

The Mongols were the quintessential pastoral nomads. Very little is known of their early history, largely because they were a small, fragmented, and powerless people living along the borderlands of southern Siberia, eastern Mongolia, and northwestern Manchuria. To their east lived the Tatars, and to their west the Uighurs and Khitai, far more powerful pastoral peoples from whom the Mongols learned many of their political and military skills. The Mongols first surface in Chinese sources during the Tang dynasty (618–907 CE). The Chinese, who feared the military capabilities of steppe peoples and were regularly invaded and even conquered by those peoples, had little fear of the Mongols at this time, regarding them as an insignificant community far from the empire's northern frontier. The Mongols were well known, however, for raiding, looting, and violence toward outsiders and among themselves.

Few individuals have had a greater impact on world history than the founder of the Mongol state, Temüjin (c. 1162–1227). His youthful travails hardened him as a warrior and made him a leader. Having lost his father at a young age and being the eldest of his siblings, he, along with his mother, endured a harsh existence. But as an adult, he unified warring Mongol clans and defeated the Mongols' enemies, either assimilating them to the Mongol way of life or exterminating them if they refused his leadership. In 1206, as a result of his spectacular military successes, he took the name Chinggis Khan, meaning Supreme Ruler. Not only did he bring most of Inner Asia under his rule, but his armies pushed southward into Manchuria and northern China and west toward central Asia and the Islamic states. At his death in 1227, he divided his vast territorial conquests among the four sons of his first wife, Borte. These men and their successors created four Mongol states, called khanates, loosely linked as an empire: Yuan China; the Khanate of the Golden Horde; the northern steppe (Khanate of the Chagatai); and Persia, known as the Il-Khanate.

The Mongols established their rule over settled societies in China, Iran, central Asia, and Russia, but then had to decide how to rule over sedentary populations. Specifically, the issue facing Mongol rulers was whether to foster close relations with the ruling classes of the conquered societies or stay apart, relying on military force. In truth, the Mongol empire fragmented and each state was ruled in manifestly different ways. Yet one quality underlay all of the Mongol states—the dominant presence of the Mongol military and the high prestige that attached to being a Mongol. Commonly, pastoral nomads who conquered sedentary peoples kept their distance from those settled societies with their cities, bureaucracies, artisans, and priests, instead extracting tribute

not impose rough steppe-land ways on the "civilized" urbanite Chinese. While non-Chinese outsiders took political control, they were a conquering elite that ruled over a vast Han majority. The result was a divided ruling system in which incumbent Chinese elites governed locally, while the newcomers managed the unifying central dynasty and collected taxes for the Mongols.

Southeast Asia also felt the whiplash of Kublai Khan's conquest. Circling Song defenses in southern China, the Mongols galloped southwest and conquered from them while maintaining their own distinctive way of life. For example, Chinggis forbade his followers to live in towns, and the Golden Horde Mongols lived separate from the peoples they conquered, maintaining their pastoral norms, content to receive tribute payments.

Early on, some of Chinggis's followers wanted to annihilate the northern Chinese population and turn the region into pure pastureland. Ogodei, Chinggis's third son and successor as the Great Khan, was opposed to Chinggis's merciless and destructive practices and ordered that "no peaceable inhabitants of the country be killed and forbade arbitrary pillage." One of Ogodei's successors, Kublai, became the founder of the Yuan dynasty in China, claiming for himself the Chinese mandate of heaven. Even so, Kublai cherished his Mongol identity, never learned Chinese, never consulted a book in Chinese, and "never identified with the values of the Chinese cultural legacy other than to recognize

the utility of systemic and reasoned explanation in the Chinese pattern." Moreover, the Yuan rulers divided the populations under their rule into four ranked tiers: the first of which were the Mongols themselves; the second, the non-Han Chinese of the western parts of Inner Asia, mainly nomads like themselves; the third, the northern Chinese, conquered early in the Mongol expansion; and the fourth, the southern Chinese, once the domain of the Song dynasty and the center of Confucian culture. In such a fashion, the Yuan dynasty, although centered in China proper—the heartland of urbanization and high culture—did not allow itself to be swallowed up by the Han population or its culture.

Thus, the Mongol empire, which lasted for more than two centuries, made an uneasy accommodation with sedentary populations, with its rulers partially embracing the institutions of the sedentary peoples, but never fully renouncing their pastoral, nomadic ways.

Questions for Analysis

- How did nomads and sedentary peoples view one another?
- Why might one consider the Mongols in general, and Temüjin in particular, to be unlikely conquerors?
- In what ways did different Mongol leaders negotiate the difference between pastoral and sedentary ways?

Explore Further

Di Cosmo, Nicola, Allen J. Frank, and Peter Golden (eds.), *The Cambridge History of Inner Asia: The Chinggisid Age* (2009).

Khazanov, Anatoly M., *Nomads and the Outside World*, 2nd ed., trans. Julia Crookurden, with a foreword by Ernest Gellner (1994).

Mote, Frederick W., *Imperial China, 900–1800* (1999).

Rossabi, Morris, *A History of China* (2014).

Tanner, Harold M., *China: A History* (2009).

Sources: Nicola Di Cosmo, Allen J. Frank, and Peter Golden (eds.), *The Cambridge History of Inner Asia: The Chinggisid Age* (New York: Cambridge University Press, 2009), p. 9; Anatoly M. Khazanov, *Nomads and the Outside World*, 2nd ed., trans. Julia Crookurden, with a foreword by Ernest Gellner (Madison: University of Wisconsin Press, 1994), p. 245; Frederick W. Mote, *Imperial China, 900–1800* (Cambridge, MA: Harvard University Press, 1999), p. 451.

states in Yunnan and in Burma. From there, in the 1270s, the armies headed directly back east into the soft underbelly of the Song state. In this sweep, portions of mainland Southeast Asia became annexed to China for the first time. Kublai Khan used the conquered Chinese fleets to push his expansionism onto the high seas—meeting with failure during his unsuccessful 1274 and 1281 invasions of Japan from Korea. An ill-fated Javanese expedition to extend Mongol reach beyond the South China Sea in 1293 was Kublai Khan's last.

Mongol Warriors This miniature painting is one of the illustrations for *History* by Rashid al Din, the most outstanding scholar under the Mongol regimes. Note the relatively small horses and strong bows used by the Mongol soldiers.

In the end, the Mongol Empire reached its outer limits. In the west, the Egyptian Mamluks stemmed the advancing Mongol armies and prevented Egypt from falling into their hands. In the east, the waters of the South China Sea and the Sea of Japan foiled Mongol expansion into Java and Japan. Better at conquering than governing, the Mongols struggled to rule their vast possessions in makeshift states. Bit by bit, they yielded control to local administrators and rulers who governed as their surrogates. There was also frequent feuding among the Mongol rulers themselves. In China and in Persia, Mongol rule collapsed in the fourteenth century. Ultimately, the Mongols would meet a deadly adversary even more brutal than they were: the plague of the fourteenth century (see Chapter 11).

Mongol conquest reshaped Afro-Eurasia's social landscape. Islam would never again have a unifying authority like the caliphate or a powerful center like Baghdad. China, too, was divided and changed by the Mongols' introduction of Persian, Islamic, and Byzantine influences into China's architecture, art, science, and medicine. The Yuan policy of benign tolerance brought elements from Christianity, Judaism, Zoroastrianism, and Islam into the Chinese mix. The Mongol thrust also facilitated the flow of fine goods, traders, and technology from China to the rest of the world. Finally, the Mongol conquests encouraged an unprecedented Afro-Eurasian interconnectedness, surpassing even the Hellenistic connections that Alexander's conquests had brought in the late fourth century BCE (see Chapter 6). Out of Mongol conquest and warfare would come centuries of trade, migration, and increasing contacts among Africa, Europe, and Asia.

Conclusion

Between 1000 and 1300 CE, Afro-Eurasia was forming large cultural spheres. As trade and migration spanned longer distances, these spheres prospered and became more integrated. In central Afro-Eurasia, Islam was firmly established, and its merchants, scholars, and travelers acted as commercial and cultural intermediaries joining the landmass together as they spread their universalizing faith. As seaborne trade expanded, India, too, became a commercial crossroads. Merchants in its port cities welcomed traders arriving from Arab lands to the west, from China, and from Southeast Asia. China also boomed, pouring its manufactures into trading networks that reached throughout Eurasia and even into Africa. Christian Europe had two centers—at Rome and at Constantinople—both of which were at war with Islam.

Neither sub-Saharan Africa nor the Americas saw the same degree of integration, but trade and migration in these areas had profound effects. Certain African cultures flourished as they encountered the commercial energy of trade on the Indian Ocean. Africans' trade with one another linked coastal and interior regions in an ever more integrated world. American peoples also built cities that dominated cultural areas and thrived through trade. American cultures shared significant features: reliance on trade, maize, and the exchange of goods such as shells and precious feathers. And larger areas honored the same spiritual centers.

By 1300, trade, migration, and conflict were connecting Afro-Eurasian worlds in unprecedented ways. When Mongol armies swept into China, into Southeast Asia, and into the heart of Islam, they applied a thin coating of political integration to these widespread regions and built on existing trade links. At the same time, most people's lives remained quite localized, driven by the need for subsistence and governed by spiritual and governmental representatives acting at the behest of distant authorities.

Still, locals noticed the evidence of cross-cultural exchanges everywhere—in the clothing styles of provincial elites, such as Chinese silks in Paris or quetzal plumes in northern Mexico; in enticements to move (and forced removals) to new frontiers; in the news of faraway conquests or advancing armies. Worlds were coming together within themselves and across territorial boundaries, while remaining apart as they sought to maintain their own identities and traditions. In Afro-Eurasia especially, as the movement of goods and peoples shifted from ancient land routes to sea-lanes, these contacts were more frequent and far-reaching. Never before had the world seen so much activity connecting its parts, nor had there ever been so much cultural similarity within those parts. By the time the Mongol Empire arose, the regions composing the globe were those that we now recognize as the cultural spheres of today's world.

Focus On
Foundational Cultural Spheres

The Islamic World

- The Islamic world undergoes a burst of expansion, prosperity, and cultural diversification but remains politically fractured.

- Arab merchants and Sufi mystics spread Islam over great distances and make it more appealing to other cultures, helping to transform Islam into a distinct cultural sphere.

- Islam travels across the Sahara Desert; the powerful gold- and slave-supplying empire of Mali arises in West Africa.

China

- The Song dynasty reunites China after three centuries of fragmented rulership, reaching into the past to re-establish a sense of a "true" Chinese identity as the Han through a widespread print culture and denigration of outsiders.

- Agrarian success and advances in manufacturing—including the production of both iron and porcelain—fuel an expanding economy, complete with paper money.

India

- India remains a mosaic under the canopy of Hindu-ism despite cultural interconnections and increasing prosperity.

- The invasion of Turkish Muslims leads to the Delhi Sultanate, which rules over India for three centuries, strengthening cultural diversity and tolerance.

Christian Europe

- Roman Catholicism becomes a "mass" faith and helps to create a common European cultural identity.

- Feudalism organizes the elite-peasant relationship, while manorialism forms the basis of the economy.

- Europe's growing confidence is manifest in its efforts, including the Crusades and the reconquering of Iberia, to drive Islam out of "Christian" lands.

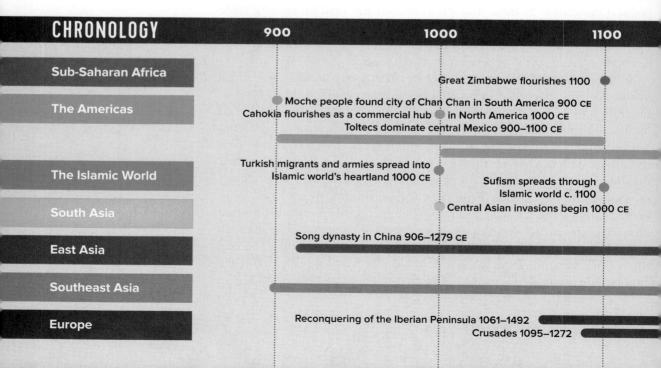

CHRONOLOGY

	900	1000	1100
Sub-Saharan Africa			Great Zimbabwe flourishes 1100
The Americas	Moche people found city of Chan Chan in South America 900 CE		
	Cahokia flourishes as a commercial hub in North America 1000 CE		
	Toltecs dominate central Mexico 900–1100 CE		
The Islamic World	Turkish migrants and armies spread into Islamic world's heartland 1000 CE	Sufism spreads through Islamic world c. 1100	
South Asia		Central Asian invasions begin 1000 CE	
East Asia	Song dynasty in China 906–1279 CE		
Southeast Asia			
Europe	Reconquering of the Iberian Peninsula 1061–1492		
		Crusades 1095–1272	

THINKING ABOUT GLOBAL CONNECTIONS

- **Thinking about *Worlds Together, Worlds Apart*** From 1000 to 1300 CE, a range of social and political developments contributed to the consolidation of four cultural spheres that still exist today: Europe, the Islamic world, India, and China. In what ways did these spheres interact with one another? In what ways was each sphere genuinely distinct from the others? To what extent were sub-Saharan Africa and the Americas folded into these spheres and with what result?

- **Thinking about Transformation & Conflict and Becoming the World** As the four cultural spheres of Afro-Eurasia consolidated, shocking examples of conflict between them began to take place. Whether Pope Urban II's call in 1095 to reclaim the "holy land" from Muslims or the Mongol Hulagu's brutal sack of Baghdad in 1258, this period was marked by large-scale

warfare between rival cultural spheres. To what extent was such conflict inevitable? In what ways did conflict transform the groups involved?

- **Thinking about Crossing Borders and Becoming the World** Major innovations facilitated economic exchange in the Indian Ocean and in Song China. The magnetic needle compass, better ships, and improved maps shrank the Indian Ocean to the benefit of traders. Similarly, paper money in Song China changed the nature of commerce. How did these developments shift the axis of Afro-Eurasian exchange? What evidence suggests that bodies of water and the routes across them became more significant than overland exchange routes in binding together Afro-Eurasia? What might be the longer-term implications of these developments?

Key Terms

Cahokia p. 473	entrepôts p. 446	Mali Empire p. 468	Sufism p. 450
Chimú Empire p. 471	flying cash p. 459	manorialism p. 463	Toltecs p. 472
Delhi Sultanate p. 454	*jizya* p. 449		

 Go to **INQUIZITIVE** to see what you've learned—and learn what you've missed—with personalized feedback along the way.

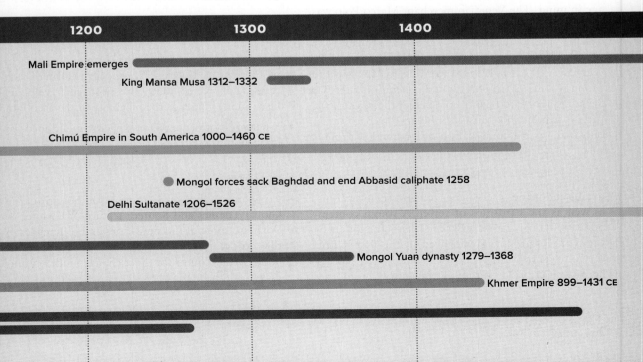

1200   **1300**   **1400**

Mali Empire emerges

King Mansa Musa 1312–1332

Chimú Empire in South America 1000–1460 CE

Mongol forces sack Baghdad and end Abbasid caliphate 1258

Delhi Sultanate 1206–1526

Mongol Yuan dynasty 1279–1368

Khmer Empire 899–1431 CE

Global Themes and Sources

Comparing "World" Travelers Over Time

The maritime revolution described in this chapter, along with the Silk Roads across Inner Eurasia, facilitated travel for trade, diplomacy, and religious pilgrimage on a scale previously unseen. While earlier travelers, like the Spanish nun Egeria or the Buddhist monks Faxian and Xuanzang, had covered great distances and for reasons similar to those of some of the travelers whose accounts you'll read here, the sheer distances traveled by Bar Sāwmā or Ibn Battuta eclipse the journeys of their centuries-earlier counterparts. Like the earlier pilgrims, however, several travelers who moved between the worlds of Afro-Eurasia in this period left records of their stunning journeys or were written about by others.

As we saw at the start of this chapter, Bar Sāwmā traveled primarily along land routes from Yuan dynasty China all the way to modern-day France in the late thirteenth century. A Nestorian Christian monk, Bar Sāwmā appears to have made his journeys, which were recorded in a Syriac text shortly after his death in 1294, with both diplomacy and religious pilgrimage in mind. The Venetian merchant Marco Polo was traveling at nearly the same time as Bar Sāwmā, but in the opposite direction. Long after his travels were completed, Marco Polo recounted his twenty-four year voyage (1271–1295), including his time in the Mongol court of China. About a generation after Bar Sāwmā and Marco Polo completed their journeys, the North African Muslim scholar Ibn Battuta set out to traverse a combination of land and sea routes through much of Africa, Southwest Asia, Southeast Asia, and East Asia between 1325 and 1354. Writing after his travels were completed, Ibn Battuta offered details about the places he visited and their customs, as well as the hardships of travel. A rough contemporary of Ibn Battuta, a Syrian Islamic historian by the name of al-Umari who lived in the first half of the fourteenth century, provides the fourth passage here, a description of the pilgrimage of yet another

famous traveler, Mansa Musa, King of Mali, in 1324–1325. The final "world" traveler represented here is the Chinese naval commander Zheng He, whose voyages came later (1405–1433; see Chapter 11) but can be usefully compared with those of Bar Sāwmā, Marco Polo, Ibn Battuta, and Mansa Musa. In a series of expeditions, Zheng He's fleet sailed from China through Southeast Asia, to Sri Lanka, into the northern Indian Ocean, and even to the Persian Gulf and the Red Sea, leaving stone inscriptions at many of the sites he visited.

The records of these travelers—Bar Sāwmā, Marco Polo, Ibn Battuta, Mansa Musa, and Zheng He—allow us to study the realities of pilgrimage and exploration in this period, but also to analyze how they are similar and how they change over time. Together with what you've learned in this chapter about the political situations across Afro-Eurasia, you can begin to explain the similarities and differences in patterns of "world" travel over hundreds of years and to think about the historical significance of those journeys.

Analyzing Comparisons of World Travelers

- Based on these excerpts, what sorts of details seem to interest each traveler? How does the form of each text (life of revered holy figure, post-trip travelogue, inscription) influence the reliability of the account?

- What sorts of dangers are explicitly mentioned, or implied, in these texts?

- What in the texts suggests the exchange of goods and ideas?

- Compare these travel accounts with those from the Global Themes and Sources feature of Chapter 8. What are some of the similarities and differences in the "world" travels of these two groups of individuals? What accounts for those changes and continuities over time?

Pilgrimage to Jerusalem (c. 1300), Bar Sāwmā

This passage illustrates the realities of travel for Bar Sāwmā and his travel companion Markōs in the late thirteenth century. Setting out from the Mongol capital Khan-balik, they enter the territory of Mar Denha (or Mar Catholicus), the Patriarch of the Nestorian Church, who, after greeting them warmly, sends them on their way to visit holy sites. Just in this one passage, we can see the territory these pilgrims covered, starting in Khan-balik, arriving at Maraghah (in the territory of modern Azerbaijan), continuing on to Baghdad, and then into Armenia and Georgia. Many of the interactions and travel issues they describe resonate with those of the Spanish nun Egeria. (Titles of sites have been capitalized, as in the original translation.)

....

- What are some of the practical travel issues Bar Sāwmā and his travel companion face?

- How do Bar Sāwmā and his companion interact with people and places on their travels?

- How do those travel issues and interactions compare with those of the Spanish nun Egeria, 900 years earlier?

....

And having enjoyed the conversation of those brethren they set out to go to ADHÔRBÎJÂN . . . so that they might travel from there to BAGHDÂD, to MÂR DENHÂ, the Catholicus. . . . Now it happened that Mâr Catholicus had come to MÂRÂGHÂH [a town of ADHÔRBÎJÂN, the capital of HÛLÂGÛ KHÂN], and they met him there. And at the sight of him their joy grew great, and their gladness was increased. . . . And when [Mar Catholicus] asked them, "Whence [come] ye?" they replied, "From the countries of the East, from KHÂN BÂLÎK, the city of the King of Kings [KÛBLÂI] KHÂN. We have come to be blessed by you, and by the Fathers (i.e. Bishops), and the monks, and the holy men of this quarter of the world. And if a road [openeth] to us, and God hath mercy upon us, we shall go to JERUSALEM."

. . . [Catholicus] comforted them and said unto them, "Assuredly, O my sons, the Angel of Providence shall protect you on this difficult journey, and he shall be a guide unto you until the completion of your quest." . . .

[After a few days, Bar Sāwmā and his companion] request [of Mar Catholicus]: "If we have found mercy (i.e. favour) in the eyes of Mâr our Father, let him permit us to go to BAGHDÂD, in order that we may receive a blessing from the holy sepulchers (or relics?) of MÂR MÂRÊ, . . . the Apostle, the teacher of the East, and those of the Fathers that are there. And from there we would go to the monasteries that are in the country of BÊTH GARMAI and in NISIBIS that we may be blessed there also, and demand assistance."

And when the Catholicus saw the beauty of their object, and the innocence of their minds, and the honesty of their thoughts, he said unto them, "Go ye, my sons, and may Christ, the Lord of the Universe, grant unto you your petition." . . . And he wrote for them a *pêthîkhâ* (i.e. a letter of introduction) to these countries so that they might be honourably entreated whithersoever they went; and he sent with them a man to show them the way, and to act as a guide along the roads.

And they arrived in Baghdad, and thence they went to the Great Church of KÔKÊ [at Ctesiphon]. . . . And they went to the monastery of MÂR MÂRÎ, the Apostle, and received a blessing from the sepulchers (or relics?) of that country. And from there they turned back and came to the country of BÊTH GARMAI, and they received blessings from the shrine (or tomb) of MÂR EZEKIEL [the prophet, near Dâkôk], which was full of helps and healings. And from there they went to ARBÎL, and thence to MÂWSIL (i.e. Môsul on the Tigris). And they went [to] SHÎGAR (SINJÂR), and NISIBIS, and MERDÂ (MARDÎN); and were blessed by the shrine [containing] the bones of MÂR AWGÎN, the second CHRIST. And thence they went to GÂZARTÂ of BÊTH ZABHDAI, and they were blessed by all the shrines and monasteries, and the religious houses, and monks, and the Fathers (i.e. Bishops) in their dioceses. . . .

And when they arrived at the city of Animto [i.e. ANÎ, the ancient capital of Christian ARMENIA, situated on an affluent of the river Araxes], and saw the monasteries and the churches therein, they marvelled at the great extent of the buildings and at their magnificence. And thence they went towards BÊTH

GÛRGÂYÊ (i.e. the country of Georgia), so that they might travel by a clear (or safe?) road, but when they arrived there they heard from the inhabitants of the country that the road was cut because of the murders and robberies which had taken place along it.

Chapter 4. And the two monks turned back and came to Mâr Catholicus, who rejoiced [at the sight of] them, and said unto them, "This is not the time for a journey to JERUSALEM. The roads are a disturbed state, and the ways are cut. Now behold, ye have received blessings from all the Houses of God, and the shrines (or relics?) which are in them, and it is my opinion that when a man visits them with a pure heart, the service thus paid to them is in no way less than that of a pilgrimage to Jerusalem."

Source: Rabban Bar Sāwmā. *The Monks of Kublai Khan, Emperor of China, or The History of the Life and Travels of Rabban Sāwmā*, trans. E. A. Wallis Budge (London: Religious Tract Society, 1928), pp. 140–43, 145–46.

PRIMARY SOURCE 10.2

The Mongol Capital at Kanbalu (Khan-Balik) (c. 1300), Marco Polo

In the last quarter of the thirteenth century, the Venetian merchant Marco Polo, together with his father and uncle, undertook a magnificent trek eastward on the Silk Roads. They ultimately arrived at Khan-balik, capital of the Mongol Yuan dynasty (and the place from which Bar Sāwmā set out, in the previous passage). There, they encountered Kublai Khan. Long after his journey was completed, Marco Polo offered this thorough description of the city, which would ultimately become Beijing. While some scholars have questioned the veracity of Polo's travels, arguing that he may never have made it all the way to China, the detail offered in this passage suggests firsthand experience.

- What does Marco Polo emphasize in his description of Kanbalu (Khan-balik)?
- What different groups of people live in greater Khan-balik? How are they organized and distributed?
- Why do you think Marco Polo focuses on the issues that he describes?

The city of Kanbalu is situated near a large river in the province of Cathay, and was in ancient times eminently magnificent and royal. The name itself implies "the city of the sovereign;" but his majesty having imbibed an opinion from the astrologers, that it was destined to become rebellious to his authority, resolved upon the measure of building another capital, upon the opposite side of the river, where stand the palaces just described: so that the new and the old cities are separated from each other only by the stream that runs between them. The new-built city received the name of Tai-du, and all the Cathaians, that is, all those of the inhabitants who were natives of the province of Cathay, were compelled to evacuate the ancient city, and to take up their abode in the new. Some of the inhabitants, however, of whose loyalty he did not entertain suspicion, were suffered to remain, especially because the latter, although of the dimensions that shall presently be described, was not capable of containing the same number as the former, which was of vast extent.

This new city is of a form perfectly square, and twenty-four miles in extent, each of its sides being neither more nor less than six miles. It is enclosed with walls of earth, that at the base are about ten paces thick, but gradually diminish to the top, where the thickness is not more than three paces. In all parts the battlements are white. The whole plan of the city was regularly laid out by line, and the streets in general are consequently so straight, that when a person ascends the wall over one of the gates, and looks right forward, he can see the gate opposite to him on the other side of the city. In the public streets there are, on each side, booths and shops of every description. All the allotments of ground upon which the habitations throughout the city were constructed are square, and exactly on a line with each other; each allotment being sufficiently spacious for handsome buildings, with corresponding courts and gardens. One of these was assigned to each head of a family; that is to say, such a person of such a tribe had one square allotted to him, and so of the rest. Afterwards the property passed from hand to hand. In this manner the whole interior of the city is disposed in squares, so as to resemble a chessboard, and planned out with a degree of precision and beauty impossible to describe. The wall of the city has twelve gates, three on each side of the square, and over each gate and compartment of the wall there is a handsome building; so that on each side of the square there are five such buildings, containing large rooms, in which are disposed the arms of those who form the garrison of the city, every gate being guarded by a thousand men. It is not to be understood that such a force is stationed there in consequence of the apprehension of danger from any hostile power whatever, but as a guard suitable to the honour and dignity of the sovereign. Yet it must be allowed that the declaration of the astrologers has excited in his mind a degree of suspicion with regard to the Cathaians. . . .

Outside of each of the gates is a suburb so wide that it reaches to and unites with those of the other nearest gates on both sides, and in length extends to the distance of three or four miles, so that the number of inhabitants in these suburbs exceeds that of the city itself. Within each suburb there are, at intervals, as far perhaps as a mile from the city, many hotels, or caravanserais, in which the merchants arriving from various parts take up their abode; and to each description of people a separate building is assigned, as we should say, one to the Lombards, another to the Germans, and a third to the French. . . .

Guards, in parties of thirty or forty, continually patrol the streets during the course of the night, and make diligent search for persons who may be from their homes at an unseasonable hour, that is, after the third stroke of the great bell. When any are met with under such circumstances, they immediately apprehend and confine them, and take them in the morning for examination before officers appointed for that purpose, who, upon the proof of any delinquency, sentence them, according to the nature of the offence, to a severer or lighter infliction of the bastinade beating with a cudgel, usually on the soles of the feet, which sometimes, however, occasions their death. It is in this manner that crimes are usually punished amongst these people, from a disinclination to the shedding of blood, which their *baksis* or learned astrologers instruct them to avoid.

Source: Marco Polo, *The Travels of Marco Polo, The Venetian*, ed. Thomas Wright (London: George Bell and Sons, 1904), pp. 181–86. Notes in brackets added by the author.

The Holy Sites of Jerusalem (c. 1360), Ibn Battuta

Ibn Battuta's travels dwarf those of any other world traveler in this period. What began as a *hajj* became a journey of tens of thousands of miles. Traveling for more than a quarter century, Ibn Battuta was particularly interested in the role and practice of Islam in each place he visited. While he was sometimes called into action to serve as a learned Muslim *qadi* (judge) in the places he visited, his travels often took the form of engaged and devoted religious tourism, as when he visited Jerusalem, as described in the passage here.

- **What can you make out of Ibn Battuta's itinerary? What sites does he visit? What, and how, does he learn about the history of each site?**

- **How does Ibn Battuta describe mosques? Churches? What do you think accounts for the differences in his descriptions?**

- **How do Ibn Battuta's descriptions of holy sites compare with those in Bar Sāwmā's account?**

From Gaza I travelled to the city of Abraham [Hebron], the mosque of which is of elegant, but substantial, construction, imposing and lofty, and built of squared stones. At one angle of it there is a stone, one of whose faces measures twenty-seven spans. It is said that Solomon commanded the *jinn* to build it. Inside it is the sacred cave containing the graves of Abraham, Isaac, and Jacob, opposite which are three graves, which are those of their wives. I questioned the imám, a man of great piety and learning, on the authenticity of these graves, and he replied: "All the scholars whom I have met hold these graves to be the very graves of Abraham, Isaac, Jacob and their wives. No one questions this except introducers of false doctrines; it is a tradition which has passed from father to son for generations and admits of no doubt.". . .

On the way from Hebron to Jerusalem, I visited Bethlehem, the birthplace of Jesus. The site is covered by a large building; the Christians regard it with intense veneration and hospitably entertain all who alight at it.

We then reached Jerusalem (may God ennoble her!), third in excellence after the two holy shrines of Mecca and Medína, and the place whence the Prophet was caught up into heaven. Its walls were destroyed by the illustrious King Saladin and his successors, for fear lest the Christians should seize it and fortify themselves in it. The sacred mosque is a most beautiful building, and is said to be the largest mosque in the world. Its length from east to west is put at 752 "royal" cubits and its breadth at 435. On three sides it has many entrances, but on the south side I know of one only, which is that by which the imám enters. The entire mosque is an open court and unroofed, except the mosque al-Aqsá, which has a roof of most excellent workmanship, embellished with gold and brilliant colours. Some other parts of the mosque are roofed as well. The Dome of the Rock is a building of extraordinary beauty, solidity, elegance, and singularity of shape. It stands on an elevation in the centre of the mosque and is reached by a flight of marble steps. It has four doors. The space round it is also paved with marble, excellently done, and the interior likewise. Both outside and inside the decoration is so magnificent and the workmanship so surpassing as to defy description. The greater part is covered with gold so that the eyes of one who gazes on its beauties are dazzled by its brilliance, now glowing like a mass of light, now flashing like lightning. In the centre of the Dome is the blessed rock from which the Prophet ascended to heaven, a great rock projecting about a man's height, and underneath it there is a cave the size of a small room, also of a man's height, with steps leading down to it. Encircling the rock are two railings of excellent workmanship, the one nearer the rock being artistically constructed in iron, and the other of wood.

Among the grace-bestowing sanctuaries of Jerusalem is a building, situated on the farther side of the valley called the valley of Jahannam [Gehenna] to the east of the town, on a high hill. This building is said to mark the place whence Jesus ascended to heaven. In the bottom of the same valley is a church venerated by the Christians, who say that it contains the grave of Mary. In the same place there is another church which the Christians venerate and to which they come on pilgrimage. This is the church of which they are falsely persuaded to believe that it contains the grave of Jesus. All who come on pilgrimage to visit it pay a stipulated tax to the Muslims, and suffer very unwillingly various humiliations. Thereabouts also is the place of the cradle of Jesus, which is visited in order to obtain blessing.

Source: Ibn Battúta, *Ibn Battúta: Travels in Asia and Africa, 1325–1354*, trans. and ed. H. A. R. Gibb (London: George Routledge & Sons, Ltd., 1929), pp. 55–57.

The Hajj of Mansa Musa (1324–1325), al-Umari

Al-Umari was a historian who lived in the first half of the fourteenth century. While his personal life reflected the vicissitudes of court politics in Mamluk-controlled Syria (complete with a period of imprisonment when he fell out of favor), his well-researched history was much appreciated by his contemporaries. The passage included here, in which al-Umari describes the famed *hajj* of Mansa Musa, shows that al-Umari himself traveled to Cairo to gather information from local informants about Mansa Musa's sojourn in the city.

- **What are the layers of reporting in this passage? How does the traveling historian al-Umari come by his information on Mansa Musa?**

- **How does Mansa Musa's *hajj* influence the peoples with whom he and his retinue come into contact?**

- **How typical was Mansa Musa's *hajj*? Even if it is atypical, what can you generalize about the role of *hajj* in the Mediterranean and Indian Ocean worlds based on Mansa Musa's and Ibn Battuta's experiences?**

The emir Abū 'l-Ḥasan 'Alī b. Amīr Ḥajib told me that he was often in the company of sultan Mūsā the king of this country when he came to Egypt on the Pilgrimage. He was staying in [the] Qarāfa [district of Cairo] and Ibn Amīr Ḥajib was governor of Old Cairo and Qarāfa at that time. A friendship grew up between them and this sultan Mūsā told him a great deal about himself and his country and the people of the Sūdān who were his neighbours. One of the things which he told him was that his country was very extensive and contiguous with the Ocean. By his sword and his armies he had conquered 24 cities each with its surrounding district with villages and estates. It is a country rich in livestock—cattle, sheep, goats, horses, mules—and different kinds of poultry—geese, doves, chickens. The inhabitants of his country are numerous, a vast concourse, but compared with the peoples of the Sūdān who are their neighbours and penetrate far to the south they are like a white birth-mark on a black cow. He has a truce with the gold-plant people, who pay him tribute.

Ibn Amīr Ḥājib said that he asked him about the gold-plant, and he said: "It is found in two forms. One is found in the spring and blossoms after the rains in open country (ṣaḥrā'). It has leaves like the najīl grass and its roots are gold (tibr). The other kind is found all the year round at known sites on the banks of the Nīl and is dug up. . . .

Sultan Mūsā told Ibn Amīr Ḥājib that gold was his prerogative and he collected the crop as a tribute except for what the people of that country took by theft. . . .

"This sultan Mūsā, during his stay in Egypt both before and after his journey to the Noble Ḥājib, maintained a uniform attitude of worship and turning towards God. It was as though he were standing before Him because of His continual presence in his mind. He and all those with him behaved in the same manner and were well-dressed, grave, and dignified. He was noble and generous and performed many acts of charity and kindness. He had left his country with 100 loads of gold which he spent during his Pilgrimage on the tribes who lay along his route from his country to Egypt, while he was in Egypt, and again from Egypt to the Noble Hijāz and back. . . .

From the beginning of my coming to stay in Egypt I heard talk of the arrival of this sultan Mūsā on his Pilgrimage and found the Cairenes eager to recount what they had seen of the Africans' prodigal spending. . . .

This man flooded Cairo with his benefactions. He left no court emir (amīr muqarrab) nor holder of a royal office without the gift of a load of gold. The Cairenes made incalculable profits out of him and his suite in buying and selling and giving and taking. They exchanged gold until they depressed its value in Egypt and caused its price to fall. . . .

Merchants of Miṣr and Cairo have told me of the profits which they made from the Africans, saying that one of them might buy a shirt or cloak (thawb) or robe (izār) or other garment for five dinars when it was not worth one. Such was their simplicity and trustfulness that it was possible to practice any deception on them. They greeted anything that was said to them with credulous acceptance. But later they formed the very poorest opinion of the Egyptians because of the obvious falseness of everything they said to them and their outrageous behaviour in fixing the prices of the provisions and other goods which were sold to them. . . .

Muhanna' b. 'Abd al-Bāqī al-'Ujrumī the guide informed me that he accompanied sultan Mūsā when he made the Pilgrimage and that the sultan was very open-handed towards the pilgrims and the inhabitants of the Holy Places. He and his companions maintained great pomp and dressed magnificently during the journey. He gave away much wealth in alms. "About 200 mithqals of gold fell to me" said Muhanna' "and he gave other sums to my companions." Muhanna' waxed eloquent in describing the sultan's generosity, magnanimity, and opulence.

Gold was at a high price in Egypt until they came in that year. The mithqal did not go below 25 dirhams and was generally above, but from that time its value fell and it cheapened in price and has remained cheap till now. The mithqal does not exceed 22 dirhams or less. This has been the state of affairs for about twelve years until this day by reason of the large amount of gold which they brought into Egypt and spent there.

Source: al-Umari, *Corpus of Early Arabic Sources for West African History*, trans. J. F. P Hopkins (Cambridge: Cambridge University Press, 1981), pp. 267, 269–71.

PRIMARY SOURCE 10.5

The Galle Trilingual Stone Inscription (1411), Zheng He

No discussion of world travelers in this increasingly connected Afro-Eurasian world would be complete without evidence from Zheng He's travels, although he lived in a slightly later period than the other travelers discussed here (namely, during the Ming dynasty, which took the mandate of heaven from the

Mongol Yuan dynasty of China in the aftermath of the Black Death; see Chapter 11). The seven far-reaching naval expeditions undertaken by Zheng He from 1405 to 1433 illustrate Ming patronage of voyages of exploration that demonstrated their might. This trilingual inscription (in Chinese, Persian, and Tamil), set up in 1411 by Zheng He and his companions at Sri Lanka [called Ceylon in the source], demonstrates the pragmatic religious devotion of those voyaging for nonreligious aims.

....

- What range of goods does Zheng He's embassy offer? Why these specific commodities?

- Why do Zheng He, who was born and raised a Muslim, and his companions make offerings to Buddha?

- How do Zheng He's reasons for travel and what he does at this holy site compare with the other travelers in this section?

....

His Majesty, the Emperor of the Great Ming dynasty has despatched the eunuchs Ching-Ho [Zheng He], Wang Ch'ing-Lien, and others to set forth his utterance before Buddha, the World Honoured one, as follows:

"Deeply do we reverence you, Merciful and Honoured One, whose bright perfection is wide-embracing, and whose way of virtue passes all understanding, whose law enters into all human relations, and the years of whose great Kalpa (period) are like the sand of the river in number, you whose controlling influence ennobles and converts, whose kindness quickens, and whose strength discerns, whose mysterious efficacy is beyond compare! Whereas Ceylon's mountainous isle lies in the south of the ocean, and its Buddhist temples are sanctuaries of your gospel, where your miraculous responsive power imbues and enlightens. Of late, we have dispatched missions to announce our mandate

to foreign nations, and during their journey over the ocean they have been favoured with the blessing of your beneficent protection. They escaped disaster or misfortune and journeyed in safety to and fro. In everlasting recognition of your supreme virtue, we, therefore, bestow offerings in recompense, and do now reverently present before Buddha, the Honoured One, oblations of gold and silver, gold embroidered jewelled banners of variegated silk, incense burners, and flower vases, silks of many colours in lining and exterior, lamps and candles with other gifts, in order to manifest the high honour of our worship. Do you, Lord Buddha, bestow on them, your regard!"

List of Alms bestowed at the shrine of the Buddhist temple in the Mountain of Ceylon as offerings:

1000 pieces of gold; 5000 pieces of silver; fifty rolls of embroidered silk in many colours; fifty rolls of silk taffeta in many colours; four pairs of jewelled banners, gold embroidered, and of variegated silk; two pairs of the same picked in red; one pair of the same in yellow; one pair in black; five antique brass incense burners; five pairs of antique brass flower vases picked in gold on lacquer, with gold stands; five pairs of yellow brass candle-sticks, picked in gold on lacquer, with gold stand; five yellow brass lamps picked in gold on lacquer, with gold stands; five incense vessels in vermilion red, lacquered gold picked on lacquer, with gold stands; six pairs of golden lotus flowers; 2500 catties of scented oil; ten pairs of wax candles; ten sticks of fragrant incense.

The date being the seventh year of Yung-Lo (1410 a.d.) marked Chi ch'ou in the sixty years' cycle, on the Chia Hsu day of the sixty days cycle in the second moon, being the first day of the month. A reverent oblation.

Source: "Appendix I. Translation of the Chinese Inscription," trans. Edmund Backhouse, in "The Galle Trilingual Stone," *Spolia Zeylanica* 8 (Issued from the Colombo Museum; Ceylon: H. M. Richards, Acting Government Printer, 1913), pp. 125–26. Bracketed notes added by the author.

Interpreting Visual Evidence

Imagining the World

During this period when Afro-Eurasia was "becoming the world," cartographers began producing "world" maps. In 1154 al-Idrisi, a Muslim cartographer sponsored by King Roger II of Sicily, produced his *Tabula Rogeriana*. Al-Idrisi's map was accompanied by a commentary that contained information about the ten regions (numbered west to east; but note that the map was drawn so that the south is at the top) and seven climate zones (numbered south to north and following the scheme set forth by the second-century CE Greco-Roman geographer Ptolemy). In 1375, a Jewish mapmaker named Abraham Cresques, from the island of Majorca off the east coast of Spain, produced the second map included here, which is known as the *Catalan Atlas*. Cresques's map is a mixture of practical information and storytelling. The crisscrossed lines that mark compass bearings, suggestive of a nautical chart, reflect the influence of the compass on European mapmaking beginning around 1300. The ornate depictions of the Mali king Mansa Musa and the caravan of Marco Polo offer historical information. In 1459, a monk named Fra Mauro, from Venice, created his *Mappa Mundi* (Map of the World), the third map pictured here. Fra Mauro's map is striking in its detail and information. Not only does it carefully mark out shorelines, rivers, cities, and other geographic features, it also includes banners with detailed information and even drawings of the different types of ships (such as the North Atlantic cogs, Chinese junks, and Arabian dhows, discussed in this chapter) that sailed the different seas.

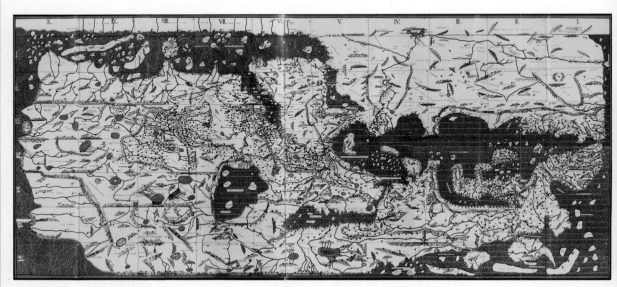

Al-Idrisi's *Tabula Rogeriana*.

Cresques's *Catalan Atlas*.

Questions for Analysis

1. Compare these maps in terms of their representations of land, water, perspective, and other features. What accounts for the maps' similarities and differences?

2. Based on the features and information on the maps, where did the cartographers get the data to create them? How might these maps have been used, and by whom?

3. What do these maps suggest about how these cartographers and their patrons understood the known world? Why are certain parts of the world emphasized and others left off?

Fra Mauro's *Mappa Mundi*.

11

Crisis and Recovery in Afro-Eurasia

1300–1500

When Mongol armies besieged the Genoese trading outpost of Caffa on the Black Sea in 1346, they not only damaged trading links between East Asia and the Mediterranean but also unleashed a devastating disease: the bubonic plague. Defeated Genoese merchants and soldiers withdrew, unknowingly taking the germs with them aboard their ships. By the time they arrived in Messina, Sicily, half the passengers were dead. The rest were dying. People waiting on shore for the ships' trade goods were horrified at the sight and turned the ships away. Desperately, the captains went to the next port, only to face the same fate. Despite these efforts at isolation, Europeans could not keep the plague (later called the Black Death) from reaching their shores. As it spread from port to port, it eventually contaminated all of Europe, killing more than half of the population.

This story illustrates the disruptive effects of both the Mongol invasions and the long-distance trade routes that the Mongols foisted on Afro-Eurasian societies. In the thirteenth and early fourteenth centuries, Mongol armies swept into and took control of vast regions of Afro-Eurasia. Although the invasions ushered in an age of intensified cultural and political contact, the channels of exchange—the land routes and sea-lanes of human voyagers—became accidental conduits for deadly microbes. These germs devastated societies far more decisively than did Mongol warfare. They were the real "murderous hordes" of world

Chapter Outline

- Collapse and Consolidation
- The Islamic Heartland
- Western Christendom
- Ming China
- Conclusion

Core Objectives

- **DESCRIBE** the nature and origins of the crises spanning Afro-Eurasia during the fourteenth century.
- **ASSESS** the impact of the Black Death on China, the Islamic world, and Europe.
- **COMPARE** the ways in which regional rulers in postplague Afro-Eurasia attempted to construct unified states and **ANALYZE** the extent and nature of their successes.
- **EXPLAIN** the role that religious belief systems played in rebuilding the Islamic world, Europe, and Ming China in the fourteenth and fifteenth centuries.
- **EXAMINE** the way art and architecture reflected the political realities of the Islamic world, Europe, and Ming China after the Black Death.
- **COMPARE** how Ottoman, Iberian, and Ming rulers extended their territories and regional influence.

history, infecting people from every community, class, and culture they encountered. So staggering was the Black Death's toll that population densities did not recover for 200 years. The most severely affected regions were those that the Mongols had brought together: settlements and commercial hubs along the old Silk Roads and around the Mediterranean Sea and the South China Sea. While segments of the Indian Ocean trading world experienced death and disruption, South Asian societies, which had escaped the Mongol conquest, also escaped the dying and political disruptions associated with the Black Death.

This chapter explores the ways in which Afro-Eurasian peoples restored what they thought was valuable from old traditions after these crises, while discarding what they thought had failed them in favor of radically new institutions and ideas. Much of the recovery had striking similarities across Afro-Eurasia, as societies reaffirmed their most deeply held and long-standing beliefs. Chinese rulers looked to Confucian thought and well-known dynastic institutions to provide guidance going forward. In the Muslim heartland, a small band of Turkish-speaking warriors—the Ottomans—channeled the energies of a revived Islam to expand their own territory and the Muslim world. Europeans also invoked their traditions. In the Iberian Peninsula, political elites used a resurgent Catholicism to spread their political power and drive Muslim communities out of Europe. Europeans also created new dynastic monarchies and looked to their distant past in Greek and Roman culture for inspiration.

Radically new institutions and ideas appeared across Afro-Eurasia in the aftermath of the Black Death. Notable among these was the outburst of cultural activity

Global Storylines

- The spread of the Black Death and the collapse of the Mongol Empire sets off crises across Afro-Eurasia, with major demographic, political, economic, and cultural consequences.

- Across Afro-Eurasia, continuity in religious beliefs and cultural institutions accompanies changes in political structures in Europe, the Muslim world, and China.

- In central Eurasia, new rulers—most notably the Ottomans—rebuild dynasties in place of the Mongols, using a blend of religion, military expansion, administrative control, and cultural tolerance.

- In western Christendom, new monarchies establish political order, and the Renaissance brings a cultural rebirth to societies devastated by plague.

- In East Asia, the Ming dynasty replaces the Mongol Yuan dynasty, using an elaborate Confucian bureaucracy to oversee infrastructure and long-distance exchange.

that took place in western Europe. Historians have called this flourishing the Renaissance (rebirth), for during this era Europeans rediscovered their Greek and Roman pasts and used inspiration drawn from classical antiquity to bring about far-reaching innovations in art, architecture, thought, and political and financial institutions. While significant changes reshaped institutions and ideas in this period, there were also many continuities. Considering how grievously people suffered and how many died, it is perhaps surprising how much of the old—particularly religious beliefs and institutions—survived the aftermath of Mongol rule and the Black Death.

Collapse and Consolidation

Although the Mongol invasions overturned political systems, the plague devastated society itself. The pandemic killed millions, disrupted economies, and threw communities into chaos. Rulers could explain to their people the assaults of "barbarians," but it was much harder to make sense of an invisible enemy. Nonetheless, in response to the upheaval, new ruling groups moved to reorganize their states. By making strategic marriages and building powerful armies, these rulers enlarged their territories, formed alliances, and built dynasties.

THE BLACK DEATH

The spread of the Black Death was the fourteenth century's most significant historical development. (See Map 11.1.) Originating in Inner Asia, the disease afflicted peoples from China to Europe and killed 25 to 65 percent of infected populations.

How did the **Black Death** move so far and so fast? One explanation may lie in climate changes. The cooler climate of this period—scholars refer to a "Little Ice Age"—may have weakened populations and left them vulnerable to disease. In Europe, for instance, beginning around 1310, harsh winters and rainy summers shortened growing seasons and ruined harvests. Exhausted soils no longer supplied the resources required by growing urban and rural populations, while nobles squeezed the peasantry in an effort to maintain their luxurious lifestyle. The ensuing famine lasted from 1315 to 1322, during which time millions of Europeans died of starvation or of diseases against which the malnourished population had little resistance. This climate change and famine laid the groundwork for the Black Death that soon followed. Another climate-related factor in the spread of the plague lay in the drying up of the central Asian steppe borderlands, where bubonic plague had existed for centuries. This drought may have forced rodents out of their usual dwelling places and pressed pastoral peoples, who carried the infectious strains, closer to settled agricultural communities. Fleas transmitted plague from rodent to rodent, and to humans. The resulting epidemic was terrifying, for its causes

THE BIG PICTURE

What crises affected fourteenth-century Afro-Eurasia and what was the range of responses to those crises?

Black Death
Great epidemic of the bubonic plague that ravaged Europe, East Asia, and North Africa in the fourteenth century, killing large numbers of people, including perhaps as much as one-third of the European population.

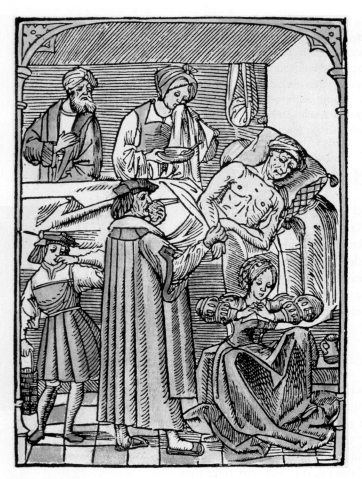

Plague Victim The plague was highly contagious and quickly led to death. Here a physician and his helper cover their noses to avoid the unbearable stench emanating from the patient.

were unknown at the time. Infected victims died quickly—sometimes overnight—and in agony, coughing up blood and oozing pus and blood from black sores the size of eggs.

But it was the trading network that spread the germs across Afro-Eurasia into famine-struck western Europe. This wider Afro-Eurasian population was vulnerable because its members had no immunity to the disease. The first outbreak in a heavily populated region occurred in the 1320s in southwestern China. From there, the disease spread through China and then continued its death march along the major trade routes. Many of these routes terminated at the Italian port cities, where ships with dead and dying people aboard arrived in 1347. From there, what Europeans called the Pestilence or the Great Mortality engulfed the western end of the landmass. Societies in China, the Muslim world, and Europe suffered the disastrous effects of the Black Death.

Plague in China China was ripe for the plague pandemic. Its population had increased under the Song dynasty (960–1279) and subsequent Mongol rule. But by 1300, hunger and scarcity spread as resources were stretched thin. The weakened population was especially vulnerable. For seventy years, the Black Death ravaged China, reduced the size of the already small Mongol population, and shattered the Mongols' claim to a mandate from heaven. In 1331, plague may have killed 90 percent of the population in Bei Zhili (modern Hebei) Province. From there it spread throughout other provinces, reaching Fujian and the coast at Shandong. By the 1350s, most of China's large cities had suffered severe outbreaks.

Even as the Black Death was engulfing China, bandit groups and dissident religious sects were undercutting the power of the last Mongol Yuan rulers. Popular religious movements warned of impending doom. Most prominent was the Red Turban movement, which blended China's diverse cultural and religious traditions, including Buddhism, Daoism, and other faiths. Its leaders emphasized strict dietary restrictions, penance, and ceremonial rituals, and made proclamations that the world was drawing to an end.

Plague in the Islamic World The plague devastated parts of the Muslim world as well. The Black Death reached Baghdad by 1347. By the next year, the plague overtook Egypt, Syria, and Cyprus, causing as many as 1,000 deaths a day according to a Tunisian report. Animals, too, were afflicted. One Egyptian writer commented: "The country was not far from being ruined. . . . One found in the desert the bodies of savage animals with the bubos under their arms. It was the same with horses, camels, asses, and all the beasts in general, including birds, even the ostriches." In the eastern Mediterranean, plague left much of the Islamic world in a state of near political and economic collapse. The great Arab historian Ibn Khaldûn (1332–1406), who lost his mother and father and a number of his teachers to the Black Death in Tunis, underscored the desolation: "Cities and buildings were laid waste, roads and way signs were obliterated, settlements and mansions became empty, dynasties and tribes grew weak," he wrote. "The entire world changed."

Plague in Europe In Europe, the Black Death first ravaged the Italian Peninsula; then it seized France, the Netherlands, Belgium, Luxembourg, Germany, and England in its deathly grip. Overcrowded and unsanitary cities were particularly vulnerable. All levels of society—the poor, craftspeople, aristocrats—were at risk, although flight to the countryside offered some protection from infection. Nearly 50 million of Europe's 80 million people perished between 1347 and 1351. After 1353, the epidemic waned, but the plague returned every seven years or so for the rest of the century and sporadically through the fifteenth century. Consequently, the European population continued to decline, until by 1450 many areas had only one-quarter the number of a century earlier.

In the face of the Black Death, some Europeans turned to debauchery, determined to enjoy themselves before they died. Others, especially in urban settings in Flanders, the Netherlands, and parts of Germany, claimed to find God's grace outside what they saw as a corrupt Catholic Church. Semimonastic orders like the Beghards and Beguines, which had begun in the century or so before the plague, expanded in its wake. These laypeople (unordained men and women) argued that people should trust their own "interior instinct" more than the Gospel as then preached. By contrast, the Flagellants were so convinced that man had incurred God's wrath that they whipped themselves to atone for human sin.

For many who survived the plague, disappointment with the clergy smoldered. Famished peasants resented priests and monks for living lives of luxury. In addition, they despaired at the absence of clergy when they were so greatly needed. While many clerics had perished attending to their parishioners during the Black Death, others had fled to rural retreats far from the ravages of the plague, leaving their followers to fend for themselves.

ASSESS the impact of the Black Death on China, the Islamic world, and Europe.

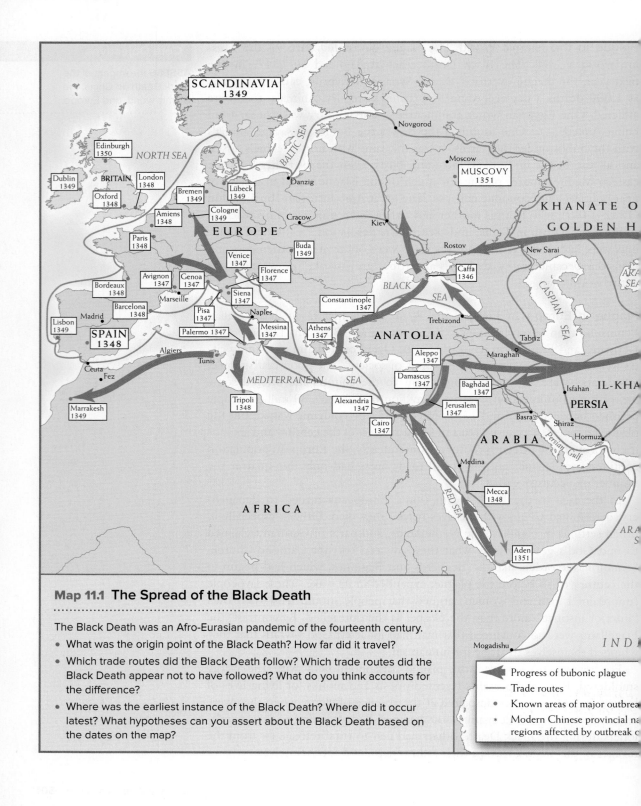

Map 11.1 The Spread of the Black Death

The Black Death was an Afro-Eurasian pandemic of the fourteenth century.

- What was the origin point of the Black Death? How far did it travel?
- Which trade routes did the Black Death follow? Which trade routes did the Black Death appear not to have followed? What do you think accounts for the difference?
- Where was the earliest instance of the Black Death? Where did it occur latest? What hypotheses can you assert about the Black Death based on the dates on the map?

Map labels:

SCANDINAVIA 1349

Edinburgh 1350
NORTH SEA
Dublin 1349
BRITAIN
London 1348
Oxford 1348
Bremen 1349
Lübeck 1349
Cologne 1349
Amiens 1348
Paris 1348
EUROPE
Buda 1349
Danzig
Cracow
Kiev
Novgorod
Moscow
MUSCOVY 1351
Rostov
New Sarai
KHANATE O
GOLDEN H
BALTIC SEA
Venice 1347
Florence 1347
Caffa 1346
CASPIAN SEA
ARA SEA
Avignon 1347
Genoa 1347
Bordeaux 1348
Marseille
Siena 1347
Pisa 1347
Naples
BLACK SEA
Constantinople 1347
Trebizond
Tabriz
Maraghah
Barcelona 1348
Madrid
Palermo 1347
Messina 1347
Athens 1347
ANATOLIA
Aleppo 1347
Baghdad 1347
Isfahan
IL-KHA
Lisbon 1349
SPAIN 1348
Algiers
Tunis
Damascus 1347
Jerusalem 1347
PERSIA
Basra
Shiraz
Hormuz
Ceuta
Fez
MEDITERRANEAN SEA
Tripoli 1348
Alexandria 1347
Cairo 1347
ARABIA
Marrakesh 1349
Medina
RED SEA
Mecca 1348
AFRICA
Aden 1351
ARA S
Mogadishu
IND

Legend:
Progress of bubonic plague
Trade routes
Known areas of major outbrea
Modern Chinese provincial na
regions affected by outbreak o

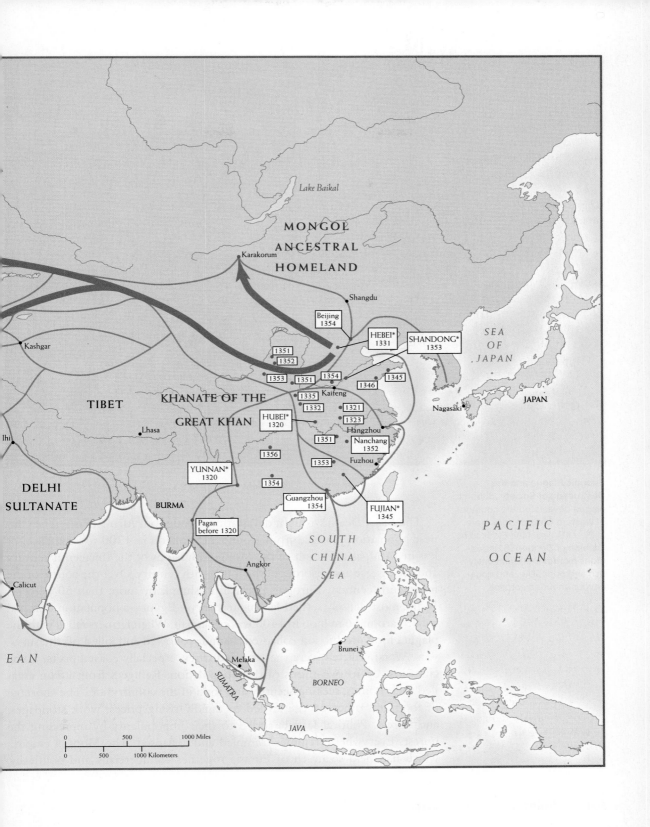

Lake Baikal

MONGOL
ANCESTRAL
HOMELAND

Karakorum

Shangdu

Beijing
1354

Kashgar

1351
1352

HEBEI*
1331

SHANDONG*
1353

SEA
OF
JAPAN

1353

1351

1354

1345

JAPAN

TIBET

KHANATE OF THE

GREAT KHAN

1335

Kaifeng

1332

1346

Nagasaki

HUBEI*
1320

1321

1323

Lhasa

Hangzhou

lhi

1351

Nanchang
1352

DELHI

1356

1353

Fuzhou

SULTANATE

YUNNAN*
1320

BURMA

1354

Guangzhou
1354

FUJIAN*
1345

PACIFIC

Pagan
before 1320

OCEAN

Calicut

Angkor

SOUTH
CHINA
SEA

EAN

Brunei

Melaka

BORNEO

SUMATRA

JAVA

| 0 | | 500 | | 1000 Miles |
| 0 | 500 | | 1000 Kilometers | |

Bubonic Plague and the Destruction of Society Bubonic plague devastated the countries of western Christendom. Here, in Pieter Bruegel the Elder's *The Triumph of Death* (1562), skeletons murder indiscriminately, rich and poor alike, and dogs devour unburied corpses.

The Black Death wrought devastation throughout Afro-Eurasia. The Chinese population plunged from around 115 million in 1200 to 75 million or less in 1400, as the result of the Mongol invasions of the thirteenth century and the disease and disorder of the fourteenth century. Over the course of the fourteenth century, Europe's population shrank by more than 50 percent. In the most densely settled Islamic territory—Egypt—a population that had totaled around 6 million in 1400 was cut in half. When farmers fell ill with the plague, food production collapsed. Famine followed and killed off the survivors. Worst afflicted were the crowded cities, especially coastal ports. Some cities lost up to two-thirds of their population. Refugees from urban areas fled their homes, seeking security and food in the countryside. The shortage of food and other necessities led to rapidly rising prices, work stoppages, and unrest. Political leaders added to their unpopularity by repressing the unrest. Everywhere, regimes trembled and collapsed. The Mongol empire, which had held so much of Eurasia together commercially and politically, disintegrated. Thus, the way was prepared for experiments in state building, religious beliefs, and cultural understandings.

REBUILDING STATES

Starting in the late fourteenth century, Afro-Eurasians began the task of reconstructing both their political order and their trading networks. By then the plague had died down, though it continued to afflict peoples for centuries. However, the rebuilding of military and civil administrations—no easy task—also required political legitimacy. With their people deeply shaken by the extraordinary loss of life, rulers needed to revive confidence in themselves and their regimes, which they did by fostering beliefs and rituals that confirmed their legitimacy and by increasing their control over subjects.

The basis for power was a political institution well known to Afro-Eurasians for centuries, the dynasty—the hereditary ruling family that passed control from one generation to the next. Like those of the past, the new dynasties sought to establish their legitimacy in three ways. First, ruling families insisted that their power derived from a divine calling: Ming emperors in China claimed for themselves what previous dynastic rulers had asserted—the "mandate of heaven"—while European monarchs claimed to rule by "divine right." From their base in Anatolia, Ottoman warrior-princes asserted that they now carried the banner of Islam. In these ways, ruling households affirmed that God or the heavens intended for them to hold power. Second, leaders attempted to prevent squabbling among potential heirs by establishing clear rules about succession to the throne. Many European states tried to standardize succession by passing titles to the eldest male heir, thus ensuring political stability at a potential time of crisis, but in practice there were countless complications and quarrels. In the Islamic world, successors could be designated by the current ruler or elected by the community; here, too, struggles over succession were frequent. Third, ruling families elevated their power through conquest or alliance—by ordering armies to extend their domains forcibly, or by marrying their royal offspring to rulers of other states or members of other elite households, a technique widely practiced in Europe. Once it established legitimacy, the typical royal family would consolidate power by enacting coercive laws and punishments and sending emissaries to govern distant territories. A ruling family would also establish standing armies and new administrative structures to collect taxes and to oversee building projects that proclaimed royal power.

As we will see in the next three sections of this chapter, the innovative state building that occurred in the wake of the plague's devastation would not have been as successful had it not drawn on older traditions. In Europe, a cultural flourishing based largely on ancient Greek and Roman models gave rise to thinkers who proposed new views of governance. The peoples of the Islamic world held fiercely to their religion as successor states, notably the Ottoman Empire, absorbed numerous Turkish-speaking groups. The Ming renounced the Mongol expansionist legacy and emphasized a return to Han rulership, consolidating control of Chinese lands and concentrating on internal markets rather than overseas trade. Many of these regimes lasted for centuries, promoting political institutions and cultural values that became deeply embedded in the fabric of their societies.

The Islamic Heartland

Core Objectives

COMPARE the ways in which regional rulers in postplague Afro-Eurasia attempted to construct unified states and **ANALYZE** the extent and nature of their successes.

The devastation of the Black Death followed hard on the heels of the Mongol destruction of Islam's most important city, Baghdad, and Islam's old political order. Nonetheless, these two catastrophes prepared the way for new Islamic states to emerge. The old, Arabic-speaking Islamic world remained vital, still at the heart of Islam geographically, but it now had to yield authority to new rulers and religious men. This new Islamic world included large Turkish- and Persian-speaking populations as well. It occupied a vast geographic triangle that stretched from Anatolia in the west to the Khurasan region of Persia and Afghanistan in the east and to Baghdad in the south.

The Ottomans, the Safavids, and the Mughals emerged as the dominant states in the Islamic world in the early sixteenth century. They exploited the rich agrarian resources of the Indian Ocean regions and the Mediterranean basin, and they benefited from a brisk seaborne and overland trade. By the mid-sixteenth century the Mughals controlled the northern Indus River valley; the Safavids occupied Persia; and the Ottomans ruled Anatolia, the Arab world, and much of southern and eastern Europe. Here we will explore in depth the Ottoman Empire, which emerged first and endured the longest of the three. (See Chapter 12 for a fuller discussion of the Mughals and Chapter 14 for more on the Safavids.)

THE OTTOMAN EMPIRE

The rise of the **Ottoman Empire** owed as much to innovative administrative techniques and religious tolerance as to military strength. Although the Mongols considered Anatolia to be a borderland region of little economic importance, their military forays in the late thirteenth century opened up the region to new political forces. The ultimate victors here were the Ottoman Turks. They transformed themselves from warrior bands roaming the borderlands between the Islamic and Christian worlds into rulers of a settled state and, finally, into sovereigns of a far-flung, highly bureaucratic empire. (See Map 11.2.)

Under their chief, Osman (r. 1299–1326), the Turkish Ottomans formalized a stern and disciplined warrior ethos. In addition to deploying their

Ottoman Empire
A Turkish warrior band that transformed itself into a vast, multicultural, bureaucratic empire that lasted from the early fourteenth century through the early twentieth century and encompassed Anatolia, the Arab world, and large swaths of southern and eastern Europe.

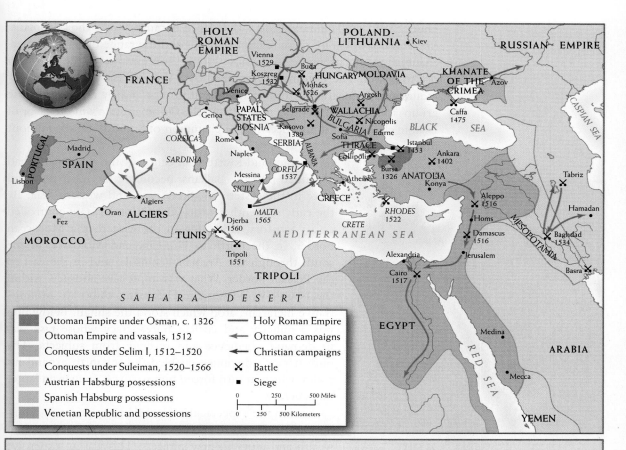

Map 11.2 The Ottoman Empire, 1300–1566

This map charts the expansion of the Ottoman state from the time of its founder, Osman, through the reign of Suleiman, the empire's most illustrious ruler.

- Where did the Ottoman Empire originate under Osman? Into what regions did the Ottomans expand between the years 1326 and 1566?
- What were the geographic limits of the Ottoman Empire?
- What governments were able to resist Ottoman expansion?

fierce warriors, knowns as *ghazis*, Osman and his son Orhan (r. 1326–1362), both Sunni Muslims, proved skilled at working with those who held different religious beliefs, including Byzantine Christians, Sufi dervishes, and Shiites. Osman and Orhan offered genuine opportunities for others to exercise power and gain wealth. While other Turkish warrior bands fought for booty under charismatic military leaders, they failed because, unlike the Ottomans, they did not integrate these religious groups and the range of artisans, merchants, bureaucrats, and clerics whose support was essential in the Ottoman rise to power. The Ottomans triumphed over their rivals by adapting techniques of administration from neighboring groups and by attracting those groups to their rule. In time, not only did the Ottoman state win the favor of Islamic clerics, but it also became the champion of Sunni Islam throughout the Islamic world.

The Fall of Constantinople The use of heavy artillery in the forty-day siege of Constantinople was instrumental to the Ottoman victory. At the center of this Turkish miniature is one such cannon, possibly of Hungarian origin, which required hundreds of men and oxen to transport and secure outside the city walls.

By the mid-fourteenth century, the Ottomans had expanded into the Balkans, becoming the most powerful force in the eastern Mediterranean and western Asia. By the early sixteenth century, the Ottoman state controlled a vast territory, stretching in the west to the Moroccan border, in the north to Hungary and Moldavia, in the south through the Arabian Peninsula, and in the east to the Persian border. What was impressive and new within the Islamic world was the Ottomans' elaborate administrative hierarchy, atop which stood the sultan. Below him was a military and civilian bureaucracy whose task was to demand obedience and revenue from subjects. The bureaucracy's discipline enabled the sultan to expand his realm, which in turn forced him to invest in an even larger bureaucracy.

The empire's spectacular expansion was primarily a military affair. To recruit followers, the Ottomans promised wealth and glory to new subjects. This was an expensive undertaking, but territorial expansion generated vast financial and administrative rewards. Moreover, by spreading the spoils of conquest and lucrative administrative positions, rulers bought off potentially unhappy subordinates. Still, without military might, the Ottomans would not have enjoyed the successes associated with the brilliant reigns of Murad II (r. 1421–1451) and his appropriately named successor, Mehmed the Conqueror (r. 1451–1481).

Mehmed's most spectacular triumph was the conquest of Constantinople, an ambition for Muslim rulers ever since the birth of Islam. Mehmed left no doubt that this was his primary goal: shortly after his coronation, he vowed to capture Constantinople, the ancient Roman and Christian capital of the Byzantine Empire, and a city of immense strategic and commercial importance, which had withstood Muslim efforts at conquest for centuries. First, Mehmed built a fortress of his own to prevent European vessels from reaching the capital. Then, by promising his soldiers free access to booty and portraying the city's conquest as a holy cause, he amassed a huge army that outnumbered the defending force of 7,000 by more than ten times. For forty days his troops bombarded Constantinople's massive walls with artillery that included enormous cannons built by Hungarian and Italian engineers. On May 29, 1453, Ottoman troops overwhelmed the surviving defenders and took Constantinople—which Mehmed promptly renamed Istanbul.

The Tools of Empire Building The Ottomans adopted Byzantine administrative practices to unify their enlarged state and incorporated many of Byzantium's powerful families into it. Their dynastic power, however, was not only military; it also rested on a firm religious foundation. At the center of this empire was the sultan, who combined a warrior ethos with an unwavering devotion to Islam. Describing himself as the "shadow of God" on earth, the sultan claimed the role of caretaker for the Islamic faith. Throughout the empire, he devoted substantial resources to the construction of elaborate mosques and to the support of Islamic schools. As self-appointed defender of the faith, the sultan assumed the role of protector of the holy cities on

The Suleymaniye Mosque Built by Sultan Suleiman in the mid-sixteenth century to crown his achievements, the Suleymaniye Mosque was designed by the architect Sinan to dominate the city. Location mattered to Suleiman. The Bosporus Strait, the vital route connecting the Mediterranean with the Black Sea, is visible beyond the mosque, and Justinian's Hagia Sophia (not visible above) is located just across a park from the mosque.

the Arabian Peninsula and of Jerusalem, while working to unite the realm's diverse lands and peoples and constantly striving to extend the borders of Islam. During the reign of Suleiman (r. 1520–1566), the Ottomans reached the height of their territorial expansion. Under his administration, the Ottoman state ruled 20 to 30 million people. By the time Suleiman died, the Ottoman Empire bridged Europe and the Arab world. Istanbul by then was a dynamic imperial hub, dispatching bureaucrats and military men to oversee a vast domain.

Istanbul's **Topkapi Palace** exhibited the Ottomans' view of governance, the sultans' emphasis on religion, and the continuing influence of Ottoman familial traditions. Laid out by Mehmed II, the palace complex projected a vision of Istanbul as the center of the world. As a way to promote the sultan's magnificent power, architects designed the complex so that the buildings containing the imperial household were nestled behind layers of outer courtyards, in a mosaic of mosques, courts, and special dwellings for the sultan's harem. The harem had its own hierarchy of thousands of women, from the sultan's mother and consorts to the slave women who waited on them, and it became a formidable political force at the heart of Ottoman power.

The growing importance of Topkapi Palace as the command post of empire represented a crucial transition in the history of Ottoman rulers. Not only was the palace the place where future bureaucrats received their training; it was also the place where the chief bureaucrat, the grand vizier, carried out the day-to-day running of the empire. Whereas the early sultans had led their soldiers into battle personally and had met face-to-face with their kinsmen, the later rulers withdrew into the sacredness of the palace, venturing out only occasionally for grand ceremonies. Still, every Friday, subjects lined up outside the palace to introduce their petitions, ask for favors, and seek justice. If they were lucky, the sultans would be there to greet them—but they did so behind grated glass, issuing their decisions by tapping on the window. The palace thus projected a sense of majestic, distant wonder, a home fit for semidivine rulers.

Diversity and Control The fact that the Ottoman Empire endured into the twentieth century owed much to the ruling elite's ability to gain the support and employ the talents of exceedingly diverse populations. After all, neither conquest nor conversion eliminated cultural differences among the empire's distant provinces. Thus, for example, the Ottomans' language policy was one of flexibility and tolerance. Although Ottoman Turkish was the official language of administration, Arabic was the primary language of the Arab provinces, the common tongue of street life. Within the empire's European lands, many people spoke their own languages. From the fifteenth century onward, the Ottoman Empire was perhaps more multilingual than any of its rivals.

In politics, as in language, the Ottomans showed flexibility and tolerance. The imperial bureaucracy permitted extensive regional autonomy. In fact,

Ottoman military cadres perfected a technique for absorbing newly conquered territories into the empire by parceling them out as revenue-producing units among loyal followers and kin. Regional appointees could collect local taxes, part of which they earmarked for Istanbul and part of which they pocketed for themselves. This approach was a common administrative device for many world dynastic empires ruling extensive domains.

Like other empires, the Ottoman state was always in danger of losing control over its provincial rulers. Local potentates—the group that the imperial center allowed to rule in their distant regions—found that great distances enabled them to operate independently from central authority. These rulers kept larger amounts of tax revenues than Istanbul deemed proper. So, to limit their autonomy, the Ottomans established the janissaries, a corps of infantry soldiers and bureaucrats who owed direct allegiance to the sultan. The system at its high point involved conscription of Christian youths from the empire's European lands. This conscription, called the **devshirme**, required each village to hand over a certain number of males between the ages of eight and eighteen. Uprooted from their families and villages, selected for their fine physiques and good looks, these young men were converted to Islam and sent to farms to build up their bodies and learn Turkish. A select few were moved on to Topkapi Palace to learn Ottoman military, religious, and administrative techniques. Some of these men later enjoyed exceptional careers in the arts and sciences—such as the architect Sinan, who designed the Suleymaniye Mosque. Recipients of the best education available in the Islamic world, trained in Ottoman ways, instructed in the use of modern weaponry, and deprived of family connections, the *devshirme* recruits were prepared to serve the sultan (and the empire as a whole) rather than the interests of any particular locality or ethnic group.

Thus, the Ottomans established their legitimacy via military skill, religious backing, and a loyal bureaucracy. They artfully balanced the decentralizing tendencies of the outlying regions with the centralizing forces of the imperial capital. Relying on a careful mixture of religious faith, imperial patronage,

devshirme
The Ottoman system of taking non-Muslim children in place of taxes in order to educate them in Muslim ways and prepare them for service in the sultan's bureaucracy.

and cultural tolerance, the sultans curried loyalty and secured political stability. Indeed, the Ottoman Empire was so strong and stable that it dominated the coveted and highly contested trading crossroads between Europe and Asia for many centuries. Thus, its consolidation had powerful consequences for Europeans' efforts to rebuild their societies after the plague; above all, it closed off their traditional overland trade routes to India and China.

Western Christendom

No region suffered more from the Black Death than western Christendom, and arguably no region made a more spectacular comeback. From 1100 to 1300, Europe had enjoyed a surge in population, rapid economic growth, and significant technological and intellectual innovations, only to see these achievements halted in the fourteenth century by famine and the Black Death. Europeans responded by creating new political and cultural forms. New dynastic states arose, competing with one another, and a movement called the Renaissance revived Europe's connections with its Greek and Roman past and produced masterpieces of art, architecture, and other forms of thought.

THE CATHOLIC CHURCH, STATE BUILDING, AND ECONOMIC RECOVERY

Core Objectives

EXPLAIN the role that religious belief systems played in rebuilding the Islamic world, Europe, and Ming China in the fourteenth and fifteenth centuries.

In the aftermath of famine and plague, the peoples of western Christendom, like those in the Muslim world, looked to their religious beliefs and institutions as foundations for recovery. The faith of many had been severely tested, and religious authorities had to struggle to reclaim their power. To begin with, the late medieval western church found itself divided at the top (at one point during this period there were three popes) and challenged from below, both by individuals pursuing alternative kinds of spirituality and by increasing demands on the clergy and church administration. Disappointment with the clergy smoldered. The peasantry despaired at the absence of clergy when they were so greatly needed during the famines and Black Death. With groups like the Beghards and Beguines challenging the clergy's right to define religious doctrine and practices, the church fought back, identifying all that was suspect and demanding strict obedience to the true faith. This response included the persecution of heretics, Jews, Muslims in the Iberian Peninsula, homosexuals, prostitutes, and "witches." During this period the church also expanded its charitable and bureaucratic functions, providing alms to the urban poor and registering births, deaths, and economic transactions. Crucially, when faced with challenges to its authority, the church associated itself with secular rulers, lending moral authority to kings who claimed to rule "by divine right."

Europe's political rulers aligned themselves with church leaders to rebuild their states and consolidate their power. One royal family, the Habsburgs, drew on their Catholic religious traditions and established a powerful, long-lasting dynasty that would rule large parts of central Europe for centuries to follow. Habsburg leaders were elected to head the federation of states known as the Holy Roman Empire almost continuously from 1438 to 1806, and for a time they ruled Spain and its New World colonies. Yet even at the height of its power in the early sixteenth century, the Habsburg monarchy never succeeded in restoring an integrated empire to western Europe.

In 1450, western Christendom had no central government, no official tongue, and only a few successful commercial centers, mostly in the Mediterranean basin. (See Map 11.3.) The feudal system of a lord's control over the peasantry (see Chapter 10), which was now in decline, left a legacy of political fragmentation and enduring elite privileges, which made the consolidation of a unified Christian Europe even more difficult to achieve. Europe's linguistic diversity reflected its political fragmentation. No single ruler or language united peoples, even when they shared a religion. Latin lost ground as rulers chose various regional dialects (e.g., French, Spanish, English) to be their official state languages, in contrast with China, whose written literary Chinese script remained a key administrative tool for the new dynasts, and the Islamic world, where Arabic was the common language of faith and Turkish the language of administration.

Those who sought to rule the emerging states faced numerous obstacles. For example, rival claimants to the throne financed threatening private armies. Also, the clergy demanded and received privileges in the form of access to land and relief from taxation; they often meddled in politics themselves, and the church became a formidable economic powerhouse. And once the printing press became more widely available in Europe in the 1460s, printers circulated anonymous pamphlets criticizing the court and the clergy. Some states had consultative political bodies—such as the Estates General in France, the Cortes in Spain, and Parliament in England—in which princes formally asked representatives of their people for advice and, in the case of the English Parliament, for consent to new forms of taxation. Such political bodies gave no voice to common men and no representation to women. But they did allow the collective expression of grievances against overbearing policies.

Out of the chaos of famine, disease, and warfare, the diverse peoples of Europe found a political way forward. This path involved the formation of centralized dynastic monarchies. While not new to this period, the political institution of **monarchy** was particularly instrumental to western Christendom in the fifteenth century. Often in competition with the new monarchies, a handful of European city-states, in which a narrow group of wealthy and influential voters selected their leaders, survived right up to the nineteenth

monarchy
Political system in which one individual holds supreme power and passes that power on to his or her next of kin.

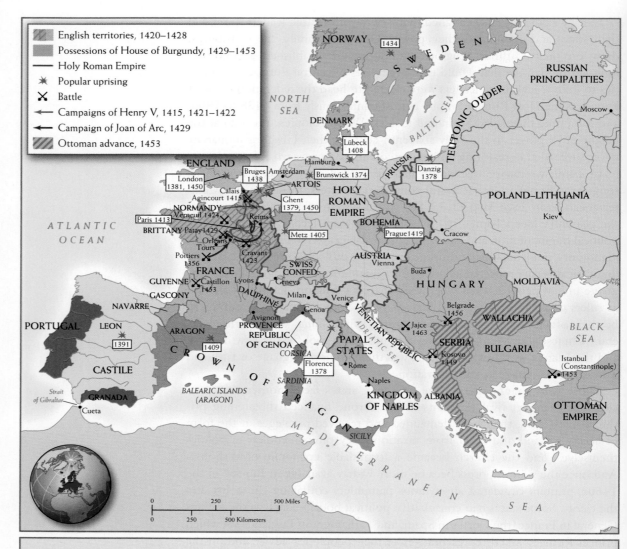

Map 11.3 Western Christendom, 1400–1500

Europe was a region divided by dynastic rivalries during the fifteenth century. Locate the most powerful regional dynasties on the map: Portugal, Castile, Aragon, France, Burgundy, England, and the Holy Roman Empire.

- Using the scale, contrast the sizes of political units in this map with those in Maps 11.2 (Ottoman Empire) and 11.4 (Ming China). Explain the significance of the differences.
- Where did popular uprisings take place? Based on your reading, why did those regions experience popular unrest?
- Based on the map, why might the Venetian Republic have been particularly engaged, both in trade and intermittent warfare, with the Ottomans?

century and in some cases into the twentieth. Consolidation of these states occurred sometimes through strategic marriages but more often through warfare, both between princely families and with local aristocratic allies and foreign mercenaries.

One striking example of this political turmoil was the Hundred Years' War (1337–1453), in which the French sought to throw off English domination. The Black Death raged in the early years of this intermittent conflict. A central figure toward the end of the war was the peasant girl Joan of Arc, whose visions of various saints inspired her to support the French monarch Charles VII and see him crowned at Reims Cathedral. While Joan was a charismatic leader of troops, commanding as many as 8,000 at the decisive battle at Orleans, eventually the French nobility turned on her, and she was captured by the English. Joan was tried for heresy and burned at the stake in Rouen in 1431. Joan's brief, but remarkable, part in the Hundred Years' War illustrates the role an exceptional woman, even a peasant girl, could play on the predominantly male, elite political stage.

Elsewhere, in southern Europe, where economies rebounded through seaborne trade with Southwest Asia, political stabilization was swifter. The stabilization of Italian city-states such as Venice and Florence, and of monarchical rule in Portugal and Spain, led to an economic and cultural flowering known as the Renaissance. In northern and western Europe, the process took longer. In England and France, in particular, internal feuding, regional warfare, and religious fragmentation delayed recovery for decades (see Chapter 12).

POLITICAL CONSOLIDATION AND TRADE IN THE IBERIAN PENINSULA

War and overseas trade played a central role in the emergence of new dynasties in Portugal and Spain. Through the fourteenth century, Portuguese Christians devoted themselves to fighting the Moors, who were Muslim occupants of North Africa, the western Sahara, and the Iberian Peninsula. After the Portuguese crossed the Strait of Gibraltar and seized the Moorish fortresses at Ceuta, in Morocco, their ships could sail between the Mediterranean and the Atlantic without Muslim interference. With that threat diminished, the Portuguese perceived their neighbor, Castile (a region in what is now Spain), as their chief foe. Under João I (r. 1385–1433), Portugal defeated the Castilians, becoming the dominant power on the Iberian peninsula. No longer preoccupied with Castilian competition, the Portuguese sought new territories and trading opportunities in the North Atlantic and along the West African coast. João's son, Prince Henrique, known later as Henry the Navigator, further expanded the royal family's domain by supporting expeditions down the coast of Africa and offshore to the Atlantic islands of Madeira and the Azores. The west and central coasts of Africa and the islands of the North and

South Atlantic, including the Cape Verde Islands, São Tomé, Principe, and Fernando Po, soon became Portuguese ports of call.

Portuguese monarchs granted the Atlantic islands to nobles as hereditary possessions on condition that the grantees colonize them, and soon the colonizers were establishing lucrative sugar plantations. In gratitude, noble families and merchants threw their political weight behind the king. Subsequent monarchs continued to cultivate local aristocrats' support for monarchical authority, thus ensuring smooth succession to the crown for members of the royal family.

In Spain, a new dynasty also emerged, though the road was difficult. Medieval Spain comprised rival kingdoms that quarreled ceaselessly. Within those kingdoms, several religions coexisted: Muslims, Jews, and Christians lived side by side in relative harmony, and Muslim armies still occupied strategic posts in the south. Over time, marriages and the formation of kinship ties among nobles and between royal lineages yielded a new political order. One by one, the major houses of the Spanish kingdoms intermarried, culminating in the wedding of Isabella of Castile and Ferdinand of Aragon (1469). This marriage linked Castile, wealthy and populous, to Aragon, which enjoyed an extended trading network in the Mediterranean. Together, the monarchs brought unruly nobles and distant towns under their control. They topped off their achievements by marrying their children into other European royal families—especially the Habsburgs, central Europe's most powerful dynasty. Thus, Spain's two most important provinces were joined, and Spain later became a state to be reckoned with.

The new Spanish rulers sent Christian armies south to push Muslim forces out of the Iberian Peninsula. By the mid-fifteenth century only Granada, a strategic linchpin overlooking the straits between the Mediterranean and the Atlantic, remained in Muslim hands. After a long and costly siege, Christian forces captured the fortress there in 1492. This was a victory of enormous symbolic importance, as joyous as the fall of Constantinople to Mehmed and the Ottomans in 1453 was depressing (for Christians).

The Inquisition and Westward Exploration Isabella and Ferdinand sought to drive all non-Catholics out of Spain. Terrified by Ottoman incursions into Europe, they launched an **Inquisition** in 1481, taking aim especially against *conversos*—converted Jews and Muslims, whom they suspected were Christians only in name. When Granada fell, the crown ordered the expulsion of all Jews from Spain. After 1499, a more tolerant attempt to convert the Moors (Muslims) by persuasion gave way to forced conversion—or emigration. All told, almost half a million people were forced to flee the Spanish kingdoms. This lack of tolerance meant that Spain, like other European states in this era, became increasingly homogeneous. With fewer groups vying for influence within their territories, rulers' attention turned outward, fueling rivalries between the various European states.

Inquisition
General term for a tribunal of the Roman Catholic Church that enforced religious orthodoxy. Several inquisitions took place over centuries, seeking to punish heretics, witches, Jews, and those whose conversion to Christianity was called into doubt.

So strong was the tide of Spanish fervor by late 1491 that the monarchs listened now to a Genoese navigator whose pleas for patronage they had previously rejected. Christopher Columbus promised them unimaginable riches that could finance their military campaigns and bankroll a crusade to liberate Jerusalem from Muslim hands. Off he sailed with a royal patent that guaranteed the monarchs a share of all he discovered. Soon the Spanish economy was reorienting itself toward the Atlantic, and Spain's merchants, missionaries, and soldiers were preparing for conquest and profiteering in what had been, just a few years before, a blank space on the map.

THE RENAISSANCE

Just as the Ming invoked Han Chinese traditions and the Ottomans looked to Sunni Islam to point the way forward, European elites drew on their own traditions for guidance as they rebuilt after the devastation of the plague. They found inspiration in ancient Greek and Roman institutions and ideas. Europe's extraordinary political and economic revival also involved a powerful outpouring of cultural achievements, led by Italian scholars and artists and financed by bankers, churchmen, and nobles. Much later, scholars coined the word **Renaissance** to characterize the cultural flourishing of the Italian city-states, France, the Netherlands, England, and the Holy Roman Empire in the period 1430–1550. What was being "reborn" was ancient Greek and Roman art and learning—knowledge that could help people understand an expanding world and support the rights of secular individuals to exert power in it.

Although the Renaissance was largely funded by popes, Christian kings, and powerful wealthy merchants, it challenged the authority of traditional religious elites, breaking the medieval church's monopoly on answers to the big questions. Religious topics and themes, such as David and Goliath, Judith and Holophernes, and various scenes from Jesus's story (annunciation of his birth to Mary, Jesus's adoration by the magi, and his baptism and crucifixion) dominated much of Renaissance art, but these themes took on new meaning as warnings to overbearing rulers and reminders to the obscenely

Ferdinand and Isabella Entering Granada This altar relief, sculpted by Felipe Vigarny in the early sixteenth century, depicts the triumphant entrance of King Ferdinand and Queen Isabella into the city of Granada after their conquest of this last Muslim stronghold in Spain.

Renaissance
Term meaning "rebirth" used by historians to characterize the cultural flourishing of European nations between 1430 and 1550, which emphasized a break from the church-centered medieval world and a new concept of humankind as the center of the world.

wealthy, who sponsored many of these works, of their place in the cosmos and the civic responsibility that stemmed from their wealth. These religious themes were also joined by classical topics, such as scenes from mythology and the ancient past. The movement valued secular forms of learning, rather than just Christian doctrine, and a more human-centered understanding of the cosmos.

The Renaissance was all about new exposure to the old—to classical texts and ancient art and architectural forms. Although some Greek and Roman texts were known in Europe and the Islamic world, the use of the printing press made others accessible to western scholars for the first time. Scholars now realized that the pre-Christian Greeks and Romans had developed powerful means of representing and caring for the human body. Having studied the world directly, without the need to square their observations with biblical information, the ancients had much to teach about geography, astronomy, and architecture and about how to govern states and armies. For Renaissance scholars it was no longer enough to understand Christian doctrine and to concern themselves with the next world. One had to go back to the original, classical sources in order to understand the human condition. This in turn required the learning of languages and history. Scholarship that attempted to return to Greek and Roman sources became known as **humanism**.

Because political and religious powers were not united in Europe (as they were in China and the Islamic world), scholars and artists seeking sponsors for their work could play one side against the other or, alternatively, could suffer both clerical and political persecution. Michelangelo (1475–1564), a leading painter, sculptor, architect, and engineer of the age, completed commissions for the famous Florentine bankers and political leaders of the Medici family, for the Florentine Wool Guild, and for Pope Julius II. Peter Paul Rubens painted for the courts of France, Spain, England, and the Netherlands, as well as selling paintings on the open market. These two painters, renowned for showing a great deal of flesh, frequently offended conservative church officials. Even so, most support for the arts came either from the church or from individual clergymen, and virtually all secular donors were devout believers who commissioned works with religious themes. The Dutch scholar Desiderius Erasmus ridiculed corrupt popes and the clergy under the patronage of English, Dutch, and French supporters while remaining a Catholic, an ordained cleric, and an opponent of Reformation doctrines. Conflicts within the Catholic Church, between the church and secular leaders, and among secular leaders and wealthy private citizens enabled artists to present challenging images and ideas with an unusual independence.

Gradually, a network of educated men and women took shape that was not wholly dependent on the church, the state, or a single princely patron. Classical knowledge gave individuals the means to challenge political, clerical, and aesthetic authority. Moreover, rivalries between Europe's relatively small

humanism
The Renaissance aspiration to develop a greater understanding of the human experience than the Christian scriptures offered by reaching back into ancient Greek and Roman texts.

Renaissance Masterpieces Leonardo da Vinci's *The Last Supper* (*left*) depicts Christ's disciples reacting to his announcement that one of them will betray him. Michelangelo's *David* (*right*) stands over seventeen feet high and was conceived as an expression of Florentine civic ideals.

states and city-states allowed many of these scholars to dodge the authorities by fleeing to neighboring communities. Of course, they could also use their learning to defend the older elites: for example, numerous lawyers and scholars continued to work for the popes in defending the papacy. At the same time, men like Erasmus and later Martin Luther (the leading figure of the Reformation in the sixteenth century) looked to secular princes to support their critical scholarship. In Florence, Niccolò Machiavelli wrote the most famous treatise on authoritarian power, *The Prince* (1513). Machiavelli argued that political leadership required mastering the rules of modern statecraft, even if in some cases this meant disregarding moral imperatives. Holding and exercising power were vital ends in themselves, he claimed; traditional ideas of civic virtue should not deter rulers, like those of the Medici family, from maintaining control over society.

With Renaissance ideas challenging traditional authority and rulers facing a range of internal and external obstacles, the new monarchies of Europe were not all immediately successful in consolidating power and unifying peoples. In France and England, for example, the great age of monarchy had yet to dawn. Even when stable states did arise in Europe, they were fairly small compared with the Ottoman and Ming empires. In the mid-sixteenth century, Portugal and Spain, Europe's two most expansionist states, had populations of 1 million and 9 million, respectively. England, excluding Wales, had a mere 3 million in 1550. Only France, with 17 million, had a population close to the Ottoman Empire's 25 million. And these numbers paled in comparison with Ming China's population of nearly 200 million in 1550. But in Europe, small could be advantageous. Portugal's relatively small population meant that the crown had fewer groups to control. In the world of finance, the most successful merchants were those inhabiting the smaller Italian city-states and, a bit later, the cities of the northern Netherlands. The Florentines developed sophisticated banking techniques, created extensive networks of agents throughout Europe and the Mediterranean, and served as bankers to the popes. At the same time, the Renaissance—which flourished in the city-states and newly stabilized monarchies—made elite European culture more cosmopolitan and independent from government authority, even if it could not unify the states and peoples who cultivated it.

Ming China

Like the Europeans, the Chinese saw their stable worldview and political order crumble under the catastrophes of human and microbial invasions. Moreover, like the Europeans, people in China had long regarded outsiders as "barbarians" and balked at being ruled by them. Together, the Mongols and the Black Death upended the political and intellectual foundations of what had appeared to be the world's most integrated society. The Mongols brought the Yuan dynasty to power; then the plague devastated China and prepared the way for the emergence of a new dynasty. The **Ming dynasty**, ruled by ethnically Han Chinese, defined itself against its foreign predecessors. Ming emperors sought to reinforce everything Chinese. In particular, they supported China's vast internal agricultural markets in an attempt to minimize dependence on merchants and foreign trade.

RESTORING ORDER

In the chaotic fourteenth century, as plague and famine ravaged China and the Mongol Yuan dynasty collapsed, only a strong military movement capable of overpowering other groups could restore order. That intervention began at the hands of a poor young man who had trained in the **Red Turban movement**: Zhu Yuanzhang, a successful warlord who had led a rebellion against the waning power of the Mongols and any others who would assert control in their wake.

It soon became clear that Zhu had a much grander design for China than the ambitions of most warlords. When he took Nanjing in 1356, he renamed it Yingtian (in response to heaven). Lifted by subsequent successful military campaigns, Zhu (r. 1368–1398) took the imperial title of Hongwu (expansive and martial) Emperor and proclaimed the founding of the Ming (brilliant) dynasty in 1368. Soon thereafter, his troops met little resistance when

Ming dynasty
Successor to the Mongol Yuan dynasty that reinstituted and reinforced Han Chinese ceremonies and ideals, including rule by an ethnically Han bureaucracy.

Red Turban movement
Diverse religious movement in China during the fourteenth century that spread the belief that the world was drawing to an end as Mongol rule was collapsing.

they seized the Yuan capital of Khan-balik (soon renamed Beijing), causing the Mongol emperor to flee to his homeland in the steppe. It would, however, take Hongwu almost another twenty years to reunify the entire country.

CENTRALIZATION UNDER THE MING

Hongwu and successive Ming emperors had to rebuild a devastated society from the ground up. Although in the past China had experienced natural catastrophes, wars, and social dislocation, the plague's legacy was devastation on an unprecedented scale. It left the new rulers with the formidable challenge of rebuilding the great cities, restoring respect for ruling elites, and reconstructing the bureaucracy.

Imperial Grandeur and Kinship The rebuilding began with the Hongwu Emperor, whose capital at Nanjing reflected imperial grandeur. When the dynasty's third emperor, the Yongle (perpetual happiness) Emperor, relocated the capital to Beijing, he flaunted an even more grandiose style, employing around 100,000 artisans and 1 million laborers to build this new capital. The city had three separate walled enclosures. Inside the outer city walls sprawled the imperial city; within its walls lay the palace compound, the Forbidden City. Traffic within the walled sections navigated through broad boulevards leading to the different gates, above which imposing towers soared. The palace compound, where the imperial family resided, had more than 9,000 rooms. Anyone standing in the front courts, which measured more than 400 yards on a side and boasted marble terraces and carved railings, would gasp at the awe-inspiring projection of power. That was precisely the effect the Ming emperors wanted, just as the Ottoman sultans did in building Topkapi Palace.

Marriage and kinship buttressed the power of the Ming imperial household, much as dynastic strategies did in Europe. The Ming dynasty's founder married the adopted daughter of a leading Red Turban rebel (her father, according to legend, was a convicted murderer), thereby consolidating his power and eliminating a threat. Empress Ma, as she was known, became Hongwu's principal wife and was praised for her compassion. Emerging as the kinder face of the regime, she tempered the harsh and sometimes cruel disposition of her spouse. He had numerous other consorts as well, including Korean and Mongol women, who bore him twenty-six sons and sixteen daughters (similar to, although on a smaller scale than, the Ottoman sultan's harem at Topkapi Palace).

Building a Bureaucracy Faced with the challenge of reestablishing order out of turmoil, Hongwu initially sought to rule through his kinsmen—by giving imperial princes generous stipends, command of large garrisons, and

Ming Fashion

Ming rulers liked to represent themselves as custodians of "civilized" Han traditions, in contrast to the "barbarian" ways of the previous Mongol Yuan dynasty. However, from governmental practices to clothing fashions, there were visible signs everywhere that the Ming, despite their rhetoric, followed in the footsteps of the Yuan and became more and more linked to an ever-growing, interconnected world. As trade with neighboring and faraway lands continued unabated and merchants and travelers kept moving, it proved to be impossible for the Ming to keep outside influences at arm's length. At the same time, the rhetoric of a return to Han traditions did generate moves to invoke antiquity in the realm of fashion. Status-conscious elites with newfound wealth eagerly purchased clothes in what they believed to be the ancient Han style, hoping to set themselves apart from the common people. Their flirtation with antiquity, however, often ended up being more of a reinvention to satisfy the surging demands of the market than a genuine return to earlier conventions.

Founder Zhu Yuanzhang set the tone of the Ming by trying to rid the

An example of headwear used by Ming officials, reputedly following the style of earlier dynasties. The beams attached to the crown of the cap indicate the official's rank, so the cap is known as a "beamed cap."

country of the close-fitting tunics worn by the Mongols. He advocated instead the wearing of the reputedly Tang-style garment of earlier times. While this measure did meet with some success, the vibrant clothing industry was hardly free of its fascination with the "exotic," such as horsehair skirts from

Korea for men. These skirts were a rare commodity when they first arrived, probably via trade missions, but by the late fifteenth century, local weavers had become so skilled in making them, and consumers so eager to obtain them, that craftspeople were caught stealing the tails of horses to satisfy the soaring demand for the raw materials. Indeed, undoubtedly to the chagrin of the first Ming emperor and his descendants, much of the Yuan style and even terminology in both male and female clothing persisted during the Ming era.

Hats for men—a convenient yet highly visible way to make a statement of social standing—were another striking example of Ming retro taste in fashion. Invoking the names of earlier dynasties were the Han cap, the Jin cap, the Tang cap, and so on. The most interesting, however, was the Chunyang hat, which allegedly drew upon both Han and Tang styles in its design but had actually become a symbol of the so-called new and strange fashion that so often attracted commentary in Ming writings. In fact, it was favored by the young, who had nothing but disdain for ancient styles!

significant autonomy in running their domains. However, when the princes' power began to threaten the court, Hongwu slashed their stipends, reduced their privileges, and took control of their garrisons. No longer dependent on these men, he established an imperial bureaucracy beholden only to him and to his successors. Its officials won appointments through their outstanding performance on a reinstated civil service examination.

In addition, Hongwu took other steps to install a centralized system of rule. He assigned bureaucrats to oversee the manufacture of porcelain, cotton, and silk products as well as tax collection. He reestablished the Confucian

The "paddy-field gown" for women might have had its origins in Buddhist robes.

Nor was the rage for fashion reserved for men only, or even for just the privileged. As one Ming writer lamented, perhaps with a hint of exaggeration: "Nowadays the very servant girls dress in silk gauze, and the singsong girls look down on brocaded silks and embroidered gowns." Respectable women, we are told, looked to the clothing and style of the courtesans of the prosperous southern region of the country for ideas and inspiration for fashion. Indeed, much of our visual knowledge of Ming women's clothing comes from paintings that probably show highly trained courtesans or the female "entertainers" that were ubiquitous in Ming urban centers. These paintings reveal the different and consistently evolving styles of clothing for Ming women—including the "paddy-field gown," which might have owed its origins to Buddhist robes—that were the focus of much criticism from those who frowned on the growing penchant for the exotic, the strange, the outrageous, and the irreverent in the realm of fashion. If nothing else, this debate about clothing certainly tells us that despite the often conservative stance and policies of the Ming regime, the everyday life of many Ming subjects was a constant exercise in negotiating the multiple impacts of both the old and the new, as well as the familiar and the foreign, in different arenas of their rapidly changing society.

Questions for Analysis

- What are some examples of Ming "retro" fashion? Why did the Ming elite cultivate an "ancient" Han style?
- How do we know about changes in women's fashion in the Ming era? Are there any dangers in using these sources to understand the dress of all Ming women?
- Flipping back through the illustrations in this chapter, what do you see of the clothing from other regions? What questions does the analysis of Ming clothing presented here raise for you as you reexamine the images of Ottomans and western Europeans?

Explore Further

Clunas, Craig and Harrison-Hall, eds., *Ming: 50 Years that Changed China* (2014).
Finnane, Antonia, *Changing Clothes in China: Fashion, History, Nation* (2008).

school system as a means of selecting a cadre of loyal officials (not unlike the Ottoman janissaries and administrators). He also set up local networks of villages to rebuild irrigation systems and to supervise reforestation projects to prevent flooding—with the astonishing result that the amount of land reclaimed nearly tripled within eight years. For water supply and flood control, over 40,000 reservoirs underwent repairs or new construction. Historians estimate that Hongwu's reign oversaw the planting around Nanjing of about 1 billion trees, which were later used in building a maritime expedition fleet in the early fifteenth century.

The Forbidden City The Yongle Emperor relocated the capital to Beijing, where he began the construction of the Forbidden City, or imperial palace compound, in the early fifteenth century. The palace was designed to inspire awe in all who saw it.

The imperial palace not only projected the image of a power center, it *was* the center of power. Every official received his appointment by the emperor through the Ministry of Personnel. Hongwu eliminated the post of prime minister (he executed the man who held the post) and ruled directly. Ming bureaucrats had to kneel before the emperor. The drawback of this centralized control, of course, was that the Ming emperor had to keep tabs on this immense system. Hongwu constantly moved his bureaucrats around, sometimes fortifying the administration, sometimes undermining it lest it become too autonomous. Over time, Hongwu nurtured a bureaucracy far more extensive than that of the Ottomans. The Ming thus established the most highly centralized system of government of all the monarchies of this period.

Religion under the Ming Just as the Ottoman sultans projected themselves as Muslim rulers, calling themselves the shadow of God, and European monarchs claimed to rule by divine right, the Ming emperors enhanced their legitimacy by drawing on ancient Chinese religious traditions. Citing the mandate of heaven, the emperor revised and strengthened the elaborate rites and ceremonies that had supported dynastic power for centuries. Official rituals, such as those related to the gods of soil and grain, reinforced political and social classes, portraying the rulers as the moral and spiritual benefactors of their subjects. In lavish ceremonies, the emperor engaged in sacrificial rites, cultivating his image as mediator between the human and the spiritual worlds. The message was clear: the gods were on the side of the Ming household.

MING RULERSHIP

Conquest and defense helped establish the Ming empire, and bureaucracy kept it functioning. The empire's scale required complex administration. (See Map 11.4.) To many outsiders (especially Europeans, whose region was in a state of constant war), Ming stability and centralization appeared to be political wizardry.

Ming rulers worried in particular about maintaining the support of ordinary people in the countryside. The emperor wished to be seen as the special guardian of his subjects. He wanted their allegiance as well as their taxes and labor. But during hard times, poor farmers were reluctant to provide resources— taxes or services—to distant officials. A popular Chinese proverb was "The mountain is high and the emperor is far away." For these reasons, and because he distrusted state bureaucrats, Hongwu preferred to entrust the management of rural communities to local leaders, whom he appointed as village chiefs, village elders, or tax captains. Within these communities, the dynasty created a social hierarchy based on age, sex, and kinship. While women's labor remained critical for the village economy, the government reinforced a gender hierarchy by promoting women's chastity and constructing commemorative arches for widows who honored their husbands by refraining from remarrying.

Like the European and Islamic states, the Ming Empire faced periodic unrest and rebellion. Rebels often proclaimed their own brand of religious beliefs and local elites resented central control. Outright terror helped stymie these threats to central authority. In a massive wave of carnage, Hongwu slaughtered anyone who posed a threat to his authority, from the highest of ministers to the lowliest of scribes. From 1376 to 1393, four of his purges condemned close to 100,000 subjects to execution. Yet, despite the emperor's immense power, the Ming Empire remained undergoverned. Indeed, as the population multiplied, there were too few loyal officials to handle local

Ming Deities The pantheon of deities worshipped during the Ming dynasty demonstrates the rich religious culture of the period.

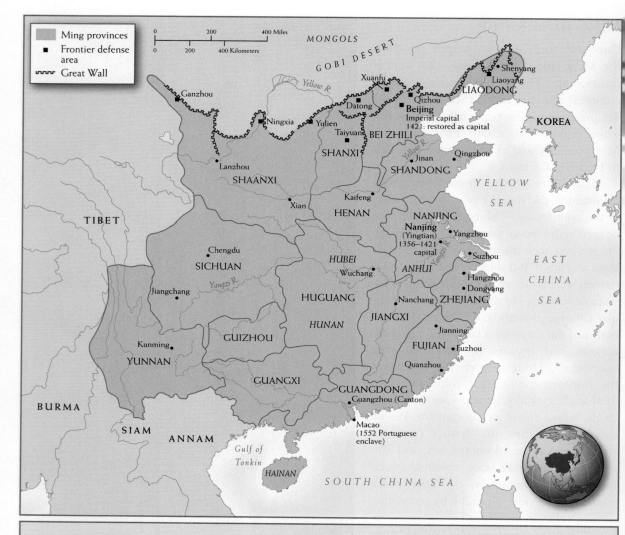

Map 11.4 Ming China, 1500s

The Ming state was one of the largest empires at this time—and the most populous. Using the scale, determine the length of its coastline and its internal borders.

- What were the two Ming capitals and the three main seaport trading cities? How far are they from one another?
- According to the map, where did the Ming rulers expect the greatest threat to their security?
- How many provinces are outlined on the map? How far is Beijing from some of the more distant provinces? What sorts of challenges might that create for the centralized style of Ming rule, and how does the chapter suggest those challenges were resolved?

affairs. By the sixteenth and early seventeenth centuries, for example, some 10,000 to 15,000 officials shouldered the responsibility of managing a population exceeding 200 million people. Nonetheless, Hongwu bequeathed to his descendants a set of tools for ruling that drew on subjects' direct loyalty to the emperor and on the intricate workings of an extensive bureaucracy. His legacy enabled his successors to balance local sources of power with the needs of dynastic rulership.

TRADE AND EXPLORATION UNDER THE MING

Gradually, the political stability brought by the Ming dynasty allowed trade to revive. Now the new dynasty's merchants reestablished China's preeminence in long-distance commercial exchange. Chinese silk and cotton textiles, as well as fine porcelains, ranked among the world's most coveted luxuries. When a Chinese merchant ship sailed into a port, trading partners and onlookers crowded the docks to watch the unloading of precious cargoes. Although Ming rulers' support for overseas ventures wavered and eventually declined, this period saw important developments in Chinese trade and exploration.

Core Objectives

COMPARE how Ottoman, Iberian, and Ming rulers extended their territories and regional influence.

Overseas Trade: Success and Suspicion During the Ming period, Chinese traders based in the three main ports—Hangzhou, Quanzhou, and Guangzhou (Canton)—were as energetic as their Muslim counterparts in the Indian Ocean. These and other ports were home to prosperous merchants and the point of convergence for vast sea-lanes. Leaving the mainland ports, Chinese vessels carried precious wares to offshore islands, the Pescadores, and Taiwan. From there, they sailed on to the ports of Southeast Asia. As entrepôts for global goods, East Asian ports flourished. Former fishing villages developed into major urban centers.

The Ming dynasty viewed overseas expansion with suspicion, however. Hongwu feared that too much contact with the outside world would cause instability and undermine his rule. In fact, he banned private maritime commerce in 1371. But enforcement was lax, and by the late fifteenth century maritime trade had once again surged. Because much of the thriving business took place in defiance of official edicts, it led to constant friction between government officials and maritime traders. Although the Ming government ultimately agreed to issue licenses for overseas trade in the mid-sixteenth century, its policies continued to vacillate. To Ming officials, unlike their counterparts in Portugal and Spain, the sea represented problems of order and control rather than opportunities.

The Expeditions of Zheng He One spectacular exception to the early Ming attitude toward maritime trade was a series of officially sponsored expeditions in the early fifteenth century. It was the ambitious third Ming emperor, the Yongle Emperor, who took this initiative. One of his loyal followers was a Muslim whom the Ming army had captured as a boy. The youth was castrated and sent to serve at the court (as a eunuch, he could not continue his family line and so theoretically owed allegiance solely to the emperor). Given the name **Zheng He** (1371–1433), he grew up to be an important military leader. The emperor entrusted him with venturing out to trade, collect tribute, and display China's power to the world.

From 1405 to 1433, Zheng He commanded the world's greatest armada and led seven naval expeditions. His larger ships stretched 400 feet in length (Columbus's *Santa Maria* was 85 feet), carried hundreds of sailors on four tiers of decks, and maneuvered with sophisticated rudders, nine masts, and watertight compartments. The first expedition set sail with 28,000 men aboard a flotilla of sixty-two large ships and over 200 lesser ones. Zheng He and his entourage aimed to establish tributary relations with far-flung territories—from Southeast Asia to the Indian Ocean ports, to the Persian Gulf, and to the east coast of Africa. (See Map 11.5.) These expeditions did not seek territorial expansion, but rather control of trade and tribute. When

Zheng He's Ships and Exotic Cargo The largest ship in Zheng He's armada had nine staggered masts and twelve silk sails. This graphic demonstrates just how large and complex Zheng He's ships were, compared with Christopher Columbus's *Santa Maria*. With ships so large, Zheng He's fleet could return to China with magnificent and exotic cargo, like the giraffes brought as tribute from Bengal in 1414 and Malindi in 1415. These tribute giraffes were recorded in several paintings, some inscribed with a poem attributed to contemporary Shen Du that described the giraffes as *qilin*, mythical creatures that appear during the rule of a great leader.

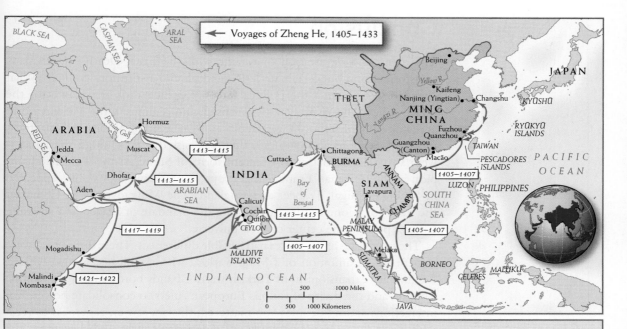

Map 11.5 Voyages of Zheng He, 1405–1433

Zheng He's voyages are some of the most famous in world history. Many have speculated about how history might be different if the Chinese emperors had allowed the voyages to continue.

- What routes did Zheng He's armada follow?
- Referring to other maps in this chapter and earlier chapters, with what peoples did Zheng He's armada come into contact?
- Using the scale on the map, estimate how far Zheng He's armada sailed. How does that distance compare with those covered by other world travelers you've encountered in this text?

the Yonge Emperor died in 1424, the expeditions lost their most enthusiastic patron. Moreover, by the mid-fifteenth century, there was a revival of military threats from the north, recalling how the maritime-oriented Song dynasty had been overrun by invaders from the north (see Chapter 10). Consequently, Ming officials withdrew imperial support for seagoing ventures and instead devoted their energies to overland ventures and defense.

Even though maritime commerce continued without official patronage, the Ming decision to forgo overseas ventures was momentous. Although China remained the wealthiest, most densely settled region of the world, with fully developed state structures and thriving markets, the empire's wariness of overseas projects deprived merchants and would-be explorers of vital support in an age when others were beginning to look outward and overseas.

Conclusion

The dying and devastation that came with the Black Death caused many transformations, but certain underlying ideals and institutions endured. What changed were mainly the political regimes, which took the blame for the catastrophes. The Yuan dynasty collapsed, and regimes in the Muslim world and western Christendom were replaced by new political forms. In contrast, universal religions and cultural systems persisted, even though they underwent vast transformations. A fervent form of Sunni Islam found its champion in the Ottoman Empire. In Europe, centralizing monarchies appeared in Spain, Portugal, France, and England. The Ming dynasts in China set the stage for a long tenure by claiming the mandate of heaven and stressing China's place at the center of their universe.

The new states and empires had notable differences. These differences were evident in the ambition of a Ming warlord who established a new dynasty, the military expansionism of Turkish warrior bands bordering the Byzantine Empire, and the desire of various European rulers to consolidate power. But interactions among peoples also mattered; this era saw an eagerness to reestablish and expand trade networks and a desire to convert unbelievers to "the true faith"—be it a form of Islam or an exclusive Christianity.

All of the dynasties surveyed in this chapter faced similar problems. They had to establish legitimacy, ensure smooth succession, deal with religious movements, and forge working relationships with nobles, townspeople, merchants, and peasants. Yet each state developed a distinctive identity. They all combined political innovation, traditional ways of ruling, and ideas borrowed from neighbors. European monarchies achieved significant internal unity, often through warfare with competing states. Ottoman rulers perfected techniques for ruling an ethnically and religiously diverse empire: they moved military forces swiftly, allowed local communities a degree of autonomy, and trained a bureaucracy dedicated to the Ottoman and Sunni Islamic way of life. The Ming fashioned an imperial system based on a Confucian bureaucracy and intense subordination to the emperor so that it could manage a mammoth population. The rising monarchies of Europe and the Ottoman state all blazed with religious fervor and sought to eradicate or subordinate the beliefs of other groups.

The new states displayed unprecedented political and economic powers. All demonstrated military prowess, a desire for stable political and social hierarchies and secure borders, and a drive to expand. Each legitimized its rule via dynastic marriage and succession, state-sanctioned religion, and administrative bureaucracies. Each supported vigorous commercial activity. The Islamic regimes, especially, engaged in long-distance commerce and, by conquest and conversion, extended their holdings.

For western Christendom, the Ottoman conquests were decisive. They provoked Europeans to establish commercial connections to the east, south, and west. The consequences of their new toeholds would be momentous—just as the Chinese decision to turn away from overseas exploration and commerce meant that China's contact with the outside world would be overland and more limited. As we shall see in Chapter 12, both decisions were instrumental in determining which worlds would come together and which would remain apart.

Focus On
Crisis and Recovery in Afro-Eurasia

Collapse and Consolidation

- Bubonic plague originates in Inner Asia and afflicts people from China to Europe.
- Climate change and famine leave people vulnerable to infection, while commerce facilitates the spread of disease.
- The plague kills 25 to 65 percent of infected populations and leaves societies in turmoil.

The Islamic Heartland

- Ottomans overrun Constantinople and become the primary Sunni regime in the Islamic world.
- The Ottomans establish their legitimacy with military prowess, religious backing, and a loyal bureaucracy.
- Sultans manage the decentralizing tendencies of outlying provinces with flexibility and tolerance, relying on religious faith, patronage, and bureaucracy.

Western Christendom

- New dynastic monarchies that claim to rule by divine right appear in Portugal, Spain, France, and England.
- The Inquisition takes aim against conversos—converted Jews and Muslims.
- A rebirth of classical learning, known as the Renaissance, originates in Italian city-states and spreads throughout western Europe.

Ming China

- The Ming dynasty replaces the Mongol Yuan dynasty and rebuilds a strong state from the ground up, claiming a mandate from heaven.
- An elaborate, centralized bureaucracy oversees the revival of infrastructure and long-distance trade.
- The emperor and bureaucracy concentrate on developing internal markets and overland trade at the expense of overseas commerce.

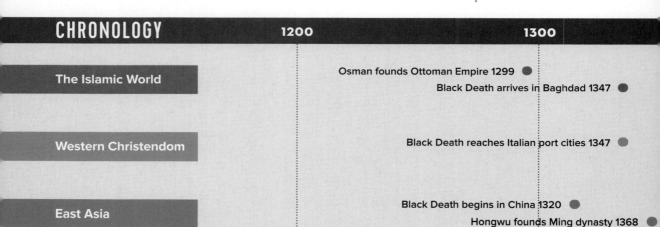

CHRONOLOGY

	1200	1300
The Islamic World		Osman founds Ottoman Empire 1299 ●
		Black Death arrives in Baghdad 1347 ●
Western Christendom		Black Death reaches Italian port cities 1347 ●
East Asia		Black Death begins in China 1320 ●
		Hongwu founds Ming dynasty 1368 ●

THINKING ABOUT GLOBAL CONNECTIONS

Thinking about Exchange Networks By the fourteenth century, most of the Afro-Eurasian landmass was bound together by multiple exchange networks that functioned on many levels—political, cultural, and commercial. How did these exchange networks facilitate the spread of the plague? In what ways did the spread of the Black Death correspond with and diverge from existing political, cultural, and commercial networks?

Thinking about Changing Power Relationships Fourteenth-century famine and plague, and the accompanying political, economic, and natural crises, together triggered powerful, often differing, responses in western Europe, the Ottoman lands, and Ming China. How did men and women at different levels of society respond to the fourteenth-century crises? How did their responses reshape their societies? Pay special attention to the relationships among ordinary men and women, elites, and imperial bureaucracies in all three regions.

Thinking about Environmental Impacts Climate change laid the groundwork for the devastation of the Black Death. What environmental developments in Europe, central Asia, and China set the stage for the Black Death?

Key Terms

Black Death p. 499
devshirme p. 511
humanism p. 518
Inquisition p. 516

Ming dynasty p. 520
monarchy p. 513
Ottoman Empire p. 506

Red Turban movement p. 520
Renaissance p. 517

Topkapi Palace p. 510
Zheng He p. 528

 Go to INQUIZITIVE to see what you've learned—and learn what you've missed—with personalized feedback along the way.

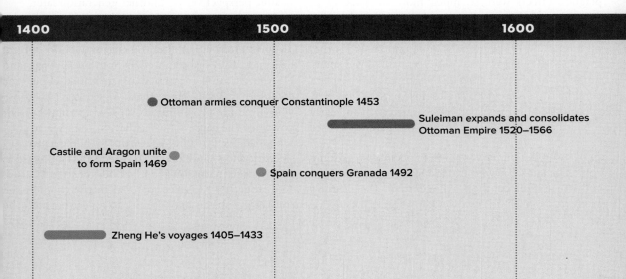

1400 — 1500 — 1600

Ottoman armies conquer Constantinople 1453

Suleiman expands and consolidates Ottoman Empire 1520–1566

Castile and Aragon unite to form Spain 1469

Spain conquers Granada 1492

Zheng He's voyages 1405–1433

Global Themes and Sources

Causes and Effects of the Black Death

The devastation wrought by the plague in Afro-Eurasia and the upheaval that followed were unprecedented and far-reaching in their impact. Families were broken as parents, spouses, and children deserted one another for fear of contagion. Religious responses varied from hopelessness to ecstatic devotion. The plague affected the economy as well, causing skyrocketing prices, diminished availability of goods and labor, and unmet demand for certain products and services. Dramatic population losses demonstrate its demographic impact: beginning in southwestern China in the 1320s, the Pestilence or Great Mortality, as it came to be known in Europe, wiped out between 25 and 65 percent of the populations it afflicted.

The plague traveled along the trade routes of Inner Eurasia, taking advantage of the connectivity that had bound the Afro-Eurasian world together and facilitated the movement of people, goods, and ideas. The plague also took advantage of an already weakened population that had experienced a "Little Ice Age" and a resulting famine in the early years of the fourteenth century. Modern scholars have scrutinized sources to determine answers to such questions as what the precise death tolls were, why the plague's effects were so much more devastating in some regions than in others, and what kind of disease it was—septicemic (blood borne and spread by fleas on rats and other animals), pneumonic (airborne, spread by the coughing that accompanied the spewing of blood that so many of the sources report), or a combination of the two. No less fascinating, however, are the attempts by writers of the fourteenth and early fifteenth centuries to understand the plague's causes and immediate effects.

The sources here offer a mix of perspectives. Some come from authors who experienced plague firsthand and others from authors who lived in the plague's aftermath and considered its causes and its effects.

There are regional accounts from two different cultural spheres: the Islamic world, particularly Syria and Egypt, and Europe. Ibn al-Wardi, from Aleppo in Syria, recorded his thoughts on what was causing the plague and described immediate responses to, and effects of, the disease. His understanding offers only the most short-term perspective because he died from the plague in 1349 and thus did not live to see the long-term aftermath. The Florentine Baldasarre de Buonaiuti experienced the plague in one of the European cities hit the hardest, and perhaps the most memorably, by the disease, given the description, with echoes of Baldasarre, in the introduction to Boccaccio's famed *Decameron*, in which elite youth withdraw from the city and entertain one another with stories having locked themselves away in a country villa to escape the sickness in the city. In his later years, Baldasarre recollected the events of 1348 in his *Florentine Chronicle*. The plague offered Ibn Khaldûn (c. 1375) an opportunity to ruminate on the patterns of civilization in his *Muqadimmah*. Written in Cairo, his historiographical masterpiece gives a North African perspective on the effects of the plague a full generation after its impact. Finally, a student of Ibn Khaldûn, al-Maqrizi, gives yet another Cairene, Islamic perspective, yet another generation later.

These sources, with their different perspectives—Christian and Islamic, contemporary and from the plague's aftermath, by chronicler and philosophical historian, European as well as Southwest Asian and North African—encourage us to think about the complexity of cause and effect. We can see how those who lived in proximity to this catastrophic event described the causes of what they, or their recent relatives, had lived through. The sources allow us to consider the short- and long-term effects of the disease as experienced in the fourteenth and fifteenth centuries. And, together with the material in the chapter, the sources give us an opportunity to reflect both on the complexity of causation, teasing out the primary and secondary causes for how the plague played out, and on the larger historical significance of the plague and its aftermath.

Analyzing the Causes and Effects of the Black Death

- How do the responses to, and the effects of, plague in the Muslim world (as reported by Ibn Khaldûn, al-Wardi, and al-Maqrizi) compare with those in Florence (as reported in the *Florentine Chronicle*)?

- What patterns in explaining causation and effects of plague do you detect in these sources? How do the various causes, and effects, explicitly or implicitly discussed in each text build on one another?

- Based on your reading of these sources, what do you think is the short- and long-term historical significance of the effects of the plague?

PRIMARY SOURCE 11.1

Plague in Southwest Asia, Ibn al-Wardi (1349)

Al-Wardi wrote two major works, one a natural history of the Islamic world and the other a history, from which this excerpt on the plague's devastation is taken. His is the most thorough extant contemporary Muslim description of the Black Death. Al-Wardi's discussion of the plague is rendered all the more poignant by the fact that he became one of its victims as the plague swept through Aleppo in 1349.

- What role does religion, and/or God, play in al-Wardi's account of the plague? How do the Sunni-Shia division and other rifts factor into al-Wardi's account?

- How does al-Wardi describe the plague's progress across Afro-Eurasia, and what does that description suggest about al-Wardi's understanding of causation?

- What are some of the attempted remedies described by al-Wardi, and what do those remedies suggest about the understanding of the plague's causes?

God is my security in every adversity. My sufficiency is in God alone. Is not God sufficient protection for His servant? Oh God, pray for our master, Muḥammad, and give him peace. Save us for his sake from the attacks of the plague and give us shelter.

The plague frightened and killed. It began in the land of darkness. Oh, what a visitor! It has been current for fifteen years. China was not preserved from it nor could the strongest fortress hinder it. The plague afflicted the Indians in India. It weighed upon the Sind. It seized with its hand and ensnared even the lands of the Uzbeks. How many backs did it break in what is Transoxiana! The plague increased and spread further. It attacked the Persians, extended its steps toward the land of Khiṭai, and gnawed away at the Crimea. It pelted Rūm with live coals and led the outrage to Cyprus and the islands. The plague destroyed mankind in Cairo. Its eye was cast upon Egypt, and behold, the people were wide-awake. It stilled all movement in Alexandria. . . .

Then, the plague turned to Upper Egypt. It, also, sent forth its storm to Barqah. The plague attacked Gaza, and it shook Asqalān severely. The plague oppressed Acre. The scourge came to Jerusalem and paid the *zakāt* [with the souls of men]. It overtook those people who fled to the al-'Aqsā Mosque, which stands beside the Dome of the Rock. If the door of mercy had not been opened, the end of the world would have occurred in a moment. It, then, hastened its pace and attacked the entire maritime plain. The plague trapped Sidon and descended unexpectedly upon Beirut, cunningly. Next, it directed the shooting of its arrows to Damascus. There the plague sat like a king on a throne and swayed with power, killing daily one thousand or more and decimating the population. It destroyed mankind with its pustules. May God the Most High spare Damascus to pursue its own path and extinguish the plague's fires so that they do not come close to her fragrant orchards.

Oh God, restore Damascus and protect her from insult.

Its morale has been so lowered that people in the city sell themselves for a grain. . . .

The plague and its poison spread to Sarmīn. It reviled the Sunni and the Shī'ī. It sharpened its spearheads for the Sunni and advanced like an army. The plague was spread in the land of the Shī'ī with a ruinous effect. To Antioch the plague gave its share. Then, it left there quickly with a shyness like a man who has forgotten the memory of his beloved. . . . The plague subjected Dhulūl and went straight through the lowlands and the mountains. It uprooted many people from their homes. Then, the plague sought Aleppo, but it did not succeed. By God's mercy the plague was the lightest oppression. . . . How amazingly does it pursue the people of each house! One of them spits blood, and everyone in the household is certain of death. It brings the entire family to their graves after two or three nights. . . .

Oh God, it is acting by Your command. Lift this from us. It happens where You wish; keep the plague from us. Who will defend us against this horror other than You the Almighty? . . .

Oh, if you could see the nobles of Aleppo studying their inscrutable books of medicine. They multiply its remedies by eating dried and sour foods. The buboes which disturb men's healthy lives are smeared with Armenian clay. Each man treated his humours and made life more comfortable. They perfumed their homes with ambergris and camphor, cyperus and sandal. They wore ruby rings and put onions, vinegar, and sardines together with the daily meal. They ate less broth and fruit but ate the citron and similar things.

If you see many biers and their carriers and hear in every quarter of Aleppo the announcements of death and cries, you run from them and refuse to stay with them. In Aleppo the profits of the undertakers have greatly increased. . . .

We ask God's forgiveness for our souls' bad inclination; the plague is surely part of His punishment. We take refuge from His wrath in His pleasure and from His chastisement in His restoring. . . .

Among the things which exasperated the Muslims and brought suffering is that our enemy, the damned people of Sis, are pleased by our trial. They act as if they are safe from the plague—that there is a treaty so that it will not approach them or that they have triumphed over it. Our Lord does not create us as an enticement for those who disbelieve. . . .

This plague is for the Muslims a martyrdom and a reward, and for the disbelievers a punishment and a rebuke. When the Muslim endures misfortune, then patience is his worship. It has been established by our Prophet, God bless him and give him peace, that the plague-stricken are martyrs. This noble tradition is true and assures martyrdom. And this secret should be pleasing to the true believer. If someone says it causes infection and destruction, say: God creates and recreates.

Source: Michael Dols, "Ibn al-Wardi's Risalah al-Naba an al-Waba, A translation of a major source for the history of the Black Death in the Middle East," in *Near Eastern Numismatics, Iconography, Epigraphy, and History: Studies in Honor of George C. Miles*, edited by Dickran K. Kouymjian (American University of Beirut, 1974), pp. 447–54.

The Florentine Chronicle: Rubric 643 (late fourteenth Century)

Marchione di Coppo Stefani (the pseudonym for Baldasarre de Buonaiuti) wrote his chronicle in the late fourteenth century after he retired from Florentine business and politics. When he was about 12 years old, in 1348, the Black Death swept through Florence. Buonaiuti's later recollection of the plague balances the practical effects of the pestilence, such as inflation, with the pathos of the plague—namely, family members deserting one another and abandoned sick people calling out for help.

- How does Buonaiuti describe the plague and its ferocity? What details does he report to support that description?

- While Buonaiuti may not directly assert an explanation for the causes of the plague, what are some indirect indicators for what those experiencing the plague thought were its causes?

- What are the effects of the plague on family? On religion? On the economy? On the population?

Concerning a Mortality in the City of Florence in Which Many People Died

In the year of the Lord 1348 there was a very great pestilence in the city and district of Florence. It was of such a fury and so tempestuous that in houses in which it took hold previously healthy servants who took care of the ill died of the same illness. Almost none of the ill survived past the fourth day. Neither physicians nor medicines were effective. Whether because these illnesses were previously unknown or because physicians had not previously studied them, there seemed to be no cure. There was such a fear that no one seemed to know what to do. When it took hold in a house it often happened that no one remained who had not died. And it was not just that men and women died, but even sentient animals died. Dogs, cats, chickens, oxen, donkeys, sheep showed the same symptoms and died of the same disease. And almost none, or very few, who showed these symptoms, were cured. The symptoms were the following: a bubo in the groin, where the thigh meets the trunk; or a small swelling under the armpit; sudden fever; spitting blood and saliva (and no one who spit blood survived it). It was such a frightful thing that when it got into a house, as was said, no one remained. Frightened people abandoned the house and fled to another. Those in town fled to villages. Physicians could not be found because they had died like the others. And those who could be found wanted vast sums in hand before they entered the house. And when they did enter, they checked the pulse with face turned away. They inspected the urine from a distance and with something odoriferous under their nose. Child abandoned the father, husband the wife, wife the husband, one brother the other, one sister the other. In all the city there was nothing to do but to carry the dead to a burial. And those who died had neither confessor nor other sacraments. And many died with no one looking after them. And many died of hunger because when someone took to bed sick, another in the house, terrified, said to him: "I'm going for the doctor." Calmly walking out the door, the other left and did not return again. Abandoned by people, without food, but accompanied by fever, they weakened. There were many who pleaded with their relatives not to abandon them when night fell. But [the relatives] said to the sick person, "So that during the night you did not have to awaken those who serve you and who work hard day and night, take some sweetmeats, wine or water. They are here on the bedstead by your head; here are some blankets." And when the sick person had fallen asleep, they left and did not return. . . .

No one, or few, wished to enter a house where anyone was sick, nor did they even want to deal with those healthy people who came out of a sick person's house. And they said to them: "He is stupefied, do not speak to him!" saying further: "He has it because there is a bubo in his house." They call the swelling a bubo. Many died unseen. So they remained in their beds until they stank. And the neighbors, if there were any, having smelled the stench, placed them in a shroud and sent them for burial. . . .

At every church, or at most of them, they dug deep trenches. . . . And those who were responsible for the dead carried them on their backs in the night in which they died and threw them into the ditch, or else they paid a high price to those who would do it for them. The next morning, if there were many [bodies] in the trench, they covered them over with dirt. And then more bodies were put on top of them, with a little more dirt over those; they put layer on layer just like one puts layers of cheese in a lasagna.

The *beccamorti* [literally, vultures] who provided their service, were paid such a high price that many were enriched by it. Many died from [carrying away the dead], some rich, some after earning just a little, but high prices continued. Servants, or those who took care of the ill, charged from one to three florins per day and the cost of things grew. . . .

Some fled to villas, others to villages in order to get a change of air. Where there had been no [pestilence], there they carried it; if it was already there, they caused it to increase. None of the guilds in Florence was working. All the shops were shut, taverns closed; only the apothecaries and the churches remained open. If you went outside, you found almost no one. And many good and rich men were carried from home to church on a pall by four *beccamorti* and one tonsured clerk who carried the cross. Each of them wanted a florin. This mortality enriched apothecaries, doctors, poultry vendors, *beccamorti*, and greengrocers who sold poultices of mallow, nettles, mercury and other herbs necessary to draw off the infirmity. And it was those who made these poultices who made a lot of money. . . .

This pestilence began in March, as was said, and ended in September 1348. And people began to return to look after their houses and possessions. And there were so many houses full of goods without a master that it was stupefying. . . .

Now it was ordered by the bishop and the Lords [of the city government] that they should formally inquire as to how many died in Florence. When it was seen at the beginning of October that no more persons were dying of the pestilence, they found that among males, females, children and adults, 96,000 died between March and October.

Source: Marchione di Coppo Stefani, Cronaca Fiorentina, edited by Niccolo Rodolico, Vol. 30 of *Rerum Italicarum Scriptores* (Citta di Castello: S. Lapi, 1903–1913). As translated by Duane Osheim.

PRIMARY SOURCE 11.3

Berbers, Arabs, and Plague in the Maghrib, from the *Muqadimmah*, Ibn Khaldûn (c. 1375)

Born in Tunis, Ibn Khaldûn came from a family that had been active in the political development of Spain and the Maghrib (North Africa) in the century before his birth. Ibn Khaldûn followed in his family's tradition of public service. In his forties, however, he stepped back from public life and composed a grand multivolume history, in the introduction to which, the *Muqadimmah*, he outlines a far-reaching analytical philosophy of history. Essential to his analysis is a theory of causation and considerations about the rise and fall of civilizations. (Ibn Khaldun offers dates according to the Muslim calendar, which marks time from Mohammad's migration from Mecca to Medina in 632. CE equivalents are provided in brackets.)

- **What are the causes of population shifts of Berbers and Arabs in the Maghrib, according to Ibn Khaldûn?**

- **What does Ibn Khaldûn say were the effects of the plague on civilization?**

- **How does Ibn Khaldûn use earlier writers of history, al-Masûdî and al-Bakrî, to explore the purpose of history? How does the plague fit into Ibn Khaldûn's ideas about history writing?**

History refers to events that are peculiar to a particular age or race. Discussion of the general conditions of regions, races, and periods constitutes the historian's

foundation. Most of his problems rest upon that foundation, and his historical information derives clarity from it. It forms the topic of special works, such as the *Murúj adh-dhahab* of al-Mas'ūdī. In this work, al-Mas'ūdī commented upon the conditions of nations and regions in the West and in the East during his period (which was) the three hundred and thirties [the nine hundred and forties]. He mentioned their sects and customs. He described the various countries, mountains, oceans, provinces, and dynasties. He distinguished between Arabic and non-Arabic groups. His book, thus, became the basic reference work for historians, their principal source for verifying historical information.

Al-Mas'ūdī was succeeded by al-Bakri who did something similar for routes and provinces, to the exclusion of everything else, because, in his time, not many transformations or great changes had occurred among the nations and races. However, at the present time–that is, at the end of the eighth [fourteenth] century–the situation in the Maghrib, as we can observe, has taken a turn and changed entirely. The Berbers, the original population of the Maghrib, have been replaced by an influx of Arabs, (that began in) the fifth [eleventh] century. The Arabs outnumbered and overpowered the Berbers, stripped them of most of their lands, and (also) obtained a share of those that remained in their possession. This was the situation until, in the middle of the eighth [fourteenth] century, civilization both in the East and the West was visited by a destructive plague which devastated nations and caused populations to vanish. It swallowed up many of the good things of civilization and wiped them out. It overtook the dynasties at the time of their senility, when they had reached the limit of their duration. It lessened their power and curtailed their influence. It weakened their authority. Their situation approached the point of annihilation and dissolution. Civilization decreased with the decrease of mankind. Cities and buildings were laid waste, roads and way signs were obliterated, settlements and mansions became empty, dynasties and tribes grew weak. The entire inhabited world changed. The East, it seems, was similarly visited, though in accordance with and in proportion to (the East's more affluent) civilization. It was as if the voice of existence in the world had called out for oblivion and restriction, and the world had responded to its call. God inherits the earth and whomever is upon it.

When there is a general change of conditions, it is as if the entire creation had changed and the whole world been altered, as if it were a new and repeated creation, a world brought into existence anew. Therefore, there is need at this time that someone should systematically set down the situation of the world among all regions and races, as well as the customs and sectarian beliefs that have changed for their adherents, doing for this age what al-Mas'ūdī did for his. This should be a model for future historians to follow. In this book of mine, I shall discuss as much of that as will be possible for me here in the Maghrib. I shall do so either explicitly or implicitly in connection with the history of the Maghrib, in conformity with my intention to restrict myself in this work to the Maghrib, the circumstances of its races and nations, and its subjects and dynasties, to the exclusion of any other region. (This restriction is necessitated) by my lack of knowledge of conditions in the East and among its nations, and by the fact that secondhand information would not give the essential facts I am after.

Source: Ibn Khaldûn, *The Muqaddimah, An Introduction to History*, Vol. 1, translated by Franz Rosenthal (New York: Pantheon Books, 1958), pp. 63–65.

PRIMARY SOURCE 11.4

Plague in Syria and Egypt (1348–1350), by al-Maqrizi (early fifteenth century)

Al-Maqrizi wrote his extensive historical works in Cairo in the early fifteenth century. His roots in Cairo were deep, but his family also had connections in Damascus, and he lived there for about ten years in his forties. Given that al-Maqrizi was so prolific a historian, it is surprising that much of what is known about him is based on writing about him by contemporaries and later biographers. Interestingly for our purposes, he was a student of Ibn Khaldûn in Cairo.

....

- **What part of the population seems to have been hardest hit by the plague? Why might the death toll from plague have been higher during Ramadan?**

- **What was the effect of the plague on religious practice?**

- **What impact did the plague have on the workforce in terms of wages, available workers, and employment opportunities?**

....

News reached [Cairo from Syria] that the plague in Damascus had been less deadly than in Tripoli, Hama, and Aleppo. From . . . [October 1348] death raged with intensity. 1200 people died daily and, as a result, people stopped requesting permits from the administration to bury the dead and many cadavers were abandoned in gardens and on the roads.

In New and Old Cairo, the plague struck women and children at first, then market people, and the numbers of the dead augmented. . . . The [ravages of the] plague intensified in . . . [November] in [New] Cairo and became extremely grave during *Ramadan* [December], which coincided with the arrival of winter. . . . The plague continued to spread so considerably that it became impossible to count how many died. . . .

In [January 1349], new symptoms developed and people began spitting up blood. One sick person came down with internal fever, followed by an unrestrained need to vomit, then spat blood and died. Those around him in his house fell ill, one after the other and in one or two nights they all perished. Everyone lived with the overwhelming preoccupation that death was near. People prepared themselves for death by distributing alms to the poor, reconciled with one another, and multiplied their acts of devotion.

None had time to consult doctors or drink medicinal syrups or take other medications, so rapidly did they die. By [January 7th,] bodies had piled up in the streets and markets; [town leaders] appointed burial brigades, and some pious people remained permanently at places of prayer in New and Old Cairo to recite funeral orations over the dead. The situation worsened beyond limits, and no solution appeared possible. Almost the entire royal guard disappeared and the barracks in the sultan's citadel contained no more soldiers.

Statistics of the dead from funerals in Cairo during . . . [November and December] attained 900,000. . . . There were 1,400 litters on which they carried the dead and soon even they did not suffice. So they began carrying dead bodies in boxes, on doors taken from stores and on plain boards, on each of which they placed two to three bodies.

People began searching for *Quran* readers for funerals, and many individuals quit their trades to recite prayers at the head of burial procession[s]. A group of people devoted themselves to applying a coat of clay to the inner sides of the graves. Others volunteered to wash corpses, and still others to carry them. Such volunteers received substantial wages. For example, a *Quran* reader earned 10 *dirhams:* the moment he finished with one funeral, he ran off to another. A body carrier demanded six *dirhams* in advance, and still it was hard to find any. A grave digger wanted 50 *dirhams* per grave. But most of them died before they had a chance to spend their earnings.

Family celebrations and marriages no longer took place. . . . No one had held any festivities during the entire duration of the epidemic, and no voice was heard singing. In an attempt to revive these activities, the *wazir* [prime minister] reduced by a third the taxes paid by the woman responsible for collecting dues on singers. The call to prayer was suspended at many locations, and even at the most important ones, there remained only a single *muezzin* [caller to prayer].

The drum batteries before most of the officers' quarters no longer functioned, and the entourage of a commander [who controlled a thousand men] was reduced now from about fifteen to three soldiers.

Most of the mosques and *zawiyas* [Sufi lodges] were closed. It was also a known fact that during this epidemic no infant survived more than one or two days after his birth, and his mother usually quickly followed him to the grave.

At [the end of February], all of Upper Egypt was afflicted with the plague. . . . According to information that arrived . . . from . . . other regions, lions, wolves, rabbits, camels, wild asses and boars, and other savage beasts, dropped dead, and were found with scabs on their bodies.

The same thing happened throughout Egypt. When harvest time arrived, many farmers had already perished [and no field hands remained to gather crops]. Soldiers and their young slaves or pages headed for the fields. They tried to recruit workers by promising them half of the proceeds, but they could not find anyone to help them gather the harvest. They threshed the grain with their horses [hoofs], and winnowed the grain themselves, but, unable to carry all the grain back, they had to abandon much of it.

Most craft workshops closed, since artisans devoted themselves to disposing of the dead, while others, not less numerous, auctioned off property and textiles [which the dead left behind]. Even though the prices of fabric and other such commodities sold for a fifth of their original value . . . they remained unsold. . . . Religious texts sold by their weight, and at very low prices.

Workers disappeared. You could not find either water carriers, or launderers or servants. The monthly salary of a horse groom rose from 30 to 80 *dirhams.* . . . This epidemic, they say, continued in several countries for 15 years.

Source: al-Maqrizi, *The Guide to the Knowledge of Dynasties and Kings,* excerpted in *The Middle East and Islamic World Reader,* edited by Marvin Gettleman and Stuart Schaar (New York: Grove Press, 2012), pp. 52–53.

Interpreting Visual Evidence

Marking Boundaries, Inspiring Loyalty

The fourteenth century witnessed the emergence of dynastic states across Afro-Eurasia that endured for centuries. The size of these new states and the ethnic and religious diversity of their populations posed formidable challenges to those in power. Rulers had to distinguish those who belonged to the community—and owed taxes or military service—from those who did not. They used a careful mixture of privilege and punishment to create a sense of unity among their subjects while at the same time justifying their own right to rule and reinforcing traditional social hierarchies. The three images below show different ways rulers approached this problem.

The first painting, from around 1500, is by the Spanish artist Pedro Berruguete. It portrays a scene

Spanish painting by Berruguete.

The *devshirme* system.

from two centuries earlier in which Spanish authorities burned people at the stake for their alleged heretical beliefs. Notice in the foreground members of the Dominican Order, who were instrumental in the administration of the Inquisition, and soldiers loyal to the crown. The second image, a miniature painting from 1558, depicts the *devshirme* system in the Ottoman Empire. Authorities took non-Muslim children from their families in Europe as a human tribute in place of cash taxes, which the poor region could not pay. The children would then be educated in Ottoman Muslim ways and prepared for service in the sultan's civil and military bureaucracy. The final image, a painting on silk by Ch'iu Ying, represents a group of Confucian scholars waiting for the results of their civil service examination. Candidates spent three days and two nights taking examinations as they sought to enter the Ming bureaucracy.

Chinese painting by Ch'iu Ying.

Questions for Analysis

1. Assess the combinations of privilege and punishment conveyed by these images. What kinds of assistance or special privileges did leaders grant, to whom did they offer this assistance, and what kinds of punishments did they impose?

2. Describe the original context for these images. Who might have created these images, for whom, and who might have seen them?

3. Interpret the role religion plays in these images. How does the artist present the relationship between religion and social order?

4. Explain how Berruguete's use of the past alters the relationship between royal authorities and traditional elites presented in the first painting, compared to the relationship between rulers and elites shown or implied by the other two images.

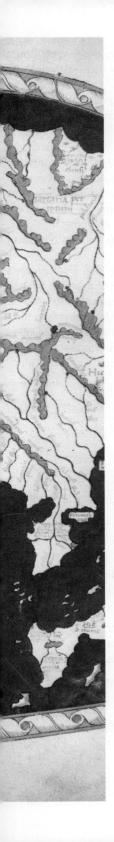

12

Contact, Commerce, and Colonization

1450-1600

At the time of Christopher Columbus's birth in 1451, the great world power on the rise was neither Spain nor Portugal, but the Ottoman Empire. For the Ottomans, unlike the other major Asian empires, the fifteenth and sixteenth centuries marked a period of frenzied territorial expansion in the Mediterranean as well as the Indian Ocean. The Ottomans were eager to fulfill what they considered to be Islam's primary mission: world dominion. Sultans Bayezid II (r. 1481–1512), Selim I (r. 1512–1520), and Suleiman the Magnificent (r. 1520–1566) continued the conquests of Mehmed the Conqueror and led the thrust into Arab lands and the Indian Ocean even while pressing ahead in Europe. Indeed, Selim I boasted that "he was the ruler of the east and the west."

As the Ottomans turned their attention to conquest of the Red Sea, the Arabian Peninsula, and North Africa, reestablishing under their own control trade routes disrupted by the Mongols and the Black Death, they forced others seeking shares in South and East Asian luxuries to seek new sea passages. European states gave the Ottomans no cause for alarm when they began to make inroads in South Asia in the mid-sixteenth century. After all, it was not Ottoman territory they were contesting, and the Ottomans, looking westward, had bigger fish to fry.

No one could have predicted that European conquests of a few South Asian trading cities were particularly significant, compared with the

Core Objectives

- **DESCRIBE** the broad patterns of world trade after 1450, and **COMPARE** major features of world trade in Asia, the Americas, Africa, and Europe.

- **ANALYZE** the factors that enabled Europeans to increase their trade relationships with Asian empires in the fifteenth and sixteenth centuries, and **ASSESS** their significance.

- **COMPARE** the practices and the impact of European explorers in Asia and the Americas.

- **ANALYZE** the social and political relationships, and **EXPLAIN** the sources of conflict within the Afro-Eurasian polities.

- **ASSESS** how European colonization of the Americas affected African and Amerindian peoples, and **DESCRIBE** their responses.

Ottomans' relentless annexations of large territories, including great stretches of southeastern Europe. Even more unpredictable, though hugely consequential, was the accidental discovery made by Christopher Columbus.

Seeking to circumvent Ottoman power in the eastern Mediterranean, Columbus opened up a "New World" about which Afro-Eurasians had no previous knowledge. Although Christopher Columbus did not intend to "discover" America when he went looking for Asia, his voyages convinced Europeans that there were still new territories to exploit and peoples to convert to Christianity. For the first time since the Ice Age migrations, large numbers of people moved from Afro-Eurasian landmasses to the Americas. So did animals, plants, commercial products, and—most momentous—deadly germs. Europeans now began building empires—but of a different nature than the land empires of Africa and Asia. Their empires were overseas. While the new colonies generated vast riches, they also brought unsettling changes to the rulers and the ruled.

Despite the significance of Europeans' activity in the Americas, most Africans and Asians were barely aware of the Americas. Asian empires continued to flourish after recovering from the Black Death. Nor was Europe's attention exclusively on the Americas, for its royal houses competed with one another for power and territory at home. Religious revolt in the form of the Protestant Reformation intensified these rivalries. In the wake of Columbus, the drive to build and protect empires across oceans began to change the terms on which people around the globe interacted with one another.

Global Storylines

- The European "discovery" of the Americas begins a complex process that changes the ways peoples around the world interact with one another.

- For the first time, major world empires are oceanic, overseas empires rather than continental empires.

- Despite the long-term significance of European activity in the Americas, most Africans and Asians are barely aware of the Americas or the expansion of long-distance trade.

- Within Europe, dynastic states concentrate attention and resources on their own internal rivalries. Religious revolts, especially the Protestant Reformation, intensify those rivalries.

- Asian empires thrive in the sixteenth century, thanks to commercial expansion and political consolidation.

Ottoman Expansion and World Trade

Ottoman expansion overland continued as European expansion overseas began. Both caused important global shifts in the organization of polities as well as in patterns of trade. The two were interconnected, as increasing Ottoman control in the eastern Mediterranean motivated Portuguese and Spanish explorers to turn toward the Atlantic in hopes of reaching the rich trading posts of China and the Indian Ocean by another route. Ottoman expansion was made possible by the Ottomans' domination of Afro-Eurasian trade routes as they recovered in the wake of the Black Death, and it was marked by the sultanate's co-optation of local elites and a relatively tolerant attitude toward other peoples and religions.

For the Europeans, in contrast, expansion overseas was quite new and experimental. Mariners and traders, searching for new routes to South and East Asia, began exploring the Atlantic coast of Africa. Lured by spices, silks, and slaves, and aided by new maritime technology, Portuguese expeditions made their way around Africa and onward to India. Although Europeans still had little to offer would-be trading partners in Asia, their developing capability in overseas trade laid the foundations for a new kind of global commerce.

Both the new and the old expansionism knitted worlds together that had previously been apart or only loosely interconnected. Together they laid the foundations for a new chapter in world history. But we must not forget that even in the midst of this global transformation, the peoples of each continent continued to focus on local, and often religious, struggles closer to their everyday lives.

THE REVIVAL OF ASIAN ECONOMIES

Trade all across Afro-Eurasia benefited enormously from China's economic dynamism, which was driven primarily by China's vast internal economy. Chinese demand for silver fueled a revival of trade across the Indian Ocean and traditional overland routes. After the Ming dynasty relocated its capital from Nanjing in the prosperous south to the northern city of Beijing, Chinese merchants, artisans, and farmers exploited the surging domestic market. Reconstruction of the Grand Canal now opened a major artery that allowed food and riches from the economically vibrant lower Yangzi area to reach the capital region of Beijing. Urban centers, such as Nanjing with a population approaching a million and Beijing at half a million, became massive and lucrative markets. Despite official restrictions on trade, merchants thrived and coastal cities remained active harbors. (See Map 12.5.)

What did foreign buyers have to trade with the Chinese? The answer was silver, which became essential to the Ming monetary system. Whereas their

THE BIG PICTURE
....
How would you describe the broad patterns of world trade after 1450?

Chinese Porcelain Box There were two distinct markets for Chinese porcelains in this period, one external and one internal, for consumption within China itself. Although it ultimately ended up in a French museum, this box was produced for the vibrant internal Chinese market, for Persian eunuchs serving the Ming court. The inscription on top, in Arabic script, says, "Strive for excellence in penmanship, for it is one of the keys of livelihood"; the inscription on the sides, in Persian, says, "Ignorance is an irremediable evil, [but] knowledge is a priceless elixir." Neither comes from the Quran, but they both express Islamic sentiments in favor of calligraphy and intellectualism glorying God and testify to extensive commercial activity in China.

predecessors had used paper money, Ming consumers and traders mistrusted anything other than silver or gold for commercial dealings. Once the rulers adopted silver as a means of tax payment in the 1430s, it became the predominant medium for larger transactions. China, however, did not produce sufficient silver for its booming economy. Indeed, silver and other precious metals were about the only commodities for which the Chinese would trade their precious manufactures. Through most of the sixteenth century, China's main source of silver was Japan, which one Florentine merchant called the "silver islands." After the 1570s, however, the Philippines, now under the control of the Spanish, became a gateway for silver coming from the New World. One-third of all silver mined in the Americas during the sixteenth and seventeenth centuries wound up in Chinese hands.

China's economic expansion contributed to the revival of Indian Ocean trade. Long-distance merchants developed a brisk commerce that tied the whole of the Indian Ocean together. Ports as far off as East Africa and the Red Sea enjoyed links with coastal cities of India, South Asia, and the Malay Peninsula. Muslims dominated this trade. India was the geographic and economic center of numerous trade routes. With a population expanding as rapidly as China's, its large cities (such as Agra, Delhi, and Lahore) each boasted nearly half a million residents. India's manufacturing center, Bengal, exported silk and cotton textiles and rice throughout South and Southeast Asia. Like China, India exported more than it imported, selling textiles and pepper in exchange for silver.

Overland commerce also thrived anew. One well-trafficked route linked the Baltic Sea, Muscovy, the Caspian Sea, the central Asian oases, and China. Other land routes carried goods to the ports of China and the Indian Ocean; from there, they crossed to the Ottoman Empire's heartland and went by land farther into Europe. Ottoman authorities took a keen interest in the caravan trade, since the state gained considerable tax revenue from it. To facilitate the caravans' movement, the government maintained refreshment and military stations along the route. The largest had individual rooms to accommodate the chief merchants and could provide lodging for up to 800 travelers, as well as care for all their animals. But gathering so many traders, animals, and cargoes could also attract marauders, especially desert tribesmen. To stop the raids, authorities and merchants offered cash payments to tribal chieftains as "protection money." This was a small price to pay in order to protect the caravan trade, whose revenues ultimately supported imperial expansion.

OTTOMAN EXPANSION

Having built the period's most powerful military forces and armed themselves with the latest maps and scientific instruments, the Ottomans began the sixteenth century in possession of Constantinople and great swaths of southeastern Europe and Anatolia. During the sultanate of Suleiman the Magnificent (r. 1520–1566), Ottoman forces carried the empire southward into Egypt, eastward to the Iranian borderlands, and westward into Europe. By 1550, the Ottoman Empire stretched from Hungary and the Crimea in the north to the Arabian Peninsula in the south, from Morocco in the west to the contested border with Safavid Iran in the east (see Map 12.1 and Chapter 13).

The Ottomans had become a world power, and their armada dwarfed that of all others at the time. It consisted of seventy-four ships, including twenty-seven large and small galleys and munitions ships, mounted with cannons. Piri Reis—an Ottoman admiral and cartographer—conducted research in the Indian Ocean, an area previously unknown to the Ottomans. Not only did he produce a map of the world, but in 1526 he presented to Sultan Suleiman

Overland Caravans and Caravanserais Muslim governments and merchants' associations constructed inns, or caravanserais, along the major trading routes. These areas were capable of accommodating a large number of traders and their animals in great comfort.

a masterpiece of geography and cartography known as *The Book of the Sea*. The book drew on Arab sources as well as Indian maps obtained from the Portuguese and offered full information on the geography of the world. In no small part thanks to Piri, the Ottomans made important gains in the Red Sea and ventured into the Indian Ocean as rivals to the Portuguese. But their main energies were devoted to the lands around the eastern Mediterranean, the Black Sea, and the Arabian Peninsula.

The conquest of Syria and Egypt in 1516–1517 was decisive in allowing Ottoman leaders to regard their Sunni state as the preeminent Muslim empire from that moment forward, even enabling some sultans to call themselves caliphs. Egypt became the Ottomans' most lucrative and important acquisition, the breadbasket of the empire and the province that provided Istanbul with the largest revenue stream. But the conquest was no easy matter. The Mamluk rulers resisted mightily, losing a bloody battle in 1516 at Marj Dabiq, north of Aleppo, after which, according to Ibn Iyas, the Arab chronicler of the age, "the battlefield was strewn with corpses and headless bodies and faces covered with dust and grown hideous." Nor did the conquest of Egypt prove any easier, for the Mamluks were determined to hold on to their most precious possession. The conquest of Constantinople and the Arab lands transformed the Ottoman Empire, creating a Muslim majority in an empire once mainly populated by conquered Christians and enabling Ottoman sultans to see themselves as heirs of a long line of empires that had ruled over these regions.

Yet on the eastern front, in conflicts with the Safavid Empire, the Ottomans encountered their earliest military failures and their most determined foe, an enemy state that plagued the Ottoman Empire until its collapse early in the eighteenth century (see Chapters 11 and 13). Blocked from eastward expansion, the Ottomans moved westward into Europe, which terrified Europeans. Having taken Constantinople in 1453, Sultan Mehmed II took Athens in 1458. The Ottomans also took large swaths of Balkan territory before turning to North Africa and Egypt and exerted more control than ever over commerce in the Mediterranean.

Ottoman conquests in southeastern and central Europe resulted in the subordination of Christians and Jews to Muslim rule. Centuries of Ottoman rule left a multiethnic legacy in places like Bosnia, including large populations of Muslims in areas later taken by the Habsburg Empire. Thus, the Ottomans, too, from the eastern end of the Mediterranean, became key players in the transformation of Europe in the age of da Gama and Columbus.

EUROPEAN EXPLORATION AND EXPANSION

The emergence of the Ottoman Empire prompted Europeans to probe unexplored links to the east in the sixteenth century. When the Ottomans took control of traditional overland trade routes from Europe to Asia, Europeans

Core Objectives

ANALYZE the factors that enabled Europeans to increase their trade relationships with Asian empires, and ASSESS their significance.

began to look south and west—and ventured across the seas. (See Map 12.1.) Taking the lead were the Portuguese, whose search for new routes to Asia led them first to Africa. Europeans had long believed that Africa was a storehouse of precious metals. In fact, a fourteenth-century map, the Catalan Atlas, had depicted a single black ruler controlling a vast quantity of gold in the interior of Africa. As the price of gold skyrocketed during and after the Black Death, ambitious men decided to venture southward in search of this commodity and its twin, silver. Having found sea routes around Africa, European merchants sought to reap the riches abounding in Asian ports, especially once Asian states were firmly established across the Indian Ocean in the seventeenth century.

Innovations in maritime technology and information from other mariners helped Portuguese sailors navigate the treacherous waters along the African coast. New vessels included the carrack, a three- or four-masted ship, developed by the Portuguese to deal with rough waters like the Atlantic Ocean and the Mediterranean. Equally important was the caravel, with specially designed triangular sails, which enabled European sailors to nose in and out of estuaries and navigate unpredictable currents and winds. By using highly maneuverable caravels and perfecting the technique of tacking (sailing into the wind rather than before it), the Portuguese advanced far along the West African coast. In addition, newfound expertise with the compass and the astrolabe helped navigators determine latitude.

Portuguese seafarers ventured from the coasts of Africa into the Indian Ocean and inserted themselves into its thriving commerce. In Asia, Portugal did not attempt to rule directly or to establish colonies. Rather, it aimed to exploit Asian commercial networks and trading systems. To do so, the Portuguese took advantage of a technology developed centuries earlier in China: gunpowder. Mounting small cannons on their warships, they bombarded ports and rival navies or merchant vessels.

The first Portuguese mariner to reach the Indian Ocean was Vasco da Gama (1469–1524). Like Columbus, da Gama was relatively unknown before his extraordinary voyage commanding four ships around the Cape of Good Hope. He found a network of commercial ties spanning the Indian Ocean, as well as skilled Muslim mariners who knew the currents, winds, and ports of call. Once established in the key ports, the Portuguese attempted to take over the trade or, failing this, to tax local merchants. From Sofala, Kilwa, and other important ports on the East African coast, from Goa and Calicut in India, and from Macao in southern China, the Portuguese soon dominated the most active sea-lanes of the Indian Ocean. The Portuguese did not interrupt the flow of luxuries among Asian and African elites; rather, their naval captains simply kept a portion of the profits for themselves, content to benefit from Asian prosperity without imposing Portuguese rule. Only with the discovery of the Americas and the conquest of Brazil did Portugal become an empire with large overseas colonies. For this to transpire, mariners would have to traverse the Atlantic Ocean itself.

The Global View

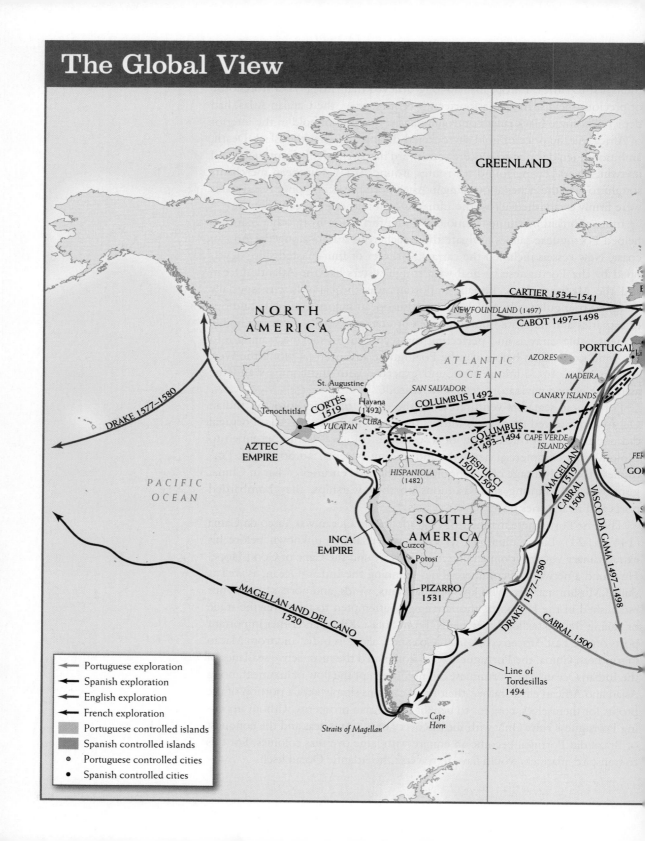

GREENLAND

NORTH AMERICA

CARTIER 1534–1541

NEWFOUNDLAND (1497)

CABOT 1497–1498

PORTUGAL Li

ATLANTIC OCEAN

AZORES

MADEIRA

CANARY ISLANDS

COLUMBUS 1492

St. Augustine

SAN SALVADOR

Havana (1492)

Tenochtitlán CORTÉS 1519

CUBA

YUCATAN

COLUMBUS 1493–1494 CAPE VERDE ISLANDS

DRAKE 1577–1580

AZTEC EMPIRE

VESPUCCI 1501–1502

HISPANIOLA (1482)

MAGELLAN 1519

CABRAL 1500

VASCO DA GAMA 1497–1498

FE

GO

PACIFIC OCEAN

SOUTH AMERICA

INCA EMPIRE

Cuzco

Potosí

PIZARRO 1531

MAGELLAN AND DEL CANO 1520

DRAKE 1577–1580

CABRAL 1500

Line of Tordesillas 1494

Straits of Magellan

Cape Horn

Portuguese exploration
Spanish exploration
English exploration
French exploration
Portuguese controlled islands
Spanish controlled islands
• Portuguese controlled cities
• Spanish controlled cities

....

the fifteenth and sixteenth centuries, sailors from Portugal, Spain, England, and France explored and mapped the pastline of most of the world. Their activities took place in the shadow of the leading empires of the day, with the ttomans, Safavids, Mughals, and Ming largely unconcerned and unthreatened by them. They established contacts and ade connections that, over time, became increasingly important.

Explain why Europeans would have chosen sea routes to reach Asia rather than land routes.

Trace the voyages that started from Portugal, and then the voyages that started from Spain. Explain why Portuguese explorers concentrated on Africa and the Indian Ocean, whereas their Spanish counterparts focused on the Americas.

Contrast the different patterns of exploration in the New World with those in the Indian Ocean and the South China Sea.

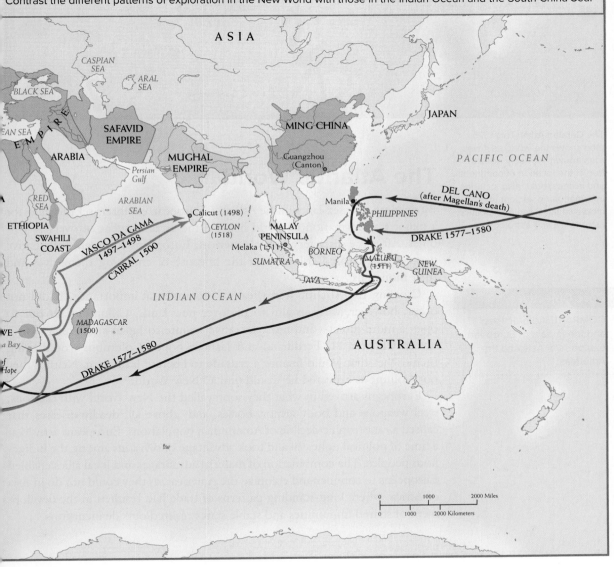

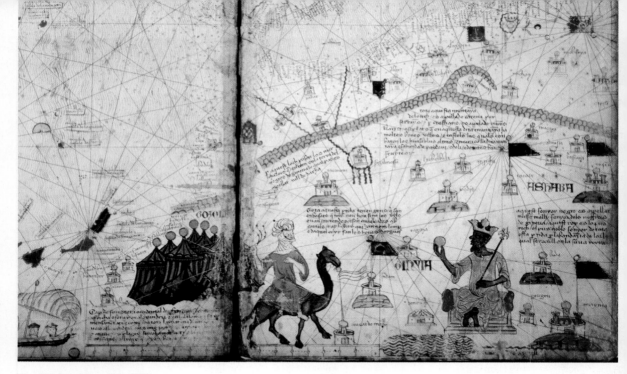

The Catalan Atlas This 1375 map shows the world as it was then known. Not only does it depict the location of continents and islands, but it also includes information on ancient and medieval tales, regional politics, astronomy, and astrology.

The Atlantic World

By opening new sea-lanes in the Atlantic, European explorers set the stage for a major transformation in world history: the establishment of overseas colonies. After the discovery of the Americas, Europeans conquered the native peoples and created colonies for the purpose of enriching themselves and their monarchs.

Crossing the Atlantic was a feat of monumental importance. It did not occur, however, with an aim to discover new lands. Columbus set out to open a more direct—and more lucrative—route to Japan and China. As we saw in Chapter 11, Ferdinand and Isabella hoped Columbus would bring them riches that would finance a crusade to liberate Jerusalem. Neither they nor Columbus expected he would find a "New World."

Europeans arrived in what they soon called the New World with cannons, steel weapons and body armor, horses, and, above all, deadly diseases that caused a catastrophic decline of Amerindian populations. Europeans arrived at a time of political upheaval and took advantage of divisions among the indigenous peoples. The combination of material advantages and local allies enabled Europeans to conquer and colonize the Americas, as they could not do in Asia or Africa, where long-standing patterns of trade had resulted in the development of shared immunities and stable states resisted outside incursions.

The devastation of the Amerindian population also resulted in severe labor shortages. Thus began the large-scale introduction of slave laborers imported from Africa, which led to the "Atlantic system" that connected Europe, the Americas, and Africa. The precious metals of the New World now gave Europeans something to offer their trading partners in Asia and enabled them to grow rich. In the process, they brought together peoples and ecosystems that had developed separately for thousands of years.

FIRST ENCOUNTERS

Christopher Columbus set sail from Spain in early 1492, stopped in the Canary Islands for supplies and repairs, and cast off into the unknown. When he stepped onto the beach of San Salvador (in the Bahamas) on October 12, 1492, the explorer ushered in a new era in world history. Once established in the Americas, Columbus and the other mariners, like other expansion-minded Europeans, aimed to Christianize the world while enriching themselves and their backers. These goals—to save souls and to make money—drove the European colonization of the Americas and the formation of an Atlantic system. They also shaped Europeans' early interactions with Amerindians and Africans captured in the slave trade.

When Columbus made landfall in the Caribbean Sea, he unfurled the royal standard of Ferdinand and Isabella and claimed the "many islands filled with people innumerable" for Spain. It is fitting that the first encounter with Caribbean inhabitants, in this case the Tainos, drew blood. Columbus noted, "I showed them swords and they took them by the edge and through

Columbus As Columbus made landfall and encountered Indians, he planted a cross to indicate the spiritual purpose of the voyage and read aloud a document proclaiming the sovereign authority of the king and queen of Spain. Quickly, he learned there was barter for precious stones and metals.

ignorance cut themselves." The Tainos had their own weapons but did not forge steel—and thus had no knowledge of such sharp edges.

For Columbus, the Tainos' naïveté in grabbing his sword symbolized the child-like primitivism of these people, whom he would mislabel "Indians" because he thought he had arrived off the coast of Asia. In Columbus's view the Tainos had no religion, but they did have at least some gold (found initially hanging as pendants from their noses). Likewise, Pedro álvares Cabral, a Portuguese mariner whose trip down the coast of Africa in 1500 was blown off course across the Atlantic, wrote that the people of Brazil had all "the innocence of Adam." He also noted that they were ripe for conversion and that the soils "if rightly cultivated would yield everything." But, as with Africans and Asians, Europeans also developed a contradictory view of the peoples of the Americas. From the Tainos, Columbus learned of another people, the Caribs, who (according to his informants) were savage, warlike cannibals. For centuries, these contrasting images—innocents and savages—structured European (mis)understandings of the native peoples of the Americas.

We know less about what the Indians thought of Columbus or other Europeans on their first encounters. Certainly they were impressed with the Europeans' appearance and their military prowess. The Tainos fled into the forest at the approach of European ships, which they thought were giant monsters; others thought they were floating islands. European metal goods, in particular weaponry, struck them as otherworldly. The Amerindians found the newcomers different not for their skin color (only Europeans drew the distinction based on skin pigmentation), but for their hairiness. Indeed, the Europeans' beards, breath, and bad manners repulsed their Indian hosts. The newcomers' inability to live off the land also stood out. In due course, the Indians realized not just that the strange, hairy people bearing metal weapons were odd trading partners, but that they meant to stay and to force the local population to labor for them. The explorers had become **conquistadors** (conquerors).

FIRST CONQUESTS

First contacts between peoples gave way to dramatic conquests in the Americas; then conquests paved the way to mass exploitation of native peoples. After the first voyage, Columbus claimed that on Hispaniola (present-day Haiti and the Dominican Republic) "he had found what he was looking for"—gold. That was sufficient to persuade the Spanish crown to invest in larger expeditions. Whereas Columbus first sailed with three small ships and 87 men, ten years later the Spanish outfitted an expedition with 2,500 men.

Between 1492 and 1519, the Spanish experimented with institutions of colonial rule over local populations on the Caribbean island that they renamed Hispaniola. Ultimately they created a model that the rest of the New World colonies would adapt. But the Spaniards faced problems that would recur. The first was Indian resistance. As early as 1494, starving Spaniards raided and pillaged Indian villages. When the Indians revolted, Spanish soldiers replied with punitive expeditions and began enslaving them to work in mines extracting gold. As the crown rewarded conquistadors with grants (*encomiend*as) giving them control over Indian labor, a rich class of **encomenderos** arose who enjoyed the fruits of the system. Although the surface gold mines soon ran dry, the model of granting favored settlers the right to coerce Indian labor endured. In return, those who received the labor rights paid special taxes on the precious metals that were extracted. Thus, both the crown and the *encomenderos* benefited. The same cannot be said of the Amerindians, who perished in great numbers from disease, malnutrition, and overwork.

As Spanish colonists saw the bounty of Hispaniola dry up, they set out to discover and conquer new territories. Finding their way to the mainlands of the American landmasses, they encountered larger, more complex, and more militarized societies than those they had overrun in the Caribbean. Great civilizations had arisen there centuries before, boasting large cities, monumental buildings, and riches based on wealthy agrarian societies. In both Mesoamerica, starting with the Olmecs (see Chapter 5), and the Andes, with the Chimú (see Chapter 10), large states had laid the foundations for the subsequent Aztec Empire and **Inca Empire**. These empires were powerful. But they had evolved untouched by Afro-Eurasian developments; as worlds apart, they were unprepared for the kind of assaults that European invaders had honed. In pre-Columbian Mesoamerica and then the Andes, warfare was more ceremonial, less inclined to wipe out enemies than to make them pay tribute. As a result, the wealth and vulnerability of these empires made them irresistible to outside conquerors.

Aztec Society   In Mesoamerica, the Mexica had created an empire known to us as "Aztec." Around Lake Texcoco, Mexica cities grew and in 1430 formed a three-city league, which then expanded through the Central Valley of Mexico to incorporate neighboring peoples. Gradually the **Aztec Empire** united numerous small, independent states under a single monarch who ruled with the help of counselors, military leaders, and priests. By the late fifteenth century, the Aztec realm may have embraced 25 million people. Tenochtitlán, situated on an immense island in Lake Texcoco, ranked among the world's largest cities.

Tenochtitlán spread in concentric circles, with the main religious and political buildings in the center and residences radiating outward. The city's outskirts connected a mosaic of floating gardens producing food for urban markets. Canals irrigated the land, waste served as fertilizer, and high-yielding produce found easy transport to markets. Entire households worked: men, women, and children all had roles in Aztec agriculture.

encomenderos
Commanders of the labor services of the colonized peoples in Spanish America.

Inca Empire
Empire of Quechua-speaking rulers in the Andean valley of Cuzco that encompassed a population of 4 to 6 million. The Incas lacked a clear inheritance system, causing an internal split that Pizarro's forces exploited in 1533.

Aztec Empire
Mesoamerican empire that originated with a league of three Mexica cities in 1430 and gradually expanded through the Central Valley of Mexico, uniting numerous small, independent states under a single monarch who ruled with the help of counselors, military leaders, and priests. By the late fifteenth century, the Aztec realm may have embraced 25 million people. In 1521, the Aztecs were defeated by the conquistador Hernán Cortés.

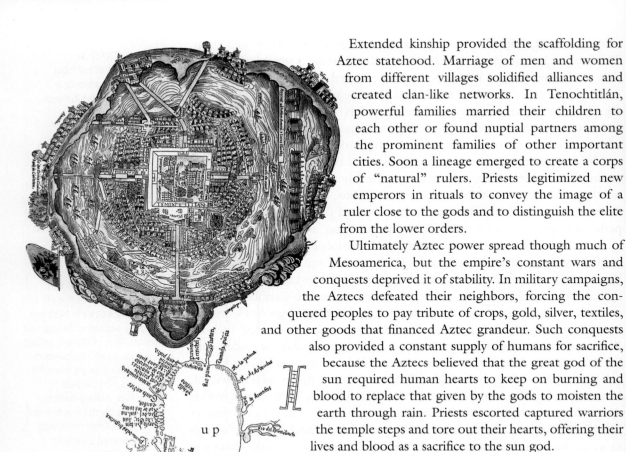

Tenochtitlán At its height, the Aztec capital, Tenochtitlán, was as populous as Europe's largest city. As can be seen from this map, it spread in concentric circles, with the main religious and political buildings in the center and residences radiating outward.

Extended kinship provided the scaffolding for Aztec statehood. Marriage of men and women from different villages solidified alliances and created clan-like networks. In Tenochtitlán, powerful families married their children to each other or found nuptial partners among the prominent families of other important cities. Soon a lineage emerged to create a corps of "natural" rulers. Priests legitimized new emperors in rituals to convey the image of a ruler close to the gods and to distinguish the elite from the lower orders.

Ultimately Aztec power spread though much of Mesoamerica, but the empire's constant wars and conquests deprived it of stability. In military campaigns, the Aztecs defeated their neighbors, forcing the conquered peoples to pay tribute of crops, gold, silver, textiles, and other goods that financed Aztec grandeur. Such conquests also provided a constant supply of humans for sacrifice, because the Aztecs believed that the great god of the sun required human hearts to keep on burning and blood to replace that given by the gods to moisten the earth through rain. Priests escorted captured warriors the temple steps and tore out their hearts, offering their lives and blood as a sacrifice to the sun god.

Those whom the Aztecs sought to dominate did not submit peacefully. From 1440, the empire faced constant turmoil as subject populations rebelled. Tlaxcalans and Tarascans waged a relentless war for freedom, holding at bay entire divisions of Aztec armies. To pacify the realm, the empire diverted more and more men and money into a mushrooming military. By the time the electoral committee chose Moctezuma II as emperor in 1502, divisions among elites and pressures from the periphery had placed the Aztec Empire under extreme stress.

Cortés and Conquest Not long after Moctezuma became emperor, news arrived from the coast of ships bearing pale, bearded men and monsters (horses and dogs). Here distinguishing fact from fiction is difficult. Some accounts left after the conquest by indigenous witnesses reported that Moctezuma consulted with his ministers and priests, and the observers wondered if these men were the god Quetzalcoatl and his entourage. Most historians dismiss the importance of these omens, describing them as the efforts of rival elites to blame Moctezuma for their own inaction. In any case, Moctezuma sent emissaries bearing gifts, but he did not prepare for a military engagement.

Cortés Meets Mesoamerican Rulers (*Left*) This colonial image depicts the meeting of Cortés (second from right) and Moctezuma (seated on the left), with Doña Marina serving as an interpreter and informer for the Spanish conquistador. Notice at the bottom what are likely Aztec offerings for the newcomer. As Mexicans began to celebrate their mixed-blood heritage, Doña Marina became the symbolic mother of the first mestizos. But she remains controversial and has also been viewed in Mexico as a traitor for the help she provided to the Spanish. (*Right*) This detail from a twentieth-century Mexican mural depicts the meeting of Cortés and the king of Tlaxcala, enemy of the Aztecs.

Aboard one of the ships was Hernán Cortés (1485–1547), a former law student from one of the Spanish provinces. He would become the model conquistador, just as Columbus was the model explorer. For a brief time, Cortés was an *encomendero* in Cuba; but when news arrived of a potentially wealthier land to the west, he set sail with over 500 men, eleven ships, sixteen horses, and artillery. When the expedition arrived near present-day Veracruz, Cortés acquired two translators, including the daughter of a local Indian noble family, who became known as Doña Marina, also known as La Malinche. With the assistance of Doña Marina and other native allies, Cortés marched his troops to Tenochtitlán. Upon entering, he gasped in wonder, "This city is so big and so remarkable [that it is] almost unbelievable." One of his soldiers wrote, "It was all so wonderful that I do not know how to describe this first glimpse of things never heard of, seen or dreamed of before."

How was this tiny force to overcome an empire of many millions with an elaborate warring tradition? Crucial to Spanish conquest was their alliance, negotiated through translators, with Moctezuma's enemies—especially the

Tlaxcalans. After decades of yearning for release from the Aztec yoke, the Tlaxcalans and other Mesoamerican peoples embraced Cortés's promise of help. The Spaniards' second advantage was their method of warfare. The Aztecs were seasoned fighters, but they fought to capture, not to kill. Nor were they familiar with gunpowder or sharp steel swords. Although outnumbered, the Spaniards killed their foes with abandon, using superior weaponry, horses, and war dogs. When Cortés arrived at Tenochtitlán, the Aztecs were still unsure who these strange men were and allowed Cortés to enter their city. With the aid of the Tlaxcalans and a handful of his own men, in 1519 Cortés captured Moctezuma, who became a puppet of the Spanish conqueror.

The Aztecs quickly changed their approach to fighting. When Spanish troops massacred an unarmed crowd in Tenochtitlán's central square while Cortés was away, they provoked a massive uprising. The Spaniards led Moctezuma to one of the palace walls to plead with his people for a truce, but the Aztecs kept up their barrage of stones, spears, and arrows—striking and killing Moctezuma. Cortés returned to reassert control; but realizing this was impossible, he gathered his loot and escaped. He left behind hundreds of Spaniards, many of whom were dragged up the temple steps and sacrificed by Aztec priests.

With the Tlaxcalans' help, Cortés regrouped. This time he bombarded Tenochtitlán with artillery, determined to defeat the Aztecs completely. Even more devastating was the spread of smallpox, brought by the Spanish, which ran through the Aztec soldiers and commoners like wildfire. In the end, starvation, disease, lack of artillery, and Cortés's ability to rally Amerindian allies to his side vanquished the Aztec forces. More died from disease than from fighting—the total number of Aztec casualties may have reached 240,000. As Spanish troops retook the capital, now in ruins, the Spaniards and their allies had to engage in house-to-house combat to secure control over Tenochtitlán. The Aztecs lamented their defeat in verse: "We have pounded our hands in despair against the adobe walls, for our inheritance, our city, is lost and dead." Cortés became governor of the new Spanish colony, renamed "New Spain." He promptly allocated *encomiendas* to his loyal followers and dispatched expeditions to conquer the more distant Mesoamerican provinces.

The Mexica experience taught the Spanish an important lesson: an effective conquest had to be swift—and it had to remove completely the symbols of legitimate authority. Their winning advantage, however, was disease. The Spaniards unintentionally introduced germs that made their subsequent efforts at military conquest much easier.

The Incas The other great Spanish conquest occurred in the Andes, where Quechua-speaking rulers, called Incas, had established an impressive state. Sometime around 1200, a band of Andean villagers settled into the valleys near what is now Cuzco, in Peru, which soon became the hub of South America's greatest empire. A combination of raiding neighbors and intermarrying into elite families raised the Incas to regional supremacy. Their power radiated along the valley routes that carved up the chain of great mountains until they finally ran up against the mighty warrior confederacy of the Chanca. After defeating the Chanca rivals around 1438, the Inca warrior Yupanqui renamed himself Pachacuti and began the royal line of Inca emperors. They eventually ruled a vast domain from what is now Chile to southern Colombia. At its center was the capital, Cuzco, with the magnificent fortress of Sacsayhuamán as its head. Built of huge boulders, the citadel was the nerve center of a complex network of strongholds that held the empire together.

As in most empires of the day, political power depended on a combination of tribute and commercial exchange to finance an extensive communication and military network. The empire developed an elaborate system of sending messages by runners who relayed up and down a system of stone highways carrying instructions to allies and roving armed divisions. None of this would have been possible without a wealthy agrarian base. Peasants paid tribute to village elders in the form of labor services to maintain public works, complex terraces, granaries, and food storage systems in case of drought or famine. In return, Inca rulers were obliged to shelter their people and allies in case of hardship. They oversaw rituals, festivals, and ceremonies to give spiritual legitimacy to their power. At their peak, the Incas may have governed a population of up to 6 million people. But as the empire stretched into distant provinces, especially into northern frontiers, ruling Incas lost touch with their base in Cuzco. Fissures began to open in the Andean empire as European germs and conquistadors appeared on South American shores.

When the Spaniards arrived in 1532, they found a divided empire, a situation they quickly learned to exploit. Francisco Pizarro, who led the Spanish campaign, had been inspired by Cortés's victory and yearned for his own glory. Commanding a force of about 600 men, he invited Atahualpa, the Inca ruler, to meet at the town of Cajamarca. There he laid a trap, intending to overpower the Incas and capture their ruler. As columns of Inca warriors and servants covered with colorful plumage and plates of silver and gold entered the main square, the Spanish soldiers were awed. One recalled, "many of us urinated without noticing it, out of sheer terror." But Pizarro's plan worked. His guns and horses shocked the Inca forces. Atahualpa himself fell into Spanish hands, later to be decapitated. Pizarro's conquistadors overran Cuzco in 1533 and then vanquished the rest of the Inca forces, a process that took decades in some areas.

The defeat of the New World's two great empires had enormous repercussions for world history. First, it set the Europeans on the road to controlling the human and material wealth of the Americas and opened a new frontier that the Europeans could colonize. Second, it gave Europeans a market for their own products—goods that found little favor in Afro-Eurasia. Now, following the Portuguese push into Africa and Asia (as well as a Russian push into northern Asia; see Chapter 13), the New World conquests introduced Europeans to a new scale of imperial expansion.

Core Objectives

ASSESS how European colonization of the Americas affected African and Amerindian peoples, and DESCRIBE their responses.

The Columbian Exchange The Spanish came to the Americas for gold and silver, but in the course of conquest and settlement they also learned about crops such as potatoes and corn. They brought with them horses, wheat, grapevines, and sugarcane, as well as devastating diseases. Historians call this transfer of previously unknown plants, animals, people, diseases, and products in the wake of Columbus's voyages the **Columbian exchange**. Over time, this exchange transformed environments, economies, and diets in both the new and the old worlds.

The first and most profound effect of the Columbian exchange was a destructive one: the decimation of the Amerindian population by European diseases. For millennia, the isolated populations of the Americas had been cut off from Afro-Eurasian microbe migrations. Africans, Europeans, and Asians had long interacted, sharing disease pools and gaining immunities; in this sense, in contrast, the Amerindians were indeed worlds apart. Sickness spread from almost the moment the Spaniards arrived. One Spanish soldier noted, upon entering the conquered Aztec capital, "The streets were so filled with dead and sick people that our men walked over nothing but bodies." As each wave of disease retreated, it left a population weaker than before, even less prepared for the next wave. The scale of death was unprecedented: imported pathogens wiped out up to 90 percent of the Indian population. A century after smallpox arrived on Hispaniola in 1519, no more than 5 to 10 percent of the island's population was alive. Diminished and weakened by disease, Amerindians could not resist European settlement and colonization of the Americas. Thus were Europeans the unintended beneficiaries of a horrifying catastrophe.

As time passed, all sides adopted new forms of agriculture from one another. After Amerindians taught Europeans how to grow potatoes and corn, the crops became staples all across Afro-Eurasia. The Chinese found that they could grow corn in areas too dry for rice and too wet for wheat, and in Africa corn gradually replaced sorghum, millet, and rice to become the continent's principal food crop by the twentieth century. (See Current Trends in World History: Corn and the Rise of Slave-Supplying Kingdoms in West Africa.) Europeans also took away tomatoes, beans, cacao, peanuts, tobacco, and squash, while importing livestock such as cattle, swine, and horses to the New World. The environmental effects of the introduction of livestock to the Americas were significant. For example, in regions of central Mexico where Native Americans had once cultivated maize and squash, Spanish settlers introduced large herds of sheep and cattle. Without natural

Columbian exchange
Movements between Afro-Eurasia and the Americas of previously unknown plants, animals, people, diseases, and products that followed in the wake of Columbus's voyages.

predators, these animals reproduced with lightning speed, destroying entire landscapes with their hooves and their foraging.

As Europeans cleared trees and other vegetation for ranches, mines, or plantations, they undermined the habitats of many indigenous mammals and birds. On the islands of the West Indies, described by Columbus as "roses of the sea," the Spanish chopped down lush tropical and semitropical forests to make way for sugar plantations. Before long, nearly all of the islands' tall trees as well as many shrubs and ground plants were gone, and residents lamented the absence of birdsong. Over ensuing centuries, the plants and animals of the Americas took on an increasingly European appearance. At the same time, the interactions between Europeans and Native Americans would continue to shape societies on both sides of the Atlantic.

THE IBERIAN EMPIRES IN THE AMERICAS

The European presence in the New World went beyond the control of commercial outposts. Unlike in the Indian Ocean—where they had to contend with stable, powerful states—European colonizers in the Americas controlled large amounts of territory, and ultimately the entire landmass (see Map 12.2). Those Native Americans who survived the original encounters were harnessed as a means to siphon tribute payments to the new masters.

By fusing traditional tribute taking with their own innovations, Spanish masters made villagers across their new American empire deliver goods and services. But because the Spanish authorities also bestowed *encomiendas*, those favored individuals could demand labor from their lands' Indian inhabitants—for mines, estates, and public works. Whereas Aztec and Inca rulers had used conscripted labor to build up their public wealth, the Spaniards did so for private gain.

Spanish migrants and their descendants preferred towns to the countryside. With the exception of ports, the major cities of Spanish America were the former centers of Indian empires. Mexico City took shape on the ruins of Tenochtitlán; Cuzco arose from the razed Inca capital. In their architecture, economy, and family life, the Spanish colonies adopted as much as they transformed the worlds they encountered.

The next European power to seize land in the Americas, the Portuguese, were no less interested in immediate riches than the Spanish were. Disappointed by the absence of tributary systems and precious metals in the area they controlled, Brazil, they found instead abundant, fertile land, which they doled out with massive royal grants. These estate owners governed their plantations like feudal lords (see Chapter 10). Failing to find established cities, the Portuguese created enclaves along the coast and lived in more dispersed settlements than the Spanish settlers did.

Corn and the Rise of Slave-Supplying Kingdoms in West Africa

New World varieties of corn spread rapidly throughout the Afro-Eurasian landmass soon after the arrival of Columbus in the Americas. Its hardiness and fast-ripening qualities made it more desirable than many of the Old World grain products. In communities that consumed large quantities of meat, it became the main product fed to livestock.

Corn's impact on Africa was as substantial as it was on the rest of Afro-Eurasia. Seeds made their way to western regions more quickly than to the south of the Sahara along two routes. One was via European merchants calling into ports along the coast; the second was via West African Muslims returning across the Sahara after participating in the pilgrimage to Mecca. The first evidence of corn cultivation in sub-Saharan Africa comes from a Portuguese navigator who identified the crop being grown on the island of Cape Verde in 1540. By the early seventeenth century, corn was replacing millet and sorghum as the main grain

being grown in many West African regions and was destined to transform the work routines and diets of the peoples living in the region's tropical rain forests all the way from present-day Sierra Leone in the east to Nigeria in the west. In many ways this area, which saw the rise of a group of powerful slave-supplying kingdoms in the eighteenth century, notably Asante, Dahomey, Oyo, and Benin, owed its prosperity to the cultivation of this New World crop. (See Chapter 14 for a fuller discussion of these states.)

The tropical rain forests of West and central Africa were thick with trees and ground cover in 1500. Clearing them so that they could support intensive agriculture was exhausting work, requiring enormous outlays of human energy and man-hours. Corn, a crop first domesticated in central Mexico 7,000 years ago, made this task possible. It added much-needed carbohydrates to the carbon-deficient diets of rain-forest dwellers. In addition, as a crop that matured more quickly than those that

were indigenous to the region (millet, sorghum, and rice) and required less labor, it yielded two harvests in a single year. Farmers also cultivated cassava, another New World native, which in turn provided households with more carbohydrate calories. Yet corn did more than produce more food per unit of land and labor. Households put every part of the plant to use—grain, leaves, stalks, tassels, and roots were made to serve useful purposes.

Thus, at the very time that West African groups were moving southward into the rain forests, European navigators were arriving along the coast with new crops. Corn gave communities of cultivators the caloric energy to change their forest landscapes, expanding the arable areas. In a select few of these regions, enterprising clans emerged to dominate the political scene, creating centralized kingdoms like Asante in present-day Ghana, Dahomey in present-day Benin, and Oyo and Benin in present-day Nigeria. These

The problem was where to find labor to work the rich lands of Brazil. Because there was no centralized government to deal with the labor shortage, Portuguese settlers initially tried to enlist the dispersed native population; but when recruitment became increasingly coercive, Indians turned on the settlers. Some Indians fought; others fled to the vast interior. Reluctant to pursue the Indians inland, the Portuguese hugged their beachheads, extracting brazilwood (the source of a beautiful red dye) and sugar from their coastal enclaves.

Silver, Sugar, and Slaves The Iberian empires in the Americas concentrated on three commodities that would transform Europe's relationship

elites transformed what had once been thinly settled environments into densely populated states, with elaborate bureaucracies, big cities, and large and powerful standing armies.

There was much irony in the rise of these states, which owed so much of their strength to the linking of the Americas with Afro-Eurasia. The armies that they created and the increased populations that the new crops allowed were part and parcel of the Atlantic slave trade. That which the Americas gave with one hand (new crops), it took back with the other in warfare, captives, and New World slavery.

Corn Plantation This nineteenth-century engraving by famed Italian explorer Savorgnan de Brazza shows women of the West African tribe Bateke working in corn plantations. Brazza would later serve as the governor general of the French colony in the Congo.

Questions for Analysis

- What were the major effects of growing corn in West Africa?
- How did the growing of corn reshape the history of the Atlantic world during this period?

Explore Further

McCann, James, *Maize and Grace: Africa's Encounter with a New World Crop, 1500–2000* (2005).

o the rest of the world: silver, sugar, and slaves. Silver enabled Spain and Portugal to enter established trade networks in Asia. The slave trade was a big business in itself: it subsidized shipbuilding and new insurance schemes. Above all, the use of slave labor made sugar cultivation fantastically profitable, fueling economic growth and political instability around the world.

The first Europeans in the Americas hoarded vast quantities of gold and silver for themselves and their monarchs. But they also introduced precious metals into the world's commercial systems, which electrified them. In the twenty years after the fall of Tenochtitlán, conquistadors took more gold and

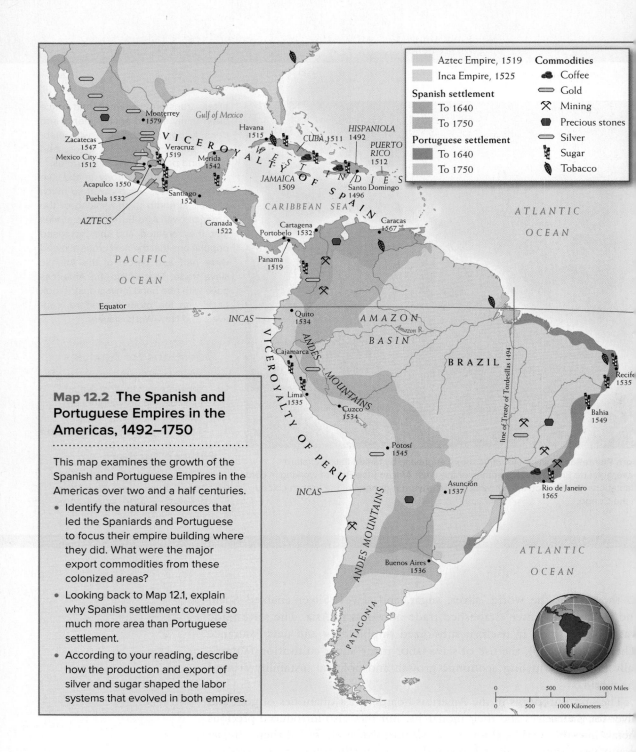

Map 12.2 The Spanish and Portuguese Empires in the Americas, 1492–1750

This map examines the growth of the Spanish and Portuguese Empires in the Americas over two and a half centuries.

- Identify the natural resources that led the Spaniards and Portuguese to focus their empire building where they did. What were the major export commodities from these colonized areas?

- Looking back to Map 12.1, explain why Spanish settlement covered so much more area than Portuguese settlement.

- According to your reading, describe how the production and export of silver and sugar shaped the labor systems that evolved in both empires.

Legend:

Aztec Empire, 1519
Inca Empire, 1525
Spanish settlement
To 1640
To 1750
Portuguese settlement
To 1640
To 1750

Commodities
Coffee
Gold
Mining
Precious stones
Silver
Sugar
Tobacco

Map labels: Monterrey 1579, Gulf of Mexico, Zacatecas 1547, Havana 1515, CUBA 1511, HISPANIOLA 1492, PUERTO RICO 1512, VICEROYALTY OF SPAIN, Veracruz 1519, Mexico City 1512, Merida 1542, WEST INDIES, Acapulco 1550, Santiago 1524, Santo Domingo 1496, Puebla 1532, JAMAICA 1509, AZTECS, Granada 1522, CARIBBEAN SEA, Caracas 1567, Cartagena 1532, Portobelo, Panama 1519, PACIFIC OCEAN, ATLANTIC OCEAN, Equator, INCAS, Quito 1534, AMAZON BASIN, Amazon R., Cajamarca, ANDES MOUNTAINS, BRAZIL, line of Treaty of Tordesillas 1494, Recife 1535, Lima 1535, Cuzco 1534, Bahia 1549, VICEROYALTY OF PERU, Potosí 1545, Asunción 1537, Rio de Janeiro 1565, INCAS, ANDES MOUNTAINS, Buenos Aires 1536, ATLANTIC OCEAN, PATAGONIA, 500 1000 Miles, 500 1000 Kilometers

Silver Silver was an important discovery for Spanish conquerors in Mesoamerica and the Andes. Conquerors expanded the customs of Inca and Aztec labor drafts to force Amerindians to work in mines, often in brutal conditions.

silver from Mexico and the Andes than all the gold accumulated by Europeans over the previous centuries.

Having looted Indian coffers, the Spanish entered the business of mining directly, opening the Andean Potosí mines in 1545. Between 1560 and 1685, Spanish America sent 25,000 to 35,000 tons of silver annually to Spain. From 1685 to 1810, this sum doubled. The two mother lodes were Potosí in present-day Bolivia and Zacatecas in northern Mexico. Silver brought bounty not only to the crown but also to a privileged group of families based in Spain's colonial capitals; thus, private wealth funded the formation of local aristocracies.

Colonial mines epitomized the Atlantic world's new economy. They relied on an extensive network of Amerindian labor, at first enslaved, subsequently drafted. Here again, the Spanish adopted Inca and Aztec practices of requiring labor from subjugated villages. Each year, under the *mita*, the local system for recruiting labor, village elders selected a stipulated number of men to toil in the shafts, refineries, and smelters. Under the Spanish, the digging, hauling, and smelting taxed human limits to their capacity—and beyond. Mortality rates were appalling. The system pumped so much silver into European commercial networks that it transformed Europe's relationship to all its trading partners, especially those in China and India. It also shook up trade and politics within Europe itself.

Along with silver, sugar emerged as the most valuable export from the Americas. It also was decisive in rearranging relations between peoples around the Atlantic. Cultivation of sugarcane had originated in India, spread to the Mediterranean region, and then reached the coastal islands of West Africa. The Portuguese, the Spanish, and other European settlers transported the

West African model to the Americas, first in the sixteenth century in Brazil, and then in the Caribbean. By the early seventeenth century, sugar had become a major export from the New World. Because Amerindians resisted recruitment and their numbers were greatly reduced by disease, European plantation owners began importing African slaves. By the eighteenth century, sugar production required continuous and enormous transfers of labor from Africa, and its value surpassed that of silver as an export from the Americas to Europe.

At first, most sugar plantations were fairly small, employing between 60 and 100 slaves. But they were efficient enough to create an alternative model of empire, one that resulted in more complete and dislocating control of the existing population. The slaves lived in wretched conditions: their barracks were miserable, and their diets were insufficient to keep them alive under backbreaking work routines. Moreover, these slaves were disproportionately men. As they rapidly died off, the only way to ensure replenishment was to import more Africans. This model of settlement relied on the transatlantic flow of slaves.

As European demand for sugar increased, the slave trade expanded. Although African slaves were imported into the Americas starting in the fifteenth century, the first direct voyage carrying them from Africa to the Americas occurred in 1525. From the time of Columbus until 1820, five times as many Africans as Europeans moved to the Americas: approximately 2 million Europeans (voluntarily) and 10 million Africans (involuntarily) crossed the Atlantic.

Well before European merchants arrived off its western coast, Africa had known long-distance slave trading. In fact, the overall number of Africans sold into captivity in the Muslim world exceeded that of the Atlantic slave trade. Moreover, Africans maintained slaves themselves. African slavery, like its American counterpart, was a response to labor scarcities. In many parts of Africa, however, slaves did not face permanent servitude. Instead, they were assimilated into families, gradually losing their servile status.

With the additional European demand for slaves to work New World plantations alongside the ongoing Muslim slave trade, pressure on the supply of African slaves intensified. Only a narrow band stretching down the spine of the African landmass, from present-day Uganda and the highlands of Kenya to Zambia and Zimbabwe, escaped the impact of African rulers engaged in the slave trade and Asian and European slave traders.

By the late sixteenth century, important pieces had fallen into place to create a new Atlantic world, one that could not have been imagined a century earlier. This was the three-cornered **Atlantic system**, with Africa supplying labor, the Americas land and minerals, and Europeans the technology and military power to hold the system together. In time, the wealth flows to Europe and the slave-based development of the Americas would alter the world balance of power.

The Transformation of Europe

Despite the flow of American silver into Spanish coffers, most European rulers and their subjects were focused on Europe, not the New World, in the sixteenth century. The period's frequent warfare centered on purely European concerns, above all on a religious split within the Roman Catholic Church, known as the Reformation. This conflict led to profound religious rifts among states and brought additional political rivalries to the continent.

Core Objectives

ANALYZE the social and political relationships, and **EXPLAIN** the sources of conflict within the Afro-Eurasian polities.

THE REFORMATION

Like the Renaissance, the **Protestant Reformation** in Europe began as a movement devoted to returning to ancient sources—in this case, to biblical scriptures. Yet returning to the sources and interpreting Christian doctrine for oneself was dangerous in the fourteenth and fifteenth centuries, for the church feared that challenges to its authority would arise if laypersons were allowed to read the scriptures as they pleased. The church was right: when Luther and his followers seized the right to read and interpret the Bible in a new way, they paved the way for a "Protestant" Reformation that split Christendom for good.

The opening challenge to the authority of the Catholic Church originated in Germany. Here a monk and a professor of theology, **Martin Luther** (1483–1546), used his knowledge of the Bible to criticize the church's ideas and practices. For Luther, God's gift of forgiveness did not depend on taking sacraments or performing good deeds. This faith was something Christians could obtain from reading the Bible—rather than by having a priest tell them what to believe. Finally, Luther concluded that Christians did not need specially appointed mediators to speak to God for them; all believers were equally bound by God's laws and obliged to minister to one another's spiritual needs.

These became the three main principles that launched Luther's reforming efforts: (1) belief that faith alone saves, (2) belief that the scriptures alone hold the key to Christian truth, and (3) belief in the priesthood of all believers. Luther also reacted against corrupt practices in the church, such as the keeping of mistresses by monks, priests, and even popes; and the selling of indulgences, certificates that would supposedly shorten the buyer's time in purgatory. In the 1510s, clerics were hawking indulgences across Europe in an effort to raise money for the sumptuous new Saint Peter's Basilica in Rome. In 1517, Luther formulated ninety-five statements, or theses, and posted them on the doors to the Wittenberg cathedral, hoping to stir up his colleagues in debate.

In response, Pope Leo X and the Habsburg emperor, Charles V, demanded that Luther take back his criticisms and theological claims. When he refused, he was declared a heretic and narrowly avoided being burned

Protestant Reformation
Religious movement initiated by sixteenth-century monk Martin Luther, who openly criticized the corruption in the Catholic Church and voiced his belief that Christians could speak directly to God. His doctrines gained wide support, and those who followed this new view of Christianity rejected the authority of the papacy and the Catholic clergy, broke away from the Catholic Church, and called themselves "Protestants."

Martin Luther
(1483–1546) A German monk and theologian who sought to reform the Catholic Church; he believed in salvation through faith alone, the importance of reading scripture, and the priesthood of all believers. His Ninety-Five Theses, which enumerated the abuses by the Catholic Church as well as his reforms, started the Protestant Reformation.

at the stake. Luther wrote many more pamphlets attacking the church and the pope, whom he now described as the anti-Christ. Luther also translated the New Testament from Latin into German so that laypersons could have direct access, without the clergy, to the word of God. This act spurred many other reformers across Europe to undertake translations of their own, and it encouraged the Protestant clergy to teach children (and adults) to read their local languages.

Spread by printed books and ardent preachers in all the common languages of Europe, Luther's doctrines and those put forward by other reformers won widespread support in some regions, particularly among urban populations. In France and Switzerland, the reformer **Jean Calvin** (1509–1564) emphasized moral regeneration through church teachings and laid out a doctrine of predestination—the notion that each person is "predestined for damnation or salvation even before birth." Those who followed the new faith of Luther and Calvin identified themselves as "Protestants." They promised that their reformed version of Christianity provided both an answer to individual spiritual needs and a new moral foundation for community life. The renewed Christian creed appealed to commoners as well as elites, especially in communities that resented rule by Catholic "outsiders." For example, Protestantism was popular among the Dutch, who resented being ruled by Philip II, an Austrian Catholic who lived in Spain. Although Protestants were rarely a majority before the seventeenth century, the new ideas gained a wide following in the German states, France, Switzerland, the Low Countries, England, and Scotland (see Map 12.3). Later, following the sociologist Max Weber (1864–1920), many European historians and economists, in their efforts to explain the origins of capitalism, would look back to these ideas—especially the emphasis on discipline, industriousness, and the individual's relation to God—as distinguishing Europeans from other peoples.

Counter-Reformation The Catholic Church responded to Luther and Calvin by embarking on its own renovation, which became known as the **Counter-Reformation**. At the Council of Trent, whose twenty-five sessions stretched from 1545 to 1563, Catholic leaders reaffirmed the church's doctrines. But the council also enacted reforms to answer the Protestants' assaults on clerical corruption. Like the Protestants, the reformed Catholics carried their message overseas—especially through an order established by a Spaniard, Ignatius Loyola (1491–1556). Loyola founded a brotherhood of priests, the Society of Jesus, or **Jesuits**, dedicated to the revival of the Catholic Church. From bases in Lisbon, Rome, Paris, and elsewhere in Europe, the Jesuits opened missions as far as South and North America, India, Japan, and China. The Reformation split European society deeply as both Catholics and Protestants vigorously promoted their faiths.

The following labels appear on the map:

PRESBYTERIAN
SCOTLAND
CALVINIST
Edinburgh
NORTH SEA
NORWAY
SWEDEN
LUTHERAN
Stockholm
FINLAND
LUTHERAN
ANGLICAN
IRELAND
Dublin
York
ENGLAND
ANGLICAN
Oxford
London
Canterbury
DENMARK
Copenhagen
NETHERLANDS
Hamburg
BALTIC SEA
TEUTONIC ORDER
LUTHERAN
LUTHERAN
PRUSSIA
RUSSIA
ATLANTIC OCEAN
Brussels
Cologne
CALVINIST
LUTHERAN
CALVINIST
BRANDENBURG
Berlin
Wittenberg
HOLY ROMAN EMPIRE
LUTHERAN
POLAND-LITHUANIA
Warsaw
CALVINIST
Paris
Orléans
Nantes
Worms
LUTHERAN
Prague
FRANCE
CALVINIST
Zurich
Augsburg
BAVARIA
Munich
LUTHERAN
Vienna
HUNGARY
LUTHERAN
CALVINIST
CALVINIST
LUTHERAN
CALVINIST
LUTHERAN
Geneva
Trent
Venice
LUTHERAN
PIEDMONT
Genoa
Avignon
Belgrade
BLACK SEA
PORTUGAL
Lisbon
NAVARRE
SPAIN
Madrid
Florence
PAPAL STATES
Rome
ADRIATIC SEA
OTTOMAN EMPIRE
MUSLIMS
Seville
CORSICA
SARDINIA
BALEARIC ISLANDS (ARAGON)
Naples
MUSLIMS
MEDITERRANEAN SEA

Map legend:
- Roman Catholic
- Protestant
- Eastern Orthodox
- Muslim

Scale: 0 — 250 — 500 Miles; 0 — 250 — 500 Kilometers

Map 12.3 Religious Divisions in Europe after the Reformation, 1590

The Protestant Reformation divided Europe religiously and politically.

- Within the formerly all-Catholic Holy Roman Empire, list the Protestant groups that took hold.
- Looking at the map, what geographic patterns can you identify in the distribution of Protestant communities?
- List the regions in which you would expect Protestant-Catholic tensions to be the most intense, and explain why.

RELIGIOUS WARFARE IN EUROPE

Holy Roman Empire
Enormous realm that encompassed much of Europe and aspired to be the Christian successor state to the Roman Empire. In the time of the Habsburg dynasts, the empire was a loose confederation of principalities that obeyed an emperor elected by elite lower-level sovereigns. Despite its size, the empire never effectively centralized power; it was split into Austrian and Spanish factions when Charles V abdicated to his sons in 1556.

The religious revival led Europe into another round of ferocious wars. Their ultimate effect was to weaken the **Holy Roman Empire**—a loose confederation of principalities that were clustered mainly in central Europe and presided over in this period by the Habsburgs (see Chapter 11)—and strengthen the English, French, and Dutch. Already in the 1520s, the circulation of books presenting Luther's ideas sparked peasant revolts across central Europe. Some peasants, hoping that Luther's assault on the church's authority would help liberate them, rose up against repressive feudal landlords. In contrast to earlier wars in which one noble's retinue fought a rival's, the defense of the Catholic mass and the Protestant Bible brought crowds of simple folk to arms. Now wars between and within central European states raged for nearly forty years.

Religious conflicts weakened European dynasties. Spain, with its massive empire and its silver mines in the New World, spent much of its new fortune waging war in Europe. Most debilitating was its costly effort to subdue recently acquired Dutch territories. After a series of wars spanning nearly a hundred years, Catholic Spain finally conceded the Protestant Netherlands its independence. Wars took their toll on the Spanish Empire, which was soon wallowing in debts; not even the riches of its American silver mines could bail out the court. In the late 1550s, Philip II could not meet his obligations to creditors, and, within two decades, Spain was declared bankrupt three times. Its decline opened the way for the Dutch and the English to extend their trading networks into Asia and the New World, and the center of power within Europe shifted to the north.

Religious conflicts also sparked civil wars. In France, the divide between Catholics and Protestants exploded in the St. Bartholomew's Day Massacre of 1572. Catholic crowds rampaged through the streets of Paris murdering Huguenot (Protestant) men, women, and children and dumping their bodies into the Seine River. The number of dead reached 3,000 in Paris and 10,000 in provincial towns. Slaughter on this scale did not break the Huguenots' spirit, but it did bring more disrepute to the monarchy for failing to ensure peace. Another round of warfare exhausted the French and brought Henry of Navarre, a Protestant prince, to the throne. To become king, Henry IV converted to Catholicism. Shortly thereafter, he issued the Edict of Nantes, a proclamation that declared France a Catholic country but also tolerated some Protestant worship.

As princes sought to resolve religious questions within their domains, states increasingly became identified with one or another form of Christian faith—and, for Protestants, with a local language. (Protestants translated the Bible from Latin so that more people could read it.) In this way, religious strife propelled forward the process of state building and the forming of national identities. At the same time, religious conflict fueled rivalries for wealth and territory overseas. Thus, Europe entered its age of overseas exploration as a collection of increasingly powerful yet irreconcilably competitive rival states, whose differences stemmed not just from language but from the ways they worshipped the Christian God.

Prosperity in Asia

While Europe was experiencing religious warfare, Asian empires were expanding and consolidating their power, and trade was flourishing. If anything, the arrival of European sailors and traders in the Indian Ocean strengthened trading ties across the region and enhanced the political power and expansionist interests of Asia's imperial regimes. The Mughal ruler of India, Akbar, and the Ottoman sultan, Suleiman the Magnificent (see Chapter 11), were effective and esteemed rulers. The Ming dynasty's elegant manufactures enjoyed worldwide renown, and its ability to govern vast numbers of highly diverse peoples led outsiders to consider China the model imperial state.

Core Objectives

COMPARE the major features of world trade in Asia, the Americas, Africa, and Europe.

MUGHAL INDIA AND COMMERCE

The **Mughal Empire** became one of the world's wealthiest empires just when Europeans were establishing sustained connections with India. These connections, however, only touched the outer layer of Mughal India, one of Islam's greatest regimes. Established in 1526, it was a vigorous, centralized state whose political authority encompassed most of modern-day India. During the sixteenth century, it had a population of between 100 and 150 million.

The Mughals' strength rested on their military power. The dynasty's founder, Babur, had introduced horsemanship, artillery, and field cannons from central Asia, and gunpowder had secured his swift military victories over northern India. Under his grandson, Akbar (r. 1556–1605), the empire enjoyed expansion and consolidation that continued (under his own grandson, Aurangzeb) until it covered almost all of India (see Map 12.4). Known as the "Great Mughal," Akbar was skilled not only in military tactics but also in the art of alliance making. Deals with Hindu chieftains through favors and intermarriage also undergirded his empire.

Mughal rulers were flexible toward their realm's diverse peoples, especially in spiritual affairs. Though its primary commitment to Islam stood firm, the imperial court also patronized other beliefs, displaying a tolerance that earned it widespread legitimacy. The contrast with Europe, where religious differences drove deep fractures within and between states, was stark. Unlike European monarchs, who tried to enforce religious uniformity, Akbar studied comparative religion and hosted regular debates among Hindu, Muslim,

Mughal Empire
One of Islam's greatest regimes. Established in 1526, it was a vigorous, centralized state whose political authority encompassed most of modern-day India. During the sixteenth century, it had a population of between 100 and 150 million.

Map 12.4 Expansion of the Mughal Empire, 1556–1707

Under Akbar and Aurangzeb, the Mughal Empire expanded and dominated much of South Asia. Yet, by looking at the trading ports along the Indian coast, one can see the growing influence of Portuguese, Dutch, French, and English interests.

- Look at the dates for each port, and identify which traders came first and which came last.

- Compare this map with Map 12.2 (showing a period that begins earlier, 1492–1750). To what extent do the trading posts shown here reflect increased European influence in the region?

- According to your reading, explain how these European outposts affected Mughal policies.

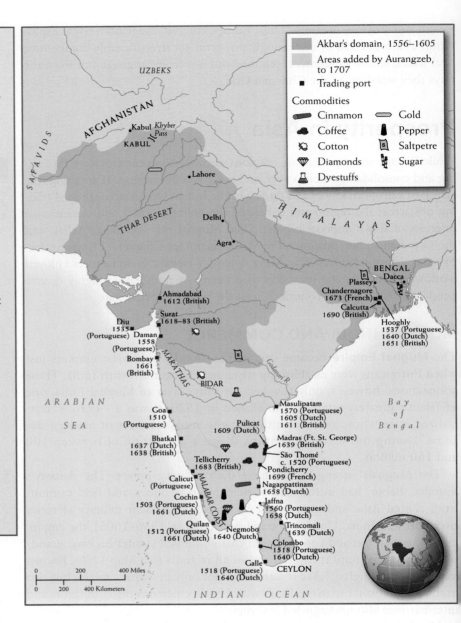

Akbar's domain, 1556–1605
Areas added by Aurangzeb, to 1707
■ Trading port

Commodities
Cinnamon — Gold
Coffee — Pepper
Cotton — Saltpetre
Diamonds — Sugar
Dyestuffs

UZBEKS

AFGHANISTAN
Kabul Khyber Pass
KABUL

SAFAVIDS

THAR DESERT

Lahore

Delhi

Agra

HIMALAYAS

BENGAL
Dacca
Plassey
Chandernagore 1673 (French)
Calcutta 1690 (British)
Hooghly 1537 (Portuguese) 1640 (Dutch) 1651 (British)

Ahmadabad 1612 (British)
Surat 1618–83 (British)
Diu 1535 (Portuguese)
Daman 1558 (Portuguese)
Bombay 1661 (British)

MARATHAS

BIDAR

Godavari R.

ARABIAN SEA

Goa 1510 (Portuguese)

Bhatkal 1637 (Dutch) 1638 (British)

Tellicherry 1683 (British)

Calicut (Portuguese)

MALABAR COAST

Cochin 1503 (Portuguese) 1661 (Dutch)

Quilan 1512 (Portuguese) 1661 (Dutch)

Negmobo 1640 (Dutch)

Masulipatam 1570 (Portuguese) 1605 (Dutch) 1611 (British)

Bay of Bengal

Pulicat 1609 (Dutch)

Madras (Ft. St. George) 1639 (British)
São Thomé c. 1520 (Portuguese)
Pondicherry 1699 (French)
Nagappattinam 1658 (Dutch)

Jaffna 1560 (Portuguese) 1658 (Dutch)
Trincomali 1639 (Dutch)
Colombo 1518 (Portuguese) 1640 (Dutch)
Galle 1518 (Portuguese) 1640 (Dutch)
CEYLON

INDIAN OCEAN

0   200   400 Miles
0   200   400 Kilometers

Jain, Parsi, and Christian theologians. His tolerance kept a multifaceted spiritual kingdom under one political roof.

During the sixteenth century, expanded trade with Europe brought more wealth to the Mughal polity, while the empire's strength limited European incursions. Although the Portuguese occupied Goa and Bombay on the Indian coast, they had little presence elsewhere and dared not antagonize the Mughal emperor. In 1578, Akbar recognized the credentials of a Portuguese ambassador and allowed a Jesuit missionary to enter his court. Thereafter, commercial ties between Mughals and Portuguese intensified, but the merchants were still restricted to a handful of ports. In the 1580s and 1590s, the Mughals ended the Portuguese monopoly on trade with Europe by allowing Dutch and English merchantmen to dock in Indian ports.

Centered in northern India, the Mughal Empire used surrounding regions' wealth and resources—military, architectural, and artistic—to glorify the court. Over time, the enhanced wealth caused friction between wealthy and poorer Indian regions, and even between merchants and rulers. Yet as long as merchants relied on rulers for their commercial gains, and as long as rulers balanced local and imperial interests, the realm maintained a formal unity and kept Europeans on its margins.

PROSPERITY IN MING CHINA

China also prospered from increased commerce in the late sixteenth century. Like the Mughals, the Ming seemed unconcerned with the increasing appearance of foreigners, including Europeans bearing silver. As in India, the Ming confined European traders to port cities. Silver from the Americas did, however, circulate widely in China. It allowed employers to pay their workers with money rather than with produce or goods, which in turn motivated those workers to produce more. China also experienced soaring production in agriculture and handicrafts. A cotton boom, for example, made spinning and weaving China's largest industry.

One measure of greater prosperity under the Ming was its population surge. By the mid-seventeenth century, China's population probably accounted for more than one-third of the total world population. Although 90 percent of Chinese people lived in the countryside, large numbers filled the cities. Beijing, the Ming capital, grew to over 1 million; Nanjing, the secondary capital, nearly matched that number. Cities offered diversions ranging from literary and theatrical societies to schools of learning, religious societies, urban associations, and manufactures from all over the empire. The elegance and material prosperity of Chinese cities dazzled European visitors. One Jesuit missionary described Nanjing as surpassing all other cities "in beauty and grandeur. . . . It is literally filled with palaces and temples and towers and bridges. . . . There is a gaiety of spirit among the people who are well mannered and nicely spoken."

Urban prosperity fostered entertainment districts where people could indulge themselves anonymously and in relative freedom. Some Ming women found a place here as refined entertainers and courtesans, others as midwives, poets, sorcerers, and matchmakers. Female painters, mostly from scholar-official families, emulated males who used the home and garden for creative pursuits. The expanding book trade also accommodated women, who were writers as well as readers, not to mention literary characters and archetypes (especially of Confucian virtues). But Chinese women made their greatest fortunes inside the emperor's Forbidden City as healers, consorts, and power brokers. The vitality that commerce brought to Ming society continued even after the dynasty's fall in 1644, laying the foundation for further population growth and territorial expansion.

ASIAN RELATIONS WITH EUROPE

Europeans' overseas expansion had originally looked toward Asia, and now the products from their New World colonies enabled them to realize some of those dreams. The Portuguese led the way, with Vasco da Gama's rounding of the Cape of Good Hope in 1497–1498. In 1557, their arrival at Macao, a port along the southern coast of China, enabled them to participate in China's expanding import-export trade. Within five years the number of Portuguese in Macao neared 1,000 (see Map 12.5).

Seeing how much the Portuguese were earning on Asian trade, the Spanish, English, and Dutch also ventured into Asian waters. With its monopoly on American silver, Spain enjoyed a competitive advantage. In 1565, the first Spanish trading galleon reached the Philippines; in 1571, after capturing Manila and making it a colonial capital, the Spanish established a brisk trade with China. Each year, ships from Spain's colonies in the Americas crossed the Pacific to Manila, bearing cargoes of silver. They returned carrying porcelain and silks for well-to-do European consumers. Merchants in Manila also procured silks, tapestries, and feathers from the China seas for shipment to the Americas, where the mining elite eagerly awaited these imports.

The year 1571 was altogether decisive in the history of the modern world. For the first time, Spanish ships were able to circle the globe from the New World to China and from China back to Europe. Silver was the commodity that linked the world commercially, the only foreign commodity for which the Chinese had an insatiable demand. From the mother lodes of the Andes and Mesoamerica, silver made the commerce of the world go round.

Other Europeans, too, wanted their share of Asia's wealth. The English and the Dutch reached the South China Sea by 1594. Five years later, 101 English investors pooled their funds and formed a joint-stock company (an association in which each member owned shares of capital) called the English East India Company. Soon this company won a royal charter

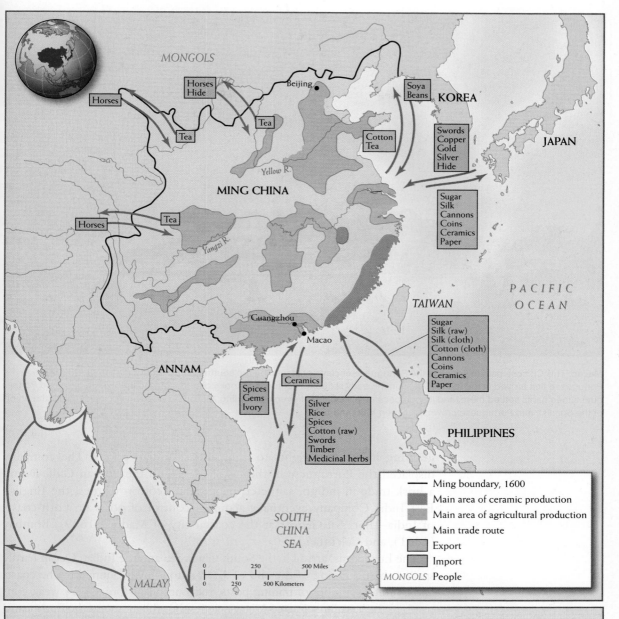

Legend
—— Ming boundary, 1600
Main area of ceramic production
Main area of agricultural production
← Main trade route
Export
Import
MONGOLS People

Map labels: MONGOLS, Horses/Hide, Beijing, Horses, Tea, Tea, Yellow R., MING CHINA, Horses, Tea, Yangzi R., Cotton/Tea, Soya Beans, KOREA, JAPAN, Swords/Copper/Gold/Silver/Hide, Sugar/Silk/Cannons/Coins/Ceramics/Paper, PACIFIC OCEAN, TAIWAN, Sugar/Silk (raw)/Silk (cloth)/Cotton (cloth)/Cannons/Coins/Ceramics/Paper, Guangzhou, Macao, ANNAM, Spices/Gems/Ivory, Ceramics, Silver/Rice/Spices/Cotton (raw)/Swords/Timber/Medicinal herbs, PHILIPPINES, SOUTH CHINA SEA, MALAY

Scale: 0 — 250 — 500 Miles / 0 — 250 — 500 Kilometers

Map 12.5 Trade and Production in Ming China

The Ming Empire in the early seventeenth century was the world's most populous state and arguably its wealthiest.

- According to this map, list the main items involved in China's export-import trade, and identify some of the regions that purchased its exports.
- Evaluate the relative importance of China's internal and overland trade, and contrast it with overseas commerce.
- Evaluate the balance between raw materials, agricultural products, and manufactured goods.

Macao This Chinese painting depicts the Portuguese enclave of Macao on the southern border of China around 1800. The Portuguese first arrived in the Indian Ocean in the early sixteenth century and took control of Macao in 1557. Chinese and Portuguese merchants settled there, and it soon became a vital hub of overseas trading. Macau's golden age coincided with the union of the Spanish and Portuguese crowns between 1580 and 1640.

granting it exclusive rights to import East Indian goods. The company displaced the Portuguese in the Arabian Sea and the Persian Gulf. Doing a brisk trade in indigo, saltpeter, pepper, and cotton textiles, the English East India Company eventually acquired control of ports on both coasts of India—Fort St. George at the coastal city of Madras (1639), Bombay (1661), and Calcutta (1690).

The Europeans' arrival in the South China Sea and the Indian Ocean hardly spelled the beginning of the end of Asian autonomy. Confined to the coasts and a limited number of trading posts, the Europeans forged very weak connections to the ruling elites of Asian societies. For the moment, the Europeans' increased presence enhanced the wealth and might of Asian dynasties.

Conclusion

In the multicentered world of the fifteenth century, Europe was a poor cousin. However, a new spirit of adventure and achievement animated its peoples, stirred up by the rediscovery of antiquity (the Renaissance), the ambitions of merchants and other elites, and the spiritual fervor of the Reformation and Counter-Reformation. Desiring Asian luxury goods, European merchants and mariners were eager to exploit trade routes leading eastward, and new navigational techniques enabled them to sail into dangerous waters. More important, Europe's location promoted expansion across the largely unknown Atlantic Ocean. With the Ottomans controlling Constantinople and the eastern Mediterranean, Atlantic sea-lanes offered an alternative route to Asia. As Europeans searched for routes around Islamic territory, they first sailed down the coast of Africa and then across the Atlantic.

Encountering the "New World" was an accident of monumental significance. In the Americas, Europeans found riches. Mountains of silver and rivers of gold gave them the currency they needed for dealing with Asian traders. Europeans also found opportunities for exchange, conquest, and colonization. Yet, establishing these transatlantic empires heightened tensions within Europe, as rivals fought over the spoils and a religious schism turned into a divisive political and spiritual struggle.

Thus, two conquests characterize this age of increasing world interconnections. The Islamic conquest of Constantinople drove Europeans to find new links to Asia. In turn, the Spanish conquest of the Aztecs and the Incas gave Europeans access to silver, which bought them an increased presence in Asian trading networks.

Amerindians also played an important role, as Europeans sought to conquer their lands, exploit their labor, and confiscate their gold and silver. Sometimes Amerindians worked with Europeans, sometimes under Europeans, sometimes against Europeans—and sometimes none were left to work at all. Then Europeans brought in African laborers, compounding the calamity of the encounter with the tragedy of slavery. Out of the catastrophe of contact, a new oceanic system arose to link Africa, America, and Europe. This was the Atlantic system. Unlike the Indian Ocean and China seas, which supported a system of tributary and trading orders, the Atlantic Ocean supported a system of formal imperial control and settlement of distant colonies. These would become more important to how worlds connected and collided in the following centuries.

Focus On
Regional Developments in the Age of Exploration

Europe

- Portugal creates a trading empire in the Indian Ocean and the South China Sea.
- Spain and Portugal establish colonies in the Americas, discover silver, and establish export-oriented plantation economies.
- The Protestant Reformation breaks out in northern and western Europe, splitting the Catholic Church.

The Americas

- Millions of Amerindians, lacking immunity to European diseases, perish in every region of the New World.

- Spanish conquest and disease destroy the two great Native American empires in Mexico (the Aztecs) and Peru (the Incas).

Africa

- Trade in African captives fuels the Atlantic slave trade, which furnishes labor for European plantations in the Americas.

Asia

- Asian empires—the Mughals in India, the Ming in China, and the Ottomans in western Asia and the eastern Mediterranean—barely notice the Americas but profit economically from enhanced global trade.

Key Terms

Atlantic system p. 568	conquistadors p. 556	Holy Roman Empire p. 572	Martin Luther p. 569
Aztec Empire p. 557	Counter-Reformation p. 570	Inca Empire p. 557	Mughal Empire p. 573
Jean Calvin p. 570	*encomenderos* p. 557	Jesuits p. 570	Protestant Reformation p. 569
Columbian exchange p. 562			

CHRONOLOGY

1500

Europe

Luther begins Protestant Reformation 1517 ●

The Americas

Columbus discovers the "New World" 1492 ●
Cortés conquers Aztec Empire 1521 ●
Pizarro conquers Inca Empire 1533 ●

South Asia

Da Gama sails to India 1498 ●
Portuguese establish bases around Indian Ocean 1508–1511 ●

East Asia

THINKING ABOUT GLOBAL CONNECTIONS

- **Thinking about Exchange Networks and the Age of Exploration** In the fifteenth and sixteenth centuries, the densest trade networks and most powerful states remained centered in Asia. How did Columbus's "discovery" of the New World alter the terms on which peoples across Afro-Eurasia interacted with one another? What commodities and trade networks brought peoples together, and on what terms? What new inequalities did those contacts create around the world?

- **Thinking about Changing Power Relationships and the Age of Exploration** The effort to expand empires and trading networks differed substantially across Afro-Eurasia and the Americas in the fifteenth and

sixteenth centuries. How did men and women at all levels of society contribute to this expansion? How did that participation shape or reshape their societies? Pay particular attention to the relationship between lower classes and elites.

- **Thinking about Environmental Impacts and the Age of Exploration** The Columbian exchange led to demographic catastrophe and environmental transformation in the New World. Why did the indigenous populations of the Americas get sick so much more often than Europeans did? Why did the plants and animals of the New World increasingly come to resemble those of Afro-Eurasia?

 Go to INQUIZITIVE to see what you've learned—and learn what you've missed—with personalized feedback along the way.

1600

Religious and dynastic wars 1520s–1570s

Expansion and consolidation of Mughal Empire 1556–1605

Portuguese establish trading port in Macao 1557

Spanish make Manila their major port in the Pacific Ocean 1571

Global Themes and Sources

Cultural Contexts in the Age of Exploration

Overseas exploration and commerce brought new contacts between Amerindians, Europeans, Africans, and Asians in the fifteenth and sixteenth centuries. The primary sources brought together here document important examples of cultural contact in this era and allow us to see how people from radically different cultures perceived one another. They also provide clues about conflict within each of the communities.

The first two documents present opposing views of the initial confrontation between the Spaniards, led by Hernán Cortés (1485–1547), and the Mexica. The third document, a selection from *The History and Description of Africa* by Leo Africanus (al-Ḥasan ibn Muḥammad al-Wazzān al-Zayyātī or al-Fāsī, born c. 1485, died c. 1554), recounts the author's travels in Egypt, Morocco, and Mali, especially Timbuktu (Tombuto), a great center of Islamic learning. The final document, from a Ming official named He Ao, complains that Europeans were untrustworthy. Such sentiments were also common among officials in subsequent centuries, even as China thrived in the commercial exchanges of an increasingly connected world.

Making sense of these sources requires careful attention to context. It's important to note how the prior experiences of the different communities shaped their responses to alien cultures, and how prior exposure to outsiders influenced the ways communities marked the boundaries between "us" and "them." You should pay just as much attention to divisions within each cultural group as to those between the groups.

Analyzing Contexts: The Age of Exploration

- How did prior experiences of different cultures shape the encounters in these sources?
- All of these documents were produced by elite men. How do you think the authors' gender and status influenced their portrayal of events?

How did the authors' gender and status shape their attribution of responsibility for the problems they identified within their societies?

- Compare Cortés's description of Tenochtitlán in his letter to Charles V with Leo Africanus's description of Timbuktu.

PRIMARY SOURCE 12.1

Mexica Views of the Spaniards (c. sixteenth century), Florentine Codex

The Florentine Codex compiled accounts of the Spanish conquest from Mexica elites a generation after the fall of Tenochtitlán. The passages about Moctezuma's response to the Spaniards are drawn largely from interviews with elites from Tenochtitlán's junior partner, the city-state of Tlatelolco, in the aftermath of the Mexica defeat.

- **What about the Spaniards most struck the authors of the Florentine Codex? Identify the factors—appearance, animals, behavior, beliefs—they used to mark the Spaniards as different.**
- **Explain why the Mexica elite (of the 1550s–1560s) might have portrayed Moctezuma as afraid. Pay special attention to local politics before the Spaniards arrived.**
- **Evaluate the claim that Moctezuma believed the Spaniards to be gods. Is it plausible?**

During this time Montezuma neither slept nor touched food. Whatever he did, he was abstracted; it seemed as though he was ill at ease, frequently sighing. He tired and felt weak. He no longer found anything tasteful, enjoyable, or amusing.

Therefore he said, "What is to come of us? Who in the world must endure it? Will it not be me [as ruler]?

My heart is tormented, as though chile water were poured on it; it greatly burns and smarts. Where in the world [are we to turn], o our lord?"

Then [the messengers] notified those who guarded [Montezuma], who kept watch at the head of his bed, saying to them, "Even if he is asleep, tell him. 'Those whom you sent out on the sea have come back.'"

But when they went to tell him, he replied, "I will not hear it here. I will hear it at the Coacalco; let them go there." And he gave orders, saying, "Let some captives be covered with chalk [for sacrifice]."

Then the messengers went to the Coacalco, and so did Montezuma. Thereupon the captives died in their presence; they cut open their chests and sprinkled blood on the messengers. (The reason they did it was that they had gone to very dangerous places and had seen, gazed on the countenances of, and spoken to the gods.)

Seventh chapter, where is told the account that the messengers who went to see the boat gave to Montezuma.

When this was done, they talked to Montezuma, telling him what they had beheld, and they showed him what [the Spaniards'] food was like.

And when he heard what the messengers reported he was greatly afraid and taken aback, and he was amazed at their food. It especially made him faint when he heard how the guns went off at [the Spaniards'] command, sounding like thunder, causing people actually to swoon, blocking the ears. And when it went off, something like a ball came out from inside, and fire went showering and spitting out. And the smoke that came from it had a very foul stench, striking one in the face. And if they shot at a hill, it seemed to crumble and come apart. And it turned a tree to dust; it seemed to make it vanish, as though someone had conjured it away. Their war gear was all iron. They clothed their bodies in iron, they put iron on their heads, their swords were iron, their bows were iron, and their shields and lances were iron.

And their deer that carried them were as tall as the roof. And they wrapped their bodies all over; only their faces could be seen, very white. Their faces were the color of limestone and their hair yellow-reddish, though some had black hair. They had long beards, also yellow-reddish. [The hair of some] was tightly curled. And their food was like fasting food, very large, white, not heavy, like chaff, like dried maize stalks, as tasty as maize stalk flour, a bit sweet or honeyed, honeyed and sweet to eat.

And their dogs were huge creatures, with their ears folded over and their jowls dragging. They had burning eyes, eyes like coals, yellow and fiery. They had thin, gaunt flanks with the rib lines showing; they were very tall. They did not keep quiet, they went about panting, with their tongues hanging down. They had spots like a jaguar's, they were vari-colored.

When Montezuma heard it, he was greatly afraid; he seemed to faint away, he grew concerned and disturbed.

Eighth chapter, where it is said how Montezuma sent witches, wizards, and sorcerers to do something to the Spaniards.

Then at that time Montezuma sent out emissaries. Those whom he sent were all bad people, soothsayers and witches. He also sent elders, strong warriors, to see to all [the Spaniards] needed as to food: turkey hens, eggs, white tortillas, and whatever they might request, and to look after them well so that they would be satisfied in every way. He sent captives in case [the Spaniards] should drink their blood. And the emissaries did as indicated.

Montezuma did this because he took them for gods, considered them gods, worshiped them as gods. They were called and given the name of gods who have come from heaven, and the blacks were called soiled gods.

They say that Montezuma sent the witches, the rainmakers, to see what [the Spaniards] were like and perhaps be able to enchant them, cast spells on them, to use conjury or the evil eye on them or hurl something else at them, perhaps addressing some words of wizardry to them so that they would take sick, die, or turn back. But when they performed the assignment they had been given concerning the Spaniards, they could do nothing; they had no power at all. Then they quickly returned to tell Montezuma what they were like, how strong they were, [saying,] "We are not their match; we are as nothing."

Source: The Florentine Codex, translated by James Lockhart, in *Victors and Vanquished: Spanish and Nahua Views of the Conquest of Mexico*, edited by Stuart B. Schwartz (Boston: Bedford/St. Martin's, 2000), pp. 96–98.

Approaching Tenochtitlán (1520), Hernán Cortés

Written in the midst of the Spanish invasion of Mexico, Cortés's Second Letter was addressed to Emperor Charles V of Spain. In it, Cortés provides an account of his meeting with Moctezuma. He also describes the capital city of Tenochtitlán and its houses of worship.

- Explain how Tenochtitlán compares to Spanish cities, in Cortés's view.

- Why does Cortés mention mosques in Tenochtitlán when there were no Muslims there?

- Analyze the relationship between respect and contempt in this source. What does Cortés admire about the Mexica, and what does he dismiss?

This great city of Tenochtitlan is built on the salt lake, and from the mainland to the city is a distance of two leagues, from any side from which you enter. It has four approaches by means of artificial causeways, two cavalry lances in width. The city is as large as Seville or Cordoba. Its streets (I speak of the principal ones) are very broad and straight, some of these, and all the others, are one half land, and the other half water on which they go about in canoes. All the streets have openings at regular intervals, to let the water flow from one to the other, and at all of these openings, some of which are very broad, there are bridges, very large, strong, and well constructed, so that, over many, ten horsemen can ride abreast. Perceiving that, if the inhabitants wished to practise any treachery against us, they had plenty of opportunity, because the said city being built as I have described, they might, by raising the bridges at the exits and entrances, starve us without our being able to reach land, as soon as I entered the city, I made great haste to build four brigantines, which I had completed in a short time, capable whenever we might wish, of taking three hundred men and the horses to land.

The city has many squares where markets are held and trading is carried on. There is one square, twice as large as that of Salamanca, all surrounded by arcades, where there are daily more than sixty thousand souls, buying and selling, and where are found all the kinds of merchandise produced in these countries, including food products, jewels of gold and silver, lead, brass, copper, zinc, stone, bones, shells, and feathers. Stones are sold, hewn and unhewn, adobe bricks, wood, both in the rough and manufactured in various ways. There is a street for game, where they sell every sort of bird, such as chickens, partridges, quails, wild ducks, fly-catchers, widgeons, turtle-doves, pigeons, reed-birds, parrots, owls, eaglets, owlets, falcons, sparrow-hawks and kestrels, and they sell the skins of some of these birds of prey with their feathers, heads, beaks, and claws. They sell rabbits, hares, and small dogs which they castrate, and raise for the purpose of eating.

***

This great city contains many mosques, or houses for idols, very beautiful edifices situated in the different precincts of it; in the principal ones of The Aztec which are the religious orders of their sect. Priests for whom, besides the houses in which they keep their idols, there are very good habitations provided. All these priests dress in black, and never cut or comb their hair from the time they enter the religious order until they leave it; and the sons of all the principal families, both of chiefs as well as noble citizens, are in these religious orders and habits from the age of seven or eight years till they are taken away for the purpose of marriage. This happens more frequently with the first-born, who inherit the property, than with the others. They have no access to women, nor are any allowed to enter the religious houses; they abstain from eating certain dishes, and more so at certain times of the year than at others.

Amongst these mosques, there is one principal one, and no human tongue is able to describe its greatness and details, because it is so large that within its circuit, which is surrounded by a high wall, a village of five hundred houses could easily be built. Within, and all around it, are very handsome buildings, in which there are large rooms and galleries, where the religious who live there are lodged. There are as many as forty very high and well-built towers, the largest having fifty steps to reach the top; the principal one is higher than the tower of the chief church in Seville. They are so well built, both in their masonry, and their wood work, that they could not be better made nor constructed anywhere; for all the masonry inside the chapels, where they keep their idols, is carved with figures, and the wood work is all wrought with designs of monsters, and other shapes. All these towers are places of burial for the chiefs, and each one of their chapels is dedicated to the idol to which they have a particular devotion. Within this great mosque, there are three halls wherein stand the principal idols of marvelous grandeur in size, and much decorated with carved figures, both of stone and wood; and within these halls there are other chapels, entered by very small doors, and which have no light, and nobody but the religious are admitted to them. Within these are the images and figures of the idols, although, as I have said, there are many outside.

The principal idols in which they have the most faith and belief I overturned from their seats, and rolled down the stairs, and I had those chapels, where they kept them, cleansed, for they were full of blood from the sacrifices; and I set up images of Our Lady, and other Saints in them, which grieved Montezuma, and the natives not a little. At first they told me not to do it, for, if it became known throughout the town, the people would rise against me, as they believed that these idols gave them all their temporal goods, and, in allowing them to be ill-treated, they would be angered, and give nothing, and would take away all the fruits of the soil, and cause the people to die of want. I made them understand by the interpreters how deceived they were in putting their hope in idols, made of unclean things by their own hands, and I told them that they should know there was but one God, the Universal Lord of all, who had created the heavens, and earth, and all things else, and them, and us, who was without beginning, and immortal; that they should adore, and believe in Him, and not in any creature, or thing.

Source: *Letters of Cortes,* translated and edited by Francis Augustus MacNutt (New York: G. P. Putnam's Sons, 1908), vol. 1, pp. 256–57, 259–61.

Leo Africanus's Travels in Africa (1550)

Published in Italian in 1550, *The History and Description of Africa* was the first European account of the geography of Africa. The author, Leo Africanus, was a Berber, born in Spanish Grenada. His family moved to Morocco when he was a young child, and he later served as a diplomat. (Archaic spelling from the original translation has been preserved.)

- **Leo describes the people of Egypt as savages. Explain how he uses the term.**

- **Explain how Leo divides up the peoples of Africa he encounters. What groups does he describe? How does he distinguish them?**

- **Does this document reveal more about Europe or Africa?**

Wherein he intreateth of the land of Negros, and of the confines of Egypt.

Our ancient Chroniclers of Africa, to wit, *Bichri* and *Meshudi* knew nothing of the land of Negros but onely the regions of Guechet and Cano: for in their time all other places of the land of Negros were vndiscouered. But in the yeere of the Hegeira 380, by the meanes of a certaine Mahumetan which came into Barbarie, the residue of the said land was found out, being as then inhabited by great numbers of people, which liued a brutish and sauage life, without any king, gouernour, common wealth, or knowledge of husbandrie. Clad they were in skins of beasts, neither had they any peculiar wiues: in the day time they kept their cattell; and when night came they resorted ten or twelue both men and women into one cottage together, using hairie skins instead of beds, and each man choosing his leman which he had most fancy vnto. Warre they wage against no other nation, ne yet are desirous to trauell out of their owne countrie. Some of them performe great adoration vnto the sunne rising: others, namely the people of Gualata, worship the fire: and some others, to wit, the inhabitants of Gaoga, approch (after the Egyptians manner) neerervnto the Christian faith. These Negros were first subject vnto king *Ioseph* the founder of Maroco, and afterward vnto the fiue nations of Libya; of whom they learned the Mahumetan lawe, and diuers needfull handycrafts: a while after when the merchants of Barbarie began to resort vnto them with merchandize, they learned the Barbarian language also. But the foresaid fiue people or nations of Libya diuided this land so among themselues, that euery third part of each nation possessed one region. Howbeit the king of Tombuto that now raigneth, called *Abuacre Izchia*, is a Negro by birth: this *Abuacre* after the decease of the former king, who was a Libyan borne, slue all his sonnes, and so vsurped the kingdome. And hauing by warres for the space of fifteene yeeres conquered many large dominions, he then concluded a league with all nations, and went on pilgrimage to Mecca, in which iournie he so consumed his treasure, that he was constrained to borrow great summes of money of other princes. Moreouer the fifteene kingdomes of Negros knowen to vs, are all situate vpon the riuer of Niger, and vpon other riuers which fall thereinto. And all the land of Negros standeth betweene two vast deserts, for on the one side lieth the maine desert betweene Numidia and it, which extendeth it selfe vnto this very land: and the south side thereof adioineth vpon another desert, which stretcheth from thence to the maine Ocean: in which desert are infinite nations vnknowen to vs, both by reason of the huge distance of place, and also in regarde of the diuersitie of languages and religions. They haue no traffique at all with our people, but we haue heard oftentimes of their traffique with the inhabitants of the Ocean sea shore.

A description of the kingdome of Gualata.

This region in regarde of others is very small: for it containeth onely three great villages, with certaine granges and fields of dates. From Nun it is distant southward about three hundred, from Tombuto northward fiue hundred, and from the Ocean sea about two hundred miles. In this region the people of Libya, while they were lords of the land of Negros, ordained their chiefe princely seate: and then great store of Barbarie-merchants frequented Gualata: but afterward in the raigne of the mighty and rich prince *Heli*, the said merchants leauing Gualata, began to resort vnto Tombuto and Gago, which was the occasion that the region of Gualata grew extreme beggerly. The language of this region is called Sungai, and the inhabitants are blacke people, and most friendly vnto strangers. In my time this region was conquered by the king of Tombuto, and the prince thereof fled into the deserts, whereof the king of Tombuto hauing intelligence, and fearing least the prince would returne with all the people of the deserts, graunted

him peace, conditionally that he should pay a great yeerely tribute vnto him, and so the said prince hath remained tributarie to the king of Tombuto vntill this present. The people agree in manners and fashions with the inhabitants of the next desert. Here groweth some quantitie of Mil-seed, and great store of a round & white kind of pulse, the like whereof I neuer saw in Europe; but flesh is extreme scarce among them. Both the men & the women do so couer their heads, that al their countenance is almost hidden. Here is no forme of a common wealth, nor yet any gouernours or iudges, but the people lead a most miserable life.

Source: Leo Africanus, *The History and Description of Africa and of the Notable Things Therein Contained*, edited by Robert Brown (London: Printed for the Hakluyt Society, Lincoln's Inn Fields W.C., 1896), pp. 819–21.

Commentary on Foreigners (c. 1420), Ming Official He Ao

He Ao was a censor, a high official in the provincial bureaucracy of the Ming Empire. The censorate was part of the central state. Responsible directly to the emperor, it was tasked with rooting out corruption at the local level. This document, in which He describes the threats posed by Europeans (called Feringis), is an official government report to his superiors.

- **Identify the factors He used to mark foreigners as different, and evaluate their relative significance. Pay special attention to his language and the terms he used.**

- **What specific threats resulting from European influence does He identify, and what remedies does he propose?**

- **Explain the distinction this document draws between the way trade was conducted in the past, in the "time of our ancestors," and in the present. What is He's view of commerce?**

The Feringis are most cruel and crafty. Their arms are superior to those of other foreigners. Some years ago they came suddenly to the city of Canton, and the noise of their cannon shook the earth [these were cannon-shots fired as a salute by the fleet of Fernão Peres]. Those who remained at the post-station [places where foreigners were lodged] disobeyed the law and had intercourse with others. Those who came to the Capital were proud and struggled [among themselves?] to become head. Now if we allow them to come and go and to carry on their trade, it will inevitably lead to fighting and bloodshed, and the misfortune of our South may be boundless.

In the time of our ancestors, foreigners came to bring tribute only at fixed periods, and the law provided for precautionary measures, therefore the foreigners who could come were not many. But some time ago the Provincial Treasurer, Wu T'ing-chü, saying that he needed spice to be sent to the Court, took some of their goods no matter when they came.

It was due to what he did that foreigner ships have never ceased visiting our shores and that barbarians have lived scattered in our departmental cities. Prohibition and precaution having been neglected, the Feringis became more and more familiar with our fair ways. And thus availing themselves of the situation the Feringis came into our port. I pray that all the foreign junks in our bay and the foreigners who secretly live (in our territory) be driven away, that private intercourse be prohibited and that our strategical defence be close, so that that part of our country will have peace.

Source: T'ien-Tse Chang, *Sino-Portuguese Trade from 1514 to 1644: A Synthesis of Portuguese and Chinese Sources* (Leyden: E. J. Brill, 1934), pp. 51–52.

Interpreting Visual Evidence

Conflict and Consent

In the fifteen and sixteenth centuries, new contacts led to conflict and, in some cases, consent. The consolidation of existing land empires, especially in Asia, required rulers to manage vast, diverse populations. They often used policies of tolerance to win the consent of their new subjects. European overseas empires, by contrast, almost immediately came into conflict with indigenous societies, decimating the Amerindian population and drafting African slaves to perform labor the remaining Amerindians refused. This resulted in societies in the Americas that initially had extremely pronounced cultural differences.

Depictions of these encounters show the dynamics between the groups involved, as well as the artist's point of view. The first image below, an anonymous Mexican painting (c. 1520), portrays Spanish soldiers in gleaming body armor with muskets firing on Amerindians, who are barely visible at the painting's edges and armed only with bows and arrows. The second, *The Conquest of the Aztecs*, was drawn by a converted Amerindian later in the sixteenth century and relied on indigenous oral histories and familiar artistic forms. It shows the Aztec (Mexica) warriors in full battle dress and also portrays their battles with other Amerindians who had sided with the Spanish. In the final image, *Akbar Hears a Petition*, the individuals gathered before Akbar represent the diversity of people who sought the assistance of the Mughal emperor. This miniature reflects the multiethnic and multireligious character of Akbar's empire and the tolerance required to maintain social cohesion.

Anonymous Mexican painting of the Spanish conquest.

The Conquest of the Aztecs, drawn by a converted Amerindian.

Akbar Hears a Petition.

Questions for Analysis

1. In the first two images, note the divisions within each camp, Spanish and Aztec. Explain how each portrays the Aztec defeat. What do the images present to explain the defeat, and what factors, emphasized in this chapter, do they both omit?

2. Interpret the artist's portrayal of Akbar's authority in the third image. Describe the audience presented in the painting. What can you tell about the different groups present?

3. Contrast the first two images with the third. Pay special attention to the center of each image. Describe which elements the artists emphasize, in visual terms. What does that say about the social order?

4. Explain who you think was the audience for each image. Were all three produced for rulers, their court, the elite in general, a particular ethno-religious or social group, or the general public?

13

Worlds Entangled

1600–1750

The leading Ottoman intellectual of the sixteenth century, Mustafa Ali, was a gloomy man, convinced that the Ottoman Empire had slipped into an irreversible decline. When he published his magnum opus, *The Essence of History* (1591), the empire's fortunes looked grim. The first half of the century had witnessed the conquest of Egypt and the reign of Suleiman the Magnificent and the Lawgiver, arguably the most successful of sultans. But by century's end, the Ottomans had lost territory to their main European adversaries; military rioting had occurred in protest against payments in debased silver coinage; and uprisings against the empire were widespread in eastern Anatolia.

Historians now know that many of these problems stemmed from a cold spell that descended on the entire world, which has come to be called the Little Ice Age. Historians have seen the seventeenth century as the most intense phase of a decline in global temperatures that spanned the adjoining centuries. Declining temperatures laid waste to agricultural and pastoral lands, spreading hunger and famines worldwide. As global empires ramped up their competition, they squeezed their peasants for resources to pay for warfare when they could least afford to contribute. A wave of suffering, peasant unrest, and political upheaval swept across Afro-Eurasia.

In spite of the turmoil, the period 1600–1750 saw the world's oceans give way to booming sea-lanes for global trading networks. Europeans conquered and colonized more of the Americas, the demand for African slaves to work New World

Chapter Outline

- Global Commerce and Climate Change
- Exchanges and Expansions in North America
- The Plantation Complex in the Caribbean.
- The Slave Trade and Africa
- Asia in the Seventeenth and Eighteenth Centuries
- Transformations in Europe
- Conclusion

Core Objectives

- **DESCRIBE** and **EXPLAIN** the impact of climate change on societies are economies across the globe.
- **IDENTIFY** and **EXPLAIN** the major steps in the integration of global trade networks in the seventeenth and eighteenth centuries, and **ANALYZE** examples of resistance to this integration.
- **ANALYZE** the consequences of the Atlantic slave trade across the Atlantic world.
- **EXPLAIN** the effects of New World silver and increased trade on the Asian empires, and their response to them.
- **COMPARE** the impact of trade and religion on state power in various regions.
- **EXPLAIN** the significance of European consumption of goods (like tobacco, textiles, and sugar) for the global economy.

plantations leaped upward, and global trade intensified, fueled by New World silver. In the Americas, Spain and Portugal faced new competitors—primarily England and France. With religious tensions added to the mix, the stage was set for decades of bloody warfare in Europe and the Americas. At the same time, in the East, rulers in India, China, and Japan enlarged their empires, while Russia's tsars incorporated Siberian territories into their domain. Meanwhile, the Ottoman, Safavid, and Mughal dynasties, though resisting most European intrusions, found their stability profoundly shaken by climate change and global commerce.

Global Storylines

- Transoceanic trade networks (on an unprecedented scale) create vast wealth and new kinds of inequality.

- Silver gives Europeans a commodity to exchange with Asians and begins to tilt the balance of wealth and power from Asia toward Europe.

- New World sugar also accelerates the shift of power in the Atlantic world from the Spanish and Portuguese to the British and French.

- European merchants and African leaders radically increase the volume and violence of the slave trade, destabilizing African societies.

- Asian rulers in India, China, and Japan and Russian tsars enlarge their empires.

- The Ottoman, Safavid, and Mughal dynasties all struggle to resist European assaults.

Global Commerce and Climate Change

In spite of the worldwide trauma brought on by the plunge in temperatures, global trade flourished during this period. Increasing economic ties brought new places and products into world markets. (See Current Trends in World History: Stimulants, Sociability, and Coffeehouses.) Closer economic contact enhanced the power of certain states and destabilized others. It bolstered the legitimacy of England and France, and it prompted strong local support of new rulers in Japan and parts of sub-Saharan Africa. But also in England, France, Japan, Russia, and Africa, linkages led to civil wars and social unrest. In the Ottoman state, outlying provinces slipped from central control; the Safavid regime foundered and then collapsed; the Ming dynasty gave way to the Qing. In India, rivalries among princes and merchants eroded the Mughals' authority, compounding the instability caused by peasant uprisings.

THE BIG PICTURE

What were the major steps in the integration of global trade networks in the seventeenth and eighteenth centuries?

EXTRACTING WEALTH: MERCANTILISM

Transformations in global relations began in the Atlantic, where the extraction and shipment of gold and silver siphoned wealth from the New World (the Americas) to the Old World (Afro-Eurasia). (See Map 13.1.) American exports were so lucrative for Spain and Portugal that other European powers wanted a share in the bounty, so they too launched colonizing ventures in the New World. Although these latecomers found few precious minerals, they devised other ways to extract wealth, for the Americas had fertile lands on which to cultivate sugarcane, cotton, tobacco, indigo, and rice.

If silver quickened the pace of global trade, sugar transformed the European diet. First domesticated in Polynesia, sugar rarely appeared in European diets before the New World plantations started exporting it. Previously, Europeans had used honey as a sweetener, but they soon became insatiable consumers of sugar. Between 1690 and 1790, Europe imported 12 million tons of sugar—approximately 1 ton for every African enslaved in the Americas.

No matter what products they supplied, colonies were supposed to provide wealth for their "mother countries"—according to the economic theory of mercantilism, which drove European empire builders. The term **mercantilism** describes a system that saw the world's wealth as fixed, meaning that any one country's wealth came at the expense of other countries. Mercantilism further assumed that overseas possessions existed solely to enrich European motherlands. Thus, colonies should ship more "value" to the mother country than they received in return. Colonies were supposed

Core Objectives

EXPLAIN the significance of European consumption of goods (like tobacco, textiles, and sugar) for the global economy.

mercantilism
Economic theory that drove European empire builders. In this economic system, the world had a fixed amount of wealth, which meant one country's wealth came at the expense of another's. Mercantilism assumed that colonies existed for the sole purpose of enriching the country that controlled the colony.

Stimulants, Sociability, and Coffeehouses

While armies, travelers, missionaries, and diseases have breached the world's main political and cultural barriers, commodities have been the least respectful of the lines that separate communities. It has been difficult for ruling elites to curtail the desire of their populations to dress themselves in fine garments, to possess jewelry, and to consume satisfying food and drink no matter where these products may originate. The history of commodities, thus, is a core area for world historical research, for products span cultural barriers and connect peoples over long distances. As the world's trading networks expanded in the seventeenth and eighteenth centuries, merchants in Europe, Asia, Africa, and the Americas distributed many new commodities. By far the most popular were a group of stimulants—coffee, cocoa, sugar, tobacco, and tea—all of which (except for sugar) were addictive and also produced a sense of well-being.

Previously, many of these products had been grown in isolated parts of the world: the coffee bean in Yemen, tobacco and cocoa in the New World, and sugar in Bengal. Yet, by the seventeenth century, in nearly every corner of the world, the well-to-do began to congregate in coffeehouses, consuming these new products and engaging in sociable activities.

Coffeehouses everywhere served as locations for social exchange, political discussions, and business activities. Yet they also varied from cultural area to cultural area, reflecting the values of the societies in which they arose.

The coffeehouse first appeared in Islamic lands late in the fifteenth century. As coffee consumption caught on among the wealthy and leisured classes in the Arabian Peninsula and the Ottoman Empire, local growers protected their advantage by monopolizing its cultivation and sale and refusing to allow any seeds or cuttings from the coffee tree to be taken abroad.

Despite some religious opposition, coffee spread into Egypt and throughout the Ottoman Empire in the sixteenth century. Ottoman bureaucrats, merchants, and artists assembled in coffeehouses to trade stories, read, listen to poetry, and play chess and backgammon. Indeed, so deeply connected were coffeehouses with literary and artistic pursuits that people referred to them as schools of knowledge.

From the Ottoman territories, the culture of coffee drinking spread to western Europe. The first coffeehouse in London opened in 1652, and within sixty years the city claimed no fewer than 500 such establishments. In fact, the Fleet Street area of London had so many that the English essayist Charles Lamb commented, "[T]he man must have a rare recipe for melancholy who can be dull in Fleet Street." Although coffeehouses attracted people from all levels of society, they especially appealed to the new mercantile and professional classes as locations where stimulating

to be closed to competitors, so that foreign traders would not drain precious resources from an empire's exclusive domain. As the mother country's monopoly over its colonies' trade generated precious metals for royal treasuries, European states grew rich enough to wage almost unceasing wars against one another. Ultimately, mercantilists believed, as did the English philosopher Thomas Hobbes (1588–1679), that "wealth is power and power is wealth."

The mercantilist system required an alliance between the state and its merchants. Mercantilists understood economics and politics as interdependent, with the merchant needing the monarch to protect his interests and the monarch relying on the merchant's trade to enrich the state's treasury. **Chartered companies**, such as the (English) Virginia Company and the Dutch East India Company were the most visible examples of the collaboration between

chartered companies
Private firms that were awarded monopoly trading rights over vast areas by European monarchs (for example, the Virginia Company and the Dutch East India Company).

beverages like coffee, cocoa, and tea promoted lively conversations. Here, too, opponents claimed that excessive coffee drinking destabilized the thinking processes and even caused conversions to Islam. But against such opposition, the pleasures of coffee, tea, and cocoa prevailed. These bitter beverages in turn required liberal doses of the sweetener sugar. A smoke of tobacco topped off the experience. In this environment of pleasure, patrons of the coffeehouses indulged their addictions, engaged in gossip, conducted business, and talked politics.

Coffee Coffee drinkers at an Ottoman banquet (*left*) and in an English coffeehouse (*right*).

Questions for Analysis

- What factors drove the consumption of stimulants like coffee on a global scale?
- What other commodities from earlier in world history played a similar role? Were there differences in the underlying factors such as scale of consumption between the different periods?

Explore Further

Hattox, Ralph S., *Coffee and Coffeehouses: The Origins of a Social Beverage in the Medieval Near East* (1985).

the state and the merchant classes. European monarchs awarded these firms monopoly trading rights over vast areas.

THE LITTLE ICE AGE

Global cooling occurred unevenly around the world. In some places, the effect of falling temperatures, shorter growing seasons, and irregular precipitation patterns was felt as early as the fourteenth century. But the impact of the **Little Ice Age** reached farther and deeper in the seventeenth century. What caused this climate change is a matter of debate. But a combination of low sunspot activity, changing ocean currents, and volcanic eruptions that filled the atmosphere with dust shocked an increasingly integrated world. While the seventeenth century was especially severe, the cold lasted well into

Little Ice Age
A period of global cooling—not a true ice age—that extended roughly from the sixteenth to the nineteenth century. The dates, especially for the start of the period, remain the subject of scientific controversy.

The Global View

ALASKA

GREENLAND

ICELAND

NETHERL

EN

L

RUPERT'S
LAND

NEWFOUND-
LAND

PORTU

Québec

NEW
FRANCE

LOUISIANA

Boston
Philadelphia
New York
THIRTEEN
COLONIES

NOVA
SCOTIA

Lisb

From North
America

Tobacco
Rice
Furs
Indigo
Meat
Timber
Grain
Taxes

Manufactures

Silk
Spices

VICEROYALTY
OF
NEW SPAIN

Zacatecas

New Orleans

From South
America

Sugar
Gold
Hides
Coffee
Diamonds
Calico
Taxes

Iron
Copper
Textiles
Cutlery
Firearms

Timbu

MEXICO
Mexico City
Acapulco

Veracruz

CURAÇAO

Slaves

ATLANTIC
OCEAN

ASA

Cartagena
Panama
VICEROYALTY
OF
GRANADA

SURINAM

FER

Quito

DUTCH
BRAZIL

PACIFIC
OCEAN

Lima

VICEROYALTY
OF BRAZIL

Recife
Bahia

Slaves

VICEROYALTY
OF PERU

Potosí

Tobacco
Sugar

Rio de Janeiro

Buenos Aires

Line of
Tordesillas
1494

Map 13.1 Trade in Silver and Other Commodities, 1650–1750

The seventeenth and eighteenth centuries were the first centuries of true global commerce. Silver was the one item that was traded all over the world.

- Trace the flows of silver from the Americas around the globe (by following the thick orange arrows), and identify the commodities that silver was exchanged for in different parts of the world.
- Explain the relationship between the trade of manufactures and natural resources.
- According to this map, how did increased trade shape European states' territorial ambitions?

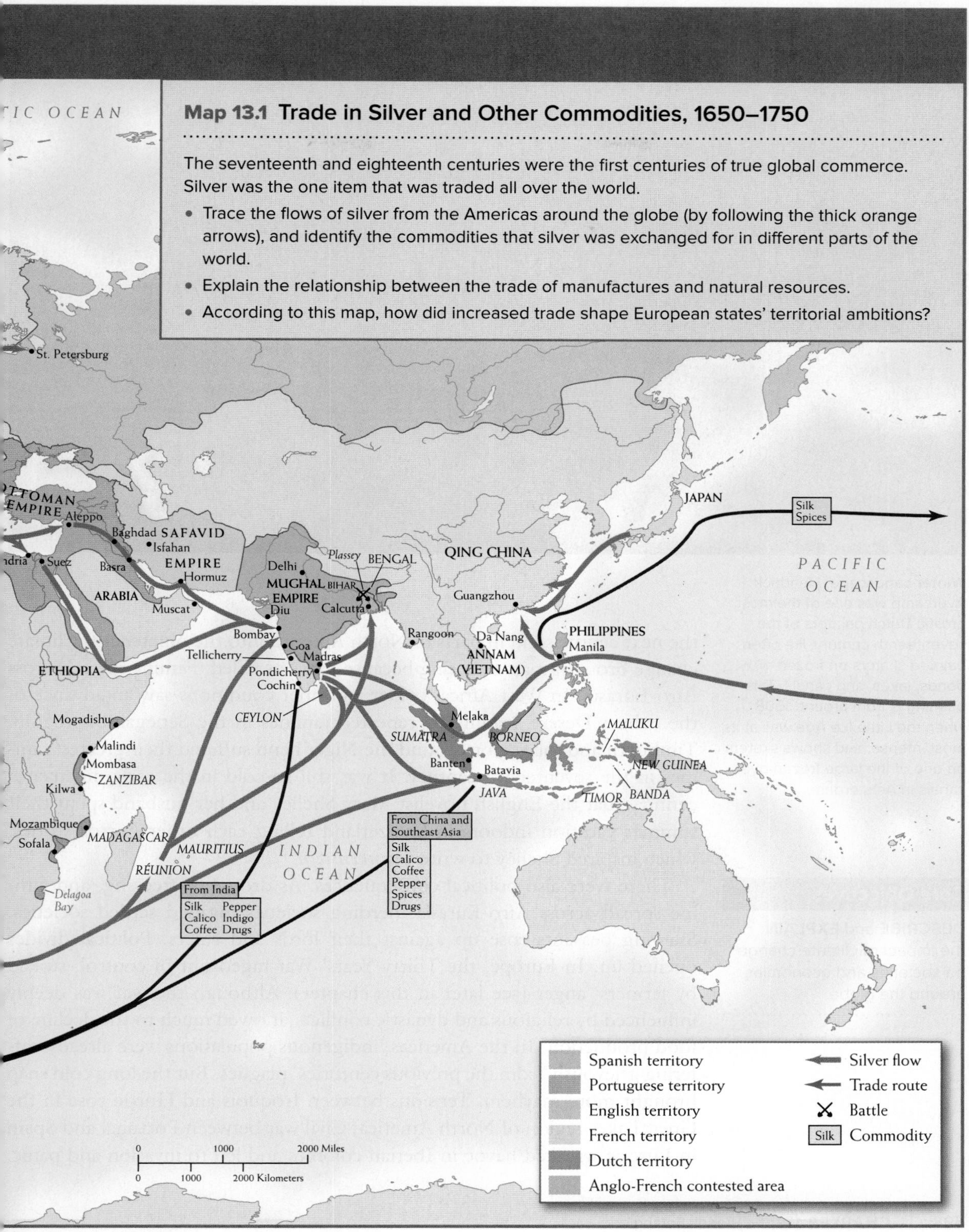

TIC OCEAN

St. Petersburg

OTTOMAN EMPIRE
Aleppo
andria · Suez
Baghdad SAFAVID
Isfahan
Basra EMPIRE
Hormuz
ARABIA
Muscat
Diu
Delhi
MUGHAL
EMPIRE
BIHAR
Plassey BENGAL
Calcutta
QING CHINA
JAPAN

Silk
Spices

PACIFIC
OCEAN

Bombay
Goa
Tellicherry
Madras
Pondicherry
Cochin
Rangoon
Da Nang
ANNAM
(VIETNAM)
Guangzhou
PHILIPPINES
Manila

ETHIOPIA

Mogadishu

CEYLON

Malindi
Mombasa
ZANZIBAR
Kilwa

Melaka
SUMATRA
BORNEO
MALUKU
NEW GUINEA
BANDA
TIMOR

Banten
Batavia
JAVA

Mozambique
Sofala
MADAGASCAR
MAURITIUS
RÉUNION

INDIAN
OCEAN

Delagoa
Bay

From China and
Southeast Asia
Silk
Calico
Coffee
Pepper
Spices
Drugs

From India
Silk   Pepper
Calico Indigo
Coffee Drugs

Spanish territory	← Silver flow
Portuguese territory	← Trade route
English territory	✗ Battle
French territory	Silk Commodity
Dutch territory	
Anglo-French contested area	

0   1000   2000 Miles

0   1000   2000 Kilometers

Winter Landscape Hendrick Avercamp was one of the most prolific Dutch painters of the seventeenth century. He often painted skaters on frozen ponds, lakes, and canals. This painting is from around 1608, when the Little Ice Age was at its most intense, and shows skaters on one of the large frozen-over canals in Amsterdam.

the next century and in parts of North America into the nineteenth. Climate change brought mass suffering because harvests failed. Famine spread across Afro-Eurasia. In West Africa, colder and drier conditions saw an advance of the Sahara Desert, leading to repeated famines in the Senegambia region. Timbuktu and the region around the Niger bend suffered their greatest famines in the seventeenth century. It was still so cold in the early nineteenth century that the English novelist Mary Shelley and her husband spent their summer vacation indoors in Switzerland telling each other horror stories, which inspired Shelley to write *Frankenstein*.

There were also political consequences. As droughts, freezing, and famine spread across Afro-Eurasia, herding societies invaded settled societies. Starving peasants rose up against their lords and rulers. Political divides opened up. In Europe, the Thirty Years' War raged out of control, stoked by farmers' anger (see later in this chapter). Although the war was deeply influenced by religious and dynastic conflicts, it owed much to the decline of food production. In the Americas, indigenous populations were already suffering grievously from the previous centuries' plagues. But the long cold snap brought more mayhem. Tensions between Iroquois and Huron rose in the Great Lakes region of North America. Civil war between Portugal and Spain in Europe wreaked havoc in Iberian colonies and led to invasion and panic.

The Ottomans faced a crippling revolt, while in China the powerful Ming regime could not deal with the climate shock. It was invaded, as was so often the case when pastures turned to dust, by Manchurian peoples from beyond the Great Wall. They installed a new regime, the Qing dynasty. The English philosopher Thomas Hobbes famously wrote in *Leviathan* (1651) that "[m]an's natural state . . . was war; and not simply war, but the war of every man against every other man." "The life of man," he continued, is "solitary, poor, nasty, brutish, and short."

The Little Ice Age had a devastating impact on populations. It is hard, however, to separate the victims of starvation from the victims of war, since warfare aggravated starvation and famine contributed to war. But in continental Europe, the Thirty Years' War carried off an estimated two-thirds of the total population, on a par with the impact of the Black Death (see Chapter 11). Elsewhere, estimates were closer to one-third. Not until the twentieth century did the world again witness such extensive warfare. For some Afro-Eurasian regimes, the global crisis led to collapse and decline; for others, it became an opportunity for renewal and reinvention.

Exchanges and Expansions in North America

As rulers in England, France, and Holland granted monopolies to merchant companies, those countries began to dominate the settlement and trade of new colonies in the Americas and compete with the established colonies of Spain and Portugal. (See Map 13.2.) Although the search for precious metals or water routes to Asia had initially spurred British, French, and Dutch efforts to establish New World colonies, colonizers soon learned that only by exploiting other resources could they generate profits.

EXPANDING MAINLAND COLONIES

While the Dutch relied primarily on commerce, the British and the French exploited natural resources in their North American colonies: the British established farms in a number of ecological zones, while the French relied primarily on the fur trade, especially in the interior.

In their colonies along the Atlantic seaboard, the English established one model for new colonies in the Americas. Although these territories failed to yield precious metals or a waterway across the continent, they did boast land suitable for growing a variety of crops. Different climates and soils made for very different agricultural possibilities: wheat, rye, barley, and oats in the Middle Colonies; tobacco in Virginia and North Carolina; and rice and indigo farther south. In all of England's North American colonies,

Map 13.2 Colonies in North America, 1607–1763

France, England, and Spain laid claim to much of North America at this time.

- Where was each of these colonial powers strongest before the outbreak of the Seven Years' War in 1756? (See p. 631 for a discussion of the Seven Years' War.)
- Which empire gained the most North American territory, and which lost the most at the end of the war in 1763?
- How do you think Native American peoples reacted to the territorial arrangements agreed to by Spain, France, and England at the Peace of Paris, which ended the war?

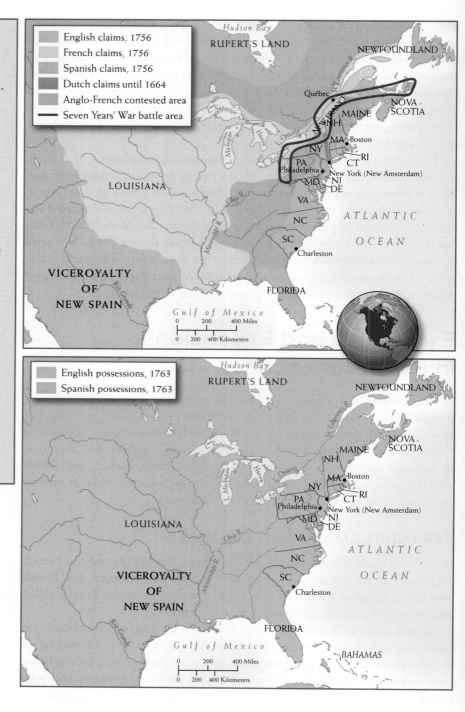

English claims, 1756
French claims, 1756
Spanish claims, 1756
Dutch claims until 1664
Anglo-French contested area
Seven Years' War battle area

English possessions, 1763
Spanish possessions, 1763

population growth fed greater hunger for farmlands, which put pressure on Indian holdings. The result: a souring of relations between Native Americans and colonists, often ferocious wars between natives and newcomers, and, over the course of the seventeenth and eighteenth centuries, the dispossession of Indians from lands between the Atlantic Ocean and the Appalachian Mountains.

By contrast, Dutch and French colonies rested not on the expulsion of natives, but on dependence on them. Holland's North American venture, however, proved short-lived, as the English took over New Netherland and renamed it New York in 1664. French claims were more enduring and extended across a vast swath of the continent, encompassing eastern Canada, the Great Lakes, and the Mississippi Valley. Crucial to the trade between Europeans and Native Americans in the northern parts of North America was the beaver, an animal for which Native Americans previously had little use.

The distinctive aspect of the fur trade was the Europeans' utter dependence on Native American know-how. After all, trapping required familiarity with the beavers' habits and habitats, which Europeans lacked. This reliance forced the French to adapt to Native American ways, which is evident in their pattern of exchange. Responding to Native American desires to use trade as an instrument to cement familial bonds, the French gave gifts, participated in Native American diplomatic rituals, and even married into Native American families. As a result, *métis* (French–Native American offspring) played an important role in New France as interpreters, traders, and guides. Thus, the French colonization of the Americas—owing to their reliance on Native Americans as trading partners, military allies, and mates—rested more on cooperation than conquest, especially compared to the empires built by their Spanish and English rivals.

As French (and English) traders introduced guns into the exchange networks, however, they initiated an arms race among Native Americans. To get more guns, Native Americans had to collect more skins, which resulted in the depletion of the beaver population in heavily trapped areas. That, in turn, pushed Native Americans to expand their hunting/trapping zones, which heightened conflicts between groups now increasingly competing for hunting territories. Alcohol, too, became a potent weapon for Europeans. It gave them a commodity that Native Americans wanted badly enough to undermine long-standing understandings of the relationship between humans and animals and to overwhelm strictures against overhunting.

The initial agricultural endeavors in the New World were modest. They relied on crops like tobacco that required relatively modest capital investments and could be profitably farmed on a small scale, with few workers. Sugar, by contrast, required major investments. It had to be processed near

The Fur Trade For Europeans in northern North America, no commodity was as important as beaver skins. For the French especially, the fur trade determined the character of their colonial regime in North America. For Native Americans, it offered access to European goods, but overhunting depleted resources and provoked intertribal conflicts.

the cane fields, which meant mills had to be built, and it required massive amounts of labor. Produced on a large scale with slave labor, sugar was enormously profitable. From the middle of the seventeenth century, the British and French devoted their energies to replicating the Portuguese sugar plantations of Brazil on the islands they controlled in the Caribbean. All was not sweet there, however.

The Plantation Complex in the Caribbean

Large European plantations in the Caribbean relied on slave labor to produce sugar for export. Sugar was a killing crop. So deadly was the hot, humid environment in which sugarcane flourished (as fertile for disease as for sugarcane) that many sugar barons spent little time on their plantations. Management fell to overseers, who worked their slaves to death. Despite having immunities to yellow fever and malaria from their homelands' similar environment, the African slaves who worked on the plantations could not withstand the regimen. Inadequate food, atrocious living conditions, and a lack of sanitation added to their miseries. Moreover, plantation managers on large sugar plantations treated their slaves as nonhumans: one English gentleman commented that slaves were like cows, "as near as beasts may be, setting their souls aside."

More than disease and inadequate rations, the work itself decimated the enslaved. Average life expectancy was three years. Six days a week slaves rose before dawn, labored until noon, ate a short lunch, and then worked until dusk. At harvest time, sixteen-hour days saw hundreds of men, women, and children doubled over to cut the sugarcane and transport it to refineries, sometimes seven days per week. Under this brutal schedule, slaves occasionally dropped dead from exhaustion.

Amid disease and toil, the enslaved resisted as they could. The most dramatic expression of resistance was violent revolt. A more common form of resistance was flight. Seeking refuge from overseers, thousands of slaves took to the hills—for example, to the remote mountains of Caribbean islands or to Brazil's vast interior. Those who remained on the plantations resisted via foot dragging, pilfering, and sabotage.

Caribbean settlements and slaveholdings were not restricted to any single European power. But it was the latecomers—especially the English and the French—who concentrated on the islands of the Caribbean. (See Map 13.3.) The English took Jamaica from the Spanish and made it the premier site of Caribbean sugar by the 1740s. When the French seized half of Santo Domingo in the 1660s (renaming it Saint-Domingue, which is present-day Haiti), they created one of the wealthiest societies based on slavery of all time. This French colony's exports eclipsed those of all the Spanish and English islands combined. By 1789, French Saint-Domingue produced nearly half of the world's supply of sugar and coffee. Its principal port city, Cap-Français, was among the richest in the Atlantic world. The colony's merchants and planters built immense mansions worthy of the highest European nobles. Thus, the Atlantic system benefited elite Europeans, who amassed new fortunes by exploiting the colonies' rich soil (which they eroded) and tropical climate and the African slaves' labor.

The Slave Trade and Africa

Although the slave trade began in the mid-fifteenth century, only in the seventeenth and eighteenth centuries did the numbers of human exports from Africa begin to soar. (See Map 13.4.) By 1820, four slaves had crossed the Atlantic for every European. Those numbers were essential to the prosperity of Europe's American colonies. At the same time, the departure of so many inhabitants depopulated and destabilized many parts of Africa.

Core Objectives

DESCRIBE the consequences of the Atlantic slave trade across the Atlantic world.

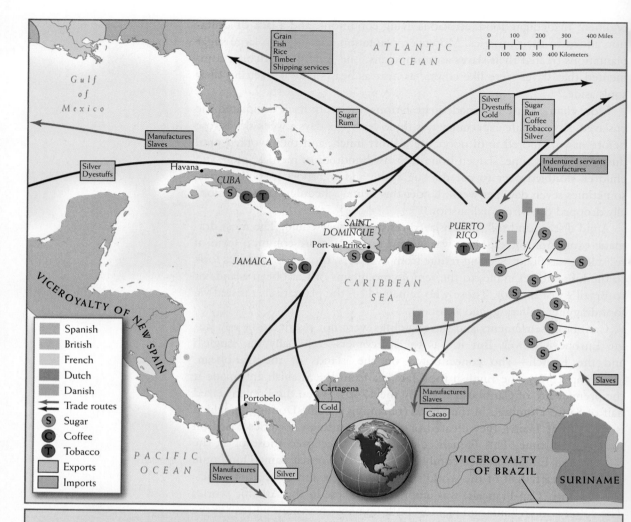

Map 13.3 Caribbean Colonies, 1625–1763

The Caribbean was a region of expanding trade in the seventeenth and eighteenth centuries.

- What were its major exports and imports?
- Who were its main colonizers and trading partners?
- According to your reading, how did the transformation of this region shape other societies in the Atlantic world?

Tobacco The cultivation of tobacco saved the Virginia colony from ruin and brought prosperity to increasing numbers of planters. The spread of tobacco plantations also pushed Native Americans off their lands and led planters to turn to Africa for a labor force.

CAPTURING AND SHIPPING SLAVES

Merchants in Europe and the New World prospered as the slave trade grew, but their fortunes depended on trading and political networks in Africa. In fact, before the nineteenth-century discovery of quinine, European slavers could not survive in the African interior. Instead they took advantage of Africans' rivalries. Using firearms supplied by Europeans, African elites controlled the capturing of slaves; their networks linked moneylenders and traders on the coast with allies in the interior.

Before the Europeans' arrival, Africa had an already existing system of slave commerce, mainly flowing across the Sahara to North Africa and Egypt and eastward to the Red Sea and the Swahili coast of East Africa. From the Red Sea and Swahili coast destinations, Muslim and Hindu merchants shipped slaves to ports around the Indian Ocean. However, the number of these slaves could not match the volume destined for the Americas once plantation agriculture began to spread. Indeed, 12.5 million Africans survived forcible enslavement and shipment to Atlantic ports from 1525 (the date of the first direct voyage from Africa to the Americas) until 1867 (when the last voyage took place).

Now the slave ports along the African coast became gruesome holding pens. Many slaves who perished did so before losing sight of Africa. Stuck in vast camps where disease and hunger were rampant, the slaves were then

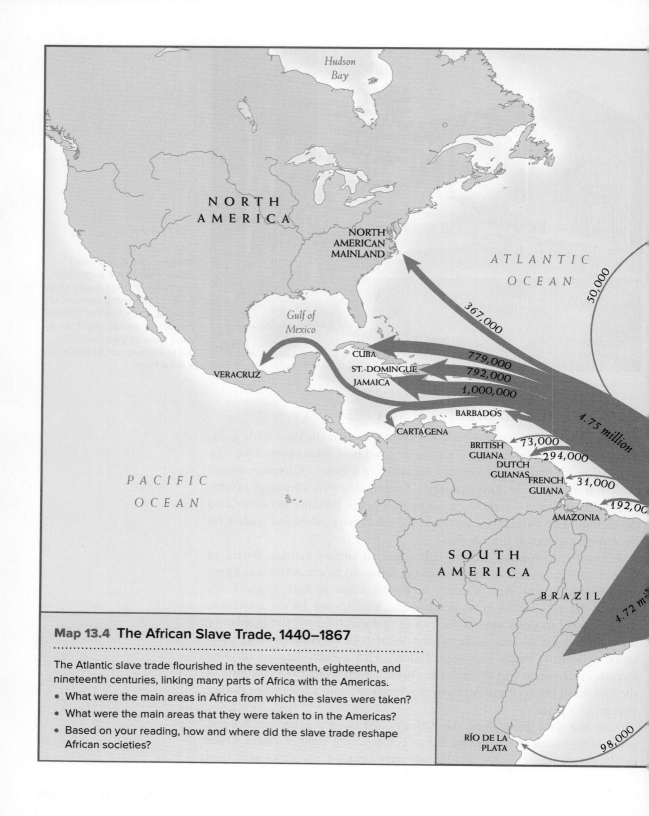

Map 13.4 The African Slave Trade, 1440–1867

The Atlantic slave trade flourished in the seventeenth, eighteenth, and nineteenth centuries, linking many parts of Africa with the Americas.

- What were the main areas in Africa from which the slaves were taken?
- What were the main areas that they were taken to in the Americas?
- Based on your reading, how and where did the slave trade reshape African societies?

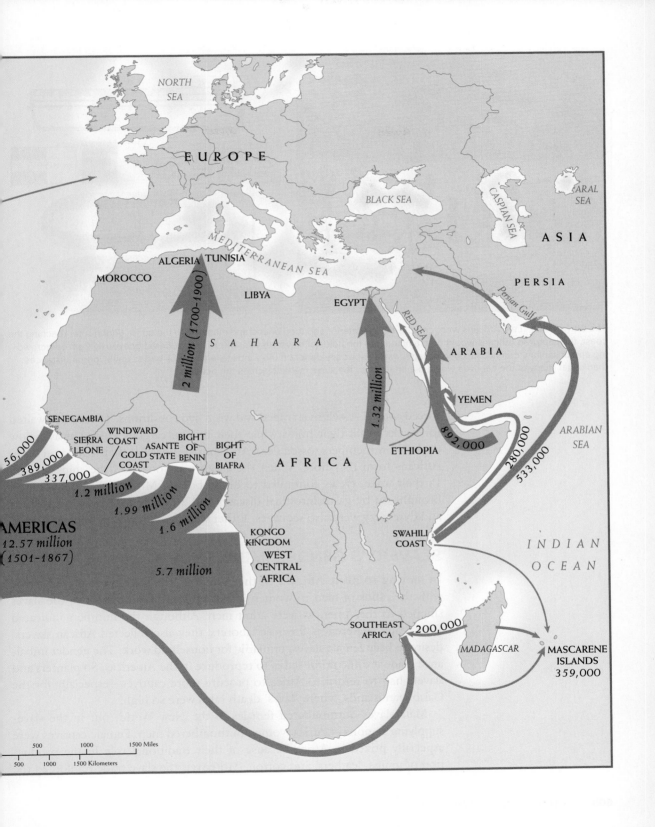

NORTH
SEA

EUROPE

BLACK SEA

ARAL
SEA

ASIA

CASPIAN
SEA

MEDITERRANEAN SEA

PERSIA

Persian Gulf

MOROCCO

ALGERIA TUNISIA

LIBYA

EGYPT

RED SEA

ARABIA

S A H A R A

2 million (1700–1900)

1.32 million

YEMEN

ARABIAN
SEA

892,000

280,000

533,000

SENEGAMBIA

56,000

SIERRA
LEONE

389,000

337,000

WINDWARD
COAST

1.2 million

ASANTE
GOLD
COAST

1.99 million

BIGHT
OF
STATE BENIN

1.6 million

BIGHT
OF
BIAFRA

ETHIOPIA

AFRICA

AMERICAS

12.57 million
(1501–1867)

KONGO
KINGDOM
WEST
CENTRAL
AFRICA

5.7 million

SWAHILI
COAST

INDIAN

OCEAN

SOUTHEAST
AFRICA

200,000

MADAGASCAR

MASCARENE
ISLANDS

359,000

500   1000   1500 Miles

500   1000   1500 Kilometers

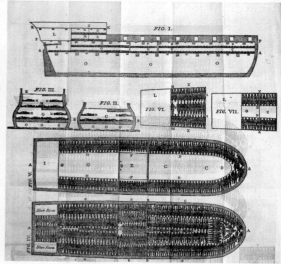

The Slave Trade (*Left*) Africans were captured in the interior and then bound and marched to the coast. (*Right*) After reaching the coast, the captured Africans would be crammed into the holds of slave vessels, where they suffered grievously from overcrowding and unsanitary conditions. Long voyages were especially deadly. If the winds failed or ships had to travel longer distances than usual, many of the captives would die en route to the slave markets across the ocean.

forced aboard vessels in cramped and wretched conditions. These ships waited for weeks to fill their holds while their human cargoes wasted away below deck. Crew members tossed dead Africans overboard as they loaded on other Africans from the shore. When the cargo was complete, the ships set sail. In their wake, crews continued to dump bodies. Most died of dehydration brought on by gastrointestinal diseases and a lack of fresh water. Smallpox and dysentery were also scourges. Either way, death was slow and agonizing.

SLAVERY'S GENDER IMBALANCE

In moving so many Africans to the Americas, the slave trade played havoc with the ratios of men to women in both places because most of the slaves shipped to the Americas were adult men. Although the numbers indicated Europeans' preferences for male laborers, they also reflected African slavers' desire to keep female slaves, primarily for household work. The gender imbalance made it difficult for slaves to reproduce in the Americas. So planters and slavers had to return to Africa to procure more captives—especially for the Caribbean islands, where slaves' death rates were so high.

Male slaves outnumbered females in the New World, but in the slave-supplying regions of Africa women outnumbered men. Female captives were especially prized in Africa because of their traditional role in the production of grains, leathers, and cotton. Moreover, the slave trade reinforced the traditional practice of polygamy—allowing relatively scarce men to take several wives, which helped minimize the loss of population.

AFRICA'S NEW SLAVE-SUPPLYING STATES

Africans did not passively let captives fall into the arms of European slave buyers; instead, local political leaders and merchants were active suppliers. This activity promoted the growth of centralized political structures, particularly in West African rain forest areas. The trade also shifted control of wealth away from households owning large herds or lands to those who profited from the capture and exchange of slaves—urban merchants and warrior elites.

In some parts of Africa, the booming slave trade created chaos as local leaders feuded over control of the traffic. In the Kongo kingdom, for example, civil wars raged for over a century after 1665, and captured warriors were sold as slaves. As members of the royal family clashed, entire provinces saw their populations vanish. Europeans fueled these conflicts and provided weapons to their African allies. Moreover, kidnapping became so prevalent that farmers worked their fields bearing weapons, leaving their children behind in guarded stockades.

As some African merchants and warlords sold other Africans, their commercial success enabled them to consolidate political power and grow wealthy. Their wealth financed additional weapons, with which they subdued

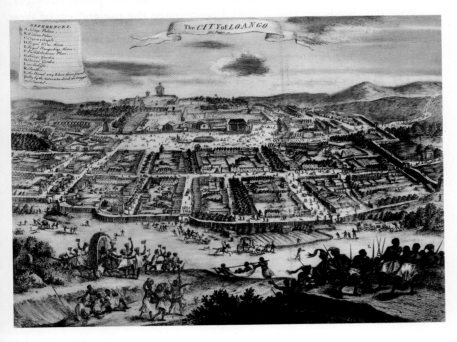

The Port of Loango Partly as a result of the profits of the slave trade, African rulers and merchants were able to create large and prosperous port cities such as Loango (pictured), which was on the west coast of south-central Africa.

neighbors and extended political control. Among the most durable new polities was the Asante state, which arose in the West African tropical rain forest in 1701 and expanded through 1750. This state benefited from its access to gold, which it used to acquire firearms (from European traders) to raid nearby communities for captives to be sold into slavery in the Americas. From its capital city at Kumasi, the state eventually encompassed almost all of present-day Ghana. Main roads spread out from the capital like spokes of a wheel, each approximately twenty days' travel from the center. Through the Asante trading networks African traders bought, bartered, and sold captives, who wound up in the hands of European merchants waiting in ports with vessels carrying manufactures and weaponry.

Slavery and the emergence of new states enriched and empowered some Africans, but they cost Africa dearly. For the princes, warriors, and merchants who organized the slave trade, their business enabled them to obtain European goods—especially alcohol, tobacco, textiles, and guns. The Atlantic system also tilted wealth away from rural dwellers and village elders and increasingly toward port cities. Across the landmass, the slave trade thinned the population. True, Africa was spared a demographic catastrophe equal to the devastation of American Indians. The introduction of American food crops—notably maize and cassava, producing many more calories per acre than the old staples of millet and sorghum—blunted the trade's depopulating aspects. Yet some areas suffered grievously from three centuries of heavy involvement in the slave trade. The Atlantic trade enhanced the warrior class, who carried out raids for captives; the dislocations, internal power struggles, and economic hardships that followed precipitated the rise and fall of West African kingdoms.

Asia in the Seventeenth and Eighteenth Centuries

Global trading networks grew as vigorously in Asia as they did in the Americas. In Asia, however, the Europeans were less dominant. Although they could gain access to Asian markets with American silver, they could not conquer Asian empires or colonize vast portions of the region. Nor were they able to enslave Asian peoples as they had Africans. The Mughal Empire continued to grow, and the Qing dynasty, which had wrested control from the Ming, significantly expanded China's borders. China remained the richest state in the world, but in some places the balance of power was tilting in Europe's direction. Not only did the Ottomans' borders contract, but by the late eighteenth century Europeans had established economic and military dominance in parts of India and much of Southeast Asia.

THE DUTCH IN SOUTHEAST ASIA

In Southeast Asia the Dutch already enjoyed considerable influence by the seventeenth century. Although the Portuguese had seized the vibrant port city of Melaka in 1511 and the Spaniards had taken Manila in 1571, neither was able to monopolize the lucrative spice trade. To challenge them, the Dutch government persuaded its merchants to charter the Dutch East India Company (abbreviated as VOC) in 1602. Benefiting from Amsterdam's position as the most efficient money market with the lowest interest rates in the world, the VOC raised ten times the capital of its English counterpart—the royal chartered English East India Company. The advantages of chartered companies were evident in the VOC's scale of operation: at its peak the company had 257 ships and employed 12,000 persons. Throughout two centuries it sent ships manned by a total of 1 million men to Asia.

The VOC's main impact was in Southeast Asia, where spices, coffee, tea, and teak wood were key exports (see again Map 13.1). The company's objective was to secure a trade monopoly wherever it could, fix prices, and replace the local population with Dutch planters. Under the leadership of Jan Pieterszoon Coen (who once said that trade could not be conducted without war and war could not be conducted without trade), the Dutch swept into the Javanese port of Jakarta in 1619 and took over the nearby Banda Islands two years later. In Banda, the traditional chiefs and almost the entire population were killed outright, left to starve, or taken into slavery. Dutch planters and their slaves replaced the decimated local population and sent their produce to the VOC. The motive for such rapacious action was the huge profit to be made by buying nutmeg at a low price in the Banda Islands and selling it at many times that price in Europe. Although this aggressive expansion met widespread resistance from the local population and other merchants involved in the region's trade, by 1670 the Dutch had also taken Melaka from the Portuguese and controlled all of the lucrative spice trade from the Maluku islands. Next, the VOC set its sights on pepper. However, the Dutch had to share this commerce with Chinese and English competitors. Moreover, since there was no demand for European products in Asia, the Dutch had to participate more in inter-Asian trade as a way to reduce their need to make payments in precious metals.

TRANSFORMATIONS IN THE ISLAMIC HEARTLAND

Compared with Southeast Asia, the major Islamic empires did not feel such direct effects of European intrusion. They did, however, face internal difficulties, which were exacerbated by trade networks that eluded state control and, in some important instances, by climate change. From its inception, the Safavid Empire had always required a powerful, religiously inspired ruler to enforce Shiite religious orthodoxy and to hold together the realm's tribal, pastoral, mercantile, and agricultural factions. With a succession of weak rulers and declining tax revenues—aggravated by a series of droughts and epidemics—the state foundered, and ultimately collapsed in 1722 (see Chapter 14). The Ottoman and Mughal Empires, in contrast, remained more resilient.

The Ottoman Empire Climate change hit the eastern Mediterranean earlier than other regions. Fierce cold and endless drought brought famine and high mortality. In 1620, the Bosporus froze over, enabling people to walk from the European side of Istanbul into the Asian side. In lands dependent on floodwaters for their well-being, such as Egypt and Iraq, food was in short supply and death rates skyrocketed. In addition, the import of New World silver led to high levels of inflation and a destabilized economy.

Having attained a high point under Suleiman (see Chapter 11), the Ottoman Empire ceased expanding. After Suleiman's reign, Ottoman armies and navies tried unsuccessfully to expand the empire's borders—losing, for example, on the western flank to the European Habsburgs. As military campaigns and a growing population strained the realm's limited resources, Ottoman intellectuals worried that the empire's glory was ebbing. A series of administrative reforms in the seventeenth century reinvigorated the state, but it never recaptured the vast power it enjoyed at its height.

Even as the empire's strength waned, by the seventeenth century its sultans faced a commercially more connected world. The introduction of New World silver into Ottoman networks of commerce and moneylending eventually destabilized the empire. Although early Ottoman rulers had avoided trade with the outside world, the lure of silver broke through state regulations. Now Ottoman merchants established black markets for commodities that eager European buyers paid for in silver—especially wheat, copper, and wool. Because these exports were illegal, their sale did not generate tax revenues to support the state's civilian and military administration. So Ottoman rulers had to rely on loans of silver from the merchants. Some European royal houses, notably the Dutch and English, would grant those who bankrolled them a say in government, which vastly increased the crown's credit and ultimately its power. Ottoman sultans, by contrast, feuded with their financiers, which undermined the sultans' authority.

More silver and budget deficits were a recipe for inflation. Prices tripled between 1550 and 1650. Runaway inflation caused hard-hit peasants in Anatolia, suffering from bad harvests and increasing taxes (used to pay off dynastic debts), to join together in uprisings that threatened the state's stability. A revolt, begun in central Anatolia in the early sixteenth century, continued in fits and starts throughout the century, reaching a crescendo in the early seventeenth century. Known as the Celali Revolt, after Shaykh Celali, who had led one of the initial uprisings, the rebellion challenged the sultan's authority with an army of 30,000 and turned much of Anatolia into a danger zone. Disorder at the center of the empire was accompanied by difficulties in the provinces, where breakaway regimes appeared.

The most threatening of the breakaway pressures occurred in Egypt beginning in the seventeenth century. In 1517, Egypt had become the Ottoman Empire's greatest conquest. As the wealthiest Ottoman territory, it was an important source of revenue, and its people shouldered heavy tax burdens. The group that asserted Egypt's political and commercial autonomy consisted of military men, known as **Mamluks** (Arabic for "owned" or "possessed"), who had ruled Egypt as an independent regime until the Ottoman

Mamluks
(Arabic for "owned" or "possessed") Military men who ruled Egypt as an independent regime from 1250 until the Ottoman conquest in 1517.

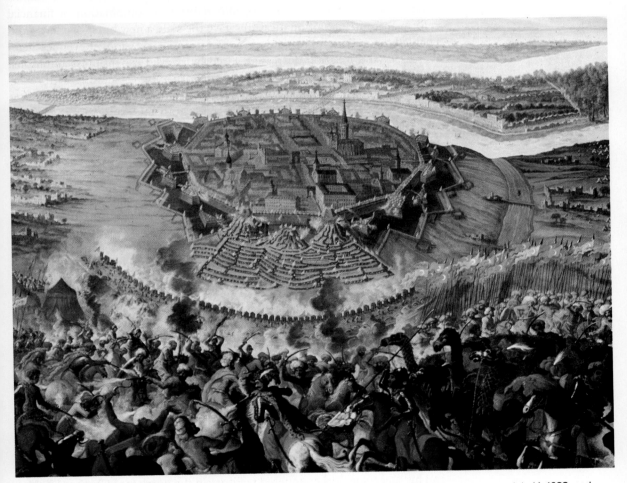

Siege of Vienna This seventeenth-century painting depicts the Ottoman siege of Vienna, which began on July 14, 1683, and ended on September 12. The city might have fallen if the Polish king, John III, had not answered the pope's plea to defend Christendom and sent an army to assist German and Austrian troops in defeating the Ottomans.

conquest. Although the Ottoman army had routed Mamluk forces on the battlefield, Ottoman governors in Egypt allowed the Mamluks to reform themselves. By the seventeenth century, these military men were nearly as powerful as their ancestors had been in the fifteenth century when they ruled Egypt independently. Mamluk leaders enhanced their power by aligning with Egyptian merchants and catering to the religious elites of Egypt, the *ulama*. Turning the Ottoman administrator of Egypt into a mere figurehead, this new provincial elite kept much of the area's fiscal resources for themselves at the expense not only of the imperial coffers but also of the local peasantry.

Amid new economic pressures and challenges from outlying territories, the Ottoman system also had elements of resilience—especially at the center, where decaying leadership provoked demands for reform from administrative elites. Known as the Köprülü reforms, a combination of financial reform and anticorruption measures gave the state a new burst of energy and enabled the military to reacquire some of its lost possessions. Revenues again increased, and inflation decreased. Fired by revived expansionist ambitions, Istanbul decided to renew its assault on Christianity—beginning with rekindled plans to seize Vienna. Although the Ottomans gathered an enormous force outside the Habsburg capital in 1683, both sides suffered heavy losses and the Ottoman forces ultimately retreated. Under the treaty that ended the Austro-Ottoman war, the Ottomans lost major European territorial possessions, including Hungary.

Thus, the Ottoman Empire began the eighteenth century dealing with serious economic and environmental challenges. Whereas in the sixteenth century rulers of the Ottoman Empire had wanted to create a self-contained and self-sufficient imperial economy, silver undermined this vision as it had elsewhere in the global economy. Indeed, the influx of silver opened Ottoman-controlled lands to trade with the rest of the world, producing breakaway regimes, widespread inflation, social discontent, and conflict between the state and its financiers. The crop shortages and population crises of the Little Ice Age made all of those problems more difficult to manage.

The Mughal Empire In contrast to the Ottomans' military reversals, the Mughal Empire reached its height in the seventeenth century. The period saw Mughal rulers extend their domain over almost all of India and enjoy increased domestic and international trade. But they, too, eventually had problems governing dispersed and resistant provinces, where many villages retained traditional religions and cultures and suffered from the effects of the Little Ice Age on their land's productivity.

Before the Mughals, India had never had a single political authority. Akbar and his successors had conquered territory in the north (see Chapter 12, Map 12.4), so now the Mughals turned to the south and gained control over most of that region by 1689. As the new provinces provided an additional source of resources, local lords, and warriors, the Mughal bureaucracy grew better at extracting services and taxes.

Imperial stability and prosperity did not depend entirely on the Indian Ocean trading system. Indeed, although the Mughals profited from seaborne trade, they never undertook overseas expansion. The main source of their wealth was land rents, which increased via incentives to bring new land into cultivation. But the imperial economy also benefited from Europeans' increased demand for Indian goods, including a sixfold rise in the English East India Company's textile purchases.

Eventually, the Mughals were victims of their own success. More than a century of imperial expansion, commercial prosperity, and agricultural development placed substantial resources in the hands of local and regional authorities. As a result, local warrior elites became more autonomous. By the late seventeenth century, many regional leaders were well positioned to resist Mughal authority. As in the Ottoman Empire, distant provinces began to challenge central rulers. Now the Indian peasants (like their counterparts in Ming China, Safavid Persia, and the Ottoman Empire) capitalized on weakening central authority. Many rose in rebellions, especially when drought and famine hit; others took up banditry.

At this point, the Mughal emperors had to accept diminished power over a loose unity of provincial states. Most of these areas accepted Mughal control in name only, administering their own affairs with local resources. Yet India still flourished, and landed elites brought new territories into agrarian production. Cotton, for instance, supported a thriving textile industry as peasant households focused on weaving and cloth production. Much of their production was destined for export as the region deepened its integration into world trading systems.

The Mughals themselves paid scant attention to commercial matters, but local rulers welcomed Europeans into Indian ports. As more European ships arrived, these authorities struck deals with merchants from Portugal and, increasingly, from England and Holland. Some Indian merchants formed trading companies of their own to control the sale of regional produce to competing Europeans; others established intricate trading networks that reached as far north as Russia. Mercantile houses grew richer and gained greater political influence over financially strapped emperors. Thus, even as global commercial entanglements enriched some in India, the effects undercut the Mughal dynasty.

FROM MING TO QING IN CHINA

Like India, China prospered in the seventeenth and eighteenth centuries; but here, too, growing wealth and climate change undermined central control and, in this case, contributed to the fall of a long-lasting dynasty.

Core Objectives

ANALYZE examples of resistance in Southeast Asia and China to the growth of global trade networks.

As in Mughal India, local power holders in China increasingly defied the Ming government. Moreover, because Ming sovereigns discouraged overseas commerce and forbade travel abroad, they did not reap the rewards of long-distance exchange. Rather, such profits went to traders and adventurers who evaded imperial edicts. Together, the persistence of local autonomy and the accelerating economic and social changes brought unprecedented challenges until finally, in 1644, the Ming dynasty collapsed.

Administrative and Economic Problems How did a dynasty that in the early seventeenth century governed the world's most economically advanced society (and perhaps a third of the world's population) fall from power? As in the Ottoman Empire, responsibility often lay with the rulers and their inadequate response to economic and environmental change. Zhu Yijun, the Wanli Emperor (r. 1573–1620), was secluded despite being surrounded by a staff of 20,000 eunuchs and 3,000 women. The "Son of Heaven" rarely ventured outside the palace compound, and when he moved within it a large retinue accompanied him, led by eunuchs clearing his path with whips. Ming emperors like Wanli quickly discovered that despite the elaborate arrangements and ritual performances affirming their position as the Son of Heaven, they had little control over the vast bureaucracy. An emperor frustrated with his officials could do little more than punish them or refuse to cooperate.

The timing of administrative breakdown in the Ming government was unfortunate, because expanding opportunities for trade led many individuals to circumvent official rules. From the mid-sixteenth century, bands of supposedly Japanese pirates ravaged the Chinese coast. Indeed, the Ming government had difficulties regulating trade with Japan and labeled all pirates as Japanese, but many of the marauders were in fact Chinese who flouted imperial authority. In tough times, the roving gangs terrorized sea-lanes and harbors. In better times, some functioned like mercantile groups: their leaders mingled with elites, foreign trade representatives, and imperial officials. What made these predators so resilient—and their business so lucrative—was their ability to move among the mosaic of East Asian cultures.

Just like in the Islamic empires, the influx of silver from the New World and Japan, while at first stimulating the Chinese economy, led to severe economic and, eventually, political problems. As we saw in Chapter 12, Europeans used New World silver to pay for their purchases of Chinese goods. As a result, by the early seventeenth century China imported more than twenty times more silver bullion (uncoined gold or silver) than it produced. Increasing monetization of the economy—which meant that silver currency became the primary medium of exchange—bolstered market activity and state revenues at the same time.

Yet the use of silver pressured peasants, who now needed that metal to pay their taxes and purchase goods. When silver supplies were abundant, the peasants faced inflationary prices. When supplies were low, the peasants could not meet their obligations to state officials and merchants, and they took up arms in rebellion.

The Collapse of Ming Authority By the seventeenth century, the Ming's administrative and economic difficulties were affecting their subjects' daily lives. This was particularly evident when the regime failed to cope with devastation caused by natural disasters, as in the northwestern province of Shanxi after a drop in average temperatures shortened growing seasons and reduced harvests.

While the Little Ice Age was not wholly responsible for the fall of the Ming, it played a major role. As the price of grain soared there in 1627–1628, the poor and the hungry fanned out to find food by whatever means they could muster. To deal with the crisis, the government imposed heavier taxes and cut the military budget. Bands of dispossessed Chinese peasants and mutinous soldiers then vented their anger at local tax collectors and officials.

Now the cycle of rebellion and weakened central authority that played out in so many other places took its predictable toll. Outlaw armies grew large under charismatic leaders. The most famous rebel leader, the "dashing prince" Li Zicheng, arrived at the outskirts of Beijing in 1644. Only a few companies of soldiers and a few thousand eunuchs were there to defend the capital's 21 miles of walls, so Li Zicheng seized Beijing easily. Two days later, the emperor hanged himself. On the following day, the triumphant "dashing prince" rode into the capital and claimed the throne.

News of the fall of the Ming capital sent shock waves around the empire. One hundred and seventy miles to the northeast, where China meets Manchuria, the army's commander received the news within a matter of days. His task in the area was to defend the Ming against their menacing neighbor, a group that had begun to identify itself as Manchu. Immediately the commander's position became precarious. Caught between an advancing rebel army on the one side and the Manchus on the other, he made a fateful decision: he appealed for the Manchus' cooperation to fight the "dashing prince," promising his new allies that "gold and treasure" awaited them in the capital. Thus, without shedding a drop of blood, the Manchus joined the Ming forces. After years of coveting the Ming Empire, the Manchus were finally on their way to Beijing. (See Map 13.5.)

The Qing Dynasty Asserts Control Despite their small numbers, the Manchus overcame early resistance to their rule and oversaw an impressive expansion of their realm. The **Manchus**—the name was first used in 1635—were descendants of a Turkic-speaking group known as the Jurchens. They emerged as a force early in the seventeenth century, when their leader claimed the title of khan after securing the allegiance of various Mongol groups in

Manchus
Descendants of the Jurchens who helped the Ming army recapture Beijing in 1644 after its seizure by the outlaw Li Zicheng. The Manchus numbered around 1 million but controlled a domain that included perhaps 250 million people. Their rule lasted more than 250 years and became known as the Qing dynasty.

Map 13.5 From Ming to Qing China, 1644–1760

Qing China under the Manchus expanded its territory significantly during this period. Find the Manchu homeland and then the area of Manchu expansion after 1644, when the Manchus established the Qing dynasty.

- Where did the Qing dynasty expand? Explain what this tells us about the priorities of the ruling elite, in particular with respect to global commerce.
- Explain the significance of the chronology of Chinese expansion. Does this qualify your answer to the first question?
- What does the chronology of Chinese expansion tell us about the evolution of the ruling elite's priorities?
- Consider the scope of Chinese territorial expansion in this period, and, based on your reading, explain the challenges this posed for central authorities.

northeastern Asia, paving the way for their eventual conquest of China. By that time, a rising Manchu population, based in Inner China and unable to feed their people in Manchuria, was posed to breach the Great Wall in search of better lands. The Manchus found a Chinese government in disarray from warfare and fiscal crisis, with central authorities overwhelmed by roving bands of peasant rebels.

When the Manchus defeated Li Zicheng and seized power in Beijing, they numbered around 1 million. Assuming control of a domain that included perhaps 250 million people, they were keenly aware of their minority status. Taking power was one thing; keeping it was another. But keep it they did. In fact, during the eighteenth century the Manchu **Qing** ("pure") **dynasty** (1644–1911) incorporated new territories, experienced substantial population growth, and sustained significant economic growth.

The key to China's relatively stable economic and geographic expansion lay in its rulers' shrewd and flexible policies. The early Manchu emperors were able and diligent administrators. They also knew that to govern a diverse population, they had to adapt to local ways. At the same time, Qing rulers were determined to convey a clear sense of their own majesty and legitimacy. Rulers relentlessly promoted patriarchal values. Widows who remained "chaste" enjoyed public praise, and women in general were urged to lead a "virtuous" life serving male kin and family. To the majority Han population, the Manchu emperor represented himself as the worthy upholder of familial values and classical Chinese civilization. However, insinuating themselves into an existing order and appeasing subject peoples did not satisfy the yearning of the Manchus to leave their imprint. They also introduced measures that emphasized their authority, their distinctiveness, and the submission of their mostly Han Chinese subjects. For example, Qing officials composed or translated important documents into Manchu and banned intermarriage between Manchu and Han, although this proved difficult to enforce.

Manchu impositions fell mostly on the peasantry, for the Qing financed their administrative structure through taxes on peasant households. In response, the peasants sought new lands to cultivate in border areas, often planting New World crops that grew well in difficult soils. This move introduced an important change in Chinese diets: while rice remained the staple of the wealthy, peasants increasingly subsisted on corn and sweet potatoes.

While officials redoubled their reliance on an agrarian base, trade and commerce flourished. Chinese merchants continued to ply the waters stretching from Southeast Asia to Japan, exchanging textiles, ceramics, and medicine for spices and rice. Although the Qing state vacillated about permitting maritime trade with foreigners in its early years, it sought to regulate external commerce more formally as it consolidated its rule. In 1720, in Canton, a group of merchants formed a monopolistic guild to trade with Europeans seeking coveted Chinese goods and peddling their own wares. Although the

Qing dynasty
(1644–1911) Minority Manchu rule over China that incorporated new territories, experienced substantial population growth, and sustained significant economic growth.

Canton system
System officially established by imperial decree in 1759 that required European traders to have Chinese guild merchants act as guarantors for their good behavior and payment of fees.

Tokugawa shogunate
Hereditary military administration founded in 1603 that ruled Japan while keeping the emperor as a figurehead; it was toppled in 1868 by reformers who felt that Japan should adopt, not reject, Western influences.

guild disbanded in the face of opposition from other merchants, it revived after the Qing restricted European trade to Canton. The **Canton system**, officially established by imperial decree in 1759, required European traders to have guild merchants act as guarantors for their good behavior and payment of fees.

Despite public disregard for certain imperial edicts, the Qing dynasty enjoyed a heyday during the eighteenth century. It forced Korea, Vietnam, Burma, and Nepal to pay tribute, and its territorial expansion reached far into central Asia, Tibet, and Mongolia. China, in sum, negotiated a century of political upheaval and climate change without dismantling established ways in politics and economics. The peasantry continued to practice popular faiths, cultivate crops, and stay close to fields and villages. Trade with the outside world was marginal to overall commercial life; like the Ming, the Qing cared more about the agrarian than the commercial health of the empire, believing the former to be the foundation of prosperity and tranquility. As long as China's peasantry could keep the dynasty's coffers full, the government was content to squeeze the merchants when it needed funds. Some historians view this practice as a failure to adapt to a changing world order, as it ultimately left China vulnerable to outsiders—especially Europeans. But this view projects later developments onto the past. By the mid-eighteenth century, Europe still needed China more than the other way around. For the majority of Chinese, no superior model of belief, politics, or economics was conceivable. Indeed, although the Qing had taken over a crumbling empire in 1644, a century later China was enjoying a new level of prosperity.

TOKUGAWA JAPAN

Integration with the Asian trading system exposed Japan to new external pressures, even as the islands grappled with internal turmoil. But the Japanese dealt with these pressures more successfully than the mainland Asian empires (Ottoman, Safavid, Mughal, and Ming), which saw political fragmentation and even the overthrow of ruling dynasties. In Japan, a single ruling family emerged. This dynastic state, the **Tokugawa shogunate**, accomplished something that most of the world's other regimes did not: it regulated foreign intrusion. While Japan played a modest role in the expanding global trade, it remained free of outside exploitation.

Unification of Japan During the sixteenth century, Japan had suffered from political instability as banditry and civil strife disrupted the countryside. Regional ruling families, called *daimyos*, had commanded private armies of warriors known as samurai. The daimyos sometimes brought order to their domains, but no one family could establish preeminence over others. Although Japan had an emperor, his authority did not extend beyond the court in Kyoto.

RUSSIAN EMPIRE

CHINA

EZO
(HOKKAIDO)

SEA OF
JAPAN

JAPAN

HONSHŪ

Edo
(Tokyo)

KOREA

Shimabara
1638
Uprising of
Christian
converts
put down

Kyoto

Osaka

YELLOW
SEA

Hirado
1609
Dutch
trading post

SHIKOKU

Nagasaki
1570
opened to
European trade

KYŪSHŪ

PACIFIC
OCEAN

DESHIMA ISLAND
1641
Dutch traders
confined there

TANEGASHIMA
1542
Portuguese
trading post

EAST
CHINA
SEA

RYŪKYŪ ISLANDS

Outer daimyos
Hereditary daimyos
Tokugawa domains

0   50   100 Miles
0   50   100 Kilometers

Map 13.6 Tokugawa Japan, 1603–1867

The Tokugawa shoguns created a strong central
state in Japan at this time.

- According to this map, how extensive was their
  control?

- Based on your reading, what foreign states were
  interested in trade with Japan?

- How, according to the chapter, did Tokugawa
  leaders attempt to control relations with foreign
  states and other entities?

Following an effort by military leaders to unify Japan, one of the daimyos, Tokugawa Ieyasu, seized power. This was a decisive moment. In 1603, Ieyasu assumed the title of shogun (military ruler), retaining the emperor in name only while taking the reins of power himself. He also solved the problem of succession, declaring that rulership would be hereditary and that his family would be the ruling household. Administrative authority shifted from Kyoto to the site of Ieyasu's domain headquarters: the castle town called Edo (later renamed Tokyo; see Map 13.6). By the time Ieyasu died, Edo had become a major urban center with a population of 150,000. This hereditary Tokugawa shogunate lasted until 1867.

The Tokugawa shoguns ensured a flow of resources from the working population to the rulers and from the provinces to the capital. Villages paid taxes to the daimyos, who transferred resources to the seat of shogunate authority. No longer engaged in constant warfare, the samurai became administrators. Peace brought prosperity. Agriculture thrived. Improved farming techniques and land reclamation projects enabled the country's population to grow from 10 million in 1550 to 16 million in 1600 and 30 million in 1700.

Foreign Affairs and Foreigners Internal peace and prosperity did not insulate Japan from external challenges. When Japanese rulers tackled foreign affairs, their most pressing concern was the intrusion of Christian missionaries and European traders. Initially, Japanese officials welcomed these foreigners out of an eagerness to acquire muskets, gunpowder, and other new technology. But once the ranks of Christian converts swelled, Japanese authorities realized

Edo in the Rain This facsimile of an *ukiyo-e* ("floating world") print by Hiroshige (1797–1858) depicts one of several bridges in the bustling city of Edo (later Tokyo), with Mount Fuji in the background.

that Christians were intolerant of other faiths, believed Christ to be superior to any authority, and fought among themselves. The government suppressed Christianity and drove European missionaries from the country.

Even more troublesome was the lure of trade with Europeans. The Tokugawa knew that trading at various Japanese ports would pull the commercial regions in various directions, away from the capital. When it became clear that European traders preferred the ports of Kyūshū (the southernmost island), the shogunate restricted Europeans to trade only in ports under Edo's direct rule in Honshū. Then, Japanese authorities expelled all European competitors. Only the Protestant (and nonproselytizing) Dutch won permission to remain in Japan, confined to an island near Nagasaki. The Dutch were allowed to unload just one ship each year, under strict supervision by Japanese authorities.

These measures did not close Tokugawa Japan to the outside world, however. Trade with China and Korea flourished, and the shogun received missions from Korea and the Ryūkyū islands. Edo also gathered information about the outside world from the resident Dutch and Chinese (who included monks, physicians, and painters). A few Japanese were permitted to learn Dutch and to study European technology, shipbuilding, and medicine (see Chapter 14). By limiting such encounters, the authorities ensured that foreigners would not threaten Japan's security.

The arrival of New World silver provided at least an initial boost to the major Asian economies. The Mughal Empire achieved its greatest influence in the seventeenth century. Despite a change in the ruling dynasty, China remained the world's center of wealth and power, although there, as elsewhere in Asia, silver caused inflation and altered relations between center and periphery. Ottoman domains shrank, and Europeans achieved important commercial footholds in parts of India and Southeast Asia.

Transformations in Europe

Between 1600 and 1750, religious conflict and the consolidation of dynastic power, spurred on by long-distance trade and climate change, transformed Europe. Commercial centers shifted northward, and Spain and Portugal lost ground to England and France. To the east, the state of Muscovy expanded dramatically to become the sprawling Russian Empire.

Core Objectives

COMPARE the impact of trade and religion on state power in Europe and the Mughal Empire.

EXPANSION AND DYNASTIC CHANGE IN RUSSIA

During this period the Russian Empire expanded to become one of the world's largest-ever states. It gained positions on the Baltic Sea and the Pacific

Ocean, and it established political borders with both the Qing Empire and Japan. These momentous shifts involved the elimination of steppe nomads as an independent force. Culturally, Europeans as well as Russians debated whether Russia belonged more to Europe or to Asia. The answer was both.

Muscovy Becomes the Russian Empire The principality of Moscow, or Muscovy, like Japan and China, used territorial expansion and commercial networks to consolidate a powerful state. This was the Russian Empire, the name given to Muscovy by Tsar Peter the Great around 1700. (*Tsar* was a Russian word derived from the Latin *Caesar* to refer to the Russian ruler.) Originally a mixture of Slavs, Finnish tribes, Turkic speakers, and many others, **Muscovy** spanned parts of Europe, much of northern Asia, numerous North Pacific islands, and even—for a time—a corner of North America (Alaska).

Like Japan, Russia emerged out of turmoil. Security concerns inspired the Muscovite regime to seize territory in the fifteenth and sixteenth centuries. Because the steppe, which stretches deep into Asia, remained a highway for nomadic peoples (especially descendants of the powerful Mongols), Muscovy sought to dominate the areas south and east of Moscow. Beginning in the 1590s, Russian authorities built forts and trading posts along Siberian rivers, and by 1639 the state's borders reached the Pacific. Thus, in just over a century Muscovy had claimed an empire straddling Eurasia and incorporating peoples of many languages and religions. (See Map 13.7.)

Much of this expansion occurred despite the dynastic chaos that followed the death of Tsar Ivan IV in 1584. Ultimately, a group of prominent families reestablished central authority and threw their weight behind a new family of rulers. These were the Romanovs, court barons who set about reviving the Kremlin's fortunes. (The Kremlin was a medieval walled fortress where the Muscovite grand princes—later, tsars—resided.) Like the Ottoman and Qing dynasts, Romanov tsars and their aristocratic supporters would retain power into the twentieth century.

Absolutist Government and Serfdom In the seventeenth and eighteenth centuries, the Romanovs created an absolutist system of government. Only the tsar had the right to make war, tax, judge, and coin money. The Romanovs also made the nobles serve as state officials. Now Russia became a despotic state that had no political assemblies for nobles or other groups, other than mere consultative bodies like the imperial senate. Indeed, away from Moscow, local aristocrats enjoyed nearly unlimited authority in exchange for loyalty and tribute to the tsar.

During this period, Russia's peasantry bore the burden of maintaining the wealth of the nobility and the monarchy. Most peasant families gathered into communes, isolated rural worlds where people helped one another deal

Map key:

- Muscovy, 1462
- Expansion, 1462–1598
- Expansion, 1598–1689
- Expansion, 1689–1795
- Occupied by Russia, 1644–1689
- Qing Empire, 1760

Map 13.7 Russian Expansion, 1462–1795

The state of Muscovy incorporated vast territories through overland expansion as it grew and became the Russian Empire.

- Using the map key, identify the different expansions the Russian Empire underwent between 1462 and 1795 and the directions it generally expanded in.
- With what countries and cultures did the Russian Empire come into contact?
- According to the text, what drove such dramatic expansion?

with the harsh climate, severe landlords, and occasional poor harvests. Communes functioned like extended kin networks in which members supported one another. In 1649, peasants were legally bound as serfs to the nobles and the tsar, meaning that, in principle, they had to perform obligatory services and deliver part of their produce to their lords.

Imperial Expansion and Migration A series of military victories in the eighteenth century made it possible to consolidate the empire and sparked significant population movements. The conquest of Siberia brought vast territory and riches in furs. Victory in a prolonged war with Sweden and then the incorporation of the fertile southern steppes, known as Ukraine, proved decisive. Peter the Great (r. 1682–1725) accomplished the victory in Sweden, after which he founded a new capital at St. Petersburg. Under Peter's successors, including the brilliant and ruthless Catherine the Great, Russia, already a harsh and colossal space, added even more territory. By the late eighteenth century, Russia's grasp extended from the Baltic Sea, Ukraine, and the Crimea on the Black Sea, and stretched eastward all the way to Siberia.

Many people migrated eastward to Siberia. Some were fleeing serfdom; others were being deported for rejecting religious reforms. Battling astoundingly harsh temperatures (falling to –40 degrees Celsius/Fahrenheit) and frigid Arctic winds, these individuals traveled on horseback and trudged on foot to resettle in the east. But the difficulties of clearing forested lands or planting crops in boggy Siberian soils, combined with extraordinarily harsh winters, meant that many settlers died or tried to return. Isolation was a problem, too. There was no established land route back to Moscow until the 1770s, when exiles completed the Great Siberian Post Road through the swamps and peat bogs of western Siberia. The writer Anton Chekhov later called it "the longest and ugliest road in the whole world."

ECONOMIC AND POLITICAL FLUCTUATIONS IN CENTRAL AND WESTERN EUROPE

During this period European economies became more commercialized, especially after the Thirty Years' War. As in Asia, developments in distant parts of the world shaped the region's economic upturns and downturns. Underlying the economic and political fluctuations taking place in Europe, especially the brutal warfare of the Thirty Years' War, was the powerful impact of the Little Ice Age. Freezing temperatures shortened agricultural growing seasons by one to two months. The result was escalating prices for essential grain products, now in short supply. Famines and death from diseases because of malnourishment followed. The cooling had a few benefits, however, including

The Thirty Years' War The mercenary armies of the Thirty Years' War were renowned for pillaging and tormenting civilians. Here the artist Jacques Collot, from Nancy in eastern France, depicts the officially sanctioned punishment of renegade soldiers before an orderly group of townspeople. The caption that appeared with the image indicted the soldiers as "damned and infamous thieves, [hanging] like bad fruit, from this tree."

the magnificent violins, still prized today, crafted by Antonio Stradivari (1644–1737) from the denser wood that freezing temperatures produced.

The Thirty Years' War For a century after Martin Luther broke with the Catholic Church (see Chapter 12), religious warfare raged in Europe. So did contests over territory, power, and trade. The **Thirty Years' War** (1618–1648) was all three of these—a war between Protestant princes and the Catholic emperor for religious predominance in central Europe; a struggle for regional control among Catholic powers (the Spanish and Austrian Habsburgs and the French); and a bid for independence (from Spain) by the Dutch, who wanted to trade and worship as they liked.

The brutal conflict began as a struggle between Protestants and Catholics within the Habsburg Empire, but it soon became a war for preeminence in Europe. It took the lives of civilians as well as soldiers. In total, fighting, disease, and famine wiped out a third of the German states' urban population and two-fifths of their rural population. Ultimately the Treaty of Westphalia (1648) stated that as there was a rough balance of power between

> **Thirty Years' War**
> (1618–1648) Conflict begun between Protestants and Catholics in Germany that escalated into a general European war fought against the unity and power of the Holy Roman Empire.

Protestant and Catholic states, they would simply have to put up with each other. The Dutch won their independence, but the war's enormous costs provoked severe discontent in Spain, France, and England. Central Europe was so devastated that it did not recover in economic or demographic terms for more than a century.

The Thirty Years' War transformed war making. Whereas most medieval struggles had been sieges between nobles leading small armies, centralized states fielding standing armies now waged decisive, grand-scale campaigns. The war also changed the ranks of soldiers: local enlisted men defending their king, country, and faith gave way to hired mercenaries or criminals doing forced service. Even officers, who previously obtained their stripes by purchase or royal decree, now had to earn them. Gunpowder, cannons, and muskets became standardized. By the eighteenth century, Europe's wars featured huge standing armies boasting a professional officer corps, deadly artillery, and long supply lines bringing food and ammunition to the front. The costs—material and human—of war began to soar.

Western European Economies In spite of the toll that warfare took on economic activity, the European states enjoyed significant commercial expansion in the seventeenth century. Northern Europe gained more than did the south, however. Spain, for example, started losing ground to its rivals as the costs of defending its empire soared and merchants from Northern Europe cut in on its trading networks. The weighty costs of its involvement in the Thirty Years' War dealt the Spanish economy a final, disastrous blow.

As European commercial dynamism shifted northward, the Dutch led the way with innovative commercial practices and a new mercantile elite. They specialized in shipping and in financing regional and long-distance trade. Their famous *fluitschips* carried heavy, bulky cargoes (like Baltic wood) with relatively small crews. Now shipping costs throughout the Atlantic world dropped as Dutch ships transported their own and other countries' goods. Amsterdam's merchants founded an exchange bank, established a rudimentary stock exchange, and pioneered systems of underwriting and insuring cargoes.

England and France also became commercial powerhouses, establishing aggressive policies to promote national business and drive out competitors. By stipulating that only English ships could carry goods between the mother country and its colonies, the English Navigation Act of 1651 protected English shippers and merchants—especially from the Dutch.

Economic development was not limited to port towns: the countryside, too, enjoyed breakthroughs in production. Most important was expansion in the production of food. In northwestern Europe, investments in water drainage, larger livestock herds, and improved cultivation practices generated much greater yields. Also, a four-field crop rotation involving wheat, clover, barley, and turnips kept nutrients in the soil and provided year-round fodder for livestock. As a result (and as we have seen many times before), increased agricultural output supported a growing urban population.

Production rose most where the organization of rural property changed. In England, in a movement known as **enclosure**, landowners took control of lands that traditionally had been common property serving local needs. Claiming exclusive rights to these lands, the landowners planted new crops or pastured sheep with the aim of selling the products in distant markets—especially cities. The largest landowners put their farms in the hands of tenants, who hired wage laborers to till, plant, and harvest. Thus, in England, peasant agriculture gave way to farms run by wealthy families who exploited the marketplace to buy what they needed (including labor) and to sell what they produced. In this regard, England led the way in a Europe-wide process of commercializing the countryside.

Dynastic Monarchies: France and England European monarchs had varying success with centralizing state power. In France, Louis XIII (r. 1610–1643) and especially his chief minister, Cardinal Richelieu, concentrated power in the hands of the king. Instead of sharing power with the aristocracy, much less commoners, the king and his counselors wanted him to rule free of external checks, to create an **absolute monarchy**. The ruler was not to be a tyrant, but his authority was to be complete and thorough, and his state free of bloody disorders. The king's rule would be lawful; but he, not his jurists, would dictate the last legal word. If the king made a mistake, only God could call him to account. Thus, the Europeans believed in the "divine right of kings," a political belief not greatly different from that of imperial China, where the emperor was thought to rule with the mandate of heaven.

In absolutist France, privileges and state offices flowed from the king's grace. All patronage networks ultimately linked to the king: these included financial supports the crown provided directly, as well as tax exemptions and a wide array of permissions—such as consent for a writer to publish a book or for people ranging from lawyers and professors to apothecaries, bookbinders, and butchers to work in a regulated trade. The great palace Louis XIV built at Versailles teemed with nobles from all over France seeking favor, dressing according to the king's expensive fashion code, and attending the latest tragedies, comedies, and concerts.

The French dynastic monarchy provided a model of absolute rule for other European dynasts, like the Habsburgs of the Holy Roman Empire, the Hohenzollerns of Prussia, and the Romanovs of Muscovy. The king and his ministers controlled all public power, while other social groups, from the nobility to the peasantry, had no formal body to represent their interests. Nonetheless, French absolutist government was not as absolute as the king would have wished. Pockets of stalwart Protestants practiced their religion secretly in the plateau villages of central France, despite Louis XIV's

enclosure
A movement in which landowners took control of lands that traditionally had been common property serving local needs.

absolute monarchy
Form of government in which one body, usually the monarch, controls the right to tax, judge, make war, and coin money. The term *enlightened absolutist* was often used to refer to state monarchies in seventeenth- and eighteenth-century Europe.

Versailles Louis XIV's Versailles, just southwest of Paris, was a hunting lodge that was converted at colossal cost in the 1670s–1680s into a grand royal chateau with expansive grounds. Much envied and imitated across Europe, the palace became the epicenter of a luxurious court life that included entertainments such as plays and musical offerings, state receptions, royal hunts, boating, and gambling. Thousands of nobles at Versailles vied with each other for closer proximity to the king in the performance of court rituals.

discriminatory measures against them. Peasant disturbances continued. Criticism of court life, wars, and religious policies filled anonymous pamphlets, jurists' notebooks, and courtiers' private journals. Members of the nobility also grumbled about their political misfortunes, but since the king had suppressed the traditional advisory bodies they had dominated, they had no formal way to express their concerns.

England might also have evolved into an absolutist regime, but there were important differences between England and France. Queen Elizabeth (r. 1558–1603) and her successors used many policies similar to those of the French monarchy, such as control of patronage and elaborate court festivities. Above all, the English Parliament remained an important force. Whereas the French kings did not consult the Estates-General to enact taxes, the English monarchs had to convene Parliament to raise money.

Under Elizabeth's successors, fierce quarrels broke out over taxation, religion, and royal efforts to rule without parliamentary consent. Tensions ran high between Puritans (who preferred a simpler form of worship and more egalitarian church government) and Anglicans (who supported the state-sponsored, hierarchically organized Church of England headed by the king). Those tensions erupted in the 1640s into civil war that saw the victory of the largely Puritan parliamentary army and the beheading of the king, Charles I. Although the monarchy was restored a dozen years later, in 1660, the king's relation to Parliament and the relationship between the crown and religion remained undecided (in particular the right of Protestants to assume the throne).

Subsequent monarchs who aspired to absolute rule came into conflict with Parliament, whose members insisted on shared sovereignty and the right of Protestant succession. This dispute culminated in the Glorious Revolution of 1688–1689. In a bloodless upheaval, King James II fled to France and Parliament offered the crown to William of Orange and his wife, Mary (both Protestants). The outcome of the conflict established the principle that English monarchs must rule in conjunction with Parliament. Although the Church of England was reaffirmed as the official state church, Presbyterians and Jews were allowed to practice their religions. Catholic worship, still officially forbidden, was tolerated as long as the Catholics kept quiet. By 1700, then, England's nobility and merchant classes had a guaranteed say in public affairs and assurance that state activity would privilege the propertied classes as well as the ruler. As a result, English rulers could borrow money much more effectively than their rivals could.

Mercantilist Wars The rise of new powers in Europe, especially France and England, intensified rivalries for control of Atlantic trade. As conflicts over colonies and sea-lanes replaced earlier religious and territorial struggles, commercial struggles became worldwide wars. Across the globe, European empires constantly skirmished over control of trade and territory. English and Dutch trading companies took aim at Portuguese outposts in Asia and the Americas, and then at each other. Ports in India suffered repeated assaults and counterassaults. In response, European powers built huge navies to protect their colonies and trade routes and to attack their rivals.

After 1715, a series of wars occurred mainly outside Europe, as empires feuded over colonial possessions. These conflicts were especially bitter in border areas, particularly in the Caribbean and North America. Each round of warfare ratcheted up the scale and cost of fighting.

The **Seven Years' War** (known as the French and Indian War in North America) marked the culmination of this rivalry among European empires around the globe. Fought from 1756 to 1763, it saw Native Americans, African slaves, Bengali princes, Filipino militiamen, and European foot

Seven Years' War
(1756–1763) Also known as the French and Indian War; worldwide war that ended when Prussia defeated Austria, establishing itself as a European power, and when Britain gained control of India and many of France's colonies through the Treaty of Paris.

soldiers dragged into a contest over imperial possessions and control of the seas. The battles in Europe were relatively indecisive (despite being large), except in the hinterlands. After all, what sparked the war was a skirmish of British colonial troops (featuring a lieutenant colonel named George Washington) allied with Seneca warriors against French soldiers in the Ohio Valley (see Map 13.2 for North American references). In India, the war had a decisive outcome, for here the East India Company trader Robert Clive rallied 850 European officers and 2,100 Indian recruits to defeat the French (there were but 40 French artillerymen) and their 50,000 Maratha allies—men from an independent Indian empire in northern India—at Plassey. The British seized the upper hand, over everyone. Not only did the British drive off the French from the rich Bengali interior, but they also crippled Indian rulers' resistance against European intruders (see Map 12.4 for India references).

The Seven Years' War changed the balance of power around the world. Britain emerged as the foremost colonial empire. Its rivals, especially France and Spain, took a pounding; France lost its North American colonies, and Spain lost Florida (though it gained the Louisiana Territory west of the Mississippi in a secret deal with France). In India, as well, the French were losers and had to acknowledge British supremacy in the wealthy provinces of Bihar and Bengal. But overwhelmingly, the biggest losers were indigenous peoples everywhere. With the rise of one empire over all others, it was harder for Native Americans to play the Europeans off against each other. Maratha princes faced the same problem. Clearly, as worlds became more entangled, the gaps between winners and losers grew more pronounced.

Conclusion

A radical decline in temperatures worldwide made the seventeenth century a time of famine, dying, epidemic disease, and political turmoil that contributed to regime change in China, Persia, and England and threatened the rulers of the Ottoman and Mughal Empires. But by the 1750s, the world's regions were more economically connected than they had been a century and a half earlier. The process of integrating the resources of previous worlds apart that had begun with Christopher Columbus's voyages intensified during this period. Traders shipped a wider variety of commodities—from Baltic wood to Indian cotton, from New World silver and sugar to Chinese silks and porcelain—over longer distances. People increasingly wore clothes manufactured elsewhere, consumed beverages made from products cultivated in far-off locations, and used imported guns to settle local conflicts.

Everywhere, this integration and the consumer opportunities that it made possible came at a heavy price. Nowhere was it more costly than in the

Americas, where colonization and exploitation led to the expulsion of Native Americans from their lands and the decimation of their numbers. The cost was also very high for the millions of Africans forced across the Atlantic to work New World plantations and for the millions more who did not survive the journey.

Silver was the product from the Americas that most transformed global trading networks and that showed how greater entanglements could both enrich and destabilize. Although Spanish colonizers mined New World silver and shipped it to western Europe and Asia, it was Spain's main competitors in Europe that gained the upper hand in the seventeenth and eighteenth centuries. Nearly one-third of the silver from the New World ended up in China as payment for products like porcelains and silks that consumers still regarded as the world's finest manufactures. But if China's economy remained vibrant, silver did play a part in the fall of one dynasty and the rise of another. For the Ottoman and Mughal Empires, the influx of silver created rampant inflation and undermined their previous economic autonomy.

Certain societies coped with increased commercial exchange, environmental change, and internal challenges more successfully than others did. The Safavid and Ming dynasties could not withstand the pressures; both collapsed. The Spanish, Ottoman, and Mughal dynasties managed to survive but faced increasing pressure from aggressive rivals. For newcomers to the integrating world, the opportunity to trade helped support new dynasties. Japan, Russia, and England emerged on the world stage. But even in these newer regimes, commerce and competition did not erase conflict. To the contrary, while the world was more fully integrated in economic terms than ever before, greater prosperity for some hardly translated into peace for most.

Focus On
Regional Impact of World Trade

The Americas
- England, France, and Holland join Spain and Portugal as colonial powers in the Americas.
- The English and French colonies in the Caribbean become the world's major exporters of sugar.

Africa
- The Atlantic slave trade increases to record proportions, creating gender imbalances, impoverishing some regions, and elevating the power of slave-supplying states.

Southeast Asia
- The Dutch East India Company takes over the major islands of Southeast Asia.

The Islamic World
- World trade destabilizes the Safavid, Ottoman, and Mughal Empires.

East Asia
- The Ming dynasty in China loses the mandate of heaven and is replaced by the Qing.
- The Tokugawa shogunate unifies Japan and limits the influence of Europeans in the country.

Europe
- Tsarist Russia expands toward the Baltic Sea and the Pacific Ocean and becomes the largest state in the world.
- Europe recovers from the Thirty Years' War (1618–1648), with Holland, England, and France emerging as economic powerhouses.

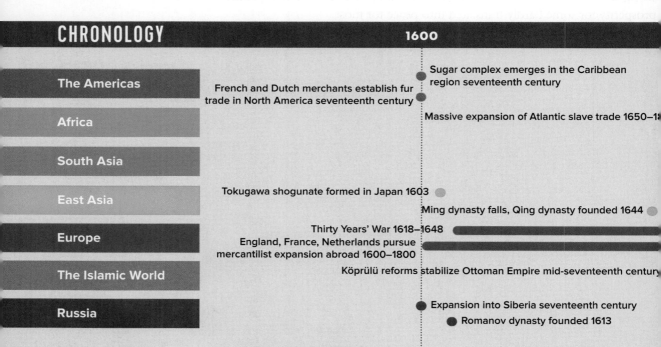

CHRONOLOGY

1600

The Americas
French and Dutch merchants establish fur trade in North America seventeenth century
Sugar complex emerges in the Caribbean region seventeenth century

Africa
Massive expansion of Atlantic slave trade 1650–18

South Asia

East Asia
Tokugawa shogunate formed in Japan 1603
Ming dynasty falls, Qing dynasty founded 1644

Europe
Thirty Years' War 1618–1648
England, France, Netherlands pursue mercantilist expansion abroad 1600–1800

The Islamic World
Köprülü reforms stabilize Ottoman Empire mid-seventeenth century

Russia
Expansion into Siberia seventeenth century
Romanov dynasty founded 1613

THINKING ABOUT GLOBAL CONNECTIONS

- **Thinking about Exchange Networks and World Trade** How did silver, and then sugar, transform world trade? What political and cultural forces benefited from the development of long-distance trading networks? Which groups suffered and how? Contrast the effects of long distance trade in major world regions.

- **Thinking about Changing Power Relationships and World Trade** The seventeenth and eighteenth centuries witnessed the rise of new powers in England, Japan, and Russia, as well as regional powers on the west coast of Africa. Several established empires continued to expand but confronted powerful new challenges to their authority. How did leaders of the Ottoman, Mughal, and Qing Empires respond to

challenges to their authority? What major challenges did they face? How would you characterize the new powers that emerged around the world in this period?

- **Thinking about the Impact of World Trade on Gender Relations** The Atlantic slave trade wreaked havoc on sex ratios both in Africa and in the slave societies of the New World because most slaves taken from Africa were men. How did this affect social life on New World plantations? What strategies did African communities utilize to mitigate the loss of so many men? Elsewhere around the world, increased trade challenged established social hierarchies. How did ruling elites mobilize gender to reinforce their authority?

Key Terms

absolute monarchy p. 629

Canton system p. 620

chartered companies p. 594

enclosure p. 629

Little Ice Age p. 595

Mamluks p. 613

Manchus p. 617

mercantilism p. 593

Muscovy p. 624

Qing dynasty p. 619

Seven Years' War p. 631

Thirty Years' War p. 627

Tokugawa shogunate p. 620

 Go to **INQUIZITIVE** to see what you've learned—and learn what you've missed—with personalized feedback along the way.

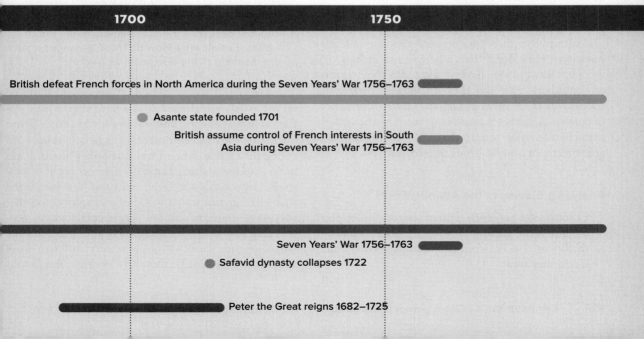

	1700	1750

British defeat French forces in North America during the Seven Years' War 1756–1763

Asante state founded 1701

British assume control of French interests in South Asia during Seven Years' War 1756–1763

Seven Years' War 1756–1763

Safavid dynasty collapses 1722

Peter the Great reigns 1682–1725

Global Themes and Sources

Comparing Perceptions on Slavery in the Atlantic World

The documents gathered here present different aspects of slavery in the Atlantic world. For African slaves, the Atlantic system was an abomination. For slave owners, merchants, and political leaders—in Africa and Europe—the slave trade was a business. Each document highlights a different aspect and presents a different perspective on Atlantic slavery.

In the first document, Olaudah Equiano describes the horrifying conditions captives endured on the African coast as they awaited the arrival of slaving ships from the point of view of a captive. In the second, Richard Ligon explains the absence of slave revolts from the planters' perspective, while in the third, the Baron de Wimpffen, a Swiss aristocrat and explorer, describes the centrality of race, as opposed to family lineage or nobility, in the colonial society of Saint-Domingue. The final three documents show data from the 1835 household census for Santiago do Iguape, Bahia, a parish in the heart of a sugar plantation region in Brazil. Created by Portuguese colonial authorities for their own purposes, the census records provide basic demographic statistics about the region's population, over half of which was enslaved.

Collectively, these documents raise comparative questions: How did different people and groups view the same institution, slavery? How did they perceive one another? How did they distinguish people like themselves from others? The statistical information, in particular, makes it possible to see how the composition of plantation society changed—to identify cause and effect—in a sugar-producing region.

Analyzing Slavery in the Atlantic World

- Compare the way each written source divides people into racial groups. How do the sources mark the boundaries between communities? What criteria do they use?

- Contrast de Wimpffen's account of Saint-Domingue with Ligon's history of Barbados. What are their biggest fears?

- Does the evidence from the graphs support or undermine the claims of the written sources?

PRIMARY SOURCE 13.1

The Interesting Narrative of the Life of Olaudah Equiano (1789), Olaudah Equiano

Taught to read and write by his masters, Olaudah Equiano (c. 1745–1797) published *The Interesting Narrative of the Life of Olaudah Equiano, or Gustavus Vassa, the African* (1789) after purchasing his freedom in 1766. Known as Gustavus Vassa during his lifetime, he was active in the British abolitionist movement.

- **Explain the significance of nation (or community) in this document.**

- **What part of his captivity most troubled Equiano, and how did he cope?**

- **Equiano describes the punishment meted out to whites. Explain why. How do those passages shape the meaning of the document as a whole?**

The first object which saluted my eyes when I arrived on the coast, was the sea, and a slave ship, which was then riding at anchor, and waiting for its cargo. These filled me with astonishment, which was soon converted into terror, when I was carried on board. I was immediately handled, and tossed up to see if I were sound, by some of the crew; and I was now persuaded that I had gotten into a world of bad spirits, and that they were going to kill me. Their complexions, too, differing so much from ours, their long hair, and the language they spoke (which was very different from any I had ever heard), united to confirm me in this belief. Indeed, such were the horrors of my views and fears at the moment, that, if ten thousand worlds had been my own, I would have freely parted with them all to have exchanged my condition with that of the meanest slave in my own country. When I looked round the ship too, and saw a large furnace of copper boiling, and a multitude of black people of every description chained together, every one of their countenances expressing dejection and sorrow, I no longer doubted of my fate; and, quite overpowered with horror and anguish, I fell motionless on the deck and fainted. When I recovered a little, I found some black people about me, who I believed were some of those who had brought me on board, and had been receiving their pay; they talked to me in order to cheer me, but all in vain. . . .

I now saw myself deprived of all chance of returning to my native country, or even the least glimpse of hope of gaining the shore, which I now considered as friendly; and I even wished for my former slavery in preference to my present situation, which was filled with horrors of every kind, still heightened by my ignorance of what I was to undergo. I was not long suffered to indulge my grief; I was soon put down under the decks, and there I received such a salutation in my nostrils as I had never experienced in my life; so that, with the loathsomeness of the stench, and crying together, I became so sick and low that I was not able to eat, nor I had the least desire to taste anything. . . .

In a little time after, amongst the poor chained men, I found some of my own nation, which in a small degree gave ease to my mind. I inquired of these what was to be done with us? They gave me to understand, we were to be carried to these white people's country to work for them. I then was a little revived, and thought, if it were no worse than working, my situation was not so desperate; but still I feared I should be put to death, the white people looked and acted, as I thought, in so savage a manner; for I had never seen among any people such instances of brutal cruelty; and this not only shown towards us blacks, but also to some of the whites themselves. One white man in particular I saw, when we were permitted to be on deck, flogged so unmercifully with a large rope near the foremast, that he died in consequence of it; and

they tossed him over the side as they would have done a brute. This made me fear these people the more; and I expected nothing less than to be treated in the same manner. . . .

At last, when the ship we were in, had got in all her cargo, they made ready with many fearful noises, and we were all put under deck, so that we could not see how they managed the vessel. But this disappointment was the least of my sorrow. The stench of the hold while we were on the coast was so intolerably loathsome, that it was dangerous to remain there for any time, and some of us had been permitted to stay on the deck for the fresh air; but now that the whole ship's cargo were confined together, it became absolutely pestilential. The closeness of the place, and the heat of the climate, added to the number in the ship, which was so crowded that each had scarcely room to turn himself, almost suffocated us. This produced copious perspirations, so that the air soon became unfit for respiration, from a variety of loathsome smells, and brought on a sickness among the slaves, of which many died. . . . The shrieks of the women, and the groans of the dying, rendered the whole a scene of horror almost inconceivable. Happily perhaps, for myself, I was soon reduced so low here that it was thought necessary to keep me almost always on deck; and from my extreme youth I was not put in fetters. In this situation I expected every hour to share the fate of my companions, some of whom were almost daily brought upon deck at the point of death, which I began to hope would soon put an end to my miseries.

Source: Olaudah Equiano, *The Interesting Narrative of the Life of Olaudah Equiano, or Gustavus Vassa, the African, Written by Himself* (New York: Norton, 2001), pp. 38–41.

A True and Exact History of the Island of Barbadoes (1673), Richard Ligon

Richard Ligon (c. 1585–1662) lost most of his fortune in the English Civil War (1642–1651). He bought half a sugar plantation on the English island of Barbados to recover from his losses and rebuild his fortune.

....

- **How does Ligon distinguish slaves from slave owners?**

- How does Ligon explain the absence of slave revolts?

- Analyze the role of religion in this document.

It has been accounted a strange thing that the Negroes, being more than double the numbers of the Christians that are there, and they accounted a bloody people where they think they have power or advantages; and the more bloody by how much they are more fearful than others: that these should not commit some horrid massacre upon the Christians, thereby to enfranchise [empower] themselves and become Masters of the Island. But there are three reasons that take away this wonder; the one is, They are not suffered [allowed] to touch or handle any weapons: The other, That they are held in such awe and slavery as they are fearful to appear in any daring act; and seeing the mustering of our men and hearing their Gun-shot (that which nothing is more terrible to them), their spirits are subjugated to so low a condition as they dare not look up to any bold attempt. Besides these, there is a third reason, which stops all designs [plans] of that kind, and that is, They are fetch'd from several parts of Africa, who speak several languages, and by that means one of them understands not another: For, some of them are fetch'd from Guinny and Binny, some from Cutchew, some from Angola, and some from the River of Gambia. And in some of these places where petty Kingdoms are, they sell their Subjects and such as they take in Battle, whom they make slaves; and some mean men sell their Servants, their Children, and sometimes their Wives; and think all good traffic [acceptable trade] for such commodities as our Merchants send them. When they are brought to us, the Planters buy them out of the Ship where they find them stark naked and therefore cannot be deceived in any outward infirmity. They choose them as they do Horses in a Market; the strongest, youthfulest, and most beautiful, yield the greatest prices. Thirty pound sterling is a price for the best man Negro; and twenty five, twenty six, or twenty seven pound for a Woman; the Children are at easier rates. . . .

When any of them die, they dig a grave, and at evening they bury him, clapping and wringing their hands and making a doleful sound with their voices.

They are a people of a timorous and fearful disposition, and consequently bloody when they find advantages [opportunities]. If any of them commit a fault, give him present [immediate] punishment, but do not threaten him; for if you do, it is an even lay, he will go and hang himself to avoid the punishment. What their other opinions are in matter of Religion, I know not; but certainly they are not altogether of the sect of the Sadduces [Hebrew sect (second century BCE–first century CE) that rejected belief in the resurrection of the soul]: For, they believe a Resurrection and that they shall go into their own Country again and have their youth renewed. And lodging this opinion in their hearts, they make it an ordinary practice, upon any great fright or threatening of their Master, to hang themselves. But Colonel Walrond, having lost three or four of his best Negroes this way, and in a very little time, caused one of their heads to be cut off and set upon a pole a dozen foot high; and having done that, caused all his Negroes to come forth and march round about this head and bid them look on it, whether this were not the head of such an one that hang'd himself. Which they acknowledging, he then told them, That they were in a main error in thinking they went into their own Countries after they were dead; for, this man's head was here, as they all were witnesses of; and how was it possible the body could go without a head. Being convinc'd by this sad yet lively spectacle, they changed their opinions; and after that, no more hanged themselves.

Source: Richard Ligon, *A True and Exact History of the Island of Barbadoes* (London: Peter Parker, 1673), excerpts available online at http://nationalhumanitiescenter.org/pds/amerbegin/power/text8/LigonBarbadosSlavery.pdf.

A Voyage to Saint Domingue (1797), Alexandre-Stanislas, Baron de Wimpffen

Alexandre-Stanislas, Baron de Wimpffen, served as a captain under the French general Count Rochambeau in 1781–1782 and was an aristocratic military figure and explorer. He served in the West Indies and resigned in 1788.

- Analyze the significance of "intimacy" in this document.
- What does de Wimpffen mean by the "compulsatory precautions arising from the prejudice of colour"?
- Explain the relationship between "whites from Europe" and "white Creoles."

Although the distance between the slave and the free man is immense, yet, to avoid subdivisions, and minute distinctions, I have adopted the division of color, as the most simple. For I must further observe to you, that the male and female negroes, as well as the male and female mulattos, in spite of the acquisition of liberty, remain in a state of abjectness, which not only disqualifies them from any public employ, but forbids them to contract with the whites a sufficient degree of intimacy, I will not say to sleep with them, but even to eat. If I visit a rich mulatto, he will call me Sir, and not master, like the rest. I call him friend, dear friend, &c. he will ask me to dinner; but if he be correct, he will not presume to sit at table with me.

Such, Sir, is the total division. Each of the three classes has besides its shades—such as those which, in despite of complexion, separate the governor from the other whites, the mulatto from the free negro, &c. &c.

The compulsatory precautions arising from the prejudice of colour, have procured for the inhabitants two advantages, which in some degree compensate for the ridiculousness of it. They render the government more circumspect in its arbitrary proceedings; and they imprint on the colonists a character of haughty independence, from which despotic administrators have more than once experienced a resistance so inflexible, that the court has been finally obliged to recall a governor, whom the habit of playing the nabob [a European who returned from India having made a fortune] in the East, has daily tempted to transgress the bounds of his authority.

The natural consequence of the order of things which prevails here, is, that all those titles of honour which are elsewhere the *pabula* [source] of emulation, of rivalry and of discord; which inspire so much pride, and create so many claims in some; so much ambition and envy in others; shrink to nothing, and entirely disappear before the sole title of WHITE. It is by your skin, however branded it may be, and not by your parchment [titles of nobility], however worm-eaten, that your pretensions to gentility are assessed. Thus you see that vanity, which on your side of the water torments and turns herself a thousand ways, to impose on the public, and usurp the tribute of respect which it accords to the claims of birth, would here lose both her time and her labor.

Each of the different classes of the inhabitants of St. Domingo has, as you will readily imagine, a turn of thinking, a style of living, more or less approximate or distinct; which, after all, has little resemblance to what you will find elsewhere; because the climate, the regimen, the manners, the wants, the occupations, the degree of reciprocal dependency, establish here connections of the slightest nature; very different from those which, with you, Sir, bind together the members of the same society. . . .

The first thing that strikes every traveller who arrives here with the faculty of observation, is, that in spite of the conformity of origin, colour and interests, the whites from Europe, and the white Creoles, form two classes, which, by their reciprocal pretentions, are so widely foundered, that necessity alone can bring them together. The former, with more breeding, more politeness, and more knowledge of the world, affect over the latter a superiority which is far from contributing to unite them. Yet, if the Creoles were a little more cautious than they are at present in their too early connections with women; if they cultivated with more care their extraordinary propensities to excel in all bodily exercises; if they seconded by a better method of education the natural facility of their genius; I am persuaded, that not having to struggle against the influence of the climate under which they were born, nor against the habitudes of a kind of life, differing essentially from that to which a European is obliged to submit himself on his arrival here, I am persuaded, I say, that all the advantages would be on their side. Nothing is wanting to the Creole, but a sufficient degree of good sense, to enable him to use, without abusing, the faculties with which nature has endued [*sic*] him.

Source: Francis Alexander Stanislaus, Baron de Wimpffen, *A Voyage to Saint Domingue, in the Years 1788, 1789, and 1790*, translated by J. Wright (London: T. Cadell, Junior, and W. Davies, 1797), pp. 62–65.

Population Statistics of the Bahia Sugar Plantations, Brazil (1835)

These documents show data from the 1835 household census for Santiago do Iguape, Bahia, a parish in the heart of a sugar plantation region in Brazil. They provide basic demographic statistics about the region's population, over half of which was enslaved. Created by colonial authorities for their own purposes, the census records make it possible to reconstruct the experience of people who left no written records themselves.

Population pyramids are graphs that present a population's composition by age and sex, and, here, by racial classification as well. A pyramid equally divided between men and women with a wide base represents an expanding population with a large proportion of children and young adults. Iguape's free and freed populations follow this pattern, but the enslaved population does not.

- Compare the data for each racial group in the first graph, and consider why the Brazilian state organized its records according to racial categories. How do you think the demands of sugar production shaped the racial categories Brazilian officials used to sort the local population?

- Considering the second two graphs, on the free and enslaved populations, how was plantation society changing? Which groups managed to achieve a level of stability, and which did not?

- Describe the challenges slaves would have faced in establishing families on the sugar plantations of Santiago do Iguape, and contrast their experience with the experiences of freed people of different racial classifications.

Source: Katherine Holt, "Population by Racial Classification, Santiago do Iguape 1835," "Free and Freed Population by Racial Classification, Iguape 1835," and "Enslaved Population by Place of Birth, Santiago do Iguape, 1835," The Bahian History Project: The 1835 Santiago do Iguape Household Census Database, http://www.mappingbahia.org/project/.

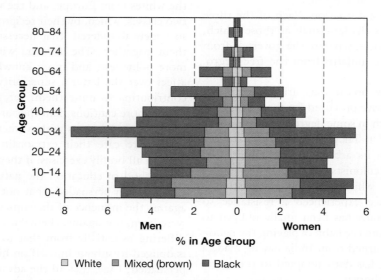

Population by Racial Classification in 1835, Santiago do Iguape

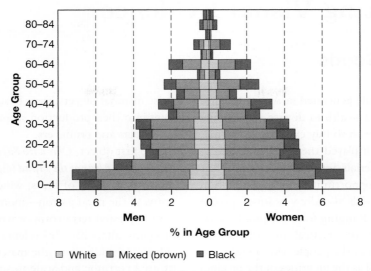

Free and Freed Population by Racial Classification in 1835, Santiago do Iguape

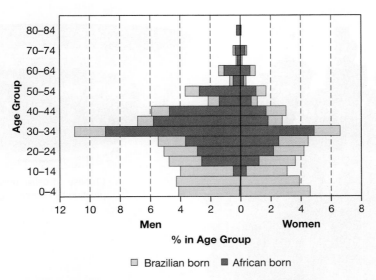

Enslaved Population by Place of Birth in 1835, Santiago do Iguape

Interpreting Visual Evidence

A World of Goods

As overseas trade generated new wealth, elites displayed this wealth in diverse ways. Some used new wealth to buy expensive local materials, while others displayed their power by incorporating foreign materials into local designs. Near commercial centers, opportunities for consumption and display of new goods also drew ordinary people into market activities. Ranging from the purely ornamental to the modest and practical, material objects reflected the identities of the people who bought and displayed them, as well as the identities of the producers who made them. They reinforced and sometimes altered status hierarchies as people's appreciation of these material objects, their beauty, and the skill that went into their production shaped the status of both consumers and producers.

The first object, *Oba with Sacrificial Animals from the Ezomo's Altar of the Hand* (eighteenth–nineteenth century), is made of brass, which signified the elite status of the royal patron—more modest men would have requested terra-cotta or wood. In the kingdom of Benin, altars like this celebrated exceptional individuals. In addition to the materials chosen, the artist used costume and scale to show the status of the figures depicted. The king, Ehenua, dressed in full military regalia, appears in the center of a group of

Chinese porcelain bowl, with painting by Francis Hayman.

Oba with Sacrificial Animals from the Ezomo's Altar of the Hand.

smaller soldiers, aids, and priests. Two rows of musketeers above the frieze include Portuguese soldiers, showing the support Europeans provided Benin's leaders. The second object is a porcelain bowl produced in China for the British market, with a painting of a cricket match by the English painter Francis Hayman (1708–1776). The third object, a Chinese lacquer tray from the Qing dynasty, likely crafted for the internal Chinese market, portrays a pastoral scene. The final object, a British-manufactured teapot, was made for middle-class consumers who could not afford imported porcelain from China. This example, with a handle, was intended to match European decorative style; the factory left off the handle for "Oriental" designs.

Tray (lacquer and mother of pearl), Chinese School, Qing dynasty.

Questions for Analysis

1. Describe how these objects were used. What functions did they serve?

2. Analyze the relationship between display and function in these objects. What impression do you think these objects made on people who saw them?

3. Explain the significance of these works for the people who produced them. What roles do you think artistry, craft skill, and financial gain played for the artists and artisans who produced them?

4. How did the conditions in which these objects were produced relate to the identities consumers sought to project? Consider also the relationship between the production of commodities—such as the tea and sugar associated with the final object—and consumer identity.

British-manufactured teapot.

14

Cultures of Splendor and Power

1500–1780

In 1664, a sixteen-year-old girl from the provinces of New Spain asked her parents for permission to attend the university in the capital. Although she had mastered Greek logic, taught Latin, and become a proficient mathematician, she had two strikes against her: she was a woman, and her thinking ran against the grain of the Catholic Church. So keen was she to pursue her studies that she proposed to disguise herself as a man. But her parents denied her requests, and instead of attending the university she entered a convent in Mexico City, where she would spend the rest of her life. The convent turned out to be a sanctuary for her. There she studied science and mathematics and composed remarkable poetry. Sor (Sister) Juana Inés de la Cruz was her name, and she spoke for a new world where people mixed in faraway places, where new wealth created new customs, and where new ideas began to take hold.

Sor Juana's story attests to the conflicts between new ideas and old orders that occurred as commerce and the consolidation of empires intensified contact between diverse cultures. On the one hand, global commerce created riches that supported arts, architecture, and scientific ventures. On the other, experiments with new ways caused discomfort among defenders of the old order and provoked backlashes against innovation.

Chapter Outline

- Trade and Culture
- Culture in the Islamic World
- Culture and Politics in East Asia
- African Cultural Flourishing
- The Enlightenment in Europe
- Creating Hybrid Cultures in the Americas
- The Influence of European Culture in Oceania
- Conclusion

Core Objectives

- **EXPLAIN** the connections between cultural growth and the creation of a global market.

- **DESCRIBE** and **COMPARE** how each culture in this period reflected the ideas of the state in which it was produced.

- **ANALYZE** the different responses to foreign cultures across Afro-Eurasia in the period from 1500 to 1780.

- **DESCRIBE** how hybrid cultures emerged in the Americas, and **EXPLAIN** the connection between these cultures and Enlightenment ideology.

- **ANALYZE** the role that race and cultural difference played in the process of global integration.

This chapter explores how global commerce enriched and reshaped cultures in the centuries after the Americas ceased to be worlds apart from Afro-Eurasia. As New World commodities invigorated global trade and states consolidated power, rulers and merchants on both sides of the Atlantic displayed their power by commissioning fabulous works of art and majestic palaces and sprawling plazas. These cultural splendors were meant to impress, which they surely did. They also demonstrated the growing connections between distant societies, reflecting how foreign influences could blend with domestic traditions. Book production and consumption soared, with some publications finding their way around the world. The spread of books and ideas and increasing cultural contact led to experiments in religious toleration and helped foster cultural diversity. Yet even as Europeans, who were the greatest beneficiaries of New World riches, claimed to advance new universal truths, cultures around the globe still showed the resilience of inherited traditions.

Global Storylines

- Growing global commerce enriches rulers and merchants, who express their power through patronage for the arts.

- Distinctive cultures flourish in the major regions of the world, blending new influences with local traditions to varying degrees.

- While the Islamic and Asian worlds confidently retain their own belief systems, the Americas and Oceania increasingly face European cultural pressures.

Trade and Culture

New wealth amassed by global commerce in the aftermath of Columbus's "discovery" created the conditions for cultural dynamism in the centuries after 1500. With newfound wealth, rulers promoted learning and the arts in order to legitimize their power and show their sophistication. In Europe, monarchs known as enlightened absolutists restricted the clergy and nobility and hired loyal bureaucrats who championed the knowledge of the new age. Mughal emperors, Safavid shahs, and Ottoman sultans glorified their regimes by bringing artists and artisans from all over the world to give an Islamic flavor to their major cities and buildings. Rulers in China and Japan also looked to artists to extol their achievements. In Africa, the wealth garnered from slave trading underwrote cultural productions of extraordinary merit.

Some rulers were more eager for change than others. Moreover, certain societies—in the Americas and the South Pacific, for example—found that contact, conquest, and commerce undermined indigenous cultural life. Although Europeans and native peoples often exchanged ideas and practices, these transfers were not equal. Native Americans, for example, adapted to European missionizing by creating mixed forms of religious worship—but only because they were under pressure to do so. And as the Europeans swallowed up new territories, it was *their* culture that spread and diversified. Indeed, the Europeans absorbed much from Native Americans and African slaves but offered them little share of sovereignty or wealth in return.

Despite the unifying aspects of world trade, each society retained core aspects of its individuality. Ruling classes disseminated values based on cherished classical texts and long-established moral and religious principles. They used space in new ways to establish and project their power. They mapped their geographies and wrote their histories according to their traditional visions of the universe.

It is not surprising that in 1500 the world's most dynamic cultures remained in Asia, in areas profiting from the Indian Ocean and China Sea trades. It was in China and the Islamic world that the spice and luxury trades first flourished; here, too, rulers had successfully established political stability and centralized control of taxation, law making, and military force. Although older ways did not die out, both trade and empire building contributed to the spread of knowledge about distant people and foreign cultures.

THE BIG PICTURE

What are the connections between cultural growth and the creation of a global market?

Culture in the Islamic World

As the Ottoman, Safavid, and Mughal Empires gained greater expanses of territory in the sixteenth and seventeenth centuries, they acquired new resources to fund cultural development. Rulers supported new schools and building projects, and the elite produced books, artworks, and luxury goods. Cultural life was connected to the politics of empire building, as emperors and elites sought greater prestige by patronizing intellectuals and artists.

Forged under different empires, Islamic cultural and intellectual life now reflected three distinct worlds. In place of an earlier Islamic cosmopolitanism, unique cultural patterns prevailed within each empire. Although the Ottomans, the Safavids, and the Mughals shared a common faith, each developed a relatively autonomous form of Muslin culture.

THE OTTOMAN CULTURAL SYNTHESIS

Core Objectives

DESCRIBE and **COMPARE** how each Islamic culture in this period reflected the ideas of the state in which it was produced.

By the sixteenth century, the Ottoman Empire enjoyed a remarkably rich culture that reflected a variety of mixing influences. As the Ottoman Empire absorbed more cultures and territories, its blend of ethnic, religious, and linguistic elements exceeded the diversity of previous Islamic empires. It also balanced the interests of military men and administrators with those of clerics. Finally, it allowed autonomy to the minority faiths of Christianity and Judaism. That ability to balance a wide array of local traditions and interests and yet maintain authority in the center, supported by new revenues drawn from global trade, constituted the Ottoman synthesis.

Religion and Education A sophisticated educational system was crucial for the empire's religious and intellectual integration and for its cultural achievements. Here, as in religious affairs, the Ottomans tolerated difference. They encouraged three educational systems that produced three streams of talent—civil and military bureaucrats, *ulama*, and Sufi religious masters. The administrative elite attended hierarchically organized schools that culminated in the palace schools at Topkapi (see Chapter 11). In the religious sphere, an equally elaborate system took students from elementary schools (where they learned reading, writing, and numbers) on to higher schools, or *madrasas* (where they learned law, religion, the Quran, and the natural sciences). These graduates became *ulama* who served as judges, experts in religious law, or teachers. Yet another set of schools, *tekkes*, taught the devotional strategies and religious knowledge for students to enter Sufi orders.

Science and the Arts During this period, the Ottomans integrated some foreign elements into their culture, especially in science and philosophy, while furthering their own traditions in architecture, literature, and music. Most of the foreign influences came from Europe, with which the Ottomans were in constant contact. The Ottomans' most impressive effort to spread European knowledge occurred when a Hungarian convert to Islam, Ibrahim Muteferrika, set up a printing press in Istanbul in 1729. Muteferrika published works on science, history, and geography. One included sections on

The Ottomans and the Tulip The Ottomans used tulip motifs to decorate tiles in homes and mosques and pottery wares, as on the plate shown here.

geometry; others included the works of Copernicus, Galileo, and Descartes and a plea to the Ottoman elite to learn from Europe. When his patron was killed, however, the *ulama* promptly closed off this avenue of contact with western learning.

The Ottomans combined inherited traditions with new elements in art as well. For example, portraiture became popular after the Italian painter Gentile Bellini visited Istanbul and painted a portrait of Mehmed II. In other areas, though, the Ottomans kept their own styles. The magnificent architectural monuments built in the sixteenth through eighteenth centuries, including mosques, gardens, tombs, forts, and palaces, showed scant western influence. Nor were the Ottomans interested in western literature or music. For the most part, they believed that God had given the Islamic world a monopoly on truth and enlightenment and that their military successes proved his favor.

The Ottomans' capacity to celebrate their well-being and prosperity spread from elites to the broader public during the so-called Tulip Period, which occurred in the 1720s. The elite had long admired the tulip's bold colors and graceful blooms, and for centuries the flower served as the sultans' symbol.

In fact, both Mehmed the Conqueror and Suleiman the Magnificent grew tulips in the most secluded and prestigious courtyards at Topkapi Palace in Istanbul. And many Ottoman warriors heading into battle wore undergarments embroidered with tulips to ensure victory. By the early eighteenth century, tulip designs appeared on tiles, fabrics, and public buildings, and authorities sponsored elaborate tulip festivals. Indeed, Ottoman enjoyment of luxury goods (including lemons, soap, pepper, metal tools, coffee, and wine) grew so extensive that a well-traveled diplomat looked askance at the supposed wealth of Europe. He wrote, "In most of the provinces [of Europe], poverty is widespread, as a punishment for being infidels. Anyone who travels in these areas must confess that goodness and abundance are reserved for the Ottoman realms." Thus, despite challenges from western Europe and fears that their best days were behind them, the Ottomans' cultural traditions flourished into the eighteenth century and beyond.

SAFAVID CULTURE, SHIITE STATE

If global trade ultimately strengthened Safavid rivals both within the empire and without (see Chapter 13), it also provided the wherewithal for a period of spectacular artistic and architectural creativity, especially at the height of Safavid power in the seventeenth century. The Safavid Empire in Persia (1501–1722) was not as long-lived as the Ottoman Empire, but it was significant for giving the Shiite branch of Islam a home base and a location for displaying Shiite culture. The brilliant culture that emerged during the Safavid period provided a unique blend of Shiism and Persia's distinctive historical identity.

The Safavids created a mixed political and religious system based on Shiism and loyalty to the royal family. The most effective architect of a cultural life based on Shiite religious principles and Persian royal absolutism was Shah Abbas I (r. 1587–1629). The location that he chose to display the wealth and royal power of his state, its Persian and Shiite heritages, and its artistic sensibility was Isfahan, the capital city from its creation in 1598 until the empire's end in 1722.

Architecture and the Arts The Safavid shahs were unique among Afro-Eurasian rulers of this era, for they sought to project both absolute authority and accessibility. Their dwellings were unlike those of other rulers—such as Topkapi Palace in Istanbul, the Citadel in Cairo, and the Red Forts of the Mughals. Those were enclosed and fortified buildings, designed to enhance rulers' power by concealing them from their subjects. In contrast, the buildings of Isfahan were open to the outside, demonstrating the Safavid rulers' desire to connect with their people. Isfahan's centerpiece was the great plaza next to the royal palace and the royal mosque at the heart of the capital.

Other aspects of intellectual life reflected the elites' aspirations, wealth, and commitment to Shiite principles. Safavid artists perfected the illustrated book, the outstanding example being *The King's Book of Kings*, which contained 250 miniature illustrations. Here, artists demonstrated their mastery of three-dimensional representation and their ability to harmonize different colors. Weavers produced ornate silks and carpets for trade throughout the world; artisans painted tiles in vibrant colors and created mosaics that adorned mosques and other buildings. Moreover, the Safavids developed an elaborate calligraphy that was the envy of artists throughout the Islamic world. All of these works celebrated Shiite visions of the sacred while at the same time reinforcing the authority and prestige of the empire's ruling elite.

POWER AND CULTURE UNDER THE MUGHALS

Like the Safavids and the Ottomans, the Mughals fostered a lavish high culture, supported primarily by taxes on agriculture but reliant on silver for its currency and, at its high point, open to global trade. Because the Mughals ruled over a large non-Muslim population, the culture they developed in South Asia was initially broad and open, welcoming non-Muslims into its circle. Thus, while Islamic traditions dominated the empire's political and judicial systems, Hindus shared with Muslims the flourishing of learning, music, painting, and architecture, especially from the middle of the sixteenth century to the middle of the seventeenth.

Religion, Architecture, and the Arts In the sixteenth and early seventeenth centuries, Mughal culture mixed diverse elements from within South Asia and the broader Islamic world. The promise of an open Islamic high culture found its greatest fulfillment under the Mughal emperor Akbar (r. 1556–1605). This skillful military leader was also a popular ruler who allowed common people as well as nobles from all ethnic groups to converse with him at court. His quest for universal truths outside the strict *sharia* led him to develop a religion of his own, which incorporated many aspects of Hindu belief and ritual practice (see Chapter 12).

In architecture, too, the Mughals produced masterpieces that blended styles. This was already evident as builders combined Persian, Indian, and Ottoman elements in tombs and mosques built by Akbar's predecessors. But

Akbar Leading Religious Discussion This miniature painting from 1604 shows Akbar receiving Muslim theologians and Jesuits. The Jesuits (in the black robes on the left) hold a page relating, in Persian, the birth of Christ. A lively debate will follow the Jesuits' claims on behalf of Christianity.

Taj Mahal

Royal palace of the Mughal Empire, built by Shah Jahan in the seventeenth century in homage to his wife, Mumtaz.

Akbar enhanced this mixture in the elaborate city he built at Fatehpur Sikri, beginning in 1571. The buildings included residences for nobles (whose loyalty Akbar wanted), gardens, a drinking and gambling zone, and even an experimental school devoted to studying language acquisition in children.

Akbar's descendant Shah Jahan was also a lavish patron of architecture and the arts. In 1630, Shah Jahan ordered the building in Agra of a magnificent white marble tomb for his beloved wife, Mumtaz Mahal. Like many other women in the Mughal court, she had been an important political counselor. Designed by an Indian architect of Persian origin, this structure, the **Taj Mahal**, took twenty years and 20,000 workers to build. The 42-acre complex included a main gateway, a garden, minarets, and a mosque. The translucent marble mausoleum lay squarely in the middle of the structure, enclosed by four identical façades and crowned by a majestic central dome rising to 240 feet. The stone inlays of different types and hues, organized in geometrical and floral patterns and featuring Quranic verses inscribed in Arabic calligraphy, gave the surface an appearance of delicacy and lightness. Blending Persian and Islamic design with Indian materials and motifs, this poetry in stone represented the most splendid example of Mughal high culture and the combining of cultural traditions.

Foreign Influences versus Islamic Culture Although later emperors were less tolerant than Akbar, Mughal culture remained vibrant. Well into the eighteenth century, the Mughal nobility lived in unrivaled luxury. The presence of foreign scholars and artists enhanced the courtly culture, and the elite eagerly consumed exotic goods from China and Europe. Foreign trade also brought in more silver, advancing the money economy and supporting the nobles' sumptuous lifestyles. In addition, the Mughals assimilated European military technology: they hired Europeans as gunners and military engineers in their armies, employed them to forge guns, and bought guns and cannons from them.

For all their openness to outside influences, the Mughals, like the Ottomans, remained supremely confident of their own traditions. The centers of the Islamic world were still Istanbul, Cairo, and Delhi. Even while incorporating a few new European elements into their cultural mix, most Muslims regarded Europeans as rude barbarians. Elites in Persia, India, and the Ottoman Empire looked to China and the east, not to Europe and the west, for inspiration.

Culture and Politics in East Asia

In East Asia, prosperity, facilitated by China's vast importation of silver from Japan and the Americas, promoted cultural dynamism in the sixteenth through eighteenth centuries. Still, it was China's booming internal market, more than global trade, that fueled a Chinese culture inspired mainly by its own traditions. China had long been a renowned center of learning, with its emperors and elites supporting artists, poets, musicians, scientists, and teachers. But in late Ming and early Qing China, a growing population and extensive commercial networks propelled the circulation of ideas as well as goods.

In Japan, too, economic growth supported elite and popular culture. Because of its giant neighbor across the sea, the Japanese people had always been aware of outside influences. Like the Chinese government, the Tokugawa shogunate tried to promote Confucian notions of a social hierarchy organized on the basis of social position, age, gender, and kin. It also tried to shield the country from egalitarian ideas that would threaten the strict social hierarchy. But the forces that undermined governmental control of knowledge in China proved even stronger in Japan.

CHINA: THE CHALLENGE OF EXPANSION AND DIVERSITY

While China had become increasingly connected with the outside world in the sixteenth and seventeenth centuries, the sources for its cultural flourishing during the period came primarily from within. The circulation of books spread ideas among the literate, and religious rituals instilled cultural values among the broader population. Advances in cartography reflected the distinctive worldview of Chinese elites.

Publishing and the Transmission of Ideas The decentralization of book production and the domestic market helped circulate ideas within China. Woodblock and movable type printing had been present in China for centuries. Although initially the state had spurred book production by printing Confucian texts, before long the economy's increasing commercialization weakened government controls over what got printed. Even as officials clamped down on unorthodox texts, there was no centralized system of censorship, and unauthorized opinions circulated freely.

By the late Ming era, a burgeoning publishing sector catered to the diverse social, cultural, and religious needs of educated elites and urban populations. European visitors admired the vast collections of printed materials housed in Chinese libraries, describing them as "magnificently built" and "finely adorn'd." Perhaps more important, books and other luxury goods were now more affordable. Increasingly, publishers offered a mix of wares: guidebooks for patrons of the arts, travelers, or merchants; handbooks for performing rituals, choosing dates for ceremonies, or writing proper letters; almanacs and encyclopedias; morality books; medical manuals; and, above all, study guides.

Study aids for the civil service examination dominated the literary marketplace. In 1595, Beijing reeled with scandal over news that the second-place

Core Objectives

ANALYZE the different responses to foreign cultures across Afro-Eurasia in the period from 1500 to 1780.

graduate had reproduced verbatim several model essays published by commercial printers. Ironically, then, the increased circulation of knowledge led critics to bemoan a decline in real learning; instead of mastering the classics, they charged, examination candidates were simply memorizing the work of others.

Elite women also joined China's literary culture. Women's poetry was especially popular, not only in anthologies published for the general market but in volumes produced for limited circulation to celebrate the refinement of the writer's family. Men of letters soon recognized the market potential of women's writings; some also saw women's less regularized style (usually acquired through family channels rather than state-sponsored schools) as a means to challenge stifling stylistic conformity. On rare occasions, women even served as publishers themselves.

Although elite women enjoyed success in the world of culture, the period brought increasing restrictions on their lives. The practice of footbinding (which elite women first adopted at least as far back as the twelfth century) continued to spread among common people, as small, delicate feet came to signify femininity and respectability. The thriving publishing sector indirectly promoted stricter morality by printing plays and novels that echoed the government's conservative attitudes.

Popular Culture and Religion Important as the book trade was, it had only an indirect impact on most men and women in late Ming China. Those who could not read well or at all absorbed cultural values through oral communication, ritual performance, and daily practices.

Villagers participated in various religious and cultural practices, such as honoring local guardian spirits, patronizing Buddhist and Daoist temples, or watching performances by touring theater groups. At the grassroots level, there was little distinction among Buddhist, Daoist, and local cults. The Chinese believed in cosmic unity, and although they celebrated spiritual forces, they did not consider any of them to be a Supreme Being who favored one sect over another. They believed it was the emperor, rather than any religious group, who held the mandate of heaven. (See Current Trends in World History: The Political Uses of Space.) Unless sects posed an obvious threat, the emperor had no reason to regulate their spiritual practices. This situation promoted religious tolerance and avoided the sectarian warfare that plagued post-Reformation Europe.

Technology and Cartography Belief in cosmic unity did not prevent the Chinese from devising technologies to master nature's operations in this world. For example, the magnetic compass, gunpowder, and the printing press were all Chinese inventions. Chinese astronomers also compiled accurate records of eclipses, comets, novae, and meteors. In part, the emperor's

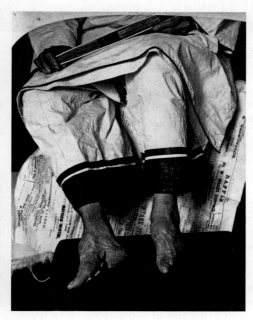

Footbinding Two images of bound feet: (*left*) as an emblem of feminine respectability when wrapped and concealed, as on this well-to-do Chinese woman; (*right*) as an object of curiosity and condemnation when exposed for the world to see.

needs drove their interest in astronomy and calendrical science. It was the emperor's job as the Son of Heaven, and thus mediator between heaven and earth, to determine the best dates for planting, holding festivities, scheduling mourning periods, and convening judicial court sessions.

Convinced that their sciences were superior, Christian missionaries in China tried to promote their own knowledge in areas such as astronomy and cartography (mapmaking). In 1583, the Jesuit missionary Matteo Ricci brought European maps to China, hoping to impress the elite with European learning. Challenging their belief that the world was flat, his maps demonstrated that the earth was spherical—and that China was just one country among many others. Chinese critics complained that Ricci treated the Ming Empire as "a small unimportant country." As a concession, he placed China closer to the center of the maps and provided additional textual information. Still, his maps had a negligible impact, as neither the earth's shape nor precise scale was particularly important to most Chinese geographers.

Before the nineteenth century, the Chinese had fairly incomplete knowledge about foreign lands despite a long history of contact. Chinese writers, for example, often identified groups of other people through distinctive and,

The Political Uses of Space

The use of space for political purposes is a theme we can trace across world history. In the early modern period, many kings and emperors opted to build grand palaces to create lavish power centers, from which they could project their influence over their kingdoms; petitioners and potential rivals would have to come to *them* to ask for favors or to complete their business. Monarchs sculpted these environments, creating a series of spaces, each of them open to a smaller and smaller number of the king's favorites. Both palaces and their surrounding grounds were ornate and splendid, were expensive to construct, and involved the best craftsmen and artists available, which often meant borrowing ideas and designs from neighboring cultures. Palace complexes of this type, built in Beijing, in Istanbul, in Isfahan, and just outside of Paris, used space to project the rulers' power and to show who was boss.

The **Forbidden City of Beijing** was the earliest of these impressive sites of royal power (see illustration on p. 524). Its construction took about four years—from 1416 to 1420—although the actual name "Forbidden City" did not appear until 1576. The entrance of the city was straddled by the Meridian Gate, the tallest structure of the entire complex, which towered over all other buildings at more than 115 feet above the ground. It was from this lofty position that the emperor extended his gaze toward his empire, as he oversaw various court ceremonies, including the important annual proclamation of the calendar that governed the entire country's agricultural and ritual activities. Foreign emissaries received by the court were also often allowed to use one of the passageways through the gate, where they were expected to be duly awed. As for the officials' daily audience with the emperor, they had to line up outside the Meridian Gate around 3 a.m. before proceeding to the Hall of Supreme Harmony. It was typical of the entire construction project that this impressive hall with vermilion walls and golden tiles was built at considerable cost. For the columns of the hall, fragrant hardwood had to be found in the tiger-ridden forests of the remote southwest, while the mountain forests of the south and southwest were searched for other timbers that eventually made their way to the capital through the Grand Canal.

The Topkapi Palace in Istanbul, capital of the Ottoman Empire, began to take shape in 1458 under Mehmed II and underwent steady expansion over the years (see illustration on p. 511). Topkapi projected royal authority in much the same way as the Forbidden City emphasized Chinese emperors' power: governing officials worked enclosed within massive walls, and monarchs rarely went outside their inner domain.

More than two centuries later, in the 1670s and 1680s, the French monarch Louis XIV built the **Palace of Versailles** on the site of a royal hunting lodge 11 miles from Paris, the French capital (see illustration on p. 630). This enormously costly complex was built to house Louis's leading clergymen and nobles, who were obliged to visit at least twice a year. Louis hoped that by taking wealthy and powerful men and women away from their local power bases, and by diverting them with entertainments, he could keep them from plotting new forms of religious schism or challenging his right to rule. Going to Versailles also allowed him to escape the pressures and demands of the population of Paris. Many European monarchs—including Russia's Peter the Great—would build palace complexes modeled on Versailles.

If in China, the Ottoman Empire, and France, emperors built what were essentially private spaces in which to conduct and dominate state business, Shah Abbas (r. 1587–1629) of the Safavid Empire chose to create a great new public space instead. In the early seventeenth century, Shah Abbas oversaw

Forbidden City of Beijing
Palace city of the Ming and Qing dynasties.

to them, odd physical features. A Ming geographical publication portrayed the Portuguese as "seven feet tall, having eyes like a cat, a mouth like an oriole, an ash-white face, thick and curly beards like black gauze, and almost red hair." Chinese elites glorified their "white" complexions against the peasants' dark skin; against the black, wavy-haired "devils" of Southeast Asia; and

Isfahan On the great plaza at Isfahan, markets and government offices operated in close proximity to the public Shah Abbas Mosque, shown here, and the shah's private mosque. This structure represented Shah Abbas's desire to unite control of trade, government, and religion under one leader.

exchange of ideas. World history is full of palaces and plazas (the Piazza San Marco in Venice might be compared to the royal plaza at Isfahan); we can still visit and admire them. But when we do, we should also remember that space, and the architecture that either opens up to the public or sets aside privileged spaces, has always had political as well as cultural functions.

Questions for Analysis

- Choose one of the places discussed in this feature. Explain how the architectural layout shaped the political power exercised by that space.
- Contrast private spaces, like the palace at Versailles, with public spaces, like the great plaza at Isfahan. What political goals could be accomplished by each?

Explore Further

Babaie, Sussan, *Isfahan and Its Palaces: Statecraft, Shi'ism and the Architecture of Conviviality in Early Modern Iran* (2008).

Necipoğlu, Gülru, *Architecture, Ceremonial, and Power: The Topkapi Palace in the Fifteenth and Sixteenth Centuries* (1991).

the construction of the **great plaza at Isfahan**, a structure that reflected his desire to bring trade, government, and religion together under the authority of the supreme political leader. An enormous public mosque, the Shah Abbas Mosque, dominated one end of the plaza, which measured 1,667 feet by 517 feet. At the other end were trading stalls and markets. Along one side sat government offices; the other side offered the exquisite Mosque of Shaykh Lutfollah. If the other rulers of this era devoted their (considerable) income to creating rich private spaces, Shah Abbas used the vast open space of the plaza to open up his city to all comers, keeping only the Mosque of Shaykh Lutfollah for his personal use.

The royal use of space says a great deal about how monarchs in this era wished to be seen and remembered and about how they wanted to rule. While some wanted to retreat from the rest of society, Shah Abbas wanted to create an open space for trade and the

against the Europeans' "ash-white" pallor. Qing authors in the eighteenth century confused France with the Portugal known during Ming times, and they characterized England and Sweden as dependencies of Holland. During this period of cultural flourishing, in short, most Chinese did not feel compelled to revise their view of the world.

Palace of Versailles

The palace complex, 11 miles away from the French capital of Paris, built by Louis XIV in the 1670s and 1680s to house and entertain his leading clergymen and nobles, with the hopes of diverting them from plotting against him.

great plaza at Isfahan

The center of Safavid power in the seventeenth century created by Shah Abbas (r. 1587–1629) to represent the unification of trade, government, and religion under one supreme political authority.

CULTURAL IDENTITY AND TOKUGAWA JAPAN

The culture that developed in Japan in this period drew on local traditions and, increasingly, foreign influences from China and Europe. Chinese cultural influence had long crossed the Sea of Japan, but under the Tokugawa shogunate there was also interest in European culture. This interest grew via the Dutch presence in Japan and limited contacts with Russians. At the same time, there was a surge in the study of Japanese traditions and culture. Thus, Tokugawa Japan engaged in a three-cornered conversation among time-honored Chinese ways, European teachings, and distinctly Japanese traditions.

Native Arts and Popular Culture Elite and popular culture featured elements that were distinctly Japanese. Until the seventeenth century, the main patrons of Japanese culture were the imperial court in Kyoto, the hereditary shogunate, religious institutions, and a small upper class. These groups developed an elite culture of theater and stylized painting. Samurai (former warriors turned bureaucrats) and daimyos (regional lords) favored a masked theater, called Noh and an elegant ritual for making tea and engaging in contemplation.

Alongside the elite culture arose a rougher urban one that artisans and merchants patronized. Urban dwellers could purchase works of fiction and colorful prints made from carved wood blocks, and they could enjoy the company of female entertainers known as geisha. These women were skilled (*gei*) in playing the three-stringed instrument (*shamisen*), storytelling, and performing; some were also prostitutes. Geisha worked in the cities' pleasure quarters, which were famous for their geisha houses, public baths, brothels, and theaters. Kabuki—a type of theater that combined song, dance, and skillful staging to dramatize conflicts between duty and passion—became wildly popular. This art form featured dazzling acting, brilliant makeup, and sumptuous costumes.

Much popular entertainment chronicled the world of the common people rather than politics or high society. The urbanites' pleasure-oriented culture was known as "the floating world" (*ukiyo*), and the woodblock prints depicting it as *ukiyo-e* (*e* meaning "picture"). Here, the social order was temporarily turned upside down. Those who were usually considered inferior—actors, musicians, courtesans, and others seen as possessing low morals—became idols.

Literacy in Japan now surged, especially among men. The most popular novels sold 10,000 to 12,000 copies. In the late eighteenth century, Edo had some sixty booksellers and hundreds of book lenders. In fact, the presence of so many lenders allowed books to spread to a wider public that previously could not afford to buy them. By the late eighteenth century, as more books circulated and some of them criticized the government, officials tried to censor certain publications. The government's response testified to the uncommon power wielded by people of modest means and the relative significance of popular culture in Japan.

Religion and Chinese Influence In the realm of higher culture and religion, China loomed large in the Tokugawa world. Japanese scholars wrote imperial histories of Japan in the Chinese style, and Chinese law codes and other books attracted a significant readership. Some Japanese traveled south to Nagasaki to meet Zen Buddhist masters and Chinese residents there. Buddhism originally came to Japan from China and remained associated with Chinese monks. A few of those monks even won permission to found monasteries outside Nagasaki and to give lectures and construct temples in Kyoto and Edo.

Although Buddhist temples grew in number, they did not displace the native Japanese practice of venerating ancestors and worshipping gods in nature. Later called Shintō ("the way of the gods"), this practice boasted a network of shrines throughout the country. Shintō developed from time-honored beliefs in spirits, or *kami*, who were associated with places (mountains, rivers, waterfalls, rocks, the moon) and activities (harvest, fertility). Seeking healing or other assistance, adherents appealed to these spirits in nature and daily life through incantations and offerings. Some women under Shintō served as *mikos*, a kind of shaman with special divinatory powers.

Reacting to the influence of Chinese Buddhism and desiring to honor their own country's greatness, some thinkers promoted intellectual traditions from Japan's past. These efforts stressed "native learning," Japanese texts, and Japanese uniqueness. In so doing, they formalized a Japanese religious and cultural tradition, and they denounced Buddhism as a foreign contaminant.

European Influences Not only did Chinese intellectual influences compete with revived native learning, but by the late seventeenth century Japan was also tapping other sources of knowledge. By 1670, a guild of Japanese interpreters in Nagasaki who could speak and read Dutch accompanied Dutch merchants on trips to Edo. As European knowledge spread to high circles in Edo, in 1720 the shogunate lifted its ban on foreign books. Thereafter European ideas, called "Dutch learning," circulated more openly. Scientific, geographical, and medical texts appeared in Japanese translations and in

Artist and Geisha at Tea The erotic, luxuriant atmosphere of Japan's urban pleasure quarters was captured in a new art form, the *ukiyo-e*, or "pictures from a floating world." In this image set in Tokyo's celebrated Yoshiwara district, several geisha flutter about a male artist.

some cases displaced Chinese texts. A Japanese-Dutch dictionary appeared in 1745, and the first official school of Dutch learning followed. Students of Dutch and other European teachings remained a limited segment of Japanese society, but the demand for translations intensified.

Japan's internal debates about what to borrow from the Europeans and the Chinese illustrate the changes that the world had undergone in recent centuries. A few hundred years earlier, products and ideas generally did not travel beyond coastal regions and had only a limited effect (especially inland) on local cultural practices. By the eighteenth century, though, expanded networks of exchange and new prosperity made the integration of foreign ideas feasible and, sometimes, desirable. The Japanese did not consider the embrace of outside influences as a mark of inferiority or subordination, particularly when they could put those influences to good use. This was not the case for the cultures that thrived within the great Asian land-based empires, which were eager lenders but hesitant borrowers.

African Cultural Flourishing

The wealth that spurred artistic achievement and displays of power in Asia and the Islamic world did not bypass African states. Proceeds from the slave trade enabled African upper classes to fund cultural activities and invigorate strong artisanal and artistic traditions that dated back many centuries. African artisans, like those in East Asia, maintained local forms of cultural production, such as wood carving, weaving, and metalworking.

Cultural traditions in Africa varied from kingdom to kingdom, but there were patterns among them. For example, all West African elites encouraged craftsmen to produce carvings, statues, masks, and other objects that would glorify the power and achievements of rulers. (Royal patrons in Europe, Asia, and the Islamic world did the same with architecture and painting.) There was also a widespread belief that rulers and their families had the blessing of the gods. Arts and crafts not only celebrated royal power but also captured the energy of a universe that people believed was suffused with spiritual beings. Starting in the sixteenth century and continuing through the eighteenth century when the slave trade reached its peak, African rulers who benefited from that trade had even more reason—and means—to support cultural pursuits.

THE ASANTE, OYO, AND BENIN CULTURAL TRADITIONS

The kingdom of Asante led the way in cultural attainments, and the Oyo Empire and Benin also promoted rich artistic traditions.

The Asante kingdom's access to gold and the revenues that it derived from selling captives made it the richest state in West Africa, perhaps even in the whole of sub-Saharan Africa. The citizens of Asante accorded the highest respect to entrepreneurs who made money and were able to surround themselves with retainers and slaves. The adages of the age were inevitably about becoming rich: "money is king" or "nothing is as important as money" or "money is what it is all about."

Asante's artisans celebrated these traditions through the crafting of magnificent seats or stools coated with gold as symbols of authority; the most ornate were reserved for the head of the Asante federation, the Asantehene, who ruled this far-flung empire from the capital city of Kumasi. By the eighteenth century, these monarchs ventured out from the secluded royal palace only on ceremonial and feast days, when they wore sumptuous silk garments featuring many dazzling colors and geometric patterns all joined together in interwoven strips. Known as Kente cloth, this fabric could be worn only by the rulers. Kings also had a golden elephant tail, which was carried in front of them. It symbolized the highest level of wealth and power. Also held aloft on these celebratory occasions were maces, spears, staffs, and other symbols of power fashioned from the kingdom's abundant gold supplies. These reminded the common people of the Asantehene's connection to the gods.

Equally resplendent were rulers of the Oyo Empire and Benin, located in the territory that now constitutes Nigeria. Elegant, refined metalwork in the form of West African bronzes reflects these rulers' power and their peoples' high esteem. In the Oyo Empire, the Yoruba people drew on craft and artistic traditions dating back to the first millennium CE. The bronze heads of Ife, capital city of the Yoruba Oyo Empire, are among the world's most sophisticated pieces of art. According to one commentator, "[L]ittle that Italy or Greece or Egypt ever produced could be finer, and the appeal of their beauty is immediate and universal." Artisans fashioned the best known of these works in the thirteenth century (before the slave trade era), but the tradition continued and became more elaborate in the seventeenth and eighteenth centuries.

Stunning bronzes were produced in Benin as well. Although historical records have portrayed Benin as one of Africa's most brutal slave-trading regimes, it produced art of the highest order. Whether Benin's reputation for brutality was deserved or simply part of Europeans' desire to label African rulers as "savage" in order to justify their intervention in African affairs, it cannot detract from the splendor of its artisans' creations.

Brass Oba Head The brass head of an Oba, or king, of Benin. The kingdom's brass and bronze work was among the finest in all of Africa.

Although supported by funds from the Atlantic slave trade, the cultural traditions of western Africa remained little influenced by intellectual and artistic influences from the wider world. African culture during this period was relatively autonomous, even as Africa became increasingly entangled in the global webs of economic exchange and political domination.

The Enlightenment in Europe

An extraordinary cultural flowering also blossomed in Europe during the seventeenth and eighteenth centuries, driven by trade and internal commerce. Often the **Enlightenment** is defined purely in intellectual terms as the spreading of faith in reason and in universal rights and laws, but this era encompassed broader developments, such as the expansion of literacy, the spread of critical thinking, and the decline of religious persecution. Contact between Europe and the wider world after the fifteenth century played a formative role in Europeans' view of the world and their place in it. They quickly became eager consumers of other people's goods and practices. From Amerindian trapping methods to African slaves' cultivation techniques, from Chinese porcelain to New World tobacco and chocolate, contact with others influenced Europe in the seventeenth and eighteenth centuries. The more they learned, the more European intellectuals became convinced not only that their culture was superior—for that was hardly rare—but that they had discovered a set of universal laws that applied to everyone, everywhere around the world.

Abandoning the Christian belief in divine intervention, Enlightenment thinkers sought universal, objective knowledge that did not reflect any particular religion, political view, class, gender, or culture. These scholars struggled to formulate universal, natural laws, although most of these thinkers were unaware of how culture-bound their vision was. They ignored the extent to which European, upper-class male perspectives colored their "objective" knowledge.

THE NEW SCIENCE

Interest in scientific discoveries increased gradually over the seventeenth and eighteenth centuries. While the sixteenth century had brought new prosperity, the seventeenth century produced civil and religious wars, dynastic conflicts, and famines that devastated central Europe. These events bankrupted the Spanish, caused chaos in France, led to the execution of the English king and saw the Dutch break free from Spanish control. They also contributed to the spread of Protestantism in Europe. At the same time, the crises made some intellectuals wish to turn their backs on religious strife and develop useful ways for understanding and improving *this* world—by imposing order on the chaos and instability they saw around them. By 1750, in some western countries, a significant minority of the population was eager to join in these discussions, which concentrated on the natural sciences, especially physics and astronomy.

The search for new, testable knowledge began centuries before the Enlightenment, in the efforts of Nicolaus Copernicus (1473–1543) and Galileo Galilei (1564–1642) to understand the behavior of the heavens. These men were both astronomers and mathematicians. Making their own mathematical calculations and observations of the stars and planets, they came to conclusions that contradicted age-old assumptions. This entailed considerable risk: when Galileo confirmed Copernicus's claims that the earth revolved around the sun, he was tried for heresy.

In the seventeenth century, a small but influential group of scholars committed themselves, similarly, to experimentation, calculation, and observation. They adopted a method for "scientific" inquiry laid out by the philosopher Sir Francis Bacon (1561–1626), who claimed that real science entailed the formulation of hypotheses that could be tested in carefully controlled experiments. Bacon was chiefly wary of classical and medieval authorities, but his principle also applied to traditional knowledge that European scientists were encountering in the rest of the world. Confident of their calculations performed according to the new **scientific method**, scientists like Isaac Newton (1642–1727) sought universal laws that applied to all matter and motion; they criticized older conceptions of nature (from Aristotelian ideas to folkloric and foreign ones) as absurd and obsolete. Thus, in his *Principia Mathematica* (1687) Newton set forth the laws of motion—including the famous law of gravitation, which simultaneously explained falling bodies on earth and planetary motion.

Most historians no longer call these changes a scientific revolution, for European thinking did not change overnight. Only gradually did thinkers come to see the natural world as operating according to inviolable laws that experimenters could figure out, like gravity and inertia. But by the late seventeenth century, many rulers had developed a new interest in science, and they established royal academies to encourage research. This patronage, of course, had a political function. By incorporating the British Royal Society in 1662, for example, Charles II hoped to show not only that the crown backed scientific progress but also that England's great minds backed the crown. Similar reasoning lay behind Louis XIV's founding of the French Royal Academy of Sciences.

Gradually, the new science expanded beyond the court to gain popularity among elite circles. Marquise de Châtelet-Lomont built a scientific laboratory in her home and translated Newton's *Principia* into French, which her lover, Voltaire, one of the most influential of the Enlightenment figures, popularized. By about 1750, even artisans and journalists were applying Newtonian mechanics to their practical problems and inventions. In Italy, numerous female natural philosophers emerged, and the genre of scientific literature

scientific method
Method of inquiry based on experimentation in nature. Many of its principles were first laid out by the philosopher Sir Francis Bacon (1561–1626), who claimed that real science entailed the formulation of hypotheses that could be tested in carefully controlled experiments.

for "ladies" took hold. A consensus emerged among proponents of the new science that useful knowledge came from collecting data and organizing them into universally valid systems, rather than from studying revered classical texts.

By no means, however, did the scientific worldview dominate European thinking. Most people still understood their relationships with God, nature, and fellow humans via Christian doctrines and local customs. Although literacy was increasing, it was far from universal; schools remained church-governed or elite, male institutions. All governments employed censors and punished radical thinkers, peasants still suffered under arbitrary systems of taxation, and judicial regimes were as harsh as during medieval times. Nonetheless, the promise of universal scientific truths inspired Enlightenment thinkers, who in turn held them out as an ideal.

ENLIGHTENMENT THINKERS

Enlightenment thinkers, called **philosophes** in France, applied scientific reasoning to human interaction and society as opposed to nature. Such thinkers included the French writers Voltaire (1694–1778) and Denis Diderot (1713–1784) and the Scottish moral philosopher and political economist Adam Smith (1723–1790). These writers also called attention to the evils and flaws of human society: Voltaire criticized the torture of criminals, Diderot denounced the despotic tendencies of the French kings Louis XIV and Louis XV, and Smith exposed the inefficiencies of mercantilism. Other Enlightenment thinkers, similarly, criticized contemporary European conditions, and they often suffered imprisonment or exile for writing about what they considered to be superstitious beliefs and corrupt political structures.

The Enlightenment touched all of Europe, but the extent of its reach varied. In France and Britain, enlightened learning spread widely; in Spain, Poland, and Scandinavia, enlightened circles were small and had little influence on rulers or the general population. Enlightened thought flourished in commercial centers like Amsterdam and Edinburgh and in colonial ports like Philadelphia and Boston.

Popular Culture In the emerging marketplace for new books and new ideas, some of the most popular works were not from high intellectuals. Pamphlets charging widespread corruption, fraudulent stock speculation, and insider trading circulated widely. Sex, too, sold well. Works like *Venus in the Cloister, or the Nun in a Nightgown* racked up as many sales as the now-classic works of the Enlightenment. Bawdy and irreligious, these vulgar best-sellers exploited consumer demand—but they also seized the opportunity to mock authority figures, such as nuns and priests. Some even dared to go after the royal family, portraying Marie Antoinette as having sex with her court confessor. Such works displayed the seamier side of the Enlightenment, but they also revealed a willingness on the part of high- and low-brow intellectuals alike to challenge established beliefs and institutions and to undermine royal authority.

The reading public itself helped generate new cultural institutions and practices. In Britain and Germany, book clubs and coffeehouses sprang up to cater to sober men of business and learning; here, aristocrats and well-to-do commoners could read news sheets or discuss stock prices, political affairs, and technological novelties. The same sort of noncourtly socializing occurred in Parisian salons, where aristocratic women presided. The number of female readers, and writers, soared, and the relatively new genre of the novel, as well as specialized women's journals, appealed especially to them. A public sphere emerged that was radically democratic and beyond the control of kings or any corporate body: all it took to participate was the ability to read and the willingness to debate the issues of the day.

Challenges to Authority and Tradition Even though they took the aristocracy's money, many Enlightenment thinkers tried to overturn the status distinctions that characterized European society. They emphasized merit rather than birth as the basis for status. In his *Treatise on Human Understanding* (1690), John Locke claimed that man was born with a mind that was a clean slate (*tabula rasa*) and acquired all his ideas through experience. Locke stressed that cultural differences were the result not of unequal natural abilities but of unequal opportunities to develop one's abilities. Similarly, in *The Wealth of Nations* (1776), Adam Smith remarked that there was little difference (other than education) between a philosopher and a street porter: both were born, he claimed, with the ability to reason, and both should be free to rise in society according to their talents. Yet Locke and Smith still believed that a mixed set of social and political institutions was necessary to regulate relationships among ever-imperfect humans. Moreover, they did not believe that women could act as independent, rational individuals in the same way that all men, presumably, could. Although educated women like Mary Wollstonecraft and Olympe de Gouges took up the pen to protest these inequities (see Chapter 15 for further discussion), the Enlightenment did little to change the subordinate status of women in European society.

Universal Laws and Religious Tolerance Efforts to discover the "laws" of human behavior linked up with criticism of existing governments. Explaining the laws of economic relations was chiefly the work of Adam Smith, whose book *The Wealth of Nations* described universal economic principles. According to Smith, all people have what he called the propensity to truck, barter, and exchange— an innate desire to trade with one another. He complained that mercantilist controls and guild restrictions stifled economic growth and argued instead that a division of labor, spurred on by free and fair competition, provided the best conditions for producing wealth (though he did not advocate completely free, unregulated markets). Assuming that all people, everywhere, shared Protestant notions of thrift and discipline, Smith claimed that by pursuing their own rational self-interest, virtuous individuals would advance the common good without meaning to do so—as if, as he put it, by an "invisible hand." Smith was conscious of growing economic gaps between "civilized and thriving" nations and "savage" ones. Yet he believed that until the poorer nations learned to abide by nature's laws and behaved virtuously, they could not expect a happy fate.

One of the most controversial areas for applying universal laws was religion. Although few Enlightenment thinkers were atheists (people who do not believe in any god), most of them called for religious toleration. They insisted that the use of reason, not force, was the best way to create a community of believers and morally good people. Governments often reacted by censoring books or exiling writers who criticized the authority of the church, but the arguments managed to persuade some rulers. Thus, in the late eighteenth century, governments from Denmark to Austria passed acts offering religious minorities some freedom of worship. However, toleration did not mean full civil rights—especially for Catholics in England or Jews anywhere in Europe. Religious minorities enjoyed much greater freedom in this period in the Ottoman Empire than they did in any European country.

The Enlightenment produced numerous works that attempted to encompass universal knowledge. Most important was the French *Encyclopédie*, which ultimately comprised twenty-eight volumes containing essays by nearly 200 intellectuals. It was popular among the elite despite its political, religious, and intellectual radicalism. Its purpose was "to collect all the knowledge scattered over the face of the earth" and to make it useful to men and women in the present and future. Indeed, the *Encyclopédie* offered a wealth of information about the rest of the world, including more than 2,300 articles on Islam. Here, the authors typically praised Arab culture for preserving and extending Greek and Roman science—and in doing so, preparing the way for scientific advances in Europe. But at the same time, the authors portrayed Islam with the same ill will that they applied to other organized religions, condemning Muhammad for promoting a bloodthirsty religion and Muslim culture in general for not rejecting superstition.

CONSEQUENCES OF THE ENLIGHTENMENT

The Enlightenment—or, more properly, Enlightenments, as there was much variation across Europe—was a movement with numerous ambivalent consequences, both for religious and political institutions and for Europe's relationship with the rest of the world.

Religion and the Enlightenment Although few Enlightenment thinkers were atheists, most criticized what they perceived to be the irrational rituals,

The *Encyclopédie* Originally published in 1751, the *Encyclopédie* was the most comprehensive work of learning of the French Enlightenment. (*Top*) The title page features an image of light and reason being dispersed throughout the land. The title itself identifies the work as a dictionary, based on reason, that deals not just with the sciences but also with the arts and occupations. It identifies two of the leading men of letters (*gens de lettres*), Denis Diderot and Jean le Rond d'Alembert, as the primary authors of the work. Contributors to the *Encyclopédie* included craftsmen as well as intellectuals. (*Bottom*) The detailed illustrations of a pin factory and the processes and machinery employed in pin making are from a plate in the fourth volume of the *Encyclopédie* and demonstrate its emphasis on practical information.

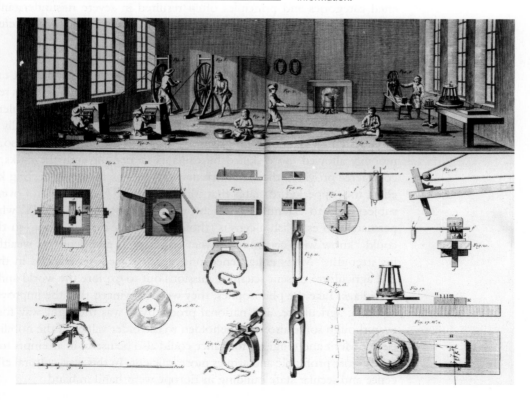

superstitions, persecutions, and expenditures defended by clergy. The Scottish philosopher and historian David Hume attacked biblical miracles, and Voltaire underscored the bloodiness of the Crusades. They insisted that the use of reason, rather than force or rote repetition of formulas, was the best way to create a community of believers and morally good people. Some governments bowed to clerical pressure and censored the most radical books or exiled writers, but many absolutist monarchs saw an advantage in reducing the church's power and introducing at least some measure of tolerance of religious minorities into their realms.

Tolerance did not mean full civil rights—for Catholics in England, for example, or for Jews anywhere in Europe. Tolerance simply meant a loosening of religious uniformity, and the population as a whole often resented even this. Few Europeans entirely lost their faith as a result of the spread of enlightened ideas and critiques. But it is unquestionably the case that the Enlightenment succeeded in spreading the suspicion of religious authorities and the distaste for religious persecution, and it did create new forms of religious belief and practice.

The application of enlightened ideas to non-European religions had conflicting effects. On the one hand, enlightened thinkers sought information about other religions and wrote books discussing similarities between Christian and non-Christian practices and beliefs. But their imposition of enlightened categories and principles often resulted in severe misunderstandings, as differences were increasingly explained as others' "backward" refusal to evolve along European lines.

The Enlightenment and Politics Absolutist governments did not entirely reject enlightened ideas, which included ideas that were in most cases reformist or critical of religious authorities rather than directly political. Rulers, like astronomers, recognized the virtues of universality (as in a universally applicable system of taxation) and precision (as in a well-drilled army). Also, social mobility allowed more skilled bureaucrats to rise through the ranks, while commerce provided the state with new riches. The idea of collecting knowledge, too, appealed to states that wanted to have greater control over their subjects and to extend their reach overseas. Consider Louis XIV, who was persuaded to establish a census (though he never carried it out) so that he could "know with certitude in what consists his grandeur, his wealth, and his strength." Many enlightened princes supported innovations in the arts and agriculture or sent scientific missions out to explore the world and plant their flags. Like the philosophes, they were convinced that the improvement of trade, agriculture, and national productivity was the right way forward, even though some also were beholden to the older values of the nobility and clergy. Merit and religious tolerance could also be useful in attempts to make states more profitable and armies more efficient. In this way, cultural efflorescence and secular state building in Europe went hand in hand.

The Enlightenment and the Origins of Racial Thought The Enlightenment introduced new ways of thinking about human difference. Scientists sought objective, rational ways to classify peoples and cultures in the same way that botanists classified plants—indeed, many leaders in this field were botanists. To do so, they relied on new concepts of race.

Before the eighteenth century, the word *race* referred to a swift current in a stream or a test of speed; sometimes it meant a family lineage (mainly that of a royal or noble family). The Frenchman François Bernier, who had traveled in Asia, may have been the first European to attempt to classify the peoples of the world. He used a variety of criteria, including those that were to become standard from the late eighteenth century down to the present, such as skin color, facial features, and hair texture. Bernier published these views in his *New Division of the Earth by the Different Groups or Races Who Inhabit It* (1684). In addition, the Swedish naturalist Carolus Linnaeus (1707–1778), the French scholar Georges Louis Leclerc, the comte de Buffon (1707–1788), and the German anatomist Johann Friedrich Blumenbach (1752–1840) also were among the first to use racial principles to classify humankind.

In his *Systema Naturae* (first published in 1735), Europe's most accomplished naturalist, Carolus Linnaeus, identified five subspecies of *Homo sapiens*, or "wise man." He gave each of the continents a subspecies: there was *Homo europaeus*, *Homo americanus*, *Homo afar*, and *Homo asiaticus*, to which he added a fifth category, *Homo monstrosus*, for "wild" men and "monstrous" types. He believed that each of these groups was marked by distinctive social and intellectual characteristics, contrasting light-skinned Europeans, who he believed were governed by laws, to "sooty" Asians, who were governed by opinion. Custom governed copper-skinned Americans, while only personal whim ruled Africans, whom he consigned to the lowest rung of the human ladder.

Linnaeus thought these categories were malleable, both under environmental pressure and through mixing to create new species. Skin color, facial features, and hair type did not directly and permanently correlate to intelligence or morality—this was far removed from the racial thought that emerged a century later. But the idea that human beings could be classified in a few large groups proved enormously influential both in scientific discourse and popular opinion, and the categories he devised were profoundly marked by the biases of his European upbringing.

THE EUROPEAN ENLIGHTENMENT IN GLOBAL PERSPECTIVE

Europe's new science and enlightened thought arose in reaction both to Europe's expanding interaction with the rest of the world and to the period's environmental, religious, and political chaos. But why Europe? Why not China or the Islamic world? As we have seen, Chinese and Muslim scholars could boast rich traditions of scientific and technological development and literary production. Why, then, did Chinese literati and, perhaps more important, Muslim scholars, who still had the most advanced knowledge of the natural sciences even as late as the fourteenth century, let the Europeans assume the lead in understanding the natural world? Answers are difficult to provide, but some suggestions are now coming to light.

For Islam, the rise of Sufi orders and Sufi mysticism posed a challenge to the dominance that the *ulama* believed that they should have over all fields of thought and principles of belief. The *ulama* responded to this threat in conservative, even fundamentalist ways, reiterating the importance of the religious sciences, which included studies of the Quran, the sayings of the Prophet (*hadith*), the *sharia* (religious law), theology, poetry, and the Arabic language, and questioning the value of the foreign sciences and the study of the natural world. Occasionally scholars were able to challenge the *ulama*'s monopoly on learning and to look outward for inspiration, but such efforts relied on reformist patrons, who were not in great abundance. While in Europe a diverse set of quarreling and competing churches and patrons made possible the articulation of new and more secular sciences, in Ottoman lands the established authorities and ideas could not so easily be dislodged.

Matteo Ricci Adapts to Chinese Culture This image depicts Jesuit father Matteo Ricci. Behind him stands a painting of the Madonna and baby Jesus with a text in literary Chinese, demonstrating Ricci's commitment to adapting Christianity and European culture to the text-oriented Chinese cultural world.

Chinese elites welcomed European learning, but they did so on their own terms. The two first Jesuit missionaries to reach China, Michele Ruggieri (1543–1607) and Matteo Ricci (1552–1610), arrived in China in 1582 and 1583, respectively. As was the case with many Jesuits at this time, both were brilliantly educated not just in religious and theological matters but in Europe's evolving new science. At the time of their arrival, China was in the midst of debates over its solar calendar, which now was out of sync with the seasons and causing difficulties coordinating ceremonial rites and rituals. Thus, Chinese officials were eager to employ Jesuit knowledge of mathematics and astronomy—based on Copernican and Galilean heliocentrism—to assist them in bringing ceremonial dates and political and economic activities into a better relationship with the seasons.

For their part, the Jesuits participated in Confucian ceremonies, hoping to win favor with the emperor and arguing that the rites were compatible with Catholicism. But, to the Jesuits' great disappointment, the Chinese did not accept their religious and theological tenets, and the men made only a very small number of converts. When Pope Clement XI issued a papal bull in 1715 condemning the missionaries' participation in the rites, the project of cultural exchange broke down. Offended, the Kangxi emperor, who had once been sympathetic to the Jesuits, banned Christian missionaries from practicing in China. His successor went even further, ordering the closing of all churches and the expulsion of Jesuits from China. Thus, starting in the mid-eighteenth century, the European window on China and the Chinese window on Europe were closed. China turned away from European contact, most notably Europe's new science that had once intrigued Chinese ruling classes.

Creating Hybrid Cultures in the Americas

As European empires expanded in the Americas, mingling between colonizers and native peoples, as well as African slaves, produced hybrid cultures. But the mixing of cultures grew increasingly unbalanced as Europeans imposed authority over more of the Americas. In addition to guns and germs, many European colonizers brought Bibles, prayer books, and crucifixes. With these, they set out to Christianize and "civilize" Amerindian and African populations in the Americas. Yet missionary efforts produced uneven and often unpredictable outcomes. Even as Amerindians and African slaves adopted Christian beliefs and practices, they often retained older religious practices too.

Core Objectives

DESCRIBE how hybrid cultures emerged in the Americas, and EXPLAIN the connection between these cultures and Enlightenment ideology.

European colonists likewise borrowed from the peoples they subjugated and enslaved. This was especially true in the sixteenth and seventeenth centuries, when the colonists' survival in the New World often depended on adapting. New sorts of hierarchies emerged, and elites in Latin America and North America increasingly followed the tastes and fashions of European aristocrats. Yet, even as they imitated Old World ways, these colonials forged identities that separated them from Europe.

SPIRITUAL ENCOUNTERS

Although the Jesuits had little impact in China and the Islamic world, Christian missionaries in the Americas had armies and officials to back up their insistence that Native Americans and African slaves abandon their own deities and spirits for Christ. Nonetheless, their attempts to force conversions were rarely a complete success, and some European settlers became interested in Amerindian culture.

European missionaries, especially Catholics, used numerous techniques to bring Amerindians within the Christian fold. They smashed idols, razed temples, and whipped backsliders. Catholic orders (principally Dominicans, Jesuits, and Franciscans) also learned what they could about Indian beliefs and rituals—and then exploited that knowledge to make converts to Christianity. For example, many missionaries found it useful to demonize local gods, subvert indigenous spiritual leaders, and transform Indian iconography into Christian symbols.

Neither gentle persuasion nor violent coercion produced the results that missionaries desired. When conversions did occur, the Christian practices that resulted were usually syncretic: mixed forms in which indigenous deities and rituals merged with Christian ones. Those who did convert saw Christian spiritual power as an addition to, not a replacement for, their own religions.

Europeans also attempted to Christianize slaves from Africa, though many slave owners doubted the wisdom of converting persons they regarded as mere property. Sent forth with the pope's blessing, Catholic priests targeted slave populations in the American colonies of Portugal, Spain, and France. Applying many of the same techniques that missionaries used with Indian "heathens," these priests produced similarly mixed results.

More distressing to missionaries than the blending of beliefs or outright defiance were the Amerindians' successes in assimilating captured colonists. It deeply troubled the missionaries that quite a few captured colonists adjusted to their situation, accepted adoptions into local societies, and refused to return to colonial society when given the chance. Moreover, some Europeans voluntarily chose to live among the Amerindians. Comparing the records of cultural conversion, one eighteenth-century colonist suggested that "thousands of Europeans are Indians," yet "we have no examples of even one of those Aborigines having from choice become European." (Aborigines are original, native inhabitants of a region, as opposed to invaders, colonizers, or later peoples of mixed ancestry.) While this calculation was no doubt exaggerated, it shows that despite the missionaries' intentions, cultural exchange went in more than one direction.

INTERMARRIAGE AND CULTURAL MIXING

In the early stages of colonization, Europeans mixed with Amerindians in part because there were many more men than women among the colonists. Almost all the early European traders, missionaries, and settlers were men (although the British North American settlements saw more women arrive relatively early on). In response to the scarcity of women and as a way to help Amerindians accept the newcomers' culture, the Portuguese crown authorized intermarriage between Portuguese men and local women. These

Racial Mixing (*Left*) This *casta* painting shows racial mixing in colonial Mexico—the father is a Spaniard, the mother an Amerindian, and the child a mestizo. (Like the word *caste*, *casta* refers to a group within a social hierarchy, in this case defined by race and racial mixing.) The image indicates that Indians who married whites achieved elevated status. (*Right*) Here, too, we see a racially mixed family. The father is a Spaniard, the mother is an African, and the child is what was then called a mulatto (a term for a person of mixed white and black ancestry that is considered offensive today). Observe, however, the less aristocratic and markedly less peaceful nature of this family.

relations often amounted to little more than rape, but longer-lasting relationships developed in places where Amerindians kept their independence—as among French fur traders and Amerindian women in Canada, the Great Lakes region, and the Mississippi Valley. Whether by coercion or consent, sexual relations between European men and Amerindian women resulted in offspring of mixed ancestry. In fact, the mestizos of Spanish colonies and the *métis* of French outposts soon outnumbered settlers of wholly European descent.

The increasing numbers of African slaves in the Americas complicated the mix of New World cultures even further. Unlike marriages between fur traders and Indian women, in which the women held considerable power because of their connections to Indian trading partners, sexual intercourse between European men and enslaved African women was almost always forced. Children born from such unions swelled the ranks of mixed-ancestry people in the colonial population, contributing to the new cultural mix that was emerging.

FORMING AMERICAN IDENTITIES

Over time, as European colonies in the Americas became more securely established, the colonists developed a sense of their own distinctive "American" identities. The colonization of the Americas brought Europeans, Africans, and Indians into sustained contact, though the nature of the colonies and the character of the contact varied considerably. Where European dominance was most secure, colonists imposed their ways on subjugated populations and

creoles

Persons of mixed European and African (or other) descent who were born in the Americas.

peninsulares

Spaniards who, although born in Spain, resided in the Spanish colonial territories. They regarded themselves as superior to Spaniards born in the colonies (creoles).

imported what they took to be the chief cultural and institutional attributes of the countries they had left behind. Yet Europeans were not immune to cultural influences from the groups they dispossessed and enslaved.

The Creole Identity In Spanish America, ethnic and cultural mixing produced a powerful new class, the **creoles**—people born in the Americas. By the late eighteenth century, creoles increasingly resented the control that **peninsulares**—men and women born in Spain or Portugal but living in the Americas—had over colonial society. Creoles especially resented the exclusive privileges given to peninsular rulers, like those that forbade creoles from trading with other colonial ports. Also, they disliked the fact that royal ministers gave most official posts to peninsulares.

In many cities of the Spanish and Portuguese empires, reading clubs and salons hosted energetic discussions of fresh Enlightenment ideas and contributed to the growing creole identity. The Spanish crown, recognizing the role of printing presses in spreading troublesome ideas, strictly controlled the number and location of printers in the colonies. In Brazil, royal authorities banned them altogether. Nonetheless, books, pamphlets, and simple gossip allowed new notions of science, history, and politics to circulate among literate creoles.

Anglicization In one important sense, wealthy colonists in British America were similar to the creole elites in Spanish and Portuguese America: they, too, copied European ways. For example, they constructed "big houses" (in Virginia and elsewhere—especially the Caribbean) modeled on the country estates of English gentlemen and imported opulent furnishings and fashions from the finest British stores. Imitating the British also involved tightening patriarchal authority. In seventeenth-century Virginia, men had vastly outnumbered women, which gave women some power (widows in particular gained greater control over property and more choices when they remarried). During the eighteenth century, however, sex ratios became more equal, and women's property rights diminished as British customs took precedence.

Intellectually, too, British Americans were linked to Europe. Importing enormous numbers of books and journals, these Americans played a significant role in the Enlightenment as producers and consumers of political pamphlets, scientific treatises, and social critiques. Indeed, drawing on the words of numerous Enlightenment thinkers, American intellectuals created the most famous of enlightened documents: the Declaration of Independence. It announced that all men were endowed with equal rights and were created to pursue worldly happiness. In this way, Anglicized Americans showed themselves, like the creole elites of Latin America, to be products of both European and New World cultures.

The Influence of European Culture in Oceania

In the South Pacific, as in the Americas, European influence had powerful consequences in the eighteenth century. Although in centuries past Hindu, Buddhist, and Islamic missionaries and Chinese traders had traveled to Malaysia and nearby islands, they had not ventured beyond Timor. (See Map 14.1.) Europeans began to do so in the years after 1770, turning their sights on **Oceania** (Australia, New Zealand, and the islands of the southwest Pacific). Using their new wealth to fund voyages with scientific and political objectives, Europeans invaded these remaining unexplored areas. The results were mixed: while some islands maintained their autonomy, the biggest prize, Australia, underwent thorough Anglicization.

Until Europeans colonized it in the late eighteenth century, Australia was, like the Americas before Columbus, truly a world apart. Separated by water and sheer distance from other regions, Australia's main features were harsh natural conditions and a sparse population. At the time of the European colonization, the island was home to around 300,000 people, mostly hunters and gatherers. Now the intrusion into Oceania presented Europeans with a previously unknown region that could serve as a laboratory for studying other peoples and geographical settings.

THE SCIENTIFIC VOYAGES OF CAPTAIN COOK

In Oceania and across the South Pacific, Europeans experimented with a scientific form of imperialism. The story of the region's most famous explorer, Captain James Cook (1728–1779), shows how closely related science and imperialist ventures could be. Cook's voyages and his encounter with the South Sea Islanders opened up the Pacific, particularly Australia, to European colonizers.

Captain Cook has become a legendary figure in European cultural history, portrayed as one of the saintly scientists of enlightened progress. His first voyage had two objectives. The Royal Society charged him with the scholarly task of observing the movement of the planet Venus from the Southern Hemisphere, and the British government assigned him the secret mission of finding and claiming "the southern continent" for Britain. Cook set sail in 1768, and his voyage was so fruitful that he subsequently undertook two more scientific-imperial adventures.

Cook was chosen to head the first expedition because of his scientific interests and skills. Besides Cook, the Royal Society sent along one of its members who was a botanist; a doctor and student of the renowned Swedish naturalist Carolus Linnaeus; and numerous artists and other scientists. The crew

The Global View

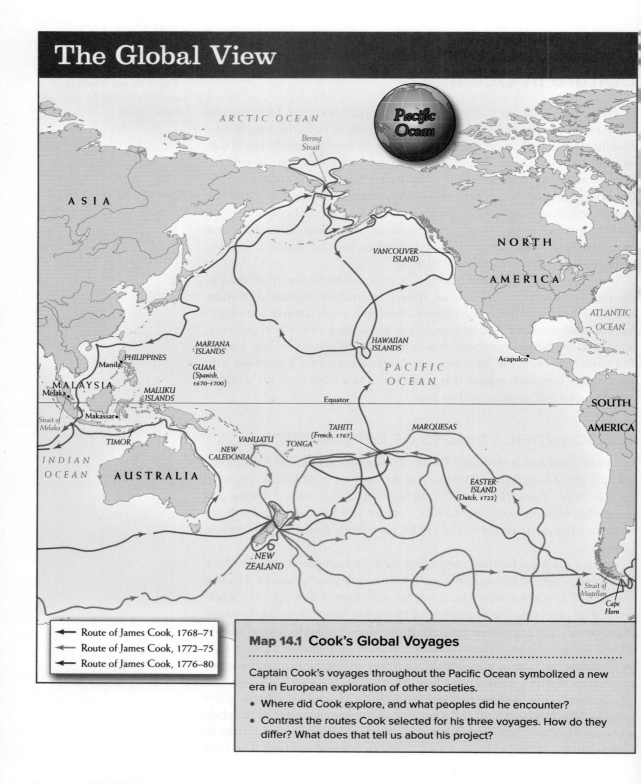

Route of James Cook, 1768–71

Route of James Cook, 1772–75

Route of James Cook, 1776–80

Map 14.1 Cook's Global Voyages

Captain Cook's voyages throughout the Pacific Ocean symbolized a new era in European exploration of other societies.

• Where did Cook explore, and what peoples did he encounter?

• Contrast the routes Cook selected for his three voyages. How do they differ? What does that tell us about his project?

The Voyages of Captain James Cook (*Left*) During his celebrated voyages to the South Pacific, Cook kept meticulous maps and diaries. Although he had little formal education, he became one of the great exemplars of enlightened learning through experience and experiment. (*Right*) Kangaroos were unknown in the west until Cook and his colleagues encountered (and ate) them on their first visit to Australia. This engraving of the animal (which unlike most animals, plants, and geographical features, actually kept the name the Aborigines had given it) from Cook's 1773 travelogue, *A Voyage Round the World in the Years 1768–1771*, lovingly depicts the kangaroo's environs and even emotions.

also carried sophisticated instruments and had instructions to keep detailed diaries. This was to be a grand data-collecting journey. Cook's voyages surpassed even the Royal Society's hopes. The scientists made approximately 3,000 drawings of Pacific plants, birds, landscapes, and peoples never seen in Europe.

ECOLOGICAL AND CULTURAL EFFECTS

More than science was at stake, however, for Australia was intended to supply Britain with raw materials. As in the Americas, extracting those materials required a labor force, and the Aborigines of Australia, like the Indians of the Americas, perished in great numbers from imported diseases. Those who survived generally fled to escape control by British masters. Thus, to secure a labor force, plans arose for grand-scale conquest and resettlement by British colonists. On his third voyage, Cook took along a wide array of animals and plants with which to turn the South Pacific into a European-style garden, with massive ecological consequences. His lieutenant later brought apples, quinces, strawberries, and rosemary to Australia; the seventy sheep imported in 1788 laid the foundations for the region's wool-growing economy. In fact, the domestication of Australia arose from the Europeans' certainty about their superior know-how and a desire to make the entire landmass serve British interests.

In 1788, a British military expedition took official possession of the eastern half of Australia. The intent was, in part, to establish a prison colony far from home. This plan belonged as well to the realm of "enlightened" dreams: removing people from an environment that did not suit them and sending them to new climes where they could be reformed, or, if they couldn't be, at least limiting problems back home. The intent was also to exploit Australia for its timber and flax and to use it as a strategic base against Dutch and French expansion. In the next decades, immigration—free and forced—increased the Anglo-Australian population from an original 1,000 to about 1.2 million by 1860. Importing their customs and their capital, British settlers turned Australia into a frontier version of home, just as they had done in British America. Yet, such large-scale immigration had disastrous consequences for the surviving Aborigines. Like the Native Americans, the original inhabitants of Australia were decimated by diseases and increasingly forced westward by European settlement. As in the Americas, European ideas and institutions proved to be far more influential and disruptive in Oceania than they were in the major land empires of Afro-Eurasia.

Conclusion

New wealth produced by commerce and state building created the conditions for a global cultural renaissance in the sixteenth, seventeenth, and eighteenth centuries. It began in the Chinese and Islamic empires and then stretched into Europe, Africa, and previous worlds apart in the Americas and Oceania. Experiments in religious toleration encouraged cultural exchange; book production and consumption soared; grand new monuments took shape; luxury goods became available for wider enjoyment.

Although the Islamic and Chinese worlds confidently retained their own systems of knowing, believing, and representing, the Americas and Oceania increasingly faced European cultural pressures. Here, while hybrid practices became widespread by the late eighteenth century, European beliefs and habits took over as the standards for judging degrees of "civilization." African cultures largely escaped this influence, though their homelands felt the impact of European expansionism because of the slave trade.

From a commercial standpoint, the world was more integrated than ever before. But the exposure and cultural borrowing that global trade promoted did not obliterate established cultural traditions. The Chinese, for instance, still believed in the superiority of their traditional knowledge and customs. Muslim rulers, confident of the primacy of Islam, allowed others to form subordinate cultural communities within their realm and adopted the Europeans' knowledge only when it served their own imperial purposes.

Only the Europeans were constructing knowledge that they believed was both universal and objective, enabling mortals to master the world of nature and all its inhabitants. This view would prove consequential, as well as controversial, in the centuries to come.

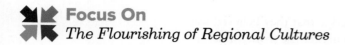

Focus On
The Flourishing of Regional Cultures

The Islamic World
- The Ottomans' unique cultural synthesis accommodates not only mystical Sufis and ultraorthodox *ulama* but also military men, administrators, and clerics.
- The Safavid state proclaims the triumph of Shiism and Persian influences in the sumptuous new capital, Isfahan.
- Mughal courtly culture values art and learning and, at its high point, welcomes non-Muslim contributions.

East Asia
- China's cultural flourishing, coming from within, is evident in the broad circulation of traditional ideas, publishing, and mapmaking.
- Japan's imperial court at Kyoto develops an elite culture of theater, stylized painting, tea ceremonies, and flower arranging.

Europe
- Cultural flourishing known as the Enlightenment yields a faith in reason and a belief in humans' ability to fathom the laws of nature and human behavior.
- European thinkers articulate a belief in unending human progress.
- Europeans expand into Australia and the South Pacific.

Africa
- Slave-trading states such as Asante, Oyo, and Benin celebrate royal power and wealth through art.

The Americas
- Even as Euro-Americans participate in the Enlightenment, their culture reflects Native American and African influences.

CHRONOLOGY

	1500	1550	1600
The Islamic World		Shah Abbas I builds Isfahan 1598–1629	
Africa			
Europe			
East Asia			
The Americas			

THINKING ABOUT GLOBAL CONNECTIONS

- **Thinking about Exchange Networks and Cultural Change** How did increased exchanges of goods and ideas change established traditions? What institutions and ideas proved most hospitable to foreign influence, even in established cultures, and why? Which fields proved more resistant to outside ideas? Why were some regions more receptive to foreign influences than others were? Consider religion, natural science, and art.

- **Thinking about Changing Power Relationships and Cultural Change** How did established cultures respond to the inclusion of the Americas in an increasingly integrated world? Which cultures flourished, and why? What relationship(s) can you see between new wealth and cultural change?

- **Thinking about Environmental Impacts and Cultural Change** The isolation of the Americas and Oceania paved the way for ecological catastrophe when Europeans arrived. How, in turn, did ecological catastrophes leave indigenous cultures vulnerable? Consider the nature of religious change in the Americas and the Afro-Eurasian core regions and population movements in Australia.

Key Terms

creoles p. 674

Enlightenment p. 662

Forbidden City of
  Beijing p. 656

great plaza at Isfahan p. 657

Oceania p. 675

Palace of Versailles p. 656

peninsulares p. 674

philosophes p. 664

scientific method p. 663

Taj Mahal p. 652

 Go to INQUIZITIVE to see what you've learned—and learn what you've missed—with personalized feedback along the way.

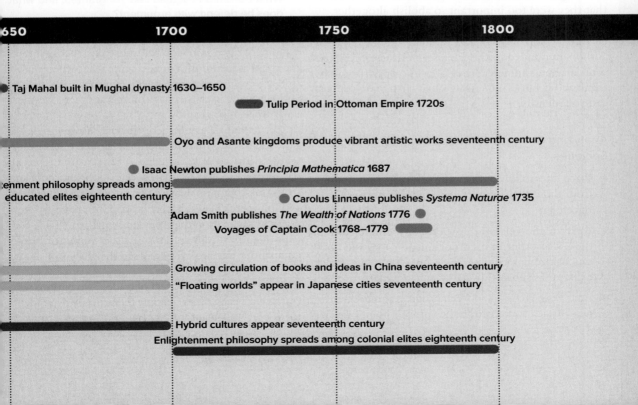

| 650 | 1700 | 1750 | 1800 |

Taj Mahal built in Mughal dynasty 1630–1650

Tulip Period in Ottoman Empire 1720s

Oyo and Asante kingdoms produce vibrant artistic works seventeenth century

Isaac Newton publishes *Principia Mathematica* 1687

Enlightenment philosophy spreads among educated elites eighteenth century

Carolus Linnaeus publishes *Systema Naturae* 1735

Adam Smith publishes *The Wealth of Nations* 1776

Voyages of Captain Cook 1768–1779

Growing circulation of books and ideas in China seventeenth century

"Floating worlds" appear in Japanese cities seventeenth century

Hybrid cultures appear seventeenth century

Enlightenment philosophy spreads among colonial elites eighteenth century

Global Themes and Sources

Comparing Changes to Global Commerce and Society

Commerce spread around the globe as never before in the centuries after 1500. Although business practices differed in different settings, the same questions confronted merchants, men of letters, and political leaders everywhere trade flourished: Was trade natural—consistent with the right order of things—or unnatural? Did it bring out the best or worst in people? Did the arrival of new wealth and goods support or undermine established cultures and social elites?

Commerce was a central issue in the European Enlightenment; the first three documents all present trade as central to modern European culture. The fourth, by a Japanese merchant named Shimai Soshitsu, instructed future generations on how to keep business interests from compromising their values. The final selection, drawn from edicts issued by the Chinese Qianlong Emperor, shows both fear about the dangers business interests posed and a recognition that they were too important to abolish altogether.

To make sense of these documents, you will need to think comparatively and evaluate how a range of authors responded to the same set of issues. Given the centrality of commerce, they offer the opportunity to think about cause and effect. What change or changes can you identify?

Analyzing Changes to Global Commerce and Societies

- Place the following documents on a continuum from those that supported commerce to those that rejected it.

- Analyze the relationship between commerce and the social order in each document. Does the document present commerce as upholding the social order or as subverting it?

- Analyze the tension between progress and backwardness in each source, from the author's point of view.

PRIMARY SOURCE 14.1

"Doux Commerce" (1748), Charles de Secondat, Baron de Montesquieu

Charles de Secondat, Baron de Montesquieu (1689–1755) was a magistrate in the *parlement* (law court) of Bordeaux and a man of letters, one of the most influential figures in the French Enlightenment. The French term *doux commerce* refers to the gentle, taming, civilizing force of commerce.

- **Explain the relationship between commerce and "barbarous behavior."**
- **Which values does trade promote, in Montesquieu's view, and which does it stifle?**
- **Identify the central assumption at work in this text. What does Montesquieu take for granted, and what does he defend with argument?**

Commerce is a cure for the most destructive prejudices; for it is almost a general rule, that wherever we find agreeable manners, there commerce flourishes; and that wherever there is commerce, there we meet with agreeable manners.

Let us not be astonished, then, if our manners are now less savage than formerly. Commerce has everywhere diffused a knowledge of the manners of all nations: these are compared one with another, and from this comparison arise the greatest advantages.

Commercial laws, it may be said, improve manners for the same reason that they destroy them. They corrupt the purest morals. This was the subject of Plato's complaints; and we every day see that they polish and refine the most barbarous.

Peace is the natural effect of trade. Two nations who traffic with each other become reciprocally dependent; for if one has an interest in buying, the other has an interest in selling; and thus their union is founded on their mutual necessities.

But if the spirit of commerce unites nations, it does not in the same manner unite individuals. We see that in countries [Holland] where the people move only by the spirit of commerce, they make a traffic of all the humane, all the moral virtues; the most trifling things, those which humanity would demand, are there done, or there given, only for money.

The spirit of trade produces in the mind of a man a certain sense of exact justice, opposite, on the one hand, to robbery, and on the other to those moral virtues which forbid our always adhering rigidly to the rules of private interest, and suffer us to neglect this for the advantage of others.

The total privation of trade, on the contrary, produces robbery, which Aristotle ranks in the number of means of acquiring; yet it is not at all inconsistent with certain moral virtues. Hospitality, for instance, is most rare in trading countries, while it is found in the most admirable perfection among nations of vagabonds.

Source: Charles de Secondat, Baron de Montesquieu, *The Spirit of the Laws* (Cambridge, England: Cambridge University Press, 1989), pp. 338–39.

PRIMARY SOURCE 14.2

"The Propensity to Truck, Barter, and Exchange" (1776), Adam Smith

Adam Smith (1723–1790) was a Scottish moral philosopher and leading figure of the Scottish Enlightenment whose 1776 book, *The Wealth of Nations*, was a pioneering work of political economy.

- According to Smith, where does the division of labor come from?
- What challenges stand in the way of economic growth, in Smith's view?
- What do you think Smith would say about economic inequality?

The division of labour, from which so many advantages are derived, is not originally the effect of any human wisdom, which foresees and intends that general opulence to which it gives occasion. It is the necessary, though very slow and gradual consequence of a certain propensity in human nature which has in view no such extensive utility; the propensity to truck, barter, and exchange one thing for another.

Whether this propensity be one of those original principles in human nature of which no further account can be given; or whether, as seems more probable, it be the necessary consequence of the faculties of reason and speech, it belongs not to our present subject to inquire. It is common to all men, and to be found in no other race of animals, which seem to know neither this nor any other species of contracts. Two greyhounds, in running down the same hare, have sometimes the appearance of acting in some sort of concert. Each turns her [the hare being hunted] towards his companion, or endeavours to intercept her when his companion turns her towards himself. This, however, is not the effect of any contract, but of the accidental concurrence of their passions in the same object at that particular time.

***

As it is by treaty, by barter, and by purchase that we obtain from one another the greater part of those mutual good offices which we stand in need of, so it is this same trucking disposition which originally gives occasion to the division of labour. In a tribe of hunters or shepherds a particular person makes bows and arrows, for example, with more readiness and dexterity than any other. He frequently exchanges them for cattle or for venison with his companions; and he finds at last that he can in this manner get more cattle and venison than if he himself went to the field to catch them. From a regard to his own interest, therefore, the making of bows and arrows grows to be his chief business, and he becomes a sort of armourer. Another excels in making the frames and covers of their little huts or movable houses. He is accustomed to be of use in this way to his neighbours, who reward him in the same manner with cattle and with venison, till at last he finds it his interest to dedicate himself entirely to this employment, and to become a sort of house-carpenter. In the same manner a third becomes a smith or a brazier, a fourth a tanner or dresser of hides or skins, the principal part of the clothing of savages. And thus the certainty of being able to exchange all that surplus part of the produce of his own labour, which is over and above his own consumption, for such parts of the produce of other men's labour as he may have occasion for, encourages every man to apply himself to a particular occupation, and to cultivate and bring to perfection whatever talent or genius he may possess for that particular species of business.

The difference of natural talents in different men is, in reality, much less than we are aware of; and the very different genius which appears to distinguish men of different professions, when grown up to maturity, is not upon many occasions so much the cause as the effect of the division of labour. The difference between the most dissimilar characters, between a philosopher and a common street porter, for example, seems to arise not so much from nature as from habit, custom, and education. When they came into the world, and for the first six or eight years of their existence, they were, perhaps, very much alike, and neither their parents nor playfellows could perceive any remarkable difference. About that age, or soon after, they come to be employed in very different occupations. The difference of talents comes then to be taken notice of, and widens by degrees, till at last the vanity of the philosopher is willing to acknowledge scarce any resemblance. But without the disposition to truck, barter, and exchange, every man must have procured to himself every necessary and conveniency of life which he wanted. All must have had the same duties to perform, and the same work to do, and there could have been no such difference of employment as could alone give occasion to any great difference of talents.

As it is this disposition which forms that difference of talents, so remarkable among men of different professions, so it is this same disposition which renders that difference useful. Many tribes of animals acknowledged to be all of the same species derive from nature a much more remarkable distinction of genius, than what, antecedent to custom and education, appears to take place among men. By nature a philosopher is not in genius and disposition half so different from a street porter, as a mastiff is from a greyhound, or a greyhound from a spaniel, or this last from a shepherd's dog. Those different tribes of animals, however, though all of the same species, are of scarce any use to one another. The strength of the mastiff is not, in the least, supported either by the swiftness of the greyhound, or by the sagacity of the spaniel, or by the docility of the shepherd's dog. The effects of those different geniuses and talents, for want of the power or disposition to barter and exchange, cannot be brought into a common stock, and do not in the least contribute to the better accommodation and conveniency of the species. Each animal is still obliged to support and defend itself, separately and independently, and derives no sort of advantage from that variety of talents with which nature has distinguished its fellows. Among men, on the contrary, the most dissimilar geniuses are of use to one another; the different produces of their respective talents, by the general disposition to truck, barter, and exchange, being brought, as it were, into a common stock, where every man may purchase whatever part of the produce of other men's talents he has occasion for.

Source: Adam Smith, *An Inquiry into the Nature and Causes of the Wealth of Nations* (London: Methuen, 1904), pp. 15, 17–18.

PRIMARY SOURCE 14.3

On Inequality (1755), Jean-Jacques Rousseau

Jean-Jacques Rousseau (1712–1778) was a political philosopher from Geneva with deep connections to the Enlightenment in France and across Europe. In the nineteenth century, his work particularly influenced Karl Marx and Sigmund Freud, among many others.

- Analyze the role of private property in this text.
- What role does competition play? Does Rousseau see competition as essential for innovation or as a problem?
- What does Rousseau mean when he says, "To be and to appear became two entirely different things"?

The first man who, having enclosed a piece of ground, thought to say *this is mine*, and found people sufficiently simple to believe him, was the true founder of civil society. How many crimes, wars, murders, how many miseries and horrors Mankind would have been spared by him who, pulling up the stakes or filling in the ditch, had cried out to his kind: Beware of listening to this impostor; You are lost if you forget that the fruits are everyone's and the Earth no one's: But in all likelihood things had by then reached a point where they could not continue as they were; for this idea of property, depending as it does on many prior ideas which could only arise successively, did not take shape all at once in man's mind: Much progress had to have been made, industry and enlightenment acquired, transmitted, and increased from one age to the next, before this last stage of the state of Nature was reached. Let us therefore take up the thread earlier, and try to fit this slow succession of events and of knowledge together from a single point of view, and in their most natural order.

***

Things having reached this point, it is easy to imagine the rest. I shall not pause to describe the successive invention of the other arts, the progress of languages, the testing and exercise of talents, the inequalities of fortune, the abuse of Wealth, nor all the details that attend them and which everyone can easily add. I shall limit myself to a brief glance at Mankind placed in this new order of things.

Here, then are all our faculties developed, memory and imagination brought into play, amour propre interested, reason become active, and the mind almost at the limit of the perfection of which it is capable. Here are all natural qualities set in action, every man's rank and fate set, not only as to the amount of their goods and the power to help or to hurt, but also as to mind, beauty, strength or skill, as to merit or talents, and, since these are the only qualities that could attract consideration, one soon had to have or to affect them; for one's own advantage one had to seem other than one in fact was. To be and to appear became two entirely different things, and from this distinction arose ostentatious display, deceitful cunning, and all the vices that follow in their wake. Looked at in another way, man, who had previously been free and independent, is now so to speak subjugated by a multitude of new needs to the whole of Nature, and especially to those of his kind, whose slave he in a sense becomes even by becoming their master; rich, he needs their services; poor, he needs their help, and moderate means do not enable him to do without them. He must therefore constantly try to interest them in his fate and to make them really or apparently find their own profit in working for his: which makes him knavish and artful with some, imperious and harsh with the rest, and places him under the necessity of deceiving all those he needs if he cannot get them to fear him and does not find it in his interest to make himself useful to them. Finally, consuming ambition, the ardent desire to raise one's relative fortune less out of genuine need than in order to place oneself above others, instills in all men a black inclination to harm one another, a secret jealousy that is all the more dangerous as it often assumes the mask of benevolence in order to strike its blow in greater safety: in a word, competition and rivalry on the one hand, conflict of interests on the other, and always the hidden desire to profit at another's expense; all these evils are the first effect of property, and the inseparable train of nascent inequality.

Before its representative signs were invented, wealth could scarcely consist in anything but land and livestock, the only real goods that men can possess. Now, once inheritances had increased in number and size to the point where they covered all the land and all adjoined one another, men could no longer aggrandize themselves except at one another's expense, and the supernumeraries whom weakness or indolence had kept from acquiring an inheritance of their own, grown poor without having lost anything because they alone had not changed while everything was changing around them, were obliged to receive or to seize their subsistence from the hands of the rich; and from this began to arise, according to the different characters of the poor and the rich, domination and servitude, or violence and plunder. The rich, for their part, had scarcely become acquainted with the pleasure of dominating than they disdained all other pleasures, and using their old Slaves to subject new ones, they thought only of subjugating and enslaving their neighbors; like those ravenous wolves which once they have tasted human flesh, scorn all other food, and from then on want to devour only men.

Source: Jean-Jacques Rousseau, Second Discourse, Part 2, in *Rousseau's Political Writings: Discourse on Inequality, Discourse on Political Economy, on Social Contract* (New York: Norton, 1988), pp. 34, 42–43.

Merchant Codes in Tokugawa Japan (1610)

Shimai Soshitsu (1539–1615) was a sake merchant in Hakata, Japan. In his testament, Shimai sets out a list of instructions, echoing military codes, to help subsequent generations remain virtuous while pursuing commerce.

- Identify the values expressed in this document.
- Analyze the merchant's relationship to money. What purpose do profits serve?
- Does commerce threaten the social order or support it, in Shimai's view?

1. Live an honest and sincere life. Respect your parents, your brothers, and your relatives, and try to live harmoniously with them all. Honor and treat with respect everyone you meet, even those you see only occasionally. Never behave discourteously or selfishly. Never lie. In fact, never say anything that even resembles a lie, even something you heard from someone else.

2. Although those who are elderly may reasonably pray about the life to come, you should ignore all such issues until you are fifty. You may follow only the Pure Land or Zen Buddhist faiths, and you must have absolutely nothing to do with the Christian religion. . . . Such a faith is an intolerable obstacle to anyone devoted to his house. Not one person in ten understands the things of this life or of the next. Birds and beasts worry only about what is immediately before them, and humans are no different. In this life they first should make certain that they do not sully their reputations. If even Buddha himself is said to have known nothing of the world to come, how can any ordinary mortal know such things? Until you reach fifty, therefore, do not worry about the future life. . . .

3. Dice, backgammon, and all other forms of gambling are strictly forbidden in this life. Even *go*, chess, the martial arts, the nō chants, and the nō dances are forbidden for people under forty. . . .

4. Until you are forty, avoid every luxury, and never act or think like one above your station in life. In matters of business and moneymaking, however, work harder than anyone else. . . . Always behave as one whose station in life is half that of yours. Although some people may suggest that you [should] be more visible and assertive, ignore all such advice and maintain a low profile. Until you turn fifty, be temperate in all things, and avoid all ostentation and finery, anything, in fact, that might call attention to yourself. Do not cultivate expensive tastes, for you should ignore such things as the tea ceremony, swords, daggers, and fine clothes. . . . Do not build a new house unless you are over fifty. Those who are that old may build what they like and can afford. Yet most people are poor by the time they die, for fewer than one in ten or twenty who build a fortune by their own talent carry it to their graves, and those who inherit their wealth are even more likely to lose it and die impoverished. Remember this.

5. Until you are forty, do not invite out others or let others invite you out. Once or twice a year you may invite out your parents, brothers, or relatives, or go out at their invitation, but—do not forget—even this you may do only occasionally. . . .

***

8. Never wander outside the shop or visit places where you have no business being. . . . Since you will generally be in the house, you yourself should tend the morning and evening cooking fires and handle the firewood and embers. You should pick up all trash inside and behind the house, chop up the pieces of rope and short bits of trash to use in plaster, and use the long pieces to make rope. Collect and clean pieces of wood and bamboo longer than five *bu* and use them as firewood. Save all paper scraps, even pieces only three or five *bu* long, to use in making fresh paper. Do as I have done, and waste absolutely nothing.

9. When you need something, go and buy it yourself, regardless of whether it is firewood, two or three *bu* of small fish or sardines, other purchases from the seaside or the town, or even timber. Bargain for the items and pay as little as you can. . . .

10. In general, use few servants, especially few female ones. . . .

11. Keep a steady supply of coarse *miso* on hand for your servants, and when you make the *miso* soup in the mornings and evenings, carefully filter the *miso*. You should add to the residue salt and cucumbers, eggplants, gourd melons, and onions, and serve this as a side dish to the servants. You can give them the stalks as well, and when rice is expensive, you may feed them some sort of hodgepodge. But if you do give your servants such a dish, you and your wife should eat it as well. Even if you intend to eat rice, first sip at least a bit of the hodgepodge, for your servants will resent it if you do not. . . .

***

13. Those with even a small fortune must remember that their duty in life is to devote themselves to their house and its business. They must not become careless, for if they buy what they want, do as they please, and, in general, live sumptuously, they will soon spend that fortune. . . . Although a samurai can draw on the produce of his tenured lands to earn his livelihood, a merchant must rely on the profit from his business, for without that profit, the money in his bags would soon disappear. No matter how much profit he makes and packs into his bags, however, if he continually wastes that money, he may as well pack it into bags full of holes. Remember this.

14. Rise early in the morning, and go to bed as soon as the sun sets, for you will waste oil if you burn lamps during evenings when you have nothing important to do. . . .

***

17. Live in harmony with your wife, for the two of you must work together diligently. Both of you should live modestly and carefully and consider always the good of the house and its business. A contentious, unhappy marriage destroys a house, for it distracts the husband and wife from their work. . . .

These seventeen articles were written not for Sōshitsu's sake but for yours. They are his testament, and you should follow them closely. They should be as important to you as the Great Constitution of Prince Shōtoku. Read them every day, or even twice a day, and be careful to forget nothing. Write a vow on the back of a votive tablet promising never to violate any of the articles and put it in my coffin when I die.

Source: Wm. Theodore de Bary, Carol Gluck, and Arthur E. Tiedemann (eds.), *Sources of Japanese Tradition*, vol. 2, *1600 to 2000*, 2nd ed. (New York: Columbia University Press, 2001), pp. 268–71.

An Edict on Trade (1793), the Qianlong Emperor

The Qianlong Emperor (1711–1799) was the sixth emperor of the Manchu-led Qing dynasty in China. In the late eighteenth century, the English East India Company sought to expand its trade with China. Here the Chinese governments seeks to regulate the activity of English merchants.

- **What was the Qianlong Emperor trying to accomplish?**
- **How does the Qianlong Emperor justify trading with foreign powers?**
- **From the emperor's point of view, what effect does trade have on the social order?**

You, O King, live beyond the confines of many seas, nevertheless, impelled by your humble desire to partake of the benefits of our civilization, you have dispatched a mission respectfully bearing your memorial. Your Envoy has crossed the seas and paid his respects at my Court on the anniversary of my birthday. To show your devotion, you have also sent offerings of your country's produce.

***

As to your entreaty to send one of your nationals to be accredited to my Celestial Court and to be in control of your country's trade with China, this request is contrary to all usage of my dynasty and cannot possibly be entertained.

***

You, O King from far, have yearned after the blessings of our civilization, and in your eagerness to come into touch with our converting influence have sent an Embassy across the sea bearing a memorial. I have already taken note of your respectful spirit of submission, have treated your mission with extreme favour and loaded it with gifts, besides issuing a mandate to you, O King, and honouring you with the bestowal of valuable presents. Thus has my indulgence been manifested.

. . . Hitherto, all European nations, including your own country's barbarian merchants, have carried on their trade with Our Celestial Empire at Canton. Such has been the procedure for many years, although Our Celestial Empire possesses all things in prolific abundance and lacks no product within its borders. There was therefore no need to import the manufactures of outside barbarians in exchange for our own produce. But as the tea, silk, and porcelain which the Celestial Empire produces are absolute necessities to European nations and to yourselves, we have permitted, as a signal mark of favour, that foreign hongs [trading firms licensed by the Chinese government] should be established at Canton, so that your wants might be supplied and your country thus participate in our beneficence. But your Ambassador has now put forward new requests which completely fail to recognize the Throne's principle to "treat strangers from afar with indulgence," and to exercise a pacifying control over barbarian tribes, the world over. . . .

Your Ambassador requests facilities for ships of your nation to call at Ningpo, Chusan, Tientsin and other places for purposes of trade. Until now trade with European nations has always been conducted at Macao, where the foreign hongs are established to store and sell foreign merchandise. Your nation has obediently complied with this regulation for years past without raising any objection. In none of the other ports named have hongs been established, so that even if your vessels were to proceed thither, they would have no means of disposing of their cargoes. Furthermore, no interpreters are available, so you would have no means of explaining your wants, and nothing but general inconvenience would result. For the future, as in the past, I decree that your request is refused and that the trade shall be limited to Macao.

Source: Gentzler J. Mason, *Changing China: Readings in the History of China from the Opium War to the Present* (New York: Praeger, 1977), pp. 23–28.

Interpreting Visual Evidence

Envisioning the World

Although maps give the impression of objectivity and geographic precision, the arrangement of names and locations, as well as the areas placed at the center and the margins, reveal the mapmakers' views of the world. In most cultures, official maps located their own major administrative and religious sites at the center of the universe and reflected local elites' ideas about how the world was organized.

There were, however, important differences. For example, Chinese maps, like the first two below, typically devoted more attention to textual explanations with moral and political messages than to locating places accurately. The Codex Xolotl presents a cartographic history, showing mountains and waterways and using hieroglyphic place-names for sites in the Valley of Mexico, marking historic conquests of an Aztec group, the Acolhuas of Texcoco. The Iranian

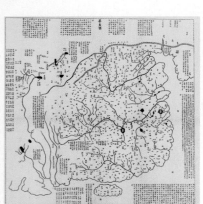

The *Huayi tu* map, 1136.

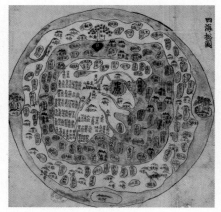

Chinese wheel map, 1760s.

Codex Xolotl, early sixteenth century.

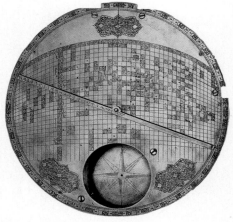

Iranian map, seventeenth century.

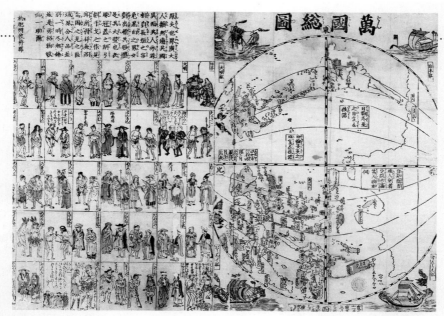

Japanese map of the world, 1761.

Waldseemüller map, 1507.

Mercator projection, 1569.

map presents an unabashedly Islamic vision, with a grid that measures the distances from any location in the Islamic world to Mecca. The Japanese map shows Dutch influence, with much information about distant lands both in the map and in the two-person images to the left. Finally, the European maps (the Waldseemüller map and the Mercator projection) appear objective at first glance, but they, too, group the rest of the world around their own territory, which they distort to make appear disproportionately large.

Questions for Analysis

1. Describe the organizing principles, and therefore priorities, of each map.

2. Compare the maps. How are they different from one another?

3. Evaluate the relative awareness each map shows of distant cultures and territories.

15

Reordering the World

1750–1850

In 1798, the French commander Napoleon Bonaparte invaded Egypt. At the time, Europeans regarded this territory as the cradle of a once-great culture, a land bridge to the Red Sea and trade with Asia, and an outpost of the Ottoman Empire. Occupying the country would allow Napoleon to introduce some of the principles of the French Revolution and to seize control of trade routes to Asia. Napoleon also hoped that by defeating the Ottomans, who controlled Egypt, he would augment his and France's historic greatness. But events did not go as Napoleon planned, for his troops faced a resentful Egyptian population. Although Napoleon soon returned to France and his dream of a French Egypt was short-lived, his invasion challenged Ottoman rule and threatened the balance of power in Europe. Indeed, Napoleon's actions in Africa, the Americas, and Europe, combined with the principles of the American and French Revolutions, laid the foundations for a new era—one based on a radically new understanding of freedom as the absence of constraint, the opposite of privileges handed down by a lord or master.

That new idea of freedom first rang out across western Europe and the Americas and reverberated around the world. It destroyed the American colonial domains of Spain, Portugal, Britain, and France; brought new nations to the stage; and challenged established elites everywhere, leading in some cases to the expansion of colonial

Core Objectives

- **DESCRIBE** the new ideas of freedom, and **EXPLAIN** how they differed from earlier understandings of this term.

- **COMPARE** political and economic developments in the Atlantic world with those of regions elsewhere around the globe during the period 1750–1850.

- **IDENTIFY** and **EXPLAIN** the key developments that constituted the industrial revolution.

- **EXPLAIN** patterns of global trade and economic growth, and **CONNECT** them to political changes during the period 1750–1850.

- **COMPARE** the groups of people who held power in each of the regions in 1750 and then in 1850, and **EXPLAIN** the changes that took place during this period in these societies.

rule. The impulse for change was a belief that governments should enact laws that apply to all people, though in practice there were significant exceptions (slaves, women, and colonized subjects). Free speech, free markets, free labor, and governments freely chosen by freeborn men, it was thought, would benefit everyone. In Europe and the Americas, though not elsewhere, the era also witnessed the emergence of the nation-state. This new form of political organization derived legitimacy from its inhabitants, often referred to as citizens, who, in theory, if not always in practice, shared a common culture, ethnicity, and language.

Yet freedom in some corners of the globe set the stage for depriving people of freedom elsewhere and led inexorably to changes in the worldwide balance of power. Even as western European countries lost their New World colonies, they gained economic and military strength, which further challenged Asian and African governments.

Global Storylines

- A new era based on radically new ideas of freedom and the nation-state emerges in the Atlantic world.
- The industrious and industrial revolutions transform communities and the global economy.
- The worldwide balance of power shifts decisively toward northwestern Europe.

Revolutionary Transformations and New Languages of Freedom

In the eighteenth century, the circulation of goods, people, and ideas created pressures for reform around the Atlantic world. As economies expanded, many people felt that the restrictive mercantilist system prevented them from sharing in the new wealth and power. Similarly, an increasingly literate public called for their states to adopt just practices, including the abolition of torture and the accountability of rulers. In several places, power holders could not stamp out these demands before they became full-scale revolutions.

Reformers wanted to expand the franchise, to enable property holders to vote. Claims of **popular sovereignty**, the idea that political power depends on "the people," became rooted in the idea of the nation: people who shared a common language, common culture, and common history. This in turn gave rise to the nation-state as a form of political organization. Over the course of the nineteenth century, political movements began to emphasize nationalism, the idea that a fully fledged nation should have a state of its own, and democracy, the idea that the people, the *demos*, should choose their own representatives and be governed by them (see Chapter 16). In this chapter, we concentrate on the first expressions of this new thinking, in thirteen of Britain's North American colonies and in France. In both places, the "nation" and the "people" toppled their former rulers.

This chapter also concentrates on far-reaching economic developments that came in tandem with revolutionary political change. Economic reformers argued that unregulated economies would produce faster economic growth. Going well beyond the work of Adam Smith, they called for **free trade** (or **laissez-faire**), unencumbered by tariffs, quotas, and fees; free markets, which would be unregulated; and free labor, which meant using paid rather than slave labor. They insisted that these economic freedoms would yield more just and more efficient societies, ultimately benefiting everyone, everywhere in the world.

Yet the same European and Euro-American elites who wanted a freer world often exploited slaves, denied women equal treatment, restricted colonial economies, and tried forcibly to open Asia's and Africa's markets to European trade and investment. In Africa, idealistic upheavals led not to free and sovereign peoples but to greater enslavement.

THE BIG PICTURE

Why did the worldwide balance of power shift during this period?

popular sovereignty
The idea that the power of the state resides in the people.

free trade (laissez-faire)
Domestic and international trade unencumbered by tariff barriers, quotas, and fees.

Core Objectives

DESCRIBE the new ideas of freedom, and **EXPLAIN** how they differed from earlier understandings of this term.

Political Reorderings

Late in the eighteenth century, revolutionary ideas spread across the Atlantic world (see Map 15.1) following the trail of Enlightenment ideas about

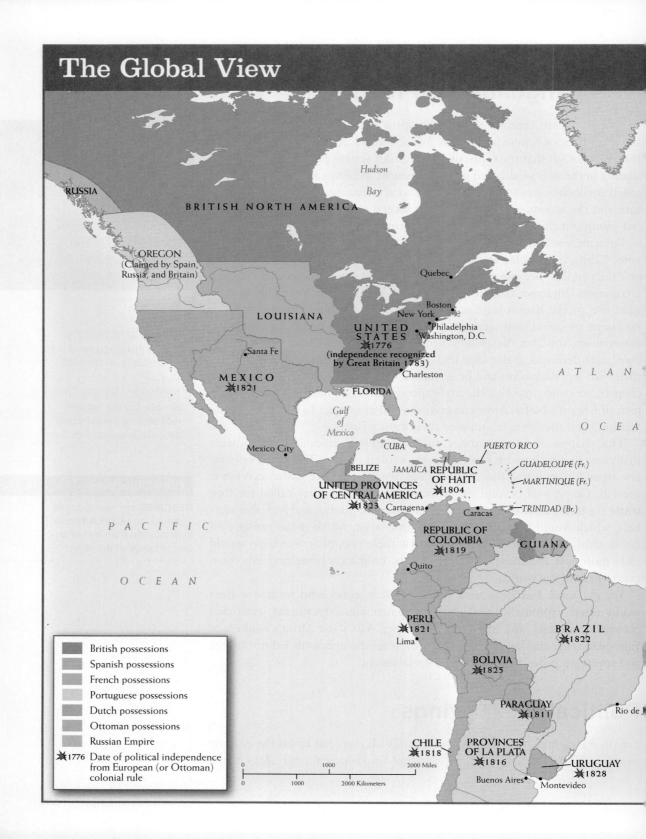

The Global View

RUSSIA

BRITISH NORTH AMERICA

Hudson
Bay

OREGON
(Claimed by Spain,
Russia, and Britain)

Quebec

LOUISIANA

Boston
New York
Philadelphia
Washington, D.C.

UNITED
STATES
✳1776
(independence recognized
by Great Britain 1783)

Santa Fe

Charleston

MEXICO
✳1821

FLORIDA

ATLAN

Gulf
of
Mexico

OCEA

Mexico City

CUBA

PUERTO RICO

BELIZE

JAMAICA

REPUBLIC
OF HAITI
✳1804

GUADELOUPE (Fr.)
MARTINIQUE (Fr.)

UNITED PROVINCES
OF CENTRAL AMERICA
✳1823   Cartagena

Caracas

TRINIDAD (Br.)

PACIFIC

REPUBLIC OF
COLOMBIA
✳1819

GUIANA

Quito

OCEAN

PERU
✳1821
Lima

BRAZIL
✳1822

BOLIVIA
✳1825

PARAGUAY
✳1811

Rio de J

	British possessions
	Spanish possessions
	French possessions
	Portuguese possessions
	Dutch possessions
	Ottoman possessions
	Russian Empire
✳1776	Date of political independence from European (or Ottoman) colonial rule

CHILE
✳1818

PROVINCES
OF LA PLATA
✳1816

URUGUAY
✳1828

Buenos Aires   Montevideo

0   1000   2000 Miles

0   1000   2000 Kilometers

SWEDEN-NORWAY

St. Petersburg

Moscow

RUSSIAN EMPIRE

DENMARK
NETHERLANDS
GREAT BRITAIN
London
Berlin
BELGIUM
GERMAN
STATES
AUSTRIAN
Paris
Vienna
EMPIRE
FRANCE

ITALIAN
Rome
STATES
GREECE
Athens
OTTOMAN
✳1829

PORTUGAL
Madrid
SPAIN
Lisbon

MEDITERRANEAN SEA

EMPIRE
Cairo
EGYPT
(occupied by
French troops
1798–1801)

AFRICA

INDIAN OCEAN

Map 15.1 Revolutions and Empires in the Atlantic World, 1776–1829

Influenced by Enlightenment thinkers and the French Revolution, colonies gained independence from European powers (and in the case of Greece, from the Ottoman Empire) in the late eighteenth and early nineteenth centuries.

- Which European powers granted independence to their colonial possessions in the Americas during this period?
- What were the first two colonial territories to become independent in the Americas?
- Based on the chronology presented in this map and on your reading, consider the relative importance of European influence and local developments in the Americas in accounting for the timing of independence in different countries. Why, in particular, did colonies in Spanish and Portuguese America obtain political independence decades after the United States won its independence?

freedom and reason. As more newspapers, pamphlets, and books circulated in European countries and American colonies, readers began to discuss their societies' problems and to believe they had the right to participate in governance.

The slogans of independence, freedom, liberty, and equality seemed to promise an end to oppression, hardship, and inequities. In the North American colonies and in France, revolutions ultimately brought down monarchies and blossomed into republics. The examples of the United States and France soon encouraged other people in the Caribbean and Central and South America to reject the rule of monarchs. In these revolutionary environments, new institutions—such as written constitutions and permanent parliaments—claimed to represent the people.

THE NORTH AMERICAN WAR OF INDEPENDENCE, 1776–1783

Core Objectives

COMPARE political and economic developments in the Atlantic world with those of regions elsewhere around the globe during the period 1750–1850.

The American Revolution ended British rule in North America. It was the first of a series of revolutions to shake the Atlantic world, inspired by new ideas of freedom.

By the mid-eighteenth century, Britain's colonies in North America swelled with people and prosperity. Bustling port cities like Charleston, Philadelphia, New York, and Boston saw inflows of African slaves, European migrants, and manufactured goods, while agricultural staples flowed out. A "genteel" class of merchants and landowning planters dominated colonial affairs.

Land was a constant source of dispute. Planters struggled with independent farmers (yeomen). Sons and daughters of farmers, often unable to inherit or acquire land near their parents, moved westward, where they came into conflict with Amerindian peoples. To defend their lands, many Amerindians allied with Britain's rival, France. After losing the Seven Years' War (see Chapter 13), however, France ceded its Canadian colony to Britain to secure the return of its much more lucrative Caribbean colonies, especially Saint-Domingue. This left many Indians no choice but to turn to the British government to help them resist the aggressive advances of land-hungry colonists. British officials did make some concessions to Indian interests, but they did not have the troops or financial strength to enforce them.

Asserting Independence from Britain Despite these tensions, Britain stood supreme in the Atlantic world in the mid-1760s, with its greatest foes defeated and its empire expanding. Political revolution in North America seemed unimaginable. And yet, a decade later, that is what occurred.

The spark came from the government of King George III, which insisted that colonists contribute to the crown that protected them, notably in the Seven Years' War (known in North America as the French and Indian War).

The king's officials imposed taxes on a variety of commodities and tried to put an end to smuggling by colonists who sought to evade mercantilist restrictions on trade. To the king's surprise and dismay, colonists objected to the new measures and protested having to pay taxes when they lacked political representation in the British Parliament.

In 1775, resistance in the form of petitions and boycotts turned into open warfare between a colonial militia and British troops in Massachusetts. Once blood was spilled, more radical voices came to the fore. Previously, leaders of the protest had claimed to revere the British Empire. Now calls for severing the ties to Britain became more prominent. Thomas Paine, a recent immigrant from England, captured the new mood in a pamphlet he published in 1776, arguing that it was "common sense" for people to govern themselves. Later that year, the Continental Congress (in which representatives from thirteen colonies gathered) adapted part of Paine's popular pamphlet for the Declaration of Independence.

The Boston Massacre Paul Revere's idealized view of the Boston Massacre of March 5, 1770. In the years after the Seven Years' War, Bostonians grew increasingly disenchanted with British efforts to enforce imperial regulations. When British troops fired on and killed several members of an angry mob in what came to be called the "Boston Massacre," the resulting frenzy stirred revolutionary sentiments among the populace.

Drawing on Enlightenment themes (see Chapter 14), the declaration written by Thomas Jefferson stated the people's "natural right" to govern themselves. It also drew inspiration from the writings of the British philosopher John Locke, notably the idea that governments should be based on a **social contract** in which the law binds both ruler and people. Locke had written nearly a century earlier that the people had the right to rebel against their government if it broke the contract and infringed on their rights. With the Declaration of Independence, the rebels announced their right to rid themselves of the English king and form their own government.

The Declaration's assertion that "all men are created equal" overturned former social hierarchies in the thirteen colonies (now calling themselves states). Thus, common men no longer automatically deferred to gentlemen of higher rank. Many women claimed that their contributions to the revolution's cause (by managing farms and shops in their husbands' absence) earned them greater equality in marriage, including property rights. However, the political arrangements Americans designed during their War of Independence gave voting rights only to white, male property owners—not women, not slaves, not Amerindians, not poor white men without property. Indeed, many slaves sided against the revolution, for it was the British who

social contract
The idea, drawn from the writings of British philosopher John Locke, that the law should bind both ruler and people.

offered them freedom most directly, in exchange for military service. Their hopes for freedom were thwarted when Britain conceded the loss of its rebellious American colonies. With the Treaty of Paris (1783), the United States gained its independence.

Building a Republican Government With independence, the former colonists had to build a new government. They generally agreed that theirs was not to be a monarchy. But what it *was* to be remained through the 1780s a source of much debate, involving heated words and sometimes heated action. As a loose confederation of relatively autonomous states, the new national state struggled to deal with local rebellions, foreign relations, and crushing levels of debt. To save the young nation from falling into "anarchy," propertied men convened the Constitutional Convention in Philadelphia in 1787.

This gathering aimed to forge a document that would create a more powerful national government and a more unified nation. After fierce debate, the convention drafted a charter for a republican government in which power would rest with representatives of the people—not with a king. When it went before the states for approval, the Constitution was controversial. Its critics, known as Anti-Federalists, feared the growth of a potentially tyrannical national government and insisted on including a Bill of Rights to protect individual liberties from abusive government intrusions. Ultimately the Constitution was ratified by the states and then amended by the Bill of Rights.

Ratification of the Constitution and the addition of the Bill of Rights did not end arguments about the scope and power of the national government of the United States. Some Americans called for the national government to abolish slavery. However, many others—especially leaders in the south, where slavery was a mainstay of the economy—argued that the national government did not have the power to do so. In an uneasy truce, political leaders agreed not to let the debate over whether to abolish slavery escalate into a cause for disunion. As the frontier pushed westward, however, the question of which new states would or would not allow slavery again posed a vexing challenge. Initially the existence of ample land postponed a confrontation. In 1800, Thomas Jefferson's election as the third president of the United States marked the triumph of a model of sending pioneers out to new lands in order to reduce conflict on old lands. In the same year, however, a Virginia slave named Gabriel Prosser raised an army of slaves to seize the state capital at Richmond and won support from white artisans and laborers for a more inclusive republic. His dream of an egalitarian revolution fell victim to white terror and black betrayal, though: twenty-seven slaves, including Prosser, went to the gallows. With them, for the moment, died the dream of a multiracial republic in which all men were truly created equal.

In the larger context of the Atlantic world, the successful defiance of Europe's most powerful empire and the establishment of a nonmonarchical, republican form of government sent shock waves through the Americas and Europe and even into distant corners of Asia and Africa. It also helped pave the way for other revolts over the next several decades.

THE FRENCH REVOLUTION, 1789–1799

Partly inspired by the American Revolution, French men and women soon began to call for liberty too—and the result profoundly shook Europe's dynasties and social hierarchies. Its impact, though, reached well beyond Europe, for the French Revolution, even more than the American, inspired rebels and terrified rulers around the globe.

Origins and Outbreak The French king himself opened the door to revolution. Eager to weaken his rival, England, Louis XVI spent huge sums in support of the American rebels—and thereby overloaded the state with debt. To restore his credit, Louis needed to raise taxes on the privileged classes; to do so, he was forced to convene the Estates-General, a medieval advisory body that had not met for over a century. Like the American colonists, French nobles argued that taxation gave them the right of representation.

When the delegates assembled in 1789, however, a procedural dispute spun out of control. The delegates of the clergy (the First Estate) and the aristocracy (the Second Estate) hoped to vote by estate and overrule the delegates representing everyone else (the Third Estate). But the Third Estate, which had more representatives than the first two estates combined, refused to be outvoted. It demanded that all delegates sit together in one chamber and vote as individuals. Soon delegates of the Third Estate declared themselves to be the "National Assembly," the body that should determine France's future.

Afraid that the king would crush the reform movement, a Parisian crowd attacked a medieval armory in search of weapons on July 14, 1789. Not only did this armory—the Bastille—hold gunpowder, but it was also an infamous prison for political prisoners. The crowd stormed the prison and murdered the commanding officer, then cut off his head and paraded it through the streets of Paris. On this day (Bastille Day), the king made the fateful decision not to call out the army, and the capital city belonged to the crowd. As news spread to the countryside, peasants torched manor houses and destroyed municipal archives containing records of feudal dues, payments they owed to landlords of specially designated properties. Barely three weeks later, the French National Assembly abolished the privileges of the nobility and the clergy. It declared a new era of liberty, equality, and fraternity. Liberty, like freedom, now meant the absence of constraint rather than a special privilege granted by the king.

The "Tennis Court Oath"
Locked out of the chambers of the Estates-General, the deputies of the Third Estate reconvened at a nearby indoor tennis court in June 1789; there they swore an oath not to disband until the king recognized the sovereignty of a national assembly.

Revolutionary Transformations The French Revolution connected the concept of a people more closely with a nation. The Declaration of the Rights of Man and of the Citizen (1789) echoed the Americans' Declaration of Independence, but in more radical terms. It guaranteed all citizens of the French nation inviolable liberties and gave all men equality under the law. It also proclaimed that "the principle of all sovereignty rests essentially in the nation." Both the rhetorical and the real war against old-regime privileges threatened to end dynastic and aristocratic rule in Europe.

Social relations changed too, as women felt that the new principles of citizenship should include women's rights. In 1791, a group of women demanded the right to bear arms to defend the revolution, but they stopped short of claiming equal rights for both sexes. In their view, women would become citizens by being good revolutionary wives and mothers, not because of any natural rights. In the same year, Olympe de Gouges composed the Declaration of the Rights of Woman and the Female Citizen, proposing rights to divorce, hold property in marriage, be educated, and have public careers. The all-male assembly did not take up these issues, believing that a "fraternity" of free *men* composed the nation.

As the revolution gained momentum, deep divisions emerged. In 1790, all clergy had to take an oath of loyalty to the new state—an action that bitterly divided the country. The most divisive, destructive turn in the revolution came in 1792, when the French declared a preemptive war against Austria, and then Prussia, Britain, and Russia. They soon had foreign armies on their soil and a civil war to contend with, when peasants outraged by the loyalty oath and city dwellers in major provincial cities rose up against the revolutionary government and its wartime demands.

The Terror In response to this self-induced crisis, elite reformers made common cause with urban radicals in Paris, who demanded price controls, direct democracy, and the violent suppression of dissent. Together, they launched the Reign of Terror. The Committee of Public Safety, including the lawyer Maximilien Robespierre, oversaw the execution of as many as 40,000 so-called enemies of the people—mostly peasants and laborers who had taken up arms against them—justified in terms of defending the Republic. If most victims were of modest means, the term *aristocrat* was often equated with treason. Even before terror was declared as government policy, Louis XVI and his wife, Marie Antoinette, had lost their heads to the guillotine (itself a novel and supposedly rational, enlightened way to execute prisoners painlessly).

By 1794 France's army numbered some 800,000 soldiers, making it the world's largest. Most French officers now came from the middle classes, some even from the lower class. Foot soldiers identified with the French fatherland. Having vowed to wage a defensive war, they now pushed foreign armies off French soil and waged a war to "liberate" the disenfranchised from their rulers across Europe.

When the military emergency ended, enthusiasm for Robespierre's measures lost popular support, and Robespierre himself went to the guillotine on 9 Thermidor (according to the new, revolutionary calendar, or July 28, 1794). His execution marked the end of the Terror but did not restore order. Several years later, following yet more political turmoil, a coup d'état brought to power a thirty-year-old general from the recently annexed Mediterranean island of Corsica.

The general, **Napoleon Bonaparte** (1769–1821), put security and order ahead of social reform. His regime retained significant revolutionary changes, especially those associated with more efficient state government. He eased religious tensions by working out an accord with the Vatican. However, Napoleon was determined not only to reform France but also to prevail over its enemies, and he retreated from republican principles. Taking the title Emperor of the French, he centralized government administration and established a system of rational tax collection. Most important, he created a civil legal code—the Napoleonic Code—that applied throughout all of France (and the French colonies).

THE NAPOLEONIC ERA, 1799–1815

Determined to extend the reach of French influence, Napoleon launched a series of military campaigns in an effort to build a vast empire. He had his armies trumpet the principles of liberty, equality, and fraternity wherever they went. Many local populations initially embraced the French, regarding them as liberators from the old order. Although Napoleon thought the entire world would take up his cause, this was not always the case.

Napoleon Bonaparte
(1769–1821) General who rose to power in a postrevolutionary coup d'état, eventually proclaiming himself emperor of France. He placed security and order ahead of social reform and created a civil legal code. Napoleon expanded his empire through military action, but after his disastrous Russian campaign, the united European powers defeated Napoleon and forced him into exile. He escaped and reassumed command of his army but was later defeated at the Battle of Waterloo.

In Portugal, Spain, and Russia, French troops faced fierce popular resistance. Portuguese and Spanish soldiers and peasants formed bands of resisters called guerrillas, and British troops joined them to fight the French in the Peninsular War (1808–1813). In Germany and Italy, as local inhabitants grew tired of paying tribute, many looked to their past for inspiration to oppose the French. Now they discovered something they had barely recognized before: *national* traditions and borders. One of the ironies of Napoleon's attempt to bring all of Europe under French rule was that it laid the foundations for nationalist strife.

In Europe, Napoleon extended his empire from the Iberian Peninsula to the Austrian and Prussian borders. (See Map 15.2.) By 1812, when he invaded Russia, however, his forces were too overstretched and undersupplied to survive the harsh winter. After his failed attack on Russia, all the major European powers united against him. At the Battle of Waterloo in Belgium in 1815, armies from Prussia, Austria, Russia, and Britain crushed his troops as they made their last stand. The stage was now set for a century-long struggle on the continent between those who wanted to restore society as it had been before the French Revolution and those who wanted to guarantee a more liberal order based on individual rights, limited government, and free trade.

REVOLUTION IN SAINT-DOMINGUE (HAITI)

France also saw colonies break away in this age of new freedoms, notably Saint-Domingue. Unlike most of British North America, revolution here came from the bottom rungs of the social ladder: slaves. In this Caribbean colony, freedom therefore meant not just liberation from Europe but emancipation from white planters. It posed a powerful question: How universal were these new rights?

At the outset of the French Revolution the island's black slave population numbered 500,000, compared with 40,000 white French settlers and about 30,000 free "people of color" (individuals of mixed black and white ancestry, as well as freed black slaves). Almost two-thirds of the slaves were relatively recent arrivals, brought to the colony to toil on its renowned sugar plantations, which were exceptional in their brutality. The slave population was an angry majority without local ties, producing wealth for rich absentee landlords of a different race.

The breakdown of authority in France unleashed conflict in Saint-Domingue, where local tensions were already high. White settlers sought self-government; they wanted to break free of the exclusive trade arrangement with France and to control the island themselves. Free blacks wanted to end racial discrimination among property holders without, initially, calling slavery into question. Slaves, by contrast, invoked revolutionary language

Map 15.2 Napoleon's Empire, 1812

Early in the first decade of the nineteenth century, Napoleon controlled almost all of Europe.

- What major states were under French control? What countries were allied to France?
- Compare this map with the European part of Map 15.1, and explain how Napoleon redrew the map of Europe. What major country was not under French control?
- According to your reading, how was Napoleon able to control and build alliances with so many states and kingdoms?

Revolution in Saint-Domingue In 1791, slaves took up arms against white planters. This engraving was based on a German report on the uprising and reflects white fears of slave rebellion as much as the actual events themselves.

to denounce their masters and air long-standing grievances. As civil war erupted, slaves fought French forces that had arrived to restore order. In 1793, the National Convention in France abolished slavery. In part, the motive was to declare the universality of liberty, equality, and fraternity within the French nation, which included colonies. In part, it was to restore order to the colony. Once liberated, the former slaves took control of the island. (See Current Trends in World History: Two Case Studies in Political Change and Environmental Degradation.)

The specter of a free country ruled by former slaves sent shudders across the Western Hemisphere, and above all in Britain and Spain, which had neighboring colonies. A version of martial law was declared in Venezuela. Thomas Jefferson, author of the Declaration of Independence and U.S. president at the time, refused to recognize Haiti. Like other American slave owners, he worried that the example of a successful slave uprising might inspire similar revolts in the United States and elsewhere in the Americas.

REVOLUTIONS IN SPANISH AND PORTUGUESE AMERICA

Revolutionary enthusiasm also spread through Spanish and Portuguese America. As in Haiti, subordinated people of color took advantage of the period's political instability; they mobilized European ideas against European colonizers and challenged the established order. (See Map 15.3.)

Even before the French Revolution, Andean Indians rebelled against Spanish colonial authority. In a major uprising in the 1780s, they demanded freedom from forced labor and compulsory consumption of Spanish wares. After an army of 40,000 to 60,000 Andean Indians besieged the ancient capital of Cuzco and nearly vanquished Spanish armies, it took Spanish forces many years to eliminate the insurgents.

After this uprising, Iberian American elites who feared their Indian or slave majorities renewed their loyalty to the Spanish or Portuguese crown. Ultimately, however, the French Revolution and Napoleonic wars shattered the ties between Spain and Portugal and their American colonies.

Brazil and Constitutional Monarchy Brazil was a prized Portuguese colony whose path to independence saw little political turmoil and no social revolution. In 1807, French troops stormed Lisbon, the capital of Portugal, but not before the royals and their associates fled to Rio de Janeiro, then the capital of Brazil. There they settled down, enacting reforms in administration, agriculture, and manufacturing and establishing schools, hospitals, and a library. Brazil now became the center of the Portuguese Empire. Furthermore, the royal family willingly shared power with the local planter aristocracy, so the economy prospered and slavery expanded.

When the king returned to Portugal in 1821, his son Pedro remained. Fearing an uprising among local elites, Pedro declared Brazil an independent state and established a constitutional monarchy. Local elites soon embraced Pedro's rule and cooperated to minimize conflict, lest a slave revolt erupt. By the 1840s, Brazil had achieved a political stability unmatched in the Americas.

Mexico's Independence When Napoleon occupied Spain, he sparked a crisis in the Spanish Empire that eventually led Mexico to secede. Because the ruling Spanish monarchy fell captive to Napoleon in 1807, colonial elites in Buenos Aires (Argentina), Caracas (Venezuela), and Mexico City (Mexico) found themselves without an emperor. After Napoleon's defeat, locally born creoles resented the fact that Spain reinstated *peninsulares* (people born in Spain) as colonial officials with the help of the royal army. Inspired by Enlightenment thinkers and chafing at the efforts to restore Iberian authority, the creoles wanted to keep their privileges and get rid of the peninsulares.

Mexico's creoles identified themselves more as Mexicans than as Spanish Americans, and as the Spanish king appeared less and less able to govern effectively, Mexican generals (with support of the creoles) proclaimed Mexican independence in 1821. Unlike the situation in Brazil, Mexican secession did not lead to stability.

Other South American Revolutions The loosening of Spain's grip on its colonies was more prolonged and militarized than Britain's separation from its American colonies. Venezuela's Simón Bolívar (1783–1830), the son of a merchant-planter family, who was educated on Enlightenment texts, dreamed of a land governed by reason. He revered Napoleonic France as a model state built on military heroism and constitutional proclamations. So did the Argentine leader General José de San Martín (1778–1850). Men like Bolívar, San Martín, and their many generals waged extended wars of independence against Spanish armies and their allies between 1810 and 1824.

What started in South America as a political revolution against Spanish colonial authority escalated into a social struggle among Indians, mestizos, slaves, and whites. The armed populace threatened the planters and

Two Case Studies in Political Change and Environmental Degradation

Overthrowing slavery and colonial domination did not necessarily halt environmental degradation. In fact, in two important New World countries, the new nations of Haiti and Brazil, the transition to independence aggravated environmental problems created by former colonial regimes.

Two hundred and fifty years ago, Haiti, which was under French colonial rule at that time and known as Saint-Domingue, was the richest colony in the Americas, perhaps even the richest colony in the world, accounting for two-thirds of France's worldwide investment. Saint-Domingue's extraordinary wealth came from large, white-owned sugar plantations that used a massive and highly coerced slave population. The slaves' lives were short and brutal, lasting on average only fifteen years; hence the wealthy planter class had to replenish their labor supplies from Africa at frequent intervals.

White planters on the island were eager to amass quick fortunes so that they could sell out and return to France. Vastly outnumbered by enslaved Africans at a time when abolitionist sentiments were gaining ground in Europe and even circulating among slaves in the Americas, the planters' families knew that their prosperity was unlikely to last. They gave little thought to sustainable growth and were not troubled that they were destroying their environment.

The planters greeted the onset of the French Revolution in 1789 with enthusiasm. They saw an opportunity to assert their independence from France, to engage in wider trading contacts with North America and the rest of the world, and thus to become even richer. They ignored the possibility that the ideals of the French Revolution—especially its slogan of liberty, equality, and fraternity—could inspire the island's free blacks and slaves. Indeed, no sooner had the white planters thrown in their lot with the Third Estate in France than a slave rebellion broke out in Saint-Domingue. From its beginnings in 1791, it led, after great loss of life to African slaves and French soldiers, to the proclamation of an independent state in Haiti in 1804, ruled by African Americans. Haiti became the Americas' second independent republican government. Although the revolt brought political independence to its black population, it only intensified the land's environmental deterioration. Not only

did sugarcane fields become scorched battlefields, but freed slaves rushed to stake out independent plots on the old plantations and in wooded areas. In both places, the new peasant class energetically cleared the land. The small country became even more deforested, and intensive cultivation increased erosion and soil depletion. Haiti fell into a more vicious cycle of environmental degradation and poverty.

The second case study of political change leading to the destruction of the environment comes from the independent Brazilian state, where the ruling elite, having achieved autonomy from Portugal, expanded the agrarian frontier. Landowners oversaw the clearing of ancient hardwood forests so that slaves and squatters could plant coffee trees. The clearing process had begun with sugarcane in the coastal regions, but it accelerated with coffee plantings in the hilly regions of São Paulo.

In fact, coffee was a worse threat to Brazil's forests than any other invader in the previous 300 years. Coffee trees thrive on soils that are neither soggy nor overly dry. Therefore, planters razed the virgin forest, which contained a balanced variety of trees and

merchants; rural folk battled against aristocratic creoles; Andean Indians fled the mines and occupied great estates. Popular armies, having defeated Spanish forces by the 1820s, fought civil wars over the new postcolonial order.

New states and collective identities of nationhood now emerged. A narrow elite led these political communities, and their guiding principles were often contradictory. Bolívar, for instance, encouraged his followers to

undergrowth, and Brazil's once-fertile soil suffered rapid depletion by a single-crop industry. Within one generation the clear-cutting led to infertile soils and extensive erosion, which drove planters farther into the frontier to destroy even more forest and plant more coffee groves. The environmental impact was monumental: between 1788 and 1888, when slavery was abolished, Brazil produced about 10 million tons of coffee and lost 300 million tons of ancient forest biomass (the accumulated biological material from living organisms).

Slaves Cutting Cane Sugar was the preeminent agricultural export from the New World for centuries. Owners of sugarcane plantations relied almost exclusively on African slaves to produce the sweetener. Labor in the fields was especially harsh, as slaves worked in the blistering sun from dawn until dusk.

Questions for Analysis

- Who intensified the deforestation and degradation in each case, and why did they do it?
- Why do you think deforestation increased in intensity after Haitians and Brazilians gained their autonomy/independence?

Explore Further

Diamond, Jared, and James A. Robinson (eds.), *Natural Experiments of History* (2010).

Geggus, David (ed.), *The Impact of the Haitian Revolution in the Atlantic World* (2001).

become "American," to overcome their local identities. He wanted the liberated countries to form a Latin American confederation, urging Peru and Bolivia to join Venezuela, Ecuador, and Colombia in the "Gran Colombia." But local identities prevailed, giving way to unstable national republics. Bolívar died surrounded by opponents; San Martín died in exile. The real heirs to independence were local military chieftains, who often forged alliances

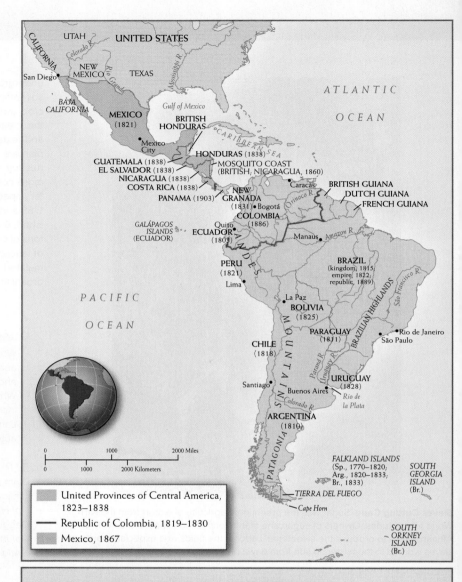

United Provinces of Central America,
1823–1838

Republic of Colombia, 1819–1830

Mexico, 1867

Map 15.3 Latin American Nation Building

Creating strong, unified nation-states proved difficult in Latin America. The map shows where boundaries were drawn in Mexico, the United Provinces of Central America, and the Republic of Colombia. In each case, the governments' territorial and nation-building ambitions failed to some degree.

• During what period did a majority of the colonies in Latin America gain independence?

• Which European countries lost the most in Latin America during this period?

• Why did all these colonies gain their independence during this time?

with landowners. Thus, the legacy of the Spanish American revolutions was contradictory and echoed developments elsewhere around the world: the triumph of wealthy elites under a banner of liberty, yet often at the expense of poorer, nonwhite, and mixed populations.

Change and Trade in Africa

Africa also was swept up in revolutionary tides, as increased domestic and world trade—including the selling of African slaves—shifted the terms of state building across the continent. The main catalyst for Africa's political shake-up was the rapid growth and then the demise of the Atlantic slave trade.

ABOLITION OF THE SLAVE TRADE

Even as it enriched and empowered some Africans and many Europeans, the slave trade became a subject of fierce debate in the late eighteenth century. Some European and American revolutionaries argued that slave labor was inherently less productive than free wage labor and ought to be abolished. At the same time, another group favoring abolition of the slave trade insisted that traffic in slaves was immoral. In London they created committees, often led by Quakers, to lobby Parliament for an end to the slave trade. Quakers in Philadelphia did likewise. Pamphlets, reports, and personal narratives denounced the traffic in people.

In response to abolitionist efforts, North Atlantic powers moved to prohibit the slave trade. Denmark acted first in its Caribbean colonies in 1803, Great Britain followed in 1807, and the United States joined the campaign in 1808. Over time, the British persuaded the French and other European governments to do likewise. To enforce the ban, Britain posted a naval squadron off the coast of West Africa to prevent any slave trade above the equator and compelled Brazil's emperor to end slave imports. After 1850, Atlantic slave shipping dropped sharply, though slavery did not end for several decades due to the continued profitability of cotton in the southern United States, sugar in the Caribbean, and coffee in Brazil. The last known Atlantic slave ship discharged its cargo in Cuba in 1867.

NEW TRADE WITH AFRICA

Even as the Atlantic slave trade died down, Europeans promoted commerce with Africa. Now they wanted Africans to export raw materials and to purchase European manufactured goods. What Europeans liked to call "legitimate" trade aimed to raise the Africans' standards of living by substituting trade in produce for trade in slaves. West Africans responded by exporting palm kernels and peanuts. The real bonanza was in vegetable oils to lubricate machinery and make candles and in palm oil to produce soap. European merchants argued that by becoming vibrant export societies, Africans would earn the wealth to profitably import European wares.

The new trade gave rise to a generation of successful West African merchants. There were many rags-to-riches stories, like that of King Jaja of Opobo (1821–1891). Kidnapped and sold into slavery as a youngster, he started out paddling canoes carrying palm oil to coastal ports. Ultimately becoming the head of a coastal canoe house, he founded the port of Opobo and could summon a flotilla of war canoes on command. Another freed slave, a Yoruba, William Lewis, made his way back to Africa and in 1828 settled in Sierra Leone (a British colony for freed slaves, notably blacks from the United States who were loyal to Great Britain). Starting with a few utensils and a small plot of land, he became a successful merchant and sent his son Samuel to England for his education. Samuel eventually became an important political leader in Sierra Leone.

However, the rise of free labor in the Atlantic world and the dwindling foreign slave trade had an unanticipated effect. It strengthened slavery within Africa. In some areas, by the mid-nineteenth century slaves accounted for more than half the population. No longer did they comfortably serve in domestic employment; instead, they toiled on palm oil plantations or, in East Africa, on clove plantations. They also served in the military forces, bore palm oil and ivory to markets as porters, or paddled cargo-carrying canoes along rivers leading to the coast. In 1850, northern Nigeria's ruling class had more slaves than independent Brazil and almost as many as the United States. As Africa ceased to be the world's supplier of slaves, it became in time the world's largest slaveholding region.

Economic Reordering

Core Objectives

IDENTIFY and EXPLAIN the key developments that constituted the industrial revolution.

Behind the political and social upheavals, profound changes were occurring in the world economy. Until the middle of the eighteenth century, global trade touched only the edges of most societies, which produced for their own subsistence. Surpluses of special goods, from porcelains to silks, entered trade arteries but did not change the cultures that produced them. A century later, by the middle of the nineteenth century, global trade networks had expanded their reach. The desire for cash, for silver or gold, drove market relations much farther than they had ever reached before. People increasingly worked to produce goods they could sell, which transformed social relations in agricultural hinterlands as well as bustling urban centers.

New Farming Technologies
Although major technological changes in agriculture emerged only late in this period, the spread of more intensive cultivation led to increased yields, especially with the introduction of synthetic fertilizers.

AN INDUSTRIOUS REVOLUTION

Many of these developments took place first in northwestern Europe and British North America. Here, as elsewhere in the world, households had always produced mainly for themselves and made available for marketplaces only meager surpluses of goods and services. But dramatic changes occurred when family members, including wives and children, decided to work harder and longer in order to produce more for the market and purchase more in the market. In these locations, households devoted less time to leisure activities and more time to working, using the additional income from hard work to purchase products produced elsewhere. Scholars recently have come to call this change an **industrious revolution**. Beginning in the second half of the seventeenth century, it gained speed in the eighteenth century and laid the foundations for the industrial revolution of the late eighteenth and early nineteenth centuries.

The willingness on the part of families to work more and an eagerness to eat more diverse foods, to wear better clothes, and to consume products that had once been available as luxuries only to the wealthy classes led in turn to a large expansion in trade. Sugar and silver were the pioneering products. But by the eighteenth century, other staples joined the long-distance trading business, including tea: its leaves came from China, the sugar to cut its bitterness from the Caribbean, the slaves to harvest the sweetener from Africa, and the ceramics to serve a proper cup from the English Midlands. Even ordinary

industrious revolution
Dramatic economic change in which households that had traditionally produced for themselves decided to work harder and longer hours in order to produce more for the market, which enabled them to increase their income and standard of living. Areas that underwent the industrious revolution shifted from peasant farming to specialized production for the market.

people could purchase imported goods with their earnings. Thus, the poor began to enjoy coffee, tea, and sugar. European artisans and farmers purchased tools, furnishings, and home decorations. Slaves and colonial laborers also used their meager earnings to buy imported cotton cloth made in Europe from the raw cotton they themselves had picked several seasons earlier.

The expansion of global trade had important social and political consequences. As new goods flowed from ever more distant corners of the globe, immense fortunes grew. To support their enterprise, traders needed new services in insurance, bookkeeping, and the recording of legal documents. Trade supported the growth of the liberal professions—accountants and lawyers. The new cities of the commercial revolution, hubs like Bristol, Bombay, and Buenos Aires, provided the homes and flourishing neighborhoods for the growing class of men and women known as the **bourgeoisie**: urban businessmen, financiers, and other property owners without aristocratic origins.

THE INDUSTRIAL REVOLUTION

Trade and finance repositioned western Europe's relationship with the rest of the world. So did the emergence of manufacturing. Like agricultural production, output of industrial commodities surged. The heart of this process was a gradual accumulation and diffusion of technical knowledge. Lots of little inventions, their applications, and their spread across the Atlantic world gradually built up a stock of technical knowledge and practice. Historians have traditionally called these changes the **industrial revolution**.

Nowhere was this industrial revolution more evident than in Britain. Britain had access to waterways, constructed a network of canals, and had large supplies of coal and iron—key materials used in manufactured products. It also had a political and social environment that allowed merchants and industrialists to invest heavily while also expanding their internal and international markets. Among their investments was the application of steam power to textile production, which enabled Britain's manufacturers to produce cheaper goods in larger quantities. Finally, Britain had access to New World lands as sources of financial investment, raw materials, and markets for manufactured goods. These factors' convergence promoted self-sustaining economic growth.

Consider the relationship between inventor and investor in the advent of the steam engine. Such engines burned coal to boil water, and the resulting steam drove mechanized devices. There were several tinkerers working on such an engine. But the most famous was James Watt (1736–1819) of Scotland, who managed to separate steam condensers from piston cylinders so that pistons could stay hot and run constantly; he joined forces with the industrialist Matthew Boulton, who marketed the steam engine and set up a laboratory where Watt could refine his device. Invented in 1769, the steam engine catalyzed a revolution in transportation. Steam-powered engines also improved sugar refining, pottery making, and other industrial processes, generating more products at lower cost than when workers had made them by hand.

Textile production was critical. Most raw cotton for the British cloth industry had come from colonial India until 1793, when the American inventor Eli Whitney (1765–1825) patented a "cotton gin" that separated cotton seeds from fiber. After that, cotton farming spread so quickly in the southern United States that by the 1850s it was producing more than 80 percent of the world's cotton supply. In turn, every black slave in the Americas and many Indians in British India were consumers of cheap, British-produced cotton shirts. The price of cotton cloth declined by nearly 50 percent between 1780 and 1850, as textiles became the world's most dynamic industry. England became the world's largest cloth producer, driving most of the other centers of textile production, notably those in the Indian subcontinent, out of business.

Wherever the industrial revolution took hold, it allowed societies to outdistance rivals in manufacturing and elevated them to a new place in the emerging global economic order. (See Map 15.4.) But why did this revolution cluster mainly in the Atlantic world? This is an important question because the unequal distribution of global wealth, the gap between the haves and have-nots, really took off in this era of revolutions. In much of Asia and Africa, technical change altered modes of production and business practices, but it was not followed by a continuous cascade of changes. The great mystery was China, the home of astronomical water clocks and gunpowder. Why did China not become the epicenter of the industrial revolution?

There are two reasons. First, China did not foster experimental science of the kind that allowed Watt to stumble onto the possibility of steam,

A Cotton Textile Mill in the 1830s The region of Lancashire became one of the major industrial hubs for textile production in the world. By the 1830s, mills had made the shift from artisanal work to highly mechanical mass production. Among the great breakthroughs was the shift from wool to cotton textiles, which were printed with designs such as paisley or calico (as in this image) and marketed to middle-class consumers.

Map 15.4 Industrial Europe around 1850

By 1850 much of western Europe was industrial and urban, with major cities linked to one another through a network of railroads.

- According to this map, what natural resources contributed to the growth of the industrial revolution? What effects did it have on urban population densities?
- Compare the course of major rivers with those of the railways.
- Why did the United Kingdom have such a large concentration of cities with more than 100,000 inhabitants? How was the United Kingdom able to support such large population centers?

or Whitney the cotton gin. Experimentation, testing, and the links between thinkers and investors were a distinctly Atlantic phenomenon. The Qing, like the Mughal and Ottoman dynasties, swept the great minds into the bureaucracy and reinforced the old agrarian system based on peasant exploitation and tribute. Second, Chinese, Mughal, and Ottoman rulers did not support the overseas expansion and trade that helped create the commercial revolution in the Atlantic world. The agrarian dynasties of China and India neither showered favors on local merchants nor effectively shut out interlopers. This made them vulnerable to cheap manufactured imports from European traders backed by their governments extolling the virtues of free trade.

The effects were profound. Historically, Europe had a trade imbalance with partners to the east—furs from Russia and spices and silks from Asia. It made up for this with silver from the Americas. But the new economic order meant that by the nineteenth century, western Europe not only had manufactures like cotton textiles to export to Asia but also had capital. One of Europe's biggest debtors was none other than the sultan of the Ottoman Empire, whose tax system could not keep up with the spending necessary to keep the realm together. More and more, Asian, African, and American governments found themselves borrowing from Europe's financiers just as their people were buying industrial products from Europe and selling their primary products to European consumers and producers.

WORKING AND LIVING

The industrial revolution brought more demanding work routines—not only in the manufacturing economies of western Europe and North America but also on the farms and plantations of Asia and Africa.

Urban Life and Work Routines Increasingly, Europe's workers made their livings in cities. London, Europe's largest city in 1700, saw its population nearly double over the next century to almost 1 million. By the 1820s, population growth was even greater in the industrial hubs of Leeds, Glasgow, Birmingham, Liverpool, and Manchester.

For most urban dwellers, cities were not healthy places. Water that powered the mills, along with chemicals used in dyeing, went directly back into waterways that provided drinking water. Overcrowded tenements shared just a few outhouses. Most European cities as late as 1850 had no running water, no garbage pickup, and no underground sewer system. The result was widespread disease. (In fact, no European city at this time had as clean a water supply as the largest towns of the ancient Roman Empire once had.)

Changes in work affected the understanding of time. Whereas most farmers' workloads had followed seasonal rhythms, after 1800 industrial settings imposed a rigid concept of work discipline. To keep the machinery operating, factory and mill owners installed huge clocks and used bells or horns to signify the workday's beginning and end. Employers also measured output per hour and compared workers' performance.

Industrialization imposed numbing work routines and paltry wages. Worse, however, was having no work at all. As families abandoned their farmland and depended on wages, being idle meant having no income. Periodic downturns in the economy put wage workers at risk, and many responded by organizing protests.

Social Protest and Emigration While entrepreneurs accumulated private wealth, the effects of the industrial revolution on working-class families raised widespread concern, sometimes leading to protests or emigration. In the 1810s in England, groups of jobless craftsmen, called Luddites, smashed the machines that had left them unemployed. Social advocates sought protective legislation for workers, including curbing child labor, limiting the workday, and, in some countries, legalizing prostitution for the sake of monitoring the prostitutes' health.

Some people, however, could not wait for legislative reform. The period saw unprecedented emigration, as unemployed workers or peasants abandoned their homes to seek their fortunes in America, Canada, and Australia. During the Irish Potato Famine of 1845–1849, at least 1 million Irish citizens left their country (and a further million or so died) when fungi attacked their subsistence crop. Desperate to escape starvation, they booked cheap passage to North America on ships so notorious for disease and malnutrition that they earned the name "coffin ships."

The industrial revolution produced wealth on an unprecedented scale, but that wealth was distributed unevenly. Enormous inequalities resulted, both within societies and between them. Free trade resulted, in the long run, not in the proliferation of ever-more-productive small workshops but in massive industrial concentration, a concentration that would prove dynamic, creative, and unstable.

Persistence and Change in Afro-Eurasia

Core Objectives

COMPARE the groups of people who held power in each of the regions in 1750 and then in 1850, and **EXPLAIN** the change that took place during this period in these societies.

Western Europe's military might, its technological achievements, and its economic strength represented a threat to the remaining Afro-Eurasian empires. Western European merchants and industrialists sought closer economic and (in some cases) political ties. They did so in the name of gaining "free" access to Asian markets and products. Rulers in Russia, the Ottoman Empire, India, and China all sought to borrow from the ideas and institutions emerging from western Europe, but they did so on their own terms, intent on defending the core of their social and political traditions.

REVAMPING THE RUSSIAN MONARCHY

Russian rulers responded to the pressures by strengthening their traditional authority through modest reforms and the suppression of domestic opposition. Tsar Alexander I (r. 1801–1825) was fortunate that Napoleon committed several blunders and lost his formidable army in the Russian snows. Yet the French Revolution and its massive armies struck at the heart of Russian political institutions, which rested upon a huge peasant population laboring as serfs. The tsars could no longer justify their absolutism by claiming that enlightened despotism was the most advanced form of government, since a new model, rooted in popular sovereignty and the concept of the nation, had arisen.

In December 1825, when Alexander died unexpectedly and childless, there was a question over succession. Some Russian officers launched a patriotic revolt. The Decembrists, as they were called, came primarily from elite families and were familiar with western European life and institutions. Some called for a constitutional monarchy to replace Russia's despotism; others favored a tsar-less republic and the abolition of serfdom. Their conspiracy failed to win over conservatives or the peasantry, who still believed in the tsar's divine right to rule. Nicholas (r. 1825–1855) became tsar and brutally suppressed the insurrectionists.

Still, Alexander's successors faced a world in which powerful European states had constitutions and national armies of citizens, not subjects. In trying to maintain absolutist rule, Russian tsars portrayed the monarch's family as the ideal historical embodiment of the nation with direct ties to the people. Nicholas himself prevented rebellion by expanding the secret police, enforcing censorship, conducting impressive military exercises, and maintaining serfdom. And in the 1830s he introduced a conservative ideology that stressed religious faith, hierarchy, and obedience. For the time being, the influence of the French Revolution was quashed in Russia.

REFORMING EGYPT AND THE OTTOMAN EMPIRE

Unlike Russia, where Napoleon's army had reached Moscow, the Ottoman capital in Istanbul never faced a threat by French troops. Still, Napoleon's invasion of Egypt shook the Ottoman Empire. Even before this trauma, Ottoman authorities faced the challenge posed by increased trade with Europe—and the greater presence of European merchants and missionaries. In addition, many non-Muslim religious communities in the sultan's empire wanted the European powers to advance their interests. In the wake of Napoleon, who had promised to remake Egyptian society, reformist energies swept from Egypt to the center of the Ottoman domain.

Reforms in Egypt In Egypt, far-reaching changes came with the rule of **Muhammad Ali**. After the French withdrawal in 1801, Muhammad Ali (r. 1805–1848) won a chaotic struggle for supreme power in Egypt and

Muhammad Ali
(r. 1805–1848) Ruler of Egypt who initiated a set of modernizing reforms that sought to make it competitive with the great powers.

Core Objectives

EXPLAIN patterns of global trade and economic growth, and **CONNECT** them to political changes during the period 1750–1850.

aligned himself with influential Egyptian families. Yet he looked to revolution-ary France for a model of modern state building. As with Napoleon (and with Simón Bolívar in Latin America), the key to his hold on power was the army.

Muhammad Ali also made reforms in education and agriculture. He estab-lished a school of engineering and opened the first modern medical school in Cairo under the supervision of a French military doctor. And his efforts in the countryside made Egypt one of the world's leading cotton exporters. A summer crop, cotton required steady watering when the Nile's irrigation waters were in short supply. So Muhammad Ali's Public Works Department, advised by European engineers, deepened the irrigation canals and con-structed a series of dams across the Nile. These efforts transformed Egypt, making it the most powerful state in the eastern Mediterranean and alarming the Ottoman state (which still controlled Egypt) and the great powers in Europe. At the same time, European merchants pressed for free access to Egyptian markets, just as they did in Latin America and Africa.

Ottoman Reforms Under political and economic pressures like those facing Muhammad Ali in Egypt, Ottoman rulers also made reforms. Indeed, military defeats and humiliating treaties with Europe were painful reminders of the sultans' vulnerability. In 1805, Sultan Selim III tried to create a new infantry trained by western European officers. But before he could bring this force up to fighting strength, the janissaries stormed the palace, killed its officers, and deposed Selim in 1807. Over the next few decades, janissary military men and clerical scholars (*ulama*) cobbled together an alliance that thwarted reformers.

Why did reform falter in the Ottoman state before it could be implemented? Reform was possible only if the forces opposed to reform—especially in the military—were weak and the reformers strong. In the Ottoman Empire, the janissary class had grown powerful, providing the main resistance to change. Ottoman authority depended on clerical support, and the Muslim clergy also resisted change. Blocked at the top, Ottoman rulers hesitated to appeal for popular support. Such an appeal, in the new age of popular sovereignty and national feeling, would be dangerous for an unelected dynast in a multiethnic and multireligious realm.

Mahmud II (r. 1808–1839) broke the political deadlock, shrewdly manip-ulating his conservative opponents. Like Muhammad Ali in Egypt, Mahmud brought in European officers to advise his forces. Here, too, military reform spilled over into nonmilitary areas. The Ottoman modernizers created a med-ical college, then a school of military sciences. To understand Europe better and to create a first-rate diplomatic corps, the Ottomans schooled their offi-cials in European languages and had European classics translated into Turkish. As Mahmud's successors extended reforms into civilian life, this era—known as the Tanzimat, or Reorganization period (1826–1839)—saw legislation that guaranteed equality for all Ottoman subjects, regardless of religion.

The reforms, however, stopped well short of revolutionary change. Reform relied too much on the personal whim of rulers, and the bureaucratic and religious infrastructure remained committed to old ways. Any effort to reform the rural sector met resistance by the landed interests. Finally, the merchant classes profited from business with a debt-ridden sultan. By preventing the empire's fiscal collapse through financial support to the state, bankers lessened the pressure for reform and removed the spark that had fired revolutions in Europe.

COLONIAL REORDERING IN INDIA

Europe's most important colonial possession in Asia between 1750 and 1850 was British India. Unlike in North America, the changes that the British fostered in Asia did not lead to political independence. Instead, India was increasingly dominated by the **East India Company**, which the crown had chartered in 1600. The company's control over India's imports and exports in the eighteenth and nineteenth centuries, however, contradicted British claims about their allegiance to a world economic system based on "free trade."

The East India Company's Monopoly In enforcing the East India Company's monopoly on trade, the British soon took control of much of the region. Initially, the British tried to control India's commerce by establishing trading posts along the coast without taking complete political control. After conquering the state of Bengal in 1757, the company began to fill its coffers and its officials began to amass personal fortunes. In spite of violent opposition, the British secured the right for the East India Company to collect tax revenues in Bengal, Bihar, and Orissa and to trade free of duties throughout Mughal territory. In return, the Mughal emperor would receive a hefty annual pension. The company went on to annex other territories, bringing much of South Asia under its rule by the early nineteenth century. (See Map 15.5.)

To rule with minimal interference required knowing the conquered society. This led to Orientalist scholarship: British scholar-officials wrote the first modern histories of South Asia, translated Sanskrit and Persian texts, identified philosophical writings, and compiled Hindu and Muslim law books. Through their efforts, the company-state presented itself as a force for revitalizing authentic Hinduism and recovering India's literary and cultural treasures. However, although the Orientalist scholars admired Sanskrit language and literature, they still supported British colonial rule and did not necessarily agree with local beliefs.

Effects in India Company rule and booming trade altered India's urban geography. By the early nineteenth century, colonial cities like Calcutta, Madras, and Bombay became the new centers at the expense of older Mughal

East India Company
(1600–1858) British charter company created to outperform Portuguese and Spanish traders in the Far East; in the eighteenth century the company became, in effect, the ruler of a large part of India.

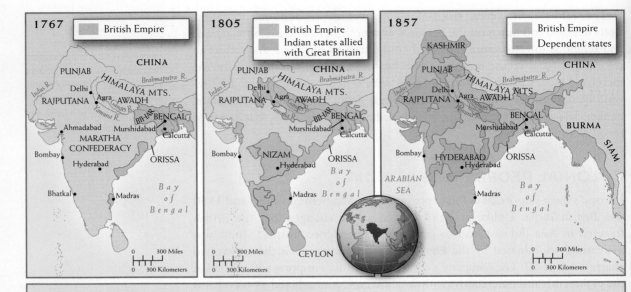

Map 15.5 The British in India, 1767–1857

Starting from locations in eastern and northeastern India, the British East India Company extended its authority over much of South Asia prior to the outbreak of the Indian Rebellion of 1857.

- What type of locations did the British first acquire in India?
- According to your reading, how did the company expand into the interior of India and administer these possessions?
- Why did it choose a strategy of direct rule over some areas and indirect rule over other areas in India?

cities like Agra, Delhi, Murshidabad, and Hyderabad. As the colonial cities attracted British merchants and Indian clerks, artisans, and laborers, their populations surged. Calcutta's reached 350,000 in 1820; Bombay's jumped to 200,000 by 1825. In these cities, Europeans lived close to the company's fort and trading stations, while migrants from the countryside clustered in crowded quarters called "black towns."

India now became an importer of British textiles and an exporter of raw cotton—a reversal of its traditional pattern of trade. In the past, India had been an important textile manufacturer, exporting fine cotton goods throughout the Indian Ocean and to Europe. But its elites could not resist the appeal of cheap British textiles. As a result, India's industrial sector declined. In addition, the import of British manufactures caused unfavorable trade balances that changed India from a net importer of gold and silver to an exporter of these precious metals.

Led by evangelical Christians and liberal reformers, the British did more than alter the Indian economy; they also advocated far-reaching changes in

Indian Resistance to Company Rule Tipu Sultan, the Mysore ruler, put up a determined resistance against the British. This painting by Robert Home shows Cornwallis, the East India Company's governor, receiving Tipu's two sons as hostages after defeating him in the 1792 war. The boys remained in British custody for two years. Tipu returned to fighting the British and was killed in the war of 1799.

Indian culture. For example, they sought to stop the practice of *sati*, by which women burned to death on the funeral pyres of their dead husbands. Now the mood swung away from the Orientalists' respect for India's classical languages, philosophies, cultures, and texts. In 1835, when the British poet, historian, and Liberal politician Lord Macaulay was making recommendations on educational policies, he urged that English replace Persian as the language of administration and that European education replace Oriental learning. The result, reformers hoped, would be a class that was Indian in blood and color but English in tastes and culture.

This was a new colonial order, but it was not stable. Most wealthy landowners resented the loss of their land and authority. Peasants, thrown to the mercy of the market, moneylenders, and landlords and subject to high taxation, were in turmoil. The non-Hindu forest dwellers and roaming cultivators, faced with the hated combination of a colonial state and moneylenders, revolted. Dispossessed artisans stirred up towns and cities. And merchants and industrialists chafed under the British-dominated economy. As freedom expanded in Europe, exploitation expanded in India.

PERSISTENCE OF THE QING EMPIRE

The Chinese empire was largely unaffected by the upheavals in Europe and America until the Opium Wars (1839–1842, 1856–1860) forced the Chinese to acknowledge their military weaknesses. The Qing dynasty, which had taken power in 1644, was still enjoying prosperity and territorial expansion as the nineteenth century dawned. Their sense of imperial splendor continued to rest on the political structure and social order inherited from the Ming (see Chapter 11). However, they could not resist European demands for access to their resources and markets.

The Qing had a talent for extending the empire's boundaries and settling frontier lands. Before 1750, they conquered Taiwan (the stronghold of remaining Ming forces), pushed westward into central Asia, and annexed Tibet. To secure these territorial gains, the Qing encouraged settlement of frontier lands like Xinjiang. New crops from the Americas aided this process—especially corn and sweet potatoes, which grow well in less fertile soils.

Like their European counterparts, Chinese peasants were on the move. But migration occurred in Qing China for different reasons. The state-sponsored westward movement into Xinjiang, for example, aimed to secure a recently pacified frontier region through military colonization, after which civilians would follow. So peasants received promises of land, tools, seed, and the loan of silver and a horse—all with the dual objectives of producing enough food to supply the troops and relieving pressure on the poor and arid northwestern part of the country. These efforts brought so much land under cultivation by 1840 that the region's ecological and social landscape completely changed.

Despite their success in expanding the empire, the Qing faced nagging problems. As a ruling minority, they looked warily at innovation, and only late in the eighteenth century did they deal with their rapidly expanding population. On the one hand, the tripling of China's population since 1300 demonstrated the realm's prosperity; on the other, a population of over 300 million severely strained resources—especially soil for growing crops and wood for fuel. In the late eighteenth and early nineteenth centuries, uprisings inspired by mystical beliefs in folk Buddhism, and at times by the idea of restoring the Ming, engulfed northern China.

By the mid-nineteenth century, extraordinary changes had made western European powers stronger than ever before, and the Qing could no longer dismiss their demands. The first clear evidence of an altered global balance of power was not the rise of Napoleon but a British-Chinese war over a narcotic. Indeed, the **Opium Wars** exposed China's vulnerability in a new era of European ascendancy.

Opium Wars
(1839–1842, 1856–1860) Wars fought between the British and Qing China over British trade in opium; the result was that China granted to the British the right to trade in five different ports and ceded Hong Kong to the British.

The Opium Wars and the "Opening" of China Europeans had been selling staples and intoxicants in China for a long time, and by the late eighteenth century opium, which had previously been used as a medicine or an aphrodisiac, was being smoked in long-stemmed pipes at every level of Chinese society. Sensing opium's economic potential, the East India Company established a monopoly over the export of opium from India in 1773 to help pay for a rapid growth in the company's purchase of tea from China. Because the Chinese showed little taste for British goods, the British had been financing their tea imports with exports of silver to China. But by the late eighteenth century, the company's tea purchases had become too large to finance with silver. Fortunately for the company, the Chinese were eager for Indian cotton and opium, and then mostly just opium.

Opium's impact on China's balance of trade was devastating. In a reversal from earlier trends, silver began to flow out of instead of into China. Once silver shortages occurred, the peasants' tax burden grew heavier. Consequently, long-simmering unrest in the countryside gained momentum. At the Qing court, some officials wanted to legalize the opium trade so as to eliminate corruption and boost revenues. (After all, as long as opium was an illegal substance, the government could not tax its traffic.) In 1838, the emperor sent a special commissioner to Canton, the main center of the trade, to eradicate the influx of opium.

When British merchants in Canton resisted, war broke out. In June 1840, British warships bombarded coastal regions near Canton and sailed upriver for a short way. On land, Qing soldiers used spears, clubs, and a few imported matchlock muskets against the modern artillery of British troops, many of whom were Indians supplied with percussion cap rifles. Along the Yangzi River, outgunned Qing forces fought fiercely, as soldiers killed their own wives and children before committing suicide themselves. But they were no match for British military technology.

The Qing ruling elite capitulated, and through the 1842 Treaty of Nanjing, the British acquired the island of Hong Kong and the right to trade directly with the Chinese in five treaty ports and to reside there.

Opium (*Left*) A common sight in late Qing China was establishments catering specifically to opium smoking. Taken from a volume condemning the practice, this picture shows opium smokers idling their day away. (*Right*) Having established a monopoly in the 1770s over opium cultivation in India, the British greatly expanded their manufacture and export of opium to China to balance their rapidly growing import of Chinese tea and silk. This picture from the 1880s shows an opium warehouse in India where the commodity was stored before being transported to China.

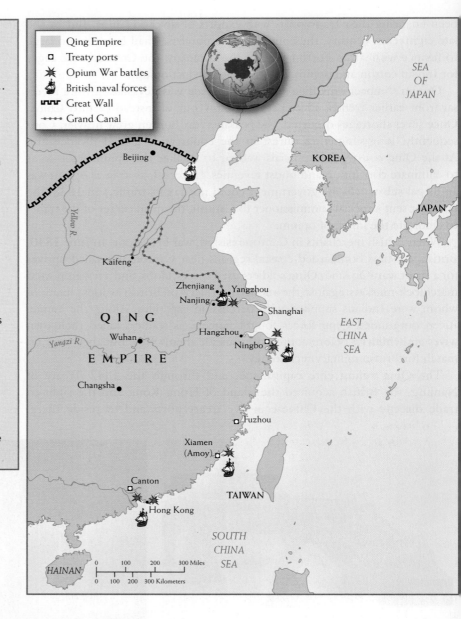

Map 15.6 The Qing Empire and the Opium Wars

The Opium Wars demonstrated the superiority of British military technology. Their victory granted the British control of Hong Kong and established a series of treaty ports, which gave Europeans access to Chinese trade and were subject to the laws of designated European countries.

- How many treaty ports were there after the Opium Wars? What was their significance?

- How were the treaty ports distributed along China's coastline?

- According to the text, how did the Opium Wars change relations between China and the western powers?

(See Map 15.6.) They also forced the Chinese to repay the costs that the British had incurred in the war.

Subsequent treaties guaranteed that the British and other foreign nationals would be tried in their own courts for crimes, rather than in Chinese courts, and would be exempt from Chinese law. Moreover, the British insisted that any privileges granted through treaties with other parties would also apply to them. Other western nations followed the British example in demanding the same right, and the arrangement thus guaranteed all Europeans and North Americans a privileged position in China.

Still, China did not become a formal colony. To the contrary, in the mid-nineteenth century Europeans and North Americans were trading only on its outskirts. Most Chinese did not encounter Europeans. Daily life for most people went on as it had before the Opium Wars. Only the political leaders and urban dwellers were beginning to feel the foreign presence and wondering what steps China might take to acquire European technologies, goods, and learning.

Conclusion

During the period 1750–1850, changes in politics, commerce, industry, and technology reverberated throughout the Atlantic world and, to varying degrees, elsewhere around the globe. By 1850, the world was more integrated economically, with Europe increasingly at the center.

In the Americas, colonial ties broke apart. In France, the people toppled the monarchy. Dissidents threatened the same in Russia. Such upheavals introduced a new public vocabulary—the language of the nation—and made the idea of revolution empowering. In the Americas and parts of Europe, nation-states took shape around redefined hierarchies of class, gender, and color. Britain and France emerged from the political crises of the late eighteenth century determined to expand their borders. Their drive forced older empires such as Russia and the Ottoman state to make reforms.

As commerce and industrialization transformed economic and political power, European governments compelled others (including Egypt, India, and China) to expand their trade with European merchants. Ultimately, such countries had to participate in a European-centered economy as exporters of raw materials and importers of European manufactures. By the 1850s, many of the world's peoples became more industrious, producing less for themselves and more for distant markets. Through changes in manufacturing, some areas of the world also made more goods than ever before. With its emphasis on free trade, Europe began to force open new markets—even to the point of colonizing them. Gold and silver now flowed out of China and India to pay for European products like opium and textiles.

However, global reordering did not mean that Europe's rulers had uncontested control over other people or that the institutions and cultures of Asia and Africa ceased to be dynamic. Some countries became dependent on Europe commercially; others became colonies. China escaped colonial rule but was forced into unfavorable trade relations with the Europeans. In sum, dramatic changes combined to unsettle systems of rulership and to alter the economic and military balance between western Europe and the rest of the world.

Focus On
The Global Effects of the "New Ideas"

The Atlantic World

- North American colonists revolt against British rule and establish a nonmonarchical, republican form of government.

- In the wake of the American Revolution, the French citizenry proclaims a new era of liberty, equality, and fraternity and executes opponents of the revolution, notably the king and queen of France.

- Napoleon's French Empire extends many principles of the French Revolution throughout Europe.

- In the midst of the French Revolution, Haitian slaves throw off French rule, abolish slavery, and create an independent state.

- Napoleon's invasion of Iberia frees Portuguese and Spanish America from colonial rule.

- The British lead a successful campaign to abolish the Atlantic slave trade and promote new sources of trade with Africa.

- An industrial revolution spreads outward from Britain to a few other parts of the Atlantic world.

Africa, India, and Asia

- In Egypt, a military leader, Muhammad Ali, modernizes the country and threatens the political integrity of the Ottoman Empire.

- The British East India Company increasingly dominates the Indian subcontinent.

- The Qing Empire persists despite major European encroachments on its sovereignty.

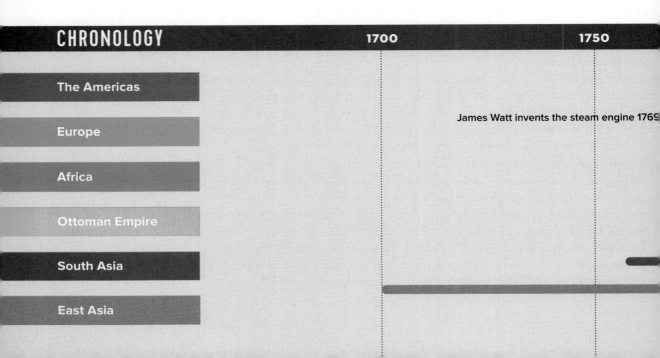

CHRONOLOGY	1700	1750
The Americas		
Europe		James Watt invents the steam engine 1769
Africa		
Ottoman Empire		
South Asia		
East Asia		

THINKING ABOUT GLOBAL CONNECTIONS

- **Thinking about Exchange Networks and Sociopolitical Change** How did established dynasties respond to pressures created by increased exchanges of goods, ideas, and peoples? To what degree did established elites respond by forging a partnership with "the people"? Who defined "the people," and on what terms?

- **Thinking about Changing Power Relationships and Sociopolitical Change** What new kinds of political organizations emerged in this period? Where did new political systems take root, and where did established elites resist most successfully?

- **Thinking about Environmental Impacts and Sociopolitical Change** Although new technologies only gradually transformed agriculture—by far the most common economic activity in the world—the spread of more intensive cultivation demanded considerable capital investment. How did the relationship between town and countryside change as a result? How did living conditions change in cities as their populations swelled?

Key Terms

Muhammad Ali p. 719

Napoleon Bonaparte p. 703

bourgeoisie p. 714

East India Company p. 721

free trade (laissez-faire) p. 695

industrial revolution p. 714

industrious revolution p. 713

Opium Wars p. 724

popular sovereignty p. 695

social contract p. 699

 Go to **INQUIZITIVE** to see what you've learned—and learn what you've missed—with personalized feedback along the way.

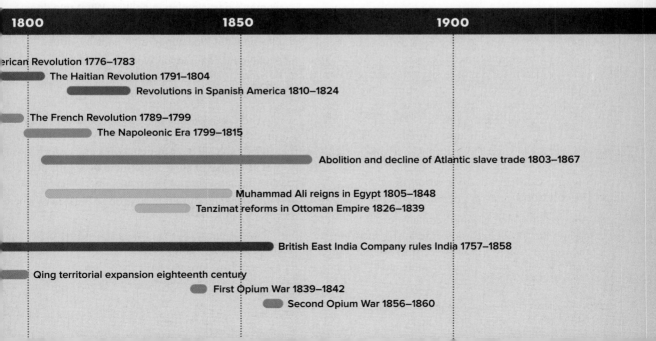

| 1800 | 1850 | 1900 |

American Revolution 1776–1783

The Haitian Revolution 1791–1804

Revolutions in Spanish America 1810–1824

The French Revolution 1789–1799

The Napoleonic Era 1799–1815

Abolition and decline of Atlantic slave trade 1803–1867

Muhammad Ali reigns in Egypt 1805–1848

Tanzimat reforms in Ottoman Empire 1826–1839

British East India Company rules India 1757–1858

Qing territorial expansion eighteenth century

First Opium War 1839–1842

Second Opium War 1856–1860

Global Themes and Sources

Revolution for Whom?

Although Enlightenment *philosophes* argued that the laws of reason applied to everyone and the American Declaration of Independence declared that all men are created equal, their ideas immediately provoked a wide range of opposition during the political reordering of the Age of Revolution. In Europe and the United States, women and the enslaved protested their exclusion, while elite men in territories occupied by western colonizers pointed to the hypocrisy of the occupiers' egalitarian rhetoric. In different ways, they all probed the central, often hidden, assumptions of European elites about hierarchy and difference.

Two of the documents were written in wealthy corners of western Europe and the United States; one was written in Egypt, then occupied by the French army; and one was written in newly independent Haiti, recently liberated from French control. One of the texts was written by a woman; the remaining three were written by men. All four were written by elites upset at their exclusion. Collectively, they highlight tensions and divisions within Europe as well as between Europeans and others. Making sense of them requires grappling with the degree to which people around the world accepted or rejected the basic premises of Enlightenment thinkers.

The sources invite you to think comparatively about the various ways that men and women viewed the same parts of the Enlightenment tradition. They also challenge you to think about whether critiques written outside Europe were similar to those from within, and which ideas resonated most deeply and why.

Analyzing Comparative Viewpoints on Revolutions

- Analyze the role of Enlightenment ideas. Do these documents challenge those ideas or seek to apply them more fully? Do they reject the Enlightenment tradition or contend that its values have not been fully realized? Which document is the most critical? Which is the least critical?

- Compare the documents written in Europe and the United States to those written in Egypt and Haiti.

- Evaluate the degree to which these documents make universal arguments and the degree to which their claims are rooted in local traditions, communities, and beliefs.

PRIMARY SOURCE 15.1

On the Rights of Women (1792), Mary Wollstonecraft

One of the founding figures of modern feminism, Mary Wollstonecraft was born in London in 1759. Her *Vindication of the Rights of Woman* (1792), written in the midst of the French Revolution, took aim at notions of women as helpless, emotional adornments, dependent by their nature on men.

- **Identify the limits Wollstonecraft places on women's participation in politics. What role does reason play in setting those limits?**

- **Explain what Wollstonecraft means by virtue.**

- **Explain the comparison Wollstonecraft draws between male superiority and the divine right of kings.**

Surely there can be but one rule of right, if morality has an eternal foundation, and whoever sacrifices virtue, strictly so called, to present convenience, or whose duty it is to act in such a manner, lives only for the passing day, and cannot be an accountable creature.

The poet then should have dropped his sneer when he says,

If weak women go astray,
The stars are more in fault than they.

For that they are bound by the adamantine chain of destiny is most certain, if it be proved that they are never to exercise their own reason, never to be independent, never to rise above opinion, or to feel the dignity of a rational will that only bows to God, and often forgets that the universe contains any being but itself and the model of perfection to which its ardent gaze is turned, to adore attributes that, softened into virtues, may be imitated in kind, though the degree overwhelms the enraptured mind.

If, I say, for I would not impress by declamation when Reason offers her sober light, if they be really capable of acting like rational creatures, let them not be treated like slaves; or, like the brutes who are dependent on the reason of man, when they associate with him; but cultivate their minds, give them the salutary, sublime curb of principle, and let them attain conscious dignity by feeling themselves only dependent on God. Teach them, in common with man, to submit to necessity, instead of giving, to render them more pleasing, a sex to morals.

Further, should experience prove that they cannot attain the same degree of strength of mind, perseverance, and fortitude, let their virtues be the same in kind, though they may vainly struggle for the same degree; and the superiority of man will be equally clear, if not clearer; and truth, as it is a simple principle, which admits of no modification, would be common to both. Nay, the order of society as it is at present regulated, would not be inverted, for woman would then only have the rank that reason assigned her, and arts could not be practiced to bring the balance even, much less to turn it.

These may be termed Utopian dreams. Thanks to that Being who impressed them on my soul, and gave me sufficient strength of mind to dare to exert my own reason, till, becoming dependent only on him for the support of my virtue, I view, with indignation, the mistaken notions that enslave my sex.

I love man as my fellow; but his sceptre, real or usurped, extends not to me, unless the reason of an individual demands my homage; and even then the submission is to reason, and not to man. In fact, the conduct of an accountable being must be regulated by the operations of its own reason; or on what foundation rests the throne of God?

It appears to me necessary to dwell on these obvious truths, because females have been insulated, as it were; and while they have been stripped of the virtues that should clothe humanity, they have been decked with artificial graces that enable them to exercise a short-lived tyranny. Love, in their bosoms, taking the place of every nobler passion, their sole ambition is to be fair, to raise emotion instead of inspiring respect; and this ignoble desire, like the servility in absolute monarchies, destroys all strength of character. Liberty is the mother of virtue, and if women be, by their very constitution, slaves, and not allowed to breathe the sharp invigorating air of freedom, they must ever languish like exotics, and be reckoned beautiful flaws in nature. Let it also be remembered, that they are the only flaw.

As to the argument respecting the subjection in which the sex has ever been held, it retorts on man. The many have always been enthralled by the few; and monsters, who scarcely have shown any discernment of human excellence, have tyrannized over thousands of their fellow-creatures. Why have men of superior endowments submitted to such degradation? For, is it not universally acknowledged that kings, viewed collectively, have ever been inferior, in abilities and virtue, to the same number of men taken from the common mass of mankind—yet have they not, and are they not still treated with a degree of reverence that is an insult to reason? China is not the only country where a living man has been made a God. *Men* have submitted to superior strength to enjoy with impunity the pleasure of the moment; *women* have only done the same, and therefore till it is proved that the courtier, who servilely resigns the birthright of a man, is not a moral agent, it cannot be demonstrated that woman is essentially inferior to man because she has always been subjugated.

Brutal force has hitherto governed the world, and that the science of politics is in its infancy, is evident from philosophers scrupling to give the knowledge most useful to man that determinate distinction.

I shall not pursue this argument any further than to establish an obvious inference, that as sound politics diffuse liberty, mankind, including woman, will become more wise and virtuous.

Source: Mary Wollstonecraft, *A Vindication of the Rights of Woman*, A Norton Critical Edition, edited by Deidre Shauna Lynch (New York: Norton, 2009), pp. 39–41.

An Egyptian Reaction to French Occupation (1798), Abd al-Rahman al-Jabarti

In 1798, revolutionary France authorized a military campaign in "the Orient," present-day Syria and Egypt, to protect French trade interests and disrupt British access to India. Napoleon Bonaparte sought to win support for the French invasion by presenting himself as a liberator and invoking the ideals of the French Revolution. Here the Cairo scholar Abd al-Rahman al-Jabarti responds.

- Describe the significance of equality in this document.
- Identify the criteria al-Jabarti uses to criticize Napoleon and the French.
- Analyze the role of religion in this document.

On Monday news arrived that the French had reached Damanhur and Rosetta [in the Nile Delta]. . . . They printed a large proclamation in Arabic, calling on the people to obey them. . . . In this proclamation were inducements, warnings, all manner of wiliness and stipulations. Some copies were sent from the provinces to Cairo and its text is:

In the name of God, the Merciful, the Compassionate. There is no god but God. He has no son nor has He an associate in His Dominion.

On behalf of the French Republic which is based upon the foundation of liberty and equality, General Bonaparte, Commander-in-Chief of the French armies makes known to all the Egyptian people that for a long time the Sanjaqs [its Mamluk rulers] who lorded it over Egypt have treated the French community basely and contemptuously and have persecuted its merchants with all manner of extortion and violence. Therefore the hour of punishment has now come.

Unfortunately, this group of Mamluks . . . have acted corruptly for ages in the fairest land that is to be found upon the face of the globe. However, the Lord of the Universe, the Almighty, has decreed the end of their power.

O ye Egyptians . . . I have not come to you except for the purpose of restoring your rights from the hands of the oppressors and that I more than the Mamluks serve God. . . .

And tell them also that all people are equal in the eyes of God and the only circumstances which distinguish one from the other are reason, virtue, and knowledge. . . . Formerly, in the lands of Egypt there were great cities, and wide canals and extensive commerce and nothing ruined all this but the avarice and the tyranny of the Mamluks.

[Al-Jabarti then challenged the arguments in the French proclamation and portrayed the French as godless invaders, inspired by false ideals.]

Here is an explanation of the incoherent words and vulgar constructions which he put into this miserable letter.

His statement "In the name of God, the Merciful, the Compassionate. There is no god but God. He has no son, nor has He an associate in His Dominion." In mentioning these three sentences there is an indication that the French agree with the three religions [Islam, Judaism, and Christianity], but at the same time they do not agree with them, nor with any religion. They are consistent with the Muslims in stating the formula "In the name of God," in denying that He has a son or an associate. They disagree with the Muslims in not mentioning the two Articles of Faith, in rejecting the mission of Muhammad, and the legal words and deeds, which are necessarily recognized by religion. They agree with the Christians in most of their words and deeds, but disagree with them by not mentioning the Trinity, and denying the mission and furthermore in rejecting their beliefs, killing the priests, and destroying the churches. Then, their statement "On behalf of the French Republic, etc.," that is, this proclamation is sent from their Republic, that means their body politic, because they have no chief or sultan with whom they all agree, like others, whose function is to speak on their behalf. For when they rebelled against their sultan six years ago and killed him, the people agreed unanimously that there was not to be a single ruler but that their state, territories, laws, and administration of their affairs, should be in the hands of the intelligent and wise men among them. They appointed persons chosen by them and made them heads of the army, and below them generals and commanders of thousands, two hundreds, and tens, administrators and advisers, on condition that they were all to be equal and none superior to any other in view of the equality of creation and nature. They made this the foundation and basis of their system. This is the meaning of their statement "based upon the foundation of liberty and equality." Their term "liberty" means that they are not slaves like the Mamluks; "equality" has the aforesaid meaning. Their officials are distinguished by the cleanliness of their garments. They wear emblems on their uniforms and upon their heads. . . .

They follow this rule: great and small, high and low, male and female are all equal. Sometimes they break this rule according to their whims and inclinations or reasoning. Their women do not veil themselves and have no modesty. . . . Whenever a Frenchman has to perform an act of nature he does so where he happens to be, even in full view of people, and he goes away as he is, without washing his private parts after defecation. . . .

His saying "[all people] are equal in the eyes of God" the Almighty is a lie and stupidity. How can this be when God has made some superior to others as is testified by the dwellers in the Heavens and on Earth? . . .

So those people are opposed to both Christians and Muslims, and do not hold fast to any religion. You see that they are materialists, who deny all God's attributes. . . . May God hurry misfortune and punishment upon them, may He strike their tongues with dumbness, may He scatter their hosts, and disperse them.

Source: Abd al-Rahman al-Jabarti, *Al-Jabarti's Chronicle of the First Seven Months of the French Occupation of Egypt,* translated by Shmuel Moreh (Leiden: E. J. Brill, 1975), pp. 39–40, 42–43, 46–47.

PRIMARY SOURCE 15.3

The Haitian Declaration of Independence (1804)

Drafted by Jean-Jacques Dessalines, a former slave who went on to become the first ruler of an independent Haiti, the Haitian Declaration of Independence was issued on January 1, 1804, in the port city of Gonaïves. The Declaration marked the end of the thirteen-year-long Haitian Revolution—the only successful slave revolution in history—and established Haiti's independence from France. Haiti was the first independent nation of Latin America and only the second in the Americas, after the United States.

- Identify the terms the Declaration uses to describe the French.
- How does the Declaration distinguish Haitians from the French? Do you think race is a factor?
- How does the Declaration explain Haiti's (temporary) defeat by the French army?

Citizens:

It is not enough to have expelled the barbarians who have bloodied our land for two centuries; it is not enough to have restrained those ever-evolving factions that one after another mocked the specter of liberty that France dangled before you. We must, with one last act of national authority, forever assure the empire of liberty in the country of our birth; we must take any hope of re-enslaving us away from the inhuman government that for so long kept us in the most humiliating torpor. In the end we must live independent or die.

Independence or death . . . let these sacred words unite us and be the signal of battle and of our reunion.

Citizens, my countrymen, on this solemn day I have brought together those courageous soldiers who, as liberty lay dying, spilled their blood to save it; these generals who have guided your efforts against tyranny have not yet done enough for your happiness; the French name still haunts our land.

Everything revives the memories of the cruelties of this barbarous people: our laws, our habits, our towns, everything still carries the stamp of the French. Indeed! There are still French in our island, and you believe yourself free and independent of that Republic, which, it is true, has fought all the nations, but which has never defeated those who wanted to be free.

What! Victims of our [own] credulity and indulgence for 14 years; defeated not by French armies, but by the pathetic eloquence of their agents' proclamations; when will we tire of breathing the air that they breathe? What do we have in common with this nation of executioners? The difference between its cruelty and our patient moderation, its color and ours the great seas that separate us, our avenging climate, all tell us plainly that they are not our brothers, that they never will be, and that if they find refuge among us, they will plot again to trouble and divide us.

Native citizens, men, women, girls, and children, let your gaze extend on all parts of this island: look there for your spouses, your husbands, your brothers, your sisters. Indeed! Look there for your children, your suckling infants, what have they become? . . . I shudder to say it . . . the prey of these vultures.

Instead of these dear victims, your alarmed gaze will see only their assassins, these tigers still dripping with their blood, whose terrible presence indicts your lack of feeling and your guilty slowness in avenging them. What are you waiting for before appeasing their spirits? Remember that you had wanted your remains to rest next to those of your fathers, after you defeated tyranny; will you descend into their tombs without having avenged them? No! Their bones would reject yours.

And you, precious men, intrepid generals, who, without concern for your own pain, have revived liberty by shedding all your blood, know that you have done nothing if you do not give the nations a terrible, but just example of the vengeance that must be wrought by a people proud to have recovered its liberty and jealous to maintain it let us frighten all those who would dare try to take it from us again; let us begin with the French. Let them tremble when they approach our coast, if not from the memory of those cruelties they perpetrated here, then from the terrible resolution that we will have made to put to death anyone born French whose profane foot soils the land of liberty.

We have dared to be free, let us be thus by ourselves and for ourselves. Let us imitate the grown child: his own weight breaks the boundary that has become an obstacle to him. What people fought for us? What people wanted to gather the fruits of our labor? And what dishonorable absurdity to conquer in order to be enslaved. Enslaved? . . . Let us leave this description for the French; they conquered but are no longer free.

Let us walk down another path; let us imitate those people who, extending their concern into the future, and dreading to leave an example of cowardice for posterity, preferred to be exterminated rather than lose their place as one of the world's free peoples.

Let us ensure, however, that a missionary spirit does not destroy our work; let us allow our neighbors to breathe in peace; may they live quietly under the laws that they have made for themselves, and let us not, as revolutionary firebrands, declare ourselves the lawgivers of the Caribbean, nor let our glory consist in troubling the peace of the neighboring islands. Unlike that

which we inhabit, theirs has not been drenched in the innocent blood of its inhabitants; they have no vengeance to claim from the authority that protects them.

Fortunate to have never known the ideals that have destroyed us, they can only have good wishes for our prosperity.

Peace to our neighbors; but let this be our cry: "Anathema to the French name! Eternal hatred of France!"

Natives of Haiti! My happy fate was to be one day the sentinel who would watch over the idol to which you sacrifice; I have watched, sometimes fighting alone, and if I have been so fortunate as to return to your hands the sacred trust you confided to me, know that it is now your task to preserve it. In fighting for your liberty, I was working for my own happiness. Before consolidating it with laws that will guarantee your free individuality, your leaders, who I have assembled here, and I, owe you the final proof of our devotion. . . .

Swear, finally, to pursue forever the traitors and enemies of your independence.

Source: Laurent Dubois and John D. Garrigus, *Slave Revolution in the Caribbean, 1789–1804: A Brief History with Documents* (Boston: Bedford/St. Martins, 2006), pp. 188–91.

PRIMARY SOURCE 15.4

"What to the Slave Is the Fourth of July?" (1852), Frederick Douglass

Frederick Douglass spent the first twenty years of his life as a slave, before becoming a leading abolitionist. In this public lecture, delivered on July 5, 1852 to the Ladies' Anti-Slavery Society in Rochester, New York, Douglass contrasts the freedoms and natural rights championed in the Declaration of Independence and celebrated on the Fourth of July with the substantial lack of freedom endured by African American slaves.

- **Analyze Douglass's use of the term *citizens*. What is the significance of citizenship?**
- **Analyze the role of patriotism in this document. Is this a patriotic speech?**
- **Explain the significance of capital punishment in this document.**

Fellow-Citizens—pardon me, and allow me to ask, why am I called upon to speak here today? What have I, or those I represent, to do with your national independence? Are the great principles of political freedom and of natural justice, embodied in that Declaration of Independence, extended to us? and am I, therefore, called upon to bring our humble offering to the national altar, and to confess the benefits, and express devout gratitude for the blessings, resulting from your independence to us? . . .

But, such is not the state of the case. I say it with a sad sense of the disparity between us. I am not included within the pale of this glorious anniversary! Your high independence only reveals the immeasurable distance between us. The blessings in which you this day rejoice, are not enjoyed in common. The rich inheritance of justice, liberty, prosperity, and independence, bequeathed by your fathers, is shared by you, not by me. The sunlight that brought life and healing to you, has brought stripes and death to me. This Fourth of July is *yours,* not *mine.* *You* may rejoice, *I* must mourn. To drag a man in fetters into the grand illuminated temple of liberty, and call upon him to join you in joyous anthems, were inhuman mockery and sacrilegious irony. Do you mean, citizens, to mock me, by asking me to speak today? If so, there is a parallel to your conduct. And let me warn you that it is dangerous to copy the example of a nation whose crimes, lowering up to heaven, were thrown down by the breath of the Almighty, burying that nation in irrecoverable ruin! I can to-day take up the plaintive lament of a peeled and woe-smitten people! . . .

Fellow-citizens; above your national, tumultuous joy, I hear the mournful wail of millions! whose chains, heavy and grievous yesterday, are, to-day, rendered more intolerable by the jubilee shouts that reach them. If I do forget, if I do not faithfully remember those bleeding children of sorrow this day, "may my right hand forget her cunning, and may my tongue cleave to the roof of my mouth!" To forget them, to pass lightly over their wrongs, and to chime in with the popular theme, would be treason most scandalous and shocking, and would make me a reproach before God and the world. My subject, then fellow-citizens, is AMERICAN SLAVERY. I shall see, this day, and its popular characteristics, from the slave's point of view. Standing, there, identified with the American bondman, making his wrongs mine, I do not hesitate to declare, with all my soul, that the character and conduct of this nation never looked blacker to me than on this 4th of July! Whether we turn to the declarations of the past, or to the professions of the present, the conduct of the nation seems equally hideous and revolting. America is false to the past, false to the present, and solemnly binds herself to be false to the future. Standing with God and the crushed and bleeding slave on this occasion, I will, in the name of humanity which is outraged, in the name of liberty which is fettered, in the name of the constitution and the Bible, which are disregarded and trampled upon, dare to call in question and to denounce, with all the emphasis I can command, everything that serves to perpetuate slavery—the great sin and shame of America! "I will not equivocate; I will not excuse"; I will use the severest language I can command; and yet not one word shall escape me that any man, whose judgment is not blinded by prejudice, or who is not at heart a slaveholder, shall not confess to be right and just. . . .

Must I undertake to prove that the slave is a man? That point is conceded already. Nobody doubts it. The slaveholders themselves acknowledge it in the enactment of laws for their government. They acknowledge it when they punish disobedience on the part of the slave. There are seventy-two crimes in the state of Virginia, which, if committed by a black man (no matter how ignorant he be) subject him to the punishment of death; while only two of these same crimes will subject a white man to the like punishment. What is this but the acknowledgment that the slave is a moral, intellectual, and responsible being. The manhood of the slave is conceded. It is admitted in the fact that southern statute books are covered with enactments forbidding, under severe fines and penalties, the teaching of the slave to read or write. When you can point to any such laws, in reference to the beasts of the field, then I may consent to argue the manhood of the slave. When the dogs in your streets, when the fowls of the air, when the cattle on your hills, when the fish of the sea, and the reptiles that crawl, shall be unable to distinguish the slave from a brute, then will I argue with you that the slave is a man!

Source: Frederick Douglass, *Narrative of the Life of Frederick Douglass, an American Slave, Written by Himself,* A Norton Critical Edition, edited by William L. Andrews and William S. McFeely (New York: Norton, 1997), pp. 123–25.

Interpreting Visual Evidence

Framing the Subject

mportant currents of Enlightenment thought (which fed into classical liberalism in the nineteenth century—see Chapter 16) stressed the autonomy of the individual. All men were thought to be created equal, endowed with reason and the ability to master nature and the world around them. European liberals celebrated individual initiative, self-control, and material success through hard work as signs of virtue. They also drew from the Enlightenment a faith that the natural world follows observable laws. This faith gave rise, as we have seen, to advances in the natural sciences and then the social sciences. In the arts, that faith corresponded to a renewed interest in representing the external world in precise, objective terms, called realism. Painters sought to capture and reflect an independent, external, stable reality—this in a period before photography.

It was a confident but also a self-centered view of the world.

Here we consider efforts to represent the individual in portraiture. Jean-Auguste-Dominique Ingres painted the French newspaper baron and businessman Louis-François Bertin, in a portrait from 1832. Bertin's *Journal des Débats* served as the recognized organ of the opposition to the Bourbon Restoration in early nineteenth-century France and helped put the constitutional July Monarchy in power. The painter Édouard Manet described Bertin as "the Buddha of the self-satisfied, well-to-to, triumphant bourgeoisie." Unlike Ingres, who painted a real historical figure, Jean-Léon Gérôme, in *Bashi-Bazouk* (1868–69), painted a model dressed in garments made of textiles he had acquired on a trip to the Near East, to represent the unpaid, irregular mercenary soldiers who lived from

Ingres, *Louis-François Bertin*.

Gérôme, *Bashi-Bazouk*.

plunder and fought in Ottoman armies. Gérôme conceived and executed this painting of an Ottoman soldier in a European studio. In the *Portrait of an Indian*, French artist Anne-Louis Girodet-Trioson painted a man in Ottoman clothing. Finally, the *Portrait of the Imperial Bodyguard Zhanyinbao* was probably sketched by a (European) Jesuit artist in the Chinese court and then transferred to a silk scroll by a Chinese master.

Girodet-Trioson, *Portrait of an Indian*.

Portrait of the Imperial Bodyguard Zhanyinbao.

Questions for Analysis

1. Create a psychological profile for each portrait. What clues does the artist give you about the men, their values, and their standing in the world?

2. What is the effect of the sparse backgrounds and the intricate detail in the foregrounds? What do you think the artists left out of these portraits that might influence your profiles?

3. Do the painters create coherent images of their subjects? What contradictions can you see—for

example, between violent aggression and delicate refinement, or between order and disorder—with respect to discipline and control?

4. Compare the two "Orientalist" paintings—the *Portrait of an Indian* and *Bashi-Bazouk*—with the other two. What does Orientalist mean in this context? How, in particular, do they differ from the *Portrait of the Imperial Bodyguard Zhanyinbao*?

16

Alternative Visions of the Nineteenth Century

By the late nineteenth century, territorial expansion in the United States confined almost all Native Americans to reservations. The buffalo that once supported many tribes disappeared: white settlers built towns, farms, and railroads throughout the buffalo's natural habitat, and Native Americans overhunted the shrinking herds. Across the American West, many Native Americans fell into despair. One was a Paiute named Wovoka. But in 1889, he had a vision of a much brighter future. In his dream, the "Supreme Being" told Wovoka that if Native Americans lived harmoniously, shunned white ways (especially alcohol), and performed the cleansing Ghost Dance, then the buffalo would return, and Native Americans, including the dead, would be reborn to live in eternal happiness.

As word spread of Wovoka's vision, Native Americans from hundreds of miles around made pilgrimages to the lodge of this new prophet. Many proclaimed him the Native Americans' messiah or the "Red Man's Christ," an impression fostered by scars on his hands. Soon, increasing numbers joined in the ritual Ghost Dance, hoping it would restore the good life that European colonialism in the Americas had extinguished. Among the hopefuls was Sitting Bull, a revered Sioux chief who was himself famous for his visions. Yet, less than two years after Wovoka's vision, Sitting Bull died at the hands of police forces on a Sioux reservation.

Chapter Outline
- Reactions to Social and Political Change
- Prophecy and Revitalization in the Islamic World and Africa
- Prophecy and Rebellion in China
- Socialists and Radicals in Europe
- Insurgencies against Colonizing and Centralizing States
- Conclusion

Core Objectives
- **DESCRIBE** the challenges to the ideals of industrial capitalism, colonialism, and nation-states in this period.
- **COMPARE** the utopian goals, immediate outcomes, and long-term influence of rebel movements around the world.
- **ANALYZE** the connections between nineteenth-century protest movements and organized religion.
- **ASSESS** the role religion played in these alternative social visions.

A few days later, on December 29, 1890, the U.S. Seventh Cavalry Regiment massacred Sioux Ghost Dancers at a South Dakota creek called Wounded Knee.

Though it failed, this movement was one of many prophetic crusades that challenged an emerging nineteenth-century order. The ideals of the French and American Revolutions in politics—equality before the law, and government for and by property-holding citizens in a world of nation-states—now provided the dominant answers to age-old questions of who should govern and how. Emerging from the industrial revolution, the ideas of free market (laissez-faire) capitalism, in which private owners competed against one another to maximize profits using new technologies and industrial organizations, provided the dominant answers to questions about how productive activity should be organized. But these political and economic answers were not powerful enough entirely to stamp out other views. A diverse assortment of political radicals, charismatic prophets, peasant rebels, and anticolonial insurgents put forward striking counterproposals to those that capitalists, colonial modernizers, and nation-state builders had developed. The people making these counterproposals were motivated by the impending loss of their existing worlds and were energized by visions of ideal, utopian futures.

This chapter presents the voices and visions of those who opposed a nineteenth-century world in which capitalism, colonialism, and nation-states held sway. It puts the spotlight on challengers who shared a dislike of global capitalism and European (and North American) colonialism. Beyond that similarity, these challengers differed in significant ways, for the alternatives they proposed reflected the local circumstances in which each of them developed. Although many of these challengers suffered devastating defeats, like the Ghost Dancers at Wounded Knee, the dreams that aroused their fervor did not always die with them. Some of these alternative visions of the nineteenth century endured to propel the great transformations of the twentieth.

Global Storylines

- Protest movements challenge the nineteenth-century order based on industrial capitalism, the nation-state, and colonization.

- Led by prophets, political radicals, and common people, the movements arise among marginal groups and regions and express visions of ideal, utopian futures.

- The movements differ markedly depending on distance from the centers of change (Europe and the Americas) and reflect local circumstances.

- Although most movements are defeated, they give voice to the views of peasants and workers and have a lasting effect on the policies of ruling elites.

Reactions to Social and Political Change

The alternatives to the emerging order of the nineteenth century varied considerably. Some rebels and dissidents called for the revitalization of traditional religions; others wanted to strengthen village and communal bonds; still others imagined a society where there was no private property and where people shared goods equally. The actions of these dissenters depended on their local traditions and the degree of contact they had with the effects of industrial capitalism, European colonialism, and centralizing nation-states.

This era of rapid social change, when differing visions of power and justice vied with one another, offers unique opportunities to hear the voices of the lower orders—the peasants and workers, whose perspectives the elites often ignored or suppressed. While there are few written records that capture the views of the illiterate and the marginalized, we do have traditions of folklore, dreams, rumors, and prophecies. Handed down orally from generation to generation, these resources illuminate the visions of common people.

Prophecy and Revitalization in the Islamic World and Africa

In regions that experienced European and North American influence but not direct colonial rule, alternative perspectives were strongest far from the main trade and cultural routes. People outside the emerging capitalist world order led these movements. In the Islamic world and Africa, leaders on the margins were especially important in articulating alternative views.

Even though much of the Islamic world and non-Islamic Africa had not been colonized and was only partially involved with European-dominated trading networks, these regions had reached turning points. By the late eighteenth century, the era of Islamic expansion and cultural flowering under the Ottomans, Safavids, and Mughals was over. Their empires had extended Muslim trading orbits, facilitated cross-cultural communication, and promoted common knowledge over vast territories. Their political and military decline, however, brought new challenges to the faithful. The sense of alarm intensified as Christian Europe's power spread from the edges of the Islamic world to its centers. While this perception of danger motivated military men in Egypt and the Ottoman sultans to modernize their states (see Chapter 15), it also bred religious revitalization movements that sought to recapture the glories of past traditions. Led by prophets who feared that the Islamic faith was in trouble, these movements spoke the language of revival and restoration as they sought to establish new religiously based governments across lands in which Muslims ruled and Islamic law prevailed.

Prophecy also exerted a strong influence in non-Islamic Africa, where long-distance trade and population growth were upending the social order. Just as Muslim clerics and political leaders sought solutions to unsettling changes by rereading Islamic classics, African communities looked to charismatic leaders who drew strength from their peoples' spiritual and magical traditions. Often uniting disparate groups behind their dynamic visions, prophetic leaders and other "big men" gained power because they were able to resolve local crises—mostly caused by drought, a shortage of arable land, or some other issue related to the harsh environment.

ISLAMIC REVITALIZATION

Movements to revitalize Islam took place on the peripheries—at a certain remove from trade networks and the changes wrought by global capitalism. (See Map 16.1.) Here, religious leaders rejected the westernizing influences they felt encroaching on their authority and way of life. Revitalization movements looked back to Islamic traditions and modeled their revolts on the life of Muhammad. But even as they looked to the past, they attempted to establish something new: full-scale theocracies. These reformers conceived of the state as the primary instrument of God's will and as the vehicle for purifying Islamic culture. (See Current Trends in World History: Islam: An Enduring Alternative in Algeria.)

Wahhabism One of the most powerful reformist movements arose on the Arabian Peninsula, the birthplace of the Muslim faith. In the Najd region, an area surrounded by mountains and deserts, a religious cleric named Muhammad Ibn Abd al-Wahhab (1703–1792) galvanized the population by attacking what he regarded as lax religious practices. His message found a ready response among local inhabitants, who felt threatened by the new commercial activities and fresh intellectual currents swirling around them. Abd al-Wahhab demanded a return to the pure Islam of Muhammad and the early caliphs.

Although Najd was far removed from the centers of the expanding world economy, Abd al-Wahhab himself was not. Having been educated in Iraq, Iran, and the Hijaz (a region on the western end of modern Saudi Arabia, on the Red Sea), he believed that Islam had fallen into a degraded state, particularly in its birthplace. He railed against the polytheistic beliefs that had taken hold of the people, complaining that in defiance of Muhammad's tenets men and women were worshipping trees, stones, and tombs and making sacrifices to false images. Abd al-Wahhab's movement stressed the absolute oneness of Allah and severely criticized Sufi sects for extolling the lives of saints over the worship of God.

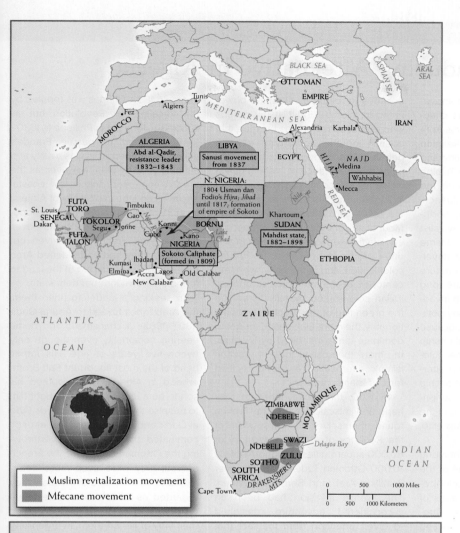

Map 16.1 Muslim Revitalization Movements in the Middle East and Africa and the *Mfecane* Movement in Southern Africa

Map 16.1 Muslim Revitalization Movements in the Middle East and Africa and the *Mfecane* Movement in Southern Africa

....

During the nineteenth century, a series of Muslim revitalization movements took place throughout the Middle East and North Africa.

- According to this map, in how many different areas did the revitalization movements occur?
- Based on their geographic location within their larger regions, did these movements occur in central or peripheral areas?
- According to your reading, were any of the same factors that led to Islamic revitalization involved in the *Mfecane* developments in southern Africa?

Islam: An Enduring Alternative in Algeria

Many of the alternative movements featured in this chapter derived their impetus from deeply held religious beliefs. Religion played a role in the Indian mutiny and in the visions that spurred the Taiping rebels. In Muslim locations far from the main currents of western influence, like the Arabian Peninsula and northern Nigeria, it generated revivalist movements. But elsewhere it became a political force, and one that developed a palpably anti-European nature as well as the power to endure long beyond the victory of European invaders. World historians like to study political and social movements because they bring into relief the relationship between the colonizer and the colonized and, in the case of these alternative movements, the relationship between peoples living on the peripheries of empires and those living in the center who are part of the ruling elite, including indigenous elites.

This was the case in particular along the old Ottoman periphery, one of the major targets for European colonization. Strikingly, in the first decades of the nineteenth century, in the Ottomans' Balkan domains of Serbia and Greece, Christianity had linked together opponents against the empire. In the decades to follow, as Ottoman power receded, it left behind it Islamic groups who also used religion as the glue that bound together otherwise diverse peoples. The following example highlights the importance of Islam in galvanizing resistance to French imperialism in Algeria. But there are examples: in the 1840s and 1850s in the Caucasus Mountains, another Ottoman periphery, Islam linked together Chechen and other groups in opposition to Russian colonization; and in the early twentieth century, Libyans attempted to oppose Italian colonization by rallying behind the green flag of the Prophet. Unquestionably, the more Europeans sought to dominate lands inhabited by Muslims, the more they called forth in reaction Islamic alternatives and a politicized form of Islamic resistance.

In 1830, through a series of mishaps and miscalculations, the French found themselves in possession of the Regency of Algiers, a territory of 60,000 square miles where previously 10,000 Ottoman Turks had ruled over 3 million Arab and Berber tribesmen. The French invasion had been an ill-considered adventure, designed to divert attention from the fact that the backward-looking French king, Charles X, had lost his legitimacy at home. In 1830, Charles was toppled by the so-called July Revolution, but his successor, King Louis Philippe (r. 1830–1848), decided to pursue France's adventure abroad. This was a risky and ultimately costly plan, however, as the French controlled only a few coastal enclaves and the capital city of Algiers; in 1831, the European civilian population was a mere 3,228. Moreover, although the French had driven out the Turks, they had emboldened Arab tribes in the western part of the land to found their own independent state.

In seeking a leader to unite them, the Arab tribes turned to Abd al-Qadir (1807–1883), a charismatic and domineering personality even though only twenty-five years of age. His father, head of the most important Sufi Brotherhood in Algeria, had groomed his son to be a leader and had taught him to despise the Ottoman overlords. Abd al-Qadir and his followers had already committed themselves to overthrowing the Ottomans, but once the French arrived, they were even more determined to rid their area of invaders they regarded as infidels who were intent on seizing their lands and imposing their way of life on them. In organizing resistance to the French, Abd al-Qadir relied on his reputation as a holy man

Wahhabism

Early eighteenth-century reform movement organized by Muhammad Ibn Abd al-Wahhab, who preached the absolute oneness of Allah and a return to the pure Islam of Muhammad.

As **Wahhabism** swept across the Arabian Peninsula, the movement threatened the Ottomans' hold on the region. Wahhabism gained a powerful political ally in the Najdian House of Saud, a leading family whose followers, inspired by the Wahhabis' religious zeal, undertook a militant religious campaign in the final years of the eighteenth century. Frightened by the Wahhabi challenge, the Ottoman sultan persuaded the provincial ruler of Egypt to send troops to the Arabian Peninsula to suppress the movement.

Abd al-Qadir in Exile, Damascus, Syria (1862) Having surrendered to a massive French army in December 1847, Abd al-Qadir was imprisoned in France. After the Revolution of 1848, the new French president, Louis-Napoleon Bonaparte (Napoleon's nephew) released Abd al-Qadir and gave him a government pension in return for the latter's promise not to disturb Algeria.

and a scholar, rather than as merely the head of one of the tribes. In preparation for battle, he called on his soldiers to follow him in a holy war (*jihad*) against Christian invaders, promising those who joined him in battle that "anyone of you who dies, will die a martyr; those of you who survive will gain glory and live happily." Tribes that might not have fought together, or fought together

so long, did so because they were united by their loyalty to a religious as well as a political leader. Abd al-Qadir succeeded in part because he was a forceful personality, but in part because he stood for Islam, which the native Algerians shared, whatever their kinship ties or loyalties to local leaders.

For fifteen years, Abd al-Qadir's forces held out, only surrendering to a massive French force of 108,000 men in 1847. Although often defeated in pitched battles, Abd al-Qadir used his superior knowledge of the terrain and his ability to wait in ambush for French columns to frustrate the French. The French government was finally compelled to send its most accomplished military man, Marshal Thomas-Robert Bugeaud, and to provide him with one-third of its entire military force to finish the job of "pacifying" Algeria.

The French conquest of Algeria marks one of the bloodiest episodes in the history of those two lands. No fewer than 300,000 Algerians perished during these years. Although the French portrayed Abd al-Qadir as a Muslim fanatic, determined to take his people back to a dark age, their message fell on deaf ears. The Algerians extolled him for resisting the French and later made him an iconic figure

of the nationalist movement. One of the first acts carried out by the independent Algerian government in 1962 was to tear down the statue of Marshal Bugeaud and to replace it with one of Abd al-Qadir. The religiously motivated resistance leader had prevailed over the secular political conquerors after all.

Questions for Analysis

- What impact did Algeria's geographic location have on its role in these revolutionary events?
- How did native Algerians view their former Ottoman rulers compared to French Europeans? What was their ultimate goal?

Explore Further

Brower, Benjamin Claude, *A Desert Named Peace: The Violence of France's Empire in the Algerian Sahara, 1844–1902* (2009).

Clancy-Smith, Julia, *Rebel and Saint: Muslim Notables, Populist Protest, Colonial Encounter (Algeria and Tunisia, 1800–1904)* (1994).

Danziger, Raphael, *Abd al-Qadir: Resistance to the French and Internal Consolidation* (1977).

The Egyptians defeated the Saudis in 1818, but Wahhabism and the House of Saud continued to represent a pure Islamic faith that attracted clerics and ordinary people throughout the Muslim world.

Usman dan Fodio and the Fulani In West Africa, Muslim revolts erupted from Senegal to Nigeria in the early nineteenth century, partly in response to increased trade with the outside world and the circulation of religious ideas from across the Sahara Desert. In this region, the Fulani people were decisive in religious uprisings that sought, like the Wahhabi movement, to re-create a supposedly purer Islamic past. The majority were cattle keepers, practicing a pastoral and nomadic way of life. But some were sedentary, living in settled communities, and people in this group converted to Islam, read the Islamic classics, and communicated with holy men of North Africa, Egypt, and the Arabian Peninsula. They concluded that West African peoples were violating Islamic beliefs and engaging in irreligious practices.

The most powerful of these reform movements flourished in what is today northern Nigeria. Its leader was a Fulani Muslim cleric, **Usman dan Fodio** (1754–1817), who ultimately created a vast Islamic empire. Dan Fodio's movement had all the trappings of the Islamic revolts of this period. It sought inspiration in the life of Muhammad and demanded a return to early Islamic practices. It attacked false belief and urged followers to wage holy war (*jihad*) against unbelievers.

Dan Fodio blamed local leaders for what he saw as their failure to respect Islamic law. He won the support of devout Muslims in the area, who agreed that the people were not properly practicing Islam. He also gained the backing of his Fulani tribes and many Hausa-speaking peasants, who had suffered under the rule of the Hausa landlord class. The revolt, initiated in 1804, resulted in the overthrow of the Hausa rulers and the creation of a confederation of Islamic emirates, almost all of which were in the hands of the Fulani allies of dan Fodio.

Fulani women of northern Nigeria made critical contributions to the success of the religious revolt. Although dan Fodio and other male leaders of the purification movement expected women to obey the *sharia* (Islamic law), being modest in their dress and their association with men outside the family, they also expected women to support the community's military and religious endeavors. In this effort, they cited women's important role in the first days of Islam. The best known of the Muslim women leaders was Nana Asma'u (1793–1864), daughter of dan Fodio. Fulani women of the upper ranks acquired an Islamic education, and Asma'u was as astute a reader of Islamic texts as any of the learned men in her society. Like other Muslim Fulani devotees, she accompanied the warriors on their campaigns, encamped with them, prepared food for them, bound up their wounds, and provided daily encouragement. According to many accounts, Asma'u inspired the warriors at their most crucial battle, hurling a burning spear into the midst of the enemy army. Her poem "Song of the Circular Journey" celebrates the triumphs of military forces that trekked thousands of miles to bring a reformed Islam to the area.

Usman dan Fodio considered himself a cleric first and a political and military man second. Although his political leadership was decisive in the revolt's success, thereafter he retired to a life of scholarship and writing. He delegated the political and administrative functions of the new empire to his brother and his son. An enduring decentralized state structure, which became known as the Sokoto caliphate in 1809, developed into a stable empire that helped spread Islam through the region. In 1800, on the eve of dan Fodio's revolt, Islam was the faith of a small minority of people living in northern Nigeria; a century later, it had become the religion of the vast majority, thanks to dan Fodio's military prowess and success in creating a stable political structure, and the increasing Fulani contacts with the broader Islamic world.

CHARISMATIC MILITARY MEN IN NON-ISLAMIC AFRICA

Non-Islamic Africa saw revolts, new states, and prophetic movements arise from the same combination of factors that influenced the rest of the world—particularly long-distance trade and population increase. Local communities here also looked to religious traditions and, as was so often the case in African history, expected charismatic clan leaders, known as "big men," to provide political leadership.

In southern Africa, early in the nineteenth century, a group of political revolts reordered the political map. Collectively known as the **Mfecane** ("the crushing" in Zulu) **movement**, its epicenter was a large tract of land lying east of the Drakensberg Mountains, an area where growing populations and land resources existed in a precarious balance (see again Map 16.1). Many branches of Bantu-speaking peoples had inhabited the southern part of the African landmass for centuries. At the end of the eighteenth century, however, their political organizations still operated on a small scale. These tiny polities could not cope with the competition for land that now dominated southern Africa. That competition intensified with the arrival of British colonizers, who fought both with Dutch settlers and indigenous African communities over natural resources. The import of European goods that flowed into southern Africa from Delagoa Bay also was a destabilizing factor. A branch of the Nguni, the Zulus, produced a fierce war leader, Shaka (1787–1828), who created a ruthless warrior state. It drove other populations out of the region and forced a shift from small clan communities to large, centralized monarchies throughout southern and central Africa.

The son of a minor chief, Shaka emerged victorious in a struggle for cattle-grazing and farming lands that arose during a severe drought. A physically imposing figure, Shaka used terror to intimidate his subjects and to overawe his adversaries. His enemies knew that the price of opposition would be a massacre, even of women and children. Nor was he kinder to his own people. Following the death of his beloved mother, he executed those who were not properly contrite and did not weep profusely. Reportedly, it took 7,000 lives to assuage his grief.

Mfecane movement
African political revolts in the first half of the nineteenth century that were caused by the expansionist methods of King Shaka of the Zulu people.

CHAKA KING OF THE ZOOLUS.

London, Published by E.Churton, 26 Holles St.

Shaka and His Zulu Regiments
(*Left*) This illustration, the only one from the time, may be an exaggeration, but it does not exaggerate the view that many had of the awesome strength and power of Shaka, the leader who united the Zulu peoples into an invincible warrior state. (*Right*) The Battle of Isandlwana (1879) was the first major encounter in the war between the British and Shaka's Zulu state. The larger Zulu army overwhelmed the British, despite the latter's superior firepower.

Shaka built a new Zulu state around his military and organizational skills and the fear that his personal ferocity produced. He drilled his men relentlessly in the use of short stabbing spears and in discipline under pressure. Like the Mongols, he had a remarkable ability to incorporate defeated communities into the state and to absorb young men into his military. His army of 40,000 men comprised regiments that lived, studied, and fought together. Forbidden from marrying until they were discharged from the army, Shaka's warriors developed an intense esprit de corps and regarded no sacrifice as too great in the service of the state. So overpowering were these forces that other peoples of the region fled from their home areas, and Shaka claimed their estates for himself and his followers. Peoples in nearby areas who weren't absorbed into the Zulu state adopted many of Shaka's military and political innovations, at first to defend themselves and then to take over new land as they fled their old areas. The new states of the Ndebele in what later became Zimbabwe and the Sotho of South Africa came into existence in this way in the mid-nineteenth century.

In turning southern Africa from a region of smaller polities into an area with larger and more powerful states, Shaka seemed very much a man of the modern, nineteenth-century world. Yet he was, in his own unique way, a familiar kind of African leader. He shared a charismatic and prophetic style with others who emerged during periods of acute social change. His new state built an enduring Zulu community and established its traditions against encroachments by outside, European forces.

Prophecy and Rebellion in China

In the mid-nineteenth century, China experienced an explosive popular rebellion that incorporated Christian beliefs into its long tradition of peasant revolts. Whereas movements promoting alternative visions in the Islamic world and Africa appeared in areas distant from western influences and drew substantially on their own traditions, China was no longer isolated. In fact, it had been conducting a brisk trade in opium with Europe. Until 1842, the Chinese had confined trade with Europeans to the port city of Canton. After the Opium War, however, westerners forced Qing rulers to open up a number of other ports to trade.

As in the Islamic world and other parts of sub-Saharan Africa, population increases in China—from 250 million in 1644 to around 450 million by the 1850s—were putting considerable pressure on land and other resources. Moreover, the rising consumption of opium, grown in India and brought to China by British traders, produced further social instability and financial crisis. As banditry and rebellions spread, the Qing rulers turned to the landed elites, the gentry, to maintain order in the countryside. But as the gentry raised its militia to suppress these troublemakers, it whittled away at the authority of the Qing Manchu rulers. Faced with these changes, the Qing dynasty struggled to maintain control.

Searching for an alternative present and future, hundreds of thousands of disillusioned peasants joined what became known as the Taiping Rebellion. Beginning in 1850, the uprising drew on China's long history of peasant revolts. Traditionally, these rebellions ignited within popular religious sects whose visions were egalitarian or **millenarian** (convinced of the imminent coming of a just and ideal society). Moreover, in contrast to orthodox institutions, here women played important roles. Inspired by Daoists, who revered a past golden age before the world was corrupted by human conventions, or by Buddhist sources, these sects threatened the established order.

THE DREAM OF HONG XIUQUAN

The story of the rebellion begins with a complex dream that inspired its founding prophet, Hong Xiuquan (1813–1864). A native of Guangdong Province in the southernmost part of the country (see Map 16.2), Hong first encountered Christian missionaries in the 1830s. He was then trying, unsuccessfully, to pass the civil service examination. After failing the exam for the third time, Hong suffered a strange "illness" in which he had visions of combating demons; these dreams included a mysterious "Old Father" and an "Elder Brother." He also began proclaiming himself the Heavenly King. Relatives and neighbors thought he might have gone mad, but Hong gradually returned to his normal state.

millenarian
Believer (usually religious) in the cataclysmic destruction of a corrupt, fallen society and its replacement by an ideal, utopian future.

Map 16.2 The Taiping Rebellion in China, 1850–1864

The Taiping Rebellion started in the southwestern part of the country. The rebels, however, went on to control much of the lower Yangzi region and part of the coastal area.

- What cities did the rebels' march start and end in?

- Why do you think the Taiping rebels were so successful in southern China and not in northern regions?

- How did western powers react to the Taiping Rebellion? Would they have been as concerned if the rebellion took place farther to the north or west?

Map labels:
SHAANXI · Zhengzhou · HENAN · JIANGSU · ANHUI · Nanjing · Suzhou · Yangzhou · Shanghai · YELLOW SEA · HUBEI · Hankou · Wuchang · Anqing · Hangzhou · ZHEJIANG · Yangzi R. · Chengdu · SICHUAN · Chongqing · Nanchang · EAST CHINA SEA · Changsha · HUNAN · JIANGXI · GUIZHOU · Guiyang · FUJIAN · Fuzhou · Guilin · Yongan · Amoy (Xiamen) · TAIWAN · YUNNAN · Jintian · GUANGXI · GUANGDONG · Guangzhou (Canton) · Nanning · Hong Kong · Macao · SOUTH CHINA SEA

Legend:
- Area controlled by rebels, c. 1861
- Hong's march to establish Heavenly Capital in Nanjing, 1850–1853
- Unsuccessful northern campaign, 1853–1854
- Advance of Western troops, 1864
- Advance of Qing troops, 1864

0   100   200   300 Miles
0   100   200   300 Kilometers

Taiping Rebellion

(1850–1864) Rebellion by followers of Hong Xiuquan and the Taiping Heavenly Kingdom against the Qing government over the economic and social turmoil caused by the Opium War. Despite raising an army of 100,000 rebels, the rebellion was crushed.

In 1843, after failing the exam for the fourth time, Hong immersed himself in a Christian tract titled *Good Words for Exhorting the Age*. Reportedly, reading this tract enabled Hong to realize the full significance of his earlier visions. All the pieces suddenly fell into place, and he began to grasp their meaning. The "Old Father," he concluded, was the Lord Ye-huo-hua (a Chinese rendering of "Jehovah"), the creator of heaven and earth. His visions of cleansing rituals in heaven foretold Hong's baptism. The "Elder Brother" was Jesus the Savior, the son of God. He, Hong Xiuquan, was the younger brother of Jesus—God's other son. Just as God had previously sent Jesus to save mankind, Hong thought, God was now sending *him* to rid the world of evil. What was once a series of dreams now became a prophetic vision.

THE REBELLION

Hong's prophecy tapped into a millenarian tradition, inspiring a movement that spread rapidly from southern China. Unlike earlier sectarian leaders whose plots for rebellion were secret before exploding onto the public arena, Hong chose a more audacious path. Once convinced of his vision, he began to preach his doctrines openly, baptizing converts and destroying Confucian idols and ancestral shrines. Such assaults on the establishment testified to his conviction that he was carrying out God's will. Hong's message of revital-ization of a troubled land and restoration of the "heavenly kingdom," imagined as a just and egalitarian order, appealed to the subordinate classes caught in the flux of social change. Drawing on a largely rural social base and asserting allegiance to Christianity, the **Taiping** ("Great Peace") **Rebellion** (1850–1864) claimed to herald a new era of economic and social justice.

Many early followers came from the margins of local society—those whose anger at social and economic dislocations caused by the Opium War was directed not at the Europeans but at the Qing gov-ernment. The Taiping identified the rul-ing Manchus as the "demons" and as the chief obstacle to realizing God's kingdom on earth. Taiping policies were strict: they prohibited the consumption of alcohol, the smoking of opium, and any indulgence in sensual pleasure. Men and women were segregated for administrative and residen-tial purposes. At the same time, in a drastic departure from dynastic practice, women joined the army in segregated units.

By 1850, Hong's movement had amassed a following of over 20,000, giving Qing rulers cause for concern. When they sent troops to arrest Hong and other rebel leaders, Taiping forces repelled them and then took their turmoil beyond the southwestern part of the country. In January 1851, Hong declared himself Heavenly King of the "Taiping Heavenly Kingdom" (or "Heavenly Kingdom of Great Peace"). By 1853, the rebels had captured major cities. Upon capturing Nanjing, the Taiping cleansed the city of "demons" by systematically killing all the Manchus they

Taiping Rebellion A painting depicting the Taiping rebels attacking a town. Had the Taip-ing succeeded in overthrowing the Qing, it would have changed the course of Chinese history and profoundly affected the rest of the world.

could find—men, women, and children. Then they established their own "heavenly" capital in the city.

But the rebels could not sustain their vision. Several factors contributed to the fall of the Heavenly Kingdom: struggles within the leadership, an excessively rigid code of conduct, and the rallying of Manchu and Han elites around the embattled dynasty. Disturbed by the Taiping's rejection of Confucianism and wanting to protect their property, landowning gentry led militias against the Taiping. Moreover, western governments also opposed the rebellion, claiming that its doctrines represented a perversion of Christianity. Thus, a mercenary army led by foreign officers took part in suppressing the rebellion. Hong himself perished as his heavenly capital fell in 1864. All told, at least 20 million people died in the Taiping Rebellion.

Like their counterparts in the Islamic world and Africa, the Taiping rebels promised to restore lost harmony. Despite all the differences of cultural and historical background, what Abd al-Wahhab, dan Fodio, Shaka, and Hong had in common was the perception that the present world was unjust. Thus, they sought to reorganize their communities—an endeavor that involved confronting established authorities. In this regard, the language of revitalization used by prophets in Islamic areas and China was crucial, for it provided an alternative vocabulary of political and spiritual legitimacy. By mobilizing masses eager to return to an imagined golden age, these prophets and charismatic leaders gave voice to those dispossessed by global change, while producing new, alternative ways of organizing society and politics.

Socialists and Radicals in Europe

Core Objectives

DESCRIBE the challenges to the ideals of industrial capitalism and nation-states in this period in Europe and the Americas.

Europe and North America were the core areas of economic growth, based on the industrial revolution and free trade, nation-state building, and colonial expansion. But there, too, the main currents of thought and activity encountered challenges. Prophets of all stripes—political, social, cultural, and religious—voiced antiestablishment values and dreamed of alternative arrangements. Radicals, liberals, utopian socialists, nationalists, abolitionists, and religious mavericks made plans for better worlds to come.

RESTORATION AND RESISTANCE

The social and political ferment of the efforts to restore the old order, known as the Restoration period (1815–1848), owed a great deal to the ambiguous legacies of the French Revolution and the Napoleonic wars. (See Map 16.3.) Kings had been toppled and replaced by republics, and then by Napoleon and his relatives; these experiments gave Restoration-era states and radicals many political options from which to choose in the years between Napoleon's downfall in 1815 and the revolutions of 1848.

Map 16.3 Civil Unrest and Revolutions in Europe, 1819–1848

Civil unrest and revolutions swept Europe after the Congress of Vienna established a peace settlement at the end of the French Revolution and Napoleon's conquests. Conservative governments had to fight off liberal rebellions and demands for change.

- How many sites of revolutionary activity can you locate on this map?
- What parts of Europe appear to have been politically stable, and what parts rebellious? Based on your reading and the map, can you explain the stability of some parts of Europe and the instability of others?

This period has often been called the Age of Ideology because revolutionary upheavals forced everyone, even those in power, to justify their vision of the social order. Appeals to tradition no longer sufficed. Those called reactionaries or conservatives wanted a return to the world that existed before the French Revolution; they rejected change. Liberals, by contrast, accepted the French Revolution's overthrow of aristocratic privilege. They wanted to hold on to the principles of 1789—above all free trade and equality before the law—without accepting the price controls and political violence of the Terror. Free markets rather than government controls, they believed, would make the most sensible decisions. These proponents of **liberalism** insisted on the individual's right to think, speak, act, and vote as he or she pleased without government interference, so long as no harm came to people or property. Both reactionaries and liberals could find elements to their taste in all the states of the post-Napoleonic world. Much more threatening to the ruling elite were the radicals who believed that the French Revolution had not gone far enough. They longed for a grander revolution that would sweep away the Restoration's political *and* economic order.

RADICAL VISIONS

Reactionaries and liberals did not form the only alternative groups of importance at this time. Most discontented of all—and most determined to effect grand-scale change—were the radicals.

The term *radicals* refers to those who favored the total reconfiguration of the old regime's state system: going to the root of the problem and continuing the revolution, not reversing it or stopping reform. In general, radicals shared a bitter hatred for the status quo and an insistence on popular sovereignty, but beyond this consensus much disagreement remained. If some radicals demanded the equalization or abolition of private property, others—like Serbian, Greek, Polish, and Italian nationalists—were primarily interested in throwing off the oppressive overlordship of the Ottoman and Austrian Empires and creating their own nation-states. It was the radicals' threat of a return to revolutions that ultimately reconciled both liberals and reactionaries to preserving the status quo.

Nationalists In the period before the revolutions of 1848, nationalism was a cause dear to both liberals and radicals, and it threatened conservative rulers who claimed to rule by divine right. The idea of popular sovereignty spread, especially during and after Napoleon's occupation of the continent, but who exactly were "the people"? The "people," or the nation, were generally considered to be those who shared a common language, culture, and history, but nationalists fought bitterly over which people counted and who decided.

All nationalists believed that governments should represent the "people" and that each people—or, at least, their people—should have a state of their own.

Each fledgling nationalist movement—whether Polish, Czech, Greek, Italian, or German—had different contours, but they all drew backers from the liberal aristocracy and the well-educated, commercially active middle classes. Most nationalist movements were, at first, weak and easily crushed, such as attempted Polish uprisings inside tsarist Russia in 1830–1831 and 1863–1864. Unable to win political power, the movements' leaders instead pursued educational and cultural programs to arouse and unite their nation for eventual statehood. By contrast, the Greeks, inspired by religious revivalism and enlightened ideas, managed to wrest independence from the Ottoman Turks after a years-long series of skirmishes, in 1832.

Other nationalist movements were suppressed or at least slowed down with little bloodshed. In places like the German principalities, the Italian states, and the Hungarian parts of the Habsburg Empire, secret societies of young men—students and intellectuals—gathered to plan bright, republican futures. Regrettably for these patriots, however, organizations like Young Italy, founded in 1832 to promote national unification and renewal, had little popular or foreign support. Censorship and a few strategic executions suppressed them. Yet many of these movements ultimately succeeded in the century's second half, when conservatives and liberals alike in western Europe employed nationalist fervor to advance their own ambitions. Kings, aristocrats, and bourgeois businessmen realized that they could mobilize popular support in their capacity as Germans, Frenchmen, or Italians, even as they limited poor people's political rights. However, in central Europe, nationalism pitted many claimants for the same territories against one another, like the Czechs, Serbs, Slovaks, Poles, and Ruthenians (Ukrainians). They did not understand why they could not have a nation-state too. Indeed, the idea of a "nation," like that of a "people," was so abstract and vague that it unleashed a series of competing claims that were incompatible with one another and would prove enormously destructive in the twentieth century.

Socialists and Communists Early socialists and communists (the terms were more or less interchangeable in the nineteenth century) insisted that political reforms offered no effective answer to the more pressing "social question": What was to be done about the inequalities so powerfully magnified by industrial capitalism? The socialists worried in particular about two things. One was the growing gap between impoverished workers and newly wealthy employers. The other concern was that the division of labor—that is, the dividing up and simplifying of tasks so that each worker performs most efficiently—might make people into soulless, brainless machines. Socialists believed that the whole free market economy, not just the state, had to be transformed to save the human race from self-destruction. Liberty and equality, they insisted, could not be separated; liberal capitalism and free markets belonged on history's ash heap, in their view, along with aristocratic privilege.

No more than a handful of radical prophets hatched revolutionary plans in the years after 1815, but they were not the only participants in strikes, riots, peasant uprisings, and protest meetings. Indeed, ordinary workers, artisans, domestic servants, and women employed in textile manufacturing all joined in attempts to answer the "social question" to their satisfaction. A few socialists and feminists—like the English thinker John Stuart Mill and his wife, Harriet—campaigned for social and political equality of the sexes. In Britain in 1819, Manchester workers at St. Peter's Field demonstrated peacefully for increased representation in Parliament, but panicking guardsmen fired on the crowd, leaving 11 dead and 460 injured in an incident later dubbed the Peterloo Massacre. In 1839 and 1842, nearly half the adult population of Britain signed the People's Charter, which called for universal suffrage for all adult males, the secret ballot, equal electoral districts, and annual parliamentary elections. Like most such endeavors, this mass movement, known as Chartism, ended in defeat. Parliament rejected the charter in 1839, 1842, and 1848.

Fourier and Utopian Socialism Despite their many defeats, the radicals kept trying. Charles Fourier's **utopian socialism** was perhaps the most visionary and influential of all Restoration-era alternative movements.

Fired by the egalitarian hopes and the cataclysmic failings of the French Revolution, Fourier (1772–1837) believed himself to be the scientific prophet of the new world to come. He was an imaginative, self-taught man who earned his keep in the cloth trade, an occupation that gave him an intense hatred for merchants and middlemen. Convinced that the division of labor and repressive moral conventions were destroying mankind's natural talents and passions, Fourier concluded that a revolution grander than that of 1789 was needed. But this utopian transformation of economic, social, and political conditions, he thought, could occur through organization, not through bloodshed. Indeed, by 1808 Fourier believed that the thoroughly corrupt world was on the brink of giving way to a new and harmonious age, of which he was the oracle.

First formulated in 1808, his "system" envisioned the reorganization of human communities into what he called phalanxes. In these harmonious collectives of 1,500 to 1,600 people, diversity would be preserved but efficiency maintained; best of all, work would become enjoyable. All members of the phalanx, rich and poor, would work, though not necessarily at the same tasks. All would work in short spurts of no more than two hours, so as to make labor more interesting and sleep, idleness, and overindulgence less attractive. Truly undesirable jobs, like sweeping out stables or cleaning

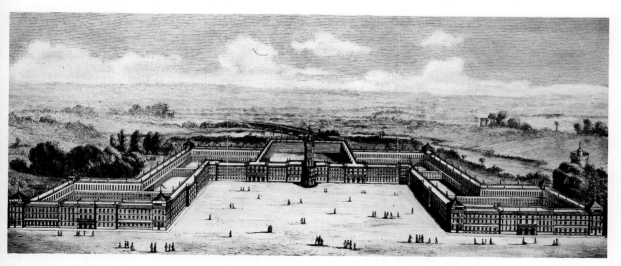

The Phalanx The phalanx, as one of Fourier's German followers envisioned it. In this rendering, the idealized home for the residents of the cooperative social system is represented as a building architecturally similar to the home of the French kings, the Louvre.

latrines, would fall to young adolescents, who, Fourier argued, actually liked mucking about in filth.

Fourier's writings gained popularity in the 1830s, appealing to radicals who supported a variety of causes. In France, women were particularly active in spreading his ideas, notably founders of the feminist press in France, including Désirée Gay and Jeanne Deroin. Longing for social and moral reforms that would address problems such as prostitution, poverty, illegitimacy, and the exploitation of workers (including women and children), some women saw in Fourier's ideas a higher form of Christian communalism. By reshaping the phalanx to accommodate monogamous families and Christian values, women helped make his work more respectable to middle-class readers. In Russia, Fourier's works inspired the imaginations of the young writer Fyodor Dostoyevsky. He and fourteen others in the radical circle to which he belonged were sentenced to death for their views (though their executions were called off at the last minute). The German thinker Karl Marx read Fourier with great care, and there are many remnants of utopian thought in his work. In *The German Ideology*, Marx describes life in an ideal communist society; in a postrevolutionary world, he predicts, people would no longer have to commit to a single profession or sphere of activity. Everyone could develop their talents in a range of areas. A well-ordered society would make it possible, as he put it in a famous phrase, "for me to do one thing today and another tomorrow, to hunt in the morning, fish in the afternoon, rear cattle in the evening, [and] criticize after dinner."

Marxism University-educated and philosophically radical, Karl Marx (1818–1883) elaborated what he called a scientific socialism. After being expelled from the university for his radical views, Marx took up a career in journalism. In that capacity, he covered legislative debates over property rights and taxation and developed an interest in economics. His understanding of capitalism, a term he was instrumental in popularizing, deepened through his collaboration with Friedrich Engels (1820–1895). Engels was a German-born radical who, after observing conditions in the factories owned by his wealthy father in Manchester, England, published a devastating indictment of industrial wage labor titled *The Condition of the Working Class in England*.

Together, Marx and Engels developed what they called "scientific socialism," which they contrasted with the "utopian socialism" of others like Fourier. Scientific socialism was rooted, they argued, in a materialist theory of history: what mattered in history were the production of material goods and the ways in which society was organized into classes of producers and exploiters. History, they claimed, consisted of successive forms of exploitative production and rebellions against them. Capitalist exploitation of the wage worker was only the latest, and worst, version of class conflict, Marx and Engels contended. In industrialized societies, capitalists owned the means of production (the factories and machinery) and exploited wage workers. Marx and Engels were confident that the clashes between industrial wage workers with nothing to sell but their labor—or **proletarians**—and capitalists would end in a colossal transformation of human society and would usher in a new world of true liberty, equality, and fraternity. These beliefs constituted the fundamentals of **Marxism**. For Marx and Engels, history moved through stages: from feudalism to capitalism, and then, finally, to socialism (or communism).

From these fundamentals, Marx and Engels issued a comprehensive critique of post-1815 Europe. They identified a whole class of the exploited—the working class. They believed that more and more people would fall into this class as industrialization proceeded and that the masses would not share in the rising prosperity that capitalists monopolized. Marx and Engels predicted that there would be overproduction, and underconsumption of goods would lead to lower profits for capitalists and, consequently, to lower wages or unemployment for workers—which would ultimately spark a proletarian revolution. This revolution would result in a "dictatorship of the proletariat" and the end of private property. With the destruction of capitalism, the men claimed, exploitation would cease and the state would wither away.

After a decade of hardship across Europe known as the hungry forties, revolutions erupted in 1848 in France, Austria, Russia, Italy, Hungary, and the German states. After hearing that revolution had broken out in France, Marx and Engels published *The Communist Manifesto*, calling on the workers of all nations to unite in overthrowing capitalism. These were not proletarian

proletarians
Industrial wage workers.

Marxism
A current of socialism created by Karl Marx and Friedrich Engels. It stressed the primacy of economics and technology—and, above all, class conflict—in shaping human history. Economic production provided the foundation, the "base" for society, which shaped politics, values, art, and culture (the superstructure). In the modern, industrial era, they believed class conflict boiled down to a two-way struggle between the bourgeoisie (who controlled the means of industrial production) and the proletariat (workers who had only their labor power to sell).

revolutions. By midcentury, modern industry had not developed beyond a few key locations, mostly in northern and western Europe. Instead the revolutions were cross-class affairs, lead by an uneasy coalition of liberal doctors, lawyers, and university professors; often-radical students and urban artisans; and a mass of poor peasants. As a group, they shared little more than a frustration with old elites and a desire for independent nations. Marx and Engels were sorely disappointed (not to mention exiled) by the reactionary crackdowns that quickly crushed the 1848 revolutions. The failure of those revolutions, however, did not doom their prophecy itself or diminish commitment to alternative social landscapes.

Insurgencies against Colonizing and Centralizing States

Outside Europe, for Native Americans and for Britain's colonial subjects in India, the greatest threat to traditional worlds was colonialism. While European radicals looked back to revolutionary legacies in imagining a transformed society, Native American insurgents and rebels in British India drew on their traditional cultural and political resources to imagine local alternatives to foreign impositions. Like the peoples of China, Africa, and the Middle East, native groups in the Americas and India met the period's challenges with prophecy, charismatic leadership, and rebellion. The insurgents all sought to defend their cultures and looked to an idealized past free from outside influences, but the new worlds they envisioned bore unmistakable marks of the present as well.

Core Objectives

DESCRIBE the challenges to the ideals of industrial capitalism in India and the Americas.

NATIVE AMERICAN PROPHETS

Like other native peoples threatened by imperial expansion, the Native Americans of North America dreamed of a world in which intrusive colonizers disappeared. Taking such dreams as prophecies, many Native Americans in the Ohio Valley flocked in 1805 to hear the revelations of a Shawnee named Tenskwatawa. Facing a dark present and a darker future, they enthusiastically embraced the Shawnee Prophet's visions, which (like those of the Paiute prophet Wovoka nearly a century later) foretold how invaders would vanish if Native Americans returned to their customary ways and traditional rites.

Early Calls for Resistance and a Return to Tradition Tenskwatawa's visions—and the anticolonial uprising they inspired—drew on a long tradition of visionary leaders. Often these prophets inspired their followers not only to engage in cleansing ceremonies but also to cooperate in violent, anticolonial uprisings. In the 1760s, for example, the preachings of the Delaware shaman Neolin encouraged Native Americans of the Ohio Valley and Great Lakes to take up arms against the British, leading to the capture of several British military posts. Although the British put down the uprising, imperial officials learned a lesson from the conflict: they assumed a less arrogant posture toward Ohio Valley and Great Lakes Native Americans, and they forbade colonists from trespassing on lands west of the Appalachian Mountains. The British, however, were incapable of restraining the flow of settlers across the mountains, and the problem became much worse for the Native Americans once the American Revolution ended. With the Ohio Valley transferred to the new United States, American settlers crossed the Appalachians and flooded into Kentucky and Tennessee.

Despite the settlers' considerable migration, much of the territory between the Appalachian Mountains and the Mississippi River, which Americans referred to as the "western country," remained a Native American country. North and south of Kentucky and Tennessee, Native American warriors more than held their own against American forces. But in 1794 Native American warriors failed to repel invading American armies, and their leaders had to surrender lands in what is now the state of Ohio to the United States. (See Map 16.4.)

Tenskwatawa: The Shawnee Prophet The Shawnees, who lost most of their land, were among the most bitter—and bitterly divided—of Native American peoples living in the Ohio Valley. Some Shawnee leaders concluded that their people's survival now required that they cooperate with American officials and Christian missionaries. This strategy, they realized, entailed wrenching changes in Shawnee culture. European reformers, after all, insisted that Native American men give up hunting and take up farming, an occupation that the Shawnees and their neighbors had always considered "women's work." Moreover, the Shawnees were pushed to abandon communal traditions in favor of private property rights.

Among the demoralized Shawnees was **Tenskwatawa** (1775–1836), whose story of overcoming personal failures through religious visions and embracing a strict moral code has parallels with that of Hong Xiuquan, the Taiping leader. In his first thirty years, Tenskwatawa could claim few accomplishments. He had failed as a hunter and as a medicine man, had blinded himself in one eye, and had earned a reputation as an obnoxious braggart. All this changed in the spring of 1805, however, after he fell into a trance and experienced a vision. In this dream, Tenskwatawa encountered a heaven where the virtuous enjoyed the traditional Shawnee way of life and a hell where evildoers suffered punishments. Additional revelations followed, and Tenskwatawa soon stitched these together into a new social gospel that urged disciples to abstain from alcohol and return to traditional customs.

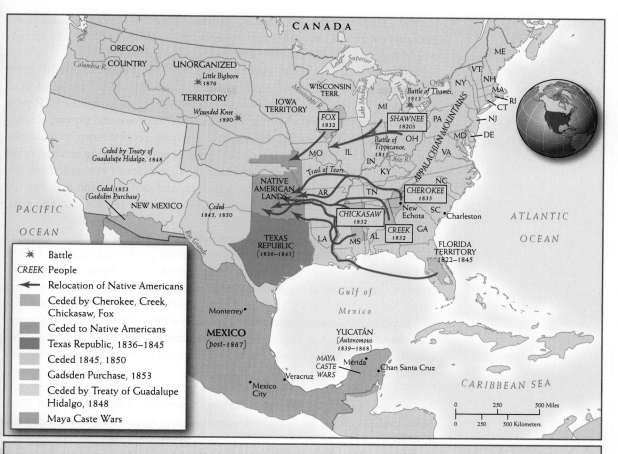

Map 16.4 Native American Revolts in the United States and Mexico

The new world order of expanding nation-states and industrial markets strongly affected indigenous peoples in North America.

- According to this map, where did the fiercest resistance to centralizing states and global market pressures occur?
- What regions of the United States were Native Americans forced to leave?
- According to your reading, to what extent, if any, did the natives' alternative visions create or preserve an alternative to the new emerging order?

Like other prophets, Tenskwatawa exhorted Native Americans to avoid contact with outside influences, to reduce their dependence on European trade goods and to sever their connections to Christian missionaries. If Native Americans obeyed these dictates, Tenskwatawa promised, the deer, which "were half a tree's length under the ground," would come back in abundant numbers to the earth's surface. Likewise, he claimed, Native Americans killed in conflict with colonial intruders would be resurrected, while evil Americans would depart from the country west of the Appalachians.

Like the Qing who responded to Hong's visions, American officials grew concerned as the Shawnee Prophet gathered followers. The spread of Tenskwatawa's message raised fears of a pan–Native American confederacy. Hoping to undermine the Shawnee Prophet's claims to supernatural power, territorial governor William Henry Harrison challenged Tenskwatawa to make the sun stand still. But Tenskwatawa one-upped Harrison. Having learned of an impending eclipse from white astronomers, Tenskwatawa assembled his followers on June 16, 1806. Right on schedule, and as if on command, the sky darkened. Claiming credit for the eclipse, Tenskwatawa saw his standing soar, as did the ranks of his disciples.

At the same time, however, Tenskwatawa had made plenty of enemies among his fellow Native Americans. His visions consigned drinkers to hell and singled out those who cooperated with colonial authorities for punishment in this world and the next. Indeed, Tenskwatawa condemned as witches those Native Americans who rejected his preaching in favor of the teachings of Christian missionaries and American authorities. (To be sure, Tenskwatawa's damnation of Christianized Native Americans was somewhat paradoxical, for missionary doctrines obviously influenced his vision of a burning hell for sinners and his crusade against alcohol.)

Tecumseh and the Wish for Native American Unity Although Tenskwatawa's accusations alienated some Native Americans, his prophecies gave heart to many more. This was particularly the case once his brother, Tecumseh (1768–1813), helped circulate the message of Native American renaissance among Native American villages from the Great Lakes to the Gulf Coast. On his journeys after 1805, Tecumseh did more than spread his brother's visions; he also wedded them to the idea of an enlarged Native American confederation. Moving around the Great Lakes and traveling across the southern half of the western country, Tecumseh preached the need for Native American unity. Always, he insisted that Native Americans resist any American attempts to get them to sell more land. In response, thousands of followers renounced their ties to colonial ways and prepared to combat the expansion of the United States.

By 1810, Tecumseh had emerged, at least in the eyes of American officials, as even more dangerous than his brother. Impressed by Tecumseh's charismatic organizational talents, William Harrison warned that this new "Indian menace" was forming "an Empire that would rival in glory" that of the Aztecs and the Incas. In 1811, while Tecumseh was traveling among southern tribes, Harrison had his troops attack Tenskwatawa's village, Prophet's Town, on the Tippecanoe River in what is now the state of Indiana.

The resulting battle was evenly fought, but the Native Americans eventually gave ground and American forces burned Prophet's Town. That defeat discredited Tenskwatawa, who had promised his followers protection from destruction at American hands. Spurned by his former disciples, including his brother, Tenskwatawa fled to Canada. Tecumseh soldiered on, supporting the British in the War of 1812 in the hope that a British victory would check American expansionism. But in 1813, with the war's outcome still in doubt and the pan–Native American confederacy still fragile, he perished at the Battle of the Thames, north of Lake Erie.

Native American Removals The discrediting of Tenskwatawa and the death of Tecumseh damaged the cause of Native American unity; then British betrayal dealt it a fatal blow. Following the war's end in 1814, the British withdrew their support and left the Native Americans south of the Great Lakes to fend for themselves against land-hungry American settlers and the armies of the United States. By 1815, American citizens outnumbered Native Americans in the western country by a seven-to-one margin, and this

Visions of Native American Unification (*Left*) A portrait of Tenskwatawa, the "Shawnee Prophet," whose visions stirred thousands of Native Americans in the Ohio Valley and Great Lakes to renounce dependence on colonial imports and resist the expansion of the United States. (*Right*) A portrait of his brother, Tecumseh, who succeeded in building a significant pan–Native American confederation, although it unraveled following his death at the Battle of the Thames in 1813 and the end of warfare between the United States and Britain the following year.

gap dramatically widened in the next few years. Recognizing the hopelessness of military resistance, Native Americans south of the Great Lakes resigned themselves to relocation. During the 1820s, most of the peoples north of the Ohio River were removed to lands west of the Mississippi River. During the 1830s, the southern tribes were cleared out, completing what amounted to an ethnic cleansing of Native American peoples from the region between the Appalachians and the Mississippi.

In the midst of these final removals, Tenskwatawa died, though his dream of an alternative to American expansion had faded for his people years earlier. Through the rest of the nineteenth century, however, other Native American prophets emerged, and their visions continued to inspire followers with the hope of an alternative to life under the colonial rule of the United States. But like Wovoka and the Ghost Dancers in 1890, these dreams failed to halt the expansion of the United States and the contraction of Native American lands.

THE CASTE WAR OF THE YUCATÁN

As in North America, the Spanish establishment of an expansionist nation-state in Mexico sparked widespread revolts by indigenous peoples. The most protracted was the Maya revolt in the Yucatán Peninsula. The revolt started in 1847, and its flames were not finally doused until the full occupation of the Yucatán by Mexican national troops in 1901.

The strength and endurance of the Maya revolt stemmed in large measure from the unusual features of the Spanish conquest in southern Mesoamerica. Because this area lacked precious metals and fertile lands, Spain and its rivals focused elsewhere—on central and northern Mexico and the Caribbean islands. As a result, the Maya Indians escaped forced recruitment for silver mines or sugar plantations. This does not mean that global processes side-stepped the Maya Indians. In fact, the production of dyes and foodstuffs for shipment to other regions drew the Yucatán into long-distance trading networks. Nonetheless, cultivation and commerce were much less disruptive to indigenous lives in the Yucatán than elsewhere in the New World.

Growing Pressures from the Sugar Trade Local developments, however, encroached on the Maya world in the nineteenth century. First, regional elites—mainly white, but often with the support of mixed-race (mestizo) populations—bickered for supremacy so long as the central authority of Mexico City remained weak. Weaponry flowed freely through the peninsula, and some combatants even appealed for Maya support. At the same time, regional and international trade spurred the spread of sugar estates, which threatened traditional corn cultivation in the Yucatán. Over the decades, plantations encroached on Maya properties. Planters used several devices to lure independent Maya to work, especially in the harvest. The most important device, debt peonage, involved giving small cash advances to Indian families, which obligated fathers and sons to work for meager wages to pay off the debts. In addition, Mexico's costly wars, culminating in a showdown with the United States in 1846, drove tax collectors and army recruiters into villages in search of revenues and soldiers.

The combination of material and physical threats was explosive. When a small band of Maya, fed up with rising taxes and ebbing autonomy, used firearms to drive back white intruders in 1847, they sparked a war that took a half century to complete. The rebels were primarily free Maya who had not yet been absorbed into the sugar economy. They wanted to dismantle old definitions of Indians as a caste—a status that deprived the Indians of legal and political equality with whites and that also subjected the Indians to special taxes. Thus, local Maya leaders, like Jacinto Pat and Cecilio Chi, upheld a republican model in the name of formal equality of all political subjects and devotion to a spiritual order that did not distinguish between Christians and non-Christians. "If the Indians revolt," one Maya rebel explained, "it is because the whites gave them reason; because the whites say they do not believe in Jesus Christ, because they have burned the cornfield."

The Caste War Horrified, the local white elites reacted to the uprising with vicious repression and dubbed the ensuing bloody conflict a caste war. In their view, the **Caste War of the Yucatán** was a struggle between forward-looking liberals and backward-looking Indians. At first, whites and mestizos were no match for the determined Maya, whose forces seized town after town. They especially targeted symbols of white power. With relish they demolished the whipping posts where Indians had endured public humiliation and punishment.

In the end, fortune, not political savvy, saved the Yucatán's whites. Settlement of the war with the United States in 1848 enabled Mexico City to rescue local elites in the Yucatán. With the help of a $15 million payment from Washington for giving up its northern provinces, Mexico could spend freely to build up its southern armies. The Mexican government soon fielded a force of 17,000 soldiers and waged a scorched-earth campaign to drive back the depleted Maya forces.

By 1849, the confrontation had entered a new phase in which Mexican troops engaged in mass repression of the Maya. Mexican armies set Indian fields and villages ablaze. Between 30 and 40 percent of the Maya population perished in the war and its repressive aftermath. The inhabitants of entire Maya cities pulled up stakes and withdrew to isolated districts protected by fortified villages. War between armies degenerated into guerrilla warfare between an occupying Mexican army and mobile bands of Maya squadrons, inflicting a gruesome toll on the invaders. As years passed, the war ground to a stalemate, especially once the U.S. funds ran out and Mexican soldiers began deserting in droves.

Caste War of the Yucatán
(1847–1901) Conflict between Maya Indians and the Mexican state over Indian autonomy and legal equality, which resulted in the Mexican takeover of the Yucatán Peninsula.

Caste War of the Yucatán
Fernando Castro Pacheco captured the violence of the Caste War in this 1974 painting.

Reclaiming a Maya Identity Warfare prompted a spiritual transformation that reinforced a purely Maya identity against the Mexican invaders' efforts to create a strong, centralized state. Thus, a struggle that began with demands for legal equality and relative cultural autonomy became a crusade for spiritual salvation and the complete cultural separation of the Maya Indians. A particularly influential group under José María Barrera retreated to a hamlet called Chan Santa Cruz. There, at the site where he found a cross shape carved into a mahogany tree, Barrera had a vision of a divine encounter. Thereafter, people in a swath of Yucatán villages around Chan Santa Cruz refashioned themselves as moral communities. Leaders created a polity, with soldiers, priests, and tax collectors pledging loyalty to the Speaking Cross. Like the followers of Hong in China's Taiping Rebellion, Indian rebels forged an alternative religion: it blended Christian rituals, faiths, and icons with Maya legends and beliefs. At the center was a stone temple, Balam Na ("House of God"), 100 feet long and 60 feet wide. Through pilgrimages to Balam Na and the secular justice of Indian judges, the Maya soon governed their domain in the Yucatán autonomously, almost completely cut off from the rest of Mexico.

The Mexican government threw its weight behind the strong-arm ruler General Porfirio Díaz (r. 1876–1911). The general sent one of his veteran commanders, Ignacio Bravo, to do what no other Mexican could accomplish: vanquish Chan Santa Cruz. When General Bravo finally entered the town, he found the once-imposing temple Balam Na covered in vegetation. Nature was reclaiming the territories of the Speaking Cross. Hunger and

Bravo's soldiers finally drove the Maya to work on white Mexican plantations; the alternative vision was vanquished. A combination of declining economic conditions and the soldiers under Ignacio Bravo brought an end to the Maya revolt.

THE REBELLION OF 1857 IN INDIA

Like Native Americans, the peoples of nineteenth-century India had a long history of opposition to colonial domination. Armed revolts had occurred since the onset of rule by the British East India Company (see Chapter 15). Nonetheless, the uprising of 1857 was unprecedented in its scale, and it posed a greater threat than had any previous rebellion.

Core Objectives

DISTINGUISH the long-term influence of protest movements from their immediate political accomplishments in Asia, Islam, and Africa.

India under Company Rule During the first half of the nineteenth century, the British rulers of India had dismantled most of the traditional powers of the nobility and the rights of peasants. Believing that the princely powers and landed aristocracies were out of date, the East India Company instituted far-reaching changes in administration. Lord Dalhousie, upon his appointment as governor-general in 1848, immediately began annexing what had been independent princely domains and stripping native aristocrats of their privileges. Swallowing one princely state after another, the British removed their former allies.

The government also decided to collect taxes directly from peasants, displacing the landed nobles as intermediaries. In disarming the landed nobility, the British threw the retainers and militia of the notables into unemployment, and by demanding high taxes from peasants, the British forced them to rely on moneylenders, who could take ownership of land when peasant proprietors failed to pay. Meanwhile, the company transferred judicial authority to an administration that was insulated from the Indian social hierarchy.

The most prized object for annexation was the kingdom of Awadh in northern India. (See Map 16.5.) Founded in 1722 by an Iranian adventurer, it was one of the first successor states to have gained a measure of independence from the Mughal ruler in Delhi. With access to the fertile resources of the Ganges plain, its opulent court in Lucknow was one place where Mughal splendor still survived. In 1765, the company imposed a treaty on Awadh under which the ruler paid an annual tribute for British troops stationed in his territory to "protect" his kingdom from internal and external enemies.

Treaty Violations and Annexation In 1856, citing misgovernment and deterioration in law and order, the East India Company violated its treaty obligations and sent its troops to Lucknow to take control of the province. Nawab Wajid Ali Shah, the poet-king of Awadh, whom the British saw as weak and immoral, refused to sign the treaty ceding control to the British.

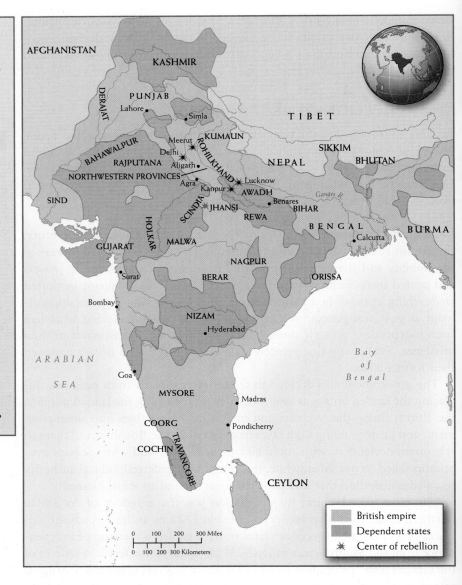

Map 16.5 Indian Rebellion of 1857

The Indian Rebellion of 1857 broke out first among the Indian soldiers of the British army. Other groups soon joined the struggle.

- According to this map, how many centers of rebellion were located in British territory and how many in dependent states?
- Why do you think the rebellion occurred in the interior of the subcontinent rather than along the coasts?
- In what way was the company's expansion into formerly autonomous areas during the first half of the nineteenth century a factor in the rebellion?

AFGHANISTAN
KASHMIR
DERAJAT
PUNJAB
Lahore
Simla
TIBET
KUMAUN
Meerut
BAHAWALPUR
Delhi
ROHILKHAND
SIKKIM
Aligarh
RAJPUTANA
NORTHWESTERN PROVINCES
NEPAL
BHUTAN
Agra
Lucknow
Kanpur
AWADH
Benares
SIND
JHANSI
Ganges R.
SCINDIA
REWA
BIHAR
HOLKAR
MALWA
BENGAL
BURMA
GUJARAT
Calcutta
NAGPUR
Surat
BERAR
ORISSA
Bombay
NIZAM
Hyderabad
ARABIAN
SEA
Bay
of
Bengal
Goa
MYSORE
Madras
COORG
Pondicherry
COCHIN
TRAVANCORE
CEYLON

0   100   200   300 Miles
0 100 200 300 Kilometers

British empire
Dependent states
✳ Center of rebellion

The annexation of princely domains and the abolition of feudal privileges formed part of the developing practices of European imperialism. To the policy of annexation, Dalhousie added an ambitious program of building railroads, telegraph lines, and a postal network to unify the disjointed territory into a single "network of iron sinew" under British control. Dalhousie saw these infrastructures as key to developing India into a productive colony—a supplier of raw materials for British industry, and a market for its manufactures.

A year after Dalhousie's departure in 1856, India went up in flames. The spark that ignited the simmering discontent into a furious rebellion—the Rebellion of 1857—was the "greased cartridge" controversy. At the end of 1856, the British army, which consisted of many Hindu and Muslim recruits (sepoys) commanded by British officers, introduced the new Enfield rifle to replace the old-style musket. To load the rifle, soldiers had to bite the cartridge open. Although manufacturing instructions stated that linseed oil and beeswax be used to grease the cartridge, a rumor circulated that cow and pig fat had been used. Biting into cartridges greased with animal fat meant violating the Hindu and Muslim sepoys' religious traditions. The sepoys became convinced that there was a plot afoot to defile them and to compel their conversion to Christianity. So a wave of rebellion spread among the 270,000 Indian soldiers, who greatly outnumbered the 40,000 British soldiers employed to rule over 200 million Indians.

Rebellion Breaks Out The mutiny broke out on May 10, 1857, at the military barracks in Meerut. The revolt soon turned from a limited military mutiny into a widespread civil rebellion that involved peasants, artisans, day laborers, and religious leaders. While the insurgents did not eliminate the power of the East India Company, which managed to retain the loyalty of princes and landed aristocrats in some places, they did throw the company into a crisis. Before long, the mutineers in Delhi issued a proclamation declaring that because the British were determined to destroy the religion of both Hindus and Muslims, it was the duty of the wealthy and the privileged to support the rebellion. To promote Hindu-Muslim unity, rebel leaders asked Muslims to refrain from killing cows in deference to Hindu sentiments.

Although the dispossessed aristocracy and petty landholders led the rebellion, leaders also appeared from the lower classes. Bakht Khan, who had been a junior noncommissioned officer in the British army, became commander in chief of the rebel forces in Delhi, replacing one of the Mughal emperor's sons. And Devi Singh, a wealthy peasant, set himself up as a peasant king. Dressed in yellow, the insignia of Hindu royalty, he constituted a government of his own, modeling it on the British administration. While his imitation of company rule showed his respect for the British bureaucracy, he defied British authority by leading an armed peasantry against the hated local moneylenders. The call

The Indian Sepoys The sepoys were drawn from indigenous groups that the British considered to be "martial races." This photograph shows two rebels hanging from a gallows following the British suppression of the rebellion, in 1858, in Lucknow, Uttar Pradesh, India.

to popular forces also marked the rebel career of Maulavi Ahmadullah Shah, a Muslim theologian. He stood at the head of the rebel forces in Lucknow, leading an army composed primarily of ordinary soldiers and people from the lower orders. Claiming to be an "Incarnation of the Deity" and thus inspired by divine will, he emerged as a prophetic leader of the common people. He voiced his undying hatred of the British in religious terms, calling on Hindus and Muslims to destroy British rule and warning his followers against betrayal by landed authorities.

Participation by the Peasantry The presence of popular leadership points to the important role of the lower classes. Although feudal chieftains often brought them into the rebellion, the peasantry made it their own. The organizing principle of their uprising was the common experience of oppression. Thus, they destroyed anything that represented the authority of the company: prisons, factories, police posts, railway stations, European bungalows, and law courts. Equally significant, the peasantry attacked native moneylenders and local power holders who were seen as benefiting from company rule.

Vigorous and militant as the popular rebellion was, it was limited in its territorial and ideological horizons. To begin with, the uprisings were local in scale and vision. Peasant rebels attacked the closest seats of administration and sought to settle scores with their most immediate and visible oppressors. They generally did not carry their action beyond the village or collection of villages. Their loyalties remained intensely local, based on village attachments and religious, caste, and clan ties. Nor did popular militants seek to undo traditional hierarchies of caste and religion.

British Response Convinced that the rebellion was the result of plotting by a few troublemakers, the British reacted with brutal vengeance. Villages were torched, and rebels were tied to cannons and blown to bits to teach Indians a lesson in power.

By July 1858, the vicious campaign to restore British control had achieved its goal. Yet, in August, the British Parliament abolished company rule and the company itself and transferred responsibility for the governing of India to the crown. In November, Queen Victoria issued a proclamation guaranteeing religious toleration, promising improvements, and allowing Indians to serve in the government. She promised to honor the treaties and agreements with princes and chiefs and to refrain from interfering in religious matters. The insurgents had risen up not as a nation but as a multitude of communities acting independently; their determination to find a new order shocked the British and threw them into a panic. Having crushed the uprising, the British resumed the work of transforming India into a modern colonial state and economy. But the desire for radical alternatives and traditions of popular insurgency, though vanquished, did not vanish.

Conclusion

The nineteenth century was a time of turmoil and transformation. Powerful forces reconfigured the world as a place for capitalism, colonialism, and nation-states, while prophets, charismatic leaders, radicals, peasant rebels, and anticolonial insurgents arose to offer alternatives. Reflecting local circumstances and traditions, the struggles of these men and women for a different future opened up spaces for the ideas and activities of the lower classes.

Conventional historical accounts either neglect these struggles or fail to view them as a whole. These individuals were not just romantic, last-ditch resisters, as some scholars have argued. Even after defeat, their messages remained alive within their communities. Nor were their actions isolated and atypical events, for when viewed on a global scale they bring to light a world that looks very different from the one that became dominant. To see the Wahhabi movement in the Arabian Peninsula together with the Shawnee Prophet in North America, the utopians and radicals in Europe with the peasant insurgents in British India, and the Taiping rebels with the Maya in the Yucatán is to glimpse a world of marginalized regions and groups. It was a world that more powerful groups endeavored to suppress but could not erase.

In this world, prophets and rebel leaders usually cultivated power and prestige locally; the emergence of an alternative political or social movement in one region did not impinge on communities and political organizations in others. As much as these individuals had in common, they envisioned widely different kinds of futures. Even Karl Marx, who called the workers of the world to unite, was acutely aware that the call for a proletarian revolution applied only to the industrialized countries of Europe. Other dissenters had even more localized horizons. A world fashioned by movements for alternatives meant a world with multiple centers and different historical timelines.

What gave force to a different mapping of the world was the fact that common people were at the center of these alternative visions, and their voices, however muted, gained a place on the historical stage. The quest for various forms of equality defined efforts to reconstitute alternative worlds. In Islamic regions, the emphasis on equality in revitalization movements was evident in their mobilization of all Muslims, not just the elites. Likewise, charismatic military leaders in Africa, for all their use of raw power, used the framework of community to build new polities. The Taiping Rebellion distinguished itself by seeking to establish an equal society of men and women in service of the Heavenly Kingdom. Operating under very different conditions, European radicals imagined a society free from aristocratic privileges and bourgeois property. Anticolonial rebels and insurgents depended on local solidarities and proposed alternative moral communities. In so doing, these movements compelled ruling elites to adjust the way they governed. The next chapter explores this challenge.

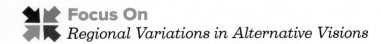

Focus On
Regional Variations in Alternative Visions

Europe
- European socialists and radicals envision a world free of exploitation and inequalities, while nationalists work to create new independent nation-states.

The Americas
- Native American prophets in the United States imagine a world restored to its customary ways and traditional rites.
- The Maya defy the central Mexican government in a rebellion known as the Caste War of the Yucatán.

The Islamic World and Africa
- Revivalist movements in the Arabian Peninsula and West Africa demand a return to traditional Islam.
- A charismatic warrior, Shaka, creates a powerful state in southern Africa.

Semi-colonial China
- An inspired prophetic figure, Hong Xiuquan, leads the Taiping Rebellion against the Qing dynasty and European encroachment on China.

Colonial India
- Indian troops mutiny against the British and attempt to restore Mughal rule.

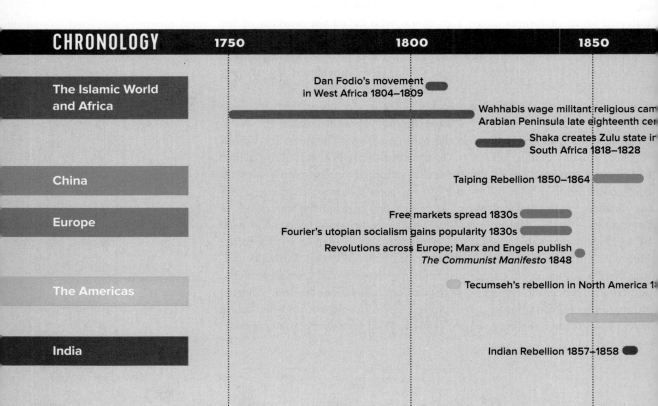

CHRONOLOGY	1750	1800	1850
The Islamic World and Africa		Dan Fodio's movement in West Africa 1804–1809	
		Wahhabis wage militant religious cam Arabian Peninsula late eighteenth cen	
			Shaka creates Zulu state in South Africa 1818–1828
China			Taiping Rebellion 1850–1864
Europe		Free markets spread 1830s	
		Fourier's utopian socialism gains popularity 1830s	
		Revolutions across Europe; Marx and Engels publish *The Communist Manifesto* 1848	
The Americas			Tecumseh's rebellion in North America 1
India			Indian Rebellion 1857–1858

THINKING ABOUT GLOBAL CONNECTIONS

- **Thinking about Exchange Networks and Alternative Visions** How did people around the world respond to the major changes of the French, American, and Industrial Revolutions? What difference did proximity to the European and American "core" make?

- **Thinking about Changing Power Relationships and Alternative Visions** What kind of challenges did the new order provoke? What kinds of traditions did those challenges draw on, and what kind of success did they have?

- **Thinking about Gender and Alternative Visions** Describe the role women played in millenarian protest movements during the nineteenth century, and explain the significance of gender to those movements.

Key Terms

Caste War of the Yucatán p. 765

Usman dan Fodio p. 746

liberalism p. 754

Marxism p. 758

Mfecane movement p. 747

millenarian p. 749

proletarians p. 758

Taiping Rebellion p. 750

Tenskwatawa p. 760

utopian socialism p. 756

Wahhabism p. 744

 Go to INQUIZITIVE to see what you've learned—and learn what you've missed—with personalized feedback along the way.

1900	1950

Ghost Dance movement in North America 1889–1890

Caste War of the Yucatán in Mexico 1847–1901

Global Themes and Sources

Comparing Alternatives to Nineteenth-Century Capitalism

While European capitalism and colonialism drove transformative changes in the nineteenth century, protest movements around the world envisioned a future based on other values. These selections provide radically different visions for the future—different from European capitalism and colonialism, and different from one another.

Tenskwatawa, Nana Asma'u, and Bahadur Shah all sought to revive local traditions, reject outside influences, and return to what they viewed as a pure, authentic past that had existed before market forces and new ideas began to unsettle the social order. The Taiping leaders, inspired by a millenarian Christianity, challenged central values of conventional Chinese society; they confronted the central role of the family and ancestral worship and urged their followers to see themselves as belonging to a single family. *The Communist Manifesto* sought nothing less than the complete transformation of society everywhere, starting from the industrial heartland of Europe and taking advantage of the technical advances of the machine age to satisfy everyone's basic needs and put an end to class conflict.

These sources highlight the causes behind the development of these alternative visions and provide an opportunity for comparison. It is particularly important to note the impact that market forces and new ideas of citizenship and equality had on these protests. Some of the protesters came in close contact with market forces and new ideas of citizenship and equality, while others flourished beyond their immediate influence. Consider how each society or group responded, and how it was shaped by the ideas and forces that emerged from the North Atlantic core in the period from 1750 to 1850. Finally, consider what common elements all of these documents share and where they part company.

Analyzing Alternatives to Nineteenth-Century Capitalism

- Analyze the influence of market forces and new ideas of equality in each document.

- Analyze the role of religion—whether explicit or implicit—in each document. Pay special attention to ideas of virtue, sin, and redemption.

- The creators of these sources all opposed capitalism and colonialism, but they reacted differently to what they viewed as outside influences. Place the authors of these sources on a continuum in terms of their rejection of those influences and their efforts to recapture an unsullied past.

PRIMARY SOURCE 16.1

Visions of the Great Good Spirit (1810), Tenskwatawa

In the first decade of the nineteenth century, the Shawnee leader Tenskwatawa recalled an earlier, happier time for the Native American peoples of the Great Lakes and Ohio Valley—it was a time before the coming of the Europeans. In this speech, Tenskwatawa recounts how contact with the "white men's goods" contaminated and corrupted the Indians. He urges them to reject the ways of white Americans and return to the pure ways of a precolonial past.

- Identify the commodities and habits that led to the Native Americans' decline.

- What rules did "Our Creator" give Tenskwatawa to help him make his people what they were before?

- Compare Tenskwatawa's view of commodities and exchange to the view expressed in *The Communist Manifesto*.

I died and went to the World Above, and saw it.

The punishments I saw terrify you! But listen, those punishments will be upon you unless you follow me through the door that I am opening for you!

Our Creator put us on this wide, rich land, and told us we were free to go where the game was, where the soil was good for planting. That was our state of true happiness. We did not have to beg for anything. Our Creator had taught us how to find and make everything we needed, from trees and plants and animals and stone. We lived in bark, and we wore only the skins of animals.

Thus were we created. Thus we lived for a long time, proud and happy. We had never eaten pig meat, nor tasted the poison called whiskey, nor worn wool from sheep, nor struck fire or dug earth with steel, nor cooked in iron, nor hunted and fought with loud guns, nor ever had diseases which soured our blood or rotted our organs. We were pure, so we were strong and happy.

For many years we traded furs to the English or the French, for wool blankets and guns and iron things, for steel awls and needles and axes, for mirrors, for pretty things made of beads and silver. And for liquor. This was foolish, but we did not know it. We shut our ears to the Great Good Spirit. We did not want to hear that we were being foolish.

But now those things of the white men have corrupted us, and made us weak and needful. Our men forgot how to hunt without noisy guns. Our women don't want to make fire without steel, or cook without iron, or sew without metal awls and needles, or fish without steel hooks. Some look in those mirrors all the time, and no longer teach their daughters to make leather or render bear oil. We learned to need the white men's goods, and so now a People who never had to beg for anything must beg for everything!

Some of our women married white men, and made half-breeds. Many of us now crave liquor. He whose filthy name I will not speak, he who was I before, was one of the worst of those drunkards. There are drunkards in almost every family. You know how bad this is.

And so you see what has happened to us. We were fools to take all these things that weakened us. We did not need them then, but we believe we need them

now. We turned our backs on the old ways. Instead of thanking the Great Spirit for all we used to have, we turned to the white man and asked them for more. So now we depend upon the very people who destroy us! This is our weakness! Our corruption! Our Creator scolded me, "If you had lived the way I taught you, the white men could never have got you under their foot!"

And that is why Our Creator purified me and sent me down to you full of the shining power, to make you what you were before!

No red man must ever drink liquor, or he will go and have the hot lead poured in his mouth!

No red man shall take more than one wife in the future. No red man shall run after women. If he is single, let him take a wife, and lie only with her.

Any red woman who is living with a white man must return to her people, and must leave her children with the husband, so that all nations will be pure in their blood.

Now hear what I was told about dealing with white men! These things we must do, to cleanse ourselves of their corruption!

Do not eat any food that is raised or cooked by a white person. It is not good for us. Eat not their bread made of wheat, for Our Creator gave us corn for our bread. Eat not the meat of their filthy swine, nor of their chicken fowls, nor the beef of their cattle, which are tame and thus have no spirit in them. Their foods will seem to fill your empty belly, but this deceives you for food without spirit does not nourish you.

There are two kinds of white men. There are the Americans, and there are the others. You may give your hand in friendship to the French, or the Spaniards, or the British. But the Americans are not like those. The Americans come from the slime of the sea, with mud and weeds in their claws, and they are a kind of crayfish serpent whose claws grab in our earth and take it from us. . . .

. . . Remember it is the wish of the Great Good Spirit that we have no more commerce with white men!

We may keep our guns, and if we need to defend ourselves against American white men, the guns will kill them because they are a white man's weapon. But arrows will kill American intruders, too! You must go to the grandfathers and have them teach you to make good bows and shape arrowheads, and you must recover the old hunting skills. . . .

We will no longer do the frolic dances that excite lust. The Great Good Spirit will teach me the old dances we did before the corruption, and from these dances we will receive strength and happiness!

Source: Elizabeth Cobbs Hoffman, Edward J. Blum, and Jon Gjerde (eds.), *Major Problems in American History*, vol. 1, *To 1877*, 3rd ed. (Boston: Wadsworth Cengage Learning, 2012), pp. 207–9.

PRIMARY SOURCE 16.2

A Female Muslim Voice in Africa (1838–1839), Nana Asma'u

The Islamic scholar, writer, and poet Nana Asma'u was the daughter of Usman dan Fodio, the leader of the Fulani Revolt in northern Nigeria at the turn of the nineteenth century. She was also deeply attached to her brother, Muhammad Bello, who succeeded their father as head of the Sokoto caliphate. Nana Asma'u composed this poem in praise of her brother, underlining his commitment to an Islamic way of life.

- Identify the values that the poet celebrates. What does she praise?

- What threats to the community does the poem identify? What is their nature, and where do they come from? Do they come from the outside world or the community's inner failings, or from some combination of these?

- What role does gender play in the poem? Why does Nana Asma'u write about her brother?

I give thanks to the King of Heaven, the One God. I invoke blessings on the Prophet and set down my poem.

The Lord made Heaven and earth and created all things, sent prophets to enlighten mankind.

Believe in them for your own sake, learn from them and be saved, believe in and act upon their sayings.

I invoke blessings on the Prophet who brought the Book, the Qur'an: he brought the *hadith* to complete the enlightenment.

Muslim scholars have explained knowledge and used it, following in the footsteps of the Prophet.

It is my intention to set down Bello's characteristics and explain his ways.

For I wish to assuage my loneliness, requite my love, find peace of mind through my religion.

These are his characteristics: he was learned in all branches of knowledge and feared God in public and in private.

He obeyed religious injunctions and distanced himself from forbidden things: this is what is known about him.

He concentrated on understanding what is right to know about the Oneness of God.

He preached to people and instructed them about God: he caused them to long for Paradise.

He set an example in his focus on eternal values: he strove to end oppression and sin.

He upheld the *shari'a*, honored it, implemented it aright, that was his way, everyone knows.

And he made his views known to those who visited him: he said to them "Follow the *shari'a*, which is sacred."

He eschewed worldly things and discriminated against anything of ill repute; he was modest and a repository of useful knowledge.

He was exceedingly level-headed and generous, he enjoyed periods of quietude: but was energetic when he put his hand to things.

He was thoughtful, calm, a confident statesman, and quick-witted.

He honored people's status: he could sort out difficulties and advise those who sought his help.

He had nothing to do with worldly concerns, but tried to restore to a healthy state things which he could. These were his characteristics.

He never broke promises, but faithfully kept them: he sought out righteous things. Ask and you will hear.

He divorced himself entirely from bribery and was totally scrupulous: He flung back at the givers money offered for titles.

One day Garange [chief of Mafora] sent him a splendid gift, but Bello told the messenger Zitaro to take it back.

He said to the envoy who had brought the bribe, "Have nothing to do with forbidden things."

And furthermore he said, "Tell him that the gift was sent for unlawful purposes; it is wrong to respond to evil intent."

He was able to expedite matters: he facilitated learning, commerce, and defense, and encouraged everything good.

He propagated good relationships between different tribes and between kinsmen. He afforded protection; everyone knows this.

When strangers came he met them, and taught about religious matters, explaining things: he tried to enlighten them.

He lived in a state of preparedness, he had his affairs in order and had an excellent intelligence service.

He had nothing to do with double agents and said it was better to ignore them, for they pervert Islamic principles.

He was a very pleasant companion to friends and acquaintances: he was intelligent, with a lively mind.

He fulfilled promises and took care of affairs, but he did not act hastily.

He shouldered responsibilities and patiently endured adversities.

He was watchful and capable of restoring to good order matters which had gone wrong.

He was resourceful and could undo mischief, no matter how serious, because he was a man of ideas.

He was gracious to important people and was hospitable to all visitors, including non-Muslims.

He drew good people close to him and distanced himself from people of ill repute.

Those are his characteristics. I have recounted a few examples that are sufficient to provide a model for emulation and benefit.

May God forgive him and have mercy on him: May we be united with him in Paradise, the place we aspire to.

For the sake of the Prophet, the Compassionate, who was sent with mercy to mankind.

May God pour blessings on the Prophet and his kinsmen and all other followers.

May God accept this poem. I have concluded it in the year 1254 AH [after *hijra*, the Muslim dating system].

Source: "Gikku Bello," in *One Woman's Jihad: Nana Asma'u, Scholar and Scribe*, by Beverly B. Mack and Jean Boyd (Bloomington: Indiana University Press, 2000), pp. 97–99.

PRIMARY SOURCE 16.3

The Azamgarh Proclamation (1857), Bahadur Shah

The Indian leaders of the Rebellion of 1857 issued numerous proclamations. The Azamgarh Proclamation, excerpted below, is one of many. The emperor, Bahadur Shah, issued it in August 1857 on behalf of the mutineers who had seized the garrison town of Azamgarh. It attacks the British for subverting Indian traditions and calls on the rebellion's followers to restore the precolonial order.

- Identify the rebels' main grievances against the English.
- Analyze the role of religion in the rebellion.
- Explain the significance of commerce and property for the rebels.

25th. August, 1857.

It is well known to all, that in this age the people of Hindoostan, both Hindoos and Mohammedans, are being ruined under the tyranny and oppression of the infidel and treacherous English. It is therefore the bounden duty of all the wealthy people of India, especially of those who have any sort of connection with any of the Mohammedan royal families, and are considered the pastors and masters of their people, to stake their lives and property for the well being of the public. With the view of effecting this general good, several princes belonging to the royal family of Delhi, have dispersed themselves in the different parts of India, Iran, Turan, and Afghanistan, and have been long since taking measures to compass their favourite end; and it is to accomplish this charitable object that one of the aforesaid princes has, at the head of an army of Afghanistan, &c., made his appearance in

India; and I, who am the grandson of Abul Muzuffer Serajuddin Bahadur Shah Ghazee, King of India, having in the course of circuit come here to extirpate the infidels residing in the eastern part of the country, and to liberate and protect the poor helpless people now groaning under their iron rule, have, by the aid of the *Majahdeens* [religious warriors], erected the standard of Mohammed, and persuaded the orthodox Hindoos who had been subject to my ancestors, and have been and are still accessories in the destruction of the English, to raise the standard of Mahavir.

Several of the Hindoo and Mussalman chiefs, who have long since quitted their homes for the preservation of their religion, and have been trying their best to root out the English in India, have presented themselves to me, and taken part in the reigning Indian crusade, and it is more than probable that I shall very shortly receive succours from the West. Therefore, for the information of the public, the present *Ishtahar*, consisting of several sections, is put in circulation, and it is the imperative duty of all to take it into their careful consideration, and abide by it. Parties anxious to participate in the common cause, but having no means to provide for themselves, shall receive their daily subsistence from me; and be it known to all, that the ancient works, both of the Hindoos and the Mohammedans, the writings of the miracle-workers, and the calculations of the astrologers, pundits, and rammals, all agree in asserting that the English will no longer have any footing in India or elsewhere. Therefore it is incumbent on all to give up the hope of the continuation of the British sway, side with me, and deserve the consideration of the Badshahi, or imperial Government, by their individual exertion in promoting the common good, and thus attain their respective ends; otherwise if this golden opportunity slips away, they will have to repent of their folly, as it is very aptly said by a poet in two fine couplets, the drift whereof is "Never let a favourable opportunity slip, for in the field of opportunity you are to meet with the ball of fortune; but if you do not avail yourself of the opportunity that offers itself, you will have to bite your finger through grief."

No person, at the misrepresentation of the well-wishers of the British Government, ought to conclude from the present slight inconveniences usually attendant on revolutions, that similar inconveniences and troubles should continue when the Badshahi Government is established on a firm basis; and parties badly dealt with by any sepoy or plunderer, should come up and represent their grievances to me, and receive redress at my hands; and for whatever property they may lose in the reigning disorder, they will be recompensed from the public treasury when the Badshahi Government is well fixed. . . .

Section II—Regarding Merchants. It is plain that the infidel and treacherous British Government have monopolized the trade of all the fine and valuable merchandise, such as indigo, cloth, and other articles of shipping, leaving only the trade of trifles to the people, and even in this they are not without their share of the profits, which they secure by means of customs and stamp fees, &c. in money suits, so that the people have merely a trade in name. Besides this, the profits of the traders are taxed, with postages, tolls, and subscriptions for schools, &c. Notwithstanding all these concessions, the merchants are liable to imprisonment and disgrace at the instance or complaint of a worthless man. When the Badshahi Government is established, all these aforesaid fraudulent practices shall be dispensed with, and the trade of every article, without exception, both by land and water, shall be open to the native merchants of India, who will have the benefit of the Government steam-vessels and steam-carriages for the conveyance of their merchandise gratis; and merchants having no capital of their own shall be assisted from the public treasury. It is therefore the duty of every merchant to take part in the war, and aid the Badshahi Government with his men and money, either secretly or openly, as may be consistent with his position or interest, and forswear his allegiance to the British Government.

Section III—Regarding Public Servants. It is not a secret thing, that under the British Government, natives employed in the civil and military services, have little respect, low pay, and no manner of influence; and all the posts of dignity and emolument in both the departments, are exclusively bestowed on Englishmen for natives in the military service, after having devoted the greater part of their lives, attain to the post of soobadar (the very height of their hopes) with a salary of 60r. or 70r. per mensem; and those in the civil service obtain the post of Sudder Ala, with a salary of 500 r. a month, but no influence, jagheer, or present. . . .

Therefore, all the natives in the British service ought to be alive to their religion and interest, and, abjuring their loyalty to the English, side with the Badshahi Government, and obtain salaries of 200 or 300 rupees per month for the present, and be entitled to high posts in future. If they, for any reason, cannot at present declare openly against the English, they can heartily wish ill to their cause, and remain passive spectators of passing events, without taking any active share therein. But at the same time they should indirectly assist the Badshahi Government, and try their best to drive the English out of the country. . . .

Section IV—Regarding Artisans. It is evident that the Europeans, by the introduction of English articles into India, have thrown the weavers, the cotton dressers, the carpenters, the blacksmiths, and the shoemakers, &c., out of employ, and have engrossed their occupations, so that every description of native artisan has been reduced to beggary. But under the Badshahi Government the native artisans will exclusively be employed in the services of the kings, the rajahs, and the rich; and this will no doubt ensure their prosperity. Therefore these artisans ought to renounce the English services, and assist the *Majahdeens*, engaged in the war, and thus be entitled both to secular and eternal happiness.

Section V—Regarding Pundits, Fakirs and other learned persons. The pundits and fakirs being the guardians of the Hindoo and Mohammedan religions respectively, and the Europeans being the enemies of both the religions, and as at present a war is raging against the English on account of religion, the pundits and fakirs are bound to present themselves to me, and take their share in the holy war. . . .

Lastly, be it known to all, that whoever, out of the above named classes, shall after the circulation of this Ishtahar, still cling to the British Government, all his estates shall be confiscated, and his property plundered, and he himself, with his whole family, shall be imprisoned, and ultimately put to death.

Source: Ainslie T. Embree (ed.), *1857 in India: Mutiny or War of Independence?* (Boston: D. C. Heath, 1963), pp. 1–3.

The Principles of the Heavenly Nature (1854), Taiping Heavenly Kingdom

In this excerpt from 1854, written after the Taiping had established a capital in Nanjing and after initial victories had given way to a decline in morale and cohesion, the Taiping leaders envision a radically new community based on the values of a messianic Christianity.

- **Explain the significance of the family. Why do the authors speak of their members as brothers and sisters?**

- **What do the authors mean by "degeneration"? What "degenerated" and why?**

- **Analyze the relationship between external challenges and internal weakness in this text.**

We marquises and chancellors hold that our brothers and sisters have been blessed by the Heavenly Father and the Heavenly Elder Brother, who saved the ensnared and drowning and awakened the deluded; they have cast off worldly sentiments and now follow the true Way. They cross mountains and wade rivers, not even ten thousand *li* being too far for them to come, to uphold together the true Sovereign. Armed and bearing shield and spear, they carry righteous banners that rise colorfully. Husband and wife, men and women, express common indignation and lead the advance. It can be said that they are determined to uphold Heaven and to requite the nation with loyalty.

In the ten thousand nations of the world everyone is given life, nourished, protected, and blessed by the Heavenly Father, the Supreme Ruler and Lord God-on-High. Thus the Heavenly Father, the Supreme Ruler and Lord God-on-High, is the universal father of man in all the ten thousand nations of the world. There is no man who should not be grateful, there is no man who should not reverently worship Him. . . .

However, worldly customs daily degenerated. There were even those who likened themselves to rulers, and, being deluded in heart and nature, arrogant yet at fault, and falsely self-exalted, forbade the prime minister and those below to sacrifice to Heaven. Then [these men] competed in establishing false gods and worshiping them, thus opening up the ways of the devilish demons. The people of the world all followed in like fashion, and this became firmly fixed in their minds. Thereupon, after a considerable time, they did not know their own errors. Hence the Heavenly Father, the Lord God, in view of mortal man's serious crime of disobedience, at his first anger, sent down forty days and forty nights of heavy rain, the vast waters spreading in all directions and drowning mortal man. Only Noah and his family had unceasingly worshiped the Heavenly Father, the Supreme Ruler and Lord God-on-High; therefore, relying on the Heavenly grace, they were fortunate and they alone were preserved. In this, the first instance of the Heavenly Father's great anger, was the great proof of his great powers displayed.

After the Flood, the devilish king of Egypt, whose ambition was mediocrity and who was possessed by the demons, envied the Israelites in their worship of God and bitterly persecuted them. Therefore, the Heavenly Father in his great anger led the Israelites out of Egypt. In this, the second instance of the Heavenly Father's great anger, was the great proof of his great powers displayed.

However, the rulers and people of that time still had not completely forgotten the Heavenly grace. But since the emergence of Daoism in the [Chinese] Qin [dynasty] and the welcoming of Buddhism in the Han [dynasty], the delusion of man by the demons has day by day increased, and all men have forgotten the grace and virtue of the Heavenly Father. . . . The Heavenly Father once again became greatly angered; yet if he were to annihilate them completely, he could not bear it in his heart; if he were to tolerate them, it would not be consonant with righteousness. At that time, the elder son of the Heavenly Father, the Heavenly Elder Brother Jesus, shouldered the great burden and willingly offered to sacrifice his life to redeem the sins of the men of the world. . . .

Let us ask your elder and younger brothers: formerly the people sacrificed only to the demons; they worshiped the demons and appealed to the demons only because they desired the demons to protect them. Yet how could they think that the demons could really protect them? . . . To worship them is of no avail. However, the men of the world sank even deeper, not knowing how to awaken themselves. Therefore, the Heavenly Father again became angry.

In the *dingyou* year [1837], our Heavenly Father displayed the heavenly grace and dispatched angels to summon the Heavenly King up to Heaven. There He clearly pointed out the demons' perversities and their deluding of the world. He also invested the Heavenly King with a seal and a sword; He ordered the Savior, the Heavenly Elder Brother, Jesus, to take command of the Heavenly soldiers and Heavenly generals and to aid the Heavenly King, and to attack and conquer from Heaven earthward, layer by layer, the innumerable demons. After their victory they returned to Heaven and the Heavenly Father, greatly pleased, sent the Heavenly King down upon the earth to become the true Taiping Sovereign of the ten thousand nations of the world and to save the people of the world. He also bade him not to be fearful and to effect these matters courageously, for whenever difficulties appeared, the Heavenly Father would assume direction and the Heavenly Elder Brother would shoulder the burden.

***

We brothers and sisters, enjoying today the greatest mercy of our Heavenly Father, have become as one family and are able to enjoy true blessings; each of us must always be thankful. Speaking in terms of our ordinary human feelings, it is true that each has his own parents and there must be a distinction in family names; it is also true that as each has his own household, there must be a distinction between this boundary and that boundary. Yet we must know that the ten thousand names derive from the one name, and the one name from one ancestor. Thus our origins are not different. Since our Heavenly Father gave us birth and nourishment, we are of one form though of separate bodies, and we breathe the same air though in different places. This is why we say, "All are brothers within the four seas." Now, basking in the profound mercy of Heaven, we are of one family. . . .

We brothers, our minds having been awakened by our Heavenly Father, joined the camp in the earlier days to support our Sovereign, many bringing parents, wives, uncles, brothers, and whole families. It is a matter of course that we should attend to our parents and look after our wives and children, but when one first creates a new rule, the state must come first and the family last, public interests first and private interests last. Moreover, as it is advisable to avoid suspicion [of improper conduct] between the inner [female] and the outer [male] and to distinguish between male and female, so men must have male quarters and women must have female quarters; only thus can we be dignified and avoid confusion. There must be no common mixing of the male and female groups, which would cause debauchery and violation of Heaven's commandments. Although to pay respects to parents and to visit wives and children occasionally are in keeping with human nature and not prohibited, yet it is only proper to converse before the door, stand a few steps apart and speak in a loud voice; one must not enter the sisters' camp or permit the mixing of men and women. Only thus, by complying with rules and commands, can we become sons and daughters of Heaven.

At the present time, the remaining demons have not yet been completely exterminated and the time for the reunion of families has not yet arrived. We younger brothers and sisters must be firm and patient to the end, and with united strength and a single heart we must uphold God's principles and wipe out the demons immediately. With peace and unity achieved, then our Heavenly Father, displaying his mercy, will reward us according to our merits. Wealth, nobility, and renown will then enable us brothers to celebrate the reunion of our families and enjoy the harmonious relations of husband and wife. Oh, how wonderful that will be! The task of a thousand times ten thousand years also lies in this; the happiness and emoluments of a thousand times ten thousand years also lie in this; we certainly must not abandon it in one day.

Source: Wm. Theodore de Bary and Richard Lufrano (eds.), *Sources of Chinese Tradition*, vol. 2, *From 1600 through the Twentieth Century*, 2nd ed. (New York: Columbia University Press, 2000), pp. 226–30.

Bourgeoisie and Proletariat (1848), Karl Marx and Friedrich Engels

At the behest of an international revolutionary organization, the Communist League, in 1847 Karl Marx and Friedrich Engels set out to draft a confession of faith. While Engels's initial draft was set in the form of a catechism, the final document, rewritten by Marx, took the following, combative, critical form. Published in January 1848, just before revolution in Paris set off rebellion across Europe, *The Communist Manifesto* foretold the inevitable overthrow of bourgeois-dominated capitalism by the working classes.

- **According to Marx and Engels, how does class conflict change over time? Pay special attention to the range of groups opposed to one another.**

- **Define the term *bourgeois*. How are the bourgeoisie different from all the prior dominant classes in history?**

- **This document was initially conceived as a declaration of faith. What role, if any, does religion play in this final version?**

A spectre is haunting Europe—the spectre of communism. . . .

The history of all hitherto existing society is the history of class struggles.

Freeman and slave, patrician and plebeian, lord and serf, guild-master and journeyman, in a word, oppressor and oppressed, stood in constant opposition to one another, carried on an uninterrupted, now hidden, now open fight, a fight that each time ended, either in a revolutionary reconstitution of society at large, or in the common ruin of the contending classes.

In the earlier epochs of history, we find almost everywhere a complicated arrangement of society into various orders, a manifold gradation of social rank. In ancient Rome we have patricians, knights, plebeians, slaves; in the Middle Ages, feudal lords, vassals, guild-masters, journeymen, apprentices, serfs; in almost all of these classes, again, subordinate gradations.

The modern bourgeois society that has sprouted from the ruins of feudal society has not done away with class antagonisms. It has but established new classes, new conditions of oppression, new forms of struggle in place of the old ones.

Our epoch, the epoch of the bourgeoisie, possesses, however, this distinct feature: it has simplified class antagonisms. Society as a whole is more and more splitting up into two great hostile camps, into two great classes directly facing each other—Bourgeoisie and Proletariat.

From the serfs of the Middle Ages sprang the chartered burghers of the earliest towns. From these burgesses the first elements of the bourgeoisie were developed. . . .

The bourgeoisie, wherever it has got the upper hand, has put an end to all feudal, patriarchal, idyllic relations. It has pitilessly torn asunder the motley feudal ties that bound man to his "natural superiors," and has left remaining no other nexus between man and man than naked self-interest, than callous "cash payment.". . .

We see then: the means of production and of exchange, on whose foundation the bourgeoisie built itself up, were generated in feudal society. At a certain stage in the development of these means of production and of exchange, the conditions under which feudal society produced and exchanged, the feudal organisation of agriculture and manufacturing industry, in one word, the feudal relations of property became no longer compatible with the already developed productive forces; they became so many fetters. They had to be burst asunder; they were burst asunder. . . .

It is enough to mention the commercial crises that by their periodical return put the existence of the entire bourgeois society on its trial, each time more threateningly. In these crises, a great part not only of the existing products, but also of the previously created productive forces, are periodically destroyed. In these crises, there breaks out an epidemic that, in all earlier epochs, would have seemed an absurdity—the epidemic of over-production. . . .

Because there is too much civilisation, too much means of subsistence, too much industry, too much commerce. The productive forces at the disposal of society no longer tend to further the development of the conditions of bourgeois property; on the contrary, they have become too powerful for these conditions, by which they are fettered, and so soon as they overcome these fetters, they bring disorder into the whole of bourgeois society, endanger the existence of bourgeois property. The conditions of bourgeois society are too narrow to comprise the wealth created by them. . . .

The weapons with which the bourgeoisie felled feudalism to the ground are now turned against the bourgeoisie itself.

But not only has the bourgeoisie forged the weapons that bring death to itself; it has also called into existence the men who are to wield those weapons—the modern working class—the proletarians. . . .

Owing to the extensive use of machinery, and to the division of labour, the work of the proletarians has lost all individual character, and, consequently, all charm for the workman. He becomes an appendage of the machine, and it is only the most simple, most monotonous, and most easily acquired knack, that is required of him. Hence, the cost of production of a workman is restricted, almost entirely, to the means of subsistence that he requires for maintenance, and for the propagation of his race. But the price of a commodity, and therefore also of labour, is equal to its cost of production. . . .

Modern Industry has converted the little workshop of the patriarchal master into the great factory of the industrial capitalist. Masses of labourers, crowded into the factory, are organised like soldiers. As privates of the industrial army they are placed under the command of a perfect hierarchy of officers and sergeants. Not only are they slaves of the bourgeois class, and of the bourgeois State; they are daily and hourly enslaved by the machine, by the overlooker, and, above all, by the individual bourgeois manufacturer himself. The more openly this despotism proclaims gain to be its end and aim, the more petty, the more hateful and the more embittering it is. . . .

But with the development of industry, the proletariat not only increases in number; it becomes concentrated in greater masses, its strength grows, and it feels that strength more. The various interests and conditions of life within the ranks of the proletariat are more and more equalised, in proportion as machinery obliterates all distinctions of labour, and nearly everywhere reduces wages to the same low level. The growing competition among the bourgeois, and the resulting commercial crises, make the wages of the workers ever more fluctuating. The increasing improvement of machinery, ever more rapidly developing, makes their livelihood more and more precarious; the collisions between individual workmen and individual bourgeois take more and more the character of collisions between two classes. Thereupon, the workers begin to form combinations (Trades' Unions) against the bourgeois; they club together in order to keep up the rate of wages; they found permanent associations in order to make provision beforehand for these occasional revolts. Here and there, the contest breaks out into riots.

Now and then the workers are victorious, but only for a time. The real fruit of their battles lies, not in the immediate result, but in the ever expanding union of the workers. This union is helped on by the improved means of communication that are created by modern industry, and that place the workers of different localities in contact with one another. It was just this contact that was needed to centralise the numerous local struggles, all of the same character, into one national struggle between classes. But every class struggle is a political struggle. And that union, to attain which the burghers of the Middle Ages, with their miserable highways, required centuries, the modern proletarian, thanks to railways, achieve in a few years. . . .

Of all the classes that stand face to face with the bourgeoisie today, the proletariat alone is a really revolutionary class. The other classes decay and finally disappear in the face of Modern Industry; the proletariat is its special and essential product. . . .

The advance of industry, whose involuntary promoter is the bourgeoisie, replaces the isolation of the labourers, due to competition, by the revolutionary combination, due to association. The development of Modern Industry, therefore, cuts from under its feet the very foundation on which the bourgeoisie produces and appropriates products. What the bourgeoisie therefore produces, above all, are its own grave-diggers. Its fall and the victory of the proletariat are equally inevitable.

Source: *The Marx-Engels Reader*, edited by Robert C. Tucker (New York: Norton, 1972), pp. 335–45.

Interpreting Visual Evidence

The Gender of Nations

Nations are abstractions. They have no material form. The scholar Benedict Anderson famously referred to them as "imagined communities," groups of people who have never met, who may not even speak the same language or worship the same god(s), and yet who come to think of themselves as sharing something profound in common, such as being an American, or an Egyptian, or Chinese. In order to create this sort of community, nationalists have had to represent their nations visually, often in human form and more often as women than as men. For every John Bull (England) or Uncle Sam (the United States), there were several Mariannes (France) or Ranis of Jhansi (India). Especially in areas where few people could read, images and iconography played a vital role in spreading the idea of nationalism to the masses.

The attributes of the chosen figures provide insight into different nationalist movements. The figures' ties to real or invented historical traditions often reflect how these movements defined themselves in opposition to established authorities. In the first image, *Liberty Leading the People* (1830), the French Romantic painter Eugène Delacroix represents a barefoot, bare-chested woman, Marianne, leading a cross-class group of rebels against King Charles X. She wears a Phrygian bonnet, which had become popular during the Revolution of 1789–1799. In the 1890s, an Egyptian Jew named Ya'qub Sanu'a published a nationalist journal in Paris called *Abu Naddara*, which helped introduce Egypt to cartoons. In one issue he presents a veiled Egypt, with France and Russia by her side, confronting Great Britain. Finally, the Rani of Jhansi was the queen of the Maratha-ruled state of Jhansi in the north-central part of India and a leading figure in the Rebellion of 1857. She later became a nationalist icon, as the twentieth-century watercolor here illustrates, and a symbol of heroic resistance against the British.

Questions for Analysis

1. Why do you think nationalists in all of these countries, unlike those in Great Britain and the United States, used female symbols for the nation? What kind of established political authority did they challenge, and how did that challenge differ from the British and American cases?

2. Why do you think Sanu'a, a cosmopolitan liberal who had criticized the subordination of women, presented Egypt as a fully covered, veiled woman? To whom do you think he was appealing?

3. To what extent does the image of the Rani of Jhansi look backward and invoke history, at least implicitly? To what extent does it look forward and make claims about the nature of contemporary India?

Delacroix, *Liberty Leading the People*.

ILLUSION DÉTRUITE

Sanu'a, cartoon in *Abu Naddara*.

The Rani of Jhansi.

17

Nations and Empires

1850–1914

In 1895, the Cuban patriot José Martí launched a rebellion against the last Spanish holdings in the Americas. The anti-Spanish struggle continued until 1898, when Spain withdrew from Cuba and Puerto Rico. Martí hoped to bring freedom to a new Cuban nation and equality to all Cubans. But even as he helped secure freedom from the declining Spanish Empire, he could not prevent military occupation and political domination of Cuba by the world's newest imperial power, the United States. Martí's hopes and frustrations found parallels around the world.

After 1850, the building of nation-states in Europe, the Americas, and Oceania and the expansion of their empires changed the map of the world, exhilarating some peoples and frustrating others. Those who benefited most were Europeans and peoples of European descent. During these decades the nation-states of Europe, now locked in intense political and economic rivalry, projected their power across the entire world. Much of the rivalry among European states intensified through disruptions in the European balance of power, caused by the unification of two new states (Italy and Germany). Across the Atlantic, the United States abandoned its anticolonial origins and annexed overseas possessions. Yet imperial expansion did not go unchallenged. It encountered resistance from communities being incorporated into the new empires. In Asia and Africa resisters struggled to repel their invaders, often demanding the right to govern themselves.

The second half of the nineteenth century witnessed the simultaneous—and entwined—advance

Core Objectives

- **IDENTIFY** the institutions that enabled elites in western Europe, the Americas, and Japan to consolidate nation-states, and **ANALYZE** the degree to which they succeeded during this period.

- **EXPLAIN** the roles that industrialization, science, and technology played in the expansion of powerful states into the rest of the world.

- **COMPARE** the reactions to imperialism in Africa and Asia, and **EVALUATE** how effective these responses were.

- **ANALYZE** the extent to which colonies contributed to the wealth and political strength of the nation-states that controlled them.

of nationalism and imperialism. These decades also saw the further expansion of industrialization. Taken together, the era's political and economic developments allowed western Europe and the United States to attain primacy in world affairs. But tensions inside these states and their empires, as well as within other states, made the new world order anything but stable.

Global Storylines

- Nation-state building and imperial expansion change the map of the world.

- Industrialization, science, and technology enable states in North America and western Europe—and, to a lesser extent, Japan—to overpower other regions politically, militarily, and economically.

- European, American, and Japanese imperialists encounter significant opposition in Africa and Asia.

Consolidating Nations and Constructing Empires

During the second half of the nineteenth century, the idea of building nation-states engulfed the globe, and nationalism became closely linked to imperialism. Enlightenment thinkers had emphasized the importance of nations, defined as peoples who shared a common past, territory, and culture. To many people it seemed natural that once absolutist rulers had fallen, governments should draw their power and legitimacy from those who lived within their borders and that the body of institutions governing each territory should be uniquely concerned with promoting the welfare of that particular people. This seemed such a natural process that little thought was given to the relationship between "nation" and "state," between the people and their government; national states were simply supposed to well up from the people's longing for liberty and togetherness.

BUILDING NATIONALISM

More often than not, however, local elites created nations. They did so by compelling diverse groups of people and regions to accept a unified network of laws, a central administration, time zones, national markets, and a single regional dialect as the "national" language. To overcome strong regional identities, state administrators broadened public education in the national language and imposed universal military service to build a national army. In this way, dominant elites spread their values and institutions outward to regions throughout each nation and beyond their borders. While a handful of nation-states were already well established in the mid-nineteenth century, two of the most important—Italy and Germany—were newly created in this period, forged through strategic military contests.

EXPANDING THE EMPIRES

The processes of nation building also required the acquisition of new territories, often overseas, a development that was called **imperialism**. Rulers measured national strength not only by their people's unity but also by their economic power and the conquest of new territories. Thus, Germany, France, the United States, Russia, and Japan challenged Britain's leadership in overseas trade by developing their industries and seizing new territories.

Imperial rule facilitated a widespread movement of labor, capital, commodities, and information. As scholars studied previously unknown tribes and races, new schools taught colonized peoples the languages, religions, scientific practices, and cultural traditions of their colonizers. Publications and

imperialism
Acquisition of new territories by a state and the incorporation of these territories into a political system as subordinate colonies.

products from the "mother country" circulated widely among indigenous elites. Yet colonies were seen as subordinate to the mother country and were given little or no representation in home governments. In this sense, nation and empire were in tension with one another.

Expansion and Nation Building in the Americas

Core Objectives

ANALYZE the degree to which elites in the Americas succeeded in consolidating nation-states.

Once freed from European control, the elites of the Americas set about creating political communities of their own. By the 1850s, they shared a desire both to create widespread loyalty to their political institutions and to expand territorial domains. This also meant finding ways to settle hinterlands that previously belonged to indigenous populations.

Although nation-states took shape throughout the world, the Americas saw the most complete assimilation of new possessions. Instead of treating outlying areas as colonial outposts, American nation-state builders turned them into new provinces. With the help of rifles, railroads, schools, and land surveys, frontiers became staging areas for the expanding populations of North and South American societies. For indigenous peoples, however, such national expansion meant the loss of traditional lands on a vast scale, and many lost lives.

THE UNITED STATES

Military might, diplomacy, and the power of numbers enabled the United States to claim territory that spanned the North American continent. (See Map 17.1.) At its independence, the new country established a barely united confederation of states. Native American resistance and Spanish and British rivalry hemmed in the Americans of European descent. At the same time, the disunited states threatened to break apart, as questions of states' rights and of slavery versus free labor intruded into national politics. Yet, rallying to the rhetoric of **Manifest Destiny**, which maintained that it was God's will for the United States to "overspread" North America, American whites pushed their territorial claims and boundaries westward. They acquired territories via purchase agreements and treaties with France, Spain, and Britain, and via warfare and treaties with diverse Native American nations and Mexico.

Manifest Destiny
Belief that it was God's will for the American people to expand their territory and political processes across the North American continent.

Civil War and States' Rights Westward expansion proved the undoing of the American nation. The question was whether newly acquired lands would be open to slavery or restricted to free labor. Following the 1860 election of Abraham Lincoln, who pledged to halt the expansion of slavery, the United States divided between North and South and plunged into a gruesome Civil War (1861–1865).

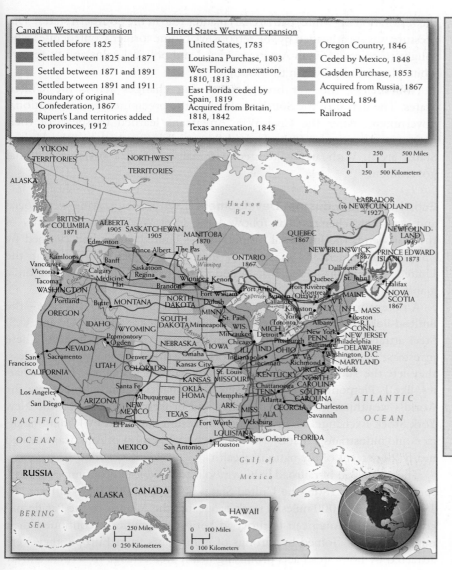

Canadian Westward Expansion

- Settled before 1825
- Settled between 1825 and 1871
- Settled between 1871 and 1891
- Settled between 1891 and 1911
- Boundary of original Confederation, 1867
- Rupert's Land territories added to provinces, 1912

United States Westward Expansion

- United States, 1783
- Louisiana Purchase, 1803
- West Florida annexation, 1810, 1813
- East Florida ceded by Spain, 1819
- Acquired from Britain, 1818, 1842
- Texas annexation, 1845
- Oregon Country, 1846
- Ceded by Mexico, 1848
- Gadsden Purchase, 1853
- Acquired from Russia, 1867
- Annexed, 1894
- Railroad

Map 17.1 U.S. and Canadian Westward Expansion, 1803–1912

....

Americans and Canadians expanded westward in the second half of the nineteenth century, aided greatly by railways.

- How do you account for the differences between the transcontinental railroads in the United States and Canada?
- When did Canada and the United States complete their respective territorial expansions? Why were these expansions not continuous, moving from east to west?
- How did territorial expansion strengthen Canadian and American nationalism?

The bloody conflict led to the abolition of slavery, and the struggle to extend voting and citizenship rights to male freed slaves qualified the Civil War as a second American Revolution. Abraham Lincoln had promised a new model of freedom for a state reborn out of bloodshed. Its cornerstone would be the incorporation of freed slaves as citizens of the United States. Yet experiments in biracial democracy during the Reconstruction period (1867–1877) were short-lived. In the decades after the Civil War, counterrevolutionary pressure led to the denial of voting rights to African Americans and the restoration of (white, patriarchal) planter rule in the Southern states. This pressure was spearheaded by the terrorism of some former Confederates who sought to reverse African Americans' legal and political gains and to restore white planters to power in the South.

Nonetheless, the war brought enduring changes across the United States. The defeat of the South established the preeminence of the national government. After the Civil War, Americans learned to speak of their nation in the singular ("the United States is" in contrast to "the United States are"). With an invigorated nationalism came a stronger national government.

Economic and Industrial Development Even more dizzying were social and economic changes that followed the Civil War. Within ten years of the war's end, the industrial output of the United States had climbed by 75 percent. Americans made such impressive industrial gains that the United States soon joined Britain and Germany atop the list of economic giants.

A potent instrument of capital accumulation appeared at this time—the **limited-liability joint-stock company**. Firms such as Standard Oil and U.S. Steel attracted money from well-to-do investors via a stock market. These investors, called shareholders, in theory owned the company; nonetheless, they left the running of these enterprises to paid managers. Intermediaries, like J. Pierpont Morgan, the New York financial giant who became the world's wealthiest man, loaned money and brokered big deals on the New York Stock Exchange. So great were the fortunes amassed by leading financiers and industrialists that by 1890 the richest 1 percent of Americans owned nearly 90 percent of the nation's wealth.

The expansion of railroad lines symbolized American economic and territorial growth. In 1865, the United States boasted 35,000 miles of track. By 1900, nearly 200,000 miles of track connected the Atlantic to the Pacific and crisscrossed the American territory in between. Americans continued their migrations west. Joined by throngs of immigrants from Europe, they were attracted by homestead acts promising nearly free acreage to settlers and by promoters from the railroads.

By now the United States had become a major world power. It boasted an economy that, despite troubles in the 1890s, had expanded rapidly over the last decades of the nineteenth century. It also was a more integrated nation after the Civil War, with an amended constitution that claimed to uphold the equality of all members of the American nation, even those men who were not white. But there was disagreement on what that equality should involve (for example, should it include women as voters?) and how the country would adjust to a new century in which the nation's "destiny" had already been fulfilled.

limited-liability joint-stock company
Company that mobilized capital from a large number of investors, called shareholders, who were not to be held personally liable for financial losses incurred by the company.

CANADA

Canadians also built a new nation, enjoyed economic success, and followed an expansionist course. Like the United States, Canada had access to a vast frontier prairie for growing agricultural exports. And as in the United States, these lands became the homes and farms of more European immigrants. However, whereas the United States had waged a war to gain independence, Canada's separation from Britain was peaceful. From the 1830s to the 1860s, Britain gradually passed authority to the colony, leaving Canadians to grapple with the task of creating a shared national community.

Building a Nation Sharp internal divisions made that task especially difficult. For one thing, there was a well-established French population. Wanting to keep their villages, their culture, their religion, and their language intact, these French Canadians did not feel integrated into the emerging Canadian national community. Nor were they eager to join the English-speaking population in settling new areas, lest such migration dilute their French-Canadian presence.

The English speakers were equally unenthusiastic about creating an independent Canadian state. Fear of being absorbed into the American republic reinforced these Canadians' loyalty to the British crown and made them content with colonial status. Indeed, when Canada finally gained its independence in 1867, it was by an Act of Parliament in London and not by revolution.

Territorial Expansion Lacking cultural and linguistic unity, Canadians used territorial expansion to build an integrated state. In response to the U.S. purchase of Alaska from Russia in 1867 and the movement of settlers onto the American plains, Canadian leaders realized that they had to incorporate their own western territories, lest these, too, fall into American hands.

The Canadian state also faced friction with indigenous peoples. Frontier warfare threatened to drive away investors and settlers, who could always find property south of the border instead. To prevent the kind of bloodletting that characterized the United States' westward expansion, the Canadian government signed treaties with indigenous peoples to ensure strict separation between natives and newcomers.

The Canadian government acquired significant powers to intervene in, regulate, and mediate social conflict between Anglo and French residents, and among both groups and the Native American population. These powers, in fact, were fuller than those of the U.S. government. But even though the state was relatively strong, the sense of a national identity was comparatively weak. Expansionism helped Canada remain an autonomous state, but it did not solve the question of what it meant to belong to a Canadian nation.

LATIN AMERICA

Latin American elites also engaged in nation-state building and expanded their territorial borders. But unlike in the United States and Canada, expansion did not always create homesteader frontiers that could help expand democracy and forge national identities. Instead, civil conflict fractured certain countries in the region (see Chapters 15 and 16), although a few, most notably Brazil and Mexico, remained united.

Much of Latin America shared a common social history. Far more than in North America, the richest lands in Latin America went to large estate holders producing exports such as sugar, coffee, or beef. As a result, privileged elites monopolized power more than in North America's young democracies.

Amerindian and peasant uprisings were a major worry in new Latin American republics. Fearing insurrections, elites devised governing systems that protected private property while limiting the political rights of the poor. Likewise, the specter of slave revolts, driven home not just by earlier, brutal events in Haiti (see Chapter 15) but also by daily rumors of rebellions, kept elites in a state of alarm. Creating strong states, it seemed to many Latin American elites, required excluding large groups of people from power.

Brazil's "Exclusive" Nation-State Brazil illustrates the process by which Latin American rulers built nation-states that excluded much of the population from both the "nation" and the "state." Through the nineteenth century, rulers in Rio de Janeiro defused political conflict by allowing planters to retain the reins of power.

The official prohibition of the importation of slaves in 1830, coupled with slave resistance, began to choke the planters' system by driving up the price of slaves within the region. Thereafter, Brazilian elites retained some former slaves as gang-workers or sharecroppers (who received tools and seeds in return for a share of the crop), and they also imported new workers— especially from Italy, Spain, and Portugal—as seasonal migrant workers or indentured tenant farmers. Indeed, European and even Japanese migration to Brazil helped planters preserve their holdings in the post-slavery era. In all, 2 million Europeans and some 70,000 Japanese moved to Brazil.

The Brazilian state was deliberately exclusive. As in the United States, elites imposed severe restrictions on suffrage and set rules that reduced political competition. However, given the greater share of the black population in Brazil, restrictions there excluded a larger share of the potential electorate than in the United States.

Brazilian Expansion and Economic Development Like Canada and the United States, the Brazilian state extended its reach to distant areas and incorporated them as provinces. The largest land grab occurred in the Amazon River basin, the world's largest drainage watershed and tropical forest. Here, the Brazilian state gave giant concessions to local capitalists to extract rubber latex. When combined with sulfur, rubber was a key raw material for tire manufacturing in European and North American bicycle and automobile industries.

For a time, Brazil became the world's exclusive exporter of rubber; as a result, its planters, merchants, and workers prospered. Rich merchants became lenders and financiers, not only to workers but also to landowners. The mercantile elite of Manaus, the capital of the Amazon region, designed and decorated their city to reflect their new fortunes. Although the streets were still paved with mud, the town's elite built a replica of the Paris Opera House, and Manaus became a regular stopover for European opera singers on the circuit between Buenos Aires and New York. Rubber workers also benefited from the boom. Mostly either Amerindians or mixed-blood people, they sent their wages home to families elsewhere in the Amazon jungle or on the northeastern coast of Brazil.

One problem was the ecosystem. Such a diversified biomass could not tolerate a regimented form of production. Cultivating rubber trees at the expense of other vegetation made the forest vulnerable to nonhuman predators. Leaf blights and ferocious ants destroyed all experiments at creating more sustainable rubber plantations.

The Brazilian rubber boom, moreover, soon went bust. As competition led to increased supplies and reduced prices, Brazilian producers went bankrupt. Merchants called in their loans, landowners forfeited their titles, and rubber workers returned to their small subsistence farms. Tropical vines crept over the Manaus Opera House, and it gradually fell into disrepair.

Throughout the Americas, nineteenth-century elites, working with outdated ideas of who should wield power, nonetheless attempted to satisfy popular demands for inclusion. While the ideal was to construct nation-states that could reconcile differences among their citizens and pave the way for economic prosperity, political autonomy did not bring prosperity, or even the right to vote, to all. As each nation-state expanded its territorial boundaries, many inhabitants were left out of the political realm.

Opera House in Manaus The turn-of-the-century rubber boom brought immense wealth to the Amazon jungle. As in many boom-and-bust cycles in Latin America, the proceeds flowed to a small elite and diminished when the rubber supply outstripped the demand. But the wealth produced was sufficient to prompt the local elite to build temples of modernity in the midst of the jungle. Pictured here is the Opera House in the rubber capital of Manaus. Like other works built by Latin American elites of the period, this one emulated the original in Paris.

Consolidation of Nation-States in Europe

Core Objectives

COMPARE the challenges elites in Europe and in the Americas faced in consolidating their nation-states, and the degrees to which they succeeded.

In Europe, no "frontier" existed into which new states could expand. Instead, nation-states took shape out of older monarchies and empires, and their borders were determined by diplomats or by battles. In the wake of the French Revolution, the idea caught on that "the people" should form the basis for the nation and that nations should share a common culture—but no one could agree on who "the people" should be. Yet, over the course of the nineteenth century, as literacy, cities, industrial production, and the number and prosperity of property owners expanded, ruling elites had no choice but to share power with a wider group of citizens. These citizens, in turn, increasingly defined themselves as, say, French or German, rather than as residents of Marseilles or subjects of the king of Bavaria.

DEFINING "THE NATION"

For a very long time, in most places, "the nation" was understood to comprise kings, clergymen, nobles—and occasionally rich merchants or lawyers—and no one else. Although some peoples, such as the English and the Spanish, were already self-conscious about their unique histories, only in the late eighteenth century were the crucial building blocks of European nationalism put in place.

Cultural changes laid the foundations of the nation. Increasingly literate urban populations met in coffeehouses and other public places to discuss the issues of the day. Their collective debates—public opinion—weighed for the first time on the decisions of kings and statesmen. During the nineteenth century, a huge expansion of the periodical press made it possible for people all across Europe to read books and newspapers in their own languages. The emerging industrial economy made merchants anxious to standardize laws, taxation policies, and weights and measures. States invested huge sums in building roads and then railroads—and these linked provincial towns and bigger cities, laying the foundations for a closer political integration.

But who were the people, and what constituted a viable nation-state? For some, the nation was a collection of all those who spoke one language; for others, it was all those who lived in a certain territory and who shared a common religious heritage. This was a particularly acute problem in multiethnic central and southeastern Europe, where many people were multilingual, rich and poor alike. But some who shared the same language objected to being lumped into one nation-state. The Irish, for example, spoke English but were predominantly Catholics and wanted to be free from Anglican rule.

UNIFICATION IN GERMANY AND ITALY

Two of Europe's fledgling nation-states came into being when the dynastic states of Prussia and Piedmont-Sardinia incorporated their smaller, linguistically related neighbors, creating the German and Italian nation-states. (See Map 17.2.) In both regions, conservative prime ministers—Count Otto von Bismarck of Prussia and Count Camillo di Cavour of Piedmont—exploited liberal, nationalist sentiment to rearrange the map of Europe.

Building Unified States The unifications of Germany and Italy, both completed in 1871, posed all the familiar problems of who should be included in the new nation-states. To begin with, German speakers were spread all across central and eastern Europe; for centuries they had lived in many different states. Similarly, Italians had lived separately in city-states and small kingdoms on the Italian Peninsula and spoke a range of dialects. The historical experiences and economic developments had made Bavarian Germans (Catholic) quite different from Prussian Germans (Protestant); likewise, the Milanese (who lived in a wealthy urban industrial center) shared little, language included, with the typical Sardinian peasant. But liberal nationalists had made the case that their high culture—especially their literary, musical, and theatrical traditions—overrode these differences, and emotional appeals by poets, composers, and orators convinced many people that this was indeed the case. Bismarck and Cavour merged this nationalist rhetoric with clever diplomacy—and the use of military force in a series of small conflicts—to forge united German and Italian nation-states.

These "unified" states rejected democracy. In the new Italy, which was a constitutional monarchy, less than 5 percent of the 25 million people could vote. The new German Empire (the Second Reich) had an assembly elected by all adult males (the Reichstag), but it had little power. The country was ruled by a combination of aristocrats and bureaucrats under a monarch. Liberals dominated in many localities, but only the emperor (the kaiser) could depose the prime minister. In fact, Bismarck continued to dominate Prussian politics for twenty-eight years, until fired in 1890 by Kaiser Wilhelm II. By that time, unification had yielded brisk economic growth both in Italy and, especially, Germany, but conflict between regions and political groups continued.

NATION BUILDING AND ETHNIC CONFLICT IN THE AUSTRO-HUNGARIAN EMPIRE

Bismarck's unification of Germany came at the expense of Habsburg supremacy in central Europe and (as we will see in the next section) of French territory and influence in the west. After Germany won a victory over the Austrian army in 1866, the Hungarian nobles who controlled the eastern Habsburg Empire forced the weakened dynasts to grant them home rule.

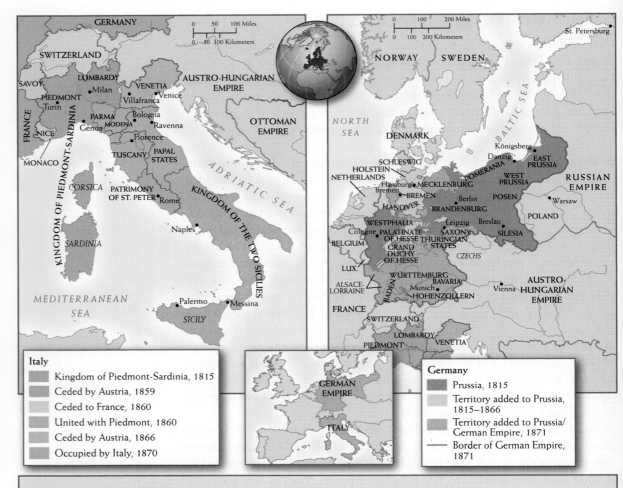

Map 17.2 Italian Unification and German Unification, 1815–1871

Italian unification and German unification altered the political map of Europe.

- What were the names of the two original states that grew to become Italy and Germany?
- Who were the big losers in these territorial transfers?
- According to your reading, what problems did the new Italian and German states face in creating strong national communities?

In the Compromise of 1867, the Habsburgs agreed that their state would officially be known as the Austro-Hungarian Empire. But this move did not solve Austria-Hungary's nationality problems. In both the Hungarian and the Austrian halves of the dual state, Czechs, Poles, and other Slavs now began to clamor for their own power-sharing "compromise" or autonomous national homelands. They would, however, have to wait until the end of World War I.

DOMESTIC DISCONTENTS IN FRANCE AND BRITAIN

Although already unified as nation-states, Britain and France faced major difficulties. For the French, dealing with defeat at the hands of the Germans was the primary national concern in the decades leading up to World War I. For the British, issues of Irish separatism, the rise of the working class, and feminists' demands troubled the political arena.

Destabilization in France The Franco-Prussian War of 1870–1871 completed the unification of Germany. Germany took the French provinces of Alsace and Lorraine, and its victory destabilized France. The German siege of Paris, which lasted for more than three months, devastated the capital. Unprepared, Parisians had no food stocks and were compelled to eat all sorts of things, including two zoo elephants. Under terrible conditions and without effective leadership, the French capital resisted until January 1871, when the government signed a humiliating peace treaty. The Germans left in place a weak provisional French government. Refusing the negotiated peace, furious Parisians vented their rage and established their own government, proclaiming the city a utopia for workers. The leftist commune they established lasted until the provisional national government's army stormed Paris a few months later. At least 25,000 Parisians died in the bloody mop-up that followed. A "Third Republic" took the place of Napoleon III's empire, but it struggled to achieve stability. In the years following the Franco-Prussian War, France saw increasing conflict between classes and the rise of anti-German nationalism.

Irish Nationalism in Great Britain Although the English had long thought of themselves as a nation, the idea that all British people belonged in the same state was much more problematic. The kingdom of England—which was originally composed of England, clearly the dominant state, and Wales—became the kingdom of Great Britain when it united with Scotland in 1707 and Ireland in 1801. It was home to peoples whose historical experiences, religious backgrounds, and economic opportunities were very different. In the nineteenth century, British leaders wrestled in particular with demands for independence from Irish nationalists and lower-class agitation, especially in England. Beginning in 1832, England responded to class conflict at home by extending political rights to most men but not women. England finally

The Irish Potato Famine Many families in Ireland were left desperate and starving in the aftermath of the potato crop failure and were forced to find sustenance wherever they could. In this engraving from the late nineteenth century, a group of people by the coast collects limpets and seaweed to eat.

established universal suffrage for all adult males after World War I, in 1918; roughly one-quarter of British women gained the right to vote at that time and the rest a decade later.

Yet Ireland remained Britain's Achilles' heel. The British government was widely condemned for its failure to relieve Irish suffering during the potato famine of 1845–1849. Over the course of the early nineteenth century, Irish peasants had planted energy-rich and easy-to-cultivate potatoes on their remaining rocky and sandy land. A relatively healthy diet of potatoes and milk had fueled population growth and put more pressure on the land. When a continent-wide potato blight ravaged the island's crops in 1845, this monoculture turned into a recipe for widespread famine. Although the blight continued to decimate harvests for the next four years, the English stuck to their laissez-faire principles and were slow to send grain to relieve Irish suffering, resulting in the death of as many as a million and the emigration of about the same number. Many of these Irish emigrants made their way to England, seeking either passage to North America or work in the English mill towns. Like their Scottish brethren, they did not assimilate easily and often got the lowliest jobs. All of this, on top of 300 years of repressive English domination, spawned a mass movement for Irish home rule that continued into the twentieth century.

Born in opposition to the old monarchical regimes, European nationalism by the end of the nineteenth century had become a means used by liberal and conservative leaders alike to unite the people behind them. But just what they meant by "the people" remained bitterly contested. Continental powers increasingly resorted to an aggressive foreign policy and imperial expansion to maintain popular support without granting political power to ordinary people. France alone, of the European great powers, had a parliamentary democracy elected by universal manhood suffrage.

Industry, Science, and Technology

A powerful combination of industry, science, and technology shaped the emerging nation-states in North America and western Europe. It also reordered the relationships among different parts of the world. One critical factor was that after 1850 western Europe and North America experienced a new phase of industrial development—essentially a second industrial revolution. Japan, too, joined the ranks of industrializing nations as its state-led program of industrial development started to pay dividends. These changes transformed the global economy and intensified rivalries among industrial societies.

NEW TECHNOLOGIES, MATERIALS, AND BUSINESS PRACTICES

New technologies and materials drove economic development in the late nineteenth century and led to new business practices. This period witnessed major technological changes with the arrival of new organic sources of power (like oil) and new ways to get old organic sources (like coal) to processing plants. These changes freed manufacturers from having to locate their plants close to their fuel sources. Not only did the most important new source of energy—electricity—permit factories to arise in areas with plenty of skilled workers, but it also slashed production costs. **Steel**, now cheaply produced because of technical innovations, became essential for shipbuilding and railways. Electricity and steel were part of a bundle of innovations that included chemicals and pharmaceuticals, which together transformed northwestern Europe, the United States, and Japan.

The breakthroughs of the second industrial revolution ushered in new business practices, especially mass production and the giant integrated firm. No longer would modest investments suffice, as they had in Britain a century earlier. Now large banks were the major providers of funds. In Europe, limited-liability joint-stock companies were as wildly successful in raising capital on stock markets as they were in the United States. Companies like Standard Oil, U.S. Steel, and Siemens mobilized investments from large numbers of shareholders. The scale of these firms was awesome. U.S. Steel alone produced over half of the world's steel ingots, castings, rails, and heavy structural shapes—and nearly half of all its steel plates and sheets, which were vital in the construction of buildings, railroads, ships, and the like.

steel
A metal more malleable and stronger than iron that became essential for industries like shipbuilding and railways.

INTEGRATION OF THE WORLD ECONOMY

Not only did industrial change concentrate power in North Atlantic societies, but it also reinforced their power on the world economic stage and created a more integrated global economy. Europe and the United States increased their exports in new products; they also grew eager to control the importation of tropical commodities such as cocoa and coffee. While the North Atlantic societies were still largely self-sufficient in coal, iron, cotton, wool, and wheat (the major commodities of the first industrial revolution), the second industrial revolution bred a need for rubber, copper, oil, and bauxite (an ore used to make aluminum), which were not available domestically. Equally important, large pools of money became available for investing overseas.

Movements of Labor and Technology Vast movements of workers took place to satisfy the labor demands of an increasingly integrated world economy. Indians moved thousands of miles from Asia to work on sugar plantations in the Caribbean, Mauritius, and Fiji; to labor in South African mines; and to build railroads in East Africa. Chinese workers constructed railroads in the western United States and toiled on sugar plantations in Cuba. The Irish, Poles, Jews, Italians, and Greeks flocked to North America to fill its burgeoning factories. Italians also moved to Argentina to harvest wheat and corn.

With steam-powered gunboats and breech-loading rifles, Europeans opened new territories for trade and conquest. At home and in their colonial possessions, imperial powers constructed networks of railroads that carried people and goods from hinterlands to the coasts. From there, steamships bore them across the seas. Completion of the Suez Canal in 1869 shortened ship voyages between Europe and Asia and lowered the costs of interregional trade. Information moved even faster than cargoes, thanks to the laying of telegraph cables under the oceans, supplemented by overland telegraph lines.

Charles Darwin and Natural Selection Although machines were the most visible evidence that humans could master the universe, perhaps the most momentous shift in the conception of nature derived from the travels of one British scientist: **Charles Darwin** (1809–1882).

Darwin's theory, articulated in his *On the Origin of Species* (1859), laid out the principles of **natural selection**. Inevitably, he claimed, populations grew faster than the food supply; this condition created a "struggle for existence" among species. In later work he showed how the passing on of individual traits was also determined by what he called sexual selection—according to which the "best" mates are chosen for their strength, beauty, or talents and the less fit fail to reproduce at comparable rates. Although Darwin's book dealt exclusively with animals (and mostly with birds), his readers immediately wondered what his theory implied for humans.

Charles Darwin
(1809–1882) British scientist who became convinced that the species of organic life had evolved under the uniform pressure of natural laws, not by means of a special, one-time creation as described in the Bible.

natural selection
Charles Darwin's theory that populations grew faster than the food supply, creating a "struggle for existence" among species. In later work he showed how the passing on of individual traits was also determined by what he called sexual selection—according to which the "best" mates are chosen for their strength, beauty, or talents. The outcome: the "fittest" survived to reproduce, while the less adaptable did not.

A passionate debate began among scientists and laymen, clerics and anthropologists. Some read Darwin's doctrine of natural selection to mean that it was natural for the strong nations to dominate the weak, or justifiable to allow disabled persons to die—something Darwin explicitly rejected. As more groups (mis)interpreted Darwin's theory to suit their own objectives, a set of beliefs known as social Darwinism legitimated the suffering of the underclasses in industrial society. In subsequent years Europeans would repeatedly suggest that they had evolved more than Africans and Asians. Extending Darwinian ideas far beyond the scientist's intent, some Europeans came to believe that nature itself gave them the right to rule others.

Imperialism and the Origins of Anticolonial Nationalism

Increasing rivalries among nations and social tensions within them produced an expansionist wave late in the nineteenth century. Although Africa became the primary focus of interest, a frenzy of territorial conquest overtook Asia as well. In China's territories, competition by foreign powers to establish spheres of influence heated up in the 1890s. And in India, imperial ambitions provoked the British to conquer Burma (present-day Myanmar). Moreover, Britain and Russia competed for preeminence from their respective outposts in Afghanistan and central Asia. In the Americas, new territories were usually incorporated as provinces of the expansionist state, making them integral parts of the nation.

In Asia and Africa, however, European and American imperialism turned far-flung territories into colonial possessions. The inhabitants of these colonial possessions were generally designated as subjects of the empire without the rights and privileges of citizens. Britain's imperial regime in India provided lessons to a generation of European colonial officials in Africa and other parts of Asia. Yet, even as Europe's colonial administrators looked to earlier imperial practices in India and the Caribbean for use in Africa, they also regarded African communities as less economically and culturally developed than Asian communities. Hence, they believed that Africans would require an extended period of colonial tutelage.

The proponents of European and North American colonization argued that colonial rule produced benefits for both the colonial peoples and the colonizers. Economically, colonies would be drawn into and profit from an emerging world economy. They would export primary products in high demand in the industrialized parts of the global economy—most notably cocoa, tea, coffee, diamonds, gold, and copper from Africa; rubber from the Dutch East Indies; huge quantities of cotton from India and Egypt; and beginning mainly after World War I, oil from the Middle East to fuel industrial economies. In return, colonial peoples would import much-needed

Core Objectives

COMPARE the different western colonial models used in various regions of the world and the responses of those regions.

manufactured commodities—clothing made from their raw cotton; processed foods made from coffee, cocoa, and tea; railway engines; and ocean-going vessels. But were the benefits evenly distributed, as some imperialist proponents claimed? A balance sheet of imperialism is difficult to construct, but the biggest beneficiaries were clearly not African and Asian peasant cultivators, as apologists asserted, or even the workers in western factories, whose wages, while rising, still remained low. Profits flowed mainly to European-run export-import firms, large global banks, and wealthy industrialists.

Not surprisingly, colonized peoples resisted the imposition of economic systems that destroyed older trading and agricultural systems and benefited only the colonial extractors. Resistance took different forms, including the demand for national self-determination. In many parts of colonial Asia, early forms of resistance, usually put down with savage reprisals, were followed by organized political protest and the formation of nationalist political parties. The African continent, the last to be colonized, at first went through an early phase of armed resistance to colonial rule, which was repressed with considerable bloodshed. After World War I, colonial critics followed in the footsteps of the Asian anticolonial nationalists. They, too, created anticolonial, mainly nonviolent, political organizations, seeking at first the redress of colonial grievances, such as lost lands. Many of these nations would have to wait until the post–World War II period to achieve full independence.

INDIA AND THE IMPERIAL MODEL

Britain's rule in India provided a model for other imperialist governments by developing the colony's infrastructure in order to maximize

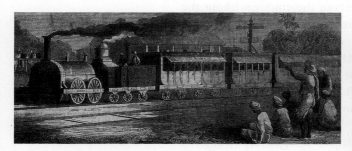

The Raj Strengthens Control (*Left*) In the aftermath of the Indian Rebellion of 1857, the British government, called the Raj (meaning "rule" in Hindi), intervened much more actively in India. It built an extensive system of railroads to develop India as a profitable colony and to maintain military security. This engraving shows the East India Railway around 1863. (*Right*) Skeletal human remains can be seen scattered among the ruins of the Palace of Secundra Bagh on the outskirts of Lucknow, after the Siege of Lucknow. The Secundra Bagh was attacked by the troops of Sir Colin Campbell in November 1857. This photograph is thought to be among the first to show casualties of war.

British profits from trade. Having suppressed the Indian Rebellion of 1857 (see Chapter 16), authorities revamped the colonial administration. From the British point of view, Indians were not to be appeased—and certainly not brought into British public life. But they did have to be governed, and the economy had to be revived. So, after replacing the East India Company's rule by crown government in 1858, the British set out to make India into a more secure and productive colony. This period of British sovereignty was known as the **Raj** ("rule").

The most urgent tasks facing the British in India were modernizing its transportation and communication systems and transforming the country into an integrated colonial state. These changes had begun under the governor-general of the East India Company, Lord Dalhousie, who oversaw the development of India's modern infrastructure. After the British suppressed the revolt, they took up the construction of public works with renewed vigor. Railways were a key element both in the pacification (they shuttled troops to danger zones) and in the later reform project. The first railway line opened in 1853, and by 1910 India had 30,627 miles of track in operation—making it the fourth-largest railway system in the world.

Construction of other public works followed. Engineers built dams across rivers to tame their force and to irrigate lands; workers installed a grid of telegraph lines that opened communication between distant parts of the region. These public works served imperial and economic purposes: India was to become a consumer of British manufactures and a supplier of primary staples such as cotton, tea, and wheat. On the hillsides of the island of Ceylon (now Sri Lanka) and the northeastern plains of India, the British established vast plantations to grow tea—which was then marketed in England as a healthier alternative to Chinese green tea. India also became an important consumer of British manufactures, especially textiles, in an ironic turnabout of its centuries-old tradition of exporting its own cotton and silk textiles.

The reform efforts of the Raj made India into a unified territory and enabled its inhabitants to begin to regard themselves as "Indians." These were the first steps to becoming a "nation" like Italy and the United States, but there were profound differences. Above all, as colonial subjects Indians did not enjoy basic civic and human rights, and even elites lacked the vote. Other European powers followed the British example in trying to modernize and integrate their colonies economically without welcoming colonial peoples into the life of the nation.

COLONIZING AFRICA

No region felt the impact of European colonialism more powerfully than Africa. In 1880, the only two large European colonial possessions there were French Algeria and two British-ruled South African states, the Cape Colony and Natal. But within a mere thirty years, seven European states had carved almost all of Africa into colonial possessions.

Partitioning the African Landmass In the context of heightened international rivalries, Portugal called for an international conference to discuss claims to Africa. Meeting in Berlin between 1884 and 1885, delegates from Europe, the United States, and the Ottoman Empire agreed to carve up Africa and to recognize the claims of the first European power that claimed control of a given territory. Colonizers rushed to plant their flags as widely as possible, lest they be outmaneuvered by their rivals.

The consequences for Africa were devastating. Nearly 70 percent of the newly drawn borders failed to correspond to older demarcations of ethnicity, language, culture, and commerce—for Europeans knew little of the landmass beyond its coast and rivers. They based their new colonial boundaries on European trading centers rather than on the location of African population groups. (See Map 17.3.)

Several motives led the European powers into their frenzied partition of Africa. Although European businesses were primarily interested in Egypt and South Africa, where their investments were lucrative, small-scale traders and investors harbored fantasies of great treasures locked in the vast uncharted interior. Politicians, publicists, and the reading public also took an interest. The writings of explorers like David Livingstone (1813–1873), a Scottish doctor and missionary, and Henry Morton Stanley (1841–1904), an adventurer in the pay of the *New York Herald*, excited readers with accounts of Africa as a continent of unlimited economic potential.

The most determined of the African empire builders was Leopold II (r. 1865–1909), king of the Belgians. (See Current Trends in World History: Africa's Newest Hunters and Gatherers: Greed, Environmental Degradation, and Resistance for Leopold's activities in central Africa and their effects on Africans and the environment.) In southern Africa, the British champion of imperialism Cecil Rhodes (1853–1902) brought the Rhodesias, Nyasaland, Bechuanaland, the Transvaal, and the Orange Free State into the British Empire as part of a design to have British territories stretching all the way from the Cape of Good Hope in South Africa to Cairo in Egypt.

Other Europeans saw Africa as a grand opportunity for converting souls to Christianity. In fact, Europe's civilizing mission was an important motive in the scramble for African territory. In Uganda, northern Nigeria, and central and western Africa, missionaries went ahead of European armies, begging the European statesmen to follow their lead.

African Resistance Africans faced two unappealing options: they could capitulate to the Europeans and negotiate to limit the loss of their autonomy, or they could fight to preserve their sovereignty. Only a few chose to negotiate.

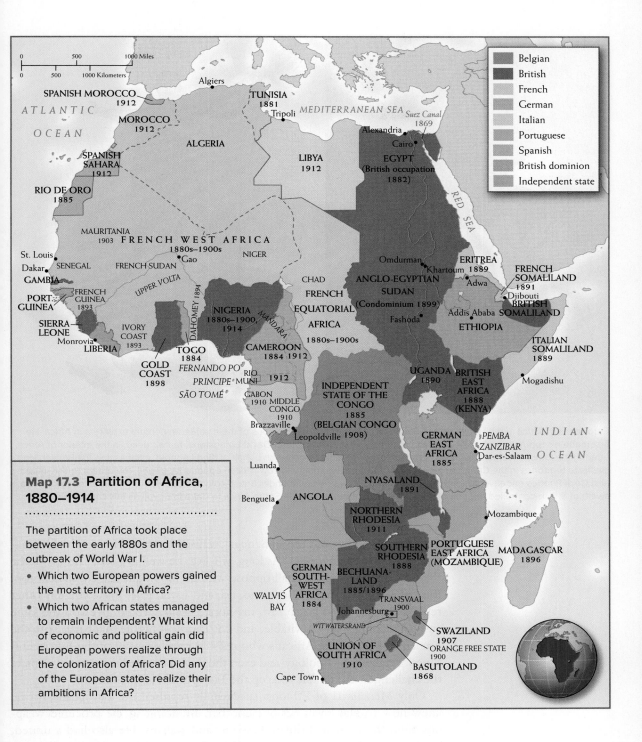

Map 17.3 Partition of Africa, 1880–1914

....

The partition of Africa took place between the early 1880s and the outbreak of World War I.

- Which two European powers gained the most territory in Africa?
- Which two African states managed to remain independent? What kind of economic and political gain did European powers realize through the colonization of Africa? Did any of the European states realize their ambitions in Africa?

Legend:

- Belgian
- British
- French
- German
- Italian
- Portuguese
- Spanish
- British dominion
- Independent state

Map labels:

SPANISH MOROCCO 1912
ATLANTIC OCEAN
Algiers
TUNISIA 1881
Tripoli
MEDITERRANEAN SEA
Suez Canal 1869
MOROCCO 1912
ALGERIA
LIBYA 1912
EGYPT (British occupation 1882)
Alexandria
Cairo
RED SEA
SPANISH SAHARA 1912
RIO DE ORO 1885
MAURITANIA 1903
FRENCH WEST AFRICA 1880s–1900s
St. Louis
Dakar
SENEGAL
GAMBIA
FRENCH SUDAN
Gao
NIGER
CHAD
ANGLO-EGYPTIAN SUDAN (Condominium 1899)
Omdurman
Khartoum
ERITREA 1889
Adwa
FRENCH SOMALILAND 1891
Djibouti
BRITISH SOMALILAND
PORT. GUINEA
FRENCH GUINEA 1893
UPPER VOLTA
DAHOMEY 1894
NIGERIA 1880s–1900, 1914
MANDARA
FRENCH EQUATORIAL AFRICA 1880s–1900s
Fashoda
Addis Ababa
ETHIOPIA
ITALIAN SOMALILAND 1889
SIERRA LEONE
Monrovia
LIBERIA
IVORY COAST 1893
GOLD COAST 1898
TOGO 1884
FERNANDO PO
PRINCIPE
SÃO TOMÉ
RIO MUNI 1912
CAMEROON 1884 1912
GABON 1910
MIDDLE CONGO 1910
Brazzaville
Leopoldville 1908
INDEPENDENT STATE OF THE CONGO 1885 (BELGIAN CONGO)
UGANDA 1890
BRITISH EAST AFRICA 1888 (KENYA)
Mogadishu
GERMAN EAST AFRICA 1885
PEMBA
ZANZIBAR
Dar-es-Salaam
INDIAN OCEAN
Luanda
ANGOLA
Benguela
NYASALAND 1891
Mozambique
NORTHERN RHODESIA 1911
GERMAN SOUTH-WEST AFRICA 1884
WALVIS BAY
SOUTHERN RHODESIA 1888
PORTUGUESE EAST AFRICA (MOZAMBIQUE)
MADAGASCAR 1896
BECHUANA-LAND 1885/1896
TRANSVAAL 1900
Johannesburg
WITWATERSRAND
SWAZILAND 1907
ORANGE FREE STATE 1900
BASUTOLAND 1868
UNION OF SOUTH AFRICA 1910
Cape Town

Europeans in Africa (*Left*) Henry Morton Stanley was one of the most famous of the nineteenth-century explorers in Africa. He first made his reputation when he located the British missionary-explorer David Livingstone, feared dead, in the interior of Africa, uttering the famous words, "Dr. Livingstone, I presume." Stanley worked on behalf of King Leopold, establishing the Belgian king's claims to territories in the Congo and often using superior weaponry to cow African opponents. (*Right*) The ardent British imperialist Cecil Rhodes endeavored to bring as much of Africa as he could under British colonial rule. He had an ambition to create a swath of British-controlled territory that would stretch from the Cape in South Africa to Cairo in Egypt, as this cartoon shows.

Lat Dior, a Muslim warlord in Senegal, refused to let the French build a railway through his kingdom. "As long as I live, be well assured," he wrote the French commandant, "I shall oppose with all my might the construction of this railway. I will always answer no, no, and I will never make you any other reply. Even were I to go to rest, my horse, *Malay*, would give you the same answer." Conflict was inevitable, and Lat Dior lost his life in a battle with the French in 1886. Most Africans who resisted were unaware of the Europeans' superior military technology, and even those who adapted their tactics to meet the challenge were unable to keep the Europeans out indefinitely.

Only Menelik II of Ethiopia successfully repulsed the Europeans, for he knew how to play rivals off one another. By doing so, he procured weapons from the French, British, Russians, and Italians. He also had a united, loyal, and well-equipped army. In 1896, his troops routed Italian forces at the Battle of Adwa, after which Adwa became a celebrated moment in African history. Its memory inspired many of Africa's later nationalist leaders.

Colonial Administrations in Africa Once the Europeans' euphoria over the gains of the partition and conquest had worn off, the power to rule the colonies fell to "men on the spot"—military adventurers, settlers, and entrepreneurs whose main goal was to get rich quick. As these individuals established little kingdoms in some areas, Africans (like Amerindians on the other side of the Atlantic) found themselves confined to territories where they could barely provide for themselves.

Eventually, these rough-and-ready systems led to violent revolts from aggrieved Africans, and in their aftermath the colonial rulers had to create more efficient administrations, dedicated to providing health care and education for the colonized. As in India, colonial powers in Africa laid the foundations for future nation-state organizations. Once information trickling out of Africa revealed that the imperial governments were not realizing their goal of bringing "civilization" to the "uncivilized" and creating easy profits, each European power implemented a new form of colonial rule, stripping the strongman conquerors of their absolute powers, monitoring them more closely, and assuming greater responsibility for the colonized peoples.

Eventually, stabilized colonies began to deliver on their economic promise. Whereas early imperialism in Africa had relied on the export of ivory and wild rubber, after these resources became depleted, the colonies pursued other exports. From the rain forests came cocoa, coffee, palm oil, and palm kernels. From the highlands of East Africa came tea, coffee, sisal (used in cord and twine), and pyrethrum (a flower used to make insecticide). Another important commodity was long-staple, high-quality cotton, grown in Egypt and the Anglo-Egyptian Sudan. Indeed, tropical commodities from all across Africa (as from India and Latin America) flowed to industrializing societies.

Thus, European colonial administrators saw Africa as fitting into the world economy in the same way that British administrators viewed India—as an exporter of raw materials and an importer of manufactures. They expected Africa to profit from this role. But, in truth, African workers gained little from participating in colonial commerce, while the price they paid in disruption to traditional social and economic patterns was substantial.

To observers, the European empires in Africa seemed solid and durable, but in fact European colonial rule there was fragile. For all of British Africa, the only all-British force was 5,000 men garrisoned in Egypt. Elsewhere, European officers depended on African military and police forces. And prior to 1914, the number of British administrative officers available for the whole of northern Nigeria was less than 500. These were hardly strong foundations for colonial rule. It would not take much to destabilize the European order in Africa.

> **Core Objectives**
>
> **ANALYZE** the extent to which colonies contributed to the wealth and political strength of the nation-states that controlled them.

Africa's Newest Hunters and Gatherers: Greed, Environmental Degradation, and Resistance

Africa was the birthplace of hunting and gathering (see Chapter 1). Ironically, although the European colonizers justified their partition of Africa on the grounds of bringing civilization to a benighted people, in fact, in their quest to enrich themselves, the first generation of colonizers exploited the most available resources of the continent, enslaved and killed huge numbers of people, and returned parts of the continent to a hunting and gathering mode of production. The most driven and greediest of these figures was Leopold II, king of the Belgians, who was determined, in spite of sweet-sounding rhetoric, to do whatever it took to line his pockets and make himself a formidable figure in European politics. King Leopold's story and others like it fascinate world historians because it conveys in stark detail the nature of the relationship between the rulers and the Africans they ruled. It also provides a point of comparison for the different models of ruling that each European power instituted in its colonies.

Even before ascending the throne in 1865, Leopold cast about for ways to become more than the constitutional monarch of a small, recently established, and neutral state. A voracious reader on colonialism, he was struck forcefully by one book: *How the Dutch Ruled Java*, published in 1861. By demonstrating how the Dutch colonial state had expropriated money from the East Indies (today called Indonesia) to spend on projects at home, the book fired his imagination. Could he not do the same? Could he not stake out a colony, take money from it to swell his own exchequer, and use some of it on public works at home—to beautify the cities of Belgium the way Paris had been beautified in the 1850s and 1860s?

Fixing his gaze on central Africa, in the 1880s Leopold manipulated the other European states into recognizing him as the sovereign head of a "Congo Free State," in which he led a European effort to "civilize" (and especially to exploit) the Congo River basin. Leopold hired the world-famous explorer Henry Stanley to "pacify" the country and ready it for economic development.

But how to make these lands pay off? They were almost entirely unexplored and unsurveyed, and though in time they would yield some of the richest mineral deposits in the world, these prospects were unknown to Leopold and his administrators at first. What the rain forests of Africa had was wild products, especially rubber and ivory. But how to get Africans, who at that point hardly participated in world trade, to tap wild rubber vines and hunt elephants? The solution here and elsewhere in similar African environments was to create large armies (known in Leopold's state as the Force Publique), fix quotas for districts to procure, and compel villagers to bring in baskets of rubber and elephant tusks.

For Leopold the results were little short of astonishing. He extracted vast

THE AMERICAN EMPIRE

The United States, like Europe, was drawn into the mania of overseas expansion and empire building. Echoing the earlier rhetoric of Manifest Destiny, the expansionists of the 1890s claimed that Americans still had a divine mission to spread their superior civilization and their Christian faith around the globe. However, America's new imperialists followed the European model of colonialism from Asia and Africa: colonies were to provide harbors for American vessels, supply raw materials to American industries, and purchase the surplus production of American farms and factories. These new territorial acquisitions were not intended for American settlement or statehood. Nor were their inhabitants to become American citizens, for nonwhite foreigners were considered unfit for incorporation into the American nation.

King Leopold Despite the inhumane way in which he funded his vast array of public buildings, Leopold is sometimes called, not unaffectionately, the "Builder King" by Belgians today.

sums from the Congo, spending lavishly on himself and on Belgium. He sank millions of francs into making the seaside city of Ostend one of the finest resorts in the world. At Tervuren, while a choir sang the new Congo anthem, Leopold laid the foundation stone of a world college for overseas colonial administration. In Brussels he spent over $5 million renovating royal palaces and constructing parks, avenues, casinos, and racecourses.

For the Congolese, Leopold's state was nothing more than a reign of terror. Forced to roam farther and farther from their home villages in search of rubber and elephants to keep pace with ever-escalating quotas, villagers suffered an immense loss of life through famine and conflicts with the Force Publique. Perhaps as many as 10 million Africans perished in a population that had been roughly 20 million before Leopold's agents arrived.

Leopold's brutality did not go unobserved, however. In 1899, the writer Joseph Conrad took the Congo as his model of rapacious European imperialism in his novella *Heart of Darkness*. African villagers rebelled, though unsuccessfully, and by the first decade of the twentieth century, rumors and then detailed reports painted a stark picture of terror and environmental degradation as the villagers rooted out almost all wild rubber and began the hunt for elephants that would ultimately render them an endangered species. In 1908, a year before his death, Leopold was compelled, against his wishes, to turn the administration of the Congo over to the Belgian parliament.

Questions for Analysis

- Why was King Leopold such an important figure in the European partition of Africa?
- While the Congo story is one of the most brutal stories of colonial exploitation and environmental degradation, which other episodes in world history does it remind you of and why?

Explore Further

Herbst, Jeffrey, *States and Power in Africa: Comparative Lessons in Authority and Control* (2000).
Hochschild, Adam, *King Leopold's Ghost* (1998).

The pressure to expand came to a head in the late 1890s, when the United States declared war on Spain and invaded the Philippines, Puerto Rico, and Cuba. The United States annexed Puerto Rico after minimal protest, but Cubans and Filipinos resisted becoming colonial subjects. Bitterness ran particularly high among Filipinos, to whom American leaders had promised independence if they joined in the war against Spain. Betrayed, Filipino rebels launched a war for independence in the name of a Filipino nation. In two years of fighting, over 5,000 Americans and perhaps 200,000 Filipinos perished. The outcome: the Philippines became a colony of the United States.

Colonies in the Philippines and Puerto Rico laid the foundations for a revised model of U.S. expansionism. The earlier pattern had been to turn Native American lands into privately owned farmsteads and to extend the Atlantic

Battle of Adwa Portrait of King Menelik, who defeated the Italian forces at the battle of Adwa in 1896, thus saving his country from European colonization.

market across the continent. But now, in this new era, the nation's largest corporations (with government support) aggressively intervened in the affairs of neighbors near and far. Following the Spanish-American War, the United States repeatedly sent troops to many Caribbean and Central American countries. The Americans preferred to turn these regimes into dependent states, rather than making them part of the United States itself (as with Alaska and Hawaii) or converting them into formal colonies (as the Europeans had done in Africa and Asia).

IMPERIALISM AND CULTURE

Europeans and Americans set out to bring "civilization" to the peoples of their colonies. At least since the Crusades, Europeans had regularly written and thought about others. These images and ideas had grown more numerous and varied as commerce and colonialism in Asia and the Atlantic world increased; they served various purposes, including those of informing, entertaining, flattering, and criticizing European culture. As Europeans and Americans grew more and more confident in their achievements, they became convinced that their arts and sciences were superior—and curiosity often turned to disdain. In time Europeans presumed that the only true modern civilization was their own; other peoples might have reigned over great empires in antiquity but had since fallen into decadence and decline. Artists and writers portrayed nonwestern peoples as exotic, sensuous, and economically backward in a genre scholars have come to call "Orientalism."

If Darwin remained ambivalent about the nature of race, his followers embraced the idea of stable racial differences that evolved only on the longest of time horizons, at a glacial pace, over thousands of years rather than decades or centuries. They ratified a view of "lower" and "higher" races, the former stuck in the past and the latter anointed by God (or in the case of social Darwinists, by nature itself) to define and dictate civilization's future. Europeans' relationship to others might now be one of condescending sympathy or of ruthless exploitation, but the result was that it was up to white Europeans and Americans to create modern culture. The darker people, social Darwinists argued, were not nearly as fully "evolved" as the Europeans and could not hope to catch up. At best they could be taught European languages, sciences, and religions, and perhaps be made to evolve more quickly.

It is telling that French colonial subjects who did well at French schools were known as *evolués*, "the evolved ones."

Celebrating Imperialism Especially in middle- and upper-class circles, Europeans celebrated their imperial triumphs. After the invention of photographic film and the Eastman Kodak camera in 1888, imperial images surfaced in popular forms such as postcards and advertisements. Imperial themes also decorated packaging materials; tins of coffee, tea, tobacco, and chocolates featured pictures highlighting the commodities' colonial origins. Cigarettes often had names like "Admiral," "Royal Navy," "Fighter," and "Grand Fleet." Some of this served as propaganda, produced by investors in imperial commodities or by colonial pressure groups.

Propaganda promoted imperialism abroad but also inspired changes at home. For example, champions of empire argued that if the British population did not grow fast enough to fill the world's sparsely settled regions, then the population of other nations would. Population was power, and the number of healthy children provided an accurate measure of global influence. "Empire cannot be built on rickety and flat-chested citizens," warned a British member of Parliament in 1905. Empire and imperialism carried European, American, and, to a lesser extent, Japanese power and culture throughout the world. In terms of the size of the populations they ruled, this era was the high point of European and Euro-American predominance.

The Women of Algiers in Their Apartment An oil painting by Eugène Delacroix (1798–1863) of Algerian women being attended by a black servant. European painters in the nineteenth century often used images of women to portray Arab Muslim society.

Pressures of Expansion in Japan, Russia, and China

Core Objectives

COMPARE the challenges elites faced in Japan, China, and Russia in consolidating nation-states to those faced by western elites.

The challenge of integrating political communities and extending territorial borders was a problem not just for western Europe and the United States. Other societies also aimed to overcome domestic dissent and establish larger domains. Japan, Russia, and China provide three contrasting models; their differing forms of expansion eventually led them to fight over possessions in East Asia.

JAPAN'S TRANSFORMATION AND EXPANSION

Starting in the 1860s, Japanese rulers tried to recast their country less as an old dynasty and more as a modern nation-state. Since the early seventeenth century, the Tokugawa shogunate had kept outsiders within strict limits and thwarted internal unrest. But after an American naval officer, Commodore Matthew Perry, entered Edo Bay in 1853 with a fleet of steam-powered ships, other Americans, Russians, Dutch, and British followed in his wake. These outsiders forced the Tokugawa rulers to sign humiliating treaties that opened Japanese ports, slapped limits on Japanese tariffs, and exempted foreigners from Japanese laws. Younger Japanese, especially among the military (samurai) elites, felt that Japan should respond by adopting, not rejecting, western practices.

In 1868, a group of reformers toppled the Tokugawa shogunate and promised to return Japan to its mythic greatness. Then Emperor Mutsuhito—the Meiji ("Enlightened Rule") Emperor—became the symbol of a new Japan.

Perry Arrives in Japan A Japanese wood-block print portraying the uninvited arrival into Edo (Tokyo) Bay on August 7, 1853, of a tall American ship, which was commanded by Matthew Perry. This arrival marked the end of Japan's ability to fully control the terms of its interactions with foreigners.

His reign (1868–1912) was called the **Meiji Restoration**. By founding schools, initiating a propaganda campaign, and revamping the army to create a single "national" fighting force, the Meiji government promoted a political community that stressed linguistic and ethnic homogeneity, as well as superiority compared to others. In this way the Meiji leaders overcame age-old regional divisions, subdued local political authorities, and mobilized the country to face the threat from powerful Europeans.

Economic Development One of the Meiji period's remarkable achievements was the nation's economic transformation. After 1871, when the government banned the feudal system and allowed peasants to become small landowners, farmers improved their agrarian techniques and saw their standard of living rise. The energetic new government unified the currency around the yen, created a postal system, introduced tax reforms, and established an advanced civil service system. In 1889, the Meiji government introduced a constitution (based largely on the German model). The following year, 450,000 people—about 1 percent of the population—elected Japan's first parliament, the Imperial Diet.

As the government sold valuable enterprises to the people who had provided strong support, it created private economic dynasties. The new large companies (such as Sumitomo, Yasuda, Mitsubishi, and Mitsui) were trusted family organizations. Fathers, sons, cousins, and uncles ran different parts of large integrated corporations—some in charge of banks, some running the trade wing, some overseeing factories. Women played a crucial role, not just as custodians of the home but also as cultivators of important family alliances, especially among potential marriage partners. In contrast to American limited-liability firms, which issued shares on stock markets to anonymous buyers, Japan's version of large-scale managerial capitalism was a personal affair.

Expansionism and Conflict with Neighbors As in many other emerging nation-states, expansion was a tempting prospect to the Japanese. It offered the promise of more markets for selling goods and obtaining staples, and it was a way to burnish the image of national superiority and greatness. The Meiji moved first to take over the kingdom of the Ry–uky–us southwest of Japan. (See Map 17.4.) A small show of force, only 160 Japanese soldiers, was enough to establish the new Okinawa Prefecture there in 1879. The Japanese regarded the people of the Ry–uky–us as an ethnic minority and refused to incorporate them into the nation-state on equal terms. In contrast with the British in India or the Americans in Puerto Rico, the Japanese conquerors refused to train a native Ry–uky–uan governing class. Meiji intellectuals insisted that the "backward" Okinawans were unfit for local self-rule and representation.

The Japanese fixed upon Korea, which put their plans on a collision course with China's. In a formal treaty, the Japanese recognized Korea as an

Map 17.4 Japanese Expansion, 1870–1910

Under the Meiji Restoration, the Japanese state built a strong national identity and competed with foreign powers for imperial advantage in East Asia.

- According to the map, what were the first areas that the Japanese Empire acquired as it started to expand?
- What two empires' spheres of influence were affected by Japan's aggressive attempts at expansion?
- According to your reading, what were the new Japanese state's objectives? How were they similar to or different from those of expansionist European states in the same period?

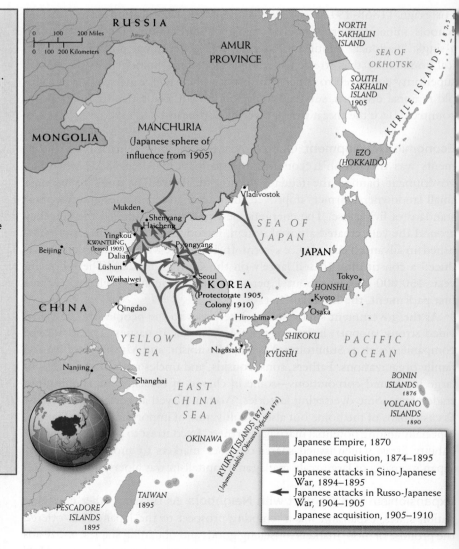

independent state (expected to be no longer dominated by China), opened Korea to trade, and won the right to apply Japanese law in Korea. As a result, the Chinese worried that soon the Japanese would try to take over Korea. These fears were well founded, for Japanese designs on Korea eventually sparked the Sino-Japanese War of 1894–1895, in which the Chinese suffered a humiliating defeat.

The Sino-Japanese War accelerated Japan's rapid transformation into a nation-state and a colonial power with no peer in Asia. Having lost the war, China ceded the province of Taiwan to the Japanese. Japan also annexed Korea in 1910 and converted Taiwan and Korea into the twin jewels of its young empire. Like the British in India, the Japanese regarded their colonial subjects as racially inferior and unworthy of the privileges of citizenship. And like other imperial powers, the Japanese expected their possessions to serve the metropolitan center.

RUSSIAN TRANSFORMATION AND EXPANSION

Russia expanded out of a sense of a civilizing mission and a need to defend against other countries expanding along its immense borders. Facing an emerging Germany, a British presence in the Middle East and Persia, a consolidating China, and an increasingly powerful Japan, Russia knew it would have to extend its already large territorial domain. So it established a number of expansionist fronts simultaneously: southwest to the Black Sea, south into the Caucasus and Turkestan, and east into Manchuria. (See Map 17.5.) Success depended on annexing territories and establishing protectorates over conquered peoples.

Modernization and Internal Reform In the 1860s, Tsar Alexander II launched a wave of "Great Reforms" to make Russia more modern and to preserve its status as a great power. In 1861, for example, a decree emancipated peasants from serfdom. Other changes included a sharp reduction in the duration of military service, a program of education for the conscripts, and the beginnings of a mass school system to teach children reading, writing, and Russian culture. Starting in the 1890s, state-sponsored industrialization led to the building of railroads and factories and stimulated the expansion of the steel, coal, and petroleum industries. But while the reforms strengthened the state, they did not enhance the lives of common people. Workers in Russia were brutally exploited, even by the standards of the industrial revolution. Also, large landowners had kept most of the empire's fertile land, and the peasants had to pay substantial redemption fees for the poorer-quality plots they received.

Before long, in the press, courtrooms, and streets, men and women denounced the regime. Revolutionaries engaged in terror and assassination. In 1881, a terrorist bomb killed the tsar. In the 1890s, following a period of famine, the radical doctrines of Marxism (see Chapter 16) gained popularity in Russia. Even aristocratic intellectuals, such as the author of *War and Peace*, Count Leo Tolstoy, lamented their despotic government.

Territorial Expansion Yet the critics of internal reform did not hold back the Russian expansionists, who believed they had to take over certain lands to keep them out of rivals' hands. So they conquered the highland people of the Caucasus Mountains to prevent Ottomans and Persians from encroaching on Russia's southern flank. And they battled the British over areas between Turkestan and British India, such as Persia (Iran) and Afghanistan. Although

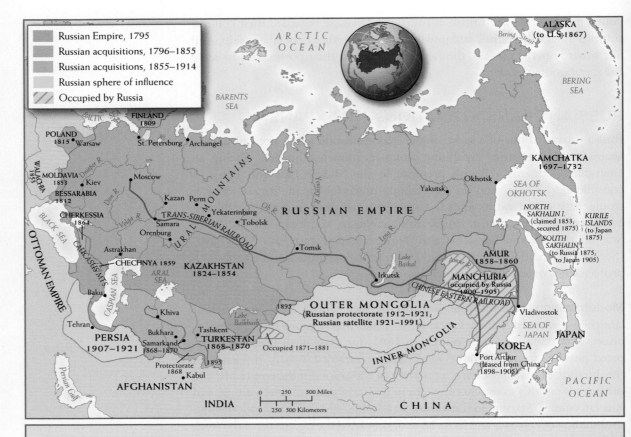

Map legend:
- Russian Empire, 1795
- Russian acquisitions, 1796–1855
- Russian acquisitions, 1855–1914
- Russian sphere of influence
- Occupied by Russia

Map 17.5 Russian Expansion, 1801–1914

The Russian state continued to expand in the nineteenth century.

- According to this map, what lands did Russia acquire during the period 1796–1855? What lands did it acquire next?

- Compare this map of Russian expansion with Map 13.7. How did the direction of Russia's expansion change in the nineteenth century?

- Which states did the expanding Russian Empire more resemble in this era, western European states (such as Great Britain) or American states (such as the United States)?

some Russians moved to these lands, they never became a majority there. The new provinces were multiethnic, multireligious communities that were only partially integrated into the Russian nation.

Perhaps the most impressive Russian expansion occurred in East Asia, where the Amur River basin offered rich lands, mineral deposits, and access to the Pacific Ocean. The Chinese also wanted to colonize this area, which lay just north of Manchuria. After twenty years of struggle, Russia claimed the land north and south of the Amur River and in 1860 founded Vladivostok, a port on the Pacific Ocean whose name signified "Rule the East." Deciding to focus on these areas in Asia, the Russian government sold its one territory in North America (Alaska) to the United States. Then, to link central Russia and the western part of the country to its East Asian spoils, the government began construction of the Trans-Siberian Railroad in the 1890s. When it was completed in 1916, the new railroad bridged the east and the west.

Governing a Diverse Empire Russia was a huge empire whose rulers were only partially effective at integrating its diverse parts into a political community. Unlike the United States, which displaced or slaughtered native populations during its expansion across an entire continent, Russia tolerated and taxed many of the new peoples. The state's approach ranged from outright repression (of Poles and Jews) to favoritism (toward Baltic Germans and Finns), although the beneficiaries of favoritism often later lost favor if they became too strong. Further, unlike the United States, which managed to pacify borders with its weaker neighbors, Russia faced the constant suspicions of Persians and Ottomans and the menace of British troops in Afghanistan. In East Asia, a clash with expansionist Japan loomed on the horizon.

CHINA UNDER PRESSURE

While the Russians and Japanese scrambled to copy European models of industrialism and imperialism, the Qing were slower to mobilize against threats from the west. Even as the European powers were dividing up China into spheres of influence, Qing officials were much more worried about internal revolts and threats from their northern borders than European incursions.

Adopting Western Learning and Skills A growing number of Chinese officials recognized the superior armaments and technology of rival powers and were deeply troubled by the threat posed by European military might. Starting in the 1860s, reformist bureaucrats sought to adopt elements of western learning and technological skills—but with the intention of keeping the core Chinese culture intact.

This so-called **Self-Strengthening movement** included a variety of new ventures: arsenals, shipyards, coal mines, a steamship company to contest the foreign domination of coastal shipping, and schools for learning foreign ways and languages. Most interesting was the dispatch abroad of about 120 schoolboys under the charge of Yung Wing. The first Chinese graduate of an American college (Yale University, 1854), Yung believed that western education would greatly benefit Chinese students, so he took his charges to Connecticut in the 1870s to attend school and live with American families. Conservatives at the Qing court were soon dismayed by reports of the

Self-Strengthening movement
A movement of reformist Chinese bureaucrats in the latter half of the nineteenth century that attempted to adopt western elements of learning and technological skill while retaining their core Chinese culture.

students' interest in Christianity and aptitude for baseball. In 1881, after the U.S. government refused to admit the boys into military academies, they summoned the students home.

Yung Wing's abortive educational mission was not the only setback for the Self-Strengthening movement, for skepticism about western technology was rife among conservative officials. Some insisted that the introduction of machinery would lead to unemployment; others worried that railways would facilitate western military maneuvers and lead to an invasion; still others complained that the crisscrossing tracks disturbed the harmony between humans and nature. The first short railway track ever laid in China was torn up in 1877 shortly after being built, and the country had only 179 miles of track prior to 1895.

Although they did not acknowledge the railroad's usefulness, the Chinese did adopt other new technologies to access a wider range of information. For example, by the early 1890s there were about a dozen Chinese-language newspapers (as distinct from the foreign-language press) published in major cities, with the largest ones having a circulation of 10,000 to 15,000. To avoid government intervention, these papers sidestepped political controversy; instead, they featured commercial news and literary contributions. In 1882, the newspaper *Shenbao* made use of a new telegraph line to publish dispatches within China.

Internal Reform Efforts China's defeat by Japan in the Sino-Japanese War (1894–1895), sparked by quarrels over Korea, prompted a more serious attempt at reform by the Qing. Known as the Hundred Days' Reform, the episode lasted only from June to September 1898. The force behind it was a thirty-seven-year-old scholar named Kang Youwei and his twenty-two-year-old student Liang Qichao. Citing rulers such as Peter the Great of Russia and the Meiji Emperor of Japan as their inspiration, the reformers urged Chinese leaders to develop a railway network, a state banking system, a modern postal service, and institutions to foster the development of agriculture, industry, and commerce. The reform failed when a group of conservative leaders placed the Dowager Cixi on the throne, rescinded the reformist laws, and executed six of the reform movement's major leaders. They did not, however, capture Kang Youwei, who fled to Japan.

But, in truth, the reforms of the Self-Strengthening movement were ineffectual: they were too modest and poorly implemented. Very few Chinese acquired new skills. Despite talk of modernizing, the civil service examination remained based on Confucian classics and still opened the only doors to government service. Governing elites were not yet ready to reinvent the principles of their political community, and they adhered instead to the traditional dynastic structure.

By the late nineteenth century, the success of the Qing regime in expanding its territories a century earlier seemed like a distant memory, as various powers repeatedly forced it to make economic and territorial concessions. Unlike Japan or Russia, however, the Qing government resisted comprehensive social reforms (until after the turn of the twentieth century), and its policies left the country vulnerable to both external aggression and internal instability.

Conclusion

Between 1850 and 1914, most of the world's people lived not in nation-states but in land empires or in the overseas colonies of nation-states. But leaders in colonial territories, often responding to popular upheavals and destabilizing economic changes, began to see independent nation-states as the most desirable form of governance for their regions.

Although the ideal of "a people" united by territory, history, and culture grew increasingly popular worldwide, it was not easy to make it a reality. Official histories, national heroes, novels, poetry, and music helped, but central to the process of nation formation were the actions of bureaucrats. Asserting sovereignty over what it claimed as national territory, the state "nationalized" diverse populations by creating a unified system of law, education, military service, and government.

Colonization beyond borders was another part of nation building in many societies. In these efforts, territorial conquests took place under the banner of nationalist endeavors. In Europe, the Americas, Japan, and to some extent Russia, the intertwined processes of nation building and territorial expansion were most effective. Expansion abroad consolidated national identities at home.

However, the integrating impulses of imperialist nation-states did not wipe out local differences, mute class antagonisms, or eliminate gender inequalities. Even as Europeans and Americans came to see themselves as chosen—by God or by natural selection—to rule the rest, they suffered deep divisions. Not everyone identified with the nation-state or the empire, or agreed on what it meant to belong or to conquer. But by the century's end, racist advocates and colonial lobbyists seem to have convinced many that their interests and destinies were bound up with their countries' unity, prosperity, and global clout.

Ironically, imperial expansion had an unintended consequence, for self-determination could also apply to racial or ethnic minorities at home and in the colonies. Armed with the rhetoric of progress and uplift, colonial authorities tried to subjugate distant people, but colonial subjects themselves often asserted the language of "nation" and accused imperial overlords of betraying their own lofty principles. As the twentieth century opened, Filipino and Cuban rebels used Thomas Jefferson's Declaration of Independence to oppose American invaders, Koreans defined themselves as a nation crushed under Japanese heels, and Indian nationalists made colonial governors feel shame for violating British standards of "fair play."

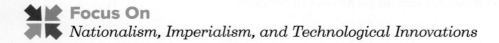

Focus On
Nationalism, Imperialism, and Technological Innovations

The Americas and Europe: Consolidating Nations

- Residents of the United States claim territory across the North American continent after fighting a bloody civil war to preserve the union and abolish slavery.

- Canadians also build a new nation and expand across the continent.

- Brazilians create a prosperous nation-state that excludes much of the population from the privileges of belonging to the "nation" and the "state."

- The dynastic states of Prussia and Piedmont-Sardinia create German and Italian nation-states at the expense of France and the Austrian Empire.

Industry, Science, and Technology on a Global Scale

- Continued industrialization transforms the global economy.

- New technologies of warfare, transportation, and communication lead to greater global economic integration.

- Charles Darwin's *On the Origin of Species* overturns previous conceptions of nature, arguing that present-day life forms evolved from simpler ones over long periods.

Empires

- After suppressing the Indian Rebellion of 1857, the British reorganize their rule in India, providing a model for other imperialist powers.

- European powers partition the entire African continent (except for Ethiopia and Liberia) despite intense African resistance.

- Americans win the Spanish-American War, annex Puerto Rico, and establish colonial rule over the Philippines.

- The expansionist aims of Japan, Russia, and China lead to clashes over possessions in East Asia, with Russia gaining much territory and Japan defeating the Chinese.

- Colonial rule spurs nationalist sentiments among the colonized.

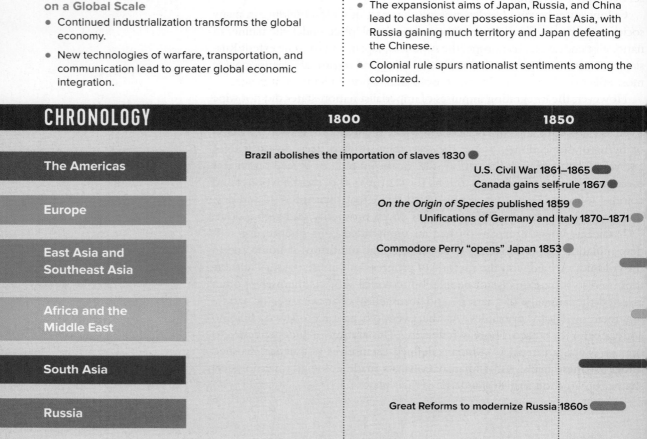

THINKING ABOUT GLOBAL CONNECTIONS

- **Thinking about Worlds Together, Worlds Apart and Nations & Empires** Compare the eighteenth-century empires of Spain, Portugal, and Britain with the new empires arising in Africa at the end of the nineteenth century. What were the sources of their wealth and power? How and to what degree were colonial territories and economies integrated with their imperialist states?

- **Thinking about Changing Power Relationships and Nations & Empires** How did the growth of western influence and Japanese power lay the basis for opposition movements in Africa and Asia? How did people respond to imperialism? Where was resistance most effective?

- **Thinking about Environmental Impacts and Nations & Empires** Describe the second industrial revolution and explain how it differed from the first industrial revolution. Pay special attention to the new technologies used in the late nineteenth century, especially the sources of power and new materials that were used.

Key Terms

Charles Darwin p. 802

imperialism p. 789

limited-liability joint-stock company p. 792

Manifest Destiny p. 790

Meiji Restoration p. 815

natural selection p. 802

Raj p. 805

Self-Strengthening movement p. 819

steel p. 801

 Go to **INQUIZITIVE** to see what you've learned—and learn what you've missed—with personalized feedback along the way.

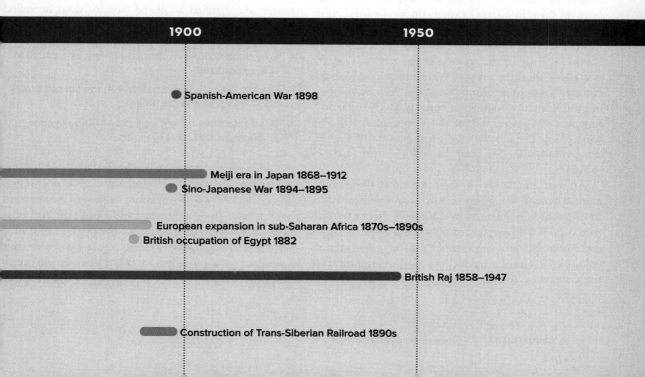

1900   1950

Spanish-American War 1898

Meiji era in Japan 1868–1912
Sino-Japanese War 1894–1895

European expansion in sub-Saharan Africa 1870s–1890s
British occupation of Egypt 1882

British Raj 1858–1947

Construction of Trans-Siberian Railroad 1890s

Global Themes and Sources

Contextualizing the Scramble for Empire

In the second half of the nineteenth century, a handful of nation-states, most but not all of them in Europe, renewed their competition for colonial territory. Class conflict at home and resistance to their efforts abroad bred a new, conflictual vision that stressed competition and struggle in nature as well as human affairs. Doubts arose about the progressive nature of the changes ushered in by the era of the French and industrial revolutions, in particular the idea that granting more people the vote and spreading free markets would lead to peace and prosperity for everyone. Colonizers increasingly believed that they must control ever-greater expanses of territory or risk defeat by rival powers.

The documents presented here show imperialist powers' efforts to explain their actions, to defend their right to rule others, and to mark boundaries of inclusion and exclusion. The sources start in the Americas: John L. O'Sullivan asserts divine support for "Anglo-Saxon" expansion westwards. Next, Count Shigenobu Okuma celebrates Japanese dynamism over the course of the prior generation. In Russia, writing in the context of the empire's expansion eastward, Prince Esper Ukhtomskii considers his country's role as a colonial power in Asia by comparing the Romanov regime to its rivals. In the final document, the General Act of the Conference of Berlin concerning the Congo, the great powers of Europe set ground rules for their competition for territory in Africa.

All written at roughly the same time, these documents demand attention to historical context. Each, in different ways, asserts its country's right to dominate others. Pay special attention to the justifications each mobilizes and the authors' efforts to distinguish colonizer from colonized, those with the right to rule from everyone else.

Analyzing the Context of the Scramble for Empire

- How do the authors justify their country's right to rule others? What kind of reasons do they present (ethnic, moral, technological)?

- Compare the efforts to divide insiders from outsiders in these documents.

- Evaluate the balance between confidence and insecurity in each source.

PRIMARY SOURCE 17.1

"Manifest Destiny" (1845), John L. O'Sullivan

John L. O'Sullivan (1813–1895) was an American newspaper columnist and editor who urged the annexation of Texas to the United States in this 1845 article. He justified it on the basis of what he called "manifest destiny."

- Why does O'Sullivan dismiss slavery as a cause for U.S. expansion?

- Explain the relationship between the United States and Mexico in this document.

- What role does technology play in O'Sullivan's justification for U.S. expansion?

No—Mr. Clay was right when he declared that Annexation was a question with which slavery had nothing to do. The country which was the subject of Annexation in this case, from its geographical position and relations, happens to be—or rather the portion of it now actually settled, happens to be—a slave country. But a similar process might have taken place in proximity to a different section of our Union; and indeed there is a great deal of Annexation yet to take place, within the life of the present generation, along the whole line of our northern border. Texas has been absorbed into the Union in the inevitable fulfilment of the general law which is rolling our population westward; the connexion of which with that ratio of growth in population which is destined within a hundred years to swell our numbers to the enormous population of *two hundred and fifty millions* (if not more), is too evident to leave us in doubt of the manifest design of Providence in regard to the occupation of this continent. It was disintegrated from Mexico in the natural course of events, by a process perfectly legitimate on its own part, blameless on ours; and in which all the censures due to wrong, perfidy and folly, rest on Mexico alone. And possessed as it was by a population which was in truth but a colonial detachment from our own, and which was still bound by myriad ties of the very heart-strings to its old relations, domestic and political, their incorporation into the Union was not only inevitable, but the most natural, right and proper thing in the world—and it is only astonishing that there should be any among ourselves to say it nay. . . .

California will, probably, next fall away from the loose adhesion which, in such a country as Mexico, holds a remote province in a slight equivocal kind of dependence on the metropolis. Imbecile and distracted, Mexico never can exert any real governmental authority over such a country. The impotence of the one and the distance of the other, must make the relation one of virtual independence; unless, by stunting the province of all natural growth, and forbidding that immigration which can alone develope its capabilities and fulfil the purposes of its creation, tyranny may retain a military dominion which is no government in the legitimate sense of the term. In the case of California this is now impossible. The Anglo-Saxon foot is already on its borders. Already the advance guard of the irresistible army of Anglo-Saxon emigration has begun to pour down upon it, armed with the plough and the rifle, and marking its trail with schools and colleges, courts and representative halls, mills and meeting-houses. A population will soon be in actual occupation of California, over which it will be idle for Mexico to dream of dominion. They will necessarily

become independent. All this without agency of our government, without responsibility of our people—in the natural flow of events, the spontaneous working of principles, and the adaptation of the tendencies and wants of the human race to the elemental circumstances in the midst of which they find themselves placed. And they will have a right to independence—to self-government—to the possession of the homes conquered from the wilderness by their own labors and dangers, sufferings and sacrifices—a better and a truer right than the artificial title of sovereignty in Mexico a thousand miles distant, inheriting from Spain a title good only against those who have none better. Their right to independence will be the natural right of self-government belonging to any community strong enough to maintain it—distinct in position, origin and character, and free from any mutual obligations of membership of a common political body, binding it to others by the duty of loyalty and compact of public faith. This will be their title to independence; and by this title, there can be no doubt that the population now fast streaming down upon California will both assert and maintain that independence.

Whether they will then attach themselves to our Union or not, is not to be predicted with any certainty. Unless the projected rail-road across the continent to the Pacific be carried into effect, perhaps they may not; though even in that case, the day is not distant when the Empires of the Atlantic and Pacific would again flow together into one, as soon as their inland border should approach each other. But that great work, colossal as appears the plan on its first suggestion, cannot remain long unbuilt. Its necessity for this very purpose of binding and holding together in its iron clasp our fast settling Pacific region with that of the Mississippi valley—the natural facility of the route—the ease with which any amount of labor for the construction can be drawn in from the overcrowded populations of Europe, to be paid in the lands made valuable by the progress of the work itself—and its immense utility to the commerce of the world with the whole eastern coast of Asia, alone almost sufficient for the support of such a road—these considerations give assurance that the day cannot be distant which shall witness the conveyance of the representatives from Oregon and California to Washington within less time than a few years ago was devoted to a similar journey by those from Ohio; while the magnetic telegraph will enable the editors of the "San Francisco Union," the "Astoria Evening Post," or the "Nootka Morning News" to set up in type the first half of the President's Inaugural, before the echoes of the latter half shall have died away beneath the lofty porch of the Capitol, as spoken from his lips.

Away, then, with all idle French talk of *balances of power* on the American Continent. There is no growth in Spanish America! Whatever progress of population there may be in the British Canadas, is only for their own early severance of their present colonial relation to the little island three thousand miles across the Atlantic; soon to be followed by Annexation, and destined to swell the still accumulating momentum of our progress. And whosoever may hold the balance, though they should cast into the opposite scale all the bayonets and cannon, not only of France and England, but of Europe entire, how would it kick the beam against the simple solid weight of the two hundred and fifty, or three hundred millions—and American millions—destined to gather beneath the flutter of the stripes and stars, in the fast hastening year of the Lord 1945!

Source: John L. O'Sullivan, "Manifest Destiny," in *The American West: A Source Book*, edited by Clark C. Spence (New York: Crowell, 1966), pp. 108–11.

PRIMARY SOURCE 17.2

Fifty Years of New Japan (1909), Count Shigenobu Okuma

Count Shigenobu Okuma (1838–1922) held high-ranking positions in the Meiji government and served as prime minister of Japan during World War I (1914–1916). The founder of Waseda University, he was an early advocate of western science and culture in Japan. In this document, he celebrates Japan's ability to draw on foreign influences.

- Identify the sources of Japan's strength, according to Okuma.

- Compare the justification for expansion in this document to the justifications in the documents by O'Sullivan and Ukhtomskii.

- Evaluate the balance in this document between internal sources of Japanese strength and borrowed foreign influences.

By comparing the Japan of fifty years ago with the Japan of today, it will be seen that she has gained considerably in the extent of her territory, as well as in her population, which now numbers nearly fifty million. Her government has become constitutional not only in name, but in fact, and her national education has attained to a high degree of excellence. In commerce and industry, the emblems of peace, she has also made rapid strides, until her import and export trades together amounted in 1907 to the enormous sum of 926,000,000 yen. Her general progress, during the short space of half a century, has been so sudden and swift that it presents a rare spectacle in the history of the world. This leap forward is the result of the stimulus which the country received on coming into contact with the civilization of Europe and America, and may well, in its broad sense, be regarded as a boon conferred by foreign intercourse. Foreign intercourse it was that animated the national consciousness of our people, who under the feudal system lived localized and disunited, and foreign intercourse it is that has enabled Japan to stand up as a world power. We possess today a powerful army and navy, but it was after Western models that we laid their foundations by establishing a system of conscription in pursuance of the principle "all our sons are soldiers," by promoting military education, and by encouraging the manufacture of arms and the art of shipbuilding. We have reorganized the systems of central and local administration, and effected reforms in the educational system of the empire. All this is nothing but the result of adopting the superior features of Western institutions. That Japan has been enabled to do so is a boon conferred on her by foreign intercourse, and it may be said that the nation has succeeded in this grand metamorphosis through the promptings and the influence of foreign civilization. For twenty centuries the nation has drunk freely of the civilizations of Korea, China, and India, being always open to the different influences impressed on her in succession. Yet we remain politically unaltered under one Imperial House and sovereign, that has descended in an unbroken line for a length of time absolutely unexampled in the world. We have welcomed Occidental civilization while preserving their old Oriental civilization. They have attached great importance to Bushido, and at the same time held in the highest respect the spirit of charity and humanity. They have ever made a point of choosing the middle course in everything, and have aimed at being always well-balanced. We are conservative simultaneously with being progressive; we are aristocratic and at the same time democratic; we are individualistic while also being socialistic. In these respects we may be said to somewhat resemble the Anglo-Saxon race.

Source: Count Shigenobu Okuma, *Fifty Years of New Japan* (*Kaikoku Gojunen Shi*), 2nd ed., edited by Marcus B. Huish, vol. 2 (London: Smith, Elder, 1910), pp. 554–55, 571–72.

PRIMARY SOURCE 17.3

Russia's Imperial Destiny (1896), Prince Esper Ukhtomskii

Prince Esper Ukhtomskii (1861–1921), a poet, publisher, and ardent advocate of eastern expansion, was a close confidant of Tsar Nicholas II of Russia. He accompanied Nicholas on an Asian tour in 1890–1891, before the latter assumed the throne. Nicholas approved each chapter of Ukhtomskii's three-volume account of the journey before publication, which was part of his preparation to assume the throne.

- How does Ukhtomskii justify Russian influence in Asia?
- What role does technology play in Russian expansion, according to Ukhtomskii?
- Which rival powers does Ukhtomskii discuss? What role do those rivalries play in Russian expansion?

Our stay at Saigon, the base of French operations in the advance against important borderlands of China, will in its turn be marked by enthusiasm in the greeting of a friendly nation. For us Russians, who scarcely ever visit the distant lands of Asia to study the powers and the means of European colonists, a visit to the central point of the "Indo-Chinese" empire governed from Paris, will be doubly instructive, doubly useful after seeing the British domains and patriarchally protected Java. This will be the more appropriate in that every figure, every vivid detail, every living fact, must and will lead us to reflect, in what a marked degree we Russians, as regards our prestige in Asia, voluntarily resign to every comer from Europe our historical part and our inherited mission as leaders of the East.

In such an abnormal state of affairs all the gain, as regards material prosperity, falls to the share of the representatives of Western principles—representatives foreign in spirit, and in reality hateful to thsoe peoples of an ancient type on whom they have forced themselves by means of their cannon. Burmah, Cambodia, and Annam are no more; Siam is on the eve of dangerous external catastrophes; Japan is on the threshold of terrible internal dissensions; China alone, standing guard over its own, and unconsciously over Russian, interests, holds its ground with the wisdom of the serpent, gathers its forces against the foe from beyond the seas, and anxiously glances towards the silent North, where is situated the only State from which the Celestial Empire, educated in autocratic principles, can expect moral support, disinterested assistance, and a practical alliance based on community of interests.

This northern land of mist, forest, and ice, the extreme east of Siberia, opened up by Khabaroff, and other bold pioneers like him, the land re-united to Russia by the genius of Mooravioff-Amoorsky—is still a realm of primitive quiet, of deepest stillness and stagnation. It is only with the end of the century, with the opening up of new ways of communication with our eastern coast, that a new era with all its unforeseen consequences may begin. Meanwhile the land bears the stamp of something unformed and sad, like the life of its original settlers. All the more attention and unprejudiced judgment, then, is required of any one who would draw a parallel between the lands of the Pacific south now opening out before us, with the emerald island of Java, the inexhaustible natural riches of the Indo-Chinese soil, the self-confident vitality of the Celestial Empire, and the marshes and retired nooks, the boundless desert borders, of the country whose mission, in spite of all this, is to be a source of light for the neighbouring expanse, with its countless population.

The tiny kingdom of Holland holds sway in Asia over more than thirty million human beings (and that, too, at the equator, in an earthly paradise), while in the third part of the same continent the most important Power in it cannot reckon up one-half the number.

European colonisers, though not without envy and enmity, have shared among them the best coast-districts of these lands. Towns of such universal commercial importance as Hong-Kong and Singapore are the most eloquent witnesses to the indefatigable enterprise of Europeans amidst the prevailing Asiatic torpor. But while drawing the juices out of this gigantic continent, and, wherever possible, holding hundreds of millions in a state of economic slavery, do the pioneers of civilisation hope for final success? Holding on to the brink and ledges of a precipice, are they not in a state of constant alarm, lest the stones should give way and hurl them into the abyss? When the whole East awakes, as it will sooner or later: when it realises its mighty power and determines to speak its mind, then threats, violence, and superficial victories will not remedy the internal discord. This is why it is Russia's part to grow in power unobserved amidst the wastes and deserts of the North in expectation of the conflict between two worlds, in which the decision will depend on neither of them.

The idea of invading a complex foreign life, of using Asia as a tool for the advancement of the selfish interests of modern, so-called civilised, mankind, was repugnant to us. For more than two hundred years we have remained at home; for our natural union with Turkestan and the region of the Amur cannot be regarded as political annexations. We have remained at home with our traditional carelessness and indolence, while the Pacific has become the arena of Western European advance against a native world with an ancient political constitution and an undoubted civilisation of its own.

The results are patent. The strangers have dethroned and oppressed the East. Coming here to live and make money, they do not find a home. (But any Asiatic borderland soon becomes a home for a Russian.) The natives are not brothers in humanity to them; for them the land is one of voluntary exile, and the people are considered as miserable and inferior beings. The latter gradually realise the meaning of these outrageous views, and repay their "masters" with intense hatred. But where and how are they to find protection and a bulwark against the foreign foe?

But the mythologising spirit is still alive amongst them. The more actively Europe presses on Asia, the brighter becomes the name of the White Tsar in popular report and tradition.

***

From that remote period when our great golden-domed Moscow, which but a little earlier was no more than a small town in an insignificant subordinate principality, received the blessing of the saints and was irradiated by the creative glow of the autocratic idea, the East, advancing on us with fire and sword, has masterfully drawn toward it the eyes of the Russians: has wakened in them sleeping powers and heroic daring: and now calls them onward to deeds of glory, to advancement beyond the bounds of a dull reality, to a bright, glorious, and ineffable future! There neither is nor ever has been a nation whose past is so closely bound up with its future, as may be seen in the growth of the Russian Empire. The man of the West (the German, the Frenchman, the Englishman, the Italian) must cross the seas to find relief from the pressure which overwhelms him at home. Far from his native land, he must build his temporal prosperity on a foundation of sand, and the more firmly he takes root there under conditions of the most favourable nature, the more evident does it become that his old home, and he the voluntary exile, belong to two perfectly alien worlds. Beyond the seas, away from the life of his native land, he may gain money and position, but cannot (except artificially and but for a short time) retain completely untouched the spirit of his people, their ideals and traditions.

Source: Prince E. Ukhtomskii, *Travels in the East of Nicholas II Emperor of Russia, When Cesarewitch 1890–1891*, vol. 2 (London: Archibald Constable and Company, 1890), pp. 142–43, 444–46.

General Act of the Conference of Berlin concerning the Congo (1885)

The Berlin Conference of 1884–1885 (also known as the Congo Conference) regulated European trade and colonization in sub-Saharan Africa in the late nineteenth century. The following selection is an excerpt from the General Act of the Conference.

- The document opens by expressing a desire for mutual understanding and a desire for economic growth. What challenges to progress and economic prosperity does the document suggest?
- Identify the priorities expressed in this document.
- What limits, if any, does this document impose on the colonizers?

In the name of Almighty God:
. . . Wishing to regulate in a spirit of good mutual understanding the conditions most favorable to the development of commerce and of civilization in certain regions of Africa, and to assure to all peoples the advantages of free navigation upon the two principal African rivers which empty into the Atlantic ocean; desirous on the other hand to prevent misunderstandings and contentions to which the taking of new possessions on the coast of Africa may in the future give rise, and at the same time preoccupied with the means of increasing the moral and material well being of the indigenous populations, have resolved, upon the invitation which has been addressed to them by the Imperial Government of Germany in accord with the Government of the French Republic, to assemble for this object a Conference at Berlin. . . .

Chapter I.

Declaration relative to the liberty of commerce in the basin of the Congo, its embouchures and neighboring country, and dispositions connected therewith.

Article 1.

The commerce of all nations shall enjoy complete liberty. . . .

Article 2.

All flags, without distinction of nationality, shall have free access to all the littoral of the territories above enumerated, to the rivers which there empty into the sea, to all the waters of the Congo and its affluents including the lakes, to all the ports situated upon the borders of these waters, as well as to all the canals which may in the future be excavated with the object of connecting together the water courses or lakes comprised in the whole extent of the territories described in Article 1. They may undertake every kind of transport and exercise the coastwise navigation by sea and river as also small boat transportation upon the same footing as the allegiants.

Article 3.

Merchandise of every origin imported into these territories, under whatever flag it may be, by route of sea or river or land, shall have to discharge no other taxes than those which may be collected as an equitable compensation for expenses useful to commerce and which, under this head, must be equally borne by the allegiants and by strangers of every nationality.

All differential treatment is prohibited in respect to ships as well as merchandise.

Article 4.

Merchandise imported into these territories shall remain free from entrance and transit dues.

The Powers reserve to themselves to decide, at the end of a period of twenty years, whether freedom of entry shall or shall not be maintained.

Article 5.

Every Power which exercises or shall exercise rights of sovereignty in the territories under consideration shall not concede there either monopoly or privilege of any kind in commercial matters.

Strangers shall enjoy there without distinction, for the protection of their persons and their goods, the acquisition and transmission of their movable and immovable property and for the exercise of the professions, the same treatment and the same rights as the allegiants.

Article 6.

Depositions relative to the protection of the natives, of missionaries and of travelers, and also to religious liberty.

All Powers exercising rights of sovereignty or an influence in the Said territories engage themselves to watch over the conservation of the indigenous populations and the amelioration of their moral and material conditions of existence and to strive for the suppression of slavery and especially of the negro slave trade; they shall protect and favor without distinction of nationality or of worship, all the institutions and enterprises religious, scientific or charitable, created and organized for these objects or tending to instruct the natives and to make them understand and appreciate the advantages of civilization.

The christian missionaries, the savants, the explorers, their escorts, properties and collections shall be equally the object of special protection.

Liberty of conscience and religious toleration are expressly guaranteed to the natives as well as to allegiants and to strangers.

The free and public exercise of all forms of worship, the right to erect religious edifices and to organize missions belonging to all forms of worship shall not be subjected to any restriction or hindrance.

* * *

Chapter II.

Declaration concerning the slave trade.

Article 9.

Conformably to the principles of the law of nations, as they are recognized by the signatory Powers, the slave trade being interdicted, and as the operations which, by land or sea, furnish slaves to the trade ought to be equally considered as interdicted, the Powers who exercise or shall exercise rights of sovereignty or an influence in the territories forming the conventional basin of the Congo declare that these territories shall not serve either for a market or way of transit for the trade in slaves of any race whatever. Each of these Powers engages itself to employ all the means in its power to put an end to this commerce and to punish those who are occupied in it.

Chapter III.

Declaration relative to the neutrality of the territories comprised in the conventional basin of the Congo.

Article 10.

In order to give a new guarantee of security to commerce and to industry and to favor, by the maintenance of peace, the development of civilization in the countries mentioned in Article 1 and placed under the regime of commercial liberty, the high signatory parties of the present Act and those who shall subsequently adhere to it engage themselves to respect the neutrality of the territories or parts of territories depending on said countries, including therein the territorial waters, so long as the Powers who exercise or shall exercise rights of sovereignty or protectorate over these territories, making use of the option to proclaim themselves neutrals, shall fulfill the duties which belong to neutrality.

* * *

Article 17.

There is instituted an International Commission charged to assure the execution of the dispositions of the present navigation Act.

The signatory Powers of this Act, as well as those who shall adhere to it hereafter, can, at all times, have themselves represented in the said Commission, each by one delegate. No delegate can dispose of more than one vote even in the case where he may represent several governments.

* * *

Article 19.

. . . In case of an abuse of power or of an injustice on the part of an agent or employé of the International Commission, the individual who shall regard himself as injured in his person or in his rights may address himself to the consular agent of his nation. The latter shall examine the complaint; if he finds it prima facie reasonable, he shall have the right to present it to the Commission. Upon his initiative, the Commission represented by at least three of its members, shall join itself to him to make an investigation touching the conduct of its agent or employé. If the consular agent considers the decision of the

Commission as giving rise to objections of right, he shall make a report of it to his government which may have recourse to the Powers represented in the Commission and invite them to come to agreement upon the instructions to be given to the Commission.

***

Chapter VI.

Declaration relative to the conditions essential to be fulfilled in order that new occupations upon the coasts of the African continent may be considered as effective.

Article 34.

The Power which henceforth shall take possession of a territory upon the coast of the African continent situated outside of its present possessions, or which, not having had such possessions hitherto, shall come to acquire them, and likewise, the Power which shall assume a protectorate there, shall accompany the respective act with a notification addressed to the other signatory Powers of the present Act, in order to put them in a condition to make available, if there be occasion for it, their reclamations.

Source: "The Treaty of Berlin," *American Journal of International Law* 3, no. 1, supplement: Official Documents (January 1909): 7–24.

Interpreting Visual Evidence

Occidentalism: Representing Western Influence

Ever since the publication of Edward Said's landmark work *Orientalism* (1978), scholars have carefully examined European and American efforts to represent nonwestern peoples in disciplines ranging from art, languages, and literature to law, biology, and philosophy. The field of postcolonial studies that emerged in Said's wake has emphasized the degree to which western descriptions of "Orientals" were really efforts to describe themselves—as the rational, disciplined opposite of the supposedly sensual Orient—and to affirm their own values. More recently, scholarly attention has turned to different peoples' efforts to make sense of European and American influences on their societies—representations that we might call "Occidentalism" (the "Occident" meaning the west).

Here we consider a range of visual materials that both reflected and shaped ordinary people's views of western influence. These depictions circulated widely; notice the combination of text and images, for those who could not read. While Japan was not colonized, the Meiji Restoration relied heavily on European models for its constitution and economic plans. In *Bake-Bake Gakkō* (School of Demons) from the series *Kyosai Rakuga* (1874), Kawanabe Kyosai satirizes the European-inspired Japanese school reforms of the Meiji Restoration. The second image, *The Beating of the (Foreign) Devils and the Burning of the (Christian) Books* (c. 1890), shows Chinese Boxer rebels attacking foreign influence. In the final image, the Mexican

Kawanabe Kyosai's *Bake-Bake Gakkō*, number 3 of the *Kyosai Rakuga* series (Kawanabe Kyosai Memorial Museum).

The Beating of the (Foreign) Devils and the Burning of the (Christian) Books.

caricaturist José Guadalupe Posada mocks American influence in *The American Mosquito* (1910–1913). Whether the mosquitoes in question represent American tourists, the Americans brought in by Mexico's President Díaz to manage railroads and mines, or the American dollar remains unclear.

The American Mosquito.

Questions for Analysis

1. Compare the representation of foreign influence in all three works. Are those influences purely oppressive? Do any local actors appear to find outside influence appealing? What is the greater threat, according to these images, internal weakness or a coercive foreign intervention?

2. Analyze the relationship between local traditions and progress in each work. Do the images present a vision of progress? From the perspective of the artists, what is the relationship, if any, between foreign influence and progress?

3. Do the artists present a homegrown vision of progress, or is progress something that comes from abroad? Is it possible, from the artists' point of view, to be Japanese, Chinese, or Mexican and modern at the same time?

4. What messages do these works convey about their own societies? Do the artists present their own people as powerless victims, as vulnerable and divided, as caught between their own autocratic rulers and outside invaders, or perhaps as unified and defiant?

18

An Unsettled World

1890–1914

In 1905 a young African man, Kinjikitile Ngwale, began to move among various ethnic groups in German East Africa, spreading a message of opposition to German colonial authorities. In the tradition of visionary prophets (see Chapter 16), Kinjikitile claimed that by anointing his followers with blessed water (*maji* in Swahili), he could protect them from European bullets and drive the Germans from East Africa. Kinjikitile's reputation spread rapidly, drawing followers from across 100,000 square miles of territory. Although German officials soon executed Kinjikitile, they could not prevent a broad uprising, called the Maji Maji Revolt (1905–1907). The Germans brutally suppressed the revolt, killing between 200,000 and 300,000 Africans.

The Maji Maji Revolt and its aftermath revealed the intensity of opposition to the world of nations and their empires. In Europe and North America, critics who felt deprived of the full benefits of industrializing nation-states—especially women, workers, and frustrated nationalists—demanded far-reaching reforms. In Asia, Africa, and Latin America, anticolonial critics and exploited classes protested European domination. In the face of so much unrest from within their nations and from their colonies, Europeans' faith in the idea of progress and the superiority of their "civilization" was shaken. Ironically, this occurred at the very moment when Europeans and people of European descent seemed to have established preeminence in world affairs.

This chapter tackles the anxieties and insecurities that unsettled the world around the turn of the

Chapter Outline

- Progress, Upheaval, and Movement
- Discontent with Imperialism
- Worldwide Insecurities
- Cultural Modernism
- Rethinking Race and Reimagining Nations
- Conclusion

Core Objectives

- **EXPLAIN** the connections between migration and the development of nationalism in this period.

- **COMPARE** Chinese responses to imperialism with responses to imperialism in Africa.

- **IDENTIFY** and **DESCRIBE** political, economic, and social crises that swept through the world in this period, and **ANALYZE** the impact they had on different regions of the world.

- **EXPLAIN** the ways in which new cultural forms at the turn of the century reflected challenges to the world order as it then existed.

- **EVALUATE** the ways in which race, nation, and religion unified populations but also made societies more difficult to govern and economies more difficult to manage.

twentieth century. It ties them in particular to several key factors: (1) the uprooting of millions of people from countryside to city and from one continent to another, (2) discontent with the poverty that many suffered even as economic production increased, and (3) resentment of and resistance to European domination. Around the globe, this tumult caused a questioning of established ideas that led to a flowering of new thinking and fresh artistic expression under the label of "modernism." This unsettling movement was a defining feature of the era.

Global Storylines

- Numerous factors lead to global instability: vast population movements, worldwide financial crises, class conflict, the rise of women's consciousness, and hatred of colonial domination.

- Class conflict, economic instability, and great power rivalry within Europe combine with growing protest from overseas to undermine Europe's dominant position in world affairs.

- New scientific thinking and artistic expression, known as cultural modernism, challenge the dominant western view of progress and open Europe and North America to the cultural achievements of nonwestern societies.

Progress, Upheaval, and Movement

Rapid economic progress in the decades leading up to 1914 brought challenges to the established order and the people in power. In Europe and the United States, radicals and middle-class reformers agitated for political and social change. In areas colonized by European countries and the United States, resentment focused on either colonial rulers or indigenous elites. Even in nations such as China, which had not been formally colonized but which faced repeated intrusions, popular discontent targeted domination by Europeans. At the same time, millions of people migrated to cities and different countries in search of a better life.

In the late nineteenth century, whole new industries fueled economic growth, especially in the industrial countries and in territories that exported vital raw materials to Europe and the United States. But industrial capitalism also spurred inequalities within industrial countries and, especially, between the world's industrial and nonindustrial regions. Periodic economic downturns left thousands out of work. This led, in some cases, to organized opposition to authoritarian regimes or to the free market system; it also provoked new critiques of the new industrial order and the values that supported it.

In Europe and North America, a generation of young artists, writers, and scientists broke with older conventions and sought new ways of seeing and describing the world. In Asia, Africa, and South America as well, many of these innovators were energized by the idea of moving beyond traditional forms of art, literature, music, and science. But this generation's exuberance worried those who were not ready to give up their cultural traditions and institutions.

THE BIG PICTURE

What are the connections between migration and the development of nationalism in this period?

PEOPLES IN MOTION

If the world was being *unsettled* by political, economic, and cultural changes, it was also being *resettled* by mass emigration. (See Map 18.1.) The emigration of throngs of Europeans to temperate zones in the Americas and Oceania began after the Napoleonic wars and gathered momentum in the 1840s, when the Irish fled their starving communities to seek better lives in North America. After 1870, the flow of Europeans became a torrent. The United States was the favored destination, with six times as many European immigrants arriving there as in Argentina (the second-place receiving country) between 1871 and 1920. The high point occurred between 1901 and 1910, when over 6 million Europeans entered the United States. This was nothing less than a demographic revolution.

Emigration, Immigration, Internal Migration Europeans were not the only peoples on the move. Between the 1840s and the 1940s, 29 million

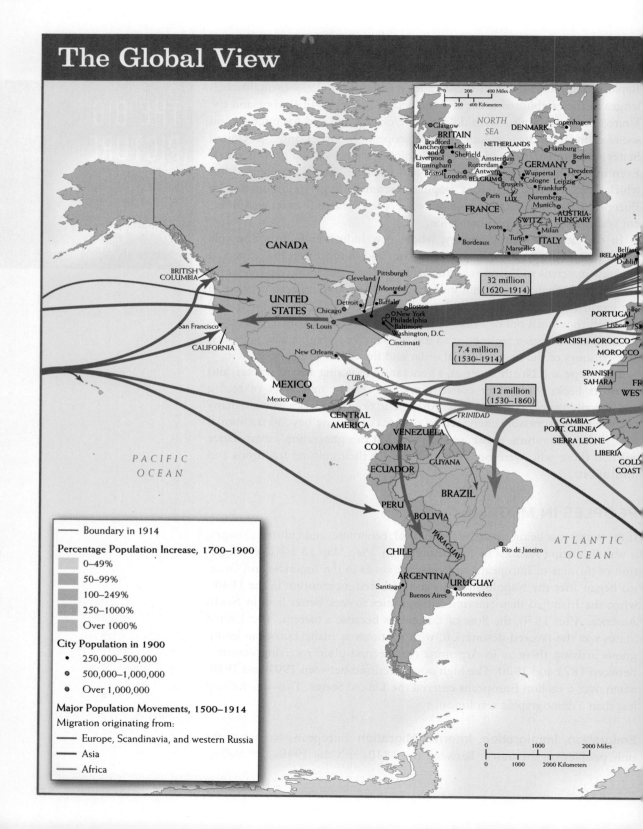

The Global View

NORTH SEA

Glasgow
BRITAIN
Bradford
Manchester Leeds
and Sheffield
Liverpool
Birmingham
Bristol London
Amsterdam
Rotterdam
Antwerp
BELGIUM
Brussels
LUX.
Paris
FRANCE
Lyons
Bordeaux
Marseilles

DENMARK
Copenhagen

NETHERLANDS
Hamburg
Berlin
GERMANY
Wuppertal Dresden
Cologne Leipzig
Frankfurt
Nuremberg
Munich
SWITZ.
Turin Milan
ITALY
AUSTRIA-
HUNGARY

IRELAND
Belfast
Dublin

CANADA

BRITISH
COLUMBIA

Cleveland Pittsburgh
Montréal
Detroit Buffalo
UNITED
STATES
Chicago
St. Louis
Boston
New York
Philadelphia
Baltimore
Washington, D.C.
Cincinnati

San Francisco

CALIFORNIA

New Orleans

MEXICO

Mexico City

CUBA

CENTRAL
AMERICA

TRINIDAD

VENEZUELA

COLOMBIA

GUYANA

ECUADOR

BRAZIL

PERU

BOLIVIA

PARAGUAY

CHILE

Rio de Janeiro

ARGENTINA
Santiago
URUGUAY
Buenos Aires Montevideo

PORTUGAL
Lisbon

SPANISH MOROCCO
MOROCCO

SPANISH
SAHARA

FR.
WEST

GAMBIA
PORT. GUINEA
SIERRA LEONE
LIBERIA
GOLD
COAST

PACIFIC
OCEAN

ATLANTIC
OCEAN

32 million
(1620–1914)

7.4 million
(1530–1914)

12 million
(1530–1860)

Legend

— Boundary in 1914

Percentage Population Increase, 1700–1900
- 0–49%
- 50–99%
- 100–249%
- 250–1000%
- Over 1000%

City Population in 1900
- • 250,000–500,000
- ◉ 500,000–1,000,000
- ◉ Over 1,000,000

Major Population Movements, 1500–1914
Migration originating from:
— Europe, Scandinavia, and western Russia
— Asia
— Africa

0   200   400 Miles
0   200   400 Kilometers

0   1000   2000 Miles
0   1000   2000 Kilometers

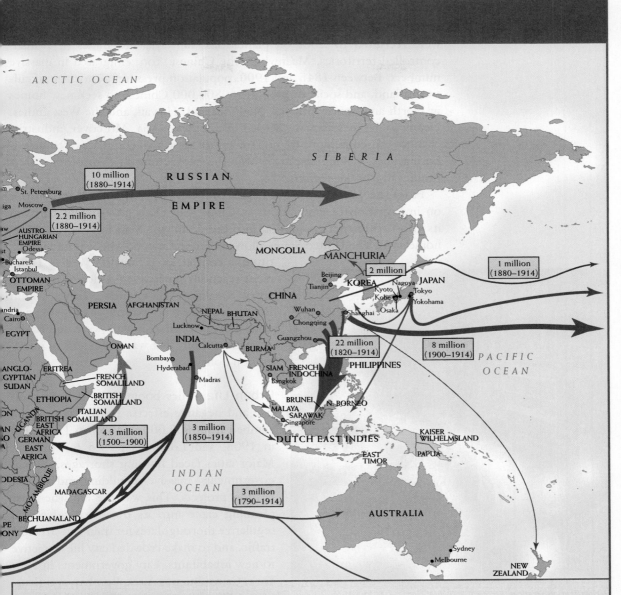

Map 18.1 labels:

ARCTIC OCEAN

10 million (1880–1914)

RUSSIAN EMPIRE

SIBERIA

St. Petersburg
Moscow

2.2 million (1880–1914)

AUSTRO-HUNGARIAN EMPIRE
Odessa
Bucharest
Istanbul
OTTOMAN EMPIRE

MONGOLIA   MANCHURIA

Beijing
Tianjin
KOREA
CHINA
Wuhan
Chongqing
Guangzhou
Shanghai

2 million

JAPAN
Nagoya
Kyoto Tokyo
Kobe Yokohama
Osaka

1 million (1880–1914)

Cairo
EGYPT

PERSIA AFGHANISTAN
Lucknow
NEPAL BHUTAN
INDIA
Calcutta
BURMA
Bombay
Hyderabad
Madras

SIAM FRENCH INDOCHINA
Bangkok

PHILIPPINES

22 million (1820–1914)

8 million (1900–1914)

PACIFIC OCEAN

ANGLO-GYPTIAN SUDAN
ERITREA
FRENCH SOMALILAND
BRITISH SOMALILAND
ETHIOPIA
ITALIAN SOMALILAND
UGANDA
BRITISH EAST AFRICA
GERMAN EAST AFRICA

OMAN

4.3 million (1500–1900)

3 million (1850–1914)

BRUNEI
MALAYA
SARAWAK
Singapore
N. BORNEO

DUTCH EAST INDIES

KAISER WILHELMSLAND
PAPUA
EAST TIMOR

MADAGASCAR

INDIAN OCEAN

3 million (1790–1914)

AUSTRALIA

MOZAMBIQUE
BECHUANALAND
PE ONY

Sydney
Melbourne

NEW ZEALAND

Map 18.1 Nineteenth-Century Migration

The nineteenth century witnessed a demographic revolution in terms of migration, urbanization patterns, and population growth. The world's population also rose from roughly 625 million in 1700 to 1.65 billion in 1900 (a two-and-a-half-fold increase).

- To what areas did most of the migrants from Europe go? What about the migrants from China, India, and Africa?

- What four areas saw the greatest population increase by 1900?

- How were migration flows and urbanization connected? What factors most accounted for these global population changes? Was internal growth more important than external migration in the case of the world's population growth? In what countries was population growth most affected by external or internal migration?

South Asians migrated into the Malay Peninsula and Burma (British colonies), the Dutch Indies (Indonesia), East Africa, and the Caribbean. Most were recruited to labor on plantations, railways, and mines in British-controlled territories. Meanwhile, the Chinese, too, emigrated in massive numbers. Between 1845 and 1900, population pressure, a shortage of cultivable land, and social turmoil drove 800,000 Chinese to seek new homes in North and South America, New Zealand, Hawaii, and the West Indies. Nearly four times as many settled in Southeast Asia. Moreover, industrial changes caused millions to migrate *within* their own countries or to neighboring ones, seeking employment in the burgeoning cities or other opportunities in frontier regions.

From the 1860s until 1914, governments imposed almost no controls on immigration or emigration. In China, the Qing government failed in its effort to restrict emigration into the dominant Manchus' northeastern homelands. The United States allowed entry to anyone who was not a prostitute, a convict, or a "lunatic"; but in 1882, racist reactions spurred legislation that barred entry to almost all Chinese. Travel within Europe required no passports or work permits; foreign-born criminals were subject to deportation, but that was the extent of immigration policy.

Urban Life Cities boomed, with both positive and negative effects. Tokyo's population climbed from 500,000 in 1863 to 1,750,000 in 1908, and London's passed 6.5 million. Major cities faced housing shortages, despite governments' massive rebuilding and beautification projects. This was the era when city planning came into its own—to widen and regularize thoroughfares for train and streetcar traffic, and to make crowded city life attractive to new inhabitants. City governments in New York, Cairo, Buenos Aires, Bombay, and Brussels spent lavishly on opera houses, libraries, sewers, and parks, hoping to ward off disease and crime and to impress others with their modernity. And yet, for all those efforts, cholera and tuberculosis remained major killers, and suicide and alcoholism became growing problems. Population movement and the growth of cities were distinct features of the later nineteenth century all over the world, opening up new opportunities to become rich or to sink into poverty.

Urban Transportation Streetcars in Tokyo, Japan's capital, are watched over by sword-bearing patrolmen in 1905, during the Russo-Japanese War. The first electric streetcar began running in Japan in 1895. Note the elevated electricity lines, which dated from the 1880s.

Discontent with Imperialism

In the decades before the Great War, opposition to European domination in Asia and Africa gathered strength. During the nineteenth century, as Europeans touted imperialism as a "civilizing mission," local prophets had voiced alternative visions contesting European supremacy (see Chapter 16). While imperialists consolidated their hold, suppression of unrest in the colonies required ever more force and bloodshed. As the cycle of resistance and repression escalated, many Europeans back home, mainly on the left and out of power, questioned the harsh means of controlling their colonies. By 1914, these questions were intensifying as colonial subjects across Asia and Africa challenged imperial domination.

UNREST IN AFRICA

Africa witnessed many anticolonial uprisings in the first decades of colonial rule. (See Map 18.2.) Violent conflicts embroiled not only the Belgians and the Germans, who paid little attention to African political traditions, but also the British, whose colonial system left traditional African rulers in place. These uprisings made Europeans uneasy. Why, they wondered, were Africans resisting regimes that had huge advantages in firepower and transport and that were bringing medical skills, literacy, and other fruits of European civilization? Some Europeans concluded that Africans were too stubborn or unsophisticated to appreciate Europe's generosity. Others, shocked by colonial cruelty, called for reform. A few radicals even demanded an end to imperialism.

The Anglo-Boer War The continent's most devastating anticolonial uprising occurred in South Africa. This unique struggle pitted two white communities against each other: the British in the Cape Colony and Natal against the Afrikaners, descendants of original Dutch settlers who lived in the Transvaal and the Orange Free State. (See Map 18.2 inset). Although two white regimes were the main adversaries, the Anglo-Boer War (1899–1902) involved the area's 4 million black inhabitants as fully as its 1 million whites.

The war's origins lay in the discovery of gold in the Transvaal in the mid-1880s. As the area rapidly became Africa's richest state, the prospect that Afrikaner republics might become the powerhouse in southern Africa was more than British imperialists could accept. Fearing that war was inevitable, the president of the Transvaal launched a preemptive strike against the British. In late 1899, Afrikaner forces crossed into South Africa. Fighting a relentless guerrilla campaign, Afrikaners waged a war that would last three years and cost Britain 20,000 soldiers and £200 million.

Map 18.2 Uprisings and Wars in Africa

The European partition and conquest of Africa were violent affairs.

- How many separate African resistance movements can you count on this map?
- Where was resistance the most prolonged?
- According to your reading, why were Ethiopians, who sustained their autonomy, able to do what other African opponents of European armies were not?

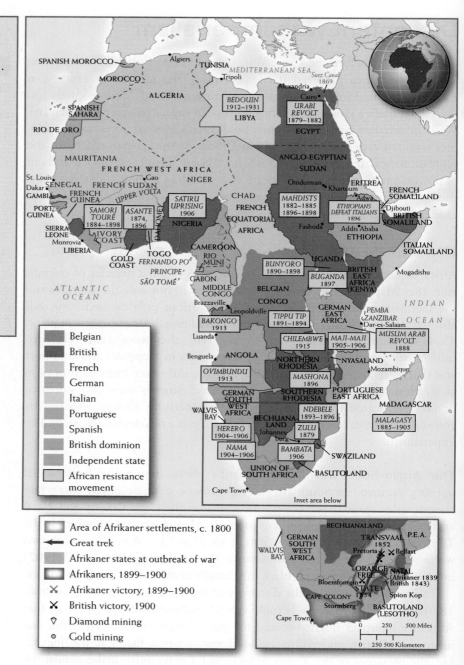

SPANISH MOROCCO
Algiers • TUNISIA
MOROCCO • Tripoli
MEDITERRANEAN SEA
Suez Canal 1869
ALGERIA
Alexandria •
BEDOUIN 1912–1931
LIBYA
URABI REVOLT 1879–1882
• Cairo
SPANISH SAHARA
RIO DE ORO
EGYPT
MAURITANIA
FRENCH WEST AFRICA
NIGER
ANGLO-EGYPTIAN SUDAN
RED SEA
St. Louis • Gao •
Dakar • SENEGAL FRENCH SUDAN
GAMBIA FRENCH GUINEA
UPPER VOLTA
Omdurman •
ERITREA
Khartoum •
FRENCH SOMALILAND
PORT. GUINEA
SATIRU UPRISING 1906
CHAD
FRENCH EQUATORIAL AFRICA
MAHDISTS 1882–1885 1896–1898
Adwa •
ETHIOPIANS DEFEAT ITALIANS 1896
• Djibouti
BRITISH SOMALILAND
SIERRA LEONE
SAMORI TOURÉ 1884–1898
ASANTE 1874, 1896
NIGERIA
Fashoda •
Addis Ababa •
ETHIOPIA
Monrovia •
IVORY COAST
LIBERIA
GOLD COAST
TOGO
DAHOMEY
FERNANDO PO
PRINCIPE
SÃO TOMÉ
CAMEROON
RIO MUNI
GABON
MIDDLE CONGO
BUNYORO 1890–1898
UGANDA
BUGANDA 1897
BRITISH EAST AFRICA (KENYA)
ITALIAN SOMALILAND
• Mogadishu
ATLANTIC OCEAN
Brazzaville •
BELGIAN CONGO
GERMAN EAST AFRICA
PEMBA
ZANZIBAR
Dar-es-Salaam •
INDIAN OCEAN
Leopoldville •
TIPPU TIP 1891–1894
BAKONGO 1913
Luanda •
CHILEMBWE 1915
MAJI-MAJI 1905–1906
MUSLIM ARAB REVOLT 1888
Benguela •
ANGOLA
NYASALAND
Mozambique •
OVIMBUNDU 1913
NORTHERN RHODESIA
MASHONA 1896
PORTUGUESE EAST AFRICA
GERMAN SOUTH WEST AFRICA
SOUTHERN RHODESIA
MADAGASCAR
WALVIS BAY
NDEBELE 1893–1896
MALAGASY 1885–1905
HERERO 1904–1906
BECHUANALAND
Johannesburg •
ZULU 1879
NAMA 1904–1906
BAMBATA 1906
SWAZILAND
UNION OF SOUTH AFRICA
BASUTOLAND
Cape Town •
Inset area below

Belgian
British
French
German
Italian
Portuguese
Spanish
British dominion
Independent state
African resistance movement

Area of Afrikaner settlements, c. 1800
← Great trek
Afrikaner states at outbreak of war
Afrikaners, 1899–1900
✕ Afrikaner victory, 1899–1900
✕ British victory, 1900
▽ Diamond mining
○ Gold mining

BECHUANALAND
GERMAN SOUTH WEST AFRICA
TRANSVAAL 1852
P.E.A.
WALVIS BAY
Pretoria • ✕ Belfast
ORANGE FREE STATE 1854
NATAL (Afrikaner 1839 British 1843)
Bloemfontein • ✕
✕ Spion Kop
CAPE COLONY
Stormberg •
BASUTOLAND (LESOTHO)
Cape Town •
0   250   500 Miles
0 250 500 Kilometers

In a frustrated effort to respond to Afrikaner hit-and-run tactics, the British instituted a terrifying innovation: the concentration camp. At one moment in the war, at least 155,000 captured men, women, and children were held in camps surrounded by barbed wire. The British rounded up Afrikaners and Africans, whom they feared would side with the "anticolonial" Dutch descendants. Ultimately, the British won the war, bringing the Transvaal and the Orange Free State—with their vast gold reserves—into their empire. But the horrors of the war traumatized the British, who regarded themselves as Europe's most enlightened and efficient colonial rulers.

Other Struggles in Colonized Africa The disgust that some Europeans felt toward imperial violence deepened after Germany's activities in Africa also went brutally wrong. Germany had established colonies in South West Africa (present-day Namibia), Cameroon, and Togo in 1884 and in East Africa in 1885. In German South West Africa, the Herero and San people resisted the Germans in the Herero Revolt, and in German East Africa (modern-day Tanzania), the Muslim Arab peoples rebelled. Between 1904 and 1906, fighting in German South West Africa escalated to such an extent that the German commander issued an extermination order against the Herero population.

According to those who favored European imperialism, however, the atrocities of the Boer War and German South West Africa, like the horrors of Leopold's Belgian Congo (see Chapter 17), were exceptions to what they considered Europeans' enlightened rule. Europeans saw Africans either as accepting subjects or childlike primitives when they resisted—as in the Maji Maji Revolt in German East Africa, described at the beginning of this chapter—and redoubled their efforts to impose colonial order. The problem, in their view, was that they had not tried hard enough to bring civilization. In many cases, the number of officials stationed in the colonies increased.

Extermination of the Herero This 1906 photograph shows a soldier guarding Herero women and children in a prison camp on the coast of German South West Africa (present-day Namibia). The Germans carried out a campaign of near-extermination against the Herero population in German South West Africa in 1904–1906. Nearly 90 percent of the Herero were killed.

THE BOXER UPRISING IN CHINA

Although not formally colonized, China too struggled against European intrusions. As the population swelled to over half a billion and outstripped the country's resources, problems of landlessness, poverty, and peasant discontent (long-standing concerns in China's modern history) left the established order vulnerable to internal revolts and foreign intervention.

The breakdown of dynastic authority originated largely with foreign pressure. For one thing, China's defeat in the Sino-Japanese War of 1894–1895 (see Chapter 17) was deeply humiliating. Japan acquired Taiwan as its first major colony, and European powers demanded that the weakened Qing government grant them specific areas within China as their respective "spheres of influence." (See Map 18.3.) The United States argued instead for maintaining an "open door" policy in China that would keep access available to all traders, while supporting missionary efforts to spread Christianity.

Unrest and Revolt The most explosive reaction to these pressures, the **Boxer Uprising,** started within the peasantry in 1899. Like colonized peoples in Africa, the Boxers violently resisted European meddling. And like the Taiping Rebellion decades earlier (see Chapter 16), the story of the Boxers was tied to missionary activities. Whereas in earlier centuries Jesuit missionaries had sought to convert the court and the elites, by the mid-nineteenth century the missionary goal was to convert commoners. After the Taiping Rebellion, Christian missionaries had streamed into China, impatient to make new converts in the hinterlands and confident of their governments' backing.

The Boxers rejected claims of western superiority. Especially in regions suffering from natural disasters and economic hardship, activists provided assistance to the dispossessed. Women played a prominent role. The so-called Red Lanterns were mostly teenage girls and unmarried women who announced their loyalty by wearing red garments. Although segregated from the male Boxers—Red Lanterns worshipped at their own altars and practiced martial arts at separate boxing grounds—they were important to the movement in counteracting the influence of Christian women. Indeed, one of the Boxers' greatest fears was that cunning Christian women would use their guile to weaken the Boxers' spirits. They claimed that the "purity" of the Red Lanterns could counter this threat. The Red Lanterns were supposedly capable of incredible feats: they could walk on water or fly through the air. Belief in their magical powers provided critical assistance for the uprising.

As the movement gained momentum, the Qing vacillated between viewing the Boxers as a threat to order and embracing them as a force to check foreign intrusion. Early in 1900, Qing troops clashed with the Boxers in an escalating cycle of violence. By spring, however, the Qing could no longer control the tens of thousands of Boxers roaming the vicinities of Beijing and Tianjin. Embracing the Boxers' cause, the empress dowager declared war against the foreign powers in June 1900.

Acting without any discernible plan or leadership, the Boxers attacked Christian and foreign symbols and persons. They harassed and sometimes killed Chinese Christians in parts of northern China, destroyed railroad tracks

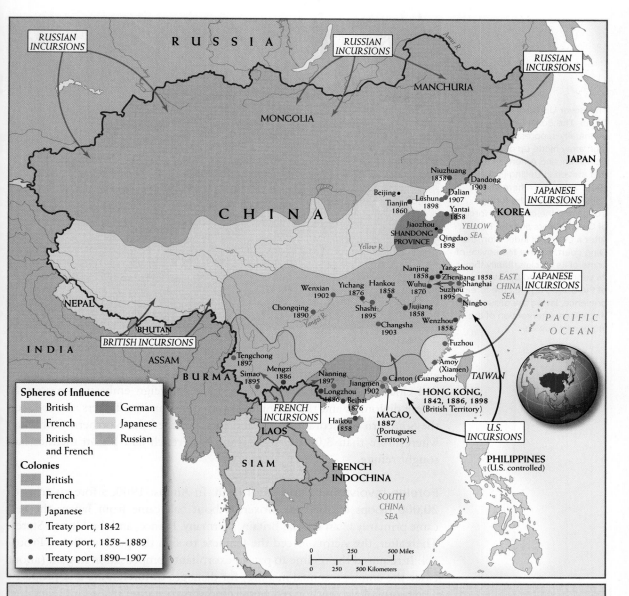

Map 18.3 Foreign Spheres of Influence in China, 1842–1907

....

While technically independent, the Qing dynasty could not prevent foreign penetration and domination of its economy during the nineteenth century.

• Which five powers established spheres of influence in China?

• At what time was the greatest number of treaty ports established?

• According to your reading, what did the foreign powers hope to achieve within their spheres of influence? What kinds of local opposition did the foreign influence inspire?

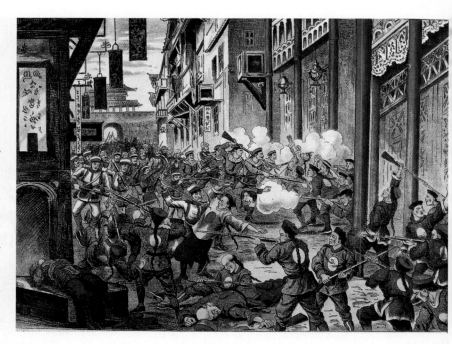

The Boxer Uprising in China The Boxer Uprising was eventually suppressed by a foreign army made up of Japanese, European, and American troops that arrived in Beijing in August 1900. The picture here shows fighting between the foreign troops and the combined forces of Qing soldiers and the Boxers. After a period of indecision, the Qing court, against the advice of some of its officials, finally threw its support behind the struggle of the Boxers against the foreign presence, laying the ground for the military intervention of the imperialist powers.

and telegraph lines, and attacked owners of foreign objects such as lamps and clocks. In Beijing, the Boxers besieged foreign embassy compounds, where diplomats and their families cowered in fear. The Boxers also reduced the Southern Cathedral to ruins and then besieged the Northern Cathedral, where more than 3,000 Catholics and 40 French and Italian marines had sought refuge.

Foreign Involvement and Aftermath In August 1900, a foreign army of 20,000 troops crushed the Boxers. About half came from Japan; the rest came primarily from Russia, Britain, Germany, France, and the United States. Thereafter, the victors forced the Chinese to sign the punitive Boxer Protocol. It required the regime to pay an exorbitant compensation in gold (about twice the empire's annual income) for damages to foreign life and property. The protocol also authorized western powers to station troops in Beijing.

Even in defeat, the Boxers' anti-western uprising showed how much had changed in China since the Taiping Rebellion. Although the Boxers were primarily peasants, even they had felt the unsettledness generated by European inroads into China. Indeed, the Europeans' commercial and spiritual reach, once confined to elites and port cities, had extended across much of China. Whereas the Taiping Rebellion had mobilized millions against the Qing, the Boxers remained loyal to the dynasty and focused their wrath on foreigners and Chinese Christians. The Boxer Uprising, like the Maji Maji

Revolt in East Africa, revealed the widespread political opposition to westernization and the willingness of disaffected populations to resist western programs.

Worldwide Insecurities

Core Objectives

IDENTIFY and **DESCRIBE** political, economic, and social crises that swept through the world in this period, and **ANALYZE** the impact they had on different regions of the world.

While news of unrest in the distant colonies and in China generally did not lead Europeans to question their ways, conflicts closer to home tore at European confidence in this era. The rise of a European-centered world deepened rivalries within Europe. Numerous factors fostered conflict, including France's smoldering resentment at its defeat in the Franco-Prussian War (see Chapter 17), and led to a buildup of military forces, especially in Britain, Germany, and France. Tensions also increased as the European states competed for raw materials and colonial footholds. Not everyone, however, supported vast expenditures on the military. Many Europeans disapproved of spending on massive steam-powered warships. Others warned that the arms race would end in a devastating war. At the same time, the booms and busts of expanding industrial economies, challenges about the proper roles of women, and problems of uncontrolled urbanization shook the established order and had an impact across the globe. (See again Map 18.1.) These changes and insecurities transformed Europe and swept through the world.

FINANCIAL, INDUSTRIAL, AND TECHNOLOGICAL CHANGE

Economic developments helped make powers "great," but they could also unsettle societies. Indeed, pride about wealth and growth coincided with laments about changes in national and international economies. To begin with, Americans and Europeans recognized that the small-scale, laissez-faire capitalism championed by Adam Smith (see Chapter 14) was giving way to an economic order dominated by huge, heavily capitalized firms. Gone, it seemed, was Smith's vision of many small producers in vigorous competition with one another, all benefiting from efficient—but not exploitative—divisions of labor.

Instead of smooth progress, the economy of Europe and North America in the nineteenth century bounced between booms and busts: long-term business cycles of rapid growth followed by countercycles of stagnation. Late in the century, the pace of economic change accelerated. Large-scale steel production, railroad building, and textile manufacturing expanded at breakneck speed, while waves of bank closures, bankruptcies, and agricultural crises ruined many small property owners, including farmers. By the century's end, European and North American economies were dominated as never before by a few large-scale firms, such as John D. Rockefeller's Standard Oil and the large banking institutions in France, Britain, Germany, and the United States. The same was true in Japan, where *zaibatsu*—large companies with banking subsidiaries for finance and industrial wings dominating different sectors of the market—like Sumitomo, Mitsui, and Mitsubishi were the engine of Japan's extraordinary economic growth.

Financial Integration and Crises These were years of heady international financial integration. More and more countries joined the world system of borrowing and lending; more and more countries were linked financially through global loans and the fact that all of the major national currencies in the world, such as the American dollar, the British pound, and the French franc were exchanged at reliable rates. At the hub of this world system were the banks of London, which since the Napoleonic wars had been a major source of capital for international borrowers.

The rise of giant banks and huge industrial corporations caused alarm, for it seemed to signal an end to free markets and competitive capitalism. Rather than longing for the return of truly free markets, many critics sought reforms that would protect people from economic instability. The solution, many economists and politicians thought, was for the state to manage the national economies.

Banking especially seemed in need of closer government supervision. Many industrial societies already had central banks (banks that issued national currencies, fixed underlying interest rates, and in general controlled monetary policy); London's Bank of England had long since overseen local and international money markets. But governments did not have the resources to protect all—or even most—investments during times of crisis. Between 1890 and 1893, 550 American banks collapsed, and only the intervention of J. P. Morgan prevented the depletion of the nation's reserves of gold that stood behind the dollar.

The road to regulation of banking and finance, however, was hardly smooth. In 1907, a more serious crisis threatened. A panic on Wall Street led to a run on the banks. Once again, J. P. Morgan rescued the American economy from financial panic—by compelling financiers to commit unprecedented funds (eventually $35 million) to protect banks and trusts against depositors' panic. Morgan himself lost $21 million and emerged from the bank panic convinced that some sort of public oversight was needed. By 1913, the U.S. Congress ratified the Federal Reserve Act, creating boards to monitor the supply and demand of the nation's money. The crisis of 1907 also showed how national financial matters could quickly become international affairs as panicked American investors withdrew their funds from other countries, many of which relied on American capital.

Industrialization and the Modern Economy Backed by big banks, industrialists extended their enterprises to new places. For example, with loans from European investors, Russia built railways, telegraph lines, and factories. By 1900, Russia was producing half of the world's oil and a considerable amount of steel. Yet industrial development remained uneven: southern Europe and the American South continued to lag behind northern regions. The gap was even more pronounced in colonial territories, which contained few industrial enterprises aside from railroad building and mining.

By 1914, the factory and the railroad had become global symbols of the modern economy—and of its positive and negative effects. Everywhere, the coming of the railroad to one's town or village was a big event: for some, it represented an exhilarating leap into the modern world; for others, a terrifying abandonment of the past. Ocean liners, automobiles, and airplanes likewise could be both dazzling and disorienting.

For ordinary people, the new economy brought benefits and drawbacks. Factories produced cheaper goods, but they belched clouds of black smoke. Railways offered faster transport, but they ruined small towns unlucky enough to be left off the branch line. Machines (when operating properly) were more efficient than human and animal labor, but workers who used them felt reduced to machines themselves. Indeed, the American Frederick Winslow Taylor proposed a system of "scientific management" to make human bodies perform more like machines, maximizing the efficiency of workers' movements. But workers did not want to be managed or to cede control of the pace of production to employers. Labor's resistance to "Taylorization" led to numerous strikes. For strikers, as for those left out of the new economy, the course of progress had taken an unsettling turn.

THE "WOMAN QUESTION"

Complicating the situation was turmoil about the "woman question." In the west, female activists demanded that women be given more rights as citizens; more radical voices called for fundamental changes to the family and the larger society. At the same time, imperialists claimed that colonial rule was bringing great improvements to women in Asia and Africa. But the "woman question" was no more easily settled there than elsewhere.

Women's Issues in the West In western countries, for most of the nineteenth century, a belief in "separate spheres" had supposedly confined women to domestic matters, while leaving men in charge of public life and economic undertakings. (In practice, only women from middle- and upper-class families avoided working outside the home for wages.) However, as economic developments created new jobs for women and greater access to education, women increasingly found work as teachers, secretaries, typists, department store clerks, social workers, and telephone operators. These jobs offered greater economic and social independence. Some educated women spearheaded efforts to improve conditions for the urban poor and to expand the government's role in regulating economic affairs. Nonetheless, much of the population continued to think that higher education and public activism were not suitable for women.

In one important change, many women began to assert control over reproduction. Although in numerous countries the use of contraceptive devices was illegal, women still found a variety of ways to limit the number of children they bore. In addition to marrying late and sleeping apart, some used spermicidal herbs, which sometimes worked but sometimes killed the woman; others relied on a variety of sponges and other barriers, had their partners use condoms, or insisted on the practice of *coitus interruptus* (withdrawal). When contraception failed, many women turned to abortion, even though it was illegal. Successful contraception, by whatever means, depended on cooperation and communication and tended to be more effective as educational levels increased.

Early in the twentieth century, the birthrate in America was half of what it had been a century before. By having fewer children, families could devote more income to education, food, housing, and leisure activities. Declining birthrates, along with improved medicine, also meant that fewer women died in childbirth; more would see their children reach adulthood.

Still, changes in women's social status did not translate into full political rights at the national level, such as the vote. By the mid-nineteenth century, women's suffrage movements had appeared in several countries, but these campaigns bore little immediate fruit. In 1868, women received the right to vote in local elections in Britain. Within a few years, Finland, Sweden, and some American states allowed single, property-owning women the right to cast ballots—again, only in local elections. Women obtained the right to vote in national elections in New Zealand in 1893, in Australia in 1902, in Finland in 1906, and in Norway in 1913.

Despite these gains, male alarmists portrayed women's suffrage and women's rights as the beginning of civilization's end. Among women, views on feminism varied. Most middle-class women in Europe and the Americas were not seeking to make women equal to men. Indeed, many bourgeois women recoiled from the close relationships between socialism and feminism. In Latin America, for example, anarchists championed a version of feminism arguing that the abolition of private property would liberate women from their misery and that the traditional family was a bourgeois convention. Other women feared becoming too "mannish," and a few worried that equality would destroy female sensuality. Most, probably, looked to reform less in terms of voting rights and more in terms of better treatment within families and local communities.

Women's Status in Colonies In the colonial world, the woman question was also a contentious issue—but it was mainly argued among men. European authorities liked to boast that colonial rule improved women's status. Citing examples of traditional societies' treatment of women, they criticized the veiling of women in Islamic societies, the binding of women's feet in China, widow burning (*sati*) in India, and female genital mutilation in Africa. Europeans believed that prohibiting such acts was a justification for colonial intervention.

And yet, colonialism only added to women's burdens. As male workers headed into the export economy, formerly shared agricultural work fell exclusively on women's shoulders. In Africa, for example, the opening of vast gold and diamond mines drew thousands of men away to work in the mines, leaving women to tend to the farmstead and to do colonial tasks that men once did. Similarly, the rise of European-owned agricultural estates in Kenya and Southern Rhodesia depleted surrounding villages of male family members, who went to work on the estates. In these circumstances, women kept the local, food-producing economy afloat.

Nor did colonial "civilizing" rhetoric improve women's political or cultural circumstances. In fact, European missionaries preached a message of domesticity to Asian and African families, emphasizing that women's place was in the home raising children and that women's education should be different from men's. Thus, males overwhelmingly dominated the new schools that Europeans built. Moreover, the chiefs who collaborated with colonial officials consistently favored men. As a result, African women often lost landholding and other rights that they had enjoyed before the Europeans' arrival.

CLASS CONFLICT

As capitalism's volatility shook confidence in free market economies and sharpened conflicts between classes, the tone of political debate was transformed as new voices called for radical change. Although living conditions for European and North American workers improved over time, widening inequalities in income and the slow pace of reform bred frustration. Most workers remained committed to peaceful agitation, but some radicals favored violence against the state and its agents.

Strikes and Revolts In the Americas and in Europe, radicals adopted numerous tactics for asserting the interests of the working class. In Europe, the franchise was gradually expanded in hopes that the lower classes would prefer voting to revolution—and indeed, most of the new political parties that catered to workers had no desire to overthrow the state. But conservatives feared them anyway, especially as they gained electoral clout. The Labour Party, founded in Britain in 1900, quickly boasted a large share of the vote. By 1912, the German Social Democratic Party was the largest party in the Reichstag, though it lacked power since the Reichstag was only an advisory body. But it was not the legally sanctioned parties that sparked violent street protests and strikes in the century's last decades. A whole array of **syndicalists** (labor activists), **anarchists** (those who opposed government altogether), royalists, and socialists sprang up in this period, making work stoppages everyday affairs.

Although the United States had similar radical groups, they were few and small. Nonetheless, American workers were organizing. The labor movement's power burst forth dramatically in 1894. Spawned by wage cuts and firings following an economic downturn, the Pullman strike (directed against the maker of railway sleeping cars, George Pullman) involved approximately 3 million workers. The strike's conclusion, however, revealed the enduring power of the status quo. After hiring replacement workers to break the strike, Pullman requested federal troops to protect his operation. After its leaders were jailed, the strike collapsed. Although strikes and protests in the United States and Europe often failed to achieve their immediate goals, they worried those in power and ultimately led to important changes.

Revolution in Mexico Perhaps the most successful turn-of-the-century revolution occurred in Mexico. This peasant uprising thoroughly transformed the country. Fueled by the unequal distribution of land and by disgruntled workers, the **Mexican Revolution** erupted in 1910 when political elites split over the succession of General Porfirio Díaz after decades of his strong-arm rule. Dissidents balked when Díaz refused to step down, and peasants and workers rallied to the call to arms.

From the north (led by the charismatic Pancho Villa) to the south (under the legendary Emiliano Zapata), peasants, farmers, and other rural workers helped topple the Díaz regime. In the name of providing land for farmers and ending oligarchic rule, peasant armies defeated Díaz's troops and proceeded to destroy many large estates. The fighting lasted for ten brutal years, during which almost 10 percent of the country's population perished.

Thereafter, political leaders had to accept popular demands for democracy, respect for the sovereignty of peasant communities, and land reform. The revolution's most lasting legacy was perhaps the creation of rural communes for Mexico's peasantry. These communal village holdings, called *ejidos*, looked back to a precolonial heritage. The revolution spawned a set of new national myths based on the heroism of rural peoples, Mexican nationalism, and a celebration of the Aztec past.

Preserving Established Orders Although the Mexican Revolution succeeded in toppling the old elite, elsewhere in Latin America the ruling establishment remained united against assaults from below. Already, in 1897, the Brazilian army had mercilessly suppressed a peasant movement in the northeastern part of the country. Moreover, in Cuba, the Spanish and then the American armies crushed tenant farmers' efforts to reclaim land from sugar estates. In Guatemala, Maya Indians lost land to coffee barons.

In Europe and the United States, the preservation of established orders did not rest on repression alone. Here, elites also grudgingly agreed to gradual change. Indeed, by the century's end, left-wing agitators, muckraking reporters, and middle-class reformers began to win meaningful social improvements. Unable to suppress the socialist movement, Otto von Bismarck, the German chancellor, defused the appeal of socialism by enacting social welfare measures in 1883–1884, insuring workers against illness, accidents, and old age and establishing maximum working hours. In the United States, it took lurid journalistic accounts of unsanitary practices in Chicago slaughterhouses (including tales of workers falling into lard vats and being rendered into cooking fat) to spur the federal government into action. In 1906, President Theodore Roosevelt signed a Meat Inspection Act that provided for government supervision of meatpacking operations. In other cases (banking, steel production, railroads), the federal government's enhanced supervisory authority served corporate interests as well. These consumer and family protection measures reflected a broader reform movement, one dedicated to creating a more efficient society and correcting the undesirable consequences of urbanization and industrialization. At local and state levels, these **progressive reformers** attacked corrupt city governments that had allegedly fallen into the hands of immigrant-dominated "political machines." The progressives also attacked other vices, such as gambling, drinking, and prostitution—all associated with industrialized, urban settings. The creation of city parks preoccupied urban planners, who hoped parks' green spaces would serve as the city's "lungs" and offer healthier forms of entertainment than houses of prostitution, gambling dens, and bars. From Scandinavia to California, the proponents of old-age pensions and public ownership of utilities put pressure on lawmakers. Thousands of associations took shape against capitalism's harsher effects, and they occasionally succeeded in changing state policies. Indeed, the period leading up to World War I was one of rapid change, in which financial crises reverberated across the globe, European and American women pressed for their rights and also agitated for the rights of Asian and African women, and elites were forced to make reforms, though they tended to be limited, in the colonial and colonializers' worlds.

Cultural Modernism

As revolutionaries and reformers wrestled with the problems of progress, intellectuals, artists, and scientists struggled to make sense of change in their own societies and beyond. What we call **modernism**—the sense of having

progressive reformers
Members of the U.S. reform movement in the early twentieth century that aimed to eliminate political corruption, improve working conditions, and regulate the power of large industrial and financial enterprises.

modernism
In the arts, modernism refers to the effort to break with older conventions and seek new ways of seeing and describing the world.

Core Objectives

EXPLAIN how European modernism drew on Afro-Asian influences and represented uncertainty about ideas inherited from the Enlightenment.

broken with tradition—came to prominence in many fields, from physics to architecture, from painting to the social sciences.

Modernist movements were notably international. Egyptian social scientists read the works of European thinkers, while French and German painters flocked to museums to inspect artifacts from Egypt and artworks from other parts of Africa, Asia, and Oceania. As education spread and political reforms enfranchised more Americans and Europeans, changes in the meaning of culture occurred, causing it to be less elitist and more popular. Yet European elites did not give up their opera houses and paintings in favor of arts and entertainments that were appealing to urban workers or colonized peoples. Instead, the arts became more abstract: musicians abandoned the comfort of harmonic and diatonic sound (the eight-tone scale standard in classical western music at the time); writers and visual artists left realistic representation behind.

Above all, modernism in arts and sciences replaced the certainties of the Enlightenment with the unsettledness of the new age. Modernists challenged claims to provide complete, coherent explanations and representations of all kinds. With growing doubts about civilizing missions or urban and industrial "progress," artists and scientists struggled to understand a world in which human reason seemed inadequate.

POPULAR CULTURE COMES OF AGE

From the late eighteenth to the late nineteenth century, production and consumption of the arts, books, music, and sports changed dramatically. The change derived mainly from new urban settings, technological innovations, mass education, and increased leisure time. Middle-class art lovers eagerly purchased mass-produced engravings; millions attended dance halls and vaudeville shows (entertainment by singers, dancers, and comedians). For the first time, sports attracted mass followings. Soccer in Europe, baseball in the United States, and cricket in India had wildly devoted middle- and working-class fans. Thus did a truly **popular culture** emerge, delivering affordable and accessible forms of art and entertainment to "the masses."

By the nineteenth century's close, the press stood as a major form of popular entertainment and information. This was partly because publishers were offering different wares to different classes of readers and partly because many more people could read, especially in Europe and the Americas. By that time, the English *Daily Mail* and the French *Petit Parisien* boasted circulations of over 1 million. In the United States, urban dwellers, many of them immigrants, avidly read newspapers—some in English, others in their native languages. Banner headlines, sensational stories, and simple language drew in readers with little education or poor English skills.

popular culture
Affordable and accessible forms of art and entertainment available to people at all levels of society.

Impressionism Emerging in Paris in the last third of the nineteenth century, impressionism was an artistic movement that was radical in its day. Its members broke away from the conventional art community and its official, academic salons. With small, visible brushstrokes, the impressionists stressed the changing qualities of light, the passage of time, and movement. Rather than compete with photography and present a facsimile of a stable, static, coherent external reality, they sought to capture perceptions of a world in rapid flux. Claude Monet's *The Gare St-Lazare* exemplifies the impressionists' ambivalent view of nineteenth-century progress.

By now the kind of culture one consumed had become a reflection of one's real (or desired) status in society. For many Latin American workers, for example, reading one's own newspaper or comic strip was part of being a worker. Argentina's socialist newspaper, *La Vanguardia*, was one of Buenos Aires's most prominent periodicals, read and debated at work and in the cafés of working-class neighborhoods. Anyone seen reading the bourgeois paper, *La Prensa*, faced heckling and ridicule by fellow workers. As the community of cultural consumers broadened and as ideas from across the globe flooded in, writers, artists, and scholars struggled to adapt.

MODERNISM IN EUROPEAN CULTURE

In intellectual and artistic terms, Europe at the turn of the twentieth century experienced perhaps its richest age since the Renaissance. Artists' work reflected their doubts about the modern world, as represented by the railroad, the big city, and the factory. While the artists and writers of the mid-nineteenth century had largely celebrated progress, the painters and novelists of the century's end took a darker view. They turned away from reason, which the Enlightenment had championed, and descriptive prose as they searched for meanings that came from instinct and emotion. The primitive came to symbolize both Europe's lost innocence and the forces that reason could not control, such as sexual drives, religious fervor, or brute strength.

Europeans began to see the world in a fundamentally different way, aided by the experience of nonwestern visual arts. The painter who led the way in incorporating nonwestern themes into modern art was Pablo Picasso (1881–1973), who found in African art forms a radically new way of expressing

New Forms of Subjectivity Jean-Auguste-Dominique Ingres, one of the great realist artists of the nineteenth century, was one of Pablo Picasso's idols. The portrait of the newspaper baron Louis-François Bertin (*left*) embodies the artist's confidence in his own ability to represent an external reality just as it appears. Picasso refined his technique by copying Ingres's works at the Louvre. He clearly used Ingres as a model for his 1910 portrait of his own art dealer, Ambroise Vollard (*right*), which built on the work of the impressionists, in an effort to challenge the two-dimensional realism of his master.

human sentiments that was shocking to most European and American observers. Other artists were inspired by the sleekness and syncopation of machines or by the irrational content of dreams. And painting was not the only art form that displayed a modern style. Arnold Schönberg (1874–1951) composed the first piece of music that rejected traditional western tonality. World-famous dancers like Isadora Duncan (1877–1927) pioneered the expressive, free-form movements that laid the foundations for modern dance.

However, the arts alone did not undermine older views of the world. Even science, in which the Enlightenment had placed so much faith, challenged the idea that the world functioned according to easily understood natural laws. After 1900, pioneering physicists and mathematicians like Albert Einstein (1879–1955) challenged the idea that a single scientific theory, like Newton's, could explain everything. They took apart the Enlightenment's conviction that man could achieve full knowledge of, and control over, nature.

In a series of papers published between 1905 and 1915, Einstein worked out the special and general theories of relativity, which demonstrated that measurements of speed and gravitational pull were not purely objective but always conditioned by the relative position and conditions of the observer. Although most scientists continued to collect data, feeling certain that they could plumb nature's depths, some of their colleagues began to question the arrogance of this view.

From the time of the Enlightenment, Europeans had prided themselves on their "reason." To be rational was to be civilized and to master irrational urges; respectable, middle-class nineteenth-century men were thought to embody these virtues. But in the late nineteenth century, faith in rationality began to falter. Perhaps reason was *not* man's highest attainment, said some; perhaps reason was impossible for man to sustain, said others. Friedrich Nietzsche (1844–1900) claimed that conventional European attempts to assert The Truth—including science and Judeo-Christian moral codes—were nothing more than life-destroying quests for power. Sigmund Freud (1856–1939) began to excavate layers of the human subconscious, where irrational desires and fears lay buried. For Freud, human nature was not as simple as it had seemed to Enlightenment thinkers. Instead, he asserted, humans were driven by sexual longings and childhood traumas. Neither Nietzsche nor Freud was well loved among nineteenth-century liberal elites. But in the new century, Nietzsche would become the prophet for many antiliberal causes, from nudism to Nazism; and Freud's dark vision would become central to the twentieth century's understanding of the self.

CULTURAL MODERNISM IN CHINA

What it meant to be modern sparked debate beyond western Europe. Europeans provided one set of answers; thinkers elsewhere offered quite different answers. Chinese artists and scientists at the turn of the century selectively engaged western ideas and transformed them. Indeed, some scholars have described the late Qing period as a time of competing cultural *modernities*, in contrast to the post-Qing era, which pursued a single, western-oriented *modernity*. These forms of modernity involved critical reflection on Chinese traditions and mixed reactions to western culture.

As in the west, Chinese writers now had a wider readership. By the late nineteenth century, more than 170 presses in China were serving a potential readership of 2 to 4 million concentrated mostly in the urban areas. These cities were more economically and culturally vibrant than the hinterlands. Not only was there an expanding body of readers, but newly rich beneficiaries of the treaty-port economy now patronized the arts.

Painters from the lower Yangzi region, collectively known as the **Shanghai School**, adopted elements from both indigenous and foreign sources.

Shanghai School
Late nineteenth-century style of painting characterized by an emphasis on spontaneous brushwork, feeling, and the incorporation of western influences into classical Chinese pieces.

Although classically trained, they appropriated new western techniques into their art.

Similarly, fantasy novels drew on both western science and indigenous supernatural beliefs. Some experimental writers explicitly addressed Chinese–western relations. Depicting China at war with western powers, the novel *New Era* (1908) celebrated conventional military themes but also introduced western inventions such as electricity-repellent clothing and bulletproof satin.

Although steamships, telegraphs, and railroads captured public attention, there was little interest in changing fundamental Chinese beliefs. Indeed, even as Chinese intellectuals recognized new modes of knowledge, many of the elite insisted that Chinese learning remain the principal source of all knowledge. What kind of balance should exist between western thought and Chinese learning, or even whether the ancient classics should keep their fundamental role, was an issue that would haunt generations to come. In this respect, the Chinese dilemma reflected a worldwide challenge to accepting the impulses of modernism.

Modernism arose at a time when intellectuals began to question the values that had sustained Europe and North America throughout most of the nineteenth century. It reflected discontent with industrialization, income inequality, and colonial repression. Even though modernism had its origins and most profound impact in Europe, in many ways, especially in art, it drew upon nonwestern traditions and spread its influence throughout Asia and Africa among the educated classes.

Rethinking Race and Reimagining Nations

Ironically, at this time of huge population transfers and shared technological modernization, many European and American elites embraced the idea that the identities of peoples and nations were deeply rooted and unchangeable and were based on physical and cultural characteristics. By the century's close, racial roots had become a crucial part of identity. People wanted to know who they (and their neighbors) were—especially in terms of *biological* ancestry. Now the idea of inheritance took on new weight, in both cultural and biological forms. Nationalists spoke of the uniqueness of the Slavic soul, the German mind, Hindu spirituality, the Hispanic race.

Nationalist and racial ideas were different in different parts of the world. In Europe and America, debates about race and national purity reflected several concerns—above all, fear of being overrun by the brown, black, and yellow peoples beyond the borders of "civilization." By contrast, in India these ideas were part of the anticolonial debate, and they helped mobilize people politically. This was also the case in China, Latin America, and the Islamic world, where discussions of identity went hand in hand with opposition to western domination and corrupt indigenous elites.

As we will see, these new impulses produced a variety of national movements, from China's anti-Qing campaign to India's Swadeshi movement. At the same time, panethnic movements looked beyond the nation-state, envisioning communities based on ethnicity. Behind these movements was the notion that political communities should be built on racial purity.

NATION AND RACE IN NORTH AMERICA AND EUROPE

Americans and Europeans greeted the end of the century with a combination of pride and pessimism, and this mood influenced attitudes about national identity, race, and religion. In the early 1890s, for example, Americans flocked to extravagant commemorations of the four-hundredth anniversary of Christopher Columbus's discovery. Yet, at the same time, Americans—like many Europeans—feared for their future.

Regulating the Environment and Immigration Americans especially worried that the United States had exhausted its supposedly infinite supply of new land and resources—as evidenced by the disappearance of the buffalo, the erosion of soils, and the depletion of timber stands by aggressive logging companies. Conservationists' alarm grew more intense with the Census Bureau's 1890 announcement that the American frontier had "closed." When Theodore Roosevelt became president of the United States in 1901, he translated concerns about conserving natural resources into government policy. The market, insisted Roosevelt and like-minded conservationists, could not be trusted to protect "nature." Instead, federal regulation was necessary. This led in 1902 to the passage of the National Reclamation Act, which provided funding for large-scale dams and irrigation projects. Three years later, the Roosevelt administration orchestrated the establishment of the National Forest Service to manage the development of millions of acres of permanent public lands.

Another issue troubled the Americans: the need to maintain the dominance of persons of European descent. As a result, the government initiated new forms of racial discrimination where old forms (like slavery) had broken down. In the American West, animosity toward Chinese workers led to the 1882 Exclusion Act, which prohibited almost all immigration from China. In the American South, where most of the nation's 7 million African Americans resided, a system of "Jim Crow" laws—enacted after Reconstruction, especially in the 1890s and later, and in force until the 1960s—upheld racial segregation and inequality.

Theodore Roosevelt with John Muir President Theodore Roosevelt and Scottish-American conservationist John Muir (to the president's left) took a camping trip in Yosemite Valley, California, in 1903. The founder of the Sierra Club, Muir took this opportunity to urge Roosevelt to set aside additional land in Yosemite and other areas in the United States for national parks.

Americans from western Europe grew even more anxious as throngs of "swarthy" immigrants entered the United States from southern and eastern Europe. Even more threatening were darker peoples who were colonial subjects in the Philippines, Puerto Rico, and Cuba. Talk of the end of white America fueled support for more restrictive immigration policies.

Across the North Atlantic, European elites engaged in similar discussions about immigration and the environment. For them, the final divvying up of Africa was in many respects equivalent to the closing of the American frontier. The Germans and Italians, in particular, complained about the lack of new territories on which to plant their flags. The French and British, by contrast, worried about how to preserve their overseas empires in a period of intense international competition; both experienced widespread nativist campaigns on their respective mainlands, and England all but closed its borders with the Aliens Act of 1905.

New Social Issues in Europe Darwinist theory provoked new anxieties about inherited diseases, racial mixing, and the dying out of white "civilizers." Sexual relations between European colonizers and indigenous women—and their mixed offspring—had always been a part of European expansionism, but as racial identities hardened, many saw racial mixing as harmful to the supposedly superior white races. In addition, medical attention focused on homosexuality, regarding it as a disease and a threat to civilization.

Some people debated whether Jews—defined by religious practice or, increasingly, by ethnicity—could be fully assimilated into European society. Even though Jews had gained rights as citizens in most European countries by the late nineteenth century, powerful prejudices persisted. In the 1880s and 1890s, violent attacks known as pogroms, often involving police complicity, targeted the large Jewish populations in the Russian Empire's western territories and pushed the persecuted farther westward. These emigrants' presence, in turn, stirred up fear and resentment, especially in Austria, Germany, and France. Rumors circulated about Jewish bankers' conspiratorial powers, and anxieties over the "pollution" of the European races became widespread.

RACE-MIXING AND THE PROBLEM OF NATIONHOOD IN LATIN AMERICA

In Latin America, debates about identity chiefly addressed ethnic intermixing and the legacy of a system of government that, unlike in much of the North

Atlantic world, excluded rather than included most people. Social hierarchies reaching back to the sixteenth century ranked whites born in Spain and Portugal at the top, creole elites in the middle, and indigenous and African populations at the bottom. Thus, the higher on the social ladder, the more likely people were to be white.

Contested Mixtures and Invented Traditions "Mixing" did not lead to a shared heritage. Nor did it necessarily lead to homogeneity. In fact, the "racial" order did not stick, since some Iberians occupied the lower ranks, while a few people of color managed to ascend the social ladder. Moreover, starting in the 1880s, the racial hierarchy saw further disruption by the deluge of poor European immigrants; they flooded into prospering Latin American countrysides or into booming cities like Buenos Aires in Argentina and São Paulo in Brazil. Latin American societies, then, did not easily become homogeneous "nations."

Latin American leaders began to exalt bygone glories as a way to promote national identity and foster unity. Inventing successful myths could make a government seem more legitimate—as the heir to a rightful struggle of the past. In Mexico, many parades celebrated Aztec grandeur, thereby creating a mythic arc from the greatness of the Aztec past to the triumphal story of Mexican independence. As the government glorified the Aztecs with pageants, statues, and pavilions, however, it continued to ignore modern Aztec descendants, who lived in squalor. Thus, race in Latin America was a more fluid category than it was in North America and Europe.

SUN YAT-SEN AND THE MAKING OF A CHINESE NATION

Just as Latin Americans celebrated their past, Chinese writers emphasized the power and depth of Chinese culture—in contrast to the Qing Empire's failing political and social strength. Here, writers used race to emphasize the superiority of the Han Chinese. Here, too, the pace of change generated a desire to trace one's roots back to secure foundations. Moreover, traditions were reinvented in the hope of saving Chinese culture threatened by modernity.

Among those who thought most intensely about the future of China was **Sun Yat-sen** (1866–1925), whose life story symbolized the challenge of nation building. Sun was part of an emerging generation of critics of the old regime. Like his European counterparts, Sun dreamed of a political community reshaped along national lines. Born into a modest rural household in southern China, he studied medicine in the British colony of Hong Kong and then turned to politics during the Sino-Japanese War. When the Qing government rejected his offer of service to the Chinese cause, he became

Sun Yat-sen
(1866–1925) Chinese revolutionary and first provisional president of the Republic of China. Sun played an important role in the overthrow of the Qing dynasty and later founded the Guomindang, the Nationalist Party of China.

Adapting to the Environment: Russian Peasants Take on the Steppe

The Eurasian steppe extends for some 5,000 miles north of the Caucasus Mountains, from northern China and Mongolia to Hungary, and below the forest belt of the original Muscovy. When historians mention these grasslands at all, it is generally to treat them as a military highway for armies of nomads that formed their own short-lived empires and harassed others. In this telling, when steppe warriors stood in the way of imperial Russian state expansion, they were wiped out or bribed to enter into bargains with the state. In the case of the powerful freebooters of the Don River basin, known as Cossacks, the Russian Empire offered grants of land and respect for Cossack self-government in exchange for the Cossacks' help in defending the empire's southern frontier. But there is another, lesser known environmental history of the steppe—one that tells of wheat fields and locusts, of snowstorms and boundless skies, and of the ways in which peasant migrants from northern, watered forests learned to adapt their farming methods to the land.

Russians first became aware of the environmental peculiarities of this region soon after Catherine the Great annexed a large swathe of the southern steppe, dubbing it "New Russia." The tsarina had hoped to use this rich earth to feed Russians living on poorer northern lands. But already by the later eighteenth century, it was clear that increased farming was not yielding great increases in food production. Why not? Catherine sent officials to investigate, and at first they blamed the land, pointing to natural vegetation, recurring droughts, and other special qualities of the steppe environment. Over time, however, they realized that the problem lay in the farmers' practices, not in the land itself. The peasants were practicing farming as they had up north, grateful for the land but ignorant of it. Gradually, painfully, peasants as well as officials learned that because the steppe was different—hot and dry—it required

different methods. The old implements did not work either: a new type of plow was needed to break the heavier-rooted plant life, especially steppe fescue (feather grass).

A breakthrough occurred when a Mennonite farmer observed topsoil blowing off his field. He planted a line of trees to break the wind and, in winter, to help retain snow for moisture. Similarly, an agronomist noticed that ravines near the river were widening and advised peasants to leave a band of steppe grasses in place as they plowed, since the grasses would help hold down the soil. At first, many peasants resisted sowing less of the land. Eventually, however, they discovered that the advice enabled them to increase crop production because of reduced erosion. In other words, environmental awareness spread—and made a difference.

The geologist Vasily Dokuchaev (1846–1903) turned the environmental awareness of the settlers and peasants into the first form of soil science.

convinced that China's rulers were out of touch with the times. Subsequently he established an organization based in Hawaii to advocate the Qing downfall and the cause of republicanism. The cornerstone of his message was Chinese—specifically, Han—nationalism. Sun blasted the feeble rule by outsiders, the Manchus, and trumpeted a sovereign political community of "true" Chinese.

Replacing the Qing and Reconstituting a Nation Realizing that reforms were necessary, the Manchu court began overhauling the administrative system and the military in the aftermath of the Boxer Uprising. Yet these

Dokuchaev's breakthrough idea was this: the problem with steppe farming was not the steppe but the farmer. He made extensive studies across Russian regions, developed a theory of soil formation in relation to climate and human usage, and created the first soil classification system. He recommended crop rotations, longer fallow periods, and lighter plowing (to preserve topsoil). He wanted peasants to become stewards, not just exploiters, of the land.

By the latter part of the nineteenth century, agriculture in the steppe had taken off. Cossacks, too, had become successful farmers. New Russia, which was also called Ukraine, became a breadbasket (which it still is to a large extent). Imperial Russia became the world's leading agricultural exporter, feeding both Germany and Britain in the run-up to World War I.

Russia's environment was transformed. And yet, the agriculture of the steppe was not what we would call "sustainable." The minimal woods in the area were depleted (peasants continued to act as if they still lived in northern forests with endless supplies of timber), and the black-earth topsoil was significantly diminished. Later, this would spur the introduction of chemical fertilizers—which would increase crop yields but once again change the steppe ecosystem, adding pollutants to rivers. Like human history, the natural history of the steppe never stands still.

Harvest in the Ukraine **(1880)** This 1880 painting by Vladimir Orlovsky shows Ukrainian peasants bringing in the rich harvest of the steppe.

Questions for Analysis

- How did the steppe lands' usefulness to the Russian Empire change during the period described above?
- How did peasants, officials, and scientists learn to think differently about steppe lands?

Explore Further

Moon, David, *The Plough That Broke the Steppes: Agriculture and Environment on Russia's Grasslands, 1700–1914* (2013).

changes came too late. The old elites grumbled, and the new class of urban merchants, entrepreneurs, and professionals (who often benefited from business with westerners) regarded the government as outmoded. Peasants and laborers resented the high cost of the reforms, which seemed to help only the rulers.

A mutiny, sparked in part by the government's nationalization of railroads and its low compensation to native Chinese investors, broke out in the city of Wuchang in central China in 1911. As it spread to other parts of the country, Sun Yat-sen hurried home from traveling in the United States. Few people rallied to the emperor's cause, and the Qing dynasty collapsed and

Diego Rivera's *History of Mexico* This is one of the most famous works of Mexican art, a history of Mexico by the radical nationalist painter Diego Rivera. Completed in 1935, this work seeks to show a people fighting constantly against outside aggressors; it winds like a grand epic from their glorious preconquest days (lower center) to the conquest, the colonial exploitation, the revolution for independence, nineteenth-century invasions from France and the United States, and the popular 1910 revolution. It culminates in an image of Karl Marx, framed by a "scientific sun" (not shown here)—pointing to a future of progress and prosperity for all, as if restoring a modern Tenochtitlán of the Aztecs. This work captured many Mexicans' efforts to return to the indigenous roots of the nation and to fuse them with modern scientific ideas.

was replaced by the Republic of China, bringing an abrupt end to a dynastic tradition of more than 2,000 years.

China was soon reconstituted, and Sun's ideas, especially those regarding race, played a central role. The original flag of the republic, for example, consisted of five colors representing the citizenry's major racial groups: red for the Han, yellow for the Manchus, blue for the Mongols, white for the Tibetans, and black for the Muslims. But Sun had reservations about this multiracial flag, believing there should be only one Chinese race. The existence of different groups in China, he argued, was the result of incomplete assimilation—a problem that the modern nation now had to confront.

NATIONALISM AND INVENTED TRADITIONS IN INDIA

British imperial rule persisted in India, but the turn of the century saw cracks in its stranglehold. Four strands had woven the territory together: the consolidation of colonial administration, the establishment of railways and telegraphs, the growth of western education and ideas, and the development of colonial capitalism. Now it was possible to speak of India as a single unit. It was also possible for anticolonial thinkers to imagine seizing and ruling India by themselves. Thus a new form of resistance emerged, different from peasant rebellions of the past. Now, dissenters talked of Indians as "a people" who had both a national past and national traditions.

A Modernizing Elite Leaders of the nationalist opposition were western-educated intellectuals from colonial cities and towns. Although a tiny minority of the Indian population, they gained influence through their access to the official world and their familiarity with European knowledge and history. This elite group used their knowledge to develop modern cultural forms. For example, they turned colloquial languages (such as Hindi, Urdu, Bengali, Tamil, and Malayalam) into standardized, literary forms for writing novels and dramas. Now the publication of journals, magazines, newspapers, pamphlets, novels, and dramas surged, facilitating communication throughout British India.

Along with print culture came a growing public sphere where intellectuals debated social and political matters. By 1885, voluntary associations in big cities had united to establish a political party, the Indian National Congress. Lawyers, prominent merchants, and local notables dominated its early leadership. The congress demanded greater representation of Indians in administrative and legislative bodies, criticized the government's economic policies, and encouraged India's industrialization.

Underlying this political nationalism, embodied by the Indian National Congress, was cultural nationalism. The nationalists claimed that Indians might not be a single race but were at least a unified people, because of their unique culture and common colonial history.

Rewriting Traditions The recovery of traditions became a way to establish a modern Indian identity without acknowledging the recent subjugation by British colonizers. So Indian intellectuals (like those in Latin America) turned to the past and rewrote the histories of ancient empires and kingdoms. In this way, Indian intellectuals promoted the idea of India as a nation-state.

To portray Indians as a people with a unifying religious creed, intellectuals reconfigured Hinduism so that it resembled western religion. This was no easy task, for traditional Hinduism did not have a supreme textual authority, like the Bible or the Quran, a monotheistic God, an organized church, or an established creed. Nonetheless, nationalist Hindu intellectuals combined various philosophical texts, cultural beliefs, social practices, and Hindu traditions into a mix that they labeled the authentic Hindu religion. While fashioning hybrid forms, revivalists also narrowed the definition of Indian traditions.

As Hindu intellectuals looked back, they identified Hindu traditions and the pre-Islamic past as the only sources of India's culture. Other contributors to the region's mosaic past were forgotten; the Muslim past, in particular, had no prominent role.

Hindu Revivalism Hindu revivalism became a powerful political force in the late nineteenth century, when the nationalist challenge to the colonial regime took a militant turn. New leaders rejected constitutionalism and called for militant agitation. The British decision to partition Bengal in 1905 into two provinces—one predominantly Muslim, the other Hindu—drew militants into the streets to urge the boycott of British goods. Rabindranath Tagore, a famous Bengali poet and future Nobel laureate, composed stirring nationalist poetry. Activists formed voluntary organizations, called Swadeshi ("one's own country") Samitis ("societies"), that championed indigenous enterprises for manufacturing soap, cloth, medicine, iron, and paper, as well as schools for imparting nationalist education. Although few of these ventures succeeded, the efforts reflected the nationalist desire to assert Indians' autonomy as a people.

Unlike the insurgents of 1857, nationalist leaders in India at the turn of the twentieth century imagined a modern national community. Invoking religious and ethnic symbols, they formed modern political associations to operate in a national public arena. They did not seek a radical alternative to the colonial order; instead, they fought for the political rights of Indians as a secular, national community. In these new nationalists, British rulers discovered an enemy not so different from themselves.

THE PAN MOVEMENTS

India and China were not the only places where activists dreamed of founding new states. Across the globe, groups had begun to imagine new communities based on ethnicity or, in some cases, religion. **Pan movements** (from the Greek *pan*, "all") sought to link people across state boundaries. The grand aspiration of all these movements—which included pan-Asianism, pan-Islamism, pan-Africanism, pan-Slavism, pan-Turkism, pan-Arabism, pan-Germanism, and Zionism—was the rearrangement of borders in order to unite dispersed communities. But such remappings posed a threat to rulers of the Russian, Austrian, and Ottoman Empires, as well as to overseers of the British and the French colonial empires.

pan movements
Groups that sought to link people across state boundaries in new communities based on ethnicity or, in some cases, religion (e.g., pan-Germanism, pan-Islamism, pan-Slavism).

Pan-Islamism Within the Muslim world, intellectuals and political leaders begged their fellow Muslims to put aside their differences and unite under the banner of Islam in opposition to European incursions. The leading spokesman for pan-Islamism was the well-traveled Jamal al-Din al-Afghani

(1839–1897). Born in Iran and given a Shiite upbringing, he nonetheless called on Muslims worldwide to overcome their Sunni and Shiite differences so that they could work together against the west. Afghani called for unity and action, for an end to corruption and stagnation, and for acceptance of the true principles of Islam.

The pan-Islamic message only added to Muslims' confusion as they confronted the west. Indeed, Arab Muslims living as Ottoman subjects had many calls on their loyalties. Should they support the Ottoman Empire to resist European encroachments? Or should they embrace the Islamism of Afghani? Most decided to work within the fledgling nation-states of the Islamic world, looking to a Syrian or Lebanese identity, for example, as the way to deal with the west and gain autonomy. But Afghani and his disciples had struck a chord in Muslim culture, and their Islamic message has long retained a powerful appeal.

Sultan Abdul Hamid II Agrees to a Constitution In 1876, the new Ottoman sultan, Abdul Hamid II, agreed to reign as a constitutional monarch. Thanks in part to war with Russia, which commenced the next year, and in part to the sultan's own dictatorial instincts, the Ottoman Empire reverted to an absolute monarchy within two years, and the sultan began to promote himself as a Muslim leader.

Pan-Germanism and Pan-Slavism Pan-Germanism found followers across central Europe, where it often competed with a pan-Slavic movement that sought to unite all Slavs against their Austrian, German, and Ottoman overlords. This area had traditionally been ruled by German-speaking elites, who owned the land farmed by Slavic peasants. German elites began to feel increasingly uneasy as Slavic nationalisms (spurred by the midcentury revivals of traditional Czech, Polish, Serbian, and Ukrainian languages and cultures) became more popular. Even more threatening was the fact that the Slavic populations were growing faster than the German population. As pogroms in the Russian Empire's borderlands in the 1880s, as well as economic opportunities, drove crowds of eastern European Jews westward, German resentment toward these newcomers also increased.

The rhetoric of pan-Germanism inspired mass, grassroots political activism. It motivated central Europeans to think of themselves as members of a German *race*, their identities determined by blood rather than defined by state boundaries. This, too, was the lesson of pan-Slavism. Both movements led extremists to take actions that were dangerous to existing states. The organization of networks of radical southern Slavs, for example, unsettled Bosnia and Herzegovina (annexed by the Austrians in 1908). Indeed, it was a

Serbian proponent of plans to carve an independent Slav state out of Austrian territory in the Balkans who assassinated the heir to the Habsburg throne in June 1914. By August, the whole of Europe had descended into mass warfare, bringing much of the rest of the world directly or indirectly into the conflict as well. Eventually, the war would fulfill the pan-Slav, pan-German, and anti-Ottoman Muslim nationalist longing to tear down the Ottoman and Habsburg Empires. Intellectuals articulated the pan movements, but aspiring political leaders and secret societies took up their ideologies, leaving Europe and much of Asia at the end of the nineteenth century boiling with ideas of how to change the borders of states and the dominance of France and Britain.

Conclusion

Ever since the Enlightenment, Europeans had put their faith in "progress." Through the nineteenth century, educated, secular elites took pride in booming industries, bustling cities, and burgeoning colonial empires. Yet by the century's end, urbanization and industrialization seemed more disrupting than uplifting, more disorienting than reassuring. Moreover, colonized people's resistance to the "civilizing mission" fueled doubts about the course of progress.

The realization that "the people" were developing ways to unseat them terrified ruling elites. In colonial settings, nationalists learned how to mobilize large populations. In Europe, socialist and right-wing leaders likewise challenged liberals by appealing to the idea of popular sovereignty. A politics that relied on closed-door negotiations between "rational" gentlemen was unprepared to deal with modern ideas and identities.

Nor were elites able to control the scope of change, for the expansion of empires had drawn ever more people into an unbalanced global economy. Everywhere, disparities in wealth appeared. Moreover, the size and power of industrial operations threatened small firms and made individuals seem insignificant. Even some cities seemed too big and too dangerous. All these social and economic challenges stretched the capacities of gentlemanly politics.

They also stimulated creative energy. Western artists borrowed nonwestern images and vocabularies; nonwestern intellectuals looked to the west for inspiration, even as they formulated anti-western ideas. The upheavals of modern experience propelled scholars to study the past and to fabricate utopian visions of the future.

Even as these changes unsettled the European-centered world, they intensified rivalries among Europe's powers themselves. Although the world had become a smaller place and travel was easier and quicker, at least for those who had wealth and came from powerful societies, this increasing global integration had its limitations and contradictions. At its center—Europe—the global order was unstable. And in the massive conflict that destroyed this era's faith in progress, Europe would ravage itself. The Great War (described in Chapter 19) would yield an age of even more rapid change—with even more violent consequences.

Focus On

Sources of Global Anxieties and Expressions of Cultural Modernism

Global Trends

- Mass migrations and unprecedented urban expansion challenge national identities.

Africa and China: Anticolonialism

- The Anglo-Boer War and violent uprisings against colonial rule in Africa call Europe's imperializing mission into question.

- The Chinese rise up against European encroachments in the Boxer Uprising.

Europe and North America: Mounting Tensions

- Intense political rivalries, financial insecurities and crises, rapid industrialization, feminism, and class conflict roil Europe and spread to the rest of the world.

Mexico: Resentment toward Elites

- The most widespread revolution from below takes place in Mexico.

Cultural Modernism

- Increased earning power gives workers in wealthy nations the leisure to enjoy music, vaudeville shows, sports, and other forms of popular culture and to read mass-circulation newspapers.

- Elite culture explores new forms in painting, architecture, music, literature, and science in order to break with the past and differentiate itself more dramatically from popular culture.

- New ideas of race emerge, as does a renewed emphasis on the nation-state and nationalism.

Key Terms

anarchists p. 852

Boxer Uprising p. 844

Mexican Revolution p. 852

modernism p. 853

pan movements p. 866

popular culture p. 854

progressive reformers p. 853

Shanghai School p. 857

Sun Yat-sen p. 861

syndicalists p. 852

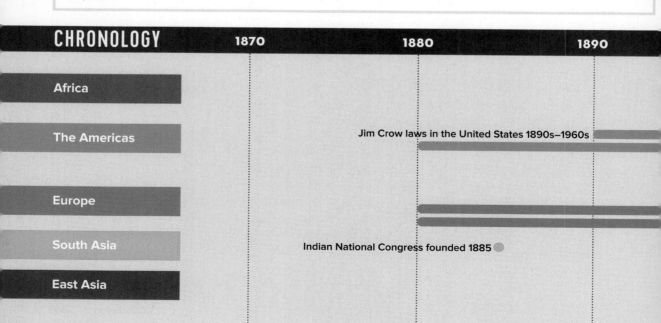

CHRONOLOGY

	1870	1880	1890
Africa			
The Americas		Jim Crow laws in the United States 1890s–1960s	
Europe			
South Asia		Indian National Congress founded 1885	
East Asia			

THINKING ABOUT GLOBAL CONNECTIONS

- **Thinking about Crossing Borders and an Unsettled World** How did mobility of different kinds unsettle established certainties in this period? Think in particular of the massive flight of farmers toward cities and the erosion of traditional social hierarchies; the prevalence of steamships and rail travel, which made long-distance journeys easier than ever before; and the emergence of the telephone and telegraph, which revolutionized communications.

- **Thinking about Changing Power Relationships and an Unsettled World** To what extent were challenges to western influence internal to the western tradition—the product of growing doubts and contradictions within the Enlightenment project—articulated by

Europeans like Nietzsche and Freud? To what degree were they external to that tradition—a reaction against the massive concentration of wealth and power centered in the west and the values that supported western dominance?

- **Thinking about Women and Gender in an Unsettled World** To what degree did the economic and technological breakthroughs of the nineteenth century improve women's lives? To what extent were women able to make claims on governments in different parts of the world? How did ordinary women take control of their bodies and their lives, and how did feminists challenge patriarchal cultures?

 Go to **INQUIZITIVE** to see what you've learned—and learn what you've missed—with personalized feedback along the way.

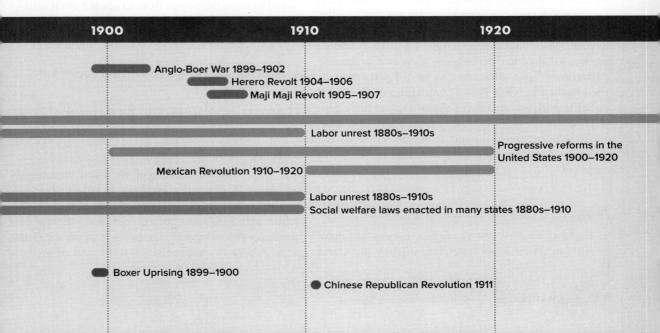

1900	1910	1920

Anglo-Boer War 1899–1902
Herero Revolt 1904–1906
Maji Maji Revolt 1905–1907

Labor unrest 1880s–1910s
Progressive reforms in the United States 1900–1920
Mexican Revolution 1910–1920
Labor unrest 1880s–1910s
Social welfare laws enacted in many states 1880s–1910

Boxer Uprising 1899–1900
Chinese Republican Revolution 1911

Global Themes and Sources

Global Feminisms

The word *feminist* first entered common usage in French in the 1890s; shortly thereafter, it appeared in English and then in a wide array of languages. Demands for women's rights, however, emerged long before that, as we have seen, and they did so around the world.

Here we present a range of women's voices on women's rights. From the middle of the nineteenth century to the early twentieth, all four women spoke up on behalf of women and basic justice. All invoked religion in their writings. But they made their cases in very different ways: they differed in particular in their appreciation (or rejection) of women's difference from men and, in varying degrees, in their views of work, education, and the importance of motherhood. A former slave turned abolitionist orator and preacher, Sojourner Truth (c. 1787–1883) was unable to read or write. However, she left an indelible mark with her speeches. In the speech reprinted here, delivered at a women's rights convention in Akron, Ohio, in 1851, she rebukes the antifeminist statements of white male ministers. The next three documents were written by privileged women. Argentine writer María Eugenia Echenique centers her argument on equality of opportunity in an article published in a feminist journal. In a public speech Qiu Jin urges Chinese women to take their destiny into their own hands and encourages those who marry to be full partners with their husbands, while Bahithat al-Badiya concentrates in her lecture on equality in the workplace for Egyptian women.

Compare these documents. Pay attention to the different ways in which they all challenge women's exclusion.

Analyzing Global Feminisms Comparatively

- Explain what women's rights means to these authors. What supports rights, in their view, and what stands in the way of rights? Do the authors agree or disagree with one another?
- What social classes did these women represent? Explain the significance of class in each document.
- Compare the opinions of marriage and motherhood expressed in these documents.
- Compare the distinctions the texts draw between the private and public life.

PRIMARY SOURCE 18.1

"Ain't I a Woman?" (1851), Sojourner Truth

Born a slave in New York State, Sojourner Truth gained her freedom in 1827 and became well known as an abolitionist speaker and advocate of women's rights. This document is an extemporaneous speech to a women's convention in Akron, Ohio, in 1851, as remembered later by Frances D. Gage.

- Why did the other women at the meeting ask Gage not to allow Sojourner Truth to speak? What were they afraid of?
- What does Truth mean when she says, "Ain't I a woman?"
- What role does religion play in this document?

Reminiscences by Frances D. Gage.

Sojourner Truth.

The leaders of the movement trembled on seeing a tall, gaunt black woman in a gray dress and white turban, surmounted with an uncouth sun-bonnet, march deliberately into the church, walk with the air of a queen up the aisle, and take her seat upon the pulpit steps. A buzz of disapprobation was heard all over the house, and there fell on the listening ear, "An abolition affair!" "Woman's rights and niggers!" "I told you so!" "Go it, darkey!"

I chanced on that occasion to wear my first laurels in public life as president of the meeting. At my request order was restored, and the business of the Convention went on. Morning, afternoon, and evening exercises came and went. Through all these sessions old Sojourner, quiet and reticent as the "Lybian Statue," sat crouched against the wall on the corner of the pulpit stairs, her sun-bonnet shading her eyes, her elbows on her knees, her chin resting upon her broad, hard palms. At intermission she was busy selling the "Life of Sojourner Truth," a narrative of her own strange and adventurous life. Again and again, timorous and trembling ones came to me and said, with earnestness, "Don't let her speak, Mrs. Gage, it will ruin us. Every newspaper in the land will have our cause mixed up with abolition and niggers, and we shall be utterly denounced." My only answer was, "We shall see when the time comes."

The second day the work waxed warm. Methodist, Baptist, Episcopal, Presbyterian, and Universalist minister came in to hear and discuss the resolutions presented. One claimed superior rights and privileges for man, on the ground of "superior intellect"; another, because of the "manhood of Christ; if God had desired the equality of woman, He would have given some token of His will through the birth, life, and death of the Saviour." Another gave us a theological view of the "sin of our first mother."

There were very few women in those days who dared to "speak in meeting"; and the august teachers of the people were seemingly getting the better of us, while the boys in the galleries, and the sneerers among the pews, were hugely enjoying the discomfiture, as they supposed, of the "strong-minded." Some of the tender-skinned friends were on the point of losing dignity, and the atmosphere betokened a storm. When, slowly from her seat in the corner rose Sojourner Truth, who, till now, had scarcely lifted her head. "Don't let her speak!" gasped half a dozen in my ear. She moved slowly and solemnly to the front, laid her old bonnet at her feet, and turned her great speaking eyes to me. There was a hissing sound of disapprobation above and below. I rose and announced, "Sojourner Truth," and begged the audience to keep silence for a few moments.

The tumult subsided at once, and every eye was fixed on this almost Amazon form, which stood nearly six feet high, head erect, and eyes piercing the upper air like one in a dream. At her first word there was a profound hush. She spoke in deep tones, which, though not loud, reached every ear in the house, and away through the throng at the doors and windows.

"Wall, chilern, whar dar is so much racket dar must be somethin' out o' kilter. I tink dat 'twixt de niggers of de Souf and de womin at de Norf, all talkin' 'bout rights, de white men will be in a fix pretty soon. But what's all dis here talkin' 'bout?

"Dat man ober dar say dat womin needs to be helped into carriages, and lifted ober ditches, and to hab de best place everywhar. Nobody eber helps me into carriages, or ober mud-puddles, or gibs me any best place!" And raising herself to her full height, and her voice to a pitch like rolling thunder, she asked, "And a'n't I a woman? Look at me! Look at my arm! (and she bared her right arm to the shoulder, showing her tremendous muscular power). I have ploughed, and planted, and gathered into barns, and no man could head me! And a'n't I a woman? I could work as much and eat as much as a man—when I could get it—and bear de lash as well! And a'n't I a woman? I have borne thirteen chilern, and seen 'em mos' all sold off to slavery, and when I cried out with my mother's grief, none but Jesus heard me! And a'n't I a woman?

"Den dey talks 'bout dis ting in de head; what dis dey call it?" ("Intellect," whispered some one near.) "Dat's it, honey. What's dat got to do wid womin's rights or nigger's rights? If my cup won't hold but a pint, and yourn holds a quart, wouldn't ye be mean not to let me have my little half-measure full?" And she pointed her significant finger, and sent a keen glance at the minister who had made the argument. The cheering was long and loud.

"Den dat little man in black dar, he say women can't have as much rights as men, 'cause Christ wan't a woman! Whar did your Christ come from?" Rolling thunder couldn't have stilled that crowd, as did those deep, wonderful tones, as she stood there with outstretched arms and eyes of fire. Raising her voice still louder, she repeated, "Whar did your Christ come from? From God and a woman! Man had nothin' to do wid Him." Oh, what a rebuke that was to that little man.

Turning again to another objector, she took up the defense of Mother Eve. I can not follow her through it all. It was pointed, and witty, and solemn; eliciting at almost every sentence deafening applause; and she ended by asserting: "If de fust woman God ever made was strong enough to turn de world upside down all alone, dese women togedder (and she glanced her eye over the platform) ought to be able to turn it back, and get it right side up again! And now dey is asking to do it, de men better let 'em." Long-continued cheering greeted this. "'Bleeged to ye for hearin' on me, and now ole Sojourner han't got nothin' more to say."

Amid roars of applause, she returned to her corner, leaving more than one of us with streaming eyes, and hearts beating with gratitude. She had taken us up in her strong arms and carried us safely over the slough of difficulty turning the whole tide in our favor. I have never in my life seen anything like the magical influence that subdued the mobbish spirit of the day, and turned the sneers and jeers of an excited crowd into notes of respect and admiration. Hundreds rushed up to shake hands with her, and congratulate the glorious old mother, and bid her God-speed on her mission of "testifyin' agin concerning the wickedness of this 'ere people."

Source: Sojourner Truth, "Ain't I a Woman?" in *History of Woman Suffrage*, vol. 1, 2nd ed., edited by Elizabeth Cady Stanton, Susan B. Anthony, and Matilda Joslyn Gage (Rochester, NY: Charles Mann, 1889), 115–17.

PRIMARY SOURCE 18.2

"The Emancipation of Women" (1876), María Eugenia Echenique

In Argentina, the young writer María Eugenia Echenique (1851–1878) advocated scientific education for women. She presented her views in a leading women's newspaper, *La Ondina del Plata*, in July 1876, in reply to a critic who celebrated women's role as mothers who were responsible for the home and could only be corrupted by public life.

- **What, according to Echenique, is the principal obstacle standing in the way of women's rights?**
- **What is the relationship between motherhood and women's rights?**
- **Explain the significance of biological difference in this document.**

When emancipation was given to men, it was also given to women in recognition of the equality of rights, consistent with the principles of nature on which they are founded, that proclaim the identity of soul between men and women. Thus, Argentine women have been emancipated by law for a long time. The code of law that governs us authorizes a widow to defend her rights in court, just as an educated woman can in North America, and like her, we can manage the interests of our children, these rights being the basis for emancipation. What we lack is sufficient education and instruction to make use of them, instruction that North American women have; it is not just recently that we have proclaimed our freedom. To try to question or to oppose women's emancipation is to oppose something that is almost a fact, it is to attack our laws and destroy the Republic.

So let the debate be there, on the true point where it should be: whether or not it is proper for women to make use of those granted rights, asking as a consequence the authorization to go to the university so as to practice those rights or make them effective. And this constitutes another right and duty in woman: a duty to accept the role that our own laws bestow on her when extending the circle of her jurisdiction and which makes her responsible before the members of her family.

This, assuming that the woman is a mother. But, are all women going to marry? Are all going to be relegated to a life of inaction during their youth or while they remain single? Is it so easy for all women to look for a stranger to defend their offended dignity, their belittled honor, their stolen interests? Don't we see every day how the laws are trodden underfoot, and the victim, being a woman, is forced to bow her head because she does not know how to defend herself, exposed to lies and tricks because she does not know the way to clarify the truth?

Far from causing the breakdown of the social classes, the emancipation of women would establish morality and justice in them; men would have a brake that would halt the "imperious need" that they have made of the "lies and tricks" of litigations, and the science of jurisprudence, so sacred and magnificent in itself but degenerated today because of abuses, would return to its splendor and true objective once women take part in the forum. Generous and abnegated by nature, women would teach men humanitarian principles and would condemn the frenzy and insults that make a battlefield out of the courtroom.

"Women either resolve to drown the voice of their hearts, or they listen to that voice and renounce emancipation." If emancipation is opposed to the tender sentiments, to the voice of the heart, then men who are completely emancipated and study science are not capable of love. The beautiful and tender girl who gives her heart to a doctor or to a scientist, gives it, then, to a stony man, incapable of appreciating it or responding to her; women could not love emancipated men, because where women find love, men find it too; in both burns the same heart's flame. I have seen that those who do not practice science, who do not know their duties or the rights of women, who are ignorant, are the ones who abandon their wives, not the ones who, concentrated on their studies and duties, barely have time to give them a caress.

Men as much as women are victims of the indifference that ignorance, not science, produces. Men are more slaves of women who abuse the prestige of their weakness and become tyrants in their home, than of the schooled and scientific women who understand their duties and are capable of something. With the former the husband has to play the role of man and woman, because she ignores everything: she is not capable of consoling nor helping her husband, she is not capable of giving tenderness, because, preoccupied with herself, she becomes demanding, despotic, and vain, and she does not know how to make a happy home. For her there are no responsibilities to carry out, only whims to satisfy. This is typical, we see it happening every day.

The ignorant woman, the one who voluntarily closes her heart to the sublime principles that provoke sweet emotions in it and elevate the mind, revealing to men the deep secrets of the All-Powerful; the woman incapable of helping her husband in great enterprises for fear of losing the prestige of her weakness and ignorance; the woman who only aspires to get married and reproduce, and understands maternity as the only mission of women on earth—she can be the wife of a savage, because in him she can satisfy all her aspirations and hopes, following that law of nature that operates even on beasts and inanimate beings.

I would renounce and disown my sex if the mission of women were reduced only to procreation, yes, I would renounce it; but the mission of women in the world is much more grandiose and sublime, it is more than the beasts', it is the one of teaching humankind, and in order to teach it is necessary to know. A mother should know science in order to inspire in her children great deeds and noble sentiments, making them feel superior to the other objects in the universe, teaching them from the cradle to become familiar with great scenes of nature where they should go to look for God and love Him. And nothing more sublime and ideal than the scientific mother who, while her husband goes to cafes or to the political club to talk about state interests, she goes to spend some of the evening at the astronomical observatory, with her children by the hand to show them Jupiter, Venus, preparing in that way their tender hearts for the most legitimate and sublime aspirations that could occupy men's minds. This sacred mission in the scientific mother who understands emancipation—the fulfillment of which, far from causing the abandonment of the home, causes it to unite more closely—instead of causing displeasure to her husband, she will cause his happiness.

The abilities of men are not so miserable that the carrying out of one responsibility would make it impossible to carry out others. There is enough time and competence for cooking and mending, and a great soul such as that of women, equal to that of their mates, born to embrace all the beauty that exists in Creation of divine origin and end, should not be wasted all on seeing if the plates are clean and rocking the cradle.

Source: María Eugenia Echenique, "The Emancipation of Women," translated by Francisco Manzo Robledo, in *Reading about the World*, vol. 2, edited by Paul Brians et al. (Boston: Harcourt Brace College Publishing, 1999).

Injustices to Chinese Women (early twentieth century), Qiu Jin

Qiu Jin (1875–1907) was a Chinese revolutionary, feminist, and writer. She left her two children and an abusive marriage behind in 1903 to travel to Japan, where she wore men's clothing and learned to make bombs. She joined a range of overseas Chinese groups that strove to overthrow the Qing Empire and was later executed for her role in an abortive nationalist uprising. In the public address reprinted here, Qiu speaks out against arranged marriages and urges women to take charge of their own future.

- According to Qiu Jin, what is the principal obstacle standing in the way of women's rights?
- On what basis does Qiu criticize arranged marriages?
- What significance, if any, does motherhood have in this document? Does Qiu demand women's rights as mothers and educators of children or on some other basis?

An Address to Two Hundred Million Fellow Countrywomen

Alas! The greatest injustice in this world must be the injustice suffered by our female population of two hundred million. If a girl is lucky enough to have a good father, then her childhood is at least tolerable. But if by chance her father is an ill-tempered and unreasonable man, he may curse her birth: "What rotten luck: another useless thing." Some men go as far as killing baby girls while most hold the opinion that "girls are eventually someone else's property" and treat them with coldness and disdain. In a few years, without thinking about whether it is right or wrong, he forcibly binds his daughter's soft, white feet with white cloth so that even in her sleep she cannot find comfort and relief until the flesh becomes rotten and the bones broken. What is all this misery for? Is it just so that on the girl's wedding day friends and neighbors will compliment him, saying, "Your daughter's feet are really small"? Is that what the pain is for?

But that is not the worst of it. When the time for marriage comes, a girl's future life is placed in the hands of a couple of shameless matchmakers and a family seeking rich and powerful in-laws. A match can be made without anyone ever inquiring whether the prospective bridegroom is honest, kind, or educated. On the day of the marriage the girl is forced into a red and green bridal sedan chair, and all this time she is not allowed to breathe one word about her future. After her marriage, if the man doesn't do her any harm, she is told that she should thank Heaven for her good fortune. But if the man is bad or if he ill-treats her, she is told that her marriage is retribution for some sin committed in her previous existence. If she complains at all or tries to reason with her husband, he may get angry and beat her. When other people find out they will criticize, saying, "That woman is bad; she doesn't know how to behave like a wife." What can she do? When a man dies, his wife must mourn him for three years and never remarry. But if the woman dies, her husband only needs to tie his queue with a blue thread. Some men consider this to be ugly and don't even do it. In some cases, three days after his wife's death, a man will go out for some "entertainment." Sometimes, before seven weeks have passed, a new bride has already arrived at the door. When Heaven created people it never intended such injustice because if the world is without women, how can men be born? Why is there no justice for women? We constantly hear men say, "The human mind is just and we must treat people with fairness and equality." Then why do they greet women like black slaves from Africa? How did inequality and injustice reach this state?

Dear sisters, you must know that you'll get nothing if you rely upon others. You must go out and get things for yourselves. In ancient times when decadent scholars came out with such nonsense as "men are exalted, women are lowly," "a virtuous women is one without talent," and "the husband guides the wife," ambitious and spirited women should have organized and opposed them. When the second Chen ruler popularized footbinding, women should have challenged him if they had any sense of humiliation at all. . . . Men feared that if women were educated they would become superior to men, so they did not allow us to be educated. Couldn't the women have challenged the men and refused to submit? It seems clear now that it was we women who abandoned our responsibilities to ourselves and felt content to let men do everything for us. As long as we could live in comfort and leisure, we let men make all the decisions for us. When men said we were useless, we became useless; when they said we were incapable, we stopped questioning them even when our entire female sex had reached slave status. At the same time we were insecure in our good fortune and our physical comfort, so we did everything to please men. When we heard that men like small feet, we immediately bound them just to please them, just to keep our free meal tickets. As for their forbidding us to read and write, well, that was only too good to be true. We readily agreed. Think about it, sisters, can anyone enjoy such comfort and leisure without forfeiting dearly for it? It was only natural that men, with their knowledge, wisdom, and hard work, received the right to freedom while we became their slaves. And as slaves, how can we escape repression? Whom can we blame but ourselves since we have brought this on ourselves? I feel very sad talking about this, yet I feel that there is no need for me to elaborate since all of us are in the same situation.

I hope that we all shall put aside the past and work hard for the future. Let us all put aside our former selves and be resurrected as complete human beings. Those of you who are old, do not call yourselves old and useless. If your husbands want to open schools, don't stop them; if your good sons want to study abroad, don't hold them back. Those among us who are middle-aged, don't hold back your husbands lest they lose their ambition and spirit and fail in their work. After your sons are born, send them to schools. You must do the same for your daughters and, whatever you do, don't bind their feet. As for you young girls among us, go to school if you can. If not, read and study at home. Those of you who are rich, persuade your husbands to open schools, build factories, and contribute to charitable organizations. Those of you who are poor, work hard and help your husbands. Don't be lazy, don't eat idle rice. These are what I hope for you. You must know that when a country is near destruction, women cannot rely on the men any more because

they aren't even able to protect themselves. If we don't take heart now and shape up, it will be too late when China is destroyed.

Sisters, we must follow through on these ideas!

Source: Qiu Jin, "An Address to Two Hundred Million Fellow Country-women," in *Chinese Civilization: A Sourcebook*, 2nd ed., edited by Patricia Buckley Ebrey (New York: Free Press, 1993), pp. 342–44.

PRIMARY SOURCE 18.4

Industrialization and Women's Freedom in Egypt (1909), Bahithat al-Badiya

Malak Hifni Nasif (1886–1918) was born into a literary, middle-class Cairo family that encouraged her education. She was a member of the first graduating class of the Girls' Section of the 'Abbas Primary School in 1901 and continued her schooling in the Saniyyah Teacher Training College but had to quit when she married. She moved to the desert and began writing under the pseudonym Bahithat al-Badiya ("Seeker in the Desert").

....

- **How does the author's social background shape her views?**
- **Analyze the relationship between public and private in this text. What is the author's view of the idea of separate spheres for men and women?**
- **Explain al-Badiya's support for the veil.**

....

A Lecture in the Club of the Umma Party

Ladies, I greet you as a sister who feels what you feel, suffers what you suffer and rejoices in what you rejoice. . . .

Our meeting today is not simply for getting acquainted or for displaying our finery but it is a serious meeting. I wish to seek agreement on an approach we can take and to examine our shortcomings in order to correct them. . . . At the moment there is a semi-feud between us and men because of the low level of agreement between us. Men blame the discord on our poor upbringing and haphazard education while we claim it is due to men's arrogance and pride. This mutual blame which has deepened the antagonism between the sexes is something to be regretted and feared. God did not create man and woman to hate each other but to love each other and to live together so the world would be populated. If men live alone in one part of the world and women are isolated in another both will vanish in time.

Men say when we become educated we shall push them out of work and abandon the role for which God has created us. But, isn't it rather men who have pushed women out of work? Before, women used to spin and to weave cloth for clothes for themselves and their children, but men invented machines for spinning and weaving and put women out of work. In the past, women sewed clothes for themselves and their households but men invented the sewing machine. The iron for these machines is mined by men and the machines themselves are made by men. Then men took up the profession of tailoring and began to make clothes for our men and children. Before women winnowed the wheat and ground flour on grinding stones for the bread they used to make with their own hands, sifting flour and kneading dough. Then men established bakeries employing men. They gave us rest but at the same time pushed us out of work. . . .

I do not mean to denigrate these useful inventions which do a lot of our work. Nor do I mean to imply that they do not satisfy our needs. But, I simply wanted to show that men are the ones who started to push us out of work and that if we were to edge them out today we would only be doing what they have already done to us.

The question of monopolising the workplace comes down to individual freedom. One man wishes to become a doctor, another a merchant. Is it right to tell a doctor he must quit his profession and become a merchant or vice versa? No. Each has the freedom to do as he wishes. . . .

Specialised work for each sex is a matter of convention. It is not mandatory. We women are now unable to do hard work because we have not been accustomed to it. . . .

Nothing irritates me more than when men claim they do not wish us to work because they wish to spare us the burden. We do not want condescension,

we want respect. They should replace the first with the second. . . .

Men criticise the way we dress in the street. They have a point because we have exceeded the bounds of custom and propriety. We claim we are veiling but we are neither properly covered nor unveiled. I do not advocate a return to the veils of our grandmothers because it can rightly be called being buried alive, not *hijab*, correct covering. The woman used to spend her whole life within the walls of her house not going out into the street except when she was carried to her grave. I do not, on the other hand, advocate unveiling, like Europeans, and mixing with men, because they are harmful to us. . . .

If we had been raised from childhood to go unveiled and if our men were ready for it I would approve of unveiling for those who want it. But the nation is not ready for it now. . . .

Veiling should not prevent us from breathing fresh air or going out to buy what we need if no one can buy it for us. It must not prevent us from gaining an education nor cause our health to deteriorate. When we have finished our work and feel restless and if our house does not have a spacious garden why shouldn't we go to the outskirts of the city and take the fresh air that God has created for everyone and not just put in boxes exclusively for men. But, we should be prudent and not take promenades alone and we should avoid gossip. We should not saunter moving our heads right and left. . . .

The imprisonment in the home of the Egyptian woman of the past is detrimental while the current freedom of the Europeans is excessive. I cannot find a better model of today's Turkish woman. She falls between the two extremes and does not violate what Islam prescribes. She is a good example of decorum and modesty. . . .

If we pursue everything western we shall destroy our own civilisation and a nation that has lost its civilisation grows weak and vanishes.

Source: Bahithat al-Badiya, "A Public Lecture for Women Only in the Club of the Umma Party," from "Industrialization and Women's Freedom in Egypt," in *Opening the Gates: A Century of Arab Feminist Writing*, edited by Margot Badran and Miriam Cooke (Bloomington: Indiana University Press, 1990), pp. 228–34, 236.

Interpreting Visual Evidence

Global Modernism

Modernism was an international cultural movement that reacted against established traditions and sought to mark a break between the old and the new. In Europe, the movement's center, modernists challenged the Enlightenment belief in stable, universal truth. They criticized realism—the attempt to reproduce the natural world and human interactions faithfully, like a photograph—as naïve and superficial; they believed realists compressed a three-dimensional reality into two and left out the passions and often-irrational urges that motivate human behavior.

When the Franco-Spanish artist Pablo Picasso first showed his painting *Les Demoiselles d'Avignon* (The Courtesans of Avignon; 1907), his friends accused him of wasting his talents, and outraged critics likened the canvas to a broken pane of glass. Picasso broke all the rules of the art academies. He abandoned

Picasso, *Les Demoiselles d'Avignon.*

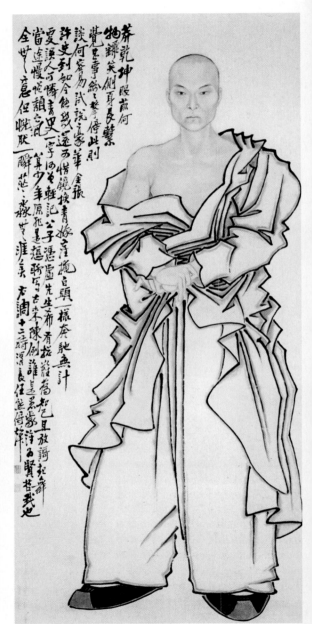

Ren Xiong, *Self-Portrait.*

perspective and proportion, distorted shapes, and borrowed from what at the time were considered primitive cultures in order to criticize the hypocrisies of bourgeois European culture. Rather than idealizing the human form of nymphs or classical goddesses, Picasso rendered it in jagged, jarring terms, presenting five common prostitutes in a brothel.

Tagore, *Bharat Mata*.

Influenced by Europe, modernists elsewhere challenged a different set of established traditions, but they too set out to redefine what it meant to be modern. For them, the problem was how to be Bengali, Chinese, or Egyptian, for example, and modern at the same time. In the self-portrait shown here (1850s), the Shanghai School artist Ren Xiong relied on old conventions in Chinese art, but the subject's pose, his facial expression, the physicality of his uncovered shoulder, and his engagement with the viewer all pointed in a new direction, as if to contrast the artist's experience with the established traditions of Chinese art.

The Indian artist Abanindranath Tagore painted a number of works that drew inspiration from Mughal art. His best known work, *Bharat Mata* (Mother India; 1905), presents a young woman with four arms, in the manner of Hindu gods, holding symbols of India's national aspirations—a book, sheaves of rice, Hindu prayer beads, and a white cloth—in an effort to create nationalist feeling in Indians across the subcontinent.

Questions for Analysis

1. Identify similarities in these works. Do you see connections in terms of the use of color or other artistic techniques? What characteristics, if any, do they share?

2. Who do you think made up the audiences for these works? With whom were the artists trying to communicate? To whom were they responding? How broad do you think they imagined their public was, compared to the audiences for the images reproduced in the Interpreting Visual Evidence section of Chapter 17?

3. What do you think each artist understood by the term *modern*, and how is this reflected in his work?

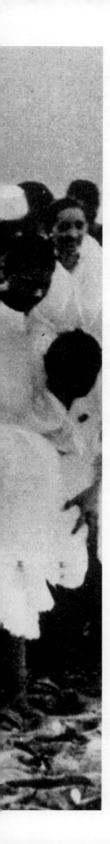

19

Of Masses and

Visions of the Modern

1910–1939

The last guns of the Great War (World War I) fell silent in a remote corner of East Africa. It took a full day for news of the armistice to reach that region, where African soldiers, under British and German officers, were battling for control of German East Africa. Here, 10,000 German-led African soldiers used guerrilla tactics to thwart the efforts of over 300,000 British-led African soldiers. Thousands of African troops died in these battles, beyond the spotlight of international opinion. Although most major battles occurred on European soil, campaigns bloodied the soil in sub-Saharan Africa, Egypt, Syria, and Turkey as well, and millions of African, Asian, and American soldiers were ferried across oceans to join the fight in Europe. The war's impact was thoroughly global.

Raging from August 1914 to November 1918, the Great War shook the foundations of the European-centered world. In addition to involving soldiers from Europe's colonies, it spread notions of freedom and self-determination and a growing disillusionment with European rule. Elsewhere, nations grappled with competing visions for building stable governments and strong economies.

This chapter deals with the Great War and its global impact. First, because the war was fought on a worldwide scale and to utter exhaustion in Europe, it required the resources of a large part of the world. It prompted production and consumption on a mass scale. Wartime leaders also used new media such as radio and film to promote

Core Objectives

- **IDENTIFY** the causes of World War I, and **ANALYZE** the effects of the war on regions both within and outside Europe.

- **EXPLAIN** how the development of modern, mass societies both caused and was affected by the Great Depression.

- **COMPARE** the ideologies of liberal democracy, authoritarianism, and anticolonialism, and **EVALUATE** the success of each in this period.

- **EXPLAIN** how access to consumer goods and other aspects of mass society influenced political conflict in Asia, Africa, and Latin America.

national loyalties and to discredit enemies—and thereby helped spread a mass culture. Second, the incomplete nature of the peace settlement contributed to the outbreak of the Great Depression. Third, political turmoil surrounding the war inflamed disputes over how to manage mass societies and build a better world. To this end, three distinct visions arose: liberal democracy, authoritarianism, and anticolonialism. These ideologies competed for preeminence in the decades leading up to World War II.

Global Storylines

- The Great War (World War I) engulfs the globe, exhausts Europe, and promotes production and consumption on a mass scale.

- The harsh terms of the peace settlement produce resentment in Germany and contribute to global economic problems.

- European countries' efforts to rebuild their economies after the Great War by cutting expenses and returning to the gold standard cause the Great Depression, which directly affects the entire global economy.

- Three strikingly different visions for building a better world arise: liberal democracy, authoritarianism, and anticolonialism.

The Quest for the Modern

When people spoke of "being modern" in the 1920s and 1930s, they disagreed about what it meant. For culture and the arts (see Chapter 18), the term *modernism* has a fairly precise meaning. It emerged in the late nineteenth century as a challenge to the supposedly conservative values of realism in Europe and to established artistic traditions elsewhere. In other fields, however, there was much less agreement. Reformers have always distinguished their ideas as modern or progressive while opposing accepted norms as backward or traditional. In the early twentieth century, most people agreed that in economic terms modernity involved mass production and mass consumption. In the west, for example, the automobile, the gramophone (record player), the cinema, and the radio reflected the benefits of economic progress and mass culture. In politics, being modern meant the involvement of the masses. Everywhere people favored strong leadership to reinvigorate their societies; some wanted more democracy to replace monarchical and colonial rule while others favored more authoritarian solutions.

The first political vision of being or becoming modern—the *liberal democratic* one—confronted economic failings that beset this period, such as the Great Depression, without sacrificing market economies or representative democracy. It widened participation in politics but also gave greater power to regulatory bureaucracies. After the Great Depression spread hard times and unemployment, this predominantly American and western European model linking capitalism and democracy no longer seemed so promising. Although many countries rejected the liberal perspective, the system survived in the United States, parts of western Europe, and several Latin American nations.

For many observers, liberal democracies failed to match the astonishing dynamism of a second perspective—*authoritarianism*. Authoritarian regimes rejected democracy, subordinated the individual to the state, managed and often owned most industries, used censorship and terror to enforce loyalty, and exalted an all-powerful leader. During this period, authoritarianism was evident in both right-wing dictatorships (including fascist Italy, Nazi Germany, dictatorial Spain and Portugal, and militaristic Japan) and a left-wing dictatorship (the Soviet Union).

The third vision—*anticolonialism*—also questioned the liberal democratic order, primarily because of its connection to colonialism. However, many anticolonialists did not reject representative democracy, private property, or free markets. Resentful of European rulers who preached democracy but practiced despotism, anticolonial leaders sought to oust their colonial rulers and then find their own path to modernity, their own vision of progress. They generally favored mixing western ideas with indigenous traditions.

THE BIG PICTURE

Identify the causes of World War I. What were the effects of the war on regions both within and outside Europe?

Authoritarian and anticolonial visions of modernity both embraced technology and economic dynamism. They sought to take advantage of economic growth and mass support and redefine what freedom meant, while rejecting what they considered the hypocrisy and weakness of liberal democracy.

The Great War

Few events were more decisive in drawing men and women worldwide into national and international politics than the **Great War (World War I)**. For over four years, millions of soldiers from Europe, as well as from its dominions and colonies, killed one another. The war's carnage shook the hierarchies of prewar society around the world. Above all, the war made clear how much the power of the state now depended on the support of the people.

The war's causes were complex. At the heart of the European tensions, however, were nationalist rivalries, which pitted a rising Germany and a conflict-ridden Austria-Hungary against Britain, France, and Russia. Through most of the nineteenth century, Britain had been the preeminent power and Russia its principle rival (in Asia). By the century's end, however, the rise of Germany—Germany's industrial output surpassed Britain's—had driven Russia and France together. In 1907, Britain affiliated with them in the Triple Entente (later called the Allied Powers after Italy joined). Germany had allied with Austria-Hungary to form the Central Powers. The two rival blocs increasingly came into conflict in the Balkans, in territory formerly controlled by the Ottoman Empire

The assassination of Archduke Franz-Ferdinand of Austria in June 1914 set off a chain reaction. The assassin, a teenage Bosnian Serb named Gavrilo Princip, hoped to trigger an independence movement that would unite South Slav territories in the Austro-Hungarian Empire (see Chapter 18) with independent Serbia. The Austro-Hungarian emperor decided to take a firm stand, and the German kaiser backed him; the Russians declared support for the Serbs in an effort to uphold state prestige and stifle domestic political opposition. The British and French sought to prevent Germany and Austria from gaining any advantage. Throughout July, diplomats sought to negotiate a deal, but no one managed to prevent the outbreak of a war that would devastate all of Europe and drag its colonies into the warfare, too.

THE FIGHTING

Despite hopes for a swift resolution, the war became infamous for its duration and horrors. The initial German offensive stalled 30 miles outside Paris at the First Battle of the Marne, in September 1914. (See Map 19.1.) A stalemate

Western Front
- ← Allied advance
- ← German advance
- — The Western Front, November 1914
- •••• German offensive, spring 1918
- – – The Western Front, March 1918
- — Armistice Line, November 1918
- ✳ Major battle

Eastern Front
- ← Russian advance
- ← German advance
- — Limit of Russian advance, 1914–1915
- – – Limit of Austro-German advances, 1915–1916
- — German penetration into Russia, June 1918
- ✳ Major battle

Allies and colonies
- ← Allied advance
- ← Central Powers' advance
- – – Maximum German Advance, 1918
- — Armistice line, Nov. 11, 1918
- — Armistice line, Treaty of Brest-Litovsk, 1918

Neutral nations that joined Allies
Central Powers
Neutral nations and empires that joined Central Powers and colonies
Neutral nations

Map 19.1 World War I: The European and Middle Eastern Theaters

Most of the fighting in World War I, despite its designation as a world war, occurred in Europe. Although millions of soldiers fought on both sides, the territorial advances were relatively small. Look at the maps above, and identify all the countries where the Allies and Central Powers made advances.

- Which countries had to fight a two-front war?
- Did the armies of the Central Powers or the Allies gain the most territory during the war?
- According to your reading, how did those territorial gains affect the war's outcome?

Trenches in World War I The expectation of a short, decisive war turned out to be an illusion; instead, armies dug trenches and filled them with foot soldiers and machine guns. To advance entailed walking into a hail of machine-gun fire. Life in the trenches meant cold, dampness, rats, disease, and boredom.

ensued. Vast land armies dug trenches along the Western Front—from the English Channel through Belgium and France to the Alps—installing barbed wire and setting up machine-gun posts. Anything but glorious, life in the trenches mixed boredom, dampness, dirt, vermin, and disease, punctuated by the terror of being ordered to "go over the top" to attack the enemy's entrenched position. Doing so meant running across a "no man's land" in which machine guns mowed down almost all attackers. The war also witnessed new instruments of warfare, including poison gas; submarines; military aircraft, used primarily for reconnaissance; and, in the latter stages, tanks.

The death toll forced governments to call up more men than ever before. More than 70 million men worldwide fought in the war, including almost all of Europe's young adult males. From 1914 to 1918, 13 million served in the German army. In Russia more than 15 million men took up arms. In France around 8 million served, roughly 80 percent of men aged fifteen to forty-nine, a greater proportion than in any other major power. The British Empire mobilized nearly 9 million soldiers, and the 5.25 million troops of the United Kingdom (England, Scotland, Wales, and Ireland) constituted almost half the prewar population of men aged fifteen to forty-nine. Lord Kitchener—who had conquered Sudan in part by unleashing the machine gun on Sudanese warriors opposing conquest—had predicted to the British cabinet that the war in Europe "will not end until we have plumbed our manpower to the last military man." Over half of all the men mobilized for World War I were killed, injured, taken prisoner, or unaccounted for. Mass mobilization also undermined traditional gender boundaries. Tens of thousands of women served at or near the front as doctors, nurses, and technicians. Even more women mobilized on the "home front," taking on previously male occupations—especially in munitions plants. But women could also turn against the state. Particularly in central Europe and Russia, the war's demands for soldiers and supplies left farms untended and caused food shortages. Bread riots and peaceful protests by women, traumatized by loss and desperate to feed their children, put states on notice that their citizens expected compensation for their sacrifices. Indeed, civilian pressure forced many states to make promises they would have to fulfill after the war, in the form of welfare provisions, expanded suffrage, and pensions for widows and the wounded.

Empire and War The war's horrors reached around the globe. (See Map 19.2.) To increase their forces, the British and the French conscripted colonial subjects: India provided 1 million soldiers, who fought exclusively in the Middle Eastern theater; over 1 million Africans fought in Africa and Europe for their colonial masters, and another 3 million transported war supplies. Even the sparsely populated British dominions of Australia, New Zealand, and Canada dispatched over a million young men to fight for the empire.

The Ottoman decision to enter the war on the side of the Central Powers proved costly. In 1915–1916, as their fortunes declined, Ottoman forces massacred or deported 1.3 million Armenians, who were accused as a group of collaborating with the Russians. Many analysts regard these attacks as the world's first genocide, the intentional elimination of a whole people. The Ottoman alliance with the Central Powers made it inevitable that the British, French, and Russians, now enemies of the Ottomans, would draw up plans for dismembering the empire. Britain and France had long coveted Arab lands that remained under Ottoman control—what would later become Syria, Iraq, Lebanon, Jordan, and Palestine. No one foresaw the full consequences of the hastily drawn-up postwar borders in places such as Iraq and Syria: they would remain in existence until the twenty-first century, then be exploded by emancipated Shiites as well as by radical Sunni Islamists—notably al-Qaeda and the Islamic State of Iraq and Syria (ISIS), also known as the Islamic caliphate.

The Russian Revolution The war destroyed entire empires. The first to go was Romanov Russia. In February 1917, Tsar Nicholas II stepped down under pressure from his generals. They wanted to quash the mass unrest in the capital, St. Petersburg, which, they believed, threatened the war effort along the Eastern Front. Some members of the Russian parliament formed a provisional government; at the same time, grassroots councils (soviets) sprang up in factories, garrisons, and towns. The irony of Russia's February Revolution,

The Global View

GREENLAND

FINLAND

NORWAY SWEDEN

DENMARK BALTIC SEA

UNITED
KINGDOM

GERMANY POLAND

CANADA

FRANCE

AUSTRIA-
HUNGARY

ROMANIA

ITALY SERBIA BULGARIA BLA

MONTENEGRO

PORTUGAL SPAIN

ALBANIA GREECE

OTTOM

EMPIR

UNITED
STATES

ATLANTIC
OCEAN

TUNISIA

MOROCCO ALGERIA

LIBYA EGYPT

BAHAMAS

RIO DE ORO

BRITISH
HONDURAS

CUBA

ANGLO-
EGYPTIAN
SUDAN

JAMAICA WEST INDIES

HONDURAS

NICARAGUA

BRITISH GUIANA

GAMBIA

NIGERIA

GUINEA

COSTA
RICA PANAMA COLOMBIA

DUTCH GUIANA

FRENCH GUIANA

SIERRA LEONE

CAMEROON

UGANDA K

VENEZUELA

GOLD COAST

GER

EA

AFF

ECUADOR

TOGO

BRAZIL

PERU

NORTHERN
RHODESIA

BOLIVIA

PACIFIC
OCEAN

PARAGUAY

GERMAN
SOUTH
WEST
AFRICA

SOUTHERN
RHODESIA

CHILE

ARGENTINA

SOUTH
AFRICA

URUGUAY

Allied Powers, colonies, and allies
Central Powers and colonies
Neutral nations throughout the war
→ Troop movements

0		1000		2000 Miles
0	1000		2000 Kilometers	

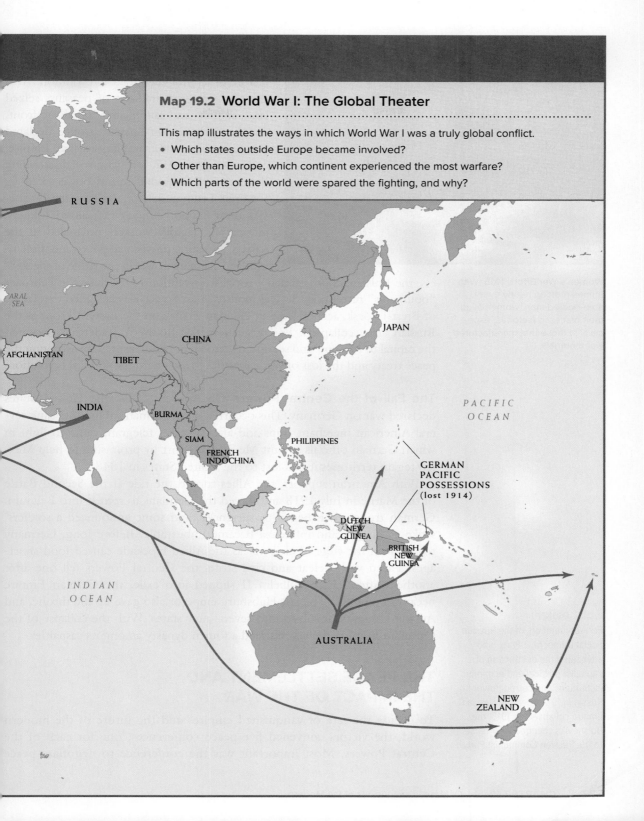

Map 19.2 World War I: The Global Theater

This map illustrates the ways in which World War I was a truly global conflict.

- Which states outside Europe became involved?
- Other than Europe, which continent experienced the most warfare?
- Which parts of the world were spared the fighting, and why?

RUSSIA

ARAL
SEA

AFGHANISTAN

TIBET

CHINA

JAPAN

INDIA

BURMA

SIAM

FRENCH
INDOCHINA

PHILIPPINES

PACIFIC
OCEAN

GERMAN
PACIFIC
POSSESSIONS
(lost 1914)

DUTCH
NEW
GUINEA

BRITISH
NEW
GUINEA

INDIAN
OCEAN

AUSTRALIA

NEW
ZEALAND

Women's War Effort, 1915 With armies drafting nearly every able-bodied man, women filled their places in factories, especially in those that manufactured war materials.

which brought an end to the monarchy, was that the military and civilian elites wanted to restore order, not encourage a revolution. With the tsar removed, millions of peasants seized land, soldiers and sailors abandoned the front, and borderland non-Russian groups declared autonomy from the crumbling Russian Empire.

In October 1917, left-wing socialists calling themselves **Bolsheviks** seized power. Led by Vladimir Lenin and Leon Trotsky, the Bolsheviks drew support among radicalized soldiers, sailors, and factory workers organized in the soviets. Arresting provisional government members and claiming power in the name of the soviets, the Bolsheviks proclaimed a socialist revolution to overtake the February "bourgeois" revolution. Several months later, Soviet Russia signed the Treaty of Brest-Litovsk, acknowledging German victory on the Eastern Front as the Russian army collapsed. For protection, the Bolshevik leadership relocated the capital to Moscow and set up a dictatorship. Lenin insisted on accepting the peace treaty and the loss of vast territories to safeguard the socialist revolution.

The Fall of the Central Powers On April 2, 1917, the United States declared war on Germany. This occurred after German submarines sank several American merchant ships and after a secret telegram came to light in which German officials sought Mexican support by promising to help Mexico regain territories it had lost to the United States in 1848.

With American support, the Allies turned the tide at the Second Battle of the Marne in July 1918 and forced the Germans to retreat into Belgium. German troops then began to surrender, and some announced a soldiers' strike as hunger and influenza became unbearable. Before long, Germany tottered on the edge of civil war as the Allied blockade caused food shortages. Faced with defeat and civil strife, the Central Powers fell one after another. After Kaiser Wilhelm II slipped into exile, the German Empire became a republic. The last Habsburg emperor also gave up the throne, and Austria-Hungary dissolved into several new states. With the collapse of the Ottoman Empire, the war claimed a fourth dynasty among its casualties.

THE PEACE SETTLEMENT AND THE IMPACT OF THE WAR

To decide the fate of vanquished empires and the future of the modern world, the victors convened five peace conferences, one for each of the Central Powers. Most important was the conference to negotiate peace

Bolsheviks
Former members of the Russian Social Democratic Party who advocated the destruction of capitalist political and economic institutions and seized power in Russia in 1917 when the Russian Empire collapsed. In 1918, the Bolsheviks changed their name to the Russian Communist Party.

with Germany, held at Versailles, France, in January 1919. Delegates drew many of their ideas from American president Woodrow Wilson's "Fourteen Points," a blueprint he had devised for making peace in Europe. Wilson especially insisted that postwar borders be redrawn by following the principle of "self-determination of nations" and that an international League of Nations be set up to negotiate further quarrels. Such high-minded ideas were appealing, but once delegates got down to the business of carving up Europe and doling out Germany's colonies, negotiations became tense and difficult. Over the objections of the Americans and British, the French insisted on a punitive treaty that assigned Germany sole blame for the war and forced it to pay reparations.

BROKEN PROMISES AND POLITICAL TURMOIL

The war's hurricane of violence followed the invention of the Maxim gun and barbed wire (originally intended to hold livestock), pogroms in imperial Russian borderlands, British concentration camps in the Boer War, and Belgian horrors in the Congo, but still proved earth shattering in its scope. Violence became an enduring part of politics.

The Russian Revolution Vladimir Lenin died just six years and three months after the October 1917 revolution, but he lived on in his writings and in images, such as in this painting by Alexander Gerassimov called *Lenin on the Stand*. Artists and propagandists helped make Lenin an icon of the new Soviet order.

The American goal of making the world safe for democracy proved illusory. The idea of self-determination created intractable problems. Although President Wilson had intended self-determination to apply principally to the ethnic minorities within the Russian and Austro-Hungarian Empires and to European peoples still under Ottoman rule, other groups expected the term to apply to themselves as well. In Europe, making ethnic and political boundaries coincide proved impossible. Suddenly, 60 million people in central and eastern Europe emerged as inhabitants of new nation-states. (See Map 19.3.) Many were unhappy, as perhaps 25 million now lived in states in which they were ethnic minorities and vulnerable to persecution in the tumultuous years after the armistice. Furthermore, colonial subjects demanded states of their own. One of them, a photographer's assistant living in Paris named Nguyen Ai Quoc, the future Ho Chi Minh, famously challenged the American delegation at Versailles to take their own principles seriously and support his people's liberation from French rule, to no avail.

Map 19.3 Outcomes of World War I in Europe, North Africa, and Some of the Middle East

....

The political map of Europe and the Middle East changed greatly after the peace treaty of 1919.

- Comparing this map with Map 19.1, which shows the European and Middle Eastern theaters of war, identify the European countries that came into existence after the war.

- What happened to the Ottoman Empire, and what powers gained control over many territories of the Ottoman state?

- What states emerged from the Austro-Hungarian Empire?

Beyond Europe, the principle of self-determination galvanized anticolonial and nationalist sentiment, but these sentiments were almost entirely dashed by France and Britain's imperial ambitions. The British, after a long-drawn-out military campaign, suppressed a 1919 rebellion in Egypt, albeit only after promising Egyptian nationalists a limited form of autonomy. The Syrians, too, did not understand why they were less deserving of self-rule than the Czechoslovaks or Yugoslavs, but the French put down a Syrian nationalist revolt. In India, similarly inspired by Wilsonian ideals, a bloody confrontation between peaceful protesters, gathered in a garden in the city of Amritsar in the Punjab, resulted in the killing of 370 Indians and the wounding of 2,000 (although Indian eyewitnesses claimed that the dead totaled more than 1,000). In China, students, offended by the minor status accorded to their country at Versailles, launched a widespread protest in the name of Wilsonianism that solidified nationalist sentiment for this generation of students and later ones.

The bloodiest of all conflicts occurred in Iraq, where nearly 600,000 people—more than 20 percent of the population—rose up against British military efforts to force them into a colonial state. The rebellion's first stages were so successful that the Iraqis established an independent state in the middle Euphrates region, one that brought together Sunni and Shiite leaders and Arab officers and soldiers who had formerly served with the Ottoman army but desired an independent Iraqi state. Ultimately, British forces totaling 73,000, of whom 63,000 were Indian soldiers, were needed to crush the rebellion.

A final set of broken promises occurred in an Arab nationalist movement led by the emir of Mecca, Sharif Husayn. Believing that he had British military and political support to create an independent Arab state in Syria, parts of Palestine, Jordan, and Iraq, Sharif Husayn led a general Arab rebellion against the Ottoman Turks. He was disabused when the Bolsheviks published secret peace agreements that had been negotiated between the British and the French during the war. One of these was the Sykes-Picot Agreement (signed in 1916 by Mark Sykes on behalf of the British and François Georges-Picot for the French), which divided the Arab east between Britain and France. (See Map 19.4.) A second promise, for a homeland for the Jews in Palestine, also angered Arab nationalists: the Balfour Declaration of November 2, 1917, took the form of a letter sent by the British foreign secretary, Arthur James Balfour, to Baron Rothschild, leader of the British Jewish community, and fulfilled a Zionist aspiration for a national homeland for the Jewish people in Palestine. The declaration did acknowledge the rights of the local residents, stating that it was "clearly understood that nothing shall be done which may prejudice the civil and religious rights of existing non-Jewish communities in Palestine, or the rights and political status enjoyed by Jews in any other country." Nonetheless, the declaration failed to reconcile competing claims, and it ultimately led to the creation of the state of Israel and numerous Arab-Israeli wars.

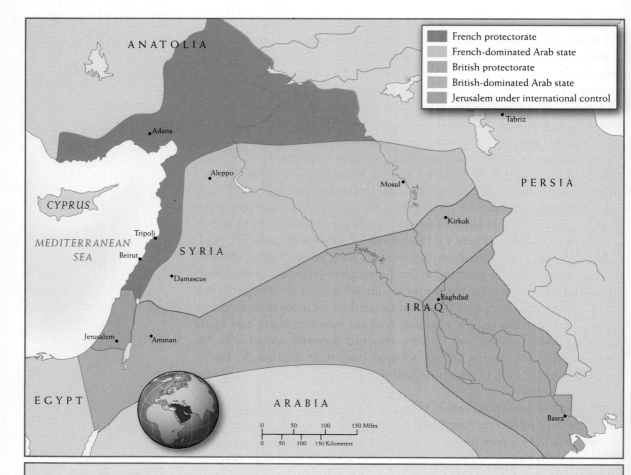

Map 19.4 The Sykes-Picot Agreement

The Sykes-Picot Agreement was negotiated between British diplomat Mark Sykes and French diplomat François Georges-Picot in 1916. While the agreement reserved protectorates for the French in Syria and the British in Iraq, it also supported the creation of a politically independent Arab state or confederation of Arab states under an Arab chief.

- Why did the British and French governments want to divide up the Arab provinces of the Ottoman Empire?
- Compare the areas that were to be the Arab confederation (though dominated by the French and the British) with the areas in the map of ISIS that appears in the Epilogue (Map E.5). How similar are the territories in both maps?
- Why do you think that Arabs in particular and Muslims in general believed that this agreement was antithetical to their wishes and was an inadequate recompense for their contributions to the war effort? Why do you think that it continues to this day to fuel powerful grievances against the west?

Mass Society: Culture, Production, and Consumption

The war dramatically extended the making of mass societies. Even before 1914, democratic regimes had begun to extend the right to vote, in many cases making non–property holders and women eligible to cast ballots. Authoritarian regimes, meanwhile, had begun to mobilize the people via rallies and mass organizations. And new technologies, such as radio, were helping to create mass cultures that spanned geographic and class divides.

MASS CULTURE

New forms of communication and entertainment contributed to the new mass culture. In an effort to mobilize populations for total war, leaders had disseminated propaganda as never before—through public lectures, theatrical productions, musical compositions, and (censored) newspapers. Indeed, the war's impact had politicized cultural activities while broadening the audience for nationally oriented information and entertainment.

Postwar *mass culture* was distinctive. First, it differed from elite culture (opera, classical music, paintings, literature) because it reflected the tastes of the working and the middle classes, who now had more time and money to spend on entertainment. Second, mass culture relied on new technologies, especially film and radio, which could reach an entire nation's population and consolidate their sense of being a single state.

Radio Radio entered its golden age after World War I. Invented early in the twentieth century, it made little impact until the 1920s, when powerful transmitters permitted stations to reach much larger audiences—often with nationally syndicated programs. Radio "broadcasts" gave listeners a sense of intimacy with newscasters and stars, addressing consumers as personal friends and drawing them in to the lives of serial heroes.

Radio also was a way to mobilize the masses, especially in authoritarian regimes. The Italian dictator Benito Mussolini pioneered the radio address to the nation; later, Soviet and Nazi propagandists used it to great effect, as did the right-wing Japanese government. But even dictatorships could not exert total control over mass culture. For example, although the Nazis regarded jazz

Josephine Baker Reacting to the Great War's carnage, many Europeans looked longingly for supposedly pristine worlds that their own corrupting civilization had not destroyed. The African American entertainer Josephine Baker was a sensation on the stage in Paris after the war. Many of her shows exoticized or even caricatured her African descent.

Core Objectives

EXPLAIN how the development of modern, mass societies both caused and was affected by the Great Depression.

as racially inferior music and the Soviets regarded it as "bourgeois," neither could prevent young or old from tuning in to foreign radio broadcasts, smuggling gramophone records over the borders, or creating their own jazz bands.

Film and Advertising Film, too, had profound effects. For traditionalists, Hollywood by the 1920s signified vulgarity and decadence because the silver screen prominently displayed modern sexual habits. Like radio, film served political purposes. Here, again, antiliberal governments took the lead. German filmmaker Leni Riefenstahl's movie of the Nazi Nuremberg rally of 1934, *Triumph of the Will*, is a key example of propagandistic cinema. Nazi-era films were comedies, musicals, melodramas, detective films, and adventure epics—sometimes framed by racial stereotypes and political goals. Soviet film studios also produced Hollywood-style musicals alongside didactic pictures about socialist triumphs.

Triumph of the Will Though later denounced, Leni Riefenstahl's propaganda film of Adolf Hitler and the Nazi Party Congress won a Golden Lion at the 1935 Venice Biennale and an award at the 1937 World's Exhibition in Paris. Its poster featured the many mass rallies that projected an image of dynamism and collective will, which Hitler claimed to embody.

In market economies, radio and film grew into big businesses, and with expanded product advertising they promoted other enterprises as well. Especially in the United States, advertising became a major industry, with radio commercials shaping national consumer tastes. Increasingly, too, American-produced entertainment, radio programs, and cinematic epics reached an international audience. Thanks to new media, America and the world began to share mass-produced images and fantasies.

MASS PRODUCTION AND MASS CONSUMPTION

The same factors that promoted mass culture also enhanced production and consumption on a mass scale. In fact, World War I had relied on industrial might, for machine technologies produced war materials with abundant and devastating effect.

Never before had armies had so much firepower at their disposal. Whereas in 1809 Napoleon's artillery had discharged 90,000 shells over two days during the largest battle waged in Europe to that point, by 1916 German guns were firing 100,000 rounds of shells per hour for twelve hours at a time in the Battle of Verdun. To sustain military production, millions of men and women worked in factories at home and in the colonies. Producing huge quantities of identical guns, gas masks, bandage rolls, and boots, these factories reflected the modern world's demands for greater volume, faster speed, reduced cost, and standardized output—key characteristics of *mass production*.

The war reshuffled the world's economic balance of power, boosting the United States as an economic powerhouse. As the United States' share of world industrial production climbed above one-third in 1929 (roughly equal to that of Britain, Germany, and Russia combined), people around the globe regarded it as a "working vision of modernity" in which not only production but also consumption boomed.

The Automobile Assembly Line The most outstanding example of the relationship between mass production and consumption in the United States was the motor car. Before World War I, the automobile had been a rich man's toy. Then came Henry Ford, who founded the Ford Motor Company in 1903. Seeking to make more cars more quickly and cheaper, Ford used mechanized conveyors to send the auto frame along a track, or assembly line, where each worker performed one simplified task. By standardizing the manufacturing process and substituting machinery for manual labor, Ford's assembly line brought a new efficiency to the mass production of automobiles.

By the 1920s, a finished car rolled off Ford's assembly line every ten seconds. Although workers complained about becoming "cogs" in a depersonalized labor process, the system boosted output and reduced costs. Altogether, nearly 4 million jobs related directly or indirectly to the automobile—an impressive total in a labor force of 45 million workers.

After World War I, automobile ownership became more common among Americans. Ford further expanded the market for cars by paying his own workers $5 per day—approximately twice the average manufacturing wage in the United States. He understood that without *mass consumption*, increased purchasing power in the middle classes, and appetite for goods there could be no mass production. Whereas in 1920 Americans owned 8 million motor cars, a decade later they owned 23 million. The automobile's rapid spread seemed to demonstrate that mass production worked.

The Great Depression Not all was easy listening and smooth motoring in countries where mass societies were taking root. On October 24, 1929—Black Tuesday—the American stock market collapsed, plunging not only the American economy and its consumers, heavily in debt, but also international financial and trading systems into crisis. This event led the world into the **Great Depression**.

The causes of the Depression went back to the Great War. The efforts by European governments to slash spending and return to the prewar gold standard stifled growth and compromised their ability to pay their war debts. Political and economic instability in Germany, the linchpin of the European economy, made matters even more difficult. The financial terms of the Versailles

Great Depression
Worldwide depression following the U.S. stock market crash on October 29, 1929.

treaty required Germany to pay reparations to compensate for the costs of the war. The German government, however, was unable or unwilling to tax citizens at the rates that prevailed in victor countries, which would have enabled it to meet its treaty obligations. It opted instead to print more money. The resulting hyperinflation destroyed both the German economy and democracy.

To restore stability, Europeans borrowed heavily from the United States. Germany borrowed more from the United States than it paid in reparations, but that assistance was insufficient and short-lived. In 1928 and 1929, American banks pulled their support. Starting in central Europe, banks began to collapse. The panic then spread to the world's stock markets, which led to the Wall Street crash of 1929, which spurred more bank closures.

Financial turmoil produced a major reduction in world trade. Striving to protect workers and investors from the influx of cheap foreign goods, governments raised tariffs against imports. After the United States enacted protective tariffs, other governments abandoned free trade in favor of protectionism. Manufacturers cut back production, laid off millions of workers, and often went out of business. By 1935, world trade had shrunk to one-third of its 1929 level. The producers of raw materials, mainly found in the less developed economies, felt the harshest effects, for their international markets shut down almost completely. For example, world prices for Argentine beef, Chilean nitrates, and Indonesian sugar all dropped sharply.

The Great Depression forced people to rethink the core of laissez-faire liberalism (see Chapter 15), the idea that free markets regulate themselves and free trade leads to economic progress. By the late 1930s, the exuberant embrace of private mass production had ceded to a new conviction: state intervention to regulate the economy was critical to prevent disaster. In 1936, the British economist John Maynard Keynes published a landmark treatise, *The General Theory of Employment, Interest, and Money*. He argued that the market could not always adjust to its own failures and that sometimes the state had to stimulate it by increasing the money supply and creating jobs. Although the "Keynesian Revolution" took years to transform economic policy, many governments had doubts whether capitalism could be saved. The Great Depression did more than any other event to challenge the belief that liberal democracy and capitalism were the best way to achieve political stability and economic progress.

Core Objectives

COMPARE the ideologies of liberal democracy, authoritarianism, and anticolonialism, and **EVALUATE** the success of each in this period.

Mass Politics: Competing Visions for Building Modern States

In the aftermath of World War I, societies grappled with the question of how to build modern, prosperous states. The war upset class, gender, and colonial relations, which were already unsettled in the prewar period. On battlefronts and home fronts, countless workers, peasants, women, and colonial subjects had sacrificed and now expected to share in the fruits of peace. Many, even in victorious nations, lost confidence in traditional authorities who had failed to prevent the cataclysm and allowed it to go on so long. Amid widespread political turmoil, the states that retained some form of democracy revised the liberal vision, while authoritarianism gained in popularity and anticolonial movements gathered steam.

LIBERAL DEMOCRACY UNDER PRESSURE

The demands of fighting a total war had a profound effect on all the European states. All of them, including the democracies in Britain and France, seized the opportunity to experiment with illiberal policies. Indeed, the war brought both the suspension of many democratic rights and an effort by governments to manage industry and distribution. States on both sides of the conflict jailed many individuals who opposed the war. Governments regulated both production and, through rationing, consumption. Above all, the war and the economic crises that followed revolutionized the size and scope of the state.

British and French Responses to Economic Crises Britain and France retained their democracies, but even here, old-fashioned liberal democracy was on the run. Strife rippled across the British Empire, and in the home isles Britain gave independence to what became the Republic of Ireland in 1922. Britain's working-class Labour Party came to power twice between 1923 and 1931; but either alone or in coalition with Liberals and Conservatives, Labour could not lift the country out of its economic crisis.

Disorder was even more pronounced in France, which had lost 10 percent of its young men and seen the destruction of vast territory. In 1932–1933, six government coalitions came and went over the course of just nineteen months. Against the threat of a rightist coup, a coalition of the moderate and radical left, including the French Communist Party, formed the Popular Front government (1936–1938). It introduced the right of collective bargaining, a forty-hour workweek, two-week paid vacations, and minimum wages.

The American New Deal In the United States, too, markets and liberalism faced challenges. When the Great Depression shattered the nation's fortunes, pressure intensified to create a more secure political and economic system.

By the end of 1930, more than 4 million American workers had lost their jobs. As President Hoover insisted that citizens' thrift and self-reliance, not government handouts, would restore prosperity, the economic situation worsened. By 1933, industrial production had dropped by a staggering

50 percent since 1929. The hard times were even worse in the countryside, where farm income plummeted by two-thirds between 1929 and 1932.

In the 1932 presidential election, a Democrat, Franklin Delano Roosevelt, won in a landslide. He promptly launched what came to be called the New Deal, a set of programs and regulations that dramatically expanded the scope of the American national government and its role in the nation's economic life. In his first hundred days in office, Roosevelt obtained legislation to provide relief for the jobless and to rebuild the shattered economy. Among his administration's experiments were the Federal Deposit Insurance Corporation to guarantee bank deposits up to $5,000, the Securities and Exchange Commission to monitor the stock market, and the Federal Emergency Relief Administration to help states and local governments assist the needy. Subsequently, in 1935, the Works Progress Administration put nearly 3 million people to work building roads, bridges, airports, and post offices. In addition, the Social Security Act inaugurated old-age pensions supported by the federal government.

Never before had the U.S. federal government expended so much on social welfare programs or intervened so directly in the national economy. Yet the Depression lingered, and before long unemployment again climbed—from 7 million in 1937 to 11 million in 1938.

The New Deal did not substantially redistribute national income. Privately owned enterprises continued to dominate American society. Roosevelt's aim was not to destroy capitalism but to save it. In this regard the New Deal succeeded, for it staved off authoritarian solutions to modern problems.

Jim Crow The American New Deal left most African Americans behind. In the rural American South, "Jim Crow" laws mandated racial segregation, with African Americans forced to use separate, and usually unequal, facilities, including schools, hotels, and theaters, such as this one in Mississippi.

During the interwar years, liberal democratic regimes respected elections and defended private property against challenges from labor movements. But they intervened in markets and regulated people's lives in ways their prewar counterparts never would have contemplated.

AUTHORITARIANISM AND MASS MOBILIZATION

Like the liberal systems they challenged, authoritarian regimes came in various stripes. Right-wing dictatorships arose in Italy, Germany, and Japan. Although differing in important respects, they all disliked the left-wing dictatorship of the Soviet Union. The Soviets, in turn, hated the fascists.

The Soviet Union and Socialism The most dramatic blow against liberal capitalism occurred in Russia when the Bolshevik Party seized power and established a socialist regime. Fearing the spread of socialist revolutions, Britain, France, Japan, and the United States sent armies to Russia to contain Bolshevism. But after executing the tsar and his family, the Bolsheviks rallied support by defending the homeland against its invaders. They also mobilized people to fight (and win) a civil war (1918–1921) in the name of defending the revolution.

To revive the economy, which had been devastated by war, revolution, and civil war, the Bolsheviks grudgingly legalized private trade and private property. In 1924, with the country still recovering from civil war, the undisputed leader of the revolution, Lenin, died. Lenin had done more than anyone to shape the institutions of the revolutionary regime, including creating expectations for a single ruler. After eliminating his rivals, **Joseph Stalin** (1878–1953) emerged as the new leader of the Communist Party and the country, which soon became the Union of Soviet Socialist Republics (USSR), or Soviet Union.

Since socialism as a fully developed social and political order did not exist anywhere in the 1920s, no one was sure how it would actually work. Stalin resolved this dilemma by defining Soviet or revolutionary socialism in opposition to capitalism. Since capitalism had "bourgeois" parliaments serving the interests of the rich, socialism, as elaborated by Stalinist leaders, would have soviets (councils) of worker and peasant deputies. Since capitalism had unregulated markets, which led to inefficiency and unemployment, socialism would have economic planning and full employment. And since capitalism relied on the "exploitation" of private ownership, socialism would outlaw private trade and private property. In short, socialism would eradicate capitalism and then invent socialist forms in housing, culture, values, dress, and even modes of reasoning.

The efforts to build a noncapitalist society required class war, and these efforts began in the heavily populated countryside. As Stalin solidified his

Joseph Stalin
(1879–1953) Leader of the Communist Party and the Soviet Union; sought to create "socialism in one country."

УДАРНУЮ УБОРКУ –
БОЛЬШЕВИСТСКОМУ УРОЖАЮ

Collectivized Agriculture Soviet plans for the socialist village envisioned the formation of large collectives supplied with advanced machinery, thereby transforming peasant labor into an industrial process, and equality between men and women. Note the woman farmer who dominates the image, and the men and women working side by side. The realities behind the images of smiling farmers—such as in this poster, proclaiming "Let's Achieve a Victorious Harvest"—were low productivity, enormous waste, and often broken-down machinery.

control over the Soviet Union in the late 1920s, he sought to combine individual farms into larger units owned and worked collectively and run by regime loyalists. Tens of thousands of urban activists and Red Army soldiers led a drive to establish these collective farms and to compel farmers to sell all their grain and livestock at state-run collection points for whatever price the state was willing to pay (often very little).

In protest, many peasants burned their crops, killed their livestock, and destroyed their farm machinery. The government responded by deporting the protesters, along with many bystanders, to remote areas. Meanwhile, harvests again declined, and famine claimed millions more lives. Grudgingly, the regime allowed the collectivized peasants to have household plots. Here they could grow their own food and take some of their produce to approved markets. But few escaped the collectives, which depended on the state for seed, fertilizers, and machinery.

The year 1928 saw the beginning of a frenzied Five-Year Plan to "catch and overtake" the leading capitalist countries. As peasants were forced onto collective farms, millions of enthusiasts (as well as deported peasants) set about building a socialist urban utopia founded on advanced technology, almost all of it purchased from the Depression-mired capitalist countries. More than 10 million people helped build or rebuild hundreds of factories, hospitals, and schools. Huge hydroelectric dams, automobile and tractor factories, and heavy machine–building plants symbolized the promise of Soviet-style modernity, which eliminated unemployment during the capitalist Great Depression. Soviet authorities also started building socialism on the borderlands, and the USSR soon included several new republics (see Map 19.5), all of which acquired their own institutions—but under central rule from Moscow.

Mass Terror and Stalin's Dictatorship The Soviet political system became more ruthless as the state expanded. Police power grew the most, partly from forcing peasants into collectives and organizing mass deportations. As the party's ranks swelled, ongoing loyalty tests also led to the removal of party members, even when they professed absolute loyalty. From 1936 to 1938, trials of supposedly treasonous "enemies of the people" resulted

Map 19.5 The Soviet Union

The Union of Soviet Socialist Republics (USSR) came into being after World War I.

- How did its boundaries compare with those of the older Russian Empire, as shown in Map 17.5?
- Identify the Soviet republics other than Russia.
- What does the large number of Soviet republics suggest about the ethnic diversity within the Soviet Union?

in the execution of around 750,000 people and the arrest or deportation of several million more. They were sent to forced-labor camps, collectively known as the Gulag. Such purges decimated the loyal Soviet elite—party officials, state officials, intelligentsia, army officers, and even members of the police who had enforced the terror. Lenin and Stalin secured a communist regime based in Russia but did so through highly coercive and deeply resented methods. Nonetheless, Stalin's efforts at heavy industrialization were to pay off when Nazi Germany invaded the Soviet Union in World War II (see Chapter 20).

Italian Fascism Disillusionment with the costs of the Great War and fear of a communist takeover like that in Russia inspired violent political movements in many European countries, above all in Italy and Germany. In Italy, mass strikes, occupations of factories, and peasant land seizures swept the country in 1919 and 1920. Amid this disorder, authoritarian nationalists seized power. Their leader was **Benito Mussolini** (1883–1945), a former socialist journalist, who coined the term **fascism**. In the wake of the Russian Revolution of 1917, fascism represented a counterrevolution. It combined mass movements, which had emerged on the political left, with an aggressive, authoritarian nationalism and antisocialist and antiliberal values.

In 1919, Mussolini sought to organize alienated veterans into a mass political movement. In the early years, black-shirted vigilante squads received money from landowners and factory owners to beat up socialist leaders. Still, the fascists presented themselves as champions of the little guy, of peasants and (nonsocialist) workers, as well as of war veterans, students, and white-collar professionals.

In 1922, Mussolini announced a march on Rome. The march was a bluff, since Mussolini had no military support, yet it intimidated the king, who opposed fascist ruffians but feared bloodshed. So the king withheld use of the army against the lightly armed marchers. When the Italian government resigned in protest, the monarch invited Mussolini to become prime minister, despite the fact that fascists had won only a small minority of seats in the 1921 elections. Soon a series of decrees transformed Italy from a constitutional monarchy into a dictatorship. Within a few years, all parties except that of the fascists had been dissolved. The regime used parades, films, radio, and visions of recapturing Roman imperial grandeur to boost support during the troubled times of the Depression. Mussolini used his personal charisma to promote the idea that as *Il Duce* (the leader), he personified the power and unity of Italy.

Mussolini's dictatorship made deals with big business and the church. He left traditional elites in place and preserved their powerful institutions; thus, his regime fell short of a total social revolution. By the mid-1930s, Italian fascism had settled into a traditional form of conservatism. Nonetheless, as the first antiliberal, antisocialist alternative, the early phase of Italian fascism served as a model for other countries.

German Nazism In Germany, too, fear of Bolshevism and anger over the war's outcome propelled a violent, authoritarian party to power. Here, the dictator was **Adolf Hitler** (1889–1945), backed by the nationalist workers' movement, whose name he changed to the National Socialist German Workers' Party (*Nationalsozialistische Deutsche Arbeiterpartei*, or **Nazis**).

Unlike Mussolini, the young Hitler was never a socialist, but the Nazi's Twenty-Five Points (1920) combined nationalism with a heavy dose of anticapitalism. The party platform called for the renunciation of the Treaty of Versailles and for discrimination against Jews. It was an assertion of Germany's grievances against the world and of the small man's grievances against those whom the Nazis perceived as the rich. At first, Hitler and the Nazis were unsuccessful, and Hitler himself was arrested. He was sentenced to five years in prison for treason but served less than a year. While in prison he wrote an autobiographical and fanatically anti-Semitic treatise called *Mein Kampf* (My Struggle, 1925), which subsequently became wildly popular among Nazis.

As the Great Depression eroded popular support for the Weimar Republic (the democratic regime that came into existence after the Treaty of Versailles), conservative leaders sought to profit from Hitler's popularity. Germany's president appointed Hitler chancellor (prime minister) in 1933, even as the Nazi movement was declining as an electoral force. Like Mussolini, Hitler came to power legally, with the help of traditional elites. Yet neither leader won an electoral majority.

Hitler's first step as chancellor was to heighten fears of communist conspiracy. The burning of the Reichstag (parliament) building in Berlin gave the Nazis an opportunity to blame the fire on the communists. They immediately suspended civil liberties, including free speech and freedom of association, and attacked and imprisoned their opponents, especially communists. By July 1933, the Nazis were the only legal party and Hitler was dictator of Germany. Like Mussolini, Hitler relied on choreographed mass rallies and new media like film and radio, as well as his own personal charisma, to mobilize a mass following.

Hitler also unleashed a campaign of persecution against Jews. Like many other right-wing Germans, he believed that a Jewish-socialist conspiracy had stabbed the German army in the back, causing its surrender in World War I, and that intermarriage with Jews was destroying the supposed purity of the Aryan race (which included northern, white Europeans). Hitler and the Nazis did not believe that religious practice defined Jewishness; instead, they held, it was transmitted biologically from parents to children. Hitler encouraged the use of terror against Jews, destroying their businesses, homes, and marriages with non-Jews and ultimately eliminating all traces of Jewish life and culture in Nazi-dominated central Europe (see Chapter 20).

The Nazis won popular support for restoring order and reviving the economy, although the economic gains had more to do with timing than Nazi policy. In any case, Germany reemerged as a great power with expansionist aspirations. Just as Mussolini reached back to ancient Rome to connect fascism to the Italian past, Hitler, too, invoked history. He called his state the Third Reich—he considered the Holy Roman Empire (or Reich) the first and the Reich created by Bismarck in 1871 the second—to bolster its legitimacy.

Militarist Japan Unlike authoritarian regimes in Europe, the right-wing movement that emerged in Japan did not spring from wounded power and pride during World War I. In fact, because wartime disruptions reduced European and American competition, Japanese products found new markets in Asia. Although the government expanded the electorate and seemed headed toward liberal democracy in the early 1920s, Japan veered to the political right in 1926 when Emperor Hirohito came to power.

Adding Manchuria to its Korean and Taiwanese colonies in 1932 (see Map 19.6), Japan established the puppet state of Manchukuo. Meanwhile, at home, "patriots" carried out a campaign of terror against uncooperative businessmen and critics of the military. Unlike Italian fascism and German Nazism, Japanese authoritarianism had an explicitly religious dimension. The state in Japan took on a sacred aura through the promotion of an official religion, Shinto, and of Emperor Hirohito's divinity. By 1940, Hirohito and his closest advisers had merged all political parties into the Imperial Rule Assistance Association, ending even the semblance of democracy, and they advocated a radical form of racial purity. The Imperial Army divided the peoples of Asia into "master races," "friendly races," and "guest races," reserving a dominant position for the Japanese "Yamato Race."

Common Features of Authoritarian Regimes All the major authoritarian regimes of this period claimed that modern economies required state direction. In Japan, the government fostered huge business conglomerates (*zaibatsu*); in Italy, it encouraged big business to form cartels. The German state also regarded the private sector as the vehicle of economic growth, but it expected entrepreneurs to support the Nazis' racial, antidemocratic, and expansionist aims. The most thorough form of economic coordination occurred in the Soviet Union, which adopted American-style mass production while eliminating private enterprise. Instead, the Soviet state owned and managed all of the country's industry.

All these states relied heavily on mass organizations. Russia, Italy, and Germany had single mass parties; Japan had various rightist groups until the 1940 merger. All promoted dynamic youth movements, such as the Hitler Youth and the Union of German Girls, the Soviet Communist Youth League, and the Italian squads marching to the anthem "Giovinezza" (Youth).

Three of the four adopted extensive social welfare policies. The Nazis emphasized full employment, built public housing, and provided assistance to needy Aryan families. The Italian National Agency for Maternity and Infancy provided services for unwed mothers and infant care. Soviet programs addressed maternity, disability, sickness, and old age. Although Japan did not enact innovative social welfare legislation, its Home Affairs Ministry

RUSSIA

AMUR PROVINCE

SAKHALIN

SEA OF OKHOTSK

KURILE ISLANDS

OUTER MONGOLIA

MANCHURIA (MANCHUKUO, 1932)

EZO (HOKKAIDŌ)

INNER MONGOLIA

JEHOL

Vladivostok

Mukden

SEA OF JAPAN

JAPAN

Beijing
Tianjin

Dalian
Lüshun (Port Arthur)
Weihaiwei
Qingdao

Seoul

KOREA

Pusan

Tokyo

HONSHŪ

Kyoto

CHINA

YELLOW SEA

RUSSIAN BALTIC FLEET

Nagasaki

SHIKOKU

KYŪSHŪ

PACIFIC OCEAN

BONIN ISLANDS

VOLCANO ISLANDS

Nanjing

Shanghai

EAST CHINA SEA

OKINAWA

RYŪKYŪ ISLANDS

0   100   200   300 Miles
0   100   200   300 Kilometers

Fuzhou

Xiamen (Amoy)

Guangzhou (Canton)

TAIWAN

PESCADORES

Hong Kong
Macao

Japanese acquisitions as of 1895
Japanese acquisitions, 1905–1910
Japanese area of influence before 1914
Japanese attack, 1914
Extension of Japanese influence after 1918
Occupied by Japan, 1920–1925
Japan forms puppet state of Manchukuo, 1932
Occupied by Japan, 1933

Map 19.6 The Japanese Empire in Asia, 1933

Hoping to become a great imperial power like the European states, Japan established numerous colonies and spheres of influence early in the twentieth century.

- What were the main territorial components of the Japanese Empire?

- How far did the Japanese succeed in extending their political influence throughout East Asia?

- According to your reading, what problems did the desire to extend Japanese influence in China present to Japanese leaders?

enlisted helpmates among civic groups, seeking to raise savings rates and improve child-rearing practices.

All these regimes, except the Soviet Union, were ambivalent about women in public roles. Even the Soviets, who claimed to support gender equality, eventually restricted abortion and rewarded mothers who had many children. Officials were eager to honor new mothers as a way to repair the loss of so many young men during the Great War. Yet many more women were also entering professional careers, and some were becoming their families' primary wage earners.

Finally, all the dictatorships used violence and terror as tools for remaking the sociopolitical order. The Italians and the Japanese were not shy about arresting political opponents, particularly in their colonies. However, it was the Nazis and especially the Soviets who filled concentration and labor camps with alleged enemies of the state, whether Jews or supposed counterrevolutionaries.

THE HYBRID REGIMES IN LATIN AMERICA

Core Objectives

EXPLAIN how access to consumer goods and other aspects of mass society influenced political conflict in Asia, Africa, and Latin America.

Latin American countries felt the same pressures that produced liberal democratic and authoritarian responses in Europe, Russia, and Japan. However, the Latin American leaders devised solutions that combined democratic and authoritarian elements.

Economic Turmoil Latin American states had stayed out of the fighting in World War I, but their export economies had suffered. As trade plummeted, popular confidence in oligarchic regimes fell, and radical agitation surged.

As in Europe, Latin American governments stepped in to manage volatile economic markets. More than in any other region, the Depression battered Latin America's trading and financial systems, as well as the standards of living of laborers, because all were so dependent on exports. Exporters of basic staples, from sugar to wheat, faced stiff competition from other exporters and evaporating demand for their commodities. The region in fact suffered doubly because it had borrowed so much money to invest in infrastructure and expansion. When the world's major banks failed, creditors called in their loans from Latin America. This move drove borrowers to default. In an effort to improve their economic prospects, Latin American governments—with enthusiastic backing from the middle classes, nationalist intellectuals, and urban workers—turned to their domestic rather than foreign markets as the main engine of growth. Here, too, the state took a much more interventionist role in market activity than in the ideal of classical liberalism.

After the war, Latin American elites confronted the mass age by establishing mass parties and encouraging interest groups to associate with them.

Collective bodies such as chambers of commerce, trade unions, peasant associations, and organizations for minorities like blacks and Indians all operated with state sponsorship. This form of modern politics, often labeled corporatist, used social groups to bridge the gap between ruling elites and the general population.

Corporatist Politics in Brazil Corporatist politics took hold especially in Brazil, where the old republic collapsed in 1930. In its place, a coalition led by the skilled politician Getúlio Vargas (1883–1954) cultivated a strong following by enacting socially popular reforms.

Dubbing himself the "father of the poor," Vargas encouraged workers to organize, erected monuments to national heroes, and supported the building of schools and the paving of roads. He made special efforts to appeal to Brazilian blacks, who had been excluded from public life since the abolition of slavery. Thus, he legalized many previously forbidden Afro-Brazilian practices, such as the ritual *candomblé* dance, whose African and martial overtones seemed threatening to white elites. Vargas also supported samba schools, organizations that not only taught popular dances but also raised funds for public works. Moreover, Vargas addressed maternity and housing policies and enfranchised women (although they had to be able to read, as did male voters). Although he condemned the old elites for betraying the country to serve the interests of foreign consumers and investors, he also arranged foreign funding and technical transfers to build steel mills and factories. However, he took this step to create domestic industry so that Brazil would not be so dependent on imports. In these and other ways, Brazil and other Latin American governments combined democratic and authoritarian institutions and methods as a response to the economic downturn of the depression.

Samba Dancers The dance started in the shantytowns of Rio de Janeiro and eventually became popular throughout the world, thanks to films, photographs, and long-playing records that featured samba music.

ANTICOLONIAL VISIONS OF MODERN LIFE

Debates over liberal-democratic versus authoritarian models engaged the world's colonial and semicolonial regions as well. But here there was a larger concern: What should be done about colonial authority? Throughout Asia, most educated people wanted to roll back the European and

Population Movements: Filling Up the Empty Spaces and Spreading Capitalism

As we have seen in Chapters 12 and 13, the European discovery of the Americas resulted in a vast movement of peoples across the Atlantic Ocean from Europe and Africa into the Western Hemisphere. These population movements, among the largest in world history up to that point, pale when measured against the long-distance migrations that occurred in the hundred years between 1840 and 1940. During these years, 150 million individuals of European and Asian descent filled up the less populated parts of the world, moving from Europe, South Asia, and China into the Americas, Southeast Asia, and northern Asia in unprecedented numbers and spreading a capitalist mode of production wherever they moved. A great many of the migrants went as laborers in the factories and on the plains of the Americas and on the rubber, sugar, tea, and coffee plantations springing up in the Dutch East Indies and East and southern Africa. They were as essential to the expansion of the capitalist system in these regions as the 12 million African captives transported to the Americas during the Atlantic slave trade were for the economic expansion of the Americas. Although the new watchword in economic relations was free labor, not all of the men and women who moved were in fact free workers. Indentured servitude—that is, agreeing to work for a certain number of years, usually between three and seven, in return for transportation to the region, food, housing, and clothing—was widely used with Chinese and Indian workers.

A good example of the movement and use of semi-coerced or indentured workers in less developed regions comes from East Africa. There, the British and Germans were engaged in a furious political rivalry to extend their control over territories, and British officials believed that constructing a railway from the coast of East Africa at the port of Mombasa to Kisumu at Lake Victoria would enhance their territorial ambitions in East Africa. They also concluded that they would be unable to recruit a sufficient supply of African workers to accomplish the task. Not surprisingly, they looked to the government of India to assist them in providing the necessary workforce.

The British government of India did more than help them. In all, it made available nearly 35,000 indentured South Asian workers on three-year contracts for the construction of what was known as the Uganda Railway, the track for which, covering a distance of 582 miles, was completed in a mere five years, from 1896 to 1901. The work was arduous and the living conditions in the work camps were horrific, yet the British official overseeing the construction concluded that had it not been for this workforce, it is doubtful that the project could have been completed in less than twenty years. The building of the Uganda Railway is one of many examples in which we see significant

American imperial presence. Some Asians even accepted Japanese imperialism as an antidote, under the slogan "Asia for the Asians." In Africa, however, where the European colonial presence was more recent, intellectuals still questioned the real meaning of colonial rule: Were the British and the French sincerely committed to African improvement, or were they obstacles to African peoples' well-being? (See Current Trends in World History: Population Movements: Filling Up the Empty Spaces and Spreading Capitalism.)

In Africa as well as Asia, then, the search for the modern encompassed demands for power sharing or full political independence. To overcome the contradictions of the democratic liberalism Europeans practiced at home and

numbers of people moving to new places and regions, sometimes by their own choosing and sometimes not, to play an important role in the expansion of the capitalist system and the rivalries between colonial powers.

The Uganda Railway Indian workers cut rock for the Uganda Railway, built in 1896 to 1901, during the Scramble for Africa.

Questions for Analysis

- Why do you think that in some cases, like the building of the Uganda Railway, governments had to be involved in forcibly moving workers to where they were needed rather than letting market forces draw the workers to where work was available?
- What do you see as some of the similarities and differences between the treatment of the African slaves and the treatment of the forced or indentured servants during this period?

Explore Further

McKeown, Adam, *Melancholy Order: Asian Migration and the Globalization of Border* (2008).

the authoritarianism they exercised in colonial areas, educated Asians and Africans proposed various forms of nationalism.

Behind the Asian and African nationalist movements were profound disagreements about how best to govern nations once they gained independence and how to define citizenship. The democratic ethos of the imperial powers appealed to many intellectuals. Others liked the radical authoritarianism of fascism and communism, with their promises of rapid change. Whatever their political preferences, most literate colonial subjects also regarded their own religious and cultural traditions as sources for political mobilization. Thus Muslim, Hindu, Chinese, and African nationalist leaders used traditional values to gain the support of the rank and file. The colonial figures involved in political and intellectual movements insisted that the societies they sought to establish were going to be modern *and* at the same time retain their indigenous characteristics.

African Stirrings Africa contained the most recent territories to come under the Europeans' control, so anticolonial nationalist movements there were quite young. The region's fate remained very much in the hands of Europeans. After 1918, however, African peoples probed more deeply for the meaning of Europe's imperial presence.

There was some room (but not much) for voicing African interests under colonialism. The French had long held to a vision of assimilating their colonial peoples into French culture. In France's primary West African colony, Senegal, four coastal cities had traditionally elected one delegate (of mixed African and European ancestry) to the French National Assembly. This practice, limiting African representation to men of mixed ancestry, lasted until 1914, when Blaise Diagne (1872–1934), an African candidate, ran for office and won the seat in the French National Assembly, invoking his African origins and garnering the African vote. While the British allowed Africans to elect delegates to municipal bodies, they refused to permit colonial representatives to sit in Parliament.

Opposition was still not widespread in Africa, for protests ran up against not only colonial administrators but also western-educated African elites. Yet even this privileged group began to reconsider its relationship to colonial authorities. In Kenya, immediately after World War I, a small contingent of mission-educated Africans called on the British to provide more and better schools and to return lands they claimed European settlers had stolen. Although defeated in this instance, the young nationalists drew important lessons from their confrontation with the authorities. Their new spokesperson, Jomo Kenyatta (1898–1978), invoked their precolonial Kikuyu traditions as a basis for resisting colonialism. These early anticolonial movements prepared the foundations for more widespread resistance to colonial rule after World War II.

Imagining an Indian Nation As Africans explored the use of modern politics against Europeans, the war and its aftermath brought full-blown challenges to British rule in India. Indeed, the Indian nationalist challenge provided inspiration for other anticolonial movements.

For over a century, Indians had heard British authorities extol the virtues of liberal democracy, yet they were excluded from participation. In 1919, the British did slightly enlarge the franchise in India and allowed more local self-government, but these moves did not satisfy Indians' nationalist longings. During the 1920s and 1930s, the nationalists, led by

Mohandas Karamchand (Mahatma) Gandhi (1869–1948), laid the foundations for an alternative, anticolonial movement.

Gandhi and Nonviolent Resistance When Gandhi returned to India in 1915, after studying law in England and gaining a reputation for working on behalf of Indian immigrants in South Africa, he immediately became the focus of the Indian nationalist movement. He spelled out the moral and political philosophy of *satyagraha*, or **nonviolent resistance**, which he had developed while in South Africa. His message to Indians was simple: develop your own resources and inner strength and control the instincts and activities that encourage participation in colonial economy and government, and you shall achieve *swaraj* ("self-rule"). Faced with Indian self-reliance and self-control pursued nonviolently, Gandhi claimed, the British eventually would have to leave.

Indian nationalists urged people to oppose cooperation with government officials, to boycott goods made in Britain, to refuse to send their children to British schools, and to withhold taxes. Gandhi added his voice, calling for an all-India *satyagraha*. He also formed an alliance with Muslim leaders and began turning the Indian National Congress from an elite organization of lawyers and merchants into a mass organization open to anyone who paid dues, even the illiterate and poor.

Gandhi and the Road to Independence (*Left*) Gandhi launched a civil disobedience movement in 1930 by violating the British government's tax on salt. Calling it "the most inhuman poll tax the ingenuity of man can devise," Gandhi, accompanied by his followers, set out on a monthlong march on foot covering 240 miles to Dandi on the Gujarat coast. The picture shows Gandhi arriving at the sea, where he and his followers broke the law by scooping up handfuls of salt. (*Right*) Gandhi believed that India had been colonized by becoming enslaved to modern industrial civilization. Indians would achieve independence, he argued, when they became self-reliant. Thus, he made the spinning wheel a symbol of *swaraj* and handspun cloth the virtual uniform of the nation.

When the Depression struck India in 1930, Gandhi singled out salt as a testing ground for his ideas on civil disobedience. Every Indian used salt, whose producer was a heavily taxed government monopoly. Thus, salt symbolized the Indians' subjugation to an alien government. To break the colonial government's monopoly, Gandhi began a 240-mile march from western India to the coast to gather sea salt for free. Accompanying him were seventy-one followers representing different regions and religions of India. News wire services and mass-circulation newspapers worldwide reported on the drama of the sixty-one-year-old Gandhi, wooden staff in hand, dressed in coarse homespun garments, leading the march. Thousands of people gathering en route were moved by the sight of the frail apostle of nonviolence encouraging them to embrace independence from colonial rule. By insisting that Indians follow their conscience (always through nonviolent protest), by exciting the masses through his defiance of colonial power, and by using symbols like homespun cloth to counter foreign, machine-spun textiles, Gandhi instilled in the people a sense of pride, resourcefulness, and Indian national awareness.

A Divided Anticolonial Movement in India Although Gandhi gained a mass following, his program met opposition from within, for many in the Indian National Congress Party did not share his vision of community as the source of public life. Cambridge-educated Jawaharlal Nehru (1889–1964), for example, believed that only by embracing science and technology could India develop as a modern nation.

Even less enamored were radical activists who wanted a revolution, not peaceful protest. In the countryside, these radicals sought to organize peasants to overthrow colonial domination. Other activists galvanized the growing industrial proletariat by organizing trade unions. Their stress on class conflict ran against Gandhi's ideals of national unity.

Religion, too, threatened to fracture Gandhi's hope for anticolonial unity. The Hindu-Muslim alliance crafted by nationalists in the early 1920s splintered over who represented them and how to ensure their political rights. The Muslim community found an impressive leader in Muhammad Ali Jinnah, who set about making the Muslim League the sole representative organization of the Muslim community. In 1940, the Muslim League passed a resolution demanding independent Muslim states in provinces where Muslims constituted a majority, on the grounds that Muslims were not a religious minority of the Indian nation but a nation themselves.

In 1937, the British belatedly granted India provincial assemblies, a national legislature with two chambers, and an executive. By then, however, India's people were deeply politicized. The Congress Party, which inspired the masses to overthrow British rule, struggled to contain the different ideologies and new political institutions, such as labor unions.

peasant associations, religious parties, and communal organizations. Seeking a path to economic modernization, Gandhi, on one side, envisioned independent India as an updated collection of village republics organized around the benevolent authority of male-dominated households. Nehru, on another side, hoped for a socioeconomic transformation powered by science and state-sponsored economic planning. Both believed that India's traditions of collective welfare and humane religious and philosophical practices set it apart from the modern west. By the outbreak of World War II, India was well on its way toward political independence, but British policies and India's divisions foretold a violent end to imperial rule (see Chapter 20).

Chinese Nationalism Unlike India and Africa, China was never formally colonized. But foreign powers' "concession areas" on Chinese soil compromised its sovereignty. Indeed, foreign nationals living in China enjoyed many privileges, including immunity from Chinese law. Furthermore, unequal treaties imposed on the Qing government had robbed China of its customs and tariff autonomy. Thus, the Chinese nationalists' vision of a modern alternative echoed that of the Indian nationalists: ridding the nation of foreign domination was the initial condition of national fulfillment. For many, the 1911 Revolution (as the fall of the Qing dynasty came to be known; see Chapter 18) symbolized the first step toward transforming a crumbling agrarian empire into a modern nation.

Despite high hopes, the new republic could not establish legitimacy. For one thing, factional and regional conflicts made the government little more than a loose alliance of rural elites, merchants, and military leaders. Its intellectual inspiration came from the ideas of Sun Yat-sen, founder of the nationalist political party, the Guomindang. Under the banner of anti-imperialism, the party sponsored large-scale organizations of workers' unions, peasant leagues, and women's associations that looked to students and workers as well as the Russian Revolution for inspiration.

In 1926, amid a renewed tide of anti-foreign agitation, **Chiang Kai-shek** (1887–1975) seized control of the party following Sun's death. Chiang launched a partially successful military campaign to reunify the country and established a new national government in 1928 with its capital in Nanjing.

Peasant Populism in China: White Wolf For many Guomindang leaders, the peasant population represented a backward class. Thus, the leadership failed to tap in to the revolutionary potential of the countryside, which was alive with grassroots movements such as that of White Wolf.

From late 1913 to 1914, Chinese newspapers circulated reports about a roving band of armed men led by a mysterious figure known as White Wolf. This figure terrified members of the elite. It is unlikely that the band,

Chiang Kai-shek
(1887–1975) Leader of the Guomindang following Sun Yat-sen's death who mobilized the Chinese masses through the New Life movement. In 1949, he lost the Chinese Revolution to the Communists and moved his regime to Taiwan.

rumored to have close to a million followers, had more than 20,000 members even at its height. But the mythology surrounding White Wolf was so widespread that the movement's impact reverberated well beyond its physical presence.

Popular myth depicted White Wolf as a Chinese Robin Hood with the mission to restore order. The band's objective was to rid the country of government injustices. Raiding major trade routes and market towns, White Wolf's followers gained a reputation for robbing the rich and aiding the poor. Stories of helping the poor won the White Wolf army many followers in rural China, where local peasants joined temporarily as fighters and then returned home when the band moved on. Although the White Wolf army lacked the power to restore order in the countryside, its presence reflected the changes that had to come in China.

A Postimperial Turkish Nation Of all the postwar anticolonial movements, none was more successful or more committed to European models than that of **Mustafa Kemal Ataturk** (1881–1938), who helped forge the modern Turkish nation-state. Until 1914, the Ottoman Empire was a colonial power in its own right. But having fought on the losing German side, it saw its realm shrink to a part of Anatolia under the Treaty of Sèvres, which ended the war between the Allies and the Ottoman Empire.

In 1920, an Ottoman army officer and military hero named Mustafa Kemal harnessed an outpouring of Turkish nationalism into opposition to Greek troops that had been sent to enforce the peace treaty. Rallying his own troops to defend the fledgling Turkish nation, Kemal reconquered most of Anatolia and the area around Istanbul and secured international recognition for the new state in 1923 in the Treaty of Lausanne. Thereafter, a vast, forcible exchange of populations occurred. Approximately 1.2 million Greek Christians left Turkey to settle in Greece, and 400,000 Muslims relocated from Greece to Turkey.

With the Ottoman Empire gone, Kemal and his followers moved to build a state based on Turkish national identity. First they deposed the sultan. Then they abolished the Ottoman caliphate and proclaimed Turkey a republic, whose supreme authority would be an elected House of Assembly. Later, after Kemal insisted that the people adopt European-style surnames, the assembly conferred on Kemal the mythic name Ataturk, "father of the Turks."

In forging a Turkish nation, Kemal looked to construct a European-style secular state and to eliminate Islam's hold over civil and political affairs. The Turkish elite replaced Muslim religious law with the Swiss civil code, instituted the western (Christian) calendar, and abolished the once-powerful dervish religious orders. They also sought to eliminate Arabic and Persian words from Turkish, substituted Roman script for Arabic letters, forbade polygamy, made wearing the fez (a brimless cap associated in Kemal's mind with old-fashioned ways) a crime, and instructed Turks to wear European-style hats. The veil, though not outlawed, was denounced as a relic. In 1934, the government enfranchised Turkish women, granted them property rights in marriage and inheritance, and allowed them to enter the professions. Schools were taken out of the hands of Muslim clerics, placed under state control, and, along with military service, became the chief instrument for making the masses conscious of belonging to a Turkish nation. Yet many villagers did not accept Ataturk's non-Islamic nationalism, remaining devoted to Islam and resentful of the prohibitions against dervish dancing.

In imitating Europe, Kemal also borrowed many of its antidemocratic models. Inspired by the Soviets, he inaugurated a five-year plan for the economy emphasizing centralized coordination by the government. During the 1930s, Turkish nationalists also drew on Nazi examples by advocating racial theories that celebrated central Asian Turks as the founders of all civilization. In another authoritarian move, Kemal occasionally rigged parliamentary elections, while using the police and judiciary to silence his critics. The Kemalist revolution in Turkey was the most far-reaching and enduring transformation that had occurred outside Europe and the Americas up to that point. It offered an important model for the founding of secular, authoritarian states in the Islamic world.

Nationalism and the Rise of the Muslim Brotherhood in Egypt Elsewhere in the Middle East, where France and Britain expanded their holdings at the Ottomans' expense, anticolonial movements borrowed from European models while putting their own stamp on nation-making and modernization campaigns. In Egypt, the British occupation predated the fall of the Ottoman Empire, but here, too, World War I energized the forces of anticolonial nationalism.

When the war ended, Sa'd Zaghlul (1857–1927), an educated Egyptian patriot, pressed for an Egyptian delegation to be invited to the peace conference at Versailles. He hoped to present Egypt's case for national independence. Instead, British officials arrested and exiled him and his most vocal supporters. When news of this action came out, Egypt burst into revolt. Rural rebels broke away from the central government, proclaiming local republics. Villagers tore up railway lines and telegraph wires, the symbols of British authority.

After defusing the conflict, British authorities tried to appease the Egyptian desire to control their own destiny. In 1922, Britain proclaimed Egypt independent, although it retained the right to station British troops on Egyptian soil. This provision was intended to protect traffic through the Suez Canal and foreign populations residing in Egypt, but it also enabled the British to continue to influence Egyptian politics. Two years later, elections placed Zaghlul's nationalist party, the Wafd, in office. But the British prevented the Wafd from exercising real power.

This subversion of independence and democracy provided an opening for antiliberal versions of anticolonialism in Egypt. During the Depression years, a fascist group, Young Egypt, garnered wide appeal. Much more influential and destined to have an enduring influence throughout the Arab world was an Islamic group founded in 1928, the Muslim Brotherhood, which attacked liberal democracy as a façade for middle-class, business, and landowning interests. The Muslim Brotherhood was anticolonial and anti-British, but its members considered mere political independence insufficient. Egyptians, they argued, must also renounce the lure of the west (whether liberal capitalism or godless communism) and return to a purified form of Islam. For the Muslim Brotherhood, Islam offered a complete way of life. A "return to Islam" through the nation-state created yet another model of modernity for colonial and semicolonial peoples.

Conclusion

The Great War and its aftermath accelerated the trend toward mass participation in a broad range of activities and the debate over how to define progress and organize the people. Because mass society meant production and consumption on a staggering scale, satisfying the populace became a pressing concern for rulers worldwide. Competing programs vied for influence in the new, broader, public domain.

Most programs fell into one of three categories: liberal democratic, authoritarian, or anticolonial. Liberal democracy defined the political and economic systems in most of western Europe and the Americas in the decade following World War I. Resting on faith in free enterprise and representative democracy (with a restricted franchise), liberal regimes had already been unsettled before the Great War. Turn-of-the-century reforms broadened electorates and brought government oversight and regulation into private economic activity. But during the Great Depression, dissatisfaction again deepened. Only far-reaching reforms, introducing greater regulation and more aggressive government intervention to provide for the citizenry's welfare, saved capitalist economies and democratic political systems in Britain, France, and North America from collapse.

Through the 1930s, liberal democracy was in retreat. Authoritarianism seemed better positioned to satisfy the masses while representing the dynamism of modernity. While authoritarians differed about the faults of capitalism, they joined in the condemnation of electoral democracy. Authoritarians mobilized the masses to put the interests of the nation above the individual. That mobilization often involved brutal repression, yet it seemed also to restore pride and purpose to a great number of people.

Meanwhile, the colonial and semicolonial world searched for ways to escape from European domination. In Asia and Africa, anticolonial leaders sought to eliminate foreign rule while turning colonies into nations and subjects into citizens. Some looked to the liberal democratic west for models of nation building, but others rejected liberalism because it was associated with colonial rule. Instead, socialism, communism, fascism, and a return to religious traditions offered more promising paths.

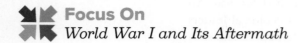

Focus On
World War I and Its Aftermath

The Great War

- The war destroys empires, starting with the Bolshevik Revolution against the tsarist regime in Russia, followed by the defeat and dissolution of the German, Austro-Hungarian, and Ottoman Empires.

- Mass mobilization sees more than 70 million men join the fighting, undermines traditional gender boundaries, and forces states to recognize their peoples' demands for compensation afterward.

- Popular culture spreads as leaders use the new media of radio and film to promote national loyalties and discredit enemies.

The Aftermath

- Liberal democracies in France, Britain, and the United States survive the Great Depression by enacting far-reaching changes in their political systems and free market economies.

- Authoritarian (communist and fascist) dictatorships with many political similarities emerge in the Soviet Union, Italy, Germany, Spain, and Portugal.

- Latin American leaders devise hybrid solutions that combine democratic and authoritarian elements.

- Peoples living under colonial rule in Asia and Africa mobilize traditional values to oppose imperial rulers.

- Key individuals emerge in the struggle to define newly independent nations: Kenyatta, Gandhi, Chiang Kai-shek, and Ataturk.

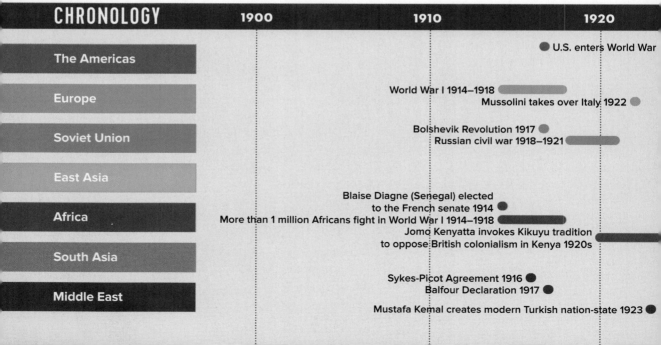

CHRONOLOGY	1900	1910	1920
The Americas			U.S. enters World War
Europe		World War I 1914–1918	Mussolini takes over Italy 1922
Soviet Union		Bolshevik Revolution 1917 Russian civil war 1918–1921	
East Asia			
Africa		Blaise Diagne (Senegal) elected to the French senate 1914 More than 1 million Africans fight in World War I 1914–1918 Jomo Kenyatta invokes Kikuyu tradition to oppose British colonialism in Kenya 1920s	
South Asia			
Middle East		Sykes-Picot Agreement 1916 Balfour Declaration 1917 Mustafa Kemal creates modern Turkish nation-state 1923	

THINKING ABOUT GLOBAL CONNECTIONS

- **Thinking about Transformation & Conflict and Visions of the Modern** What was the relationship between war and progress in the early twentieth century? What new political, social, and cultural movements grew out of the Great War? Think in particular of the role of former soldiers in politics; the adaptation in peacetime of production practices developed for the war effort; and governments' willingness and ability to regulate the economy and people's everyday lives.

- **Thinking about Changing Power Relationships and Visions of the Modern** What, if anything, was left in this period of the tradition of classical liberalism, which trusted markets to regulate themselves and believed progress would result when individuals pursued their own self-interest? What role did government intervention—in the economy and society—play for the three major traditions discussed in this chapter: liberal democratic, authoritarian, and anticolonial? How central was state intervention to their respective views of progress and modernity?

- **Thinking about Gender and Visions of the Modern** What role did women play in the social transformations of the early twentieth century, both as participants and as symbols? Pay special attention to the role of women workers in war production and, increasingly, in professional careers thereafter; to women consumers in an era of mass production; and to governments' commitment to the ideal of gender equality and their (faltering) willingness to abide by that ideal.

Key Terms

Mustafa Kemal Ataturk p. 918

Bolsheviks p. 892

Chiang Kai-shek p. 917

fascism p. 906

Mohandas Karamchand (Mahatma) Gandhi p. 915

Great Depression p. 899

Great War (World War I) p. 886

Adolf Hitler p. 906

Benito Mussolini p. 906

Nazis p. 906

nonviolent resistance p. 915

Joseph Stalin p. 903

 Go to **INQUIZITIVE** to see what you've learned—and learn what you've missed—with personalized feedback along the way.

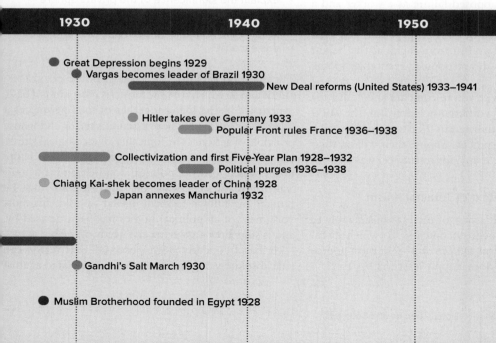

1930　　　　1940　　　　1950

● Great Depression begins 1929
● Vargas becomes leader of Brazil 1930
New Deal reforms (United States) 1933–1941

● Hitler takes over Germany 1933
Popular Front rules France 1936–1938

Collectivization and first Five-Year Plan 1928–1932
Political purges 1936–1938
● Chiang Kai-shek becomes leader of China 1928
● Japan annexes Manchuria 1932

● Gandhi's Salt March 1930

● Muslim Brotherhood founded in Egypt 1928

Global Themes and Sources

Comparing and Contextualizing Totalitarianism

The term *totalitarianism* emerged in the early twentieth century to refer to regimes that aspired to intervene more directly into people's everyday lives than previous dictatorships had done. While some writers gave the term a positive meaning, most used it critically, to condemn the erosion of basic freedoms. During the Cold War, anti-communist intellectuals in Europe and the United States linked Nazi Germany and the Soviet Union, and sometimes imperial Japan, and contrasted them with the "free world" of liberal democracies. Since the end of the Cold War, historians have largely abandoned the term, calling attention to the notable differences between Nazi Germany and the Soviet Union and to the role of ordinary people in policing one another in all the interwar dictatorships.

Hannah Arendt gave classic expression to the term *totalitarianism* in her 1951 *Origins of Totalitarianism*. The next two sources provide a more ambivalent view of state power: the letter to Marfa Gudzia shows one woman shaming another in Soviet Magnitogorsk for her husband's supposed failure as a worker and a man, while Victor Klemperer's diary shows ordinary Germans uninterested in Nazi propaganda. The final document, political graffiti from Japan at the height of the Pacific War, shows popular resistance to the militarist regime.

These sources invite you to compare and contextualize. Each provides a different window into the workings of power in authoritarian dictatorships. To what degree did the governments impose their will on their people? What space, if any, for resistance, was left?

Analyzing the Context of Totalitarianism

- How does Arendt's view of totalitarianism apply to the three subsequent documents? To which document does the term *totalitarian* seem most appropriate? To which does it apply least well?

- What role do ordinary people play in supporting or resisting the regime in the final three documents?

- Identify the nature and limits of state power in the final three documents.

The Origins of Totalitarianism (1951), Hannah Arendt

One of the most influential political philosophers of the twentieth century, Hannah Arendt (1906–1975), a Jew, fled Nazi Germany in 1933 and ultimately settled in the United States, where she received American citizenship in 1950. Her first major book, *The Origins of Totalitarianism*, linked Nazi Germany and the Soviet Union.

- Arendt claims that totalitarianism marks a fundamentally new form of politics. On what grounds does she make this claim?

- Explain the significance of the private sphere — "[t]he whole sphere of private life"—in this passage.

- What is the relationship between ruler and ruled in this excerpt?

The question we raised at the start of these considerations and to which we now return is what kind of basic experience in the living-together of men permeates a form of government whose essence is terror and whose principle of action is the logicality of ideological thinking. That such a combination was never used before in the varied forms of political domination is obvious. Still, the basic experience on which it rests must be human and known to men, insofar as even this most "original" of all political bodies has been devised by, and is somehow answering the needs of, men.

It has frequently been observed that terror can rule absolutely only over men who are isolated against each other and that, therefore, one of the primary concerns of all tyrannical government is to bring this isolation about. Isolation may be the beginning of terror; it certainly is its most fertile ground; it always is its result. This isolation is, as it were, pretotalitarian; its hallmark is impotence insofar as power always comes from men acting together, "acting in concert" ([Edmund] Burke); isolated men are powerless by definition.

Isolation and impotence, that is the fundamental inability to act at all, have always been characteristic of tyrannies. Political contacts between men are severed in tyrannical government and the human capacities for action and power are frustrated. But not all contacts between men are broken and not all human capacities destroyed. The whole sphere of private life with the capacities for experience, fabrication and thought are left intact. We know that the iron band of total terror leaves no space for such private life and that the self-coercion of totalitarian logic destroys man's capacity for experience and thought just as certainly as his capacity for action.

Source: Hannah Arendt, *The Origins of Totalitarianism* (1951; repr., San Diego: Harcourt Brace, 1973), p. 474.

Letter to Marfa Gudzia (1930s)

In this letter, a woman named Anna Kovaleva, wife of the best locomotive driver in the Soviet factory town of Magnitogorsk, writes to Marfa Gudzia, the wife of the worst, to criticize her for her husband's many shortcomings.

....

- Analyze the role of gender in this document. What is the source of Kovaleva's pride? How does she contribute to society?

- How does state power operate in this document?

- How did Kovaleva and her husband get their apartment?

....

Dear Marfa!

We are both wives of locomotive drivers of the rail transport of Magnitka. You probably know that the rail transport workers of the MMK [Magnitogorsk Metallurgical Complex] are not fulfilling the plan, that they are disrupting the supply of the blast furnaces, open hearths, and rolling shops. . . . All the workers of Magnitka accuse our husbands, saying that the rail workers hinder the fulfillment of the [overall] industrial plan. It is offensive, painful, and annoying to hear this. And moreover, it is doubly painful, because all of it is the plain truth. Every day there were stoppages and breakdowns in rail transport. Yet our internal factory transport has everything it needs in order to fulfill the plan. For that, it is necessary to work like the best workers of our country work. Among such shock workers is my husband, Aleksandr Panteleevich Kovalev. He always works like a shock worker, exceeding his norms, while economizing on fuel and lubricating oil. His engine is on profit and loss accounting. . . . My husband trains locomotive drivers' helpers out of unskilled laborers. He takes other locomotive drivers under his wing. . . . My husband receives prizes virtually every month. . . . And I too have won awards. . . .

My husband's locomotive is always clean and well taken care of. You, Marfa, are always complaining that it is difficult for your family to live. And why is that so? Because your husband, Iakov Stepanovich, does not fulfill the plan. He has frequent breakdowns on his locomotive, his locomotive is dirty, and he always overconsumes fuel. Indeed, all the locomotive drivers laugh at him. All the rail workers of Magnitka know him—for the wrong reasons, as the worst driver. By contrast, my husband is known as a shock worker. He is written up and praised in the newspapers. . . . He and I are honored everywhere as shock workers. At the store we get everything without having to wait in queues. We moved to the building for shock workers [*dom udarnika*]. We will get an apartment with rugs, a gramophone, a radio, and other comforts. Now we are being assigned to a new store for shock workers and will receive double rations. . . . Soon the Seventeenth Party Congress of our Bolshevik Party will take place. All rail workers are obliged to work so that Magnitka greets the Congress of Victors at full production capacity.

Therefore, I ask you, Marfa, to talk to your husband heart to heart, read him my letter. You, Marfa, explain to Iakov Stepanovich that he just can't go on working the way he has. Persuade him that he must work honorably, conscientiously, like a shock worker. Teach him to understand the words of comrade Stalin, that work is a matter of honor, glory, valor, and heroism.

You tell him that if he does not correct himself and continues to work poorly, he will be fired and lose his supplies. I will ask my Aleksandr Panteleevich to take your husband in tow, help him improve himself and become a shock worker, earn more. I want you, Marfa, and Iakov Stepanovich to be honored and respected, so that you live as well as we do.

I know that many women, yourself included, will say: "What business is it of a wife to interfere in her husband's work. You live well, so hold your tongue." But it is not like that. . . . We all must help our husbands to fight for the uninterrupted work of transport in the winter. OK enough. You catch my drift. This letter is already long. In conclusion, I'd like to say one thing. It's pretty good to be a wife of a shock worker. It's within our power. Let's get down to the task, amicably. I wait your answer.

Anna Kovaleva

Source: Stephen Kotkin, *Magnetic Mountain: Stalinism as a Civilization* (Berkeley: University of California Press, 1995), pp. 218–19.

PRIMARY SOURCE 19.3

Victor Klemperer's Diary (1938)

Victor Klemperer (1881–1960) was a scholar of the French Enlightenment whose diaries, published in Germany in 1995, shed light on everyday life in Nazi Germany.

- **According to Klemperer, how did the public respond to Goering's speech?**

- **Based on Klemperer's account, how would you characterize the relationship between rulers and ruled, between the Nazi state and ordinary Germans?**

- **Evaluate the influence of Nazi ideology in this document.**

September 11, Sunday

For the third time Georg has remitted 500M to me from the blocked account "of the deceased Frau Maria Kl." My joy is already no longer as great as the first two times. Because this time I was almost counting on the sum. Also it is only a very partial help; also I feel more humiliated than before, since he has not written me a single line since October and replied neither to my letter of condolence nor to my birthday greetings. Nevertheless the sum (which by the way I do not yet have in my hands, and no one knows what is going to happen tomorrow, everything is uncertain and every hour may bring new coercive measures and war), so nevertheless the money is a great relief to me at the moment. Eva was always preaching: Let the Öhlmanns come here during their holiday, then we can go for a trip with Grete. I had vacillated, the Öhlmanns' holiday came to an end, and Grete took the train to Kudowa. In view of the 500M we announced our visit to the Öhlmanns and drove to Leipzig yesterday. Luck with the weather and a very successful drive via Niederwartha, Meissen [. . .]. New rest house in Lonnewitz. Village just before Oschatz, "Long Distance Lorry Drivers' Restaurant." The huge vehicles outside, the huge portions inside. The Party Rally was coming over the loudspeaker. Announcement, the arrival of Field Marshal Goering. Introductory march, roars of triumph, then Goering's speech, about the tremendous rise, affluence, peace and workers' good fortune in Germany, about the absurd lies and hopes of its enemies, constantly interrupted by well-drilled roars of applause. But the most interesting thing about it all was the behavior of the customers, who all came and went, greeting and taking their leave with "Heil Hitler." But no one was listening. I could barely understand the broadcast because a couple of people were playing cards, striking the table with loud thumps, talking very loudly. It was quieter at other tables. One man was writing a postcard, one was writing in his order book, one was reading the newspaper. And landlady and waitress were talking to each other or to the card-players. Truly: Not one of a dozen people paid attention to the radio for even a single second, it could just as well have been transmitting silence or a foxtrot from Leipzig.

At the Öhlmanns' by two and then like the last time in early spring coffee and conversation in her little room until six. According to Trude Öhlmann's stories from the Deutsche Bücherei, where they get a great deal of official information, war is virtually certain. The air-raid precautions (we too have just had several practices, blackout, sirens), the preparations for mobilization all point to it. Mood of the public, of the workers in particular, is bad. If I talk to the butcher or the butter man here in Dresden, then there will certainly be peace, but if (as the day before yesterday) I listen to Wolf, the car man, then so many of his mates have been fetched straight from work to the army again: "Things are coming to a head now!" If I read the newspaper, see and hear the film reports, then we're doing soooo well, we love the Führer soo much and sooo unanimously—what is real, what is happening? That's how one experiences history. We know even less about today than about yesterday and no more than about tomorrow.

Source: Victor Klemperer, *I Will Bear Witness: The Diaries of Victor Klemperer*, translated by Martin Chalmers (London: Weidenfeld & Nicolson, 1998) pp. 267–68.

Political Graffiti in Imperial Japan (1941–1944)

These passages were collected by the imperial Japanese Thought Police from the walls of public and private places.

- **Are these passages evidence of the strength or weakness of the Japanese state?**
- **What can you tell about people who wrote this graffiti? What values did they share?**
- **Does this source tell us more about the opinions of ordinary Japanese people or the anxieties of the government?**

December 1941

Kill the emperor

Japan is losing in China

Why does our fatherland dare to commit aggression?
Ask the leaders why they're waging aggressive war against China.

Communism. Communism.
Workers of the world
Revolution now
. . . including the emperor

Look at the pitiful figures of the undernourished people.
Overthrow the government.
Shoot former Prime Minister Konoe, the traitor.

January 1942

Absolute opposition to the imperialist war.
Japan and Germany proclaim their domination throughout the world
But that won't make people happy.
True peace will come only when the Soviet Union obtains victory.
You laborers in military industry throughout the land—
Now is the time to become aware.

Soon we won't be able to eat.
Those who feel good being called soldiers of industry are big fools.
Win or lose, our lives won't change.
End the war (say the workers).
It's just puffing up the bourgeoisie
(says the proletariat).

March 1942

End the war.
In the end we'll lose and the people will suffer.

Her Majesty the Empress is a lecher

Sumitomo Metal is a cheating company that wrings the sweat and blood out of us workers for a pittance.
Kill those guys who decide on salaries.

June 1942

Soldiers carry weapons to kill.
What's become of things like personal character?
Ridiculous. All the more reason to commit suicide.

Capitalists are thieves, property is the fruit of
exploitation

—A Socialist

No rice. End the war.

End the war. Give us freedom.

July 1942

Capitalists ignited the war and are accumulating
wealth and hoarding it.
Give the people peace, liberty, and bread.

Destroy the aristocracy—those consuming parasites.

People's Revolution.
Japan Communist Party *banzai!*

What we believe in is nothing more than Idealism,
Liberalism, Individualism.
Become a youth of "originality."

August 1942

Overthrow the government
Raise wages

November 1942

Starvation and war dead.
The imperalist war intensified work.
Turn the war into insurrection.

Marxism *banzai*
Communist Party *banzai*

We demand repeal of the Peace Preservation Law.
We workers and farmers have been exploited as slaves
of the bourgeois landlords.
Let's throw off our submissive attitudes of the past.
Unite and overthrow Japanese imperialism and
overthrow the capitalists who have exploited and
repressed us.
Overthrow capitalism and imperialism.

No prospect of winning the war.
Kill Konoe Fumimaro.

Stop the war

December 1942

Kill the emperor
Bury the politicians, overthrow the capitalists

February 1943

Kill the dumb emperor

Don't make the farmers weep.
Kill the Minister of Agriculture
Kill Minister Ino.

Kill Tōjō

March 1943

Ridiculous to be a soldier—35 *sen* a day

May 1943

Communism *banzai*. Oppose the war.

Rid Japan of the war-mongering military.
The sword that kills one saves many.

End the war

June 1943

2,000 *yen* to whoever lops off the
emperor's head.
2,000 *yen* . . . for the empress.

Japan and the United States should cooperate for
world peace

The war is no good

July 1943

Kill the rich

Brave men! Carry out a Red revolution!
Soviet *banzai!* Japan Communist Party *banzai!*
Motherland Russia.

Attack the government's running-dog police.
You who have complaints against the government,
Join with comrades and gather under the red flag.
Anarchism. Anarchism.
Stand up, proletariat.

Destroy the bourgeoisie.

For what purpose have you all been fighting for seven years?

August 1943

Communist Party *banzai*.

Comrades of the country, band together under the flag of communism.

Do it. It's life.

Advance and overthrow the capitalists.

Concept of mutual help

Concept of joint responsibility

Concept of class struggle

. . . live with these.

September 1943

How long will the Great East Asian War last?

Three and a half years without food.

One after another, starvation. . . .

All the strong ones have perished. . . .

October 1943

Anglo-American victory, Japanese-German defeat

It's the military and bureaucrats who are profiting from the war under the beautiful name of "nation."

November 1943

To the Deity of Poverty, the Tōjō Cabinet, Liberty, and Equality:

Commoners die for the glory of a few.

For whom are we fighting this war that was started by the privileged class and the military group?

December 1943

What's wrong with liberalism and communism?

We have to reconsider this.

March 1944

Even in the Japanese empire,

Something that was bound to come has come.

What is it? Marxism.

Source: John W. Dower, *Japan in War and Peace: Selected Essays* (New York: New Press, 1993), pp. 124–28.

Interpreting Visual Evidence

Men, Machines, and Mass Production

Mass production of consumer goods reshaped economies and societies in the early twentieth century. Powered by coal and later electricity, the modern factory transformed work, first in Europe, the United States, and Japan and then, especially from 1950 onwards, around the world. The images gathered here provide several perspectives on mass production and its cult of efficiency—its efforts to streamline, to standardize productive activity, to maximize output and minimize cost—and its consequences for workers.

Large-scale manufacturing on assembly lines demands coordinated action. Engineers like Frederick Winslow Taylor (see Chapter 18) developed the field of "scientific management," the forerunner of ergonomics, to streamline the production process. Rather than shaping production to the needs and desires of skilled workers, Taylor tried to adapt machines and human bodies to one another. He and his followers broke down complex tasks into standardized, repeatable actions and then timed workers, imposing a predictable uniformity and minimizing accidents and error. Gone were the days when farmers organized their days by the light of the sun.

The French inventor-scientist Étienne-Jules Marey (1830–1904) helped prepare the way for the scientific study of labor. He developed stop-action photography in 1882, with a photographic "gun" that took twelve frames per second, which helped pave the way for modern cinema. Here we look at a series of studies of human movement that would influence Taylor and facilitate the study of labor practices around the world.

Inspired by Pablo Picasso and Karl Marx, among others, the Mexican muralist Diego Rivera (1886–1957) was fascinated by labor. His Detroit mural (1923) of the Ford Motor Company depicted workers on an assembly line, celebrating the physical force of cosmopolitan groups of industrial workers. The final two images include a photograph of a Ford assembly line in Detroit and one from a Mitsubishi electric plant in Japan in the 1930s, representing iconic examples of modern factories, with standardized, streamlined production processes powered by electricity and massive machines.

Photographs by Étienne-Jules Marey.

Mural in Detroit by Diego Rivera.

Car assembly line at Ford plant.

Mitsubishi Electric Factory.

Questions for Analysis

1. Describe the relationship between workers and machines in these images, from the point of view of the workers.

2. Explain how engineers like Taylor, who were interested in maximizing production, could also use Marey's images to improve working conditions.

3. Explain the relationship between factory production and factory workers, as depicted in these images, and mass consumption and consumers, as presented in this chapter.

4. On balance, do the images of the human body and industrial work presented here promise alienation or liberation for workers?

20

The Three-World Order

1940-1975

In February 1945, the three leaders of the World War II Allies—President Franklin Delano Roosevelt of the United States, Prime Minister Winston Churchill of Great Britain, and Premier Joseph Stalin of the Soviet Union—met to prepare for the postwar world. By then, Germany, Italy, and Japan were losing the war. But the world's postwar reordering was a source of deep contention, for the three leaders had profoundly different visions for the future. Roosevelt envisioned independent nation-states protected by an international body and had no interest in restoring the old European empires. Churchill, however, resisted decolonization of the British Empire. Stalin sought above all to secure Soviet influence in eastern Europe and to weaken Germany so that it could never again menace the Soviet Union. When the fighting stopped, the European-centered order, shocked by World War I, had been shattered by World War II. Empires lay in ruins and faced dismantling by independence movements. The nation-state had emerged as the prevailing global political organization.

With the weakening of western Europe, a new three-world order emerged. Heading the "First World," the United States championed capitalism and democracy as the best way to bring unprecedented prosperity in the decades after 1945. The Soviet Union, despite having been the United States' crucial ally during World War II, became its chief adversary in the decades that followed. As leader of the communist "Second World,"

Core Objectives

- **EXPLAIN** the relationship between World War II and the three-world order.
- **ANALYZE** the extent to which World War II was a global war.
- **ANALYZE** the roles that the United States and the Soviet Union played in the Cold War.
- **IDENTIFY** the goals of Third World states in this period, and **EVALUATE** the degree to which these goals were achieved.
- **COMPARE** the civil rights issues in the First, Second, and Third Worlds, and **ASSESS** the ways each "world" addressed these and other basic rights.

the Soviet Union contested capitalist societies' claims and trumpeted socialism's accomplishments. As their spheres of influence expanded, the Americans and the Soviets (and their respective allies) engaged in a bitter ideological rivalry, known as the **Cold War** because no direct military conflict occurred between these two superpowers. Caught in between were formerly colonized and semicolonized peoples. Lumped together as the "Third World" by western intellectuals and by Asian, Latin American, and African leaders who embraced the idea of an alternative to the two dominant blocs, these nations emerged from the war eager to seek their own ways forward.

Global Storylines

- World War II shatters the European-centered global order, weakening Europe and Japan and unsettling empires.

- The United States and its liberal democratic allies (the First World) engage in a cold war with the Soviet Union and its communist allies (the Second World).

- Decolonized states in Asia, Africa, and Latin America (the Third World) struggle to find a "third way" but find themselves caught between the rival superpowers.

World War II and Its Aftermath

World War II was truly a global conflict, a devastatingly total one. It grew out of unresolved problems connected to the Great War. World War I had not been, as many had prophesied, "the war to end all wars." Especially influential were the resentments bred by the harsh provisions and controversial state boundaries set out in the treaties signed at the war's end. World War II also resulted from the aggressive ambitions and racial theories of Germany and Japan. By the late 1930s, German and Japanese ambitions to become colonial powers brought these dictatorships (which, along with Italy, constituted the Axis powers) into conflict with France, Britain, the Soviet Union, and eventually the United States (the Allied powers). Fighting occurred in Europe, Africa, Asia, and the Atlantic and Pacific Oceans as the warring nations mobilized millions of people and placed enormous demands on civilian populations.

THE BIG PICTURE

What was the relationship between World War II and the three-world order?

THE WAR IN EUROPE

World War II began in September 1939 with Germany's invasion of Poland and Britain's and France's decision to oppose it. Before it was all over in 1945, much of Europe, including Germany, had been leveled.

Blitzkrieg and Resistance Germany's early success was staggering. Nazi troops overran Poland, France, Norway, Denmark, Luxembourg, Belgium, and the Netherlands. Within less than two years, the Germans controlled virtually all of Europe from the English Channel to the Soviet border. (See Map 20.1.) Only Britain escaped Axis control, although Nazi bombers pulverized British cities. In 1939, Germany signed a nonaggression pact with the Soviets, but in 1941, the German army broke the pact and invaded the Soviet Union with 170 divisions, 3,000 tanks, and 3.2 million men—an invasion force of a size unmatched before or since. Here, as elsewhere, the Germans fought a *blitzkrieg* (lightning war) of tank-led assaults followed by motorized infantrymen and then foot soldiers. By October 1941, the Germans had reached the outskirts of Moscow. The Soviet Union seemed on the verge of a monumental defeat.

The Nazi war was not just a grab for land and raw materials; it was also a crusade for a new order based on race. Throughout Europe, Hitler established puppet governments that complied with deportation orders against Jews and dissidents. His new order made Europe a giant police state. It gave rise to collaborators, who worked with the Germans; resistance fighters, who opposed the German occupiers for varying reasons; and a wide range of options in between, as people struggled to make their way and take care of their families as best they could.

Map 20.1 World War II: The European Theater

....

The Axis armies enjoyed great success during the early stages of World War II.

- Which parts of the European theater did the Allies control? The Axis? Which countries were neutral in 1941?
- Where did the major Allied and Axis campaigns take place?
- What was Germany's greatest geographic obstacle during World War II?

The Devastation of War In November 1942, Nazi troops entered Stalingrad, some 2,000 miles from Berlin. Hitler wanted to capture the city not only to exploit the surrounding wheat fields and the oil of the Caucasus, but also for its very name. With handheld flamethrowers and sometimes just their fists, Soviet troops drove out the Germans in February 1943.

In the east, the tide turned against the Germans and their collaborators after the ferocious battles of Stalingrad in 1942–1943 and Kursk in 1943. At the Battle of Stalingrad, the German army and its allies had 1.5 million men killed, wounded, or captured, compared with 750,000 Soviet troops suffering the same fates. Only six months later, at the Battle of Kursk, the largest tank conflict in world history, the Germans, boasting a tank force of more than 2,000, lost to a Soviet tank force twice its size. Once the Soviet army had blunted the initial German assault, it launched a massive counter-offensive. This move initiated the defeat of the German war effort on the Eastern Front, but full retreat took another two years as the Soviets drove Hitler's army slowly westward. The spectacular D-Day landing of western Allied forces in Normandy on June 6, 1944 (when the Germans had a mere 15 divisions in France, as compared with more than 300 on the Eastern Front), initiated Germany's defeat in the west. On April 30, 1945, as Soviet and Anglo-American forces converged on Berlin, Hitler committed suicide. Days later, Germany surrendered unconditionally.

The Bitter Costs of War The war in Europe had devastating human and material costs. This was particularly true in eastern Europe, where German forces leveled more than 70,000 Soviet villages, obliterated one-third of the Soviet Union's wealth, and inflicted 7 million Soviet military deaths (by contrast, the Germans lost 3.5 million soldiers) and at least 20 million civilian deaths. German bombing of British cities, such as London, took a heavy toll on civilians and buildings, as did Allied bombing of Axis war plants and cities like Dresden and Tokyo. Tens of millions were left homeless.

Europe's Jews paid an especially high price. Hitler had long talked of "freeing" Europe of all Jews. At the war's outset, the Nazis herded Jews into ghettos and labor camps, then seized their property. As the German army moved eastward, more and more Jews came under their control.

At first the Nazi bureaucrats considered deportation of Jews, but then ruled out transporting "subhumans" as too costly, and began instead to starve them and crowd them together in unsanitary ghettos. By summer 1941, special troops operating behind the army on the Eastern Front had begun mass shootings of communists and Jewish civilians, and by fall 1941, Hitler and the S.S.—the *Schutzstaffel*, or special security forces—were building a series of killing centers in the east. Cattle cars shipped Jews from all over Europe to these extermination sites, where Nazis used the latest technology, including the arsenic-based poison gas Zyklon B, to kill men, women, and children. The largest facility, Auschwitz, combined an extermination center and work camp in a single complex.

The deliberate extermination of the Jews, known as the **Holocaust**, claimed around 6 million lives. About half of this number died in the gas chambers of death camps; the others were shot, gassed in mobile vans, or succumbed to starvation or disease. The shift to a policy of extermination was both unimaginably brutal and rapid. At its core, the Holocaust was brief, intense mass murder. In mid-March 1942, roughly three-quarters of all victims of the Holocaust were still alive and one-quarter had been killed; within a year—by March 1943—the proportions were reversed, with three-quarters of the victims dead. The Nazis also turned their mass killing apparatus against Sinta and Roma (gypsies), homosexuals, communists, and Slavs, with deportations to the death camps continuing to the very end of the war.

These Nazi genocides—enormous in scale and reliant on modern, "enlightened" administrative practices—stood as a powerful challenge to European claims that science, technology, and an efficient bureaucracy would make life better for everyone. Lamenting connections between European culture and the Holocaust, German philosopher Theodor Adorno wrote that "to write poetry after Auschwitz is barbaric" (1949). Nazi crimes, he suggested, defied human understanding.

THE WAR IN THE PACIFIC

Like the war in Europe, the conflict in the Pacific transformed the military and political landscape. (See Map 20.2.) The war broke out when Japan's ambitions to dominate Asia targeted American interests and military might.

Japan's Efforts to Expand Japanese efforts to expand in Asia were already under way in the 1930s, but the outbreak of war in Europe opened opportunities for further expansion. Having fought with the Allies in World War I, Japan was granted control of the South Pacific Mandate (1919–1947) by the

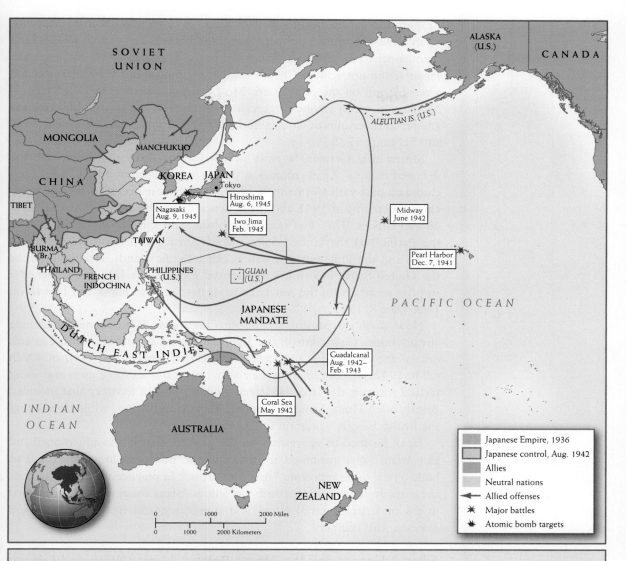

Map labels:
SOVIET UNION
ALASKA (U.S.)
CANADA
MONGOLIA
MANCHUKUO
ALEUTIAN IS. (U.S.)
CHINA
KOREA
JAPAN
Tokyo
Hiroshima Aug. 6, 1945
Nagasaki Aug. 9, 1945
Iwo Jima Feb. 1945
Midway June 1942
TIBET
TAIWAN
Pearl Harbor Dec. 7, 1941
BURMA (Br.)
THAILAND
FRENCH INDOCHINA
PHILIPPINES (U.S.)
GUAM (U.S.)
PACIFIC OCEAN
JAPANESE MANDATE
DUTCH EAST INDIES
Guadalcanal Aug. 1942– Feb. 1943
INDIAN OCEAN
Coral Sea May 1942
AUSTRALIA
NEW ZEALAND

Legend:
Japanese Empire, 1936
Japanese control, Aug. 1942
Allies
Neutral nations
Allied offenses
Major battles
Atomic bomb targets

Scale:
0   1000   2000 Miles
0   1000   2000 Kilometers

Map 20.2 World War II: The Pacific Theater

Like Germany and Italy, Japan experienced stunning military successes in the war's early years.

- In August, 1942, which areas in the Pacific theater were under the control of the Japanese, and which were under Allied control?
- What does tracing the route of the Allied offense tell you about their main strategy?
- What geographic factors influenced the American decision to drop atomic bombs on Hiroshima and Nagasaki to end the war, instead of invading Japan?

League of Nations. Japan's military forces invaded and occupied Manchuria in 1931—creating a puppet state called Manchukuo (1937–1945)—and then launched an offensive against the rest of China in 1937. Although the Japanese did not achieve China's complete submission, the invaders exacted a terrible toll on the population. Most infamous was the so-called rape of Nanjing, in which Japanese aggressors slaughtered at least 100,000 civilians and raped thousands of women in the Chinese city between December 1937 and February 1938.

Meanwhile, Germany's swift occupation of western Europe left the defeated nations' Asian colonies at the mercy of Japanese forces. After concluding a pact with Germany in 1940, the Japanese occupied French Indochina (Vietnam) in 1941 and made demands on the Dutch East Indies for oil and rubber. The chief remaining obstacle to their further expansion in the Pacific was the United States, which already had imperial interests in China and the Philippines as well as other Pacific islands. Hoping to strike the United States before it was prepared for war, the Japanese launched a surprise air attack on the American naval base at Pearl Harbor in Hawaii on December 7, 1941.

Now Japan's expansion shifted into high gear. With French Indochina already under their control, the Japanese turned against the American colony of the Philippines and against the Dutch East Indies, both of which fell in 1942. By coordinating their army, navy, and air force units and using tactical surprise, the Japanese seized a huge swath of territory that included British-ruled Hong Kong, Singapore, Malaya, and Burma while threatening the British Empire's hold on India as well.

Japan justified its aggression on the grounds that it was anticolonial and pan-Asian: Japan promised to drive out the European imperialists and to build a new order reflecting "Asia for Asians." In practice, however, the Japanese made oppressive demands on fellow Asians for resources, developed myths of Japanese racial purity and supremacy, and treated Chinese and Koreans with brutality.

Allied Advances and the Atomic Bomb Like the Germans in their war against the Soviet Union, the Japanese could not sustain their military successes against the United States. By mid-1943, U.S. forces had put the Japanese on the defensive. Fighting their way from island to island, American troops recaptured the Philippines, and a combined force of British, American, and Chinese troops returned Burma to Britain. The Allies then moved toward the Japanese mainland. By summer 1945, American bombers had all but devastated the major cities of Japan. Yet Japan did not surrender.

Anticipating that an invasion of Japan would cost hundreds of thousands of American lives, U.S. President Harry Truman unleashed the Americans' secret weapon. It was the work of a team of scientists who were predominantly

The Aftermath of the Atomic Bomb A view of Nagasaki less than half a mile from "ground zero" after the atomic bomb was dropped in August 1945. A few reinforced concrete buildings still stand.

European refugees. On August 6, 1945, an American plane dropped an atomic bomb on the city of Hiroshima, killing or maiming over 100,000 people and poisoning the air, soil, and groundwater for decades to come. Three days later, the Americans dropped a second atomic bomb on Nagasaki. Within days, Emperor Hirohito announced Japan's surrender, bringing the war to an official end. After the six years of World War II, much of East Asia and Europe lay in ruins; millions had died, and millions more were wounded, displaced, widowed, and orphaned. What the postwar world would look like, however, remained unclear.

The Beginning of the Cold War

The destruction of Europe and the defeat of Japan left a power vacuum, which the United States and the Soviet Union rushed to fill. Avoiding direct warfare, the Americans and Soviets vied for influence in postwar Europe and around the globe in a series of smaller, indirect conflicts.

Core Objectives

ANALYZE the roles that the United States and the Soviet Union played in the Cold War.

REBUILDING EUROPE

Communism and liberal democracy offered competing approaches to rebuilding states and societies in Europe after World War II. The task of

The Berlin Airlift In summer 1948, West Berlin seemed poised to become an outpost of the west inside the Soviet occupation zone. The Soviets responded by blocking western traffic into Berlin; the west countered with an airlift, forcing the Soviets to back down in May 1949 but hastening the division of Germany into two countries.

political rebuilding was daunting, for the old order had been discredited. Liberal democrats had to distance themselves from their prewar predecessors. Communism, by contrast, gained new appeal. Many eastern Europeans, reacting to the horrors of fascism and not knowing the extent of Stalin's crimes, looked to the Soviets for answers.

Europe's leftward tilt alarmed U.S. policymakers. They feared that the Soviets would use their ideological influence and the territory taken from the Nazis by the Red Army to spread communism. They also worried that Stalin might seize Europe's overseas possessions and create communist regimes outside Europe. But no one wished to fight another "hot" war. As President Truman began advocating a policy of containment to prevent the further advance of communism, an American journalist popularized the term *cold war* in 1946 to describe a new form of struggle in which both sides endeavored to avoid direct warfare.

Truman's containment policy was tested when the Soviets attempted to seize control of Berlin. Like the rest of Germany, Berlin had been partitioned into British, French, American, and Soviet zones of occupation, but the city itself was an island lying within the Soviet zone. In 1948, the Soviets attempted to cut the city off from western access by blocking routes between the western zones of Germany and the western zones of Berlin. The Allies responded with the Berlin Airlift, transporting supplies in planes to West Berlin in hope of keeping the population from capitulating to the Soviets. This crisis lasted for almost a year, until Stalin lifted the blockade in May 1949.

In that same year, occupied Germany was split into two hostile states: the democratic Federal Republic of Germany (West Germany) in the west, and the communist German Democratic Republic (East Germany) in the east. In 1961, leaders in the German Democratic Republic built a wall around West Berlin to insulate the east from capitalist propaganda and to halt a flood of émigrés fleeing communism. The Berlin Wall became the great symbol of a divided Europe and of the Cold War.

U.S. policymakers wanted to shore up democratic governments in Europe, so Truman promised American military and economic aid. Containing the spread of communism meant securing a capitalist future for Europe, a job that fell to Truman's secretary of state, General George C. Marshall. He launched the Marshall Plan, an ambitious program that provided over $13 billion in grants and credits to reconstruct Europe and facilitate an economic revival. U.S. policymakers hoped the aid would dim communism's appeal by fostering economic prosperity, muting class tensions, and integrating western European nations into an alliance of capitalist democracies.

Stalin saw the Marshall Plan as a threat to the Soviet Union and rejected the offer of support. He felt the same way about the formation in 1949 of the **North Atlantic Treaty Organization (NATO)**, a military alliance between countries in western Europe and North America. He believed that the Soviet Union, having sacrificed millions of people to the war against fascism, deserved to be dominant in eastern Europe. Soviet troops had occupied eastern European nations at the war's end, and in those nations, communists and leftist members of other parties formed Soviet-backed coalition governments. In 1955, the Soviets formally allied themselves with these communist nations in the **Warsaw Pact**, a military alliance of their own. (See Map 20.3.) The tense confrontations between NATO and the Warsaw Pact countries in Europe and in other parts of the world in the 1950s and 1960s brought the world to the brink of an atomic World War III.

WAR IN THE NUCLEAR AGE: THE KOREAN WAR

The dropping of the atomic bombs on Japan in 1945 changed military affairs forever. Spurred by the onset of the Cold War, the Soviets worked hard to

North Atlantic Treaty Organization (NATO)
International organization set up in 1949 to provide for the defense of western European countries and the United States from the perceived Soviet threat.

Warsaw Pact (1955–1991)
Military alliance between the Soviet Union and other communist states that was established in response to the creation of the North American Treaty Organization (NATO).

Map 20.3 NATO and Warsaw Pact Countries

The Cold War divided Europe into two competing blocs: those allied with the United States in the North Atlantic Treaty Organization (NATO) and those linked to the Soviet Union under the Warsaw Pact.

- Which nations had borders with nations belonging to the opposite bloc?
- Comparing this map with Map 20.1, explain how combat patterns in World War II shaped the dividing line between the two blocs.
- According to the map, where would you expect Cold War tensions to be the most intense?

U.S. and Canada are also part of NATO

Location	Marshall aid
NORWAY	$236 million
SWEDEN	$107 million
DENMARK	$273 million
IRELAND	$148 million
NETHERLANDS	$1084 million
GREAT BRITAIN	$3190 million
Luxembourg and Belgium together receive	$546 million
WEST GERMANY 1955	$1391 million
FRANCE	$2714 million
AUSTRIA	$678 million
ITALY	$1509 million
PORTUGAL	$51 million
GREECE 1952	$707 million
TURKEY 1952	$225 million

SPAIN 1982

ALBANIA until 1968

Legend:
- NATO
- Warsaw Pact
- Neutral
- U.S. $ Marshall aid recipient

catch up to the Americans, and in 1949 tested their first nuclear bomb. Thereafter, each side rushed to stockpile nuclear weapons and update its military technologies. By 1960, the explosive power of these weapons had increased so greatly that nuclear war had the potential to destroy the world without a soldier firing a single shot. This sobering realization changed the rules of the game. Each side now possessed the power to inflict total destruction on the other, a circumstance that inhibited direct confrontations but sparked smaller conflicts in parts of Asia such as Korea, where Japan's defeat resulted in an uneasy standoff between the communist North, backed by the Soviet Union, and the South, backed by the U.S.

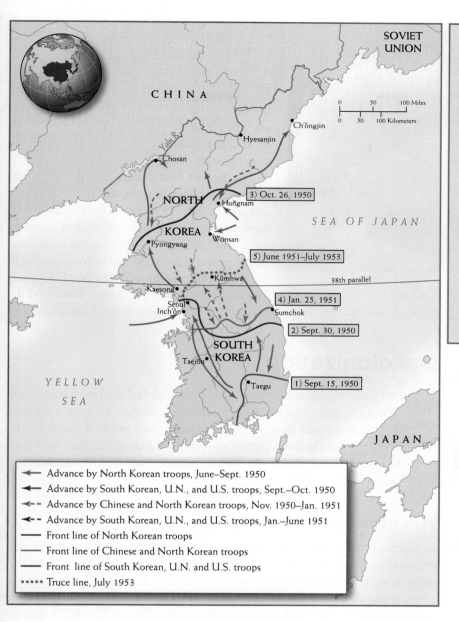

Map 20.4 The Korean War

The Korean War was an early confrontation between the capitalist and communist blocs during the Cold War era.

- What were the dates of each side's farthest advance into the other side's territory?

- Why was this peninsula strategically important?

- According to your reading, how did the outcome of the war shape political affairs in East Asia for the next several decades?

Map labels: SOVIET UNION, CHINA, NORTH KOREA, SOUTH KOREA, SEA OF JAPAN, YELLOW SEA, JAPAN, Yalu R., Ch'ŏngjin, Hyesanjin, Chosan, Hŭngnam, Pyongyang, Wonsan, Kŭmhwa, Kaesong, 38th parallel, Seoul, Inch'ŏn, Sumchok, Taejŏn, Taegu

3) Oct. 26, 1950
5) June 1951–July 1953
4) Jan. 25, 1951
2) Sept. 30, 1950
1) Sept. 15, 1950

0 50 100 Miles
0 50 100 Kilometers

Legend:

- Advance by North Korean troops, June–Sept. 1950
- Advance by South Korean, U.N., and U.S. troops, Sept.–Oct. 1950
- Advance by Chinese and North Korean troops, Nov. 1950–Jan. 1951
- Advance by South Korean, U.N., and U.S. troops, Jan.–June 1951
- Front line of North Korean troops
- Front line of Chinese and North Korean troops
- Front line of South Korean, U.N. and U.S. troops
- Truce line, July 1953

In 1950, North Korean troops invaded South Korea, setting off the Korean War. (See Map 20.4.) President Truman ordered American troops to drive back the North Koreans. The Security Council of the United Nations—an international body established in 1945 to help prevent another world war—also sent troops from fifteen nations to restore peace. Within a year, the invaders had been routed and were near collapse. When U.N. troops

Atom Bomb Anxiety This photograph shows schoolchildren taking shelter under their desks during an A-bomb drill in Brooklyn, New York, 1951. The Soviets had exploded their first test bomb in 1949. Underground bomb shelters were built in many American urban areas as places in which to survive a doomsday attack.

advanced north to the Chinese border, however, Stalin maneuvered his communist Chinese allies into rescuing the communist regime in North Korea and driving the South Korean and U.N. forces back to the old boundary in the middle of the Korean peninsula. The fighting continued until 1953, when an armistice divided the country at roughly the same spot as at the start of the war.

The Korean War energized America's anticommunist commitments and spurred a rapid increase in NATO forces. The United States now saw Japan as a bulwark against communism and resolved to rebuild Japanese economic power. Like West Germany, Japan went from being the enemy in World War II to being a valued U.S. ally as the Cold War rivalry between the United States and the Soviet Union spurred both sides to shore up alliances around the globe.

Decolonization

The unsettling of empires, including those established by Japan before and during World War II and the longer-standing colonies held by European states, inspired colonial peoples to reconsider their political futures. The resulting process of **decolonization** and nation building followed four general patterns: civil wars, negotiated independence, wars of independence, and incomplete decolonization.

THE CHINESE REVOLUTION

In China, the ousting of the Japanese occupiers intensified a civil war that eventually brought the Chinese Communist Party to power. The communist movement in China had its origins in post–World War I hostility toward the western powers. In that period, the communists had vowed to free China from colonialism, but had been outgunned by Chiang Kai-shek's nationalist regime and driven from China's cities; they retreated into the interior, where they founded base camps. In 1934, under attack by Chiang's forces, the communists, led by **Mao Zedong** (1893–1976), abandoned their bases and undertook an arduous 6,000-mile journey through the rugged terrain of northwestern China. (See Map 20.5.) In the course of this great escape, glorified in communist lore as the Long March, fewer than 10,000 of the approximately 80,000 people who started the journey reached their

decolonization
End of empire and emergence of new independent nation-states in Asia and Africa as a result of the defeat of Japan in World War II and weakened European influence after the war.

SOVIET UNION

OUTER MONGOLIA

INNER MONGOLIA

GANSU

GREAT WALL

Beijing
Tianjin

SHENYANG

SEA OF JAPAN

KOREA

JAPAN

QINGHAI

Lanzhou

Taiyuan
Yan'an
SHAANXI

Jinan

YELLOW SEA

GREAT GRASSLANDS

Xi'an

Luoyang

CHINA

Nanjing
Shanghai

EAST CHINA SEA

TIBET

SICHUAN

Chengdu

Hankou
Yichang

Yangtze R.

GREAT SNOW MT.

Chongqing

HUNAN
Changsha
Jinggangshan

JIANGXI

Nanchang

FUJIAN

INDIA

Zunyi

Guiyang

GUIZHOU

Guilin

Ruijin

Kunming

GUANGXI

GUANGDONG

Xiamen (Amoy)
Shantou

TAIWAN

YUNNAN

Guangzhou (Canton)

Hong Kong

BURMA

FRENCH INDOCHINA

SOUTH CHINA SEA

0   250   500 Miles
0   250   500 Kilometers

Map 20.5 The Long March, 1934–1935

During the Long March, which took place during the struggle for power between the nationalist Guomindang and the communists within China, communist forces traveled over 6,000 miles to save their lives and their movement.

- What route did the communist forces take?
- Why did the communists take this particular route?
- How did this movement affect the outcome of this internal struggle in the long run?

destination. Fortunately for the communists, the Japanese invasion in 1937 diverted nationalist troops and offered Mao and the survivors a chance to regroup.

Mao's followers cultivated popular support by advocating the lowering of taxes, cooperative farming, and policies aimed at women's emancipation, such as the outlawing of arranged marriages and the legalization of divorce. Like many anticolonial reformers, Mao regarded women's emancipation as a key component in building a new nation, since he considered their oppression to be both unjust and an obstacle to progress.

Communist expansion in rural areas during World War II swelled the membership of the Communist Party from 40,000 in 1937 to over a million in 1945. After Japan's surrender, China's civil war between nationalists

Mao Zedong (1893–1976)
Chinese communist leader who rose to power during the Long March (1934). In 1949, he defeated the nationalists and established a communist regime in China.

and communists resumed. But the communist forces now had the numbers, the guns (mostly supplied by the Soviet Union), and the popular support to assault nationalist strongholds and seize power, establishing the People's Republic of China in 1949.

NEGOTIATED INDEPENDENCE IN INDIA AND AFRICA

In India and most of colonial Africa, gaining independence involved little bloodshed, although the aftermath was often extremely violent. The British, realizing that they could no longer rule India without coercion, bowed to the inevitable and withdrew. The same happened in many African colonies, where nationalists also succeeded in negotiating independence from European empires, although, as we shall see, there were notable exceptions.

India Unlike China, India achieved political independence without an insurrection. But it did veer dangerously close to civil war. The leadership of the Indian National Congress Party retained tight control over the mass movement that it had mobilized in the 1920s and 1930s (see Chapter 19). Even Gandhi hesitated to leave the initiative to the common people, believing that they had not yet assimilated the doctrine of nonviolence. Gandhi and the party leadership worked hard to convince the British that they, the middle-class leaders, spoke for the nation. At the same time, the threat of a mass peasant uprising with radical aims (like the communist revolution in China) encouraged the British to transfer power quickly.

As negotiations moved forward, Hindu-Muslim unity deteriorated. Whose culture would define the new nation? The Indian nationalism that had existed in the late nineteenth century reflected the culture of the Hindu majority. Yet this movement masked the multiplicity of regional, linguistic, caste, and class differences *within* the Hindu community, just as Muslim movements that arose in reaction to Hindu-dominated Indian nationalism overlooked divisions within their own ranks. Now the prospect of defining "India" created a grand contest between newly self-conscious communities. Riots broke out between Hindus and Muslims in 1946, which increased the mutual distrust between the Congress Party and Muslim League leaders. The specter of civil war haunted the proceedings as outgoing colonial rulers decided to divide the subcontinent into two states: India and Pakistan.

On August 14, 1947, Pakistan gained independence from Britain; a day later, India did the same. The euphoria of decolonization, however, was drowned in a frenzy of brutality. Shortly after independence, as many as 1 million Hindus and Muslims killed one another. Fearing further violence, 12 million Hindus and Muslims left their homes to relocate in the new countries where they would be in the majority. Although the British departed peacefully from India, the peoples inhabiting the subcontinent engaged in open warfare over differences that haunt the relationship between India and Pakistan to this day.

Africa for Africans Shortly after Indian independence, most African states also gained their sovereignty. Except in southern Africa, where minority white rule persisted, the old colonial states gave way to indigenous rulers.

The postwar years saw Africans move to cities in search of a better life. As expanding educational systems produced a wave of primary and secondary school graduates, these educated young people and other new urban dwellers became disgruntled when attractive employment opportunities were not forthcoming. Three groups—former servicemen, the urban unemployed or underemployed, and the educated—led the nationalist agitation that began in the late 1940s and early 1950s. (See Map 20.6.)

Faced with rising nationalist demands, and too much in debt to invest more in pacifying the discontented colonies, European powers agreed to decolonize. The Soviet Union and the United States also favored decolonization. Thus, decolonization in most of Africa was a rapid and relatively sedate affair. In 1957, the Gold Coast (renamed Ghana), under Prime Minister Kwame Nkrumah, became tropical Africa's first independent state. Other British colonial territories followed in rapid succession, so that by 1963, all of British-ruled Africa, except for Southern Rhodesia, was independent.

Decolonization in much of French-ruled Africa followed a similarly smooth path, although the French were initially resistant. Instead of negotiating independence, they tried first to accord fuller voting rights to their colonial subjects, even allowing Africans and Asians to send delegates to the French National Assembly. In the end, however, the French electorate had no desire to share the privileges of French citizenship with African and Asian populations. Thus, France dissolved its political ties with French West Africa and French Equatorial Africa in 1960, having given protectorates in Morocco and Tunisia their independence in 1956. Algeria, considered an integral part of France, was a different matter. France's desperate efforts to hold onto Algeria (see below) facilitated independence movements elsewhere in Africa.

The leaders of African independence movements believed that Africa's precolonial traditions would enable the region to move from colonialism right into a special African form of socialism, escaping the ravages of capitalism. Without rejecting western culture completely, they praised the so-called African personality, exemplified by the idea of "Negritude" developed by Senegal's first president, Léopold Sédar Senghor. Negritude, they claimed, was steeped in common African traditions and able to embrace social justice and equality while rejecting the unrestrained individualism that Africans felt lay at the core of European culture.

Map 20.6
Decolonization in Africa

African decolonization occurred after World War II, largely in the 1950s, 1960s, and 1970s.

- Find at least four areas that won independence in the 1950s and identify the former colonial power that ruled each area.
- What areas took longer to gain independence?
- According to your reading, what problems and tensions contributed to this uneven process of decolonization across Africa?

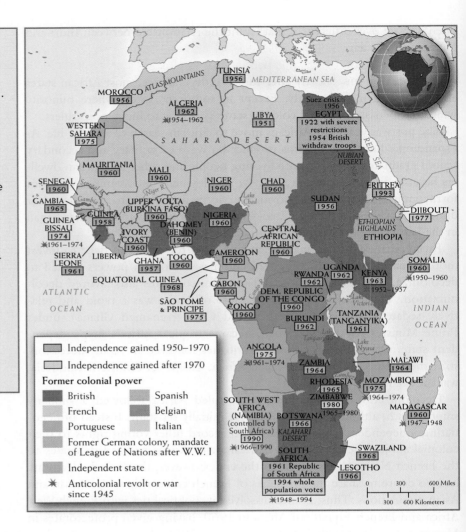

Independence gained 1950–1970
Independence gained after 1970

Former colonial power

British   Spanish
French   Belgian
Portuguese   Italian
Former German colony, mandate of League of Nations after W.W. I
Independent state
✳   Anticolonial revolt or war since 1945

VIOLENT AND INCOMPLETE DECOLONIZATIONS

Although transfers of power in most of Africa and Asia ultimately occurred peacefully, there were notable exceptions. In Palestine, Algeria, Kenya, and southern Africa, the presence of European immigrant groups created violent conflicts that aborted any peaceful transfer of power—or left the process incomplete. In Vietnam, the process was also violent and delayed, partly because of France's desire to reimpose colonial control and partly because of the power politics of Cold War competition.

Palestine, Israel, and Egypt In Palestine, Arabs and Jews had been on a collision course since the end of World War I. Before that war, a group of

European Jews, known as Zionists, had argued that only a large-scale migration from existing states to their place of origin in Palestine could lead to Jewish self-determination. Zionism combined a yearning to return to the holy lands with a fear of anti-Semitism and anguish over increasing Jewish assimilation. Zionists wanted to create a Jewish state, and they won a crucial victory during World War I when the British government, under the Balfour Declaration, promised a homeland for the Jews in Palestine. But when the British took control of Palestine after 1918, they also guaranteed the rights of Palestinian Arabs.

As more Jews settled in Palestine, tensions arose between Zionists and Palestinian Arabs, and both grew dissatisfied with British rule. Arabs resented the presence of Jews, who displaced farmers who had lived on the land for generations and who openly sought their own independent state. Zionists became especially enraged when British authorities wavered in supporting their demands for more immigration. After World War II, the pressure to allow more immigration increased as hundreds of thousands of concentration camp survivors clamored for entry into Palestine, and Zionist militants began using force to attempt to gain control of the state.

In 1947, after the British announced that they would leave negotiations over the area's fate to the United Nations, that body voted to partition Palestine into Arab and Jewish territories. The Arab states rejected the partition, and the Jewish Agency, a nongovernmental organization that supported the immigration of Jews to Israel, only reluctantly accepted it. Although the Jews were delighted to have an independent state, they were unhappy about its small size, its indefensible borders, and the fact that it did not include all the lands that had belonged to ancient Israel. For their part, the Palestinians were shocked at the partition, and they looked to their better-armed Arab neighbors to regain the territories set aside for the new state of Israel.

The ensuing Arab-Israeli War of 1948–1949 shattered the legitimacy of Arab ruling elites. Arab states entered the war poorly prepared to take on the well-run and enthusiastically supported Israeli Defense Force. By the time the United Nations finally negotiated a truce, Israel had declared its independence (May 14, 1948) and extended its boundaries; more than 1 million Palestinians had become refugees in surrounding Arab countries.

Embittered by this defeat, a group of young army officers in Egypt plotted to overthrow the Egyptian regime, which they felt was corrupt and still under European influence. One of the officers, Gamal Abdel Nasser, became the head of a secret organization of junior military officers called the Free Officers movement. These men had ties with communists and other dissident groups, including the Muslim Brotherhood, which favored a return to Islamic rule. They launched a successful coup in 1952, forcing the king to abdicate and leave the country. The new regime dissolved the parliament, banned political parties (including the communists and the Muslim Brotherhood), and stripped the old elite of its wealth.

In 1956, Nasser moved to nationalize the Suez Canal Company (an Egyptian company, mainly run by French businessmen and experts), inciting the Israelis, the British, and the French to invade Egypt and seize territory along the Suez Canal. Opposition by the United States and the Soviet Union forced the invading countries to withdraw, providing Nasser with a spectacular diplomatic triumph. As Egyptian forces reclaimed the canal, Nasser's reputation as leader of the Arab world soared. He became the chief symbol of a pan-Arab nationalism that swept across the Middle East and North Africa and especially through the camps of Palestinian refugees.

The Algerian War of Independence The appeal of Arab nationalism was particularly strong in Algeria, where a population of 1 million European settlers (the *colons*) stood in the way of decolonization. Indeed, French leaders claimed that Algeria was an integral part of France. Although the *colons* were a minority in Algeria, they held the best land and generally lived in the major cities near the coast. They controlled Algeria's finances and all of its major public institutions.

Anticolonial nationalism in Algeria gathered force after World War II. The Front de Libération Nationale (FLN) emerged as the leading nationalist party in the 1950s, using violence to provoke its opponents and to make the local population choose between supporting the nationalist cause or the *colons*. The full-fledged revolt that erupted in 1954 pitted FLN troops and guerrillas against thousands of French troops. Atrocities and terrorist acts occurred on both sides.

The war dragged on for eight years, at a cost of perhaps 300,000 lives. On the French mainland, the war came as a terrible shock, for many, though not all, French citizens had accepted the idea that Algeria was not a colonial territory but part of France itself. The *colons* insisted that they had emigrated to Algeria in response to their government's promises and that yielding power to the nationalists would be a betrayal. After an insurrection led by *colons* and army officers brought down the French government in 1958, the new French president, Charles de Gaulle, negotiated a peace accord. Shortly after the handover of power to FLN leaders, 800,000 *colons* left Algeria. By late 1962, over nine-tenths of its European and indigenous Jewish population had departed.

Southern Africa The bloody conflict in Algeria highlights a harsh reality of African decolonization: the presence of European settlers often prevented the smooth transfer of power. South Africa, which held the continent's largest and wealthiest settler population (a mixture of Afrikaans- and English-speaking peoples of European descent), defied black majority rule longer than other African states. After winning the elections of 1948, the white Afrikaner–dominated National Party enacted an extreme form of racial segregation known as apartheid. Under apartheid, laws stripped Africans, Indians, and "colored" persons (those of mixed descent) of their few political rights. Racial mixing of any kind was forbidden, and schools were strictly segregated.

The ruling party tolerated no protest. Nelson Mandela, one of the leaders of the African National Congress (ANC), a group that campaigned for an end to discriminatory legislation, was repeatedly harassed, detained, and tried by the government, even though he had at first urged peaceful resistance. After the Sharpeville massacre in 1960, in which police killed demonstrators who were peacefully protesting the oppressive laws, Mandela and the ANC decided to oppose the apartheid regime with violence. A South African court sentenced Mandela to life imprisonment, and the government banned the ANC.

Women helped keep resistance flames burning. The most dynamic of these individuals was Winnie Mandela, wife of the imprisoned Nelson Mandela. Unlike many of the ANC leaders, who opposed the regime from exile, she remained in South Africa and openly and courageously spoke out against the apartheid government. Nonetheless, whites retained external support. Through the 1950s and 1960s, western powers (especially the United States) saw South Africa as a bulwark against the spread of communism in Africa.

Vietnam The same concern to contain communism also drew the United States into support for a conservative and pro-western regime in South Vietnam. Vietnam had come under French rule in the 1880s, and by the 1920s approximately 40,000 Europeans were living among and ruling over roughly 19 million Vietnamese. To promote an export economy of rice, mining, and rubber, the colonial rulers granted vast land concessions to French companies and local collaborators while leaving large numbers of peasants landless.

The colonial system also generated a new intelligentsia. Primarily schooled in French and Franco-Vietnamese schools, educated Vietnamese worked as clerks, shopkeepers, teachers, and petty officials. Yet they had few opportunities for advancement. Discontented, they turned from the traditional ideology of Confucianism to modern nationalism. Vietnamese intellectuals overseas, notably Ho Chi Minh, one of the original founders of the French Communist Party, took the lead in imagining a new Vietnamese nation-state.

When the French tried to restore their rule in Vietnam after Japan's defeat in 1945, Ho led the resistance. War with France followed (1946–1954). The Viet Minh (League for the Independence of Vietnam) used guerrilla tactics to undermine French positions. They were most successful in the north, but even in the south their campaign bled the French. Finally, in 1954, the anti-colonial forces won a decisive military victory. At a conference held in Geneva that year, Vietnam (like Korea) was divided into two zones. Ho controlled the north, while a government with French and American support took charge in the south.

During the early 1960s, U.S. involvement in Vietnam escalated as Ho's support for the Viet Cong (Vietnamese communist) guerrillas heightened American concerns about the spread of communism. In 1965, large numbers of American troops entered the country to fight on behalf of South Vietnam, while communist North Vietnam turned to the Soviet Union for supplies. Over the next several years, the United States sent some 500,000 soldiers to fight the Vietnam War, but peasant support enabled the Viet Cong to continue fierce guerrilla fighting. Even the bombing of villages and the deployment of counterinsurgency forces failed to prevent the spread of communism in Southeast Asia. In 1975, two years after the final withdrawal of American troops, the South Vietnamese government collapsed.

Thus, the process of decolonization varied across regions. Although most of the lands in Asia and Africa had gained independence by the mid-1960s, there were significant exceptions in Africa—South Africa, Southern Rhodesia, and the Portuguese colonies—and Asia—notably Vietnam. Although the British and French realized that they no longer had the resources to stem the nationalist tide that was spreading through the Third World, they tried to use military might to support areas of European settlement, above all in Algeria.

Three Worlds

World War II and postwar decolonization created a three-world order, in which the liberal democratic and capitalist First World and the communist Second World competed for global influence, notably among the newly decolonized Third World states. The war had made the Soviet Union and the United States into superpowers. Possessing nuclear weapons, superior armies, and industrial might, they vied for global influence. As decolonization spread, the two Cold War belligerents offered new leaders their models for modernization. The decolonized, however, had their own ideas. With the communist takeover in 1949, China had shrugged off semicolonial status, but Mao soon broke from Soviet direction. Other decolonized nations in Asia and Africa had underdeveloped economies and could not leap into either capitalist or communist industrial development. They drew some elements from communist and capitalist models, but politically tended to favor single-party states. Moreover, in some places colonial rule persisted, and civilians were not allowed even relative autonomy because the colonizers remained in place.

THE FIRST WORLD

As the Cold War spread in the early 1950s, western Europe and North America became known as the First World, or "the free world." Later on, Japan joined this group. First World states sought to organize the world on the basis of capitalism and democracy. Yet, in struggling against communism, the free world sometimes aligned with Third World dictators, thereby sacrificing its commitment to freedom and democracy for the sake of propping up pro-western regimes.

Western Europe The reconstruction of western Europe after World War II was a spectacular success. By the late 1950s, most nations' economies were thriving, thanks in part to massive American economic assistance. Improvements in agriculture were particularly impressive. As industrial production boomed and wages rose, goods that had been luxuries before the war—refrigerators, telephones, automobiles, indoor plumbing—became commonplace. Prosperity and the dismantling of national military establishments allowed governments to expand social welfare systems; by the late 1950s, education and health care were within the reach of virtually all citizens.

Western Europe's economic recovery blunted the appeal of socialism and communism. At the same time, the Cold War slowed down efforts to punish fascists, Nazis, and collaborators. Although war crimes trials brought the conviction of a number of prominent Nazis, the fear was that a complete purge of former Nazis would deprive Germany of political and economic leaders, leaving it susceptible to communist subversion.

The United States While Europe lay in ruins in 1945, the United States entered a period of economic expansion and a rising standard of living. Americans could afford more consumer goods than ever before—almost always U.S. manufactures. Home ownership became more common, especially in the burgeoning suburbs.

Yet anxieties about the future of the First World abounded. Following the Soviet Union's explosion of an atomic bomb, the communist revolution in China, and the outbreak of the Korean War, fear of the communist threat prompted increasingly harsh rhetoric. Anticommunist hysteria led a Republican senator from Wisconsin, Joseph McCarthy, to initiate a campaign to uncover closet communists in the State Department and in Hollywood in the 1950s. Televised congressional hearings broadcast his views to the entire

Civil Rights Movement The 1955 arrest of Rosa Parks, for refusing to give up her seat on a Montgomery, Alabama, bus to a white passenger, led to a boycott that brought Martin Luther King Jr. to prominence and galvanized the challenge to legal racial segregation in the American South.

nation, which pressured elected officials to support a strong anticommunist foreign policy and a large military budget.

Postwar American prosperity did not benefit all citizens equally. During the 1950s, nearly a quarter of the American population lived in poverty. But many African Americans, a group disproportionately trapped below the poverty line, participated in a powerful movement for equal rights and the end of racial segregation. The National Association for the Advancement of Colored People (NAACP) won court victories that mandated the desegregation of schools. Boycotts, too, became a weapon of the growing civil rights movement, as when Martin Luther King Jr. (1929–1968) led a successful strike against injustices in the bus system of Montgomery, Alabama. Here and in subsequent campaigns against white supremacy, King borrowed his most effective weapons—the commitment to nonviolent protest and the appeal to conscience—from Gandhi. As the civil rights movement spread, the federal government gradually supported programs promoting racial equality.

The Japanese "Miracle" Japan reemerged as an economic powerhouse in the postwar period. The war had ended with Japan's unconditional surrender in 1945, its dreams of dominating East Asia dashed and its homeland devastated. But after 1945, in an attempt to incorporate Japan into the First World, American military protection, investment, and transfers of technology helped to rebuild Japanese society. The Japanese government guided economic development through directed investment, partnerships with private firms, and protectionist trade policies. By the mid-1970s, Japan, formerly a dictatorship, became a politically stable civilian regime with a thriving economy, and the power of the emperor had been replaced with a parliamentary system.

THE SECOND WORLD

The Soviet Union, with its eastern and central European allies as well as Mongolia and North Korea, constituted the communist Second World. The scourge of World War II and the shadow of the Cold War fell heavily on the Soviets. Having suffered more deaths and more damage than any other industrialized nation, the Soviet Union was determined to insulate itself from future aggression from the west. That meant turning eastern Europe into a bloc of communist buffer states.

The Appeal of the Soviet Model The Soviet model's egalitarian ideology and success with rapid industrialization made it seem a worthy alternative to capitalism. Here, there was no private property and thus, in Marxist terms, no exploitation. Workers "owned" the factories and worked for themselves. The Soviet state promised full employment, boasting that a state-run economy would be immune from upturns and downturns in business cycles. Freedom from exploitation, combined with security, was contrasted with the capitalist model of owners hoarding profits and suddenly firing loyal workers when they were not needed.

The Soviet system touted protections for workers, inexpensive mass transit, paid maternity leave, free health care, and universally available education. Whereas under the Russian Empire less than one-third of the population had been literate, by the 1950s the literacy rate soared above 80 percent. True, Soviet policies did not provide material abundance of the sort that First World nations were enjoying. But if consumer goods were often scarce, they were always cheap. Likewise, while it sometimes took ten years to obtain a small apartment through waiting lists at work, when one's turn finally came the apartment carried low annual rent and could be passed on to one's children.

Few Soviet citizens knew how people lived in the capitalist world, so it was easy to believe in the advantages of the Soviet system. Government censors skewed news about the First World and suppressed unfavorable information about the Soviet Union and the communist bloc. Critics did not typically seek to overthrow the system and restore capitalism. Rather, they wanted the Soviet regime to introduce reforms that would create "socialism with a human face."

Repression of Dissent Few people outside the Soviet sphere knew just how inhuman Soviet communism was, and few within knew the extent of its brutality. Under Stalin, anyone suspected of opposing the regime risked imprisonment, forced labor, and often torture or execution. By the time of Stalin's death in 1953, its vast Gulag (labor camp complex) confined several million people, who dug for gold and uranium and survived on hunks of bread and gruel.

In 1956, the new party leader, Nikita Khrushchev, delivered a speech at a closed session of the Communist Party Congress in which he attempted to separate Stalin's crimes from true communism. The speech was never published in the Soviet Union, but party members distributed it to party organizations abroad. The crimes that Khrushchev revealed came as a terrible shock.

Soviet Ecocide

Before the twentieth century, the spread of peasant agriculture, as well as settlement in the steppe and forest zones and the hunting of fur-bearing forest animals, brought profound changes to the Russian environment, including soil degradation, deforestation, and depopulation of species. But the environmental impact of Soviet-era industrialization was staggering. No other industrial civilization poisoned its land, air, water, and people so systematically and over so long a time. Scholars have deemed the Soviet environmental catastrophe an "ecocide."

Soviet economic planners and propagandists celebrated the plumes of purple and orange smoke in their skies as evidence of the country's huge industrial production. Pollution-control devices remained unheard of well after their 1950s introduction in Europe and the United States; even when installed in Soviet factories, they were rarely turned on so as not to depress output. Sulfur dioxide, hydrogen sulfide, and solid phenols in the water, the food supply, and the air caused epidemic levels of respiratory and intestinal ailments, blood diseases, and birth defects. The giant steel plant at Magnitogorsk, once the pride of Stalin's industrial leap, became a zone of atmospheric and soil devastation 120 miles long and 40 miles wide; inside it, chronic bronchitis, asthma, and cancers attacked the population. In agriculture, the Soviet Union continued to use the insecticide DDT long after its 1972 banning in the United States.

In the 1970s, despite the socialist country's overall development, Soviet life expectancy began to decline and infant mortality to rise. By 1989, Soviet men lived an average of 63.9 years from birth, down from 66.1 in 1965. By the late 1980s, Infant mortality rose to 25.4 per 1,000, roughly the same as in Malaysia, a developing country, and Harlem. Alcoholism also contributed mightily to adverse health trends.

The April 1986 Chernobyl nuclear disaster exposed 20 million people in Ukraine and Belarus to excess radiation. Although there was no bomb concussion, the accident spewed more radioactive material into the atmosphere than had been released by the atomic bombs over Hiroshima and Nagasaki. The Chernobyl cleanup claimed around 7,000 lives.

Few symbols of Soviet ecocide surpass the Aral Sea—once a huge saline lake at the border between Kazakhstan and Uzbekistan. Because inflow into the lake was blocked by dams built for wasteful power plants and excess irrigation for cotton production, the lake shrank by two-thirds, giving way to huge white, lifeless salt flats. Soviet cosmonauts, looking down from space in 1975, were astonished to see immense storms of dust and salt over central Asia. Toxic salt rain wreaked enormous damage on human and animal lungs. Soviet Uzbekistan, with twice the population of Soviet Belarus, was served by only one-third the hospitals.

Lake Baikal, the world's largest body of fresh water, and once among the cleanest, suffered the construction from the 1950s of factories on its perimeter, especially a cellulose

Repercussions were far-reaching. Eastern European leaders interpreted Khrushchev's speech as an endorsement for political liberation and economic experimentation. Right away, Polish intellectuals began a drive to break free from the communist ideological straitjacket. Hungarian intellectuals and students held demonstrations demanding an uncensored press, free elections with genuine alternative parties, and the withdrawal of Soviet troops. But the seeming liberalization promised by Khrushchev's speech proved short-lived.

Rather than let eastern Europeans stray, the Soviet leadership crushed dissent. In Poland, the security police massacred strikers. In Hungary, tanks from the Soviet Union and other Warsaw Pact members invaded and cord plant (for tires on Soviet bombers) and pulp plant (for paper). The threat to Baikal, as well as the Aral Sea catastrophe, sparked grassroots environmental activism in an otherwise tightly controlled Soviet society. Scientists led the way in breaking censorship taboos, and people from all walks of life turned up at unsanctioned meetings and signed their names to petitions to stop the damage and protect the environment.

Aral Sea Catastrophe What was once one of the largest lakes in the world shrank to less than 10 percent of its original size due to the aggressive Soviet construction of irrigation canals in the sixties to bolster cotton production. Here, a shipping vessel is moored on the bed of the former Aral Sea, in present-day Kazakhstan.

Questions for Analysis

- Why do you think environmental degradation was so much more severe in the Soviet Union than in western countries?
- Why do you think environmental awareness developed much sooner in the United States than in the Soviet Union?

Explore Further

Feshbach, Murray and Friendly, Alfred Jr., *Ecocide in the USSR: Health and Nation under Siege* (1992).

Micklin, Philip, Aladin, N.V., and Plotnikov, Igor, eds., *The Aral Sea: The Devastation and Partial Rehabilitation of a Great Lake* (2014).

Wiener, Douglas R., *A Little Corner of Freedom: Russian Nature Protection from Stalin to Gorbachev* (2002).

installed a new government that aimed to smash all "counterrevolutionary" activities. The Second World remained very much the dominion of the Soviet Union.

Despite its repressive policies, the Soviet Union's status surged after the launching of Sputnik, the first satellite, into space in 1957. Students from Third World countries flocked to the Soviets' excellent educational system for training as engineers, scientists, army commanders, and revolutionaries. The updated 1961 Communist Party program predicted euphorically that within twenty years the Soviet Union would surpass the United States and eclipse the First World, but reckless industrialization left terrible scars both on the population and on the landscape.

THE THIRD WORLD

Third World
A collective term used for nations of the world, mostly in Asia, Latin America, and Africa, that were not highly industrialized like First World nations or tied to the Soviet bloc (the Second World). It implies a revolutionary challenge to the existing (liberal, capitalist) order.

World Bank
International agency established in 1944 to provide economic assistance to war-torn and poor countries. Its formal title is the International Bank for Reconstruction and Development.

International Monetary Fund (IMF)
Agency founded in 1944 to help restore financial order in Europe and the rest of the world, to revive international trade, and to offer financial support to Third World governments.

In the 1950s, the French demographer Alfred Sauvy coined the term **Third World** (*tiers monde*) to describe those countries that, like the "third estate" in the 1789 French Revolution, represented the majority of the world's population but were oppressed. By the early 1960s, the term characterized a large bloc of countries in Asia, Africa, and Latin America. All had experienced colonial domination and now aimed to create more just societies than those of the First and Second Worlds by finding a "third way" between capitalism and communism.

Limits to Autonomy Charting a third way proved difficult. Both the Soviets and the Americans saw the Third World as "underdeveloped." The western powers looked to two new instruments of global capitalism, the **World Bank** and the **International Monetary Fund (IMF)**, to help them develop their economies. Both institutions raised capital from all participating nations—but the most from the United States—and provided economic guidance in the Third World. The World Bank funded loans for projects intended to lift societies out of poverty (such as providing electricity in India and building roads in Indonesia), while the IMF supported the new governments' monetary systems when they experienced economic woes (as in Ghana, Nigeria, and Egypt). Yet both institutions also intruded on these states' autonomy.

Another force that threatened Third World economic autonomy was the multinational corporation. In the rush to acquire advanced technology, Africans, Asians, and Latin Americans struck deals with multinational corporations to import their know-how. Owned primarily by American, European, and Japanese entrepreneurs, firms such as United Fruit, Firestone, and Volkswagen expanded cash-cropping and plantation activities and established manufacturing branches worldwide. But such corporations impeded the growth of indigenous firms. Although the world's nations were more economically interdependent, the west still made the decisions—and reaped most of the profits.

Whether dealing with the west or with the Soviet Union, Third World leaders had limited options because they faced pressure to choose one Cold War side or the other. In hope of adding subservient client states to its bloc, the Soviet Union backed communist insurgencies around the globe, while the United States supported almost all leaders who declared their anticommunism. With the threat of nuclear war hanging over the two superpowers, they competed through proxy states that they armed to battle one another.

Nowhere was the militarization of Third World countries more threatening to economic development than in Africa. Whereas in the colonial era African states had spent little on military forces, this trend ended abruptly once the states became independent and were drawn into the Cold War. Civil wars, like the one that splintered Nigeria between 1967 and 1970, were opportunities for the superpowers to wield influence. When the west refused to sell weapons to the Nigerian government so it could suppress the break-away eastern province of Biafra, the Soviets supplied MiG aircraft and other vital weapons, contributing to a destructive conflict and the ultimate triumph of the federal government of Nigeria.

Revolutionaries and Radicals As postcolonial states increasingly found themselves mired in debt and dependency, dissatisfaction grew. While some radicals seized power in the 1950s and 1960s, revolutionary transformation of society proved elusive.

Third World revolutionaries drew on the pioneering writings of Frantz Fanon (1925–1961). While serving as a psychiatrist in French Algeria, Fanon (who was born in a French Caribbean colony) became aware of the psychological damage of European racism. He subsequently joined the FLN and became a radical theorist of liberation. His 1961 book *The Wretched of the Earth* urged Third World peoples to achieve personal and national independence through violence against their European oppressors.

The Maoist Model While Fanon moved people with his writings, others did so by building political organizations and undertaking revolutionary social experiments. In 1958, Mao Zedong introduced the Great Leap Forward. Mao's program organized China into 24,000 social and economic units, called communes. Peasants took up industrial production in their own backyards. The campaign aimed to catapult China past the developed countries, but the communes failed to feed the people and the industrial goods were inferior. As many as 45 million people may have perished from famine and malnutrition, forcing the government to abandon the experiment in 1961.

The Cultural Revolution in China Young women were an important part of the Red Guards during the Cultural Revolution. Here, female Red Guards march in the front row of a parade in the capital city of Beijing under a sign that reads "Rise."

Fearing that China's revolution was losing spirit, Mao launched the Great Proletarian Cultural Revolution in 1966. This time Mao turned against his associates in the Communist Party and appealed to China's young people. They responded enthusiastically. Organized into "Red Guards," over 10 million of them journeyed to Beijing to participate in huge rallies, at which they pledged to cleanse the party of corrupt elements and remake Chinese society.

With help from the army, the Red Guards set out to rid society of the "four olds"—old customs, old habits, old culture, and old ideas. They ransacked homes, libraries, museums, and temples. They destroyed classical texts, artworks, and monuments. With its rhetoric of struggle against American imperialism and Soviet revisionism, the Cultural Revolution also targeted anything foreign. Knowledge of a foreign language was enough to compromise a person's revolutionary credentials. The Red Guards attacked government officials, party cadres, or just plain strangers in an escalating cycle of violence. Even family members and friends were pressured to denounce one another; all had to prove themselves faithful followers of Chairman Mao.

Given the costs of the Great Leap Forward and the Cultural Revolution, many of Mao's revolutionary policies were hard to celebrate. But radicals in much of the Third World were unaware of these costs and found the style of a rapid and massive—if deeply undemocratic—appeal to the masses attractive.

Latin American Revolution Most Third World radicals did not go as far as Mao, but they still dreamed of overturning the social order. In Latin America, such dreams excited those who wished to throw off the influence of U.S.-owned multinational corporations and local elites.

Reform programs in Latin America addressed numerous concerns. Economic nationalists urged greater protection for domestic industries and sought to curb the multinationals. Liberal reformers wanted to democratize political systems and redistribute land, lest discontent erupt into full-blown revolutions like China's. But when liberals and nationalists joined forces, as in Guatemala in the 1950s, their reforms met resistance from local conservatives and from the United States.

In Cuba, the failure of the government to address political, social, and economic concerns spurred a revolution. Since gaining its independence in the Spanish-American War of 1898, Cuba had been ruled by governments better known for their compliance with U.S. interests than with popular sentiment. In the 1930s, sugar planters, casino operators, and North American investors prospered, but middle- and working-class Cubans did not. In 1953, a group composed heavily of university students launched a botched assault on a military garrison. One of the leaders, a law student named **Fidel Castro** (1926–2016), gave a stirring speech at the rebels' trial, which made him a national hero. After his release from prison in 1955, he fled to Mexico. Several years later, he returned and started organizing guerrilla raids that brought him to power in 1959.

Castro then elbowed aside rivals and wrested control of the economy from the wealthy elite, who fled to exile. As his policies grew increasingly radical, American leaders began to plot his demise. It was over Cuba and its

Castro, Fidel (1926–2016)
Cuban communist leader who seized power in January 1959. Castro became increasingly radical as he consolidated power, announcing a massive redistribution of land and the nationalization of foreign oil refineries; he declared himself a socialist and aligned himself with the Soviet Union in the wake of the 1961 CIA-backed Bay of Pigs invasion.

radicalizing revolution that the world came closest to nuclear Armageddon in the Cuban Missile Crisis of 1962. To deter U.S. attacks, Castro appealed to the Soviet Union to install nuclear weapons in Cuba—a mere ninety miles off the coast of Florida. When U.S. intelligence detected the weapons, President John F. Kennedy ordered a blockade of Cuba, just as weapons-bearing Soviet ships were heading toward Havana. For several weeks, the world was paralyzed with anxiety as Kennedy, Khrushchev, and Castro matched threats. In the end, Kennedy succeeded in getting the Soviets to withdraw their nuclear missiles from Cuba.

By rejecting the power of capitalist industrial societies, Castro and his followers promoted revolution, not reform, as a way to achieve Third World liberation. The symbol of this new spirit was Castro's closest lieutenant, Ernesto "Che" Guevara (1928–1967). Shortly after receiving his medical degree in 1953, Guevara arrived in Guatemala in time to witness the CIA-backed overthrow of the progressive Jacobo Arbenz government. Thereafter, he became increasingly bitter about U.S. influences in Latin America. He joined Castro's forces and helped topple the pro-American regime in Cuba in 1958. After 1959, he held several posts in the Cuban government, but grew restive for more action. Latin America, he believed, should challenge the global power of the United States. Soon his casual military uniform, his patchy beard, his cigar, and his moral energy became legendary symbols of revolt.

To combat the germ of revolution, the Kennedy administration sent U.S. advisers throughout Latin America to dole out aid, explain how to reform local land systems, and demonstrate the benefits of liberal capitalism. Working with American advisers, Latin American militaries were trained to root out radicalism. Even Salvador Allende's democratically elected socialist government in Chile was not spared; the CIA and U.S. policymakers aided General Augusto Pinochet's military coup against the regime in 1973 and looked the other way while political opponents were butchered. By 1975, protesters had been liquidated in Argentina, Uruguay, Brazil, Mexico, Bolivia, and Venezuela.

Tensions within the Three Worlds

Each of the three "worlds" was beset by vulnerabilities and divisions. The United States experienced social unrest in this period on a scale not seen since the Great Depression, and other First World countries also experienced major protest movements. In the Second World, too, dissent challenged the Soviet Union's hold on world communism. In the Third World, the optimism generated at independence gave way quickly to discouragement and eventually despair. Finally, in the 1970s, the rising fortunes of oil-producing

Core Objectives

COMPARE the civil rights issues in the First, Second, and Third Worlds, and **ASSESS** the ways each "world" addressed these and other basic human rights.

nations and of Japan introduced new problems in the relations within and among worlds.

TENSIONS WITHIN THE FIRST WORLD

Although the First World enjoyed great prosperity in the decades after World War II, lingering inequality created friction within these societies.

Women's Issues, Civil Rights, and Environmental Concerns In the First World, groups that believed that they had been left behind in the surge of economic growth expressed deep unhappiness. One issue was women's economic and political opportunities. Women in Italy, France, and Belgium did not obtain the right to vote until the end of World War II. Although women made gains in employment outside the home, they still awaited a decrease in domestic responsibilities.

A second source of concern, articulated most forcefully by students in Europe, was the deployment of nuclear weapons in their countries, as well as the rigid social and educational institutions that preserved power and high culture for the elite few. Protests reached their apex in Paris in 1968, when workers joined students in a general strike and clashed violently with police.

Women Protest Sexism Insisting that "the personal is political," many women in the 1960s and 1970s argued that the problem of sexism went beyond equal rights and income equality: women's oppression began in the home, where they were treated merely as homemakers or as sex objects. At this 1971 rally in London, protesters suggested that women were being "crucified" by their association with these everyday objects: an apron, a net shopping bag, silk stockings, and an item of washing.

A rising crescendo of protests against racial discrimination in the United States propelled the U.S. federal government to enact civil rights legislation and to promote programs designed to end poverty. The Civil Rights Act of 1964 banned segregation in public facilities and outlawed racial discrimination in employment, and the Voting Rights Act of 1965 gave millions of previously disenfranchised African Americans an opportunity to exercise equal political rights. The Lyndon Baines Johnson administration also supported programs targeting social security, health, and education. Aided by impressive economic growth, these War on Poverty programs nearly halved the U.S. poverty rate.

But legacies of racism and inequality were not easy to overcome, and protest movements proliferated. In spite of Supreme Court decisions, most schools remained racially homogeneous not only in the South but across the United States, as "white flight" to the suburbs left inner-city neighborhoods and schools to minorities. Militant voices, like those of Malcolm X and the Black Panthers, became prominent. Instead of integration, these radicals advocated black separatism; instead of Americanism, they espoused embracing their African origins.

African American struggles inspired Native Americans, Mexican Americans, homosexuals, and women to initiate their own campaigns for equality and empowerment. Women now questioned a life built around taking care of home and family. In fact, the introduction of the birth control pill in 1960 and the publication of Betty Friedan's *The Feminine Mystique* in 1963 stand as watershed moments in American women's history. Because oral contraception allowed women to limit childbearing and to have sex with less fear of pregnancy, the resulting freedom helped unleash a sexual revolution. Moreover, Friedan blasted the myth of middle-class domestic contentment, describing the idealized 1950s suburban home as a "comfortable concentration camp" from which women must escape. Despite rising numbers of married women and college-educated women in the workforce, their compensation and opportunity for advancement lagged far behind those of men.

A year before Friedan authored her challenge to the subordination of women, Rachel Carson published *Silent Spring*, a book that was equally revolutionary in its attack against long-standing practices. In particular, Carson's book took on the use of synthetic pesticides such as dichlorodiphenyltrichloroethane (DDT), which she said caused cancer, devastated wildlife, and destroyed natural ecosystems. Although chemical manufacturers responded that pesticides had vastly multiplied agricultural yields, *Silent Spring* stirred opposition that ultimately led to the banning of DDT in the United States in 1972. More broadly, Carson's book spurred the development of an environmental movement that questioned many of the ideas about economic progress and material prosperity upon which the "American Dream" had rested.

The escalation of the Vietnam War prompted many white American college students to question the ideals of American society. As the United States increased troop levels there in the 1960s, it conscripted more and more men. After President Richard Nixon sent American troops into Cambodia in 1970 to root out North Vietnamese soldiers, students at over 500 campuses occupied buildings and closed down universities. At Kent State University in Ohio, National Guardsmen attempting to stop the protests killed four students. The United States withdrew from Vietnam in 1973, but not before the divisions created by the war had strained the country almost to the breaking point.

TENSIONS WITHIN WORLD COMMUNISM

The unity of the communist world also came under increasing pressure. As early as 1948, Yugoslavia had broken free of the Soviet yoke and embarked on its own road to building socialism. Other satellite states within the Soviet bloc had more trouble freeing themselves. In 1956, Poland and Hungary were forced back into line. Twelve years later, Czechoslovakia experienced the Prague Spring, in which communist authorities experimented with creating a democratic and pluralist socialist world. Workers and students rallied behind the reformist government of Alexander Dubček, calling for more freedom of expression, more autonomy for workers and consumers, and more debate within the ruling party. Once again, the Soviets crushed what they branded a "counterrevolutionary" movement. As their tanks rolled into Prague, the Czech capital, one desperate student doused himself with gasoline and lit a match—his public suicide a gesture of defiance against communist rule.

Thereafter, the Prague Spring served as a symbol for dissenters, who were divided between those who still wanted to reform socialism and those who wanted to overturn it. Underground reading groups proliferated throughout eastern Europe, and many Russians renewed their faith in Orthodox Christianity, their prerevolutionary religion. Many dissidents were exiled from the Soviet Union. Most famous by the early 1970s was the Russian novelist Alexander Solzhenitsyn. His masterwork, *The Gulag Archipelago*, rejected the notion that socialism could be reformed simply by a turn away from Stalin's policies. Yet very few people in the Soviet Union could obtain copies of Solzhenitsyn's exposé, which had been published abroad and was a best-seller in the west. In 1974, the author himself was expelled from the USSR.

Hungarian Revolt Khrushchev's secret 1956 speech denouncing Stalin's crimes unintentionally destabilized the communist bloc. Tanks of the Soviet-led Warsaw Pact forces crossed into Hungary to put down a revolt that year, restoring the Soviet-style system but damaging Soviet prestige. Some American officials and especially American-supported radio had encouraged the Hungarians to rise up but then did nothing to support them, damaging U.S. prestige. The upshot was a turn to "national communism" in the Soviet satellites as a way to promote stability and loyalty.

Still, there were important changes within the Second World. During the 1950s and 1960s, "national communism" became the rule throughout eastern Europe, even in countries that experienced Soviet invasions. National variations also arose within the Soviet Union, where Moscow conceded some autonomy to the Communist Party machines of its fifteen republics—in exchange for their fundamental loyalty. Dissidents were still persecuted, but by the 1970s, many fewer were murdered outright, and the population of the gulags declined.

Widespread dislike of the United States created a Sino-Soviet alliance in the years just after the Chinese Revolution of 1949. By the late 1950s, the Soviet Union had contributed massive military and economic aid to China. But the Chinese increasingly sought to define their own brand of Marxism and criticized Khrushchev's efforts to reduce tensions with the United States and the west. The divide raised China's profile throughout Asia and even in eastern Europe. Indeed, Romania achieved a measure of autonomy in foreign policy by playing off China and the Soviet Union. Albania declared its allegiance to China. African nations seeking Soviet aid increased their demands with subtle hints that they might consider deepening ties with China instead. Clearly, the Second World was no monolith.

TENSIONS WITHIN THE THIRD WORLD

In contrast to the First and Second Worlds, the Third World was never unified by economic, military, or political alliances. The Cold War pushed Third World states to choose between alignment with the First World or the Second. Nonetheless, radicalism nourished new hopes for unifying and empowering the Third World.

One effort at collaboration was the formation in 1960 of an alliance of oil exporters. The Organization of the Petroleum Exporting Countries (OPEC)—which included Algeria, Ecuador, Gabon, Indonesia, Iran, Iraq, Kuwait, Libya, Nigeria, Qatar, Saudi Arabia, the United Arab Emirates, and Venezuela—had little success in raising oil revenues through the 1960s, even though several members nationalized their oil fields. But after the fourth major Arab-Israeli war broke out in 1973, OPEC's Arab members decided to pressure Israel's First World allies by halting oil exports to them. Overnight, the embargo lifted oil prices more than threefold, a bonanza that enriched all oil producers and led to an oil crisis in the west. To many, the bulging treasuries of OPEC nations seemed like the Third World's revenge. Here were Saudi Arabian princes, Venezuelan magnates, and Indonesian ministers dictating world prices to industrial consumers.

But the realignment was not thorough. Third World producers of raw materials such as coffee and rubber tried unsuccessfully to duplicate OPEC's model, and OPEC itself had trouble controlling the world's oil market.

During the 1970s, oil discoveries in the North Sea, Mexico, and Canada reduced pressures on the large oil-consuming states to be more fuel efficient. With supply up, prices fell. To compensate for lost revenue, various OPEC states raised their own production, putting further downward pressure on prices.

Nor did oil revenues help overcome poverty and dependency in the Third World as a whole. To the contrary, most revenue surpluses from OPEC simply flowed back to First World banks or were invested in real-estate holdings in Europe and the United States. Some of these funds, in turn, were reloaned to the world's poorest countries in Africa, Asia, and Latin America, at high interest rates, to pay for more expensive imports—including oil! The biggest bonanza went to multinational petroleum firms, whose control over production, refining, and distribution yielded enormous profits.

For all the talk in the mid-1970s of changing the balance of international economic relations between the world's rich and poor countries, fundamental inequalities persisted. Those few Third World nations that appeared to break out of the cycle of poverty, like South Korea and Taiwan, did not achieve success through free trade and private-sector development. Rather, these nations regulated domestic markets, nurtured new industries, educated the populace, and required multinationals to work with local firms.

Conclusion

The three-world order arose on the ruins of European empires and their Japanese counterpart. First, the Soviet Union and the United States became superpowers. Second, World War II affirmed the nation-state rather than the empire as the primary form for organizing communities. Third, in spite of the rhetoric of individualism and the free market, the war and postwar reconstruction enhanced the reach and functions of the modern state. In the Third World, too, leaders of new nations saw the state as the primary instrument for promoting economic development.

The organization of the world into three blocs lasted into the mid-1970s. This arrangement fostered the economic recovery of western Europe and Japan from the wounds inflicted by war. These nations' recovery grew out of a Cold War alliance with the United States, where anti-communist hysteria accompanied an economic boom. The Cold War also cast a shadow over the citizens of the Soviet Union and eastern Europe. Gulags and political surveillance became widespread, while the Soviets and their satellite regimes mobilized resources for military purposes. The Third World, squeezed by its inability to reduce poverty on the one hand and by superpower rivalry on the other, struggled to pursue a "third way." While some states maintained democratic institutions and promoted economic development, many tumbled into dictatorships and authoritarian regimes, marked by high levels of corruption. In addition, they often suffered irreparable environmental damage.

In this context, Third World revolutionaries sought radical social and political transformation, seeking paths different from both western capitalism and Soviet communism. Though not successful, they energized considerable tensions in the three-world order. These tensions intensified in the late 1960s and early 1970s as Vietnamese communists defeated the United States, an oil crisis struck the west, and protests escalated in the First and Second Worlds. Thirty years after the end of World War II, the world order forged after 1945 was beginning to give way.

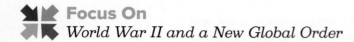

Focus On
World War II and a New Global Order

World War II

- World War II grows out of unresolved problems connected to World War I, especially the aggressive plans of Germany and Japan to expand their political and economic influence.

- The war brings huge human and material costs and ushers in an age of nuclear weapons.

- At war's end, the United States, fearing the spread of communism and Soviet influence, rebuilds war-torn Europe and Japan and creates military and political alliances to contain Soviet expansionist ambitions.

A New Global Order

- The Soviet Union and the United States become superpowers.

- Japan emerges as an economic powerhouse and a U.S. ally.

- A weakened Europe cannot resist demands for independence from Asian and African nationalists.

- Chinese communists engineer a revolution, while Indian nationalists and many African leaders achieve independence through negotiations.

- Elsewhere, especially in territories with large settler populations, decolonization is violent (Palestine, Algeria) or incomplete (southern Africa).

- Actions by Latin American reformers and revolutionaries spark counterinsurgency efforts by the United States and its regional allies.

- An insecure three-world order emerges after most Asian and African states achieve independence.

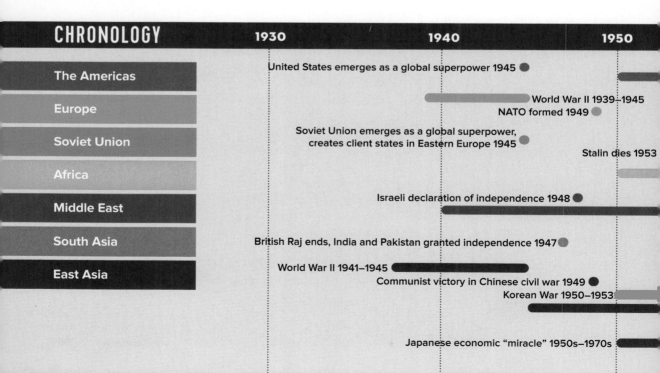

CHRONOLOGY

1930   1940   1950

The Americas

United States emerges as a global superpower 1945

Europe

World War II 1939–1945
NATO formed 1949

Soviet Union

Soviet Union emerges as a global superpower, creates client states in Eastern Europe 1945
Stalin dies 1953

Africa

Middle East

Israeli declaration of independence 1948

South Asia

British Raj ends, India and Pakistan granted independence 1947

East Asia

World War II 1941–1945
Communist victory in Chinese civil war 1949
Korean War 1950–1953

Japanese economic "miracle" 1950s–1970s

THINKING ABOUT GLOBAL CONNECTIONS

- **Thinking about Worlds Together, Worlds Apart and the Three-World Order** Explain how the collapse of a Europe-centered world changed how states interacted with one another. In what ways did the division of the globe into three rival worlds differ from the dominance of the European "great powers" that preceded it? Which world order do you think was more stable, the Europe-centered world or the three-world order that followed it? Do you think one system was more equitable than the other?

- **Thinking about Changing Power Relationships and the Three-World Order** Analyze Third World revolutionaries' ability to alter the dynamic of the Cold War. Where do you think power was located in this period?

To what degree did Washington and Moscow determine the course of world affairs, and to what degree were politicians in places like Cuba, Vietnam, and Algeria able to play the superpowers off against one another? How and to what degree were revolutionaries able to make claims on the First and Second Worlds in terms of economic, political, or military assistance?

- **Thinking about Environmental Impacts and the Three-World Order** In this period, for the first time, organized groups set out to defend the environment. What sparked their protests? Where were those organizations most fully developed? Where was ecological devastation most extreme? What force or forces opposed environmentalists?

Key Terms

Fidel Castro p. 962	Holocaust p. 938	Mao Zedong p. 947	Third World p. 960
Cold War p. 934	International Monetary	North Atlantic Treaty	Warsaw Pact p. 943
decolonization p. 946	Fund (IMF) p. 960	Organization (NATO) p. 943	World Bank p. 960

 Go to **INQUIZITIVE** to see what you've learned—and learn what you've missed—with personalized feedback along the way.

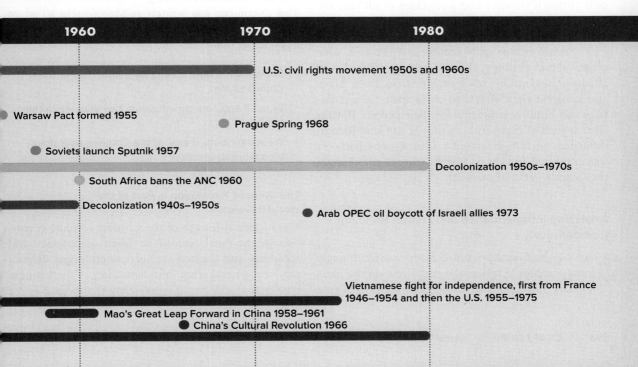

1960   1970   1980

U.S. civil rights movement 1950s and 1960s

Warsaw Pact formed 1955

Prague Spring 1968

Soviets launch Sputnik 1957

Decolonization 1950s–1970s

South Africa bans the ANC 1960

Decolonization 1940s–1950s

Arab OPEC oil boycott of Israeli allies 1973

Vietnamese fight for independence, first from France 1946–1954 and then the U.S. 1955–1975

Mao's Great Leap Forward in China 1958–1961
China's Cultural Revolution 1966

Global Themes and Sources

Comparing Independence and Nation Building

ntellectuals and political activists in the Third World sought to expel foreign colonizers and build new societies. As their nations struck out on their own, the overwhelming majority of these thinkers and leaders wanted to borrow at least some elements from their own established traditions, on the one hand, and from foreign influences, on the other.

In his "New Democracy" (1940), Mao Zedong set forth a new democratic culture—nationalistic, scientific, and mass-based—that he regarded as a transitional stage to the communist utopia of the future. Jawaharlal Nehru also celebrated science and technology in his "Note to the Members of the National Planning Committee" (1940), which sought a "third way" between capitalism and communism. In his speech on Negritude, Léopold Sédar Senghor presented a black culture different from, but not inferior to, European cultural forms. Frantz Fanon, inspired by Mao as well as Marx and Lenin, celebrated the power of violence to restore the self-respect of the colonized; only through violence and a rejection of all that the colonizers stood for, he thought, could the colonized ever truly free themselves.

These selections invite comparison. From a wide range of backgrounds, the authors represented here all drew inspiration in varying degrees from Marx and Lenin in their efforts to emancipate their countries and build new futures for their people. But for all that each of these authors sought to blend foreign influences with homegrown traditions, the balances they proposed and the pace and nature of the changes they sought differed markedly.

Analyzing Independence and Nation Building Comparatively

- All of these authors came from overwhelmingly rural societies. Explain why they drew on the ideas of Karl Marx, who famously likened peasants to a "sack of potatoes" and thought modern industry essential to end oppression of all kinds.

- Identify the balance between indigenous tradition and foreign influence in each selection. Which text draws most heavily on foreign sources and which rejects outside influences most completely?

- Analyze the relationship between the individual and the community described in each of these readings.

- Which of the readings do you consider most revolutionary and why? Do you think the idea of revolution was important to the authors?

PRIMARY SOURCE 20.1

"New Democracy" (1940), Mao Zedong

As chairman of China's Communist Party, Mao Zedong (1893–1976) ruled the People's Republic of China from its founding in 1949 until his death. This document was written as Mao sought to adapt communism to Chinese traditions and distance himself from Soviet influence.

- Explain what Mao means by democracy of the Chinese type.

- What, if any, foreign influence can you see in this text?

- What elements, if any, of the Chinese past does Mao want to preserve?

The Chinese Revolution Is Part of the World Revolution

The historical feature of the Chinese revolution consists in the two steps to be taken, democracy and socialism, and the first step is now no longer democracy in a general sense, but democracy of the Chinese type, a new and special type—New Democracy. How, then, is this historical feature formed? Has it been in existence for the past hundred years, or is it only of recent birth?

If we make only a brief study of the historical development of China and of the world, we shall understand that this historical feature did not emerge as a consequence of the Opium War but began to take shape only after the first imperialist world war and the Russian October Revolution.

After these events, the Chinese bourgeois-democratic revolution changes its character and belongs to the category of the new bourgeois-democratic revolution and, so far as the revolutionary front is concerned, forms part of the proletarian-socialist world revolution.

This "world revolution" refers no longer to the old world revolution—for the old bourgeois world revolution has long become a thing of the past—but to a new world revolution, the socialist world revolution. Similarly, to form "part" of the world revolution means to form no longer a part of the old bourgeois revolution but of the new socialist revolution. This is an exceedingly great change unparalleled in the history of China and of the world.

This correct thesis propounded by the Chinese Communists is based on Stalin's theory.

As early as 1918, Stalin wrote in an article commemorating the first anniversary of the October Revolution:

The great worldwide significance of the October Revolution chiefly consists in the fact that:

1. It has widened the scope of the national question and converted it from the particular question of combating national oppression in Europe into the general question of emancipating the oppressed peoples, colonies, and semi-colonies from imperialism.
2. It has opened up wide possibilities for their emancipation and the right path toward it, has thereby greatly facilitated the cause of the emancipation of the oppressed peoples of the West and the East, and has drawn them into the common current of the victorious struggle against imperialism.

3. It has thereby erected a bridge between the socialist West and the enslaved East, having created a new front of revolutions against world imperialism, extending from the proletarians of the West, through the Russian revolution to the oppressed peoples of the East.

Since writing this article, Stalin has again and again expounded the theoretical proposition that revolutions in colonies and semi-colonies have already departed from the old category and become part of the proletarian-socialist revolution.

The first step in, or the stage of, this revolution is certainly not, and cannot be, the establishment of a capitalist society under the dictatorship of the Chinese bourgeoisie; on the contrary, the first stage is to end with the establishment of a new-democratic society under the joint dictatorship of all Chinese revolutionary classes headed by the Chinese proletariat. Then the revolution will develop into the second stage so that a socialist society can be established in China.

New-Democratic Politics

As to the question of "political structure" [in the New Democracy], it is the question of the form of structure of political power, the form adopted by certain social classes in establishing their organs of political power to oppose their enemy and protect themselves. Without an adequate form of political power there would be nothing to represent the state. . . . But a system of really universal and equal suffrage, irrespective of sex, creed, property, or education, must be put into practice so that the organs of government elected can properly represent each revolutionary class according to its status in the state, express the people's will and direct revolutionary struggles, and embody the spirit of New Democracy. Such a system is democratic centralism. Only a government of democratic centralism can fully express the will of all the revolutionary people and most powerfully fight the enemies of the revolution.

The state system—joint dictatorship of all revolutionary classes. The political structure—democratic centralism. This is new-democratic government; this is a republic of New Democracy, the republic of the anti-Japanese united front, the republic of the new

Three People's Principles with the three cardinal policies, and the Republic of China true to its name.

New-Democratic Economy

We must establish in China a republic that is politically new-democratic as well as economically new-democratic.

Big banks and big industrial and commercial enterprises shall be owned by this republic.

Enterprises, whether Chinese-owned or foreign-owned, that are monopolistic in character or that are on too large a scale for private management, such as banks, railways, and airlines, shall be operated by the state so that private capital cannot dominate the livelihood of the people. This is the main principle of the control of capital.

This was also a solemn statement contained in the Manifesto of the First National Congress of the Nationalists during the period of the Nationalist-Communist cooperation; this is the correct objective for the economic structure of the new-democratic republic under the leadership of the proletariat. The state-operated industries are socialist in character and constitute the leading force in the national economy as a whole; but this republic does not take over other forms of capitalist private property or forbid the development of capitalist production that "cannot dominate the livelihood of the people," for China's economy is still very backward.

This republic will adopt certain necessary measures to confiscate the land of landlords and distribute it to those peasants having no land or only a little land, carry out Dr. Sun Yat-sen's slogan of "land to the tillers," abolish the feudal relations in the rural areas, and turn the land into the private property of the peasants. In the rural areas, rich peasant economic activities will be tolerated. This is the line of "equalization of land ownership." The correct slogan for this line is "land to the tillers." In this stage, socialist agriculture is in general not yet to be established, though the various types of cooperative enterprises developed on the basis of "land to the tillers" will contain elements of socialism.

New-Democratic Culture

A given culture is the ideological reflection of the politics and economy of a given society. There is in China an imperialist culture, which is a reflection of the control of imperialism over China politically and economically. This part of culture is advocated not only by the cultural organizations run directly by the imperialists in China but also by a number of shameless Chinese. All culture that contains a slave ideology belongs to this category. There is also in China a semi-feudal culture, which is a reflection of semi-feudal politics and economy and has as its representatives all those who, while opposing the new culture and new ideologies, advocate the worship of Confucius, the study of the Confucian canon, the old ethical code, and the old ideologies. Imperialist culture and semi-feudal culture are affectionate brothers, who have formed a reactionary cultural alliance to oppose China's new culture. This reactionary culture serves the imperialists and the feudal class and must be swept away.

Some Errors on the Question of the Nature of Culture

So far as national culture is concerned, the guiding role is fulfilled by Communist ideology, and efforts should be made to disseminate socialism and communism among the working class and to educate, properly and methodically, the peasantry and other sections of the masses in socialism.

A National, Scientific, and Mass Culture

New-democratic culture is national. It opposes imperialist oppression and upholds the dignity and independence of the Chinese nation. . . . China should absorb on a large scale the progressive cultures of foreign countries as an ingredient for her own culture; in the past we did not do enough work of this kind. We must absorb whatever we today find useful, not only from the present socialist or new-democratic cultures of other nations, but also from the older cultures of foreign countries, such as those of the various capitalist countries in the age of enlightenment. However, we must treat these foreign materials as we do our food, which should be chewed in the mouth, submitted to the working of the stomach and intestines, mixed with saliva, gastric juice, and intestinal secretions, and then separated into essence to be absorbed and waste matter to be discarded—only thus can food benefit our body; we should never swallow anything raw or absorb it uncritically. So-called wholesale Westernization is a mistaken viewpoint. China has suffered a great deal in the past from the formalist absorption of foreign things. Likewise, in applying Marxism to China, Chinese Communists must fully and properly unite the universal truth of Marxism with the specific practice of the Chinese revolution; that is to say, the truth of Marxism must be integrated with the characteristics of the nation and given a definite national form before it can be useful; it must not be applied subjectively as a mere formula. . . .

Communists may form an anti-imperialist and anti-feudal united front for political action with certain idealists and even with religious followers, but we can never approve of their idealism or religious doctrines. A splendid ancient culture was created during the long period of China's feudal society. To clarify the process of development of this ancient culture, to throw away its feudal dross, and to absorb its democratic essence is a necessary condition for the development of our new national culture and for the increase of our national self-confidence; but we should never absorb anything and everything uncritically.

The Twofold Task of the Chinese Revolution and the Chinese Communist Party

To complete China's bourgeois-democratic revolution (the new-democratic revolution) and to prepare to transform it into a socialist revolution when all the necessary conditions are present—that is the sum total of the great and glorious revolutionary task of the Communist Party of China. All members of the party should strive for its accomplishment and should never give up halfway. Some immature Communists think that we have only the task of the democratic revolution at the present stage but not that of the socialist revolution at the future stage; or that the present revolution or the agrarian revolution is in fact the socialist revolution. It must be emphatically pointed out that both views are erroneous. Every Communist must know that the whole Chinese revolutionary movement led by the Chinese Communist Party is a complete revolutionary movement embracing the two revolutionary stages, democratic and socialist, which are two revolutionary processes differing in character, and that the socialist stage can be reached only after the democratic stage is completed. The democratic revolution is the necessary preparation for the socialist revolution, and the socialist revolution is the inevitable trend of the democratic revolution. And the ultimate aim of all Communists is to strive for the final building of socialist society and communist society.

Source: Mao Zedong, *Selected Works*, in *Sources of Chinese Tradition*, 2nd ed., vol. 2, edited by Wm. Theodore de Bary and Richard Lufrano (New York: Columbia University Press, 2000), pp. 418–23.

"A Note to the Members of the National Planning Committee" (1940), Jawaharlal Nehru

Jawaharlal Nehru (1889–1964) was the first prime minister of India and a leading figure in Indian politics before and after independence. Here he combines a universalist, technocratic faith in planning with local traditions.

- Evaluate the balance of foreign influence and Indian tradition in this document.
- What does Nehru think planning can achieve? What risks does he want to avoid?
- What is Nehru's view of entrepreneurship and free markets?

Planning for the Future

To some it may appear that this is a most unsuitable time for planning, which is essentially a labour of peaceful co-operation. It may be argued that we should wait for better times and more stable conditions, for who knows what the outcome of the present conflict will be? On what foundation shall we build, when no man can foretell what that foundation will be? And yet though we are so uncertain of the future, this we know well that the future will be very different from the past or even from this changing present. Already we see vast political and economic changes taking shape in the womb of the future. Can we plan in India with all this doubt and uncertainty?

These considerations fill our minds, as they should, and we must give careful thought to them. And yet these very considerations lead us to a contrary conclusion. For it is this very time of change and uncertainty that demands mental activity and a vision of the future that we desire. If we are mere onlookers now, and passive and helpless agents of circumstances or the will of others, we barter away our claim to that future. Instead of preparing for it, we hand the reins to others. Every conflict ends sometime or other, every war is followed by a peace, temporary or more enduring, every work of destruction has to be followed by construction. That construction will be chaotic and wasteful unless previous thought has been given to it. A period of war and dynamic change therefore demands, even more than the static times of peace, the planned activity of the mind, so that, when time and opportunity come, this may be translated with all speed into the planned activity of the nation.

For, thinking and planning for the future is essential if that future is not to end in misdirected energy and chaos. It is foolish to imagine that when the present crisis at long last ends, a new or better arrangement of world affairs or our national affairs will automatically emerge out of it. It is equally unwise to allow matters to drift, protesting occasionally perhaps, but otherwise looking on helplessly, for fear that what we may do might involve a risk or be taken unfair advantage of by our opponents. The world is full of risks and dangers today. We cannot escape them. The greatest risk and danger is to drift and not give thought and energy to finding a way out. It is manifest that the old order has had its day and is dissolving, whether we like this or not. It has led to wars and upheavals and continuing conflicts which involve not only passion and hatred and an enormous waste of energy and resources, but also prevent us from achieving what is otherwise easily attainable. We have to understand the conflicts of forces that dominate the world today and seek to resolve these conflicts. It is certainly a possibility that the world may inevitably be led to social dissolution. We have to avoid that, if we can, but we cannot do so by shutting our eyes to the fact that the existing order is incapable of preventing this catastrophe. Something else, more in keeping with modern conditions, has to be evolved. Politics, in our country as elsewhere, dominates the scene and occupies men's minds. But the real changes that are shaping the world are deeper than politics. If we plan, we must consider them and have clear minds about them.

We shall thus have to consider, at this stage or later, the basic and fundamental policies that must govern our planning. Without a definite and clear-cut objective in view, and an understanding of the path we must pursue, we shall plan ineffectively or perhaps even in vain.

Already the NPC has given some thought to this matter and we have come to some general but fundamental decisions. It is well to recapitulate some of them. We are aiming at a free and democratic state, which has full political and economic freedom. In this state the fundamental rights of the individual and the group—political, economic, social and cultural— will be guaranteed, and the corresponding duties and obligations laid down. The state will be progressive and will utilize all scientific and other knowledge for the advancement of the people as a whole, and for the promotion of their happiness and material as well as cultural and spiritual well-being. The state will not permit the exploitation of the community by individuals or groups to the disadvantage of the former and to the injury of the nation as a whole. To realize the social objectives, the state has to plan through its representatives for the nation (whenever possible, in co-operation with other nations) and to co-ordinate the various activities of the nation so as to avoid waste and conflict and attain the maximum results. This planning will deal with production, distribution, consumption, investment, trade, income, social services, and the many other forms of national activity which act and react on each other. Briefly put, planning aims at the raising of the material and cultural standard of living of the people as a whole. In India our standards are so terribly low and poverty is so appalling that this question of raising standards is of the most vital importance. The NPC has suggested that national wealth should be increased between two and three times within the next ten years, and this should be so planned as to raise the general standard at least in a like measure.

Source: Jawaharlal Nehru, "A Note to the Members of the National Planning Committee," May 1, 1940, in *Jawaharlal Nehru: An Anthology*, edited by Sarvepalli Gopal (Delhi: Oxford University Press, 1980), pp. 304–6.

On Negritude (1959), Léopold Sédar Senghor

Léopold Sédar Senghor (1906–2001) was a Senegalese poet and politician. A leading figure in the Negritude movement, Senghor served as the first president of Senegal (1960–1980). This selection, drawn from a lecture at Oxford University and reprinted many times, presents a concise overview of the movement, which was established initially in poetry.

- Define Negritude.
- Explain the relationship between reason and emotion in this text.
- What does Senghor mean when he says that Negritude does not oppose European values but complements them?

PARADOXICALLY, it was the French who first forced us to seek its essence, and who then showed us where it lay. . . . when they enforced their policy of assimilation *and thus deepened our despair . . . Early on, we had become aware within ourselves that assimilation was a failure; we could assimilate mathematics or the French language, but we could never strip off our black skins nor root out our black souls. And so we set out on a fervent quest for the Holy Grail: our Collective Soul. And we came upon it.*

It was not revealed to us by the "official France" of the politicians who, out of self interest and political conviction defended the policy of assimilation. Its whereabouts was pointed out to us by that handful of freelance thinkers—writers, artists, ethnologists, and prehistorians—who bring about cultural revolutions in France. It was, to be quite precise, our teachers of Ethnology who introduced us to the considerable body of work already achieved in the understanding of Africa, by the University of Oxford.

What did we learn from all those writers, artists and teachers? That the early years of colonisation and especially, even before colonisation, the *slave trade* had ravaged black Africa like a bush fire, wiping out images and values in one vast carnage. That Negroid civilisation had flourished in the Upper Paleolithic Age, and that the Neolithic Revolution could not be explained without them. That their roots retained their vigour, and would one day produce new grass and green branches . . .

Negritude is *the whole complex of civilised values—cultural, economic, social and political—which characterise the black peoples*, or, more precisely, the Negro-African world.

All these values are essentially informed by intuitive reason. Because this sentient reason, the reason which comes to grips, expresses itself emotionally, through that self-surrender, that coalescence of subject and object; through myths, by which I mean the archetypal images of the collective Soul, above all through primordial rhythms, synchronised with those of the Cosmos.

In other words, the sense of communion, the gift of myth-making, the gift of rhythm, such are the essential elements of Negritude, which you will find indelibly stamped on all the works and activities of the black man. . . .

In opposition to European racialism, of which the Nazis were the symbol, we set up an "anti-racial racialism". The very excesses of Naziism, and the catastrophes it engendered, were soon to bring us to our senses. Such hatred, such violence, above all, such weeping and such shedding of blood produced a feeling of revulsion—it was so foreign to our continent's genius: our *need to love*.

And then the anthropologists taught us that there is no such thing as a pure race: scientifically speaking, races do not exist. They went one better and forecast that, with a mere two hundred million people, we would in the end disappear as a "black race", through miscegenation.

At the same time they did offer us some consolation. "The focal points of human development", wrote Teilhard de Chardin, in 1939, "always seem to coincide with the points of contact and anastomosis of several nerve paths", that is, in the ordinary man's language, of several races.

If then we were justified in fostering the values of Negritude, and arousing the energy slumbering within us, it must be in order to pour them into the mainstream of cultural miscegenation (the biological process taking place spontaneously). They must flow towards the meeting point of all Humanity; they must be our contribution to the Civilisation of the Universal.

Biological miscegenation, then, takes place spontaneously, provoked by the very laws which govern Life, and in the face of all policies of Apartheid. It is a different matter in the realm of culture. Here, we remain wholly free to cooperate or not, to provoke or prevent the synthesis of cultures. This is an important point. For, as certain biologists point out, the psychological mutations brought about by education are incorporated in our genes, and are then transmitted by heredity. Hence the major role played by *Culture*.

Seen within this prospect of the Civilisation of the Universal, the colonial policies of Great Britain and France have proved successful complements to each other, and black Africa has benefited.

The policies of the former tended to reinforce the traditional native civilisation. As for France's policy, although we have often reviled it in the past, it too ended with a credit balance, through forcing us actively to assimilate European civilisation. This fertilised our sense of Negritude.

Today, our Negritude no longer expresses itself as opposition to European values, but as a *complement* to them. Henceforth, its militants will be concerned, as I have often said, *not to be assimilated, but to assimilate*. They will use European values to arouse the slumbering values of Negritude, which they will bring as their contribution to the Civilisation of the Universal.

Nevertheless, we still disagree with Europe: not with its values any longer (with the exception of Capitalism) but with its theory of the Civilisation of the Universal. . . .

In the eyes of the Europeans, the "exotic civilisations" are static in character, being content to live by means of archetypal images, which they repeat indefinitely. The most serious criticism is that they have no idea of the *pre-eminent dignity of the human person*.

My reply is this. Just as much as black Africa, taking this as an example, Europe and its North American offspring live by means of archetypal images. For what are Free Enterprise, Democracy, Communism, but *myths*, around which hundreds of millions of men and women organise their lives?

Negritude itself is a myth (I am not using the word in any pejorative sense), but a living, dynamic one, which evolves with its circumstances into a form of humanism.

Actually, our criticism of the [European] thesis is that it is monstrously anti-humanist. For if European civilisation were to be imposed, unmodified, on all Peoples and Continents, it could only be by force. That is its first disadvantage. A more serious one is that it would not be *humanistic*, for it would cut itself off from the complementary values of the greater part of humanity. As I have said elsewhere, it would be a universal civilisation; it would not be the Civilisation of the Universal.

Whereas our revised Negritude is humanistic. I repeat, it welcomes the complementary values of Europe and the white man, and indeed, of all other races and continents.

But it welcomes them in order to fertilise and re-invigorate its own values, which it then offers for the construction of a civilisation which shall embrace all Mankind.

The *Neo-Humanism* of the twentieth century stands at the point where the paths of all Nations, Races and Continents cross, where the Four Winds of the Spirit blow.

Source: Léopold Sédar Senghor, "What is Negritude?" *Negro Digest* (April 1962), 3–6.

On Decolonization (1961), Frantz Fanon

Frantz Fanon (1925–1961) was a psychiatrist and writer from the Caribbean island of Martinique. Fanon joined the Algerian Front de Libération Nationale and treated torture victims during the Algerian War of Independence (1954–1962). This selection, written at the very end of his life, drew on his wartime experience.

- **Analyze the role of religion in this passage.**

- **Is this text Eurocentric?**

- **What role do traditional Muslim religious leaders ("the caids and the customary chiefs") play in this text?**

In decolonization, there is therefore the need of a complete calling in question of the colonial situation. If we wish to describe it precisely, we might find it in the well-known words: "The last shall be first and the first last." Decolonization is the putting into practice of this sentence. That is why, if we try to describe it, all decolonization is successful.

The naked truth of decolonization evokes for us the searing bullets and bloodstained knives which emanate from it. For if the last shall be first, this will only come to pass after a murderous and decisive struggle between the two protagonists. That affirmed intention to place the last at the head of things, and to make them climb at a pace (too quickly, some say) the well-known steps which characterize an organized society, can only triumph if we use all means to turn the scale, including, of course, that of violence.

You do not turn any society, however primitive it may be, upside down with such a program if you have not decided from the very beginning, that is to say from the actual formulation of that program, to overcome all the obstacles that you will come across in so doing. The native who decides to put the program into practice, and to become its moving force, is ready for violence at all times. From birth it is clear to him that this narrow world, strewn with prohibitions, can only be called in question by absolute violence.

* * *

As soon as the native begins to pull on his moorings, and to cause anxiety to the settler, he is handed over to well-meaning souls who in cultural congresses point out to him the specificity and wealth of Western values. But every time Western values are mentioned they produce in the native a sort of stiffening or muscular lockjaw. During the period of decolonization, the native's reason is appealed to. He is offered definite values, he is told frequently that decolonization need not mean regression, and that he must put his trust in qualities which are well-tried, solid, and highly esteemed. But it so happens that when the native hears a speech about Western culture he pulls out his knife—or at least he makes sure it is within reach. The violence with which the supremacy of white values is affirmed and the aggressiveness which has permeated the victory of these values over the ways of life and of

thought of the native mean that, in revenge, the native laughs in mockery when Western values are mentioned in front of him. In the colonial context the settler only ends his work of breaking in the native when the latter admits loudly and intelligibly the supremacy of the white man's values. In the period of decolonization, the colonized masses mock at these very values, insult them, and vomit them up.

* * *

But it so happens that for the colonized people this violence, because it constitutes their only work, invests their characters with positive and creative qualities. The practice of violence binds them together as a whole, since each individual forms a violent link in the great chain, a part of the great organism of violence which has surged upward in reaction to the settler's violence in the beginning. The groups recognize each other and the future nation is already indivisible. The armed struggle mobilizes the people; that is to say, it throws them in one way and in one direction.

The mobilization of the masses, when it arises out of the war of liberation, introduces into each man's consciousness the ideas of a common cause, of a national destiny, and of a collective history. In the same way the second phase, that of the building-up of the nation, is helped on by the existence of this cement which has been mixed with blood and anger. Thus we come to a fuller appreciation of the originality of the words used in these underdeveloped countries. During the colonial period the people are called upon to fight against oppression; after national liberation, they are called upon to fight against poverty, illiteracy, and underdevelopment. The struggle, they say, goes on. The people realize that life is an unending contest.

We have said that the native's violence unifies the people. By its very structure, colonialism is separatist and regionalist. Colonialism does not simply state the existence of tribes; it also reinforces it and separates them. The colonial system encourages chieftaincies and keeps alive the old Marabout confraternities. Violence is in action all-inclusive and national. It follows that it is closely involved in the liquidation of regionalism and of tribalism. Thus the national parties show no pity at all toward the caids and the customary chiefs. Their destruction is the preliminary to the unification of the people.

At the level of individuals, violence is a cleansing force. It frees the native from his inferiority complex and from his despair and inaction; it makes him fearless and restores his self-respect. Even if the armed struggle has been symbolic and the nation is demobilized through a rapid movement of decolonization, the people have the time to see that the liberation has been the business of each and all and that the leader has no special merit. From thence comes that type of aggressive reticence with regard to the machinery of protocol which young governments quickly show. When the people have taken violent part in the national liberation they will allow no one to set themselves up as "liberators." They show themselves to be jealous of the results of their action and take good care not to place their future, their destiny, or the fate of their country in the hands of a living god. Yesterday they were completely irresponsible; today they mean to understand everything and make all decisions. Illuminated by violence, the consciousness of the people rebels against any pacification. From now on the demagogues, the opportunists, and the magicians have a difficult task. The action which has thrown them into a hand-to-hand struggle confers upon the masses a voracious taste for the concrete. The attempt at mystification becomes, in the long run, practically impossible.

Source: Frantz Fanon, *The Wretched of the Earth*, trans. Constance Farrington (Grove Press, 1963), 37, 43, 93–95.

Interpreting Visual Evidence

War and Propaganda

Both the Allies and the Axis powers made major efforts to mobilize consent and win support, not only among soldiers but on the home front as well. Governments used propaganda—information and ideas that are spread in order to promote a certain political point of view—to shape public opinion during World War II. While Joseph Goebbels and the Nazi Ministry for Public Enlightenment and Propaganda were the most famous for their efforts to demonize the enemy and foster a sense of solidarity at home and among Germany's allies, they had analogs in Washington, London, Moscow, and Tokyo. Propaganda offices around the world enlisted journalists, cartoonists, and other visual artists, as well as radio and film, to spread their messages.

The first image, "Victory or Bolshevism," a poster by Hans Schweitzer, known as Mjölnir (the name of the Norse god Thor's hammer), contrasts a wholesome German community with the bleak prospect of a Soviet occupation after the German defeat at Stalingrad (1942–1943). The next two images show European propaganda that celebrates the loyalty of colonial subjects in their empires' war efforts. A recruitment poster for the British army shows seven uniformed soldiers from across the empire, prepared to fight for a common future. The photograph shows Free French

German poster, "Victory or Bolshevism."

British poster, "Together."

Free French troops train in Bouar.

troops—Resistance fighters who supported the Allies and opposed collaborationist Vichy France—marching in Bouar, French Equatorial Africa (today the Central African Republic). The final image shows a Japanese representation of the United States. It depicts a demonic Franklin Delano Roosevelt with grasping hands and an evil smile.

Japanese poster portraying a villainous President Roosevelt.

Questions for Analysis

1. Contrast the stereotypes presented to celebrate cooperation with those presented to demonize enemies. Do they differ in any meaningful ways?

2. Does the medium—poster, caricature, or photograph—shape the message these images convey? Is the photograph similar to or different from the posters and caricature? Do they appeal to audiences in the same way?

3. Analyze the role of gender in these images. How do the artists use masculine and feminine imagery, and to what effect?

21

Globalization

1970-2000

In the thirteenth century, few people could imagine moving beyond their local regions. The Venetian explorer Marco Polo, who traveled through China, and the Arab scholar Ibn Battuta, who traversed the Islamic world, were rare exceptions. In contrast, by the late twentieth century, people traversed in a matter of hours the distances that it took Marco Polo and Ibn Battuta years to cover. Many others staying at home could "travel" the world via the Internet, books, newspapers, and television.

But not all travelers moved about so comfortably. Many migrants—desperate to escape political chaos, persecution, or poverty—slipped across borders in the dark of night, traveled as human cargo inside shipping containers, or fled their homelands on foot. Billions of other people still had no access to the global age's technological wonders and economic opportunities. Thus, while the development of integrated worldwide cultural and economic structures—known as **globalization**—created new possibilities for some, it also caused deeper inequalities.

The forces driving global integration—and inequality—were no longer the political empires of old. By the mid-twentieth century, the European empires had lost their sway. The Cold War and decolonization movements that had produced the three-world order no longer influenced world affairs. Power structures in the First World, under stress in the 1970s, did not crack. But those in the Second World did. Thus, the Cold War ended with the implosion of the Soviet bloc. The Third World also splintered, with some areas becoming highly

Core Objectives

- **DESCRIBE** the relationship between global migration, new technologies, and the spread of cultural influences during and after the Cold War.

- **EVALUATE** the degree to which globalization after the end of the Cold War changed societies, and **COMPARE** that globalization with earlier forms of globalization.

- **DESCRIBE** how globalization and population changes affected the environment, and vice versa.

- **IDENTIFY** the transnational forces that eroded the power of the nation-state in the last third of the twentieth century, and **EXPLAIN** how they did so.

globalization
Development of integrated worldwide cultural and economic structures.

advanced and others falling into deep poverty. To be sure, nation-states remained essential for establishing democratic institutions and protecting human rights, but supranational organizations—institutions that transcended nation-state borders, like the European Union and the International Monetary Fund (IMF)—often impinged on their autonomy. A new global order emerged with a unified marketplace and unhindered flows of capital, commerce, culture, and labor.

Global Storylines

- Following the collapse of the three-world order, new global markets and communications networks integrate the world but also create deep inequalities.

- New technologies and vast population movements make global culture more homogeneous.

- Globalization, supranational organizations (like the World Bank, the European Union, and the United Nations), and religious fundamentalism erode the power of the nation-state.

Removing Obstacles to Globalization

The collapse of the Soviet Union brought the Cold War to an end. At the same time, the capitalist First World gave up its last colonial possessions and the remnants of white settler supremacy disintegrated. But as this occurred, the formerly colonized Third World's dream of a "third way" also vanished. As empires withdrew, they revealed a world integrated by markets for capital and labor, culture, and technology, rather than forced loyalties to imperial masters or rival superpowers.

ENDING THE COLD WAR

A world divided between two hostile factions limited the prospects for a global exchange of peoples, ideas, and resources. There was widespread exchange within each of the rival blocs, but for other countries, the pressure from the Soviet Union and the United States to align with a superpower imposed limits to their interactions, even with neighboring states. Pushing against the Cold War superpower framework, however, were strong nationalist aspirations and religious movements, which the superpowers tried to control—or in some cases inflame—at great cost.

Mounting Costs Rivalry was enormously costly to the superpowers. The 1970s and 1980s saw the largest peacetime accumulation of arms in history. Despite myriad treaties and summits, the United States and the Soviet Union stockpiled nuclear and conventional weaponry. Furthermore, in 1983, U.S. president Ronald Reagan unveiled the Strategic Defense Initiative (nicknamed "Star Wars"), an elaborate and expensive plan to use satellites and space missiles to insulate the United States from incoming nuclear bombs. For both sides, these military spending sprees brought economic troubles.

Other pressures within and outside the United States and the Soviet Union also strained the Cold War order. The Soviet Union sent troops to prop up a puppet regime in Afghanistan, only to fall into a bloody war against insurgents financed and armed by the United States. The resulting stalemate undermined the image of the mighty Soviet armed forces, and mothers of Soviet soldiers protested their government's involvements abroad. In Europe and North America, the antinuclear movement rallied millions to the streets, while western industrialists worried about competition from Japan, which had been plowing money into rapid industrialization rather than arms. Political leaders also grappled with distressingly high unemployment rates. Thus, both sides shared a common crisis: fatigue from the Cold War, and an economic challenge from East Asia.

THE BIG PICTURE

What were the transnational forces that eroded the power of the nation-state in the last third of the twentieth century? How did they do so?

The Soviet Bloc Collapses In the end, the Soviet bloc collapsed. (See Map 21.1.) Even though planned economies employed the entire Soviet population, they failed to fill stores with sufficient consumer goods. Socialist health care and benefits lagged behind those provided in wealthy, capitalist countries. Authoritarian political structures in the Soviet bloc relied on deception and coercion rather than elections and civic activism. Although communists had promised to beat capitalism by building socialism on the way to achieving full communism, the communist paradise was nowhere on the horizon.

Events in Poland were one catalyst in socialism's undoing. In 1978, the Catholic Church appointed a new pope, John Paul II, who

Lech Wałęsa A Polish electrician from the Lenin Shipyard in the Baltic port city of Gdańsk, Walesa spearheaded the formation of Solidarity, a mass independent trade union of workers who battled the communist regime that ruled in their name. He later was elected president of post-communist Poland.

came from Poland—the first non-Italian pope in over 450 years. The pope supported mass strikes at the Lenin Shipyard in Gdańsk, which led to the formation of the Soviet bloc's first independent trade union, Solidarity. As Communist Party members in Poland defected to its side, the union became a society-wide movement; it aimed not to reform socialism (as in Czechoslovakia in 1968; see Chapter 20) but to overcome it. A crackdown by the Polish military and police put most of Solidarity's leadership in prison and drove the movement underground, but Soviet intelligence officials secretly worried that Solidarity could not be easily eradicated.

The most consequential factor in the collapse of the Soviet superpower was the reform effort launched by Mikhail Gorbachev, who became general secretary of the Soviet Communist Party in 1985. Under this effort (known as *perestroika*, meaning "reconstruction"), Gorbachev permitted competitive elections for Communist Party posts, relaxed censorship, allowed civic associations, legalized small nonstate businesses, granted autonomy to state firms, and encouraged the Soviet republics to be responsible for their own affairs within the Soviet Union. These reforms were linked with dramatic arms-control initiatives to ease the superpower burden on the Soviet Union. Gorbachev then began withdrawing troops from Afghanistan and informed eastern European leaders that they could not count on Moscow's armed intervention to prop up their regimes.

Having set out to improve socialism, however, Gorbachev instead destabilized it. Civic groups called not for reform of the system, but for its liquidation. Eastern European states declared their intention to leave the Soviet orbit, and some of the Soviet republics began to push for independence. In response, disgruntled factions within the Communist Party and the Soviet

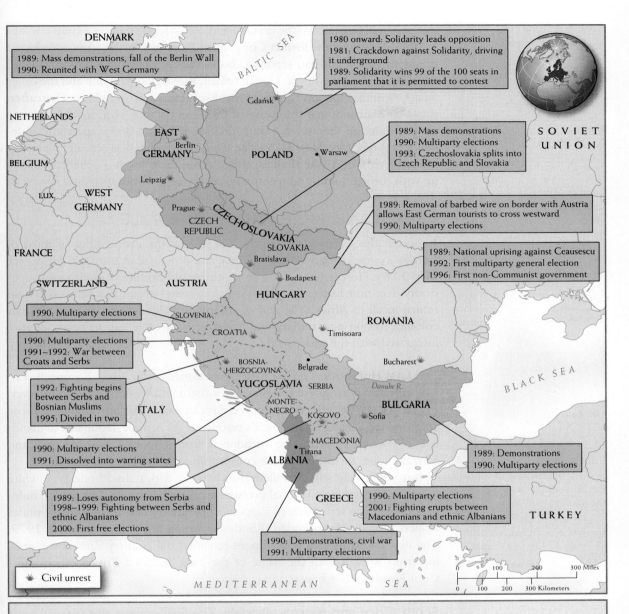

1989: Mass demonstrations, fall of the Berlin Wall
1990: Reunited with West Germany

1980 onward: Solidarity leads opposition
1981: Crackdown against Solidarity, driving it underground
1989: Solidarity wins 99 of the 100 seats in parliament that it is permitted to contest

1989: Mass demonstrations
1990: Multiparty elections
1993: Czechoslovakia splits into Czech Republic and Slovakia

1989: Removal of barbed wire on border with Austria allows East German tourists to cross westward
1990: Multiparty elections

1989: National uprising against Ceausescu
1992: First multiparty general election
1996: First non-Communist government

1990: Multiparty elections

1990: Multiparty elections
1991–1992: War between Croats and Serbs

1992: Fighting begins between Serbs and Bosnian Muslims
1995: Divided in two

1990: Multiparty elections
1991: Dissolved into warring states

1989: Demonstrations
1990: Multiparty elections

1989: Loses autonomy from Serbia
1998–1999: Fighting between Serbs and ethnic Albanians
2000: First free elections

1990: Multiparty elections
2001: Fighting erupts between Macedonians and ethnic Albanians

1990: Demonstrations, civil war
1991: Multiparty elections

* Civil unrest

Map 21.1 Collapse of the Communist Bloc in Europe

The Soviet Union's domination of eastern Europe ended precipitously in 1989. The political map of eastern and central Europe took on a different shape under European integration.

- What significant event in many communist countries signaled the collapse of communism?
- In what part of eastern and central Europe did the most political instability and conflict occur?
- According to your reading, why did the end of communist rule cause the reshuffling of political boundaries in the region?

military tried to preserve the destabilized old order by staging a coup attempt in 1991. However, the former Communist Party boss of Moscow and elected president of the Russian republic, Boris Yeltsin, rallied the opposition and faced down the hard-liners. Under Yeltsin, Russia, like Ukraine and the other Soviet republics, became a refuge for discontented Soviet elites. Thereafter, those elites abandoned the cause of the Soviet Union and divided up state property among themselves. Thus, the Soviet Union broke apart into independent states. (See Map 21.2.) The Cold War, which began as a tense stand-off between World War II allies, ended when the eastern bloc failed to keep up with the economic and technological development of its rivals.

AFRICA AND THE END OF WHITE RULE

Although the aftermath of World War II saw the dismantling of most of Europe's empires, remnants of colonial rule remained in southern Africa (see Map 20.6). Here, whites clung to centuries-old notions of their racial superiority over non-Europeans. Final decolonization meant that self-rule would return to all of Africa. The end of colonialism also set the stage for former colonies to find new trading and investment partners and to become more integrated with the wider world.

The Last Holdouts The last African territories under direct European control were the Portuguese colonies of southern and western Africa. However, by the mid-1970s, efforts to suppress African nationalist movements in those colonies had exhausted Portugal's resources. As African nationalist demands led to a hurried Portuguese withdrawal from Guinea-Bissau, Angola, and Mozambique, formal European colonialism in Africa came to an end.

But white rule still prevailed elsewhere in Africa. In Rhodesia, a white minority resisted international pressure to allow black rule. In the end, independent African states helped support a liberation guerrilla movement under Robert Mugabe. Surrounded, Rhodesian whites finally lost control in 1979. The new constitutional government renamed the country Zimbabwe, erasing from Africa's map the name of the long-deceased British expansionist Cecil Rhodes (see Chapter 17).

South Africa and Nelson Mandela The final outpost of white rule was South Africa, where the European minority was larger, richer, and more entrenched than elsewhere in the region. Yet in the countryside and cities, defiance of white rule was growing. Black South Africans lobbed rocks and crude bombs at tanks and organized mass strikes against the multinational-owned mines.

At the same time, pressures from abroad to end the racist apartheid system were mounting. The International Olympic Committee banned South

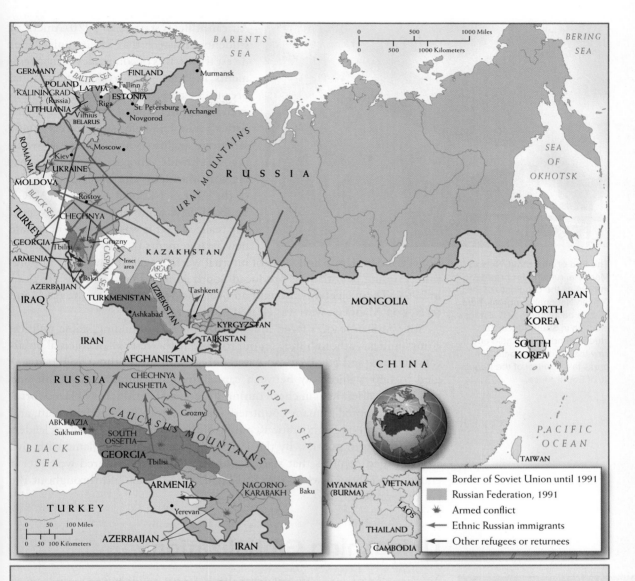

Map 21.2 The Breakup of the Soviet Union

The Soviet Union broke apart in 1991. Compare this map with Map 17.5, which illustrates Russian expansion in the nineteenth century.

- Which parts of the old Russian Empire remained under Russian rule, and which of its territories established their own states?
- In what areas did large migrations accompany the breakup, and for what reasons?
- According to your reading, how did the breakup of the Soviet Union change Russia's status in Europe and Asia?

The End of Apartheid Nelson Mandela, running for president in 1994 as the candidate of the African National Congress, here casts a ballot in the first all-races election in South Africa. This election ended apartheid and saw the African National Congress take control of the Republic of South Africa.

African athletes starting in 1970. American students insisted that their universities divest themselves of companies with investments in South Africa. As international pressures grew, foreign governments—even that of the United States, once South Africa's staunchest ally—applied economic sanctions against South Africa. A swelling worldwide chorus demanded that **Nelson Mandela**, the imprisoned leader of the African National Congress (ANC), be freed. The white political elite eventually realized that it was better to negotiate new arrangements than to endure international condemnation and years of internal warfare against a majority population. Ensuing negotiations produced South Africa's first free, mass elections in 1994. These elections brought an overwhelming victory to the ANC and to Nelson Mandela, who was elected president.

Still, African leaders faced immense problems in building stable political communities. Although they set out to destroy the vestiges of colonial political structures and build African-based public institutions, those leaders struggled to find a third way between capitalism and communism. Ethnic and religious rivalries, held in check during the colonial period, now blazed forth. Civil wars erupted in many countries—most violently in Nigeria, Sudan, and Zaire (later called Democratic Republic of the Congo)—and military leaders were drawn into politics. By the 1990s, the continent was aflame with civil strife. Armed conflicts that started with the Cold War endured well after it ended, even though white rule had finally come to an end throughout the entire continent.

Unleashing Globalization

Core Objectives

DESCRIBE the relationship between global migration, new technologies, and the spread of cultural influences during and after the Cold War.

As obstacles to international integration began to dissolve, capital, commodities, people, and culture crossed borders with ever-greater freedom. Even though these movements had occurred throughout history, their scale changed dramatically in these years. Never had there been such unequal access to the fruits of exchange. Many Third World countries, as well as those of the former eastern communist bloc—which came to be collectively called the **developing world**—were largely left out. Several factors contributed to increasing integration and to new power arrangements: international banking, expanded international trade, population migrations, and technical breakthroughs in communications.

FINANCE AND TRADE

The increase in the international flow of goods and capital was well under way in the 1970s, but the end of the Cold War removed many impediments to globalization. During the 1990s, even the strongest nation-states felt the effects of economic globalization.

Global Finance and Deregulated Markets Major transformations in the world's financial system occurred in the 1970s. America's budget and trade deficits prompted president Richard Nixon to take the dollar off the gold standard, an action that enabled the yen, the lira, the pound, the franc, and other national currencies to cut their ties to the American dollar. Now international financiers enjoyed greater freedom from national regulators and found fresh business opportunities.

The primary agents of the heightened global financial activity were banks. Based mainly in London, New York, and Tokyo, big banks attracted large amounts of capital for lucrative ventures around the world. Revenues from oil producers provided a large infusion of cash into the global economy in the 1970s. At the same time, banks joined forces to issue mammoth loans to developing countries.

No international financial organization was more influential than the International Monetary Fund (IMF), which came into existence after World War II with a view to raising capital from all of the participating states so as to be able to lend funds to states in need. During the 1980s, it emerged as a central player, especially in response to debt crises in poor countries that emerged as the prospect of finding a third way between the superpower blocs began to fade. Throughout the 1970s, European, Japanese, and North American banks had loaned money on very easy terms to cash-strapped Third World and eastern-bloc borrowers. But what was once good business soon turned sour. In 1982, a wave of defaults, in which governments and other borrowers found themselves unable to repay their loans, threatened to overrun Latin America in particular. Throughout the 1980s, international banks and the IMF kept heavily indebted customers solvent. The IMF offered short-term loans to governments on condition that recipients produce balanced budgets, compel civilian populations to give up subsidies on essential products, and cease to import far more than they exported. Latin Americans led the way in reorganizing their finances and thus pioneered the process of expanding domestic production while at the same time engaging in robust international trade. All across the world, tariffs and other barriers to foreign trade crumbled, state enterprises became private firms, and foreign banks and multinational companies took a great interest in investing in these newly reformed economies.

Effects of Integrated Networks New technologies and institutions enabled many more financial investors and traders to participate in the integrated

Nelson Mandela (1918–2013)
Leader of the African National Congress (ANC) who was imprisoned for more than two decades by the apartheid regime in South Africa for his political activities, until worldwide protests led to his release in 1990. In 1994, Mandela won the presidency in South Africa's first free mass elections.

developing world
Term applied to poor countries of the Third World and the former eastern communist bloc seeking to develop viable nation-states and prosperous economies. The term has come under sustained criticism for suggesting that there is a single path of economic growth that countries everywhere follow. It has been replaced by equally problematic terms like "advanced economy" and "emerging markets."

networks of world finance. The Internet and online trading accelerated the movement of capital across borders. Rapid changes in financial and currency markets soon created problems, however. When the Mexican economy went into paralysis in 1994, the crisis was so extreme that not even the IMF could bail it out; the U.S. Treasury issued the largest international loan in history to pull Mexico out of its economic tailspin. Despite acting as the lender in that instance, the United States emerged in the new financial order as the world's largest borrower because it imported far more than it exported. Early in the new millennium, its net foreign debt soared past $2 trillion—a 700 percent increase since the early 1990s. Much of this debt was owed to China, which had a huge trade surplus with the United States.

Globalization increased commercial, as well as financial, interdependence. The total value of goods and services exchanged through world trade increased nearly tenfold between 1973 and 1998, and trade in Asia grew even faster. Whereas an American would once have worn American-made clothes (Levi's), driven an American car (a Ford), and watched an American television (made by Zenith), such was rarely the case by the century's end. Increasingly, American consumers bought foreign goods and services and sold a greater share of their own output abroad. This pattern had always been true of smaller regions like Central America and southern Africa. But in the 1980s, it intensified as countries with cheap and skilled labor, like China, India, and Brazil, were able to undersell their competitors in world markets.

International trade also shifted the international division of labor. After World War II, Europeans and North Americans dominated manufacturing, while Third World countries supplied raw materials. But by the 1990s this was no longer the case. Brazil became a major airplane maker, South Korea exported millions of automobiles, and China emerged as the world's largest source of textiles, footwear, and electronics.

The most remarkable global shift involved East Asian industry and commerce. Manufactured goods, including high-technology products, now came from the eastern fringe of Afro-Eurasia as often as from its western fringe. Japan blazed the Asian trail: between 1965 and 1990, its share of world trade doubled to almost 10 percent. China, too, flexed its economic muscle. When Deng Xiaoping took power in 1978, China was already a growing economy. Under Deng, China started to become an economic powerhouse. For the next two decades, China chalked up astounding 10 percent annual growth rates, swelling its share of world GDP (gross domestic product, the value of goods and services produced) from 5 percent to 12 percent.

For East Asia, the share of exports doubled in the same period. Smaller states whose governments subsidized economic development, like Singapore, Taiwan, South Korea, and Hong Kong, became mini-powerhouses. By the early 1990s, these countries and Japan were also major investors abroad.

As East Asia's share of world production quickly increased, the U.S. and European shares decreased.

Regional Trade Blocs and Growing Inequalities The industrialization of poor countries, combined with lower trade barriers, increased the pressures of world competition on national economies. Some areas responded by establishing regional trade blocs in an effort to create larger markets for themselves and stay competitive in an ever more integrated world economy.

The most complete regional integration occurred in Europe, where states slashed trade barriers and harmonized their commercial policies toward the rest of the world. In 1993, the Maastricht Treaty established the **European Union (EU)** under its current name, and what had been conceived as a trading and financial bloc began to evolve into a political union as well, a supranational organization that encroached on the sovereignty of its member states. In 2002, a number of the European Union states deepened their economic interdependence by adopting a single currency, the euro. A few of the EU states—most notably the United Kingdom—did not want to give up control of their own national currency. By 2012, the European Union had twenty-seven members, with seventeen members using the euro.

Although international trade increased during this period, it also became increasingly unequal. High-technology and high-value goods now occupied an ever-greater share of the manufacturing and exports of the world's richest countries. For rich countries as a whole, about half of total GDP reflected the production and distribution of goods such as computers, software, and pharmaceuticals and services such as insurance and banking, which, collectively, gave those countries a competitive advantage. Poor nations, by contrast, generally remained locked in the production of low-tech goods and the export of raw materials. Increasingly, technology and knowledge divided the world into affluent, technically sophisticated countries and poor, technically underdeveloped regions.

MIGRATION

Migration, a constant feature of world history, became more pronounced in the twentieth century. (See Map 21.3.) Although after 1970 fewer Europeans were on the move, many more Asians, Africans, and Latin Americans were, chasing jobs in the richer countries. By 2000, there were 120 million migrants scattered across 152 countries, up from 75 million in 1965.

Patterns of Migration Migratory flows often followed the contours of past colonial and political ties. Where North America and Europe had had colonies or dependencies, their political withdrawal left tracks for migrants to follow. Indians and Pakistanis moved to Britain; so did Jamaicans. Dominicans,

European Union (EU)
International body organized after World War II as an attempt at reconciliation between Germany and the rest of Europe. It initially aimed to forge closer industrial cooperation. Eventually, through various treaties, many European states relinquished some of their sovereignty, and the cooperation became a full-fledged union with a common parliament. Some EU members adopted a single currency, the euro.

The Global View

Map 21.3 World Migration, 1918–1998

The world's population continued to grow and move around in the twentieth century.

- Looking at this map, identify the countries that had the greatest increase in foreign-born people as a percentage of total population.

- Then compare the areas of most rapid population growth during the nineteenth century with those parts of the world that, according to this map, had the highest percentage of foreign-born people in the twentieth century. What are the similarities and differences?

- During the twentieth century, which parts of the world were the sending areas, and which were the receiving territories? See also Map 18.1.

East Europeans 1918–1919

East Europeans 1918–1919

Russian Jews to USA 1980s and 1990s

European Jews to USA 1930s

CANADA

UNITED STATES

Jamaicans, Haitians, and Dominicans to USA 1990–

West Indians to Britain

Spaniards to Mexico 1936

Algerian colons to France 19__

1950–

MOROCCO

1950–

1960–

MEXICO

CUBA

BELIZE

HAITI

1960–1980

ATLANTIC OCEAN

GUATEMALA

NICARAGUA

COLOMBIA

PACIFIC OCEAN

BRAZIL

IVORY COAST

197_

1980

ARGENTINA

Foreign-born people as percentage of total population (latest available year)

- Less than 1.5%
- 1.5%–2.9%
- 3.0%–7.5%
- More than 7.5%
- Data not available
- ← Migration

0   1000   2000 Miles

0   1000   2000 Kilometers

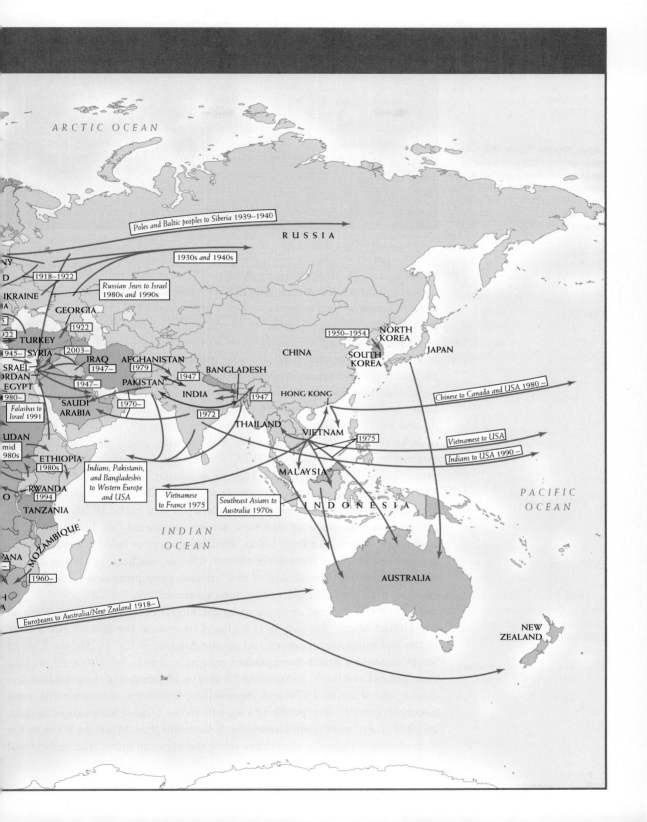

ARCTIC OCEAN

Poles and Baltic peoples to Siberia 1939–1940

RUSSIA

1930s and 1940s

NY

1918–1922

IKRAINE

Russian Jews to Israel
1980s and 1990s

GEORGIA

1922

1922

TURKEY

2003–

1945

SYRIA

IRAQ
1947–

AFGHANISTAN
1979

BANGLADESH

1950–1954

NORTH
KOREA

SOUTH
KOREA

JAPAN

CHINA

ISRAEL
ORDAN
EGYPT

1947–

PAKISTAN

1947

INDIA

1947

HONG KONG

Chinese to Canada and USA 1980 –

1980–

1970–

1972

Falashas to
Israel 1991

SAUDI
ARABIA

THAILAND

VIETNAM

1975

Vietnamese to USA

Indians to USA 1990 –

UDAN
mid
980s

ETHIOPIA
1980s

Indians, Pakistanis,
and Bangladeshis
to Western Europe
and USA

MALAYSIA

RWANDA
1994

TANZANIA

Vietnamese
to France 1975

Southeast Asians to
Australia 1970s

I N D O N E S I A

PACIFIC
OCEAN

ANA

MOZAMBIQUE

INDIAN
OCEAN

1960–

AUSTRALIA

Europeans to Australia/New Zealand 1918–

NEW
ZEALAND

Lagos, Nigeria During the twentieth century, Lagos was one of the fastest-growing and most crowded cities in Africa. Note the market and the mosque in the foreground, and the skyscrapers far in the distance.

Haitians, and Mexicans went to the United States. Algerians and Vietnamese moved to France. Where emerging rich societies cultivated close diplomatic ties, these relations opened migratory gates. This was true of Germany's relationship with Turkey, of Japan's with South Korea, and of Canada's with Hong Kong.

International migration was often an extension of regional and national migration from poorer rural areas to urban centers. In Nigeria, for example, rural-urban migration intensified after 1970. In 1900, Nigeria's capital at the time, Lagos, had a population of 41,847. At the century's end, Lagos had more than 10 million people, and this number was predicted to double by 2025. The key to Lagos's boom in the 1970s was the existence of large oil reserves in the country and the high prices that oil fetched in international markets. When OPEC sent oil prices soaring, money poured into Nigeria. The government kept most of that money in its largest city. That, in turn, spurred people to move to Lagos. This rural-urban migration increased Lagos's population by 14 percent per year in the 1970s and 1980s. No government—least of all a new, weakly supported one like Nigeria's—could cope with such a huge influx. Electricity supplies failed regularly in and around Lagos. There were never enough schools, teachers, or textbooks. But the city burst with the vitality of new arrivals, prompting one immigrant to exclaim, "It's a terrible place; I want to go there!"

One of the biggest changes in world migration patterns took place in the United States. Having all but closed its coastal borders on the Pacific in the late nineteenth century and on the Atlantic in the 1920s, the United States enacted a major immigration reform in 1965. By 2000, 27 million immigrants lived there, accounting for almost 10 percent of the population—double the share in 1970 and approaching levels not seen since the early twentieth century. The profile of migrants to the United States also changed. In 1970, there were more Canadians or Germans than Mexicans living in the United States. Over the next thirty years, the Mexican influx rose tenfold and by 2000 accounted for almost one-third of immigrants in the United States. The flow of legal and illegal immigrants from Mexico and Central America had an especially dramatic impact on the border states. The numbers migrating from Asia also surged, accounting for over 40 percent of all immigrants to the United States in the 1990s.

Temporary Migrants Some migrants moved for temporary sojourns—or at least that was their original intent. Into the 1950s and 1960s, southern Europeans moved northward; but when Spain, Portugal, Greece, and Italy also became wealthy societies, not only did the exodus decline, but these countries became magnets for Middle Eastern, North African, and later, eastern European migrants. The economic downturn in Europe in the 1970s and the resulting high unemployment rate, however, made their integration into European society difficult. Most migrants from Asia and Africa went initially to Europe in search of temporary jobs as "guest workers." With time, they and their families who followed them settled in their host countries, often living in dilapidated public housing projects, isolated from city centers and public services. The existence of welfare programs made them less likely to leave and return "home" than were earlier generations of labor migrants.

In Japan, too, immigrants were not easily incorporated. Tokyo's immigration policy in the 1970s resembled a guest-worker program. Discouraging permanent settlement and immigration, Japan encouraged itinerant workers to move to the country temporarily, yet its expanding economy required increasing numbers of these temporary migrants. Indeed, Japan's deep reluctance to recruit large numbers of foreign workers, for fear of their settling down, led to dire labor shortages. After Japan, the economic tigers of Hong Kong, Taiwan, and Malaysia all became hosts for temporary migrants. Millions of guest workers moved there, and ultimately those migrants sank deeper roots, especially once their children entered school.

Resident Noncitizens and Refugees Arguments in Los Angeles over schools and health care for resident noncitizens became part of a global debate over the rights and protections afforded to migrants. In Argentina, up to 500,000 undocumented Peruvians, Bolivians, and Paraguayans lived without rights as citizens. Even more staggering were the numbers of migrants— between 3 and 8 million—who moved from Mozambique, Zimbabwe, and Botswana to South Africa. In some Middle Eastern countries, like Saudi Arabia and Kuwait, foreign-born workers constituted over 70 percent of the workforce. In general, migrants were only partially accommodated by their host societies, while many were fully excluded. Thus, even though population movements flowed across political, kinship, and market networks, this demographic reshuffling heightened national concerns about the ethnic makeup of political communities.

Forced migrations remained a major problem. In contrast to earlier centuries' forced migration of slaves from Africa, this period's involuntary flows involved refugees fleeing civil war and torture. Many suffered for weeks, months, or years in refugee camps on the periphery of violence. The greatest concentration of refugees occurred in the world's poorest region—Africa. Many Africans were caught up in ethnic and religious conflicts that generated vast refugee camps, where their survival depended on the generosity of host governments and international contributions.

Whether migrants traveled in search of work or fled persecution, they posed a series of challenges for host countries. If migrants crossed borders easily, they often struggled to receive basic rights. Especially during economic downturns, discrimination often led to violent conflicts among recent immigrants, long-time residents (often themselves of immigrant origin), and the host country's security forces. Conflicts erupted over religion and culture, notably in French efforts to prevent women from wearing Muslim headscarves in public and the English-only movement in the United States. Governments in immigrant-receiving countries everywhere grappled with the challenge of extending citizenship to newcomers and then respecting their desires to dress, worship, and celebrate traditions as they did in their families' homelands.

GLOBAL CULTURE

Migrations and new technologies helped create a more global entertainment culture. In this domain, globalization is often equated with Americanization. Yet American entertainments themselves reflected artistic practices from across the globe as one mass culture met another. On the global scale, there was less cultural diversity in 2000 than in 1300; but in terms of individuals' everyday experience, the potential for experiencing cultural diversity, if one could afford the technology to do so, increased.

New Media Technology was key in spreading entertainment. In the 1970s, for example, cassette tapes became the dominant medium for popular music, sidelining the long-playing record and the short-lived eight-track tape. Television was another globalizing force, as American producers bundled old dramas and situation comedies for stations worldwide. Brazilian soap operas began to appear in Spanish-language TV markets throughout the Americas in the 1980s, often inducing Mexican viewers to rush home from work to catch the latest episode. Latin American television shows and music were distributed in the United States in areas with large Spanish-speaking populations. Bombay also produced its fair share of programs for viewers of British television and today produces roughly twice as many films per year as Hollywood. (See Current Trends in World History: Urbanization as a Global Phenomenon.) In terms of box-office revenues, Hollywood remains the leading producer of films in the world, helped in no small measure by its ability to send movies across borders and also by the actors from around the world who star in its films.

Television's globalizing effects were especially evident in sports. Soccer (known as football outside the United States) became an international passion, with devoted national followings for national teams. Indeed, by the 1980s, soccer was *the* world sport, with television ratings increasingly determining its schedule. Organizers of the 1986 World Cup in Mexico insisted that big soccer matches take place at midday so that the games could be televised live at prime time in Europe, even though teams had to play under the scorching sun. In many parts of the globe, major American sports also made particularly deep inroads as more people participated in them and as television broadcast American games in other countries. The National Basketball Association (along with the athletic footwear firm Nike) was particularly successful in international marketing; in the process, it made Michael Jordan the world's best-known athlete in the late twentieth century.

Cultural Exchanges Technology was not the only driving force of world cultures; migration and exchange were also important. For example, as people moved around, they brought their own musical tastes with them and borrowed others. Reggae, born in the 1960s among Jamaica's Rastafarians, became a sensation in London and Toronto, where large West Indian communities had migrated. Reggae's lyrics and realist imagery invoked a black countercultural spirit and a call for a return to African roots. Soon, Bob Marley and the Wailers, reggae's flagship band, played to audiences worldwide. In northeastern Brazil, where African culture was emerging from decades of disdain, Bob Marley became a folk hero. In Soweto, South Africa, populated by black workers, he was a symbol of resistance.

Reggae propelled a shift in black American music. In broadcasting reggae, DJs often merged sounds and chanted lyrics over a beat, a "talkover" form that soon characterized rap music as well. This was a disruptive concept in the late 1970s, but within ten years rap had become mainstream. Rap lyrics emulated reggae's realism by focusing on black problems, but they also opened a new domain of controversies by reflecting gang worldviews. On the world stage, Latino rappers stressed multicultural themes, often in "Spanglish." Asian rap stressed the genre as a vehicle for cross-cultural sharing and epitomized the ability of new cultural forms to bring peoples together.

Local Culture World cultures may have become more integrated and homogeneous, but they did not completely replace national and local cultures. Indeed, technology and migration often reinforced the appeal of "national" cultural icons as national celebrities gained popularity among emigrant groups abroad. Inexpensive new technology introduced these stars to more

Urbanization as a Global Phenomenon: Transforming Bombay into Mumbai

The city has played a pivotal role in world history since it first emerged thousands of years ago along the Tigris and Euphrates Rivers in Mesopotamia (modern-day Iraq). People have flocked to cities ever since for the social and economic advantages that these locations offer. By the end of the twentieth century, the proportion of people living in cities—usually defined as places having populations over 5,000 or 10,000—exceeded 50 percent in the wealthiest countries and was approaching that proportion in the less developed countries.

Of the burgeoning cities in the developing world, one of the most dynamic is Mumbai, in the state of Maharashtra, India. Acquired in the sixteenth century by the Portuguese, who then transferred its control to the English East India Company, Bombay (as it was named at the time) developed as a port city for colonial commerce. It profited from the cotton trade, developed a vibrant textile industry, attracted migrants from the countryside, and acquired a cosmopolitan image. India gained its independence from Britain in 1947, and in 1996 Bombay was renamed "Mumbai." It still epitomizes the modern face of the nation, and its increasingly heterogeneous population reflects the larger Indian melting pot.

Beginning in the 1980s, however, the nature of the city's relationship with the world economy started to change. The cotton textile industry, Bombay's economic backbone, went into a decline. Industrial employment fell sharply. The share of informal household enterprises, small shops, petty subcontractors, and casual labor rose, along with employment in banking and insurance. Economic liberalization removed hurdles for foreign businesses and brought the city directly into the global economy.

Today Mumbai occupies a strategic place in transnational geography. This is evident in the increasing presence of financial institutions, trading organizations, insurance companies, telecommunications corporations, and information technology enterprises with worldwide operations. Even the city's vibrant film industry addresses a global, not just a national, audience. Rather appropriately, Bombay cinema has been nicknamed "Bollywood." The city, however, still attracts a large number of poor migrants who live in slums or call the pavements their home. The gap between Mumbai's rich and poor has grown alarmingly. The millions who eke out a miserable living stand in stark contrast to a tiny elite enriched by the global economy.

Globalization has also affected Mumbai residents' identity. In the 1990s, the

and more people. In Egypt, the most popular singer of the Nasser years was Umm Kalthum, who became the favorite of Arab middle classes via radio. In 1975, she was given a state funeral, the likes of which had rarely been seen.

Nonetheless, as the market for world cultures grew increasingly competitive, performers increasingly employed a wider array of styles and also challenged biases and conventions. Among the breakthroughs that have occurred since the 1970s are the triumphs of black performers (Bob Marley, Dorothy Masuka), black athletes (Pelé, Michael Jordan), and black writers (Toni Morrison, Chinua Achebe). Competition also shattered some sexual biases. Women performers such as Madonna became popular icons. So did gay performers, starting with the Village People, whose campy multicultural anthem "YMCA" created a place for a new generation of gay, lesbian, and bisexual artists. Of course, beyond Europe and North America, challenging sexual conventions had its limits. In the Middle East, women video artists continued to wear veils—but

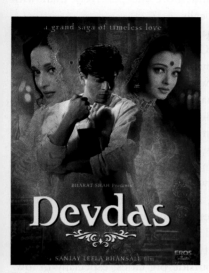

Bollywood Bombay cinema, or Bollywood, has an increasing global presence. This poster advertises *Devdas*, a three-hour romance that won awards in India and around the world.

political party then in power in Maharashtra was the Shiv Sena, a nativist regional party named after a seventeenth-century Maratha chieftain who opposed the Mughal Empire. As the industrial economy and trade unions gave way to the service sector and unorganized labor, the Shiv Sena utilized the social and political fluidity produced by globalization to win support for its nativist ideology. Mumbai's cosmopolitan image went up in smoke in 1992–1993, when the Shiv Sena led pogroms against the city's Muslim residents. In response, a Muslim underworld don, according to police investigations, engineered a series of bomb blasts in March 1993. Since then the city has experienced episodes of violence, none more gruesome than the terrorist attacks on two luxury hotels, a crowded railway station, and a Jewish center in November 2006. Ironically, the terrorists chose to attack Mumbai because of its economic importance and reputation as a cosmopolitan city.

Mumbai today illustrates the uneven effects of globalization. The society is sharply divided, economic disparities are great, and the city's politics is a cauldron of conflicting identities. These are the local forms in which this vast and influential city experiences globalization.

Questions for Analysis

- Contrast migration to Mumbai, as described here, with that to other parts of the world, notably western Europe and Japan, as described in the body of the chapter.
- How does Mumbai fit into the larger theme of "Worlds Together, Worlds Apart"?

Explore Further

Mehta, Suketu, *Maximum City: Bombay Lost and Found* (2005).
Prakash, Gyan, *Mumbai Fables* (2010).

now they swung their hips. Relatively homogeneous national cultures, often dominated by men representing the ethnic majority, gave way to a wider variety of entertainers and artists who broke loose from confining local cultures.

COMMUNICATIONS

Computer technology drove a revolution in global communications networks. In the late 1980s, while working in Switzerland, the British physicist Tim Berners-Lee devised a way to pool data stored on various computers. Whereas previous electronic links had existed only between major universities and research stations, Berners-Lee made data more accessible by creating the World Wide Web. With each use, each connection, and each datum entered, however, the Web grew unmanageably crowded and difficult to navigate. The early 1990s saw the first commercial browsers used in navigating the

Bob Marley In the 1970s, young Europeans and North Americans began to listen to music from the Third World. Among the most popular was Jamaican-based reggae, and its most renowned artist, Bob Marley. Marley's music combined rock and roll with African rhythms and lyrics about freedom and redemption for the downtrodden of the world.

Web. Suddenly people were communicating across global networks more easily than with neighbors and more inexpensively than with local phone calls.

These changes created a new generation of wealth. CEOs of top companies like General Motors, Royal Dutch Shell, and Merck now had less net worth than Michael Dell (computer hardware maker), Bill Gates (software maker), and Jeff Bezos (creator of online retailer Amazon.com). Shares of Internet firms, known as dot-coms, swept the world's stock markets. Money from these companies flowed globally as they established offices worldwide. Software and Internet technology firms developed enormous economies of scale, and thus those industries became prone to monopolization as they took over smaller companies.

While the Internet revolution provided new means to share and sell information, it also reinforced hierarchies between haves and have-nots. Great swaths of the world's population living outside big cities, especially in low-income countries, had no access to the Internet. The have-nots were poor not just from lack of capital, but from lack of access to knowledge and new media.

Characteristics of the New Global Order

Core Objectives

EVALUATE the degree to which globalization after the end of the Cold War changed societies and **COMPARE** that globalization with earlier forms of globalization.

While providing access to an unimaginable array of goods and services, globalization also deepened world inequalities. Family structures changed, and life spans increased. Education and good health determined one's status in society as never before. Populations expanded dramatically, requiring greater industrial and agricultural output from all parts of the world. While many parts of the world consumed more than ever before, others struggled with famine and the consequences of environmental change.

THE DEMOGRAPHY OF GLOBALIZATION

It took 160 years (1800–1960) for the world's population to increase from 1 billion to 3 billion; over the next 40 years (1960–2000), it jumped from 3 billion to over 6 billion. Behind this steepening curve were two important developments: a decline in mortality, especially among children, and a rise in life expectancy.

Population growth was hardly equal worldwide. (See Map 21.4.) In Europe, population growth peaked around 1900, and it moved upward only

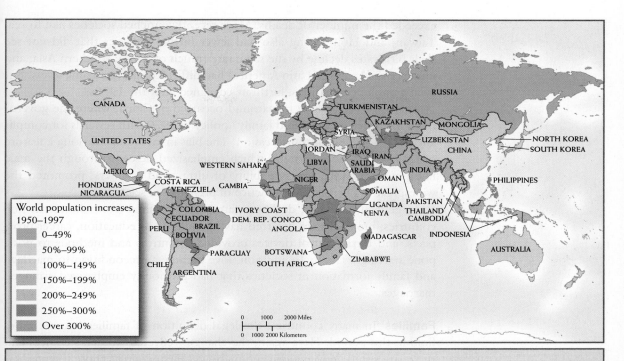

Map 21.4 World Population Increases, 1950–1997

World population increases, 1950–1997

- 0–49%
- 50%–99%
- 100%–149%
- 150%–199%
- 200%–249%
- 250%–300%
- Over 300%

The world's population more than doubled between 1950 and 1997, rising from approximately 2.5 billion to nearly 6 billion.

- Which countries had the largest population increases over these five decades?
- Why do you suppose these countries experienced such high population increases?
- According to your reading, why did western Europe and Russia have the lowest population increases during this period?

gradually, from 400 million to 730 million, during the twentieth century, with little growth after the 1970s. North America's population quadrupled over the same period, mainly because of immigration. The other population booms in the twentieth century occurred in Asia (whose population grew by 400 percent), Africa (550 percent), and Latin America (700 percent). China and India each passed the billion-person mark. Population increases were greatest in cities. By the 1980s, the world's largest cities were Asian, African, and Latin American. Greater Tokyo-Yokohama had 30 million inhabitants, while Mexico City had 20 million, São Paulo 17 million, Cairo 16 million, Calcutta 15 million, and Jakarta 12 million.

Population growth slowed most dramatically in richer societies. For some, like Italy, the growth rate declined to zero, as the number of births no longer exceeded the number of deaths. More recently enriched societies like Korea, Taiwan, and Hong Kong also had fewer births. Societies that did not see their birthrates decline by the same rate (much of Africa, southern Asia, and impoverished parts of Latin America) had difficulty raising income levels. But even among poor nations, birthrates declined after the 1970s.

The most remarkable turnaround occurred in China, where the government instituted a "one-child family" policy in 1979 with rewards for compliance and penalties for transgression. The bias in favor of sons (long a feature of China's patrilineal system, which emphasized descent through the male line), together with the availability of ultrasound scanners, promoted the widespread—albeit illegal—practice of prenatal sex selection.

In general, however, declining family size resulted from choice. In rich countries, more women deferred having children as education, career prospects, and birth-control devices provided incentives and methods to postpone starting a family. In addition, love became a precondition to marriage and family formation in societies that had previously emphasized arranged marriages.

Families In many countries, the legal definition of families became more fluid in this period. Here again, the changes reflected women's choices and the relationship between love and marriage. First, couples chose to end their marriages at unprecedented rates. In Belgium and Britain late in the twentieth century, fewer than half of all marriages survived. China's divorce rate soared too. In Beijing, by century's end, it approached 25 percent—double the 1990 rate. As of 2000, women initiated more than 70 percent of divorces.

As marriages became shorter-lived, new forms of child-rearing proliferated. Europeans, including the supposedly more traditional Italians and Greeks, abandoned nuclear family conventions. In those European countries where divorce remained difficult, more couples lived together without getting married. In the United States, out-of-wedlock births constituted one-third of all births in the late 1990s, and only about half of American children were living in households with both parents (compared with nearly three-quarters of children in the early 1970s).

Aging Average life spans grew longer as more infants survived childhood and lived to be old. The populations of industrialized nations "grayed" considerably as their median ages increased and the percentages of populations over age sixty-five grew. In western Europe and Japan, this graying was especially pronounced. Japan's birthrate plummeted, and the citizenry aged at such a rate that the population began to decrease. From a population of 127 million in 2000, estimates forecast a decline to 105 million by 2050.

Aging populations presented new challenges for families. For centuries, being a parent meant providing for children until they could be self-sufficient.

Old age, the period of relatively unproductive labor, was brief. Communities and households absorbed the cost of caring for the elderly. Household savings became family bequests to future, not to older, generations. But as populations aged, retirees needed their own and society's savings to survive. So public and private pension funds swelled to accumulate pools of money to fund future care for the aged. In Germany, over 30 percent of the government's social policy spending went into the state pension fund.

In Africa, where publicly supported pension funds were rare, the aged faced bleaker futures. Whereas in earlier times the elderly were respected founts of wisdom, colonial rule and the postcolonial world elevated the status of the young—especially those with western educations and lifestyles. Then, in the 1970s, as birthrates soared, the demand on family resources for infant and child care rose at the very moment when societies' resource bases began to shrink. The elderly could no longer work, but neither could they rely on the household's support.

INEQUALITY AND ENVIRONMENTAL DEGRADATION

Health The spread of contagious diseases also reflected inequities in the globalized world. Although microbes have no respect for borders, the effects of public health regulations, antibiotics, and vaccination campaigns reduced the spread of contagions in some countries. By the late twentieth century, not only did nutrition and healthy habits determine social status (as they always had), but access to medicines did too.

What used to be universal afflictions in previous centuries now affected only certain peoples. Water treatment and proper sewerage, for example, had banished cholera from most urban centers by the mid-twentieth century. More recently, however, its deadly grip again reached across Asia and into the eastern Mediterranean, parts of Latin America and the Caribbean, and much of sub-Saharan Africa. Thus, diseases proliferated where urban squalor was most acute—in cities with the greatest post-1970s population growth.

In the 1970s, entirely new diseases began to devastate the world's population. Consider **HIV/AIDS**, an epidemic that, in its first two decades, killed 12 million people. Acquired immunodeficiency syndrome (AIDS) is caused by the human immunodeficiency virus (HIV), which spreads through blood and other body fluids. The virus may remain dormant in the bodies of infected people for some time, but eventually attacks the immune system, leaving them unable to fight off even the most common microbes. First detected in 1981, HIV/AIDS was initially stigmatized as a "gay cancer" (as it then appeared primarily in gay men) and received little attention. But as it spread to heterosexuals and public awareness about it increased, new campaigns urged the practice of safe sex, control of blood supplies, and restrictions on sharing hypodermic needles.

HIV/AIDS
An epidemic of acquired immunodeficiency syndrome (AIDS) caused by the human immunodeficiency virus (HIV), which compromises the ability of the infected person's immune system to ward off other diseases. First detected in 1981, AIDS killed 12 million people in the two decades that followed.

In Europe and North America, where the campaigns intensified and new drugs were eventually developed to keep the virus inactive, HIV/AIDS rates stabilized. The new drugs were very expensive, however, leaving the poor and disadvantaged still vulnerable to developing AIDS. By 2000, 33 million people had AIDS (the vast majority in poor countries) and even more were infected with HIV. (See Map 21.5.) At least two-thirds of those with AIDS lived in sub-Saharan Africa. In India, 7 million carried HIV; in China, the figure topped 1 million.

Education Access to education increasingly separated the haves from the have-nots. Moreover, because educational opportunities usually favored men, schooling shaped economic opportunities available to men and women. In sub-Saharan Africa and in India, for example, literacy rates as of 2000

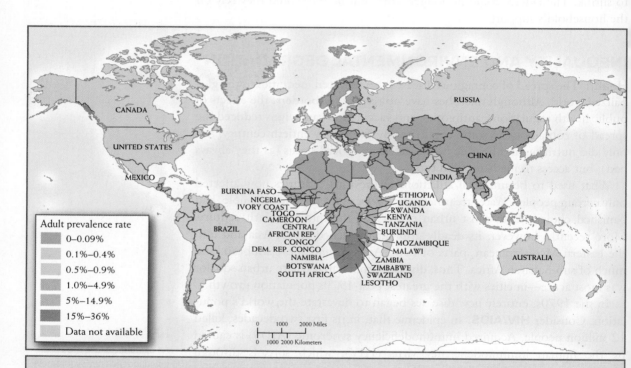

Map 21.5 HIV Infection across the World, 1999

....

HIV, which leads to AIDS, spread across the whole world within two decades, providing further evidence of global interconnectedness. The outbreak began in Africa.

- Where in Africa have the highest rates of HIV infection occurred?
- Which countries *outside* the African continent have had the highest rates of infection, and why is this so?
- Which countries have the lowest rates of HIV infection, and why is this so?

were, respectively, 63 and 64 percent for men and only 39 and 40 percent for women. In the Arab world, the literacy gap between men and women had decreased somewhat by the end of the twentieth century. Yet low levels of literacy overall and the depressed levels for women continued to impede each region's efforts to combat poverty.

Gender bias also remained in rich societies. For decades, however, women and girls pressed for equal access to education, with some astounding results. In the United States, by the late 1980s, more than half of all college degrees went to women. Chinese women made even greater strides, although roadblocks persisted. Ironically, with China's market reforms (described later in this chapter), women's access to basic education regressed as families, particularly in rural areas, reverted to spending their limited resources on educating sons. Thus, in 2000, up to 70 percent of China's 140 million illiterate people were female.

African Women and Education Though women's education lagged behind that of men in Africa, a number of women, like Stella Kenyi, pictured here, graduated from African high schools and attended universities at home or abroad. Kenyi taught business skills to men and women in Sudan after completing an undergraduate degree at Davidson College in North Carolina.

Women and Work Although more women held jobs outside the home, they lacked full equality at work. Limited by job discrimination and the burdens of child-rearing, women's participation in the workforce reached a fairly stable level by the 1980s. The percentage of women at the top of the corporate pyramid was considerably lower than their proportion in the labor force or their college graduation rates. Women worldwide had difficulties breaking through the "glass ceiling"—the seemingly invisible barrier that kept them from advancing to these high-level positions. Consequently, while the difference between men's and women's incomes narrowed, a significant gap persisted.

Working outside the home led to a problem inside the home: Who would take care of the children? Changing gender norms in rich countries sparked major migration streams. Jamaican and Filipino women, for example, migrated by the thousands in the 1970s and 1980s to Canada and Australia to work as nannies to raise money to send back home, where they had often left their own children. In South Africa and Brazil, local women worked as domestic servants and nannies. They were doing the jobs that once belonged to middle- and upper-class homemakers, women who now wanted the same rights as men: to parent *and* to work.

The deeply ingrained inequality between men and women prompted calls for change. Feminist movements arose mainly in Europe and North America in the 1960s, then became global in the 1970s. In 1975, the first truly international women's forum took place in Mexico City. But becoming global did not necessarily imply overturning local customs. What feminists called for was not the abolition of gender differences, but equal treatment—equal pay and equal opportunities for jobs and advancement.

Women took increasingly active stances against discrimination in government and in the workplace. Indeed, as economic integration intensified as a result of regional trade pacts (usually negotiated by men in the interest of male-owned and male-run firms), women struggled to ensure that globalization did not cut them out of new opportunities. For instance, after Argentina, Uruguay, Paraguay, and Brazil negotiated the Mercosur free trade pact, member governments built new highways and bridges, and traffic across South American borders soared. But as government efforts to foster approved trade grew, so did efforts to monitor illegal commerce. Women were responsible for one kind of illicit commerce: for generations, they had transported goods across the river separating Argentina and Paraguay. When customs officers tried to stop this practice in the mid-1990s, Argentine and Paraguayan women locked arms to occupy the new bridge that male truckers were using to ship Mercosur products, protesting the restrictions on their age-old enterprise.

The rising tide of global feminism culminated in the Fourth World Conference on Women, held in Beijing in 1995. Delegates from more than 180 governments attended the conference to produce "a platform for action" regarding women's rights in politics, business, education, and health. Alongside the official conference was the NGO Forum, a parallel conference for nearly 30,000 grassroots activists, who represented 2,000 nongovernmental organizations from every corner of the globe. Representatives planned strategies and coordinated programs for improving women's living and working conditions. What emerged from the conference were associations and groups that pledged to lobby for the rights of women and girls worldwide. One effect was to spotlight the ongoing shortage of opportunities for the advancement of women leaders.

Core Objectives

DESCRIBE how globalization and population changes affected the environment, and vice versa.

Agricultural Production The most immediate challenge facing many societies was how to feed their increasing populations. Yet changing agrarian practices resulted in a huge increase in food production. Starting in the 1950s, the "green revolution," which relied on chemical fertilizers, herbicides, and pesticides, produced dramatically larger harvests. Then, in the 1970s, biologists began developing genetically engineered crops, which multiplied yields at an even faster rate.

But these breakthroughs were not evenly distributed. American farmers, the biggest innovators, were also the greatest beneficiaries. For example, by century's end, they produced approximately one-ninth of the world's wheat and two-fifths of its corn. American exports accounted for about one-third of the world's international wheat trade and four-fifths of all corn exports. The most dramatic transformation of agriculture, however, occurred in China. Beginning in the late 1970s, the Chinese government broke up some of the old collective farms and restored the individual household as the basic economic unit in rural areas. Thereafter, agricultural output surged by roughly 9 percent per year and nearly doubled between 1978 and 1986.

While biology and chemistry allowed farmers in some countries to get more out of their land, others simply opened up new lands to cultivation. The most notorious frontier expansion occurred in the Amazon River basin. Migrants flocked to the Amazon frontier, largely from impoverished areas in northeastern Brazil. They cleared (by fire) cheap land, staked their claims, and, like nineteenth-century American homesteaders, tried to get ahead by cultivating crops and raising livestock. But the promise of bounty failed: the soils were poor and easily eroded, and land titles provided little security, especially once large speculators moved into the area. So the frontiersmen moved farther inland to repeat the cycle. By the 1980s, migrants to the Amazon River basin had burned away much of the rain forest, contaminated the environment, reduced the stock of diverse plant and animal life, and fostered social conflict in the Brazilian hinterland.

Not even "breadbasket" areas were always able to feed exploding populations. This was especially true in Africa from the 1970s onward, when domestic food production could not keep pace with population growth. (See Map 21.6.) Food shortages increased in frequency and duration, wiping out large numbers of people in sub-Saharan Africa. Children with protruding ribs became a clichéd image of the region.

What explained Africa's famines? As the Indian economist and Nobel laureate Amartya Sen observed, famines—and their increasing frequency—are not natural disasters; they are human-made. Food shortages in Africa stemmed largely from governments that ignored the rural sector and its politically unorganized farmers. Unable to persuade their governments to raise prices for their crops, the farmers lacked incentives to expand production. Food shortages were also by-products of global inequalities. At the urging of the IMF, African countries devoted hefty chunks of their economies to crops that could be exported to repay debts incurred in the 1970s. This focus left them without enough foodstuffs domestically, and thus they actually became food importers.

Natural Resources and the Environment The consumption of water, oil, and other natural resources became matters of international concern late in the twentieth century. So did pollution control and the disposal of waste products. Part of this internationalization reflected the recognition that individual nations could not solve environmental problems on their own. Air and water, after all, do not stop flowing at political boundaries.

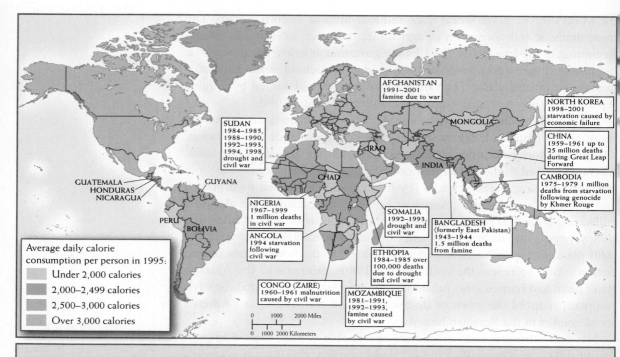

Map 21.6 Food Consumption and Famine since the 1940s

There is perhaps no better indicator of the division of the world into rich and poor, haves and have-nots, than average food consumption and famine.

- Which parts of the world have had the most difficulty in feeding their populations?
- What have been some of the causes of famine and malnourishment in these regions?
- How much have famine and malnourishment been due to human actions, and how much to climate and other matters over which human beings have little control?

Americans consumed a disproportionate share of the world's natural resources. By 2000, they were using water at a per capita rate three times the world's average. Indeed, extensive irrigation was crucial to California's agricultural sector, the most productive and profitable in the world. And piping water to desert cities like Los Angeles allowed them to grow.

In the United States and Canada, attempts to curb energy consumption saw little success, and the United States grew more dependent on imported oil. In the late 1990s, North American demand for fuel-guzzling sport utility vehicles intensified the demand for oil imports. Dependence on foreign sources locked oil importers into recurring clashes with oil exporters.

As Canadians saw their northern lakes fill up with acid rain (precipitation laced with sulfur, mainly from coal-fired power plants), they urged their

southern neighbor to curb emissions. Reciprocal agreements between Canada and the United States to cut sulfur emissions took shape in the 1980s. Europeans, also beset by acid rain, likewise negotiated regional environmental treaties. But some polluting industries simply moved overseas to poorer and less powerful nations. As the west cleaned up its environment, the rest of the world paid the price.

Other problems crossed national borders as well. These included **global warming:** increases in temperatures worldwide caused by the release of carbon into the atmosphere, mainly by the burning of fossil fuels. Global warming has the potential to change precipitation rates, sea level, and storm strength, and to shift the life cycles and migration patterns of flora and fauna—effects referred to collectively as **climate change.** International meetings in Rio de Janeiro and Kyoto in the 1990s urged restrictions on carbon emissions to avoid climate change, but a global accord proved impossible to achieve.

Ecological Crisis in the Amazon Farmers and ranchers cut and burned the Amazon rain forest at a ferocious rate on frontier lands. In these remote regions, it was hard for local authorities to enforce conservation laws.

The response to these environmental crises has been uneven at best. Carbon emissions continued to grow with the rise in automobile traffic in cities like Tokyo, Mexico City, and Los Angeles. Where environmentalists acquired political power, they forced regulators to curb carbon emissions. But controls on emissions depended on power and wealth, for it was hard to impose restrictions in societies where high energy use seemed a necessity of economic life. Even the Japanese, pioneers of clean fuel as early as the 1960s, were polluters in other spheres long thereafter. For example, with increasing controls at home, Japanese industrialists went abroad to unload hazardous waste. U.S. industrialists did the same, sending hazardous waste to Mexico. Argentina and Canada sent their nuclear waste not abroad, but to poor provinces desperate for jobs.

At the end of the twentieth century, even though some states had enacted measures to protect the environment, global guidelines for regulating the impact of human activities on the environment had eluded the world's leaders. At the same time, inequalities between and within societies grew more pronounced. The most glaring were between the rich and poor countries, despite the well-to-do middle classes that emerged everywhere in the world and tended to congregate in the big cities.

global warming
Upward temperature trends worldwide due to the release of carbon into the air, mainly by the burning of fossil fuels and other human activities.

climate change
A wide range of phenomena caused by global warming. These changes encompass not only rising temperatures, but also changes in precipitation patterns; ice mass loss on mountain glaciers around the world; shifts in the life cycles and migration patterns of flora and fauna; extreme weather events; and sea level rise.

Citizenship in the Global World

Since the nineteenth century, people had assumed that nation-states defined and protected the rights of citizens. But after the 1970s, people increasingly realized that international and supranational organizations often had more influence over their lives than did their own national governments, especially in the developing world. However, these organizations failed to stop the violence that erupted in many regions during this period. Religion also undermined the influence of nation-states as religious groups came into conflict with one another and with secular principles.

SUPRANATIONAL ORGANIZATIONS

New organizations with goals and responsibilities that transcended national boundaries took shape after World War II for the purpose of facilitating global activities. These **supranational organizations**, which were intended to facilitate globalization and manage crisis situations, impinged on the autonomy of all but the most powerful states.

Among the most prominent supranational organizations were the World Bank and the International Monetary Fund, which provided vital economic assistance to poorer nations. The World Bank, originally named the International Bank for Reconstruction and Development, was designed primarily to provide financial assistance for big development projects. In contrast, the IMF provided funds and technical assistance to countries whose economies were in trouble. A good example of the World Bank's agenda was the financial support that it gave to the government of Ghana in the 1960s for the Volta River project, which was intended to create an electrical grid for that country. Nonetheless, both the World Bank and the IMF required that recipient governments implement far-reaching economic reforms, such as devaluation of the currency and the privatization of public-sector companies; these reforms were often deeply unpopular and led to charges that these international groups were agents of a new kind of imperialism.

Another set of supranational bodies, international nongovernmental organizations (NGOs), also stepped forward late in the twentieth century. Many championed human rights or highlighted environmental problems. Others, like the International Committee of the Red Cross, once dedicated to war relief, became more active in peacetime, sheltering survivors of natural disasters or providing food for famine victims. What united NGOs was not so much their goals, but the way they pursued them: autonomously, rather than through state power.

International NGOs reached a new level of influence in the 1970s because most nation-states at that time were still not democracies. Of the 121 countries in the world in 1980, only 37 were democracies, accounting for only 35 percent of the globe's population. People found it difficult to rely on authoritarians to uphold their rights as citizens. Indeed, despite adopting a Universal Declaration of Human Rights in 1948, the United Nations (another international organization created after World War II and intended to provide a forum for settling international problems) was a latecomer to enforcing human rights provisions, largely because its own members were the selfsame authoritarians.

NGOs, then, took the lead in trying to make the language of human rights stick. The brutality of military regimes in Latin America inspired the emerging network of international human rights organizations to take action. After the overthrow of Chile's Salvador Allende in 1973, political groups created by the Catholic Church protested the military junta's harsh repression. When the Argentine military began killing tens of thousands of innocent civilians in 1976 and news of their torture techniques leaked out, human rights organizations again took action. Prominent among them was Amnesty International. Formed in 1961 to defend prisoners of conscience (detained for their beliefs, color, sex, ethnic origin, language, or religion), Amnesty International catalogued human rights violations worldwide. By 2000, an extensive network of NGOs was informing the public, lobbying governments, and pressuring U.N. member nations to live up to commitments to respect the rights of citizens.

VIOLENCE

Supranational organizations and NGOs could play only a limited role in preserving peace and strengthening human rights. The end of the Cold War left entire regions in such turmoil that even the most effective humanitarian agencies could not prevent mass killings.

Consider the Balkans in the 1990s. In the territorial remains of Yugoslavia, groups of Serbs, Croats, Bosnians, ethnic Albanians, and others fought for control. Former neighbors, fueled by opportunistic leaders' rhetoric, no longer saw themselves as citizens of diverse political communities. Instead, demagogues trumpeted the superiority of ethnically defined states. Ethnic Serbians took up arms against their Croat neighbors, and vice versa. When international agencies moved in to try to bolster public authority, they failed, and Yugoslavia's ethnic mosaic imploded into civil war and ethnic cleansing.

Some of the most gruesome scenes of political violence occurred in Africa, where many nation-states struggled to uphold the rule of law for all citizens. Here, tension often erupted into conflict between ethnic groups. The failure of African agriculture to sustain growing populations, as well as unequal access to resources like education, made ethnic rivalries worse. Droughts, famine, and corruption fanned the rivalries into riots and killings—even into bitter civil wars and the breakdown of centralized authority.

Events in Rwanda reflected Africa's horrifying experience with political violence. Friction grew between the majority Hutus (agrarian people, often

Rwandan Refugees Perhaps as many as 800,000 Tutsis were killed in Rwanda in 1994 as the Hutu leadership turned against the country's Tutsi population.

very poor) and the minority Tutsis (herders, often with better education, wealthier, and chosen by the Belgians to rule over the Hutus) after the two peoples had intermarried and lived side by side for many generations. Some resentful Hutus blamed the Tutsis for all their woes. As tensions mounted, the United Nations dispatched peacekeeping troops. Moderate Hutus urged continued peaceful coexistence, only to be shouted down by government forces in command of radio stations and a mass propaganda machine. Although alerted to the impending problem, U.N. forces, fearing a clash and uncertain of their mandate, failed to prevent the violence.

The failure on the part of the international community, including the United States, which did not have troops on the ground and which had no clear policy toward Rwanda, gave the Hutu government a green light to wipe out its opponents. In 100 days of carnage in 1994, Hutu militias massacred 800,000 Tutsis and moderate Hutus. This was not, as many proclaimed, the militarization of ancient ethnic rivalries, for many Hutus were butchered as they tried to defend Tutsi friends, relatives, and neighbors. Meanwhile, the ensuing refugee crisis destabilized neighboring countries. The Rwanda genocide sent riptides across eastern and central Africa, creating a whole new generation of conflicts. This catastrophe is the starkest example of the failure of supranational organizations to deal with a crisis before it mushroomed into a genocide. Elsewhere, in famine areas and big development projects, supranational relief agencies enjoyed more success.

Some societies tried to put political violence behind them. In Argentina, El Salvador, Guatemala, and South Africa, the transition to democracy compelled elected rulers to establish commissions to inquire into past rulers' human rights abuses. These **truth commissions** were vital for creating a new aura of legitimacy for democracies and for promising to uphold the rights of individuals. In South Africa, many blacks backed the new president, Nelson Mandela, but also demanded a reckoning with the punitive experience of the apartheid past. To avoid a backlash against the former white rulers, the South African leadership opted to record the past events rather than avenge them. The long-term consequences of these efforts to address violent atrocities remain uncertain.

truth commissions
Commissions established to inquire into human rights abuses by previous regimes. In Argentina, El Salvador, Guatemala, and South Africa, these commissions were vital for creating a new aura of legitimacy for democracies and for promising to uphold the rights of individuals.

RELIGIOUS FOUNDATIONS OF POLITICS

Secular concerns for human rights and international peace were not the only foundations for politics after the Cold War. In many regions, people wanted religion to define the moral fabric of political communities. Very often, religion provided a way to reimagine the nation-state just as globalization was undermining national autonomy.

Hindu Nationalism In India, Hindu nationalism offered a communal identity for a country being rapidly transformed by globalization. In the 1980s, India freed market forces, privatized state firms, and withdrew from its role as welfare provider. Economic reforms under the ruling Congress Party sparked economic growth, thereby creating one of Asia's largest, best-educated, and most affluent middle classes. But because these changes also widened the gap between rich and poor, lower classes and castes formed political parties to challenge the traditional elites. With established hierarchies and loyalties eroding, Hindu nationalists argued that religion could now fill the role once occupied by a secular state. Claiming that the ideology of *Hindutva* (Hinduness) would bring the help that secular nationalism had failed to give, Hindu militants trumpeted the idea of India as a nation of Hindus (the majority), with minorities relegated to a lesser status. The chief beneficiary of the politics established by economic liberalization was a Hindu nationalist party, the Bharatiya Janata Party (BJP), or Indian People's Party. It was the political arm of an alliance of Hindu organizations devoted to establishing India as a Hindu state. In 1998 a BJP coalition came to power and sought to transform the nation-state into a moral community, but without challenging the economic forces of globalization.

Islamic Conservatism In some cases, religion provided a way to resist seemingly American-dominated globalization. One of the most spirited challenges arose in the Islamic Middle East, where many people believed that modernizing and westernizing programs were leading their societies toward rampant materialism and unchecked individualism. Critics included both traditional clerics and young western-educated elites whose job prospects seemed bleak and who felt that the promise of modernization had failed. Having criticized modernizing processes since the nineteenth century, Islamic conservatives flourished once more in the 1970s as global markets and social tensions undermined secular leadership.

The most revolutionary Islamic movement arose in Iran, where clerics forced the shah, the country's ruler, from power in 1979. The revolt pitted a group of religious officials possessing only pamphlets, tracts, and tapes against the military arsenal and the vast intelligence apparatus of the Iranian state. Shah Mohammad Reza Pahlavi had enjoyed U.S. technical and military support since the Americans helped place him on the throne in 1953. His bloated army and police force, as well as his brutally effective intelligence service, had crushed all challenges to his authority. The shah had also benefited from oil revenues, which soared after 1973. Yet the uneven distribution of income, the oppressive police state, and the royal family's ostentatious lifestyle fueled widespread discontent.

The most powerful critique came from the mullahs (Muslim scholars or religious teachers), who found in the Ayatollah Ruhollah Khomeini a courageous leader. Khomeini used his traditional Islamic education and his training in Muslim ethics to accuse the shah's government of gross violations of Islamic norms. He also identified the shah's ally, America, as the Great Satan. With opposition to his rule mounting, the shah fled the country in 1979. In his wake, Khomeini established a theocratic state ruled by a council of Islamic clerics. Although some Iranians grumbled about aspects of this return to Islam, they prided themselves on having inspired a revolution based on principles other than those drawn from the west.

Religious Conservatism in the United States The search for religious foundations for politics in the global age reached into western societies. Indeed, in the United States, religion became a potent force after the 1970s as the membership and activism of conservative, fundamentalist Protestant churches eclipsed that of mainstream denominations. Insisting on a literal interpretation of the Bible, Protestant fundamentalists argued against secularizing trends in American society. This traditionalist crusade took up a broad range of cultural and political issues. Religious conservatives (predominantly evangelical Protestants, but also some Catholics and Orthodox Jews) attacked many of the social changes that had emerged from the liberation movements of the 1960s. Shifting sexual and familial relations were sore points, but the religious conservatives especially targeted public leaders who, they felt, had abandoned the moral purpose of authority by legalizing abortion and supporting secular values.

Tiananmen Square
Largest public square in the world and site of the pro-democracy demonstrations in 1989 that ended with the killing of as many as a thousand protesters by the Chinese army.

ACCEPTANCE OF AND RESISTANCE TO DEMOCRACY

New sources of power and new social movements drastically changed politics in the global age. Increasingly, supranational organizations were decisive in defining the conditions of democratic citizenship. Perhaps most remarkable was how much democracy spread toward the end of the twentieth century. In South Africa, Russia, and Guatemala, elections now decided politicians' fates. In this sense, the world's societies embraced the idea that people had a right to choose their own representatives. Nevertheless, democracy did not triumph everywhere.

An important holdout was China. Mao Zedong died in 1976, and within a few years, his successor, Deng Xiaoping, opened the nation's economy to market forces. But Deng and other Chinese Communist Party leaders resisted multiparty competition. Instead of turning to capitalism and western-style democracy, they maintained that China should follow its own path to modernity. By the late 1980s, economic reforms had produced spectacular increases in production and rising standards of living for most of China's people. But the widening gap between rich and poor, together with increasing public awareness of corruption within the party and the government, triggered popular discontent. Worker strikes and slowdowns, peasant unrest, and student activism spread.

On April 22, 1989, some 100,000 people gathered in **Tiananmen Square** at the heart of Beijing in silent defiance of a government ban on assembling. The regime responded by declaring martial law. Two huge protest demonstrations followed, and residents erected barricades to defend the city against government troops. As the protest's momentum waned, a twenty-eight-foot icon, partly inspired by the Statue of Liberty, was unveiled at the square, capturing the imagination of the crowd and the attention of the cameras. But by then the government had assembled troops to crush the movement. In a night of terror that began at dusk on June 3, the People's Liberation Army turned its guns against the people. Estimates of the death toll range from hundreds into the thousands.

In Mexico, democracy finally triumphed, as the single party that had dominated the country for seventy-one years fell after the election of Vicente

Tiananmen Square This white plaster and Styrofoam statue, inspired in part by the Statue of Liberty and dubbed the Goddess of Democracy, was created by students in Beijing in the spring of 1989. It was brought to Tiananmen Square and unveiled at the end of May in an attempt to reinvigorate the democracy movement and the spirits of the protesters. For five days it captured worldwide attention, until it was toppled by a tank on June 4 and crushed as the Chinese People's Liberation Army cleared the square of its democracy advocates.

Protests in Mexico After generations of oppression and exclusion, peasants of Chiapas, in southern Mexico, called for democracy and respect for their right to land. When Mexican authorities refused to bend, peasants took up arms. While they knew that they posed no military threat to the Mexican army, the Zapatista rebels used the world media and international organizations to embarrass the national political establishment into allowing reforms.

Fox in 2000. Until that time, Mexican rulers had combined patronage and rigged elections to stay in office. By the 1980s, corruption and abuse permeated the system. The abuse of democratic rights fell hardest on poor communities, especially those with large numbers of indigenous people.

These events in Mexico, South Africa, and China showed that men and women in every corner of the earth yearned to choose their own leaders. In 1994, millions of previously disenfranchised South Africans lined up for hours to cast a vote for their new black African president, Nelson Mandela. That same year, Zapatista rebels drew worldwide attention to the plight of poor indigenous communities when militants occupied six towns in central and eastern Chiapas, Mexico, to protest the North American Free Trade Agreement. In China, the ruling Communist Party had to call in the army to prevent regime change and democratic reforms.

Conclusion

In the thirteenth century (and long before), a few travelers like Ibn Battuta and Marco Polo ventured over long distances to trade, to explore, and to convert souls; yet communications technology was rudimentary, making long-distance mobility and exchange expensive, rare, and perilous. The world was much more a series of communities set apart than a world bound together by culture, capital, and communications networks.

By the late twentieth century, that balance had changed. Food, entertainment, clothing, and even family life were becoming more similar worldwide. To be sure, some local differences remained. In 2000, local cultures lived on, and in some cases were revived, through challenges to the authority of nation-states. No longer did the nation-state or any single level of community life define collective identities. At the same time, worldwide purveyors of cultural and commercial resources offered all local communities the same kinds of products, from aspirin to Nike shoes. Exchanges across local and national boundaries became easier. For the first time, many of the world's peoples felt they belonged to a global culture.

New technologies, new methods of production and investment, and the greater importance of personal health and education created new possibilities—and greater inequalities. Indeed, the gaps between haves and have-nots in 2000 were astonishing. For as humanity harnessed new technologies to accelerate exchanges across and within cultures, an ever-larger gulf separated those who participated in global networks from those on the margins. This inequality produced a range of different political and cultural forms after the collapse of the three-world order. Thus, as the world became more integrated, it also grew apart along ever-deeper lines.

TRACING THE GLOBAL STORYLINES

 **Focus On**
Globalization

Removing Obstacles to Globalization

- Communism's fall and the end of the Cold War improve prospects for global exchange of peoples, ideas, and resources.
- Final decolonization in Angola, Mozambique, and Guinea-Bissau and the end of apartheid in South Africa return self-rule throughout Africa.

Unleashing Globalization

- Financial deregulation and the end of the gold standard allow money to move freely across borders but lead to a Third World debt crisis.
- Widespread migrations occur as people in Africa, Asia, and Latin America move to Europe and America, following the tracks of their former colonizers.

- Revolutions in culture and communications make cultural diversity more possible for those who can afford it.

The New Global Order

- Globalization leads to dramatic population expansion, requiring greater agricultural and industrial output.
- Family structure changes, life spans increase, and more goods are available, yet inequalities deepen as education and good health determine social status as never before.
- As globalization erodes the power of the nation-state, greater violence occurs between and within states. Nongovernmental organizations (NGOs) and religion become resources for dealing with violence and inequality and for reimagining the nation-state.

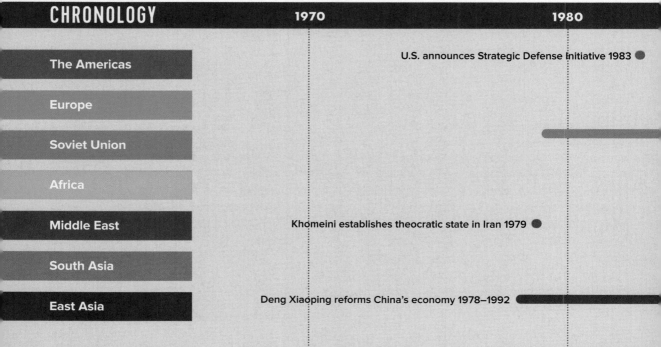

CHRONOLOGY — 1970 — 1980

The Americas — U.S. announces Strategic Defense Initiative 1983

Europe

Soviet Union

Africa

Middle East — Khomeini establishes theocratic state in Iran 1979

South Asia

East Asia — Deng Xiaoping reforms China's economy 1978–1992

- **Thinking about Worlds Together, Worlds Apart and Globalization** How did globalization shape patterns of inequality? After the Cold War, trade, migration, and communications reshaped the terms on which peoples interacted with one another around the world. Industry, agriculture, culture, and the arts all linked peoples and regions together in different ways. Consider differences in all these domains. What kinds of inequalities were most significant?

- **Thinking about Changing Power Relationships and Globalization** What kind of resistance movements did globalization generate, both within the world's wealthiest societies and elsewhere? How did the feminist, labor, and environmental reform movements resemble and differ from their predecessors? How did Hindu nationalism and religious conservatism differ from each other and from earlier nationalist and religious or pan movements?

- **Thinking about Environmental Impacts and Globalization** Explain the relationship between globalization, climate change, and the environment. The consumption of water, oil, and other natural resources became major national and international issues in this period. How did the organization of agricultural and industrial production change, and what influence did those changes have on global warming, acid rain, and pollution? Identify efforts to limit damage to the environment and evaluate their success.

Key Terms

climate change p. 1013

developing world p. 993

European Union (EU) p. 995

globalization p. 986

global warming p. 1013

HIV/AIDS p. 1007

Nelson Mandela p. 993

supranational organizations p. 1014

Tiananmen Square p. 1018

truth commissions p. 1017

 Go to INQUIZITIVE to see what you've learned—and learn what you've missed—with personalized feedback along the way.

1990   **2000**

● North American Free Trade Agreement approved 1992
● Zapatista rebellion in Mexico 1994

● Eastern European communist regimes collapse 1989
Yugoslavia dissolves, ethnic cleansing ensues 1989–1995
● European Union formed 1993, replacing the European Economic Community

● Soviet war in Afghanistan 1979–1989
● Gorbachev assumes power 1985
● Chernobyl nuclear accident 1986
● Dissolution of the Soviet Union 1991
● Mandela released from prison 1990
● Free elections in South Africa 1994
● Genocide in Rwanda 1994

BJP heads up government in India 1998 ●

● Chinese state cracks down on Tiananmen Square protests 1989

Global Themes and Sources

Comparing the Power of Grassroots Democracies

Despite the enormous economic and technological advances of the past 200 years, famine and dire poverty remain problems in many places. These problems have been particularly severe where unrepresentative, authoritarian leaders prevent foreign aid from reaching the needy and ordinary people from achieving self-sufficiency. Self-sufficiency has been further undermined by pervasive discrimination against women, which has limited their access to education and has therefore compromised economic growth for everyone, men and women alike.

Written by a dissident dramatist (and future politician) in 1978, the first document, excerpted from a long essay in political philosophy, explores the possibility for individuals to maintain their independence and dignity, and ultimately to undermine the communist dictatorships of eastern Europe. In the second document, from the General Council of the Zapatista Army for National Liberation (EZLN), a group of mostly Amerindians living in a jungle region in Chiapas, Mexico, seeks international support for its conflict with Mexican authorities. In the third, researchers for the World Bank report that better education, and especially better education for girls, improves economic development among the poor. The final selection, from economist and Nobel laureate Amartya Sen (1933–), argues that no major famine has occurred in a democratic country with a free press.

The selections presented here all call attention to the importance of grassroots democracy and equality in responding to political, economic, and ecological disasters and achieving at least a measure of autonomy. They raise big questions about the nature and location of power and the possibility of change. While there is an important comparative dimension to these selections—each understands the promise of grassroots democracy differently—they are all the product of a common context, a common reaction against monolithic, authoritarian forms of rule. Collectively, they call for both comparison and contextualization.

Analyzing the Power of Grassroots Democracies Comparatively and Contextually

- On what basis do the authors of these documents claim authority? In whose name do they speak? What goals do they seek to attain?

- What does justice mean from the perspectives of these four documents? Do the authors agree or disagree on what is just?

- What is the relationship between individual and collective rights in these documents? To what degree does each text consider individual liberties essential or harmful to the common good? Pay special attention to differences between the first document and the next three.

PRIMARY SOURCE 21.1

"The Power of the Powerless" (1978), Václav Havel

Václav Havel (1936–2011) was a Czech dramatist, founder of Charter 77, a civic initiative under communism (1976–1982) that defended human rights, and president of Czechoslovakia (1989–1992) and then the Czech Republic (1993–2003). His essay *The Power of the Powerless*, originally written in 1978, provided a model of what he called "living within the truth," a form of resistance against communism.

- What does Havel mean by "living within the truth"?
- Explain the significance of law in this document.
- Compare this selection with Friedrich Engels' and Karl Marx's *Bourgeoisie and Proletariat* (16.5). Is Havel's view of politics compatible with the manifesto?

A spectre is haunting eastern Europe: the spectre of what in the West is called "dissent." This spectre has not appeared out of thin air. It is a natural and inevitable consequence of the present historical phase of the system it is haunting. It was born at a time when this system, for a thousand reasons, can no longer base itself on the unadulterated, brutal, and arbitrary application of power, eliminating all expressions of nonconformity. What is more, the system has become so ossified politically that there is practically no way for such nonconformity to be implemented within its official structures.

***

And so the post-totalitarian system behaved in a characteristic way: it defended the integrity of the world of appearances in order to defend itself. For the crust presented by the life of lies is made of strange stuff. As long as it seals off hermetically the entire society, it appears to be made of stone. But the moment someone breaks through in one place, when one person cries out, "The emperor is naked!"—when a single person breaks the rules of the game, thus exposing it as a game—everything suddenly appears in another light and the whole crust seems then to be made of a tissue on the point of tearing and disintegrating uncontrollably.

When I speak of living within the truth, I naturally do not have in mind only products of conceptual thought, such as a protest or a letter written by a group of intellectuals. It can be any means by which a person or a group revolts against manipulation: anything from a letter by intellectuals to a workers' strike, from a rock concert to a student demonstration, from refusing to vote in the farcical elections, to making an open speech at some official congress, or even a hunger strike, for instance. If the suppression of the aims of life is a complex process, and if it is based on the multifaceted manipulation of all expressions of life, then, by the same token, every free expression of life indirectly threatens the post-totalitarian system politically, including forms of expression to which, in other social systems, no one would attribute any potential political significance, not to mention explosive power.

***

Like ideology, the legal code is an essential instrument of ritual communication outside the power structure. It is the legal code that gives the exercise of power a form, a framework, a set of rules. It is the

legal code that enables all components of the system to communicate, to put themselves in a good light, to establish their own legitimacy. It provides their whole game with its "rules" and engineers with their technology. Can the exercise of post-totalitarian power be imagined at all without this universal ritual making it all possible, serving as a common language to bind the relevant sectors of the power structure together? The more important the position occupied by the repressive apparatus in the power structure, the more important that it functions according to some kind of formal code. . . .

If the exercise of power circulates through the whole power structure as blood flows through veins, then the legal code can be understood as something that reinforces the walls of those veins. Without it, the blood of power could not circulate in an organized way and the body of society would haemorrhage at random. Order would collapse.

A persistent and never-ending appeal to the laws—not just to the laws concerning human rights, but to all laws—does not mean at all that those who do so have succumbed to the illusion that in our system the law is anything other than what it is. They are well aware of the role it plays. But precisely because they know how desperately the system depends on it—on the "noble" version of the law, that is—they also know how enormously significant such appeals are. Because the system cannot do without the law, because it is hopelessly tied down by the necessity of pretending the laws are observed, it is compelled to react in some way to such appeals. Demanding that the laws be upheld is thus an act of living within the truth that threatens the whole mendacious structure at its point of maximum mendacity.

Over and over again, such appeals make the purely ritualistic nature of the law clear to society and to those who inhabit its power structures. They draw attention to its real material substance and thus, indirectly, compel all those who take refuge behind the law to affirm and make credible this agency of excuses, this means of communication, this reinforcement of the social arteries outside of which their will could not be made to circulate through society. They are compelled to do so for the sake of their own consciences, for the impression they make on outsiders, to maintain themselves in power (as part of the system's own mechanism of self-preservation and its principles of cohesion), or simply out of fear that they will be reproached for being "clumsy" in handling the ritual. They have no other choice: because they cannot discard the rules of their own game, they can only attend more carefully to those rules.

***

Hope for those who would liberate themselves, therefore, lies in a symbiosis of the moral and the social, of humanity and democracy, in the realization of a social order in which the formalized and functionalized structure of society will be regulated and controlled by this "newly discovered" spontaneous civic activity, which will be a permanent and essential source of social self-awareness, while the bureaucracies ruling society shrink to assume merely compliant executive roles.

Source: Václav Havel, "The Power of the Powerless," in *The Power of the Powerless: Citizens against the State in Central-Eastern Europe*, ed. John Keane (Armonk, NY: M. E. Sharpe, 1985), 23, 42–43, 74–77, 108–109.

PRIMARY SOURCE 21.2

Declaration of War against the Mexican Government (1993), EZLN

The Zapatista Army of National Liberation (EZLN) is a revolutionary political organization based in Chiapas, the southernmost state in Mexico. On January 1, 1994, it took up arms against the government, calling for a restoration of the principles of the Mexican Revolution and protesting the confiscation of poor people's land rights. This document, released in 1993, issues a call to arms.

- The document opens, "We are a product of 500 years of struggle." Who is "we"? Who does the document include as insiders, and whom—whether individuals or broad social forces—does it exclude?

- On what basis do the authors speak for the nation?

- What is the relationship between this declaration and the rule of law? Do the authors claim to uphold the law, or do they reject it and seek to overthrow it?

To the People of Mexico: Mexican Brothers and Sisters:

We are a product of 500 years of struggle: first against slavery, then during the War of Independence against Spain led by insurgents, then to avoid being absorbed by North American imperialism, then to promulgate our constitution and expel the French empire from our soil, and later the dictatorship of Porfirio Diaz denied us the just application of the Reform laws and the people rebelled and leaders like Villa and Zapata emerged, poor men just like us. We have been denied the most elemental preparation so they can use us as cannon fodder and pillage the wealth of our country. They don't care that we have nothing, absolutely nothing, not even a roof over our heads, no land, no work, no health care, no food nor education. Nor are we able to freely and democratically elect our political representatives, nor is there independence from foreigners, nor is there peace nor justice for ourselves and our children.

But today, we say ENOUGH IS ENOUGH.

We are the inheritors of the true builders of our nation. The dispossessed, we are millions and we thereby call upon our brothers and sisters to join this struggle as the only path, so that we will not die of hunger due to the insatiable ambition of a 70 year dictatorship led by a clique of traitors that represent the most conservative and sell-out groups. They are the same ones that opposed Hidalgo and Morelos, the same ones that betrayed Vicente Guerrero, the same ones that sold half our country to the foreign invader, the same ones that imported a European prince to rule our country, the same ones that formed the "scientific" Porfirista dictatorship, the same ones that opposed the Petroleum Expropriation, the same ones that massacred the railroad workers in 1958 and the students in 1968, the same ones [that] today take everything from us, absolutely everything.

To prevent the continuation of the above and as our last hope, after having tried to utilize all legal means based on our Constitution, we go to our Constitution, to apply Article 39 which says:

> "National Sovereignty essentially and originally resides in the people. All political power emanates

from the people and its purpose is to help the people. The people have, at all times, the inalienable right to alter or modify their form of government."

Therefore, according to our constitution, we declare the following to the Mexican federal army, the pillar of the Mexican dictatorship that we suffer from, monopolized by a one-party system and led by Carlos Salinas de Gortari, the maximum and illegitimate federal executive that today holds power.

According to this Declaration of War, we ask that other powers of the nation advocate to restore the legitimacy and the stability of the nation by overthrowing the dictator.

We also ask that international organizations and the International Red Cross watch over and regulate our battles, so that our efforts are carried out while still protecting our civilian population. We declare now and always that we are subject to the Geneva Accord, forming the EZLN as our fighting arm of our liberation struggle. We have the Mexican people on our side, we have the beloved tri-colored flag highly respected by our insurgent fighters. We use black and red in our uniform as our symbol of our working people on strike. Our flag carries the following letters, "EZLN," Zapatista National Liberation Army, and we always carry our flag into combat.

Beforehand, we refuse any effort to disgrace our just cause by accusing us of being drug traffickers, drug guerrillas, thieves, or other names that might be used by our enemies. Our struggle follows the constitution which is held high by its call for justice and equality.

Therefore, according to this declaration of war, we give our military forces, the EZLN, the following orders:

First: Advance to the capital of the country, overcoming the Mexican federal army, protecting in our advance the civilian population and permitting the people in the liberated area the right to freely and democratically elect their own administrative authorities.

Second: Respect the lives of our prisoners and turn over all wounded to the International Red Cross.

Third: Initiate summary judgments against all soldiers of the Mexican federal army and the political police that have received training or have been paid by foreigners, accused of being traitors to our country, and against all those that have repressed and treated badly the civil population and robbed or stolen from or attempted crimes against the good of the people.

Fourth: Form new troops with all those Mexicans that show their interest in joining our struggle, including those that, being enemy soldiers, turn themselves in without having fought against us, and promise to take orders from the General Command of the Zapatista National Liberation Army.

Fifth: We ask for the unconditional surrender of the enemy's headquarters before we begin any combat to avoid any loss of lives.

Sixth: Suspend the robbery of our natural resources in the areas controlled by the EZLN.

To the People of Mexico: We, the men and women, full and free, are conscious that the war that we have declared is our last resort, but also a just one. The dictators are applying an undeclared genocidal war against our people for many years. Therefore we ask for your participation, your decision to support this plan that struggles for work, land, housing, food, health care, education, independence, freedom, democracy, justice and peace. We declare that we will not stop fighting until the basic demands of our people have been met by forming a government of our country that is free and democratic.

Join the Insurgent Forces of the Zapatista National Liberation Army.

General Command of the EZLN
1993

Source: "First Declaration from the Lacandon Jungle," http://struggle.ws /mexico/ezln/ezlnwa.html (http://struggle.ws/mexico.html).

Why Gender Matters (2000), World Bank

The *World Development Report* is an annual report published since 1978 by the International Bank for Reconstruction and Development. The report for 2000–2001, which included this selection, was devoted to the topic "Attacking Poverty."

- Describe the effect of tuition on girls' school attendance.
- Evaluate the relative importance of barriers to girls' education posed by culture on the one hand and poverty on the other.
- What effect does expanding educational opportunity for girls have on boys?

Using Subsidies to Close Gender Gaps in Education

Evaluations of recent initiatives that subsidize the costs of schooling indicate that demand-side interventions can increase girls' enrollments and close gender gaps in education. A school stipend program established in Bangladesh in 1982 subsidizes various school expenses for girls who enroll in secondary school. In the first program evaluation girls' enrollment rate in the pilot areas rose from 27 percent, similar to the national average, to 44 percent over five years, more than twice the national average. After girls' tuition was eliminated nationwide in 1992 and the stipend program was expanded to all rural areas, girls' enrollment rate climbed to 48 percent at the national level. There have also been gains in the number of girls appearing for exams and in women's enrollments at intermediate colleges. While boys' enrollment rates also rose during this period, they did not rise as quickly as girls'.

Two recent programs in Balochistan, Pakistan, illustrate the potential benefits of reducing costs and improving physical access. Before the projects there were questions about whether girls' low enrollments were due to cultural barriers that cause parents to hold their daughters out of school or to inadequate supply of appropriate schools. Program evaluations suggest that improved physical access, subsidized costs, and culturally appropriate design can sharply increase girls' enrollments.

The first program, in Quetta, the capital of Balochistan, uses a subsidy tied to girls' enrollment to support the creation of schools in poor urban neighborhoods by local NGOs. The schools admit boys as long as they make up less than half of total enrollments. In rural Balochistan the second program has been expanding the supply of local, single-sex primary schools for girls by encouraging parental involvement in establishing the schools and by subsidizing the recruitment of female teachers from the local community. The results: girls' enrollments rose 33 percent in Quetta and 22 percent in rural areas. Interestingly, both programs appear to have also expanded boys' enrollments, suggesting that increasing girls' educational opportunities may have spillover benefits for boys.

Source: The World Bank, from "Using subsidies to close gender gaps in education," World Bank. 2001. *World Development Report 2000–2001: Attacking Poverty*, p. 122, Box 7.2. © World Bank. http://openknowledge.worldbank.org/handle/10986/11856 License: Creative Commons Attribution license (CC BY 3.0).

PRIMARY SOURCE 21.4

"Democracy as a Universal Value" (1999), Amartya Sen

This selection is drawn from Sen's work on the economics and politics of famines as well as political philosophy. In many famines, Sen has shown, food supplies remained adequate, while unemployment, rising prices, and unresponsive governments led to catastrophe. The current selection comes from a keynote address delivered in New Delhi, titled "Building a Worldwide Movement for Democracy."

- What does Sen mean by democracy?
- What, according to Sen, is the relationship between democracy and economic dynamism?
- Explain the significance of famines to Sen's argument.

In the summer of 1997, I was asked by a leading Japanese newspaper what I thought was the most important thing that had happened in the twentieth century. . . .

I did not, ultimately, have any difficulty in choosing one as the preeminent development of the period: the rise of democracy.

***

It is often claimed that nondemocratic systems are better at bringing about economic development. This belief sometimes goes by the name of "the Lee hypothesis," due to its advocacy by Lee Kuan Yew, the leader and former president of Singapore. He is certainly right that some disciplinarian states (such as South Korea, his own Singapore, and postreform China) have had faster rates of economic growth than many less authoritarian ones (including India, Jamaica, and Costa Rica). The "Lee hypothesis," however, is based on sporadic empiricism, drawing on very selective and limited information, rather than on any general statistical testing over the wide-ranging data that are available. A general relation of this kind cannot be established on the basis of very selective evidence. For example, we cannot really take the high economic growth of Singapore or China as "definitive proof" that authoritarianism does better in promoting economic growth, any more than we can draw the opposite conclusion from the fact that Botswana, the country with the best record of economic growth in Africa, indeed with one of the finest records of economic growth in the whole world, has been an oasis of democracy on that continent over the decades. We need more systematic empirical studies to sort out the claims and counterclaims.

There is, in fact, no convincing general evidence that authoritarian governance and the suppression of political and civil rights are really beneficial to economic development. Indeed, the general statistical picture does not permit any such induction. . . . The directional linkage seems to depend on many other circumstances, and while some statistical investigations note a weakly negative relation, others find a strongly positive one. If all the comparative studies are viewed together, the hypothesis that there is no clear relation between economic growth and democracy in *either* direction remains extremely plausible. Since democracy and political liberty have importance in themselves, the case for them therefore remains untarnished. . . .

We must go beyond the narrow confines of economic growth and scrutinize the broader demands of economic development, including the need for economic and social security. In that context, we have to look at the connection between political and civil rights, on the one hand, and the prevention of major economic disasters, on the other. Political and civil rights give people the opportunity to draw attention forcefully to general needs and to demand appropriate public action. The response of a government to the acute suffering of its people often depends on the pressure that is put on it. The exercise of political rights (such as voting, criticizing, protesting, and the like) can make a real difference to the political incentives that operate on a government.

I have discussed elsewhere the remarkable fact that, in the terrible history of famines in the world, no substantial famine has ever occurred in any independent and democratic country with a relatively free press. We cannot find exceptions to this rule, no matter where we look: the recent famines of Ethiopia, Somalia, or other dictatorial regimes; famines in the Soviet Union in the 1930s; China's 1958–61 famine with the failure of the Great Leap Forward; or earlier still, the famines in Ireland or India under alien rule. China, although it was in many ways doing much better economically than India, still managed (unlike India) to have a famine, indeed the largest recorded famine in world history: Nearly 30 million people died in the famine of 1958–61, while faulty governmental policies remained uncorrected for three full years. The policies went uncriticized because there were no opposition parties in parliament, no free press, and no multiparty elections. Indeed, it is precisely this lack of challenge that allowed the deeply defective policies to continue even though they were killing millions each year. The same can be said about the world's two contemporary famines, occurring right now in North Korea and Sudan.

Famines are often associated with what look like natural disasters, and commentators often settle for the simplicity of explaining famines by pointing to these events: the floods in China during the failed Great Leap Forward, the droughts in Ethiopia, or crop failures in North Korea. Nevertheless, many countries with similar natural problems, or even worse ones, manage perfectly well, because a responsive government intervenes to help alleviate hunger. Since the primary victims of a famine are the indigent, deaths can be prevented by recreating incomes (for example, through employment programs), which makes food accessible to potential famine victims. Even the poorest democratic countries that have faced terrible droughts or floods or other natural disasters (such as India in 1973, or Zimbabwe and Botswana in the early 1980s) have been able to feed their people without experiencing a famine.

Famines are easy to prevent if there is a serious effort to do so, and a democratic government, facing elections and criticisms from opposition parties and independent newspapers, cannot help but make such an effort. Not surprisingly, while India continued to have famines under British rule right up to independence (the last famine, which I witnessed as a child, was in 1943, four years before independence), they disappeared suddenly with the establishment of a multiparty democracy and a free press. . . .

The issue of famine is only one example of the reach of democracy, though it is, in many ways, the easiest case to analyze. The positive role of political and civil rights applies to the prevention of economic and social disasters in general. When things go fine and everything is routinely good, this instrumental role of democracy may not be particularly missed. It is when things get fouled up, for one reason or another, that the political incentives provided by democratic governance acquire great practical value.

Source: Amartya Sen, "Democracy as a Universal Value," *Journal of Democracy* 10, no. 3 (1999): 3–17, pp. 3, 6–9.

Interpreting Visual Evidence

Chimerica

The term "Chimerica" refers to the idea that the People's Republic of China and the United States of America make up a single, dominant economic entity. It was coined by the historian Niall Ferguson and the economist Moritz Schularick to describe the interdependent relationship that began in the last two decades of the twentieth century and has extended into the first decades of the twenty-first century. China began to open its economy in the early 1980s, and its exports of manufactured goods, especially to the United States—which rose from $51.5 billion in 1996 to $102 billion in 2001—eventually fueled the world economy. Combined, the two countries make up roughly 13 percent of the world's land surface, a quarter of its population, more than a third of its economic production, and, by some estimates, nearly half of all economic growth in the first decade of the new millennium. Chimerica is also a play on the word *chimera*: a fire-breathing female monster in Greek mythology, or an unrealizable dream, an illusion.

Modern Beijing.

Foxconn factory with suicide nets.

Retirement community near Phoenix, Arizona.

Walmart Supercenter.

Like Japan and Germany after World War II, China in this period concentrated on export-led industrial growth. But unlike those countries, China refused to let workers' wages rise as the economy grew, and its leaders refused to apply international standards to workplace safety, intellectual property, or environmental protections. In developed economies, where those protections applied and wages were higher, production costs were higher. As a result, competition from China cost millions of jobs in developed countries, including 2.9 million jobs in the United States alone from 2001 to 2012. Chinese leaders instead invested the surplus revenues abroad, mostly in the United States, where the influx of Chinese investment kept interest rates low. U.S. consumers used the resulting easy credit to purchase homes, cars, and goods like tablets and mobile phones, many of them manufactured in China.

The images presented here portray different aspects of what Ferguson and Schularick call Chimerica. The first shows modern Beijing, with massive new buildings, roadways, and smog; it shows both the robust growth of the Chinese economy—notice how new the buildings are—and its environmental costs. The second photograph shows protective nets around a factory run by Foxconn, one of Apple's leading suppliers in China, after a series of suicides in 2010 drew world attention to the company's labor practices. This image reflects some of the dire costs of producing consumer goods at low prices. The third image shows a massive retirement community near Phoenix, Arizona, filled with homes purchased at low interest rates, thanks to Chinese investment. The fourth image shows a Walmart superstore in Albany, New York, filled with inexpensive goods, many of them produced in China. Such "big-box" retail stores provide many jobs, but at much lower wages than the industrial jobs that

have disappeared. The final image shows an unofficial Apple store in Tehran, Iran; it shows the dominance of global brands for Chinese-made consumer items.

Unofficial Apple Store in Tehran.

Questions for Analysis

1. Explain the relationship between China and the United States presented by these images. How has each country benefited from this relationship, and what sacrifices has each made?

2. Looking at the first two images, identify the sacrifices ordinary Chinese people have made as a result of the policies that enabled their country to invest in the United States. What group or groups in China do you think benefited from these policies, and how?

3. With the second, third, and fourth images in mind, analyze the tradeoffs for ordinary Americans that have resulted from Chinese investment in the United States.

4. Examine the final image and consider the likely consequences of the growth of Chimerica for ordinary consumers and workers around the world.

Epilogue

2001–THE PRESENT

The new millennium closed the chapter on the bloody wars and ideological rivalries of the twentieth century. Although the Cold War was over, and global integration seemed greater than ever before in human history, the twentieth-first century brought new explosive hostilities and fresh economic and political challenges.

On September 11, 2001, nineteen hijackers commandeered four commercial airplanes. The hijackers slammed two of the planes into the World Trade Center in New York City and a third into the Pentagon, home of the U.S. Department of Defense, in Washington, D.C. The fourth plane was diverted from its intended target—the White House or the Capitol—and crashed in a field in southwestern Pennsylvania. A still rather unknown Muslim militant organization, al-Qaeda, headed by an equally little known Saudi, Osama bin Laden, claimed responsibility for the attacks, which took the lives of more than 3,000 Americans. What followed was a predictable and determined American military response: the invasions of Iraq, incorrectly blamed for engineering the attacks, and Afghanistan, where a fundamentalist Islamic government provided a haven for bin Laden and his al-Qaeda affiliates.

Economic turmoil added to the turbulence of terrorism and wars. The global economy and new technologies had brought the world together as never before, but the benefits of integration were unequally distributed. Consequently, when an economic crisis broke out in 2008, its effects were felt globally, but experienced unequally. An angry, populist politics of despair swept many parts of the world fighting back against the perceived negative effects of globalization. This wave of populism led to national election victories for conservative populist candidates, such as Donald Trump in the United States and Recep Tayyip Erdogan in Turkey. Populist political parties, including the right-wing Alternative für Deutschland (AfD) in Germany, gained substantial ground in national assemblies, and in Great Britain, a majority of voters opted for the so-called Brexit: leaving the European Union (EU).

Global Challenges

WAR ON TERROR

The terrorist attack of 9/11 repulsed people around the world. Anger focused on Osama bin Laden and al-Qaeda, the loosely organized militant network of Islamist groups that had organized the attack. The militants claimed that it was a response

9/11 With the North Tower already aflame, this photograph captures a second hijacked jet an instant before it crashed into the South Tower of New York's World Trade Center on September 11, 2001.

to America's imperialist policies in the Middle East and retribution for American troops' presence in Saudi Arabia (during the first Iraq War). In the months and years that followed, countries grappled with a "war on terror," conflicts with militant Islamic groups, and a global economic crisis. George W. Bush, who had become president after a close and disputed election the year before the attack, gained broad public support for his tough talk about bringing terrorists to justice. Domestically, Bush pushed for security measures to curb future terrorist violence.

Internationally, President Bush declared a "global war on terror." With the backing of the majority of the American people, as well as strong support from many nations, Bush unsuccessfully sent American forces to Afghanistan to hunt down bin Laden, destroy al-Qaeda training camps, and topple the Taliban government that had provided a haven for the terrorists. Expanding the battlefront of the war on terror, the Bush administration ordered an invasion of Iraq in 2003, falsely charging its dictator, Saddam Hussein, with abetting the terrorist assault of 9/11 and producing weapons of mass destruction. As in Afghanistan, the initial offensive went well, but defeating the Iraqi army and finding Hussein proved easier than restoring order to the country or winning popular support.

In Afghanistan, U.S.-led coalition forces soon found themselves in a quagmire. Early successes collapsed as local warlords pursued their own goals and as the revitalized Taliban was able to regroup in neighboring Pakistan.

While the campaigns in Iraq and Afghanistan faltered, the United States accelerated its efforts to hunt down terrorist leaders. Under President Barack Obama, a daring operation in Pakistan ended with the death of Osama bin Laden in 2011. Even so, the American image suffered internationally as news of programs of extensive surveillance (including that of U.S. citizens), "rendition" of suspected militants to sites where they could be tortured to extract information, the inhumane treatment of Iraqi prisoners at the Abu Ghraib prison, and the harsh and indefinite detention of suspected terrorists at Guantanamo spread. The prospect that the new century would be one of peace and prosperity under an American order seemed increasingly remote.

CRISIS AND INEQUALITY IN THE GLOBAL ECONOMY

In 2008, the world economy fell into crisis. The problem began the previous year in the financial sector, the most globally interlinked sector of all. Seeking new sources of profits, investors from around the world had poured their money into riskier and riskier investments—many of which were so complex that not even the regulators in charge of monitoring the financial sector could understand them.

One of the most enticing of these risky bets was real estate in the United States, where a frenzy of investment in the early 2000s created a price "bubble." The bubble eventually burst, leading to a plunge in property values. By the summer of 2008, there was a worldwide panic, and the banking system nearly collapsed. As it became more difficult to borrow money and consumers stopped spending, factories shut down and stores went bankrupt.

The financial crisis brought signs of gathering discontent. In Europe, where, at last, economic and political integration within the European Union had seemed to promise an end to conflict between states, the crisis created new tensions. In Greece, radical new parties arose to protest austerity measures or to take out frustrations on immigrants, and many blamed the richer nations, especially the Germans, for having profited from the creation of the EU at the expense of the poorer nations. For the first time in decades, vehement nationalist slogans came into wide circulation, and politicians of the left and right hostile to the European project were elected. Some commentators predicted that the common currency (the euro)—and perhaps even the European Union in its current form—would not last, as exemplified by Great Britain's decision to leave the European Union. In the Americas, Mexico elected a trade skeptic, Andrés Manuel López Obrador. In the United States, the Trump administration pulled out of the Trans-Pacific Partnership (a trade agreement with twelve nations), sought to renegotiate the North American Free Trade Agreement with Mexico and Canada, and, in the name of national security, imposed restrictions on the importation of aluminum and steel.

Even as economies emerged from the crisis, economic inequality among individuals and regions led to new challenges. The very same ongoing integration of the world economy that globalized the economic crisis also produced fresh wealth across the world. Capital, technology, and media brought the world together ever more closely. The movement of ideas and images across national borders accelerated. Social media like Facebook provided new lines of communication and connections, particularly among the young. New aspirations for employment, prosperity, consumption, and political expression appeared.

These global economic and political stirrings were full of paradoxes and contradictions. The growth of prosperity and wealth around the world was highly unequal and accompanied by an unprecedented rise in the power and influence of corporations and financial institutions. Even as a global middle class came into being, inequality deepened. This sparked a range

Global Capitalism and the Great Contraction of 2008

According to the economic historian Charles Kindleberger, the twentieth century witnessed seven of the world's ten greatest global financial panics since the eighteenth century. To those crises now must be added the Great Contraction of 2008, a financial crisis almost as severe and long lasting as the Great Depression of 1929 (see Chapter 19). Although billions of people have been pulled out of poverty during the twentieth and twenty-first centuries, economic growth has come with a heavy price, namely, dramatic and alarming economic crises that have spread rapidly throughout the world, now tightly linked because of increased global integration. According to Kindleberger, "the years since the early 1970s are unprecedented in terms of volatility in the prices of commodities, currencies, real estate and stocks, and the frequency and severity of financial crises."

Many policymakers and economists believed that the lessons learned during the Great Depression rendered anything as severe as the losses of wealth and income, the high unemployment rates, and the sharp drop in consumer purchasing power in that period a thing of the past. Except for a few crying Cassandras, decision makers in the developed world were utterly unprepared for the financial crisis that was triggered by the bursting of a real-estate bubble in 2008, which in turn led to the implosion of some of the most powerful financial houses and manufacturers in the United States and throughout the world.

The signals of an approaching financial disaster were apparent to many, but were ignored, in part because Alan Greenspan, the guru of monetary policy at the Federal Reserve—America's central bank—and an ardent economic libertarian and free marketer, argued that the marketplace would bring about necessary corrections. In reality, risk and indebtedness were at record levels. Commercial and investment banks and insurance companies had tripled their indebtedness over the three decades leading up to 2008. Even when the Hongkong and Shanghai Banking Corporation (HSBC), based in London since 1991 and the seventh largest bank in the world in terms of assets, reported massive losses in its subprime housing loans, and Countrywide Business Credit filed for bankruptcy, the George W. Bush administration and Congress did not react. Only when Bear Stearns collapsed in March 2008 because of its heavy exposure to subprime mortgage loans did the U.S. Treasury intervene, providing a loan of nearly $30 billion to J. P. Morgan Chase to buy out Bear Stearns. But no support was forthcoming on September 18, 2008, when Lehman Brothers, a firm that had been in existence since 1850 and had survived the Civil War, World Wars I and II, and the Great Depression, filed for bankruptcy. Had the Treasury provided anywhere from $12 to $60 billion, the roiling financial crisis might have been averted. But it did not, and what had already been a dramatic economic and financial meltdown in the United States, the United Kingdom, Ireland, Spain, and Iceland now spread rapidly throughout Europe, Asia, Latin America, and parts of Africa. Millions lost their livelihoods and homes, corporations failed, trillions of dollars of wealth were destroyed, "and the once mighty US economy [was brought] to its knees, [leaving] all levels of government gasping for tax revenue."

The Great Contraction of 2008 did not last as long as the Great Depression of 1929. The unemployment rate

of protest movements outside conventional political and institutional forms like political parties and trade unions—none more powerful and dramatic than Occupy Wall Street (OWS), a movement that started in September 2011 in New York and was organized by a Canadian anarchist group called Adbusters, using social media to mobilize young people. It highlighted growing social and economic inequality and challenged the power of banks and corporations.

in the United States cratered out at 10 percent, not 25 percent, and hundreds of banks, not thousands, failed. The financial downturn of 2008 was not as sharp and did not persist as long as the 1929 depression largely because of the innovative policies championed by Ben Bernanke—Greenspan's successor at the Federal Reserve—and officials at the U.S. Treasury. It was perhaps fortuitous that Bernanke was at the Fed and Christina Romer was a high-ranking economic adviser in the Obama administration. Both had studied the Great Depression during their academic careers and were committed to monetary and financial policies that they believed would have pulled the United States out of the depression. Specifically, they thought it essential to protect the big banks, stimulate the economy, resist protectionism, and promote international cooperation. In keeping with these policies, the Treasury bailed out fourteen financial firms, including such heavy-hitters as Goldman Sachs, Morgan Stanley, Merrill Lynch, Bank of America, Citigroup, and J. P. Morgan Chase, as well as two automobile manufacturers, General Motors and Chrysler. They did so by pressuring a rather unwilling Congress to set aside the stupendous sum of $700 billion in a program labeled TARP (Troubled Assets Relief Program). Although the majority of Americans thought the program was wrong-headed, rewarding the banks that had brought on the financial disaster, TARP was, according to Alan Blinder, an expert economist, "among the most successful—but least understood—economic policy innovations in our nation's history." In fact, the Treasury disbursed only $430 billion of the allocated $700 billion and eventually turned a profit of $25 billion as the businesses that received the funds repaid the equity injected into their companies.

Are financial crises likely to be with us in the future? Probably so, for it is the nature of humankind to become inordinately ebullient about financial gains to be made and to take on more debt than can be sustained. It would appear that financial bubbles, panics, manias, contractions, and even catastrophic depressions are an inevitable part of world capitalism.

Explore Further

Blinder, Alan S., *After the Music Stopped: The Financial Crisis, the Response, and the Work Ahead* (2013).

Eichengreen, Barry J., *Hall of Mirrors: The Great Depression and the Great Recession, and the Uses—and Misuses—of History* (2015).

Friedman, Milton and Schwartz, Anne Jacobson, *A Monetary History of the United States, 1867–1960* (1963).

Guillen, Mauro F., *The Architecture of Collapse: The Global System in the 21st Century* (2015).

Kindleberger, Charles P. and Aliber, Robert, *Manias, Panics, and Crashes: A History of Financial Crises*, 5th edition (2005).

Reinhart, Carmen M. and Rogoff, Kenneth S., *This Time Is Different: Eight Centuries of Financial Folly* (2009).

Sources: Charles P. Kindleberger and Robert Aliber, *Manias, Panics, and Crashes: A History of Financial Crises*, 5th edition (Hoboken, NJ: John Wiley & Sons, 2005), p. 1; Alan S. Blinder, *After the Music Stopped: The Financial Crisis, the Response, and the Work Ahead* (New York: Penguin, 2013), pp. 4, 178.

CLIMATE CHANGE

As the world population continues to grow and as more areas industrialize, the pressure on vital natural resources (especially oil and water) has inspired calls for greater conservation and more environmentally sustainable economic development. But the U.S. government's resistance to global regulations, as well as a rising demand for resources (especially by China and India), has made the future of the earth's environment uncertain.

Occupy Wall Street Inspired by other stirrings around the world, this largely national movement was fueled by methods as novel as social media and as traditional as sit-ins. Here, an Occupy Wall Street rally joins a labor union demonstration outside the New York County Courthouse in 2011.

Climate change has emerged as one of the most pressing issues for the new millennium. Despite difficulties in achieving a consensus on policy, scientists and environmental experts agree that the planet needs remedial action. Thus, when the Group of Eight (G8), a forum of leaders from Canada, France, Germany, Italy, Japan, Russia, the United Kingdom, and the United States, met in 2007, a key topic was climate change. It acknowledged that humankind is contributing to, if not causing, global warming through its emissions of greenhouse gases—especially by burning coal and oil for electricity, but also by clearing vegetation for farming, development, and timber. The result is climate change: rising temperatures, melting ice caps, drought in some regions, and more severe storms elsewhere. The effects on populations living close to sea level can be catastrophic. Hurricane Katrina in 2005, for example, left much of New Orleans and the Mississippi Gulf Coast in ruins. Hurricane Sandy had similar catastrophic effects on the shorelines of New Jersey and New York in 2013; and in 2018, Hurricane Maria devastated Puerto Rico. Elsewhere, prolonged drought has led to agrarian crises and food shortages; this situation crept up on Syria over many years and led to an outburst of opposition to the despotic government of Bashar al-Assad and a bloody civil war. The resulting refugee crisis has spilled over into Turkey and Europe.

A major breakthrough occurred in Paris in 2015 when, under the sponsorship of the United Nations Framework on Climate Change, most of the nations of the world gathered to hammer out an agreement that would limit the emission of greenhouse gases and hold down the increase in global temperature. The accord, scheduled to go into effect in 2020, aims to achieve a less than 1.5°C increase in global temperature. The two heaviest polluters, China and the United States, are crucial signatories. Yet the implementation of the agreement is left to the individual nations, each of which must file reports with the United Nations. Donald Trump, the American president elected in 2016, has repudiated American participation in the Paris accord and asserted that the entire science of climate change and global warming is a hoax.

The United States, the European Union, and Japan

Although the global challenges of the twenty-first century have touched virtually every corner of the world, local contexts continue to weigh heavily. Countries and regions have experienced globalizing forces in very different ways.

THE UNITED STATES

In the United States, the Obama administration sought to cope with the economic crisis while introducing health care reform. It encountered a conservative backlash in the shape of the Tea Party movement, which espoused the ideals of small government and market freedom and contributed to a stinging defeat of the Democrats in the 2010 congressional elections. From the opposite side of the ideological spectrum arose the Occupy Wall Street movement in 2011. Claiming to speak on behalf of 99 percent of Americans against the wealthiest 1 percent, the Occupy activists, consisting largely of young people, railed against the banks and financial institutions that the federal government had rescued from bankruptcy. Although the movement ran out of steam by the end of the year, it succeeded in inserting the nation's growing inequality into political discussions.

More stunning was the 2016 election, in which candidate Donald Trump, who had never held political office, inveighed against "inner-city" crime, immigrants, international trade, and long-standing American alliances and security arrangements. Although few pundits gave Trump much chance against a field of well-established and well-financed Republican Party opponents, his platform resonated with primary voters and gained him the party's nomination. Facing Hillary Clinton in the general election, Trump once more defied pollsters by winning a majority in the Electoral College (though losing the popular vote by nearly 3 million). Coming on the heels of Brexit, Trump's victory reflected the rising populist and nationalist tide against globalization.

A CHANGING WESTERN EUROPE

The American invasion of Iraq in 2003 created fractures in the alliance between the United States and western Europe. During the 1990s, the collapse of the Soviet Union and the development of the EU had caused some rumblings about the future of NATO, but disagreements remained muted at that time. In fact, in the immediate wake of 9/11, European allies rallied behind the United States. But as the American military entered Iraq, leaders in France and Germany sharply criticized U.S. foreign policy.

Far more serious divisions emerged over the fate of NATO and of the EU, whose membership peaked at twenty-eight countries, including ten that had formerly been part of the Soviet bloc. In a 2016 referendum on EU membership in Britain, in which voters could choose "Leave" or "Remain," "Leave" secured a majority. The trend toward EU expansion, whereby member states relinquished a significant degree of sovereignty as an answer to the legacies of war, ethnic cleansing, and genocide, was reversed over the issues of free integration within the union and the unlimited jurisdiction of the European Court of Justice.

Has *Homo sapiens* Entered a New Epoch— the Anthropocene?

The Earth came into being more than 4 billion years ago, and the first life forms appeared around 2 billion years ago. From the nineteenth century onward, geologists, earth scientists, evolutionary biologists, and others have been fine-tuning a time scale of Earth history, which they divide into eons, four of which have thus far existed and each of which spans hundreds and thousands of millions of years. The eons themselves are subdivided into eras, periods, epochs, and ages. Earth scientists base their geological divisions of the earth's history on the major changes that have taken place in the environment and climate of our planet and its life forms. Using these categories, they have created a geological time scale (GTS). Today, we live in the Cenozoic Era and the Holocene Epoch. The Cenozoic Era, which began roughly 65 million years ago with the extinction of the dinosaurs, has been called the Age of Mammals because the largest land animals of the era have been mammals. The Holocene Epoch, which began about 12,000 years ago, after the last major ice age, has had a stable climate and has been increasingly dominated by *Homo sapiens*. The term *Holocene* itself, meaning whole and recent, was first proposed by the British scientist Charles Lyall in 1833, and was adopted by the International Geological Congress in 1885 as the title for our epoch.

However, two scientists, Paul J. Crutzer and Eugene F. Stoemer, believe that we have entered a new geological epoch, dominated by the impact of humankind on the earth's environment, particularly its stratosphere. They first proposed the term "Anthropocene" to represent humankind's dominance in this new epoch. Their proposal appeared in an article published in May 2000 in the newsletter of the International Geosphere-Biosphere Programme (IGBP). Although their statement was only a short one, these authors dealt with virtually all of the factors that led them and their followers to assert that the environmental and geological impact of *Homo sapiens* has been so decisive that the world has indeed entered a new geological age. They stressed human population growth, the extinction of other species, the increase in atmospheric greenhouse gases, notably carbon dioxide and methane, and the destruction of rain forests. They concluded their essay by observing that "it seems to us more than appropriate to emphasize the central role of mankind in geology and ecology by proposing the term 'anthropocene' for the current geological epoch." Evidence from glacial ice cores showing a dramatic rise in greenhouse gas concentrations since the latter part of the eighteenth century caused them to argue that the Anthropocene began at the time of the industrial revolution.

Thus far, it has been mainly environmental historians who have taken up the challenge of studying the impact of humankind on the environment, though only a few have used the term "Anthropocene" proposed by Crutzer and Stoemer. They have, however, elaborated on the factors that Crutzer and Stoemer first laid out. Two environmental historians, J. R. McNeill and Peter Engelkes, in their essay "Into the Anthropocene: People and Their Planet," contend that "a new history of the earth has begun, that the Holocene is over, and something new has begun: the Anthropocene." They prefer the twentieth century rather than Crutzer's and Stoemer's claim for the later eighteenth century as the starting point of this epoch and conclude "that humankind emerged as the most powerful influence upon the global ecology." They cite the enormous expansion of the human population: a tenfold increase over three centuries, producing the present world population of 7.6 billion. The growth of the human population was exceedingly slow up to the beginning of the nineteenth century— only about 0.05 per year—but reached a full 2 percent per year in 1970. In their view, "no primate, perhaps no mammal, has ever engaged in such a frenzy of reproduction." As for the loading of the atmosphere with carbon dioxide, three-quarters of this loading took place during the most recent six and half decades (between 1945 and 2011). The number of vehicles increased from 40 million to 800 million during the same period. Moreover, the number of residents of cities expanded from about 200 million to 3.5 billion. Until it became possible to use fossil fuels such as coal, oil, and natural gas for energy, human beings relied on their own muscles to do most work. Fossil fuels have led to rapid economic progress throughout the world, but have also created problems of smog, general pollution, and the thinning of the ozone layer in the atmosphere that shields the earth from harmful radiation, as well as the critical problem of global warming.

Crutzer and Stoemer were optimistic in 2000 that world leaders would pay attention to the evidence, revealed by earth scientists, that human beings were upsetting the ecology and environment of the earth. Short of "an enormous volcanic eruption, an unexpected epidemic, a large scale nuclear war, an asteroid impact, a new ice age, or continued plundering of Earth's resources, [they expected] . . . mankind [to] remain a major geological force for many millennia, maybe millions of years to come." Yet, are earth scientists and well-informed political leaders and ruling elites nearly so sanguine these days?

Explore Further

Crutzer, Paul J. and Stoemer, Eugene F., "The Anthropocene," *IGBP Newsletter*, no. 41 (May 2000), pp. 17–18.

McNeill, J. R., *Something New under the Sun: An Environmental History of the Twentieth Century* (2000).

McNeill, J. R. and Engelkes, Peter, "Into the Anthropocene: People and Their Planet," in *Global Interdependence: The World after 1945*, ed. Akira Iriye (2014).

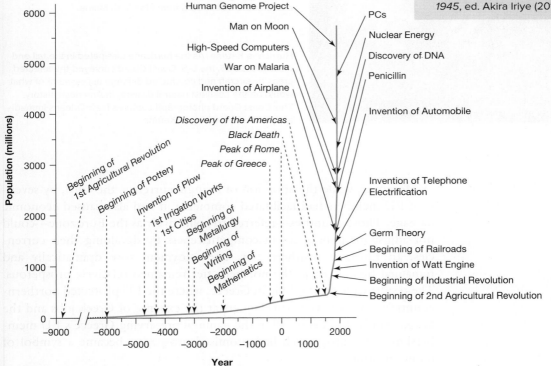

Population and Technology This graph tracks the world's increasing population over time alongside major technological developments. Where one skyrockets, so does the other, suggesting a starting point for the Anthropocene.

Source: J. R. McNeill and Peter Engelkes, "Into the Anthropocene: People and Their Planet," in *Global Interdependence: The World after 1945*, ed. Akira Iriye (Cambridge, MA: Belknap Press of Harvard University Press, 2014), 365–533.

Destruction by Hurricane Sandy on Ortley Beach, New Jersey Hurricane Sandy, moving ashore in New Jersey on October 29, 2012, was the second-costliest hurricane in U.S. history. Its high winds struck twenty-four states, including the entire eastern seaboard from Florida to Maine.

Hurricane Katrina As the hurricane dissipated in the tail end of August 2005, the U.S. Coast Guard surveyed the affected areas by aircraft and conducted damage assessment of what would be the costliest natural disaster in American history. This Coast Guard photograph captures New Orleans immediately after the passing of Katrina.

Moreover, while the adoption of a single currency, the euro, by seventeen EU members had facilitated commerce, it had also caused economic damage. Those countries—referred to collectively as the Eurozone—could not adjust for imbalances in competitiveness by devaluing their currencies. In Europe's southern tier, unemployment rose dramatically and remained high, even as the northern tier remained relatively prosperous. The results were most visible in Greece, where the EU protected northern-country (especially German) lenders at the expense of Greek jobs and the Greek standard of living, all in the name of preserving Greece's EU membership. The euro, which had promised prosperity, became a symbol of immiserization.

In addition, the EU's signature identity, democratic institutions, experienced significant erosion, beginning in Hungary and then Poland before spreading to much of the rest of Europe. Italy, which hosted the conference that led to the EU's founding Treaty of Rome (1958), elected a government in 2018 that was deeply critical of the Union. Europe's malaise put the long-term future of integration to the test.

DEMOGRAPHIC ISSUES

One threat to future peace and prosperity in Europe—and in the United States and Japan as well—comes from the interlocking issues of aging and immigration. Women in the European Union would have to bear two children on average to maintain its population of 500 million, but women in the EU now average only 1.5 children. Adding to the problem is the graying of the European population. With the percentage of elderly Europeans rising rapidly, sustaining the present ratio of workers to retirees and paying for the region's burgeoning number of pensioners will require the EU to attract around 15 million immigrants annually.

That number of immigrants has not been reached. European populations have been boosted by millions of immigrants, many of them Muslims, but sustainable economic growth has proved elusive. Islam has become the fastest-growing religion in Europe. The presence of Muslims in Europe's large cities threatens those who still equate Europe with Christendom and challenges those who believe that European integration requires complete cultural assimilation of all inhabitants.

Europe is not alone in confronting the problems of an aging population and the integration of immigrants. As its post–World War II baby boom generation ages, the United States faces a similar imbalance between retirees and workers that endangers its Social Security system. Likewise, the increase in immigration, particularly from Asia and Latin America, continues to shift the nation's ethnic composition. Donald Trump, who pledged to "build a wall" across the U.S.-Mexico border, made control of immigration central to his campaign for the presidency in 2016. (For a global look at population growth and life expectancies, see Maps E.1 and E.2.)

In many respects, the problem of an aging population presses hardest today on Japan. Like Europeans and North Americans, the Japanese are marrying later and having fewer children. Japan's female population now averages barely 1.37 children, compared with nearly 3.7 in 1950. At the same time, Japanese life expectancy has reached eighty-five, the highest in the world, which further tilts the nation's age pyramid. In 1970, the elderly (those over age sixty-five) represented around 7 percent of the population; in 2014, they made up more than 25 percent and are expected to hit 40 percent by 2050. Japan's population peaked at around 128 million and might decline to perhaps 120 million by 2050, with a substantial proportion over the working age. Such a downturn bodes ill for Japan's economy.

Like Europe and North America, Japan relies on immigrants to fill out its labor force. In the 1960s, the nation's booming economy led to labor shortages, but neither the government nor major corporations chose to invite in foreign laborers. By the 1980s, however, deepening labor shortages and the yen's rising value led to an expanded dependence on immigrant workers.

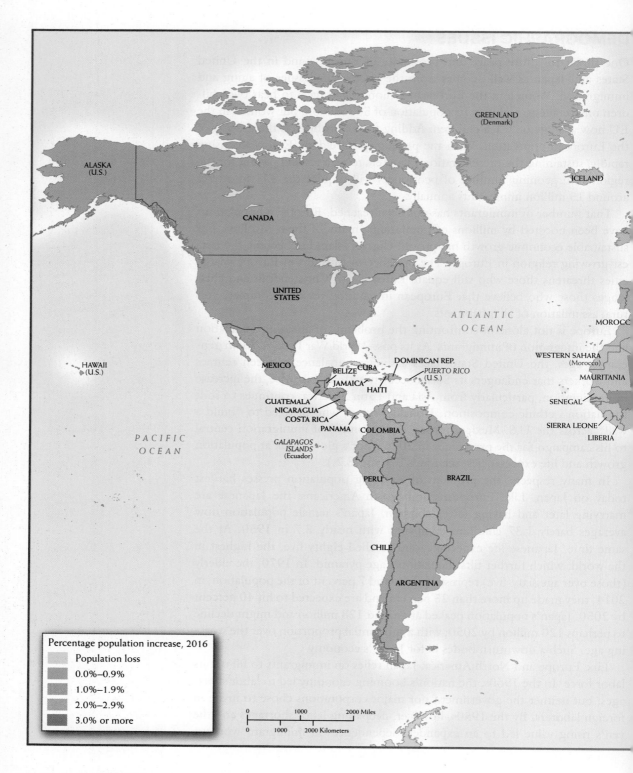

Percentage population increase, 2016

- Population loss
- 0.0%–0.9%
- 1.0%–1.9%
- 2.0%–2.9%
- 3.0% or more

ATLANTIC OCEAN

PACIFIC OCEAN

GREENLAND
(Denmark)

ICELAND

ALASKA
(U.S.)

CANADA

UNITED
STATES

HAWAII
(U.S.)

MEXICO

BELIZE CUBA
JAMAICA
GUATEMALA
NICARAGUA
COSTA RICA
PANAMA

DOMINICAN REP.
PUERTO RICO
(U.S.)

HAITI

COLOMBIA

GALAPAGOS
ISLANDS
(Ecuador)

PERU

BRAZIL

CHILE

ARGENTINA

MOROCC

WESTERN SAHARA
(Morocco)

MAURITANIA

SENEGAL

SIERRA LEONE

LIBERIA

0   1000   2000 Miles

0   1000   2000 Kilometers

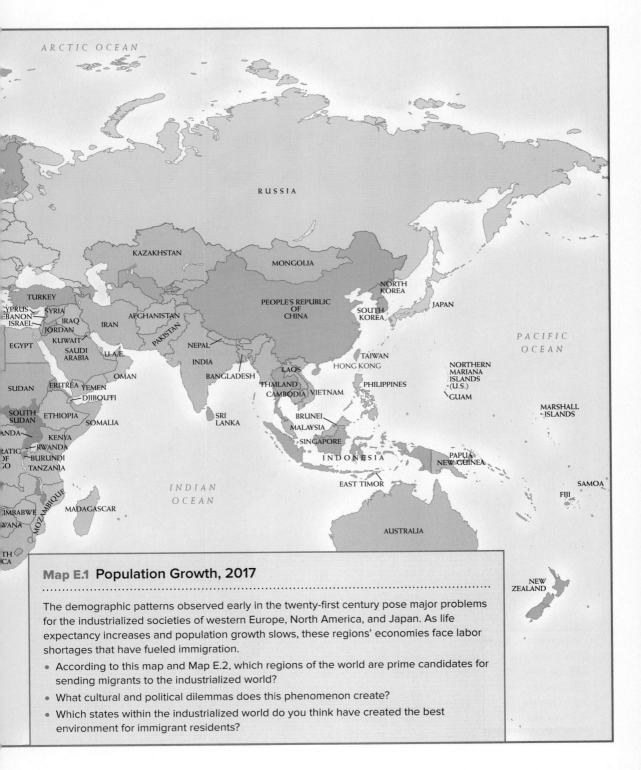

Map E.1 Population Growth, 2017

The demographic patterns observed early in the twenty-first century pose major problems for the industrialized societies of western Europe, North America, and Japan. As life expectancy increases and population growth slows, these regions' economies face labor shortages that have fueled immigration.

- According to this map and Map E.2, which regions of the world are prime candidates for sending migrants to the industrialized world?
- What cultural and political dilemmas does this phenomenon create?
- Which states within the industrialized world do you think have created the best environment for immigrant residents?

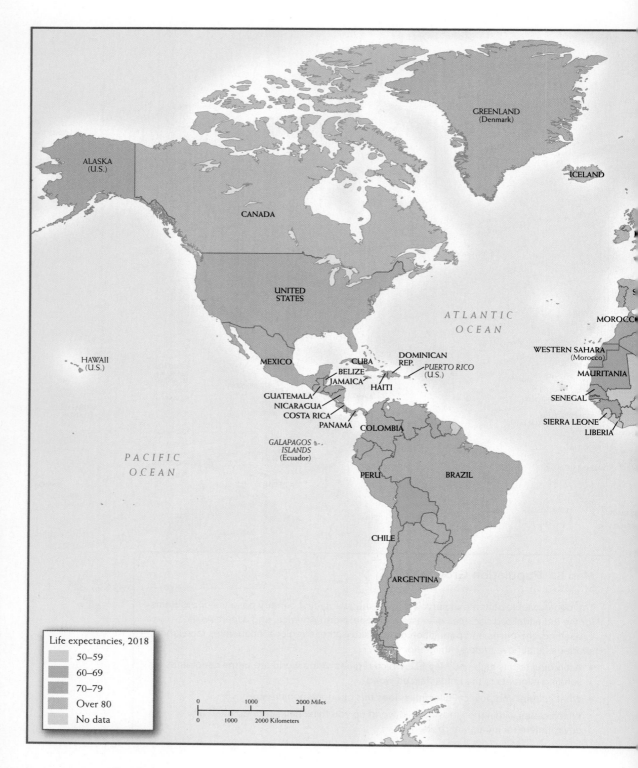

Life expectancies, 2018
- 50–59
- 60–69
- 70–79
- Over 80
- No data

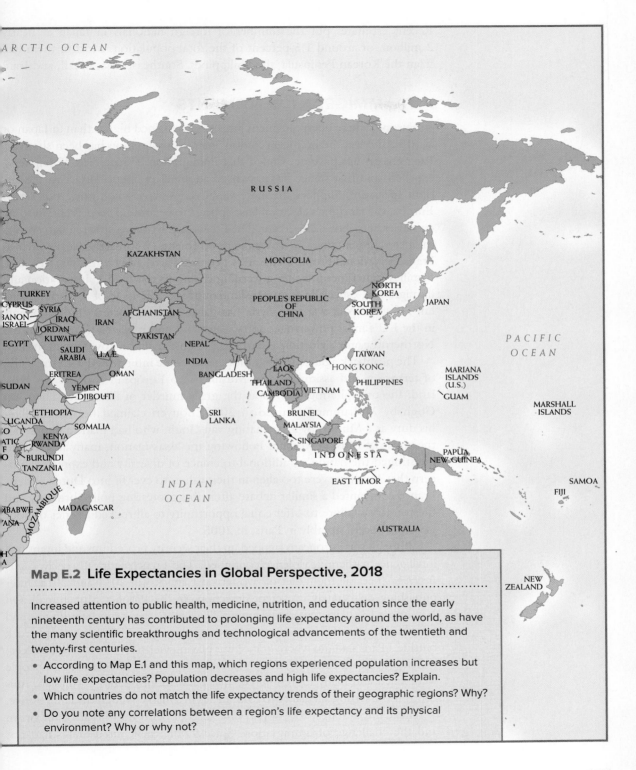

Map E.2 Life Expectancies in Global Perspective, 2018

Increased attention to public health, medicine, nutrition, and education since the early nineteenth century has contributed to prolonging life expectancy around the world, as have the many scientific breakthroughs and technological advancements of the twentieth and twenty-first centuries.

- According to Map E.1 and this map, which regions experienced population increases but low life expectancies? Population decreases and high life expectancies? Explain.

- Which countries do not match the life expectancy trends of their geographic regions? Why?

- Do you note any correlations between a region's life expectancy and its physical environment? Why or why not?

Recent estimates put the number of foreign nationals in Japan at nearly 2 million, or around 1.5 percent of the total population. Most of them hail from the Korean Peninsula, the Philippines, Southeast Asia, Brazil, and Iran.

ANTI-IMMIGRANT SENTIMENTS

In Europe, where unemployment rates have remained higher than in Japan or North America, the political reaction against immigration has been sharpest. Far-right groups have demanded that immigration be halted or "foreigners" expelled, and that stance has now been adopted by politicians across the far-right spectrum. Support for these views varies among countries, but across Europe, the far right's electoral base appears to be around 15 percent; in some countries, it is above 25 percent. The Freedom Party in Austria regularly places cabinet representatives in coalition governments. Ultra-right forces such as France's National Front, Denmark's People's Party, and the League of Polish Families sometimes pressure governing coalitions to slow EU integration and immigration, especially from Muslim countries. The issue of accepting Muslim refugees from war-torn Syria has galvanized supporters and opponents in the EU's most powerful country, Germany, and it played a key role in the Northern League's election as part of a populist coalition government in Italy.

The pushback against immigration has become intertwined with the issues of terrorism and assimilation of Muslims into European societies. In Holland, the precipitating event was the grisly murder of filmmaker Theo van Gogh by Mohammed Bouyeri in 2004. Bouyeri claimed he was fulfilling his duty as a Muslim by assassinating van Gogh, who had made a film about the abuse of Muslim women. Following the assassination, many in Holland questioned the nation's traditional tolerance of diversity and expressed concern that Muslims were too alien in their values to ever fit into Dutch society. France confronted a similar debate after riots protesting police brutality and the country's failure to offer equal opportunity to all rocked a series of poor neighborhoods, notably in Paris, in 2005.

Although the Europeans stepped up their security procedures and intensified intelligence gathering, violence continued. The French satirical weekly *Charlie Hebdo* became the target of two terrorist attacks (in 2011 and 2015) after publishing deliberately irreverent depictions of the Prophet Muhammad. On November 13, 2015, terrorists claiming allegiance to the Islamic State in Iraq and Syria (ISIS) carried out a series of coordinated attacks: while one group struck outside a Paris stadium where France was playing Germany in a football (soccer) match, others attacked restaurants, cafes, and a concert hall. In all, 130 people were killed and many more injured. Just a few months later, a Tunisian, Anis Amri, also asserting allegiance to ISIS, struck in a market in Berlin, killing twelve.

The United States, too, was trying to cope with the threat of terrorism and the challenge of immigration. Since 9/11, the United States had not

"No Muslim Ban" Protesters against the U.S. Supreme Court's decision to uphold President Donald Trump's ban on travel from several mostly Muslim countries expressed their indignation on June 26, 2018, in New York.

suffered another major attack, but smaller attacks raised the level of public alarm. While Americans often described themselves as a nation of immigrants, anti-immigrant sentiments also gathered popular support, fueled by candidate (and then President) Trump's nativist attacks on immigrants and refugees. Among its early, signature measures, the Trump administration imposed restrictions on immigration from Muslim countries (the so-called Muslim ban); separated children from parents who crossed the U.S.-Mexico border illegally; and sought to end the Deferred Action for Childhood Arrivals (DACA) policy of his predecessor, Barack Obama, which allowed some immigrants to remain and work in the United States.

In just a few years, the mood of the world's most advanced industrial societies has shifted decisively. The triumphant atmosphere that ushered in the new millennium has given way to a pessimistic outlook. In the year 2000, talk of the blessings of global integration dominated the political and economic scene; two decades later, prognosticators warn about the dangers emanating from disaffected members of their societies and from radicals, especially Islamic radicals, willing and able to unleash terror anywhere in the world.

Russia, China, and India

Fueling the anti-immigrant fires in Europe, Japan, and North America is the increasing number of jobs being "outsourced" to China, India, and other countries. In the past, businesses had turned to immigrants to fill low-wage positions (and to keep all wages down). But by the end of the twentieth century, it had become more economical to relocate manufacturing to places where cheap labor was already available.

ECONOMIC GLOBALIZATION AND POLITICAL EFFECTS

In the twenty-first century, business mobility has not been limited to low-skill and low-wage jobs. Technological advances—particularly in computers and communication—have enabled all sorts of enterprises to operate from almost any point on the globe. No longer do educated workers have to leave India or China for employment in Europe or North America, because it is increasingly cost-effective for corporations to shift certain operations to those countries. The globalized market economy has leveled the playing field in the competition for jobs, although countries with vast labor reserves, such as China, India, and Russia, still have a long way to go to achieve the per capita income levels enjoyed in the older capitalist societies. Nonetheless, Russia, China, and India have had healthy economic growth in the first years of the new century.

While Russia's economy was opening to the world, thanks to high oil prices, its political system seemed to be closing in on itself. President Vladimir Putin presided over a rebuilding of the central Russian state, which was widely welcomed in Russia. But the means used by Putin to reassert central state power led, once again, to personal rule. The president forcibly repossessed the two principal television stations from their billionaire owners and reassigned other valuable private properties, especially oil and gas companies, to the state, to be run by his former colleagues from the Soviet-era political police, the KGB. The Gorbachev-Yeltsin era's promise of a real legislature, an independent judiciary, and an end to arbitrary rule gave way, in the yearning for order and stability, to aggressive nationalism and an authoritarian executive.

Child Labor Girls in a Javanese village work in a factory transferring bundles of cotton yarn to bobbins to be used in hand-looms.

As in Russia, leaders in China have encouraged market reforms while quashing political liberalization. Their economic strategies seem to be successful. Over the last three decades, China's economy has maintained an average growth rate of over 9 percent annually, although it has recently shown signs of slowing down. Consumer goods made in China dominate so many markets that it is virtually impossible, as several newspaper reporters have found, to supply an American family's needs with a "China-free" shopping list. Indeed, the Chinese economy has been the second largest in the world since late 2010, and some projections suggest that it will be the largest by midcentury, even though China's per capita income will still lag behind that of the United States.

In many ways, China's fortunes illustrate both the promises and the pitfalls of the economic reforms undertaken by many developing countries in the era of globalization. On the one hand, China's entry into the World Trade Organization (WTO) in 2001 signified its full integration into the global capitalist economy. On the other hand, the reforms have caused political, social, and environmental problems that defy easy solutions. A 2016 report from Peking University found that 1 percent of Chinese households controlled a third of the country's assets, while the poorest 25 percent of households owned just 1 percent of the country's wealth.

There are concerns, both at home and abroad, about the environmental impact of China's economic development. China's homes and factories, for instance, use 40 percent more coal than those in the United States, and Chinese city dwellers suffer from some of the world's worst smog and poorest air quality. But as its energy consumption and economy have soared, so has China's global standing.

China has embarked on an ambitious infrastructure program. Dubbed the "Belt and Road Initiative," the plan seeks to spread Chinese economic and political influence to some sixty countries, principally in Asia and Europe but also in Oceania and eastern Africa. By the early twenty-first century, China had become the number one trading partner with almost every country in Asia, displacing the United States. It has even become the top trading partner with Brazil, as well as with many countries in Africa. China has also replaced the United States as the number one customer for Saudi Arabian oil. Chinese-Indian economic relations have strengthened, too. Although China faces numerous challenges, it has regained the enormous global weight it held for centuries up until the eighteenth century.

India has also registered impressive economic growth in the new millennium. Since the 1990s, the Indian economy has become increasingly open. The nation's information technology sector boomed, and India became a favorite destination for global corporations, attracted by its sizable English-speaking population. Per capita income rose by 20 percent annually, and poverty declined by an average of over 2 percent annually, between 2004 and 2014.

Yet the benefits of economic liberalization were unequally experienced. High inflation hit the income of the salaried class hard. Inequality and poverty

Chinese Environmental Concerns Despite its prosperity, Hong Kong, like other major Chinese cities, suffers from severe air pollution, which threatens its future as a hub of international commerce. This picture shows part of the city's waterfront shrouded in smog.

Hindu-Muslim Tensions In 2002, Gujarat was consumed by sectarian riots, set off by a train fire in which sixty Hindu pilgrims died. Although an Indian government investigation concluded that the fire was accidental, the incident sparked an orgy of violence by Hindu mobs against Muslims. Shown here is an angry right-wing Hindu Party activist.

remain acute problems. In an effort to boost the capitalist economy, the government declared an open season on land acquisition for real estate development, industrial parks, and mining, leading to the eviction of farmers and forest dwellers. The displaced people responded with armed insurgencies. In addition, the booming economy and new wealth created opportunities for corrupt practices. Riding on the widespread revulsion against corruption, the Bharatiya Janata Party (BJP), under Narendra Modi, swept the national elections and came to power in 2014.

Internal divisions and external rivalries have threatened to undo many benefits of economic globalization in India, China, and Russia. This is most clearly apparent in India, where the BJP, while advocating for the free market, has also aggressively championed *Hindutva* (Hinduness) as the bedrock of Indian identity.

Violence erupted in the state of Gujarat in February 2002 after sixty Hindu pilgrims perished in a fire that consumed a train compartment. Although the circumstances of the fire remain disputed, a rumor immediately spread that Muslims and a "foreign hand" were responsible. For the next few months, Hindu mobs went on a rampage, burning Muslim homes and hacking the residents to death. Over 2,000 Muslims lost their lives.

The ongoing tension with neighboring Pakistan poses further problems. Flexing its nationalist muscle, the Indian government exploded a nuclear device in 1998. Pakistan responded by exploding its own bombs, casting an ominous shadow over the two nations' unresolved conflict over Kashmir. In that contested province, terrorist violence repeatedly disturbed the peace and brought the nuclear-armed neighbors close to a potentially devastating war. The tension between the two countries escalated in 2008 when a small band of terrorists from Pakistan carried out raids in Mumbai, slaughtering many civilians and security personnel before being subdued.

The Middle East, Africa, and Latin America

In the Middle East, radical changes have been brought about by the Arab Spring and the growth of Islamic militancy, while more than a few countries

in Africa have begun to achieve economic progress and gained political stability through democratic elections.

THE ARAB SPRING

The trigger for what became known as the Arab Spring was a seemingly futile act
of protest. On December 17, 2010, Mohammed Bouazizi, a twenty-six-year-
old Tunisian vegetable vendor and father of eight, set himself on fire outside a
provincial office to protest the constant police harassment he had undergone.
This singular act aroused the entire population of Tunisia against the ruling
elite. Not only had the police confiscated Bouazizi's vegetable stand, and not
for the first time, but a policewoman had slapped him in the face. In explaining
his decision to take his life, his sister exclaimed, "In Sidi Bouzidi [where he
resided] those with no connections and no money for bribes are humiliated and
insulted and not allowed to live." As the story circulated through the country,
crowds poured into the streets, demanding an end to the long-term dictatorship of Zine al-Abidine Ben Ali, who had taken over from Habib Bourguiba,
Tunisia's president from independence in 1956 until 1978. The catchword
of the protesters was "*dégage*" (get out). With the army refusing to suppress
the dissenters and the security police overwhelmed, Ben Ali took the only way
open to him: he departed for Saudi Arabia on January 14, 2011.

Young Egyptian radicals watched events in Tunisia with growing interest. If the Tunisians could get rid of their dictator, why not the Egyptians? On January 25, 2011—ironically, a holiday to honor Egypt's police

Arab Spring Day and night,
Egyptians of all ages went to
Cairo's Tahrir Square to protest
the ongoing military rule after
the ousting of Mubarak. Here,
protestors burn the midnight oil
to decry the dissolution of the
parliament by Egypt's Supreme
Constitutional Court, a move to
consolidate power in the hands
of military generals. Note the
man documenting the heated
demonstration with his video
camera (bottom left), whose
footage would probably have
found its way to a wide array of
social media sites for discussion
and further dissemination.

forces—Egyptians of all backgrounds and ages assembled in Cairo's major plaza, Tahrir (Liberation) Square, to let Egypt's president, Hosni Mubarak, know that he was no longer wanted. On February 11, 2011, just three weeks after the first mass demonstration, Mubarak left office, turning the reins of power over to the Supreme Command of the Armed Forces.

The ouster of Ben Ali and Mubarak sent shock waves throughout the Arab world and sparked an outpouring of protest in all of its major cities. The protesters' demands were consistent: the end of repression, the establishment of democratic institutions, and the ousting of rulers who had stayed in power too long and who did not represent the will of the people. The results were astonishing. Monarchs in Jordan and Morocco promised new constitutions. Bahraini Shiites successfully demanded a new constitution from their Sunni king, and Ali Saleh, ruler of Yemen since 1978, fled the country. Even Muammar Qaddafi, the Libyan strongman, in power since ousting King Idris in 1969, felt the sting of protest, though his ouster and eventual execution on October 20, 2011, owed as much to NATO air power as it did to the rebel army that rose up to unseat him.

Where did the uprisings come from? In the first place, the Arab people, most of whom were young and had known only authoritarian rule, resented the fact that the wave of democratic reforms that had swept other regions had passed them by. They saw no reason why they, too, should not have leaders who represented their wishes, rather than rigged elections and fraudulent referendums that supported the wishes of the ruling elites. The young came to be known as the generation in waiting—waiting for jobs that never seemed to appear; waiting to have enough money to move out of their parents' homes; waiting to get married and start families. The fact that Hafez al-Assad of Syria had passed power to his son, Bashar al-Assad, and that Hosni Mubarak in Egypt was grooming his son, Gamal, to succeed him, heightened their rage. Although the uprisings often took names that suggested peaceful protest—such as the Jasmine Revolution in Tunisia and the White Revolution in Egypt—in reality these outbursts reflected deep-seated and long-standing fury at rulers who were repressive, corrupt, and unresponsive to their people.

Dictatorships and monarchies lost control over the media. The Qatari television station and newspaper *Al Jazeera*, founded in 1995, became an open forum for all kinds of opinions. One of its most dramatic and widely quoted programs featured an intense discussion about whether the Arab people had the right, like those in the west, to criticize their leaders. In addition, mobile phones, Facebook, Twitter, and other social media helped dissenters communicate with one another and enabled groups to organize large assemblies outside the purview of the state.

The early results led euphoric protesters to believe that they could create new and more open societies. Dictators were ousted, free elections were held, and new constitutions were promised. But the progress was hard to sustain. In Tunisia, which thus far had accomplished more than the other states, a moderate Muslim Brotherhood party, Al-Nahda, won control of the parliament. Egypt, too, held elections that were won by the Muslim Brotherhood party, Justice and Development, but nullified by the courts. It also elected a Muslim Brotherhood president, Muhammad Morsi. Yet President Morsi failed to establish an inclusive government and was ousted by Egypt's military leader, General Abdel-Fattah el-Sisi. On June 4, 2014, el-Sisi was elected president, promising to restore order to Egypt and imprisoning a large number of Muslim Brothers. Rebels in Sinai and the western desert, drawing inspiration from the rise of ISIS (discussed shortly), have challenged Sisi's government. The liberals and secularists who initiated the revolt against Mubarak have seen their aspirations dashed.

By far, the most lethal outcome of the Arab Spring has occurred in Syria. Beginning on March 15, 2011, protesters demanded the ouster of President Bashar al-Assad, formed a Free Syrian Army, gained international recognition for their movement from the United States and European states, and led protests that resulted in violent confrontation with Assad's forces, which resorted to the use of chemical weapons (sarin gas and chlorine bombs). In August 2012, U.S. President Obama declared that the use of chemical weapons would cross a "red line." A year later, on August 21, 2013, the Syrian military killed nearly 1,500 civilians in Damascus. Video footage showed people with bodies twitching, foaming at the mouth after exposure to sarin gas. Since 2013, thousands of Syrians have been injured and hundreds killed in chemical attacks. By the summer of 2014, when the United Nations stopped officially counting, more than 400,000 Syrians had lost their lives in the conflict and 12 million had been displaced, of whom 5 million sought refuge in Turkey, Lebanon, and Jordan. Another 1 million risked their lives on rickety boats bound for Europe. Even while the Americans and many others considered Assad's days to be numbered, the Syrian president defied the protesters and his western critics by gaining financial aid from Iran and crucial—indeed, regime-saving—military support from Hezbollah (a Shiite party established in Lebanon) and Russia.

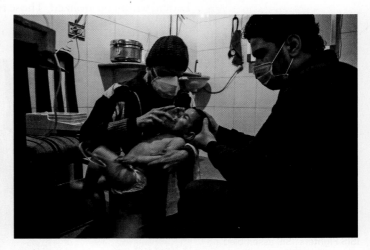

Syrian Chemical Weapons Use A child receives treatment after an alleged gas attack on the Sakba and Hammuriye areas in Eastern Ghouta, Syria on March 7, 2018.

Although Bashar al-Assad remains in power, and a general rules Egypt, at this writing, the forces unleashed by the Arab Spring are still at work. The ideals enunciated by the protesters—open societies representative of the people, which promote economic progress—are still vibrant in the region.

ISLAMIC MILITANCY

Islamic militancy, dominated by al-Qaeda in the 1990s and the first decade of the twenty-first century, changed significantly with the emergence of ISIS in the early 2000s. As the Americans clipped the power of al-Qaeda, killing many of its important leaders, ISIS rose to take its place, becoming an even more formidable opponent.

Al-Qaeda's agenda was based on the belief that the west, and especially the United States, was the main force standing in the way of Islam's rise. Thus, the first order of business was to challenge American power: hence the attack on the World Trade Center and the Pentagon. The leaders of al-Qaeda (notably the Saudi Osama bin Laden and the Egyptian Ayman al-Zawahiri) came from elite families and were gradualists in their vision of liberating the Muslim world from western influence, believing that an Islamic state could emerge only after American power had been eroded. They were also uncomfortable with the kinds of violence that more radical Islamists, like the founders of ISIS, urged upon their followers. U.S. Navy Seals killed Osama bin Laden where he was hiding out, though really in plain sight, in Abbottabad, Pakistan, but the United States has yet to find Zawahiri in spite of offering $25 million for information concerning his whereabouts.

The founder of ISIS, Abu Musab al-Zarqawi, was an unlikely leader. A heavy drinker, a brawler, and a high school dropout, he found religion—in his case, militant Islam—which became his salvation and the purpose of his life. Al-Zarqawi made his way to Afghanistan in the 1990s to meet Osama bin Laden, whom he idolized. Those meetings did not generate much enthusiasm,

ISIS Fighters ISIS assembled a powerful group of soldiers, many from foreign countries (including the United States and Europe), and created a territorial state in western Syria and northern Iraq.

probably because al-Qaeda's leadership considered him too violent and hot-headed. Nonetheless, some high-ranking members of al-Qaeda accepted him into their ranks. When the Americans chased al-Zarqawi out of Afghanistan, he made his way to Iraq, anticipating that the Americans would invade and that he could put his form of radical and militant Islam into action there.

As the American occupation of Iraq faltered, al-Zarqawi's vision of a violent jihadi world rose to prominence. Here, because of his willingness to employ extreme violence, such as beheading prisoners and burning them alive, he earned the nickname "the Sheikh of the Slaughterers." As much as al-Zarqawi hated Americans, his rage against Iraqi Shiites was even more intense. In a country where Sunnis had exercised power for centuries in spite of being a minority, the dominance of Shiites in the new American-supported government enraged al-Zarqawi and his Sunni followers.

Although American troops killed al-Zarqawi in June 2006, the movement he led resurrected itself and became known as ISIS. Its unlikely new leader, Abu Bakr al-Baghdadi, had neither military nor bureaucratic experience when he assumed leadership of ISIS in May 2010. He was an Islamic scholar, trained in some of the minor Iraqi Muslim schools, eventually gaining his doctorate by writing an exegesis of the Quran. But he had something that the parent organization, al-Qaeda, lacked: a territorial state, based in northern and central Iraq, which became even more formidable following the departure of American forces from the country. After moving into war-torn Syria and conquering Mosul in northern Iraq in 2014, ISIS also took the name Islamic Caliphate, and Baghdadi announced to the world that he was the new state's first caliph.

At its height, after the conquest of Mosul in 2014, ISIS controlled territories in central Syria and northern Iraq equivalent in area to the United Kingdom. It also had a population of between 6 and 9 million; an army of 30,000; a capital city, Raqqa, in Syria; and large financial resources, amassed though oil revenues, looting, and taxes. (For a look at the territory held by the Islamic State and the population of Shiite Muslims in the Middle East, see Map E.3 and Table E.1.) By August 2016, ISIS was reported to operate in eighteen countries around the world, including Afghanistan and Pakistan.

The territories under its control rapidly diminished thereafter. In 2017, American military sources claimed that 98 percent of territory ISIS controlled had been recaptured. The Iraqi government declared its war against ISIS over, and Russia announced a partial withdrawal of Russian troops from Syria. Whether ISIS can regroup and realize its global ambitions seems doubtful. But radical, militant Islam is here to stay.

THE IRANIAN NUCLEAR DEAL

In mid-June 2015, Iran and the United States, Russia, China, Britain, France, Germany, and the European Union reached an agreement on an issue that

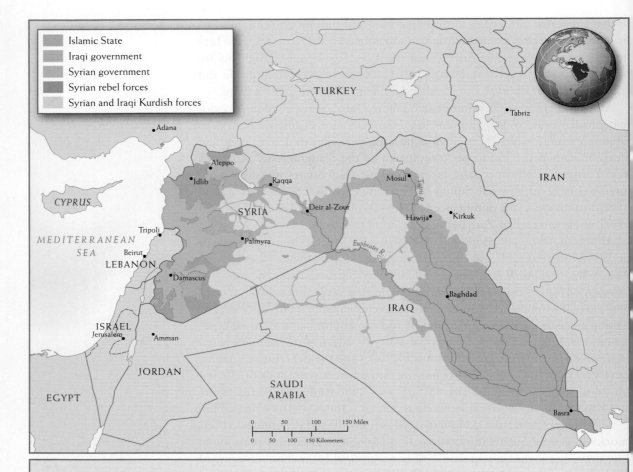

Map E.3 Warring Factions in Iraq and Syria, March 27, 2017

. . . .

This map shows the territories held by Kurdish fighters, ISIS, rebel Syrian fighters, and the Iraqi and Syrian governments.

- Compare the territories held by ISIS with the map of the boundaries set by the Sykes-Picot agreement (see Map 19.4). How similar are the territories that ISIS held in March 2017 to those that Sykes-Picot reserved for an Arab confederation?

- ISIS contends that the British-French agreements for the division of the Arab world after World War I need to be abolished. Why does ISIS hold these views?

- Why would the Turkish, Iraqi, and Syrian governments be dismayed that the Kurds have become the strongest militia fighting against ISIS?

Table E.1 Population of Shiite Muslims, 2009

	Estimated 2009 Shiite population	Approximate percentage of Muslim population that is Shiite
Iran	66–70 million	90–95
Iraq	19–22 million	65–70
Yemen	8–10 million	35–40
Azerbaijan	5–7 million	65–75
Syria	3–4 million	15–20
Lebanon	1–2 million	45–55
Kuwait	500,000–700,000	20–25
Bahrain	400,000–500,000	65–75
World total	154–200 million	10–13

Source: Mapping the Global Muslim Population (Washington, D.C.: Pew Research Center, October 7, 2009).

has troubled Iran's relations with the outside world for more than a decade and that resulted in the placing of severe economic sanctions on Iran. The agreement dealt with Iran's nuclear program, which the Iranians claimed was entirely for civil use; but the United States and many other countries believed that the Iranians were seeking to create nuclear weapon capability. The U.S. government, along with five other states, negotiated a nuclear agreement that was to run for ten years and would allow inspections of the Iranian nuclear facilities while permitting the Iranians to enrich uranium for civil, but not military, uses. The negotiating foreign powers agreed to lift the financial and economic sanctions, thus permitting Iran to engage in trade with the rest of the world and to gain access to its substantial financial resources, tied up in western banks.

Not everyone was pleased with the agreement. Benjamin Netanyahu, the Israeli prime minister, believed that the Iranians would subvert the treaty and build nuclear weapons. As a presidential candidate, Donald Trump called the agreement the worst ever signed; in 2018, as president, he pulled the U.S. out of the agreement. Trump further distanced the U.S. from its allies by agreeing to meet with North Korean dictator Kim Jong-un and accepting the latter's pledge to denuclearize without a timetable, an agreed-upon definition of what counts as denuclearization, or any measures of independent verification.

POVERTY, DISEASE, GENOCIDE

In much of the developing world, poverty, disease, and violence persist. The new millennium did not begin auspiciously for the peoples of Africa. The region remained the poorest in the world and suffered the uncontrolled and uncontrollable spread of HIV/AIDS. (For a global look at hunger and disparities in income, see Maps E.4 and E.5.)

Of the thirty-eight sub-Saharan African countries surveyed in the *World Bank Development Report* for 2009, all but seven were low-income countries. The poorest of the poor (Burundi, the Republic of the Congo, and Liberia) reported per capita incomes of U.S. $150 or less. Botswana, which enjoyed Africa's second-highest per capita income at $6,120 (behind only mineral-rich Gabon), was so devastated by HIV/AIDS that its average life expectancy, once the highest in Africa at close to seventy years, had tumbled to fifty-one years by 2007 and was one of the lowest in the world. (For a global look at HIV incidence, see Map E.6.) As Asian economies have prospered, Africa's share of global poverty has increased. In 2013, more than half of the people living in extreme poverty lived in Africa.

There have, however, been signs of progress. Ghana embraced parliamentary and presidential elections. Civil strife ended in Mozambique and Angola. South Africa convened a Truth and Reconciliation Commission to put the trauma of apartheid behind it and to stay on the course of parliamentary democracy while addressing the gross income inequality between whites and blacks that was a legacy of the twentieth century.

But these countries have been exceptions to the rule in a region where political instability has wrought misery and devastation. Many of Africa's countries (Liberia, Sierra Leone, Mali, the Ivory Coast, and the Central African Republic) were torn asunder by ethnic and personal rivalries, and the resulting conflicts required foreign interventions. Nigeria finally rid itself of its unwanted military dictatorship and moved to a civil, parliamentary system. But Nigeria's democratically elected presidents have barely been able to hold the country together. The people of the Niger Delta in the south of the country continue to rebel and to demand a larger share of the oil wealth their region produces, while in the impoverished northeast, a Muslim group calling itself Boko Haram (meaning no western learning) has carried out acts of shocking violence.

In 2011, just when Africa's longest-running civil war, pitting the animists and Christians of southern Sudan against the Muslim peoples of the north, had seemingly been resolved through the creation of a new state for the southerners, known as South Sudan, an ongoing dispute in western Sudan kept the Sudanese government in civil strife. In the region of Darfur, the state allowed local horse-riding nomads to carry out ethnic cleansing campaigns against settled agriculturalists. Thus, as in Rwanda in the 1990s (see Chapter 21), genocide has once more visited Africa. The conflict has also led to one of Africa's worst cases of displacement: as of 2018, over 4 million refugees have fled government terror and civil war to huddle in vast, miserable camps. But there is some reason for hope. In the West African country of Liberia, after years of pitiless civil war, the belligerents agreed to put down their guns in 2004. In 2005, remarkable elections swept Africa's first woman president, Ellen Johnson-Sirleaf, into office.

DEEPENING INEQUALITIES

Globalization has contributed to economic inequality in some of the poorest parts of the world. Compared with sub-Saharan Africa, Latin America's situation is not so bleak, but the divide between haves and have-nots has widened across the region, which has historically been the world's most unequal. The very rich in Buenos Aires live like the very rich in Boston; magnates of Mexico City drive the same cars, eat the same food, read the same books, and vacation in the same spots as their social cousins from New York. They send their children to private schools in the United States and the United Kingdom to join a cosmopolitan upper class. To Latin American elites, globalization has been a boon, as it has increased their wealth and has facilitated their integration into the international circulation of goods, ideas, and people. Many, in fact, identify less and less with a particular place in the world.

Some of the same features hold for the social bottom. Being disadvantaged and poor in southern Mexico looks a lot like being on the losing end in southern Africa: people cling to tiny parcels of land, migrate long distances for seasonal jobs, and fight against insensitive authorities for their basic needs. In many cases, the best solution to their problems is to leave—to move to cities or across borders in search of opportunities elsewhere.

Latin Americans have responded to these challenges in many ways. One sweeping trend is the election of left-wing governments. Most of these new leaders are not like the rebel firebrands of the 1960s. Instead, in Brazil, Chile, Argentina, and Uruguay, left-wing governments have offered policies designed to soften the blows of globalization and meet basic needs for land, schools, and decent housing. However, the same pressures of globalization that contribute to leftist electoral triumphs limit what these fledgling governments can do. Elsewhere, a more nationalist and populist brand of politics has emerged, one that rejects globalization altogether. Rather than softening the effects of globalization, its leaders promise to reverse them.

The appeal of anti-globalist politics is not limited to Latin America, or even to the developing nations. In the most advanced industrial societies, as well as in rapidly rising nations like China and India, programs to check globalization or buffer people from its destabilizing effects have found receptive

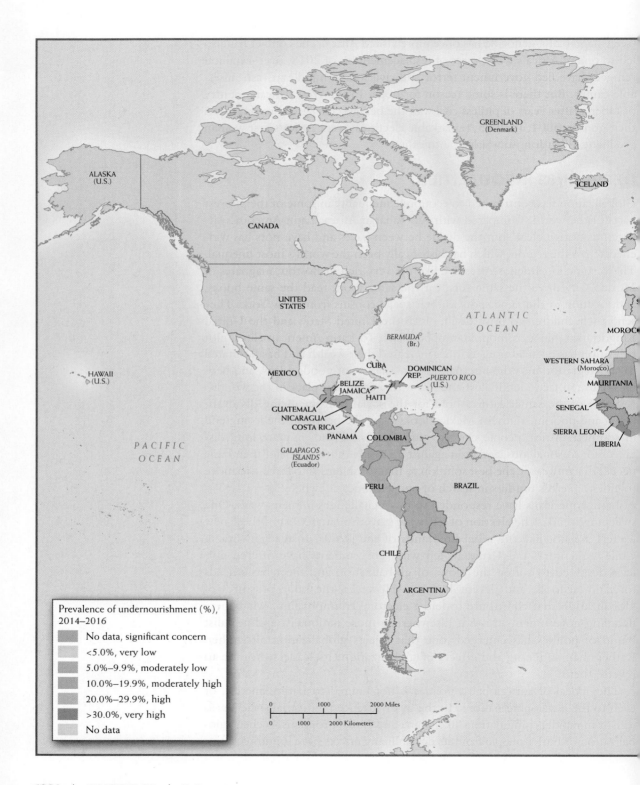

Prevalence of undernourishment (%), 2014–2016

- No data, significant concern
- <5.0%, very low
- 5.0%–9.9%, moderately low
- 10.0%–19.9%, moderately high
- 20.0%–29.9%, high
- >30.0%, very high
- No data

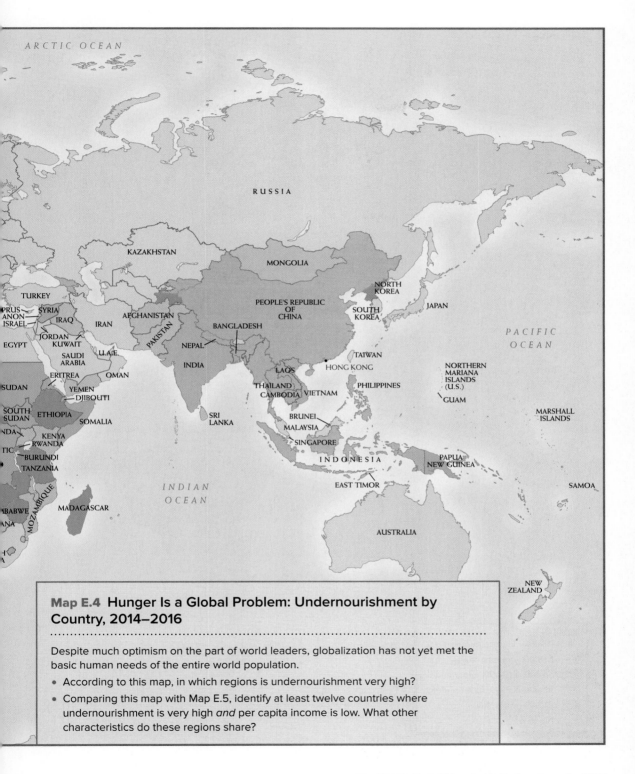

Map E.4 Hunger Is a Global Problem: Undernourishment by Country, 2014–2016

Despite much optimism on the part of world leaders, globalization has not yet met the basic human needs of the entire world population.

- According to this map, in which regions is undernourishment very high?

- Comparing this map with Map E.5, identify at least twelve countries where undernourishment is very high *and* per capita income is low. What other characteristics do these regions share?

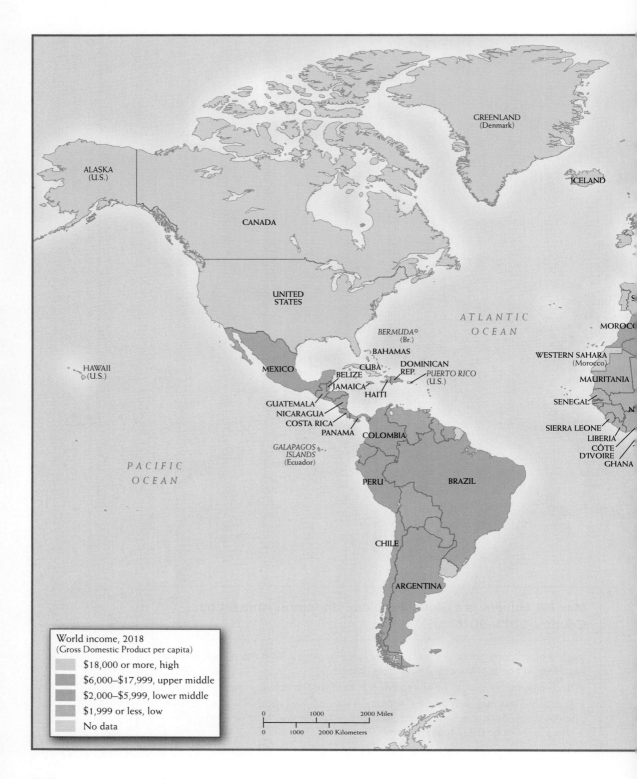

World income, 2018
(Gross Domestic Product per capita)

- $18,000 or more, high
- $6,000–$17,999, upper middle
- $2,000–$5,999, lower middle
- $1,999 or less, low
- No data

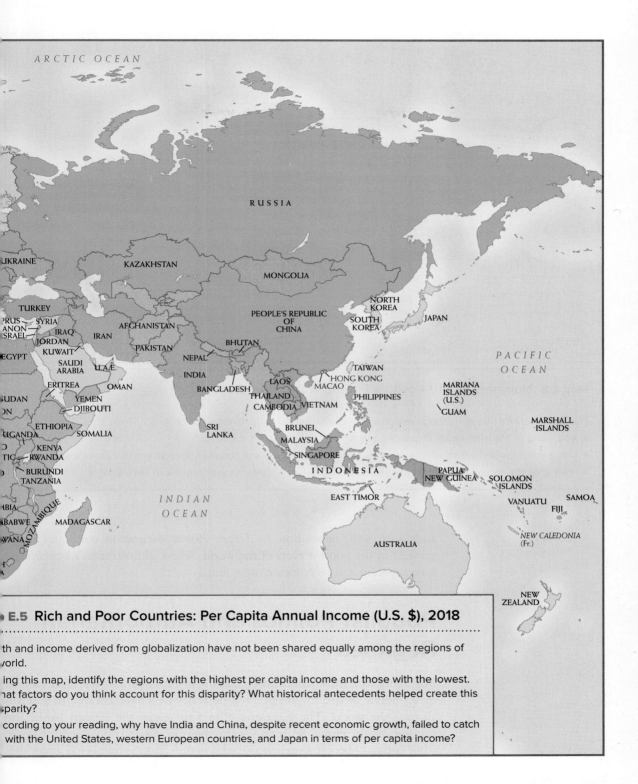

ARCTIC OCEAN

RUSSIA

UKRAINE

KAZAKHSTAN

MONGOLIA

NORTH
KOREA

TURKEY

PRUS   SYRIA
ANON   IRAQ
ISRAEL   JORDAN
                KUWAIT
EGYPT   SAUDI
         ARABIA   U.A.E.

AFGHANISTAN

IRAN

PAKISTAN

NEPAL

INDIA

PEOPLE'S REPUBLIC
OF
CHINA

SOUTH
KOREA

JAPAN

BHUTAN

TAIWAN
HONG KONG
MACAO

PACIFIC
OCEAN

ERITREA   OMAN
SUDAN   YEMEN
ON   DJIBOUTI

BANGLADESH

LAOS
THAILAND
CAMBODIA   VIETNAM

PHILIPPINES

MARIANA
ISLANDS
(U.S.)
GUAM

MARSHALL
ISLANDS

ETHIOPIA
UGANDA   SOMALIA
TIC   RWANDA
       KENYA
       BURUNDI
TANZANIA

SRI
LANKA

BRUNEI
MALAYSIA
SINGAPORE

INDONESIA

PAPUA
NEW GUINEA

SOLOMON
ISLANDS

SAMOA

VANUATU
FIJI

MBIA   MOZAMBIQUE
BABWE
WANA   MADAGASCAR

INDIAN
OCEAN

EAST TIMOR

AUSTRALIA

NEW CALEDONIA
(Fr.)

NEW
ZEALAND

E.5 Rich and Poor Countries: Per Capita Annual Income (U.S. $), 2018

th and income derived from globalization have not been shared equally among the regions of
vorld.

ing this map, identify the regions with the highest per capita income and those with the lowest.
nat factors do you think account for this disparity? What historical antecedents helped create this
sparity?

cording to your reading, why have India and China, despite recent economic growth, failed to catch
with the United States, western European countries, and Japan in terms of per capita income?

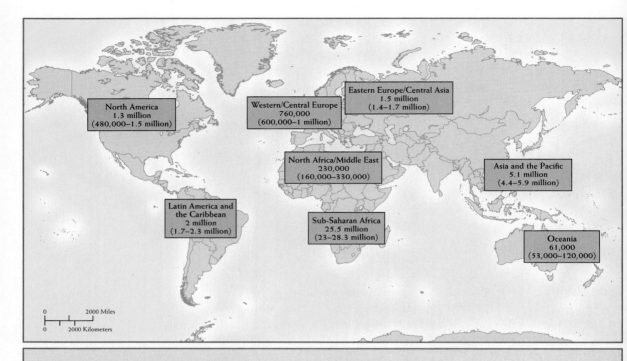

Map E.6 Numbers of HIV-Positive People Worldwide, 2016

The spread of HIV threatens the development of human capital in the twenty-first century.

- According to this map, which region has the highest rate of HIV infection?
- Using Maps E.4 and E.5 for reference, what connections do you see between poverty and HIV prevalence?
- How does the spread of HIV compromise economic development in poorer regions of the world?

audiences. Still, opposition to deeper global integration continues to be greatest in the poorest parts of the world, where globalization's benefits are least apparent and its costs are often lethal.

Populist Politics and Authoritarian Regimes

Beginning with the financial crisis of 2008, groups that have felt marginalized by economic inequality and political powerlessness have asserted themselves all over the world. The successful efforts to rescue the biggest banks and investors of the global financial system, many of which had caused the crisis, while ordinary people largely became its victims, led to widespread anger that

Inequality in São Paulo, Brazil
An aerial view of one of São Paulo's biggest slums, Favela Morumbi, which borders one of the city's richest neighborhoods, also called Morumbi.

was initially ignored—until political entrepreneurs perceived an opportunity. The last decade has experienced a resurgence of populist political sentiments that pit "the people" against their enemies. This politics of "us versus them" directs discontent and anger against illegitimate "others"—elites, immigrants, ethnic and religious minorities—that are portrayed as enemies of the nation. This kind of populism has taken many forms. In some countries, it has been highly autocratic. In democracies like those of Britain, Europe, and the United States, it has seen the rise of ethnic nationalists and the election or emergence of strong right-wing parties. In Britain, it also fueled the vote to leave the European Union.

In India, Prime Minister Narendra Modi rose to become that nation's strongman, claiming to embody the interests of the nation. With opposition parties dispirited and weak, he skillfully used social media to portray himself as a leader working tirelessly to advance India's interests against its foreign and domestic enemies. Taking a cue from their leader's aggressive nationalism, BJP politicians and Hindu vigilante groups targeted minorities, particularly Muslims.

In Turkey, similar religious and autocratic tendencies emerged under the presidency of Recep Tayyip Erdogan, who founded the Justice and Development Party (AKP) in 2001. Erdogan served as prime minister from 2003

Prime Minister Modi Meets with President Erdogan President Recep Tayyip Erdogan (*right*), of Turkey, met with the Indian Prime Minister, Narendra Modi, on November 16, 2015. Both men have used religion to enhance their popularity and the parties that they head, Erdogan fostering Islamism and Modi, Hinduism.

Families at the Border U.S. Border patrol agents stand at an open gate on the fence along the U.S.-Mexico border to allow Luis Eduardo Hernandez-Bautista to hug Ty'Jahnae Williams and his father, Eduardo Hernandez (not in view), as part of Universal Children's Day at the Border Field State Park, California, November 19, 2016.

until 2014 and thereafter as president, championing a party and movement that won an overwhelming majority in the parliamentary election in its first effort in 2001 and has been in control of Turkey's politics ever since. Although as mayor of Istanbul from 1994 to 1998, and then as prime minister, he promoted liberal and democratic policies, Erdogan embraced Islamist and authoritarian policies in the later years of his prime ministership (and especially after he became president). He intimidated journalists and intellectuals who opposed his efforts, and he curtailed freedom of speech, the press, and assembly. On July 15, 2016, a segment of the military attempted a coup d'état against the government, but their attempt failed, emboldening Erdogan to purge the country of people who favored liberal, secular policies. He obtained sweeping powers the following year in a referendum that shifted power decisively from the parliament to the executive, and in 2018 he was reelected president. Although Erdogan's Turkey is not an Islamic theocracy like Iran or a militant state like that of the Taliban in Afghanistan (and although it has joined the battle against ISIS), its shift toward Islamism and authoritarianism has been notable and has rendered its once-desired admission to the European Union impossible.

Nowhere did the rise of populism play out more dramatically than in the United States with the election of Donald Trump, an heir to a real estate fortune who became a celebrity thanks to television and new media such as Twitter. Even as he lost the popular vote, Trump won the U.S. presidency in 2016 by a majority of 77,000 combined votes in three hotly contested states, Pennsylvania, Michigan, and Wisconsin, which delivered his majority in the decisive Electoral College. Trump campaigned against immigration and free trade. Most fundamentally, he was supported by people who felt ignored in the national conversation and overlooked by the mainstream media and political establishment.

In many ways, Trump's campaign to "Make America Great Again" mirrored developments in Russia, even beyond the American president's profuse admiration for Russia's strongman leader. In Russia, too, a powerful sense of aggrieved nationalism, accusations of deception by the western media, contempt for any limits on executive power, and charges that the open, rules-based international order was rigged galvanized a wide following. The difference is that whereas Russia has always called into question the liberal world system, America created that system; U.S. withdrawal from that system therefore raises big questions about its future.

Conclusion: Globalization and Its Discontents

Globalization has had transforming effects, many of them decidedly good for large segments of the world's population, but some of them unsettling. Freer markets and international trade have created a global middle class, pulling nearly half a million Chinese out of poverty, as well as equally huge proportions of the poor in India, Southeast Asia, Egypt, Nigeria, South Africa, and many other communities around the world. Members of the new international middle class communicate with one another, read the same newspapers

Steelworkers Protest
Protestors demonstrate outside a rally for Republican presidential candidate Donald J. Trump at Ambridge Area Senior High School on October 10, 2016, in Ambridge, Pennsylvania. Ambridge, named after the American Bridge Company, a steel fabricating plant that once employed 60,000 workers, is traditionally a Democratic stronghold, but it shifted Republican as a shrinking tax base and lost jobs devastated the former industrial community. Donald Trump would carry Beaver County, PA, with nearly 60 percent of the vote.

and journals, see the same films, wear the same clothes, and eat the same foods. Nor is everything made in America, as the Nobel Prize in Literature, the leading film actors of the world, and the major commentators on increasingly international television and radio networks demonstrate. The extremely high economic growth rates enjoyed by states once regarded as part of the developing world could not have been achieved without international trade networks and significant free trade agreements.

Nonetheless, the negative effects of globalization have been much in evidence, especially since the financial crisis of 2008. While major banks and large multinational corporations were bailed out, the less well off suffered grievously. In America, the hardest hit were white workers between the ages of forty-five and fifty-four who lacked a high school education. Their death rates became alarmingly high as the result of suicide, drug addiction and overdosing, and alcoholism, bringing about for the first time an overall decline in the average life span of white males. The marginalized no longer remained silent, however. They voted overwhelmingly for Brexit (Britain's departure from the European Union) and contributed to the rise of Islamic militancy, Hindu nationalism, Turkey's turn toward Islamism and authoritarianism, and the increasing popularity of right-wing, ethnic nationalist parties in Europe, many of which oppose immigrant communities and balk at allowing refugees into their countries. In the United States, they elected Donald Trump, thereby turning away from the economic and security agreements that were central to American leadership in the post–World War II period and the initial efforts to contain climate change. In short, globalization has drawn the world more closely together, enhancing the life prospects of many, but threatening those groups who, deprived of education and marketable skills, are ill equipped to take advantage of globalism's opportunities.

Further Readings

Chapter 10: Becoming "The World," 1000–1300 CE

Allsen, Thomas, *Commodity and Exchange in the Mongol Empire: A Cultural History of Islamic Textiles* (1997). A study that uses golden brocade, the textile most treasured by Mongol rulers, as a lens through which to analyze the vast commercial networks facilitated by the Mongol conquests and control.

———, *Culture and Conquest in Mongol Eurasia* (2001). A work that emphasizes the cultural and scientific exchanges that took place across Afro-Eurasia as a result of the Mongol conquest.

Bagge, Svere, Michael Gelting, and Thomas Lundkvist (eds.), *Feudalism: New Landscapes of Debate* (2011). A collection of essays on interpretations of feudalism by experts on the topic.

Bartlett, Robert, *The Making of Europe: Conquest, Colonization and Cultural Change, 950–1350* (1993). The modes of cultural, political, and demographic expansion of feudal Europe along its frontiers, especially in eastern Europe.

Bay, Edna G., *Wives of the Leopards: Gender, Politics, and Culture in the Kingdom of Dahomey* (1998). A work that stresses the role of women in an important West African society and dips into the early history of this area.

Beach, D. N., *Shona and Zimbabwe, 900–1850: An Outline of Shona History* (1980). A good place to start for exploring the history of Great Zimbabwe.

Brooks, George E., *Landlords and Strangers: Ecology, Society, and Trade in Western Africa, 1000–1630* (1993). A survey assembled from primary sources of early West African history that stresses trans-regional connections.

Bulliet, Richard W., *Cotton, Climate, and Camels in Early Islamic Iran* (2009). An analysis of the upswing of the Iranian plateau economy after the Muslim conquest and its subsequent decline as a result of climate change.

Buzurg ibn Shahriyar of Ramhormuz, *The Book of the Wonders of India: Mainland, Sea and Islands*, ed. and trans. G. S. P. Freeman-Greenville (1981). A collection of stories told by sailors, both true and fantastic; they help us imagine the lives of sailors of the era.

Chappell, Sally A. Kitt, *Cahokia: Mirror of the Cosmos* (2002). A thorough and vivid account of the "mound people"; it explores not just what we know of Cahokia but how we know it.

Christian, David, *A Short History of Russia, Central Asia, and Mongolia*, vol. 1, *Inner Eurasia from Prehistory to the Mongol Empire* (1998). Essential reading for students interested in interconnections across the Afro-Eurasian landmass.

Curtin, Philip, *Cross-Cultural Trade in World History* (1984). A groundbreaking book on intercultural trade with a primary focus on Africa, especially the cross-Saharan trade and Swahili coastal trade.

Dawson, Christopher, *Mission to Asia* (1980). Accounts of China and the Mongol Empire brought back by Catholic missionaries and diplomats after 1240.

Di Cosmo, Nicola, Allen J. Frank, and Peter Golden (eds.), *The Cambridge History of Inner Asia: The Chinggisid Age* (2009). A definitive study of the Mongol period, written by the leading scholars of this period.

Ellenblum, Ronnie, *The Collapse of the Eastern Mediterranean: Climate Change and the Decline of the East, 950–1072* (2012). An analysis of the impact of freezing temperatures and drought on the societies of the eastern Mediterranean.

Foltz, Richard C., *Religions of the Silk Road: Overland Trade and Cultural Exchange from Antiquity to the Fifteenth Century* (1999). A study of the populations and the cities of the Silk Road as transmitters of culture across long distances.

Franklin, Simon, and Jonathan Shepherd, *The Emergence of Rus: 750–1200* (1996). The formation of medieval Russia between the Baltic and Black Seas.

Gibb, Hamilton A. R., *Saladin: Studies in Islamic History,* ed. Yusuf Ibish (1974). A sympathetic portrait of one of Islam's leading political and military figures.

Goitein, S. D., *Letters of Medieval Jewish Traders* (1973). The classic study of medieval Jewish trading communities based on the commercial papers deposited in the Cairo Geniza (a synagogue storeroom) during the tenth and eleventh centuries; it explores not only commercial activities but also the personal lives of the traders around the Indian Ocean basin.

————, *A Mediterranean Society: An Abridgment in One Volume,* rev. and ed. Jacob Lassner (1999). A portrait of the Jewish merchant community with ties across the Afro-Eurasian landmass, based largely on the documents from the Cairo Geniza (of which Goitein was the primary researcher and interpreter).

————, "New Light on the Beginnings of the Karim Merchant," *Journal of Social and Economic History of the Orient* 1 (1958). Goitein's description of Egyptian trade.

Goitein, S. D., and Mordechai A. Friedman, *India Traders of the Middle Ages: Documents from the Cairo Geniza* (2008). Collection of documents (translated into English) and authoritative essays that explore the eleventh- and twelfth-century trade conducted by several prominent Jewish families along the Mediterranean and Indian Ocean routes.

Harris, Joseph E., *The African Presence in Asia: Consequences of the East African Slave Trade* (1971). One of the few books that looks broadly at the impact of Africans and African slavery on the societies of Asia.

Hartwell, Robert, "Demographic, Political, and Social Transformations of China, 750–1550," *Harvard Journal of Asiatic Studies* 42 (1982): 365–442. A pioneering study of the demographic changes that overtook China during the Tang and Song dynasties, which

are described in light of political reform movements and social changes in this crucial era.

Historical Relations across the Indian Ocean: Report and Papers of the Meeting of Experts Organized by UNESCO at Port Louis, Mauritius, from 15 to 19 July, 1974 (1980). Excellent essays on the connections of Africa with Asia across the Indian Ocean.

Hitti, Philip, *An Arab-Syrian Gentleman and Warrior in the Period of the Crusades: Memoirs of Usāmah ibn-Munqidh* (1929). The Crusaders seen through Muslim eyes.

Hodgson, Natasha, *Women, Crusading, and the Holy Land in Historical Narrative* (2007). A book dealing with the Crusades and focusing on the place of women in them.

Holt, P. M., *The Age of the Crusades: The Near East from the Eleventh Century to 1517* (1984). The Crusades period as seen from the eastern Mediterranean and through the lens of a leading British scholar of the area.

Huff, Toby E., *The Rise of Early Modern Science* (2009). A bold attempt to look at the rise of scientific work in the Islamic world, premodern China, and Europe, seeking to explain why the scientific revolution occurred in Europe rather than the Islamic world or China.

Hymes, Robert, and Conrad Schirokauer (eds.), *Ordering the World: Approaches to State and Society in Sung Dynasty China* (1993). A collection of essays that traces the intellectual, social, and political movements that shaped the Song state and its elites.

Ibn Battuta, *The Travels of Ibn Battuta,* trans. H. A. R. Gibb (2002). A readable translation of the classic book, originally published in 1929.

Ibn Fadlan, Ahmad, *Ibn Fadlan's Journey to Russia: A Tenth Century Traveler from Baghdad to the Volga River,* translated with commentary by Richard Frye (2005). A coherent summary of the observations of an envoy who traveled from Baghdad to Russia.

Irwin, Robert, *The Middle East in the Middle Ages: The Early Mamluk Sultanate, 1250–1582* (1986). Egypt under Mamluk rule.

Jeppie, Shamil, and Souleymane Bachir Diagne (eds.), *The Meanings of Timbuktu* (2008). New materials on the ancient Muslim city of Timbuktu by scholars who have been preserving its manuscripts and writing about its historical importance.

Khazanov, Anatoly M., *Nomads and the Outside World,* 2nd ed., trans. Julia Crookurden, with a foreword by Ernest Gellner (1994). A classic overview of nomadism, based on years of research, covering all of the nomadic communities of Afro-Eurasia.

Lancaster, Lewis, Kikun Suh, and Chai-shin Yu (eds.), *Buddhism in Koryo: A Royal Religion* (1996). A description of Buddhism at its height in the Koryo period, when the religion made significant contributions to the development of Korean culture.

Levtzion, Nehemia, and Randall L. Pouwels (eds.), *The History of Islam in Africa* (2000). A useful general survey of the place of Islam in African history.

Lewis, Bernard (trans.), *Islam: From the Prophet Muhammad to the Capture of Constantinople,* vol. 2, *Religion and Society* (1974). A fine collection of original sources that portray various aspects of classical Islamic society.

Lopez, Robert S., *The Commercial Revolution of the Middle Ages, 950–1350* (1976). An account focusing on the development around the Mediterranean of commercial practices such as the use of currency, accounting, and credit.

Lyons, Malcolm C., and D. E. P. Jackson, *Saladin: The Politics of the Holy War* (1984; reprint, 2001). The fundamental revisionist work on one of the more important historical figures of the time.

Maalouf, Amin, *The Crusades through Muslim Eyes*, trans. Jon Rothschild (1984). The European Crusaders as seen by the Muslim world.

Marcus, Harold G., *A History of Ethiopia* (2002). An authoritative overview of the history of this great culture.

Mass, Jeffrey, *Yoritomo and the Founding of the First Bakufu: The Origins of Dual Government in Japan* (1999). A revisionist account of how the Kamakura military leader Minamoto Yoritomo established the "dual polity" of court and warrior government in Japan.

McDermott, Joseph, *A Social History of the Chinese Book: Books and Literati Culture in Late Imperial China* (2006). The history of the book in China since the Song dynasty, with comparisons to the book's role in other civilizations, particularly the European.

McEvitt, Christopher, *The Crusaders and the Christian World of the East: Rough Tolerance* (2008). Excellent work on the relations of religious groups in the Crusader kingdoms.

McIntosh, Roderik, *The Peoples of the Middle Niger: The Island of Gold* (1988). A historical survey of an area often omitted from other textbooks.

Moore, Jerry D., *Cultural Landscapes in the Ancient Andes: Archaeologies of Place* (2005). The most recent and up-to-date analysis of findings based on recent archaeological evidence, emphasizing the importance of local cultures and diversity in the Andes.

Mote, Frederick W., *Imperial China, 900–1800* (1999). Still the best work on this period, written by an expert on the full scope of Chinese history. The chapter on the Mongols is superb.

Niane, D. T. (ed.), *Africa from the Twelfth to the Sixteenth Century*, vol. 4 of *General History of Africa* (1984). The fourth volume of UNESCO's history of Africa covers four centuries of African history. This work features the scholarship of Africans.

Oliver, Roland (ed.), *From c. 1050 to c. 1600*, vol. 3 of *The Cambridge History of Africa*, ed. J. D. Fage and Roland Oliver (1977). Another general survey of African history. This volume draws heavily on the work of British scholars.

Peters, Edward, *The First Crusade* (1971). The Crusaders as seen through their own eyes.

Petry, Carl F. (ed.), *Islamic Egypt, 640–1517*, vol. 1 of *The Cambridge History of Egypt* (1998). A solid overview of the history of Islamic Egypt up to the Ottoman conquest.

Polo, Marco, *The Travels of Marco Polo*, ed. Manuel Komroff (1926). A solid translation of Marco Polo's famous account.

Popovic, Alexandre, *The Revolt of African Slaves in Iraq in the 3rd/9th Century*, trans. Leon King (1999). The account of a massive revolt against their slave masters by African slaves taken to labor in Iraq's mines and fields.

Rossabi, Morris, *A History of China* (2014). Part of the Blackwell History of the World series and an excellent overview of Chinese history.

Scott, Robert, *Gothic Enterprise: A Guide to Understanding the Medieval Cathedral* (2003). The meaning and social function of religious building in medieval cities in northern Europe.

Shaffer, Lynda Norene, *Maritime Southeast Asia to 1500* (1996). A history of the peoples of the southeast fringe of the Eastern Hemisphere, up to the time that they became connected to the global commercial networks of the world.

Shimada, Izumi, "Evolution of Andean Diversity: Regional Formations (500 BCE–CE 600)," in Frank Salomon and Stuart Schwartz (eds.), *South America*, vol. 3 of *The Cambridge History of the Native Peoples of the Americas* (1999), pt. 1, pp. 350–517. A splendid overview that contrasts the varieties of lowland and highland cultures.

Steinberg, David Joel, et al., *In Search of Southeast Asia: A Modern History, rev. ed.* (1987). An account of the emergence of the modern Southeast Asian polities of Cambodia, Burma, Thailand, and Indonesia.

Tanner, Harold M., *China: A History* (2009). Along with Rossabi, an excellent overview of the full history of China.

Tyerman, Christopher, *God's War: A New History of the Crusades* (2006). The balance of religious and nonreligious motivations in the Crusades.

Waley, Daniel, *The Italian City-Republics*, 3rd ed. (1988). The structures and culture of the new cities of medieval Italy.

Watson, Andrew, *Agricultural Innovation in the Early Islamic World: The Diffusion of Crops and Farming Techniques, 700–1100* (1983). An impressive study of the spread of new crops throughout the Muslim world.

West, Charles, *Reframing the Feudal Revolution: Political and Social Transformation between Marne and Moselle, c. 800–c. 1100* (2013). Big change seen through an intensely studied region.

Wickham, Chris, *Sleepwalking into a New World: The Emergence of Italian City Communes in the Twelfth Century* (2015). Origins of the city democracies of medieval Italy.

Chapter 11: Crises and Recovery in Afro-Eurasia, 1300–1500

Barkey, Karen, *Empire of Difference: The Ottomans in Comparative Perspective* (2008). A revisionist view of the rise and flourishing of the Ottoman Empire.

Bois, Guy, *The Crisis of Feudalism: Economy and Society in Eastern Normandy, c. 1300–1550* (1984). A good case study of a French region that illustrates the turmoil in fourteenth-century Europe.

Brook, Timothy, *Praying for Power: Buddhism and the Formation of Gentry Society in Late Ming China* (1994). An analysis of the role of a significant religious force in the political and social developments of the Ming.

Clunas, Craig, and Jessica Harrison-Hall (eds.), *Ming: 50 Years That Changed China* (2014). Developed to accompany an exhibition at the British Museum, this catalog includes richly illustrated scholarly essays that explore clothing, jewelry, courtly objects, and commerce during the Ming dynasty.

Dardess, John, *A Ming Society: T'ai-ho County, Kiangsi, Fourteenth to Seventeenth Centuries* (1996). A work that covers the different changes and developments of a single locality in China through the centuries.

Dols, Michael W., *The Black Death in the Middle East* (1977). One of the few scholarly works to examine the Black Death outside Europe.

Dreyer, Edward, *Early Ming China: A Political History, 1355–1435* (1982). A useful account of the early years of the Ming dynasty.

Faroqhi, Suraiya N., and Kate Fleet (eds.), *The Cambridge History of Turkey*, vol. 2, *The Ottoman Empire as a World Power, 1453–1603* (2013). An overview of this crucial period in Ottoman history, written by experts in the field.

Finkel, Caroline, *Osman's Dream: The Story of the Ottoman Empire, 1300–1923* (2005). The most authoritative overview of Ottoman history.

Hale, John, *The Civilization of Europe in the Renaissance* (1994). A beautifully crafted account of the politics, economics, and culture of the Renaissance period in western Europe.

He, Yuming, *Home and the World: Editing the "Glorious Ming" in Woodblock-Printed Books of the Sixteenth and Seventeenth Centuries* (2013). An insightful exploration of Ming society through a close look at its vibrant print culture and market for books.

Hodgson, Marshall, *The Venture of Islam: Conscience and History in a World Civilization*, vol. 3 (1974). A good volume on the workings of the Ottoman state.

Hoffman, Philip T., *Why Did Europe Conquer the World?* (2015). Makes an interesting case for the importance of Europe's use of gunpowder technologies.

Itzkowitz, Norman, *Ottoman Empire and Islamic Tradition* (1972).

Another good book on the Ottoman state.

Jackson, Peter, *The Delhi Sultanate* (1999). A meticulous, highly specialized political and military history.

Jackson, Peter, and Lawrence Lockhart (eds.), *The Cambridge History of Iran*, vol. 6 (1986). A volume that deals with the Timurid and Safavid periods in Iran.

Jones, E. L., *The European Miracle* (1981). A provocative work on the economic and social recovery from the Black Death.

Kafadar, Cemal, *Between Two Worlds: The Construction of the Ottoman State* (1995). A thorough reconsideration of the origins of one of the world's great land empires.

Karamustafa, Ahmed, *God's Unruly Friends: Dervish Groups in the Islamic Later Middle Period, 1200–1550* (1994). A book that describes the unorthodox Islamic activities that were occurring in the Islamic world prior to and alongside the establishment of the Ottoman and Safavid empires.

Levathes, Louise, *When China Ruled the Seas: The Treasure Fleet of the Dragon Throne, 1405–33* (1994). A book that provides a lively account of the Zheng He expeditions.

Lowry, Heath W., *The Nature of the Early Ottoman State* (2003). New perspectives on the rise of the Ottomans to prominence.

McNeill, William, *Plagues and Peoples* (1976). A pathbreaking work with a highly useful chapter on the spread of the Black Death throughout the Afro-Eurasian landmass.

Morgan, David, *Medieval Persia, 1040–1797* (1988). Contains an informative discussion of the Safavid state.

Peirce, Leslie, *The Imperial Harem: Women and Sovereignty in the Ottoman Empire* (1993). A work that describes the powerful place that imperial women had in political affairs.

Pirenne, Henri, *Economic and Social History of Medieval Europe* (1937). A classic study of the economic and social recovery from the Black Death.

Reid, James J., *Tribalism and Society in Islamic Iran, 1500–1629* (1983). A useful account of how the Mongols and other nomadic steppe peoples influenced Iran in the era when the Safavids were establishing their authority.

Schäfer, Dagmar, *The Crafting of the 10,000 Things: Knowledge and Technology in Seventeenth-Century China* (2011). An innovative study of the philosophy of technology and crafts in the late Ming period with important implications for the global history of science.

Singman, Jeffrey L. (ed.), *Daily Life in Medieval Europe* (1999). An introductory description of the social and material world experienced by Europeans of different walks of life.

Tuchman, Barbara W., *A Distant Mirror: The Calamitous Fourteenth Century* (1978). A book that shows, in a vigorous way, how war, famine, and pestilence devastated Europeans in the fourteenth century.

Wittek, Paul, *The Rise of the Ottoman Empire* (1958). A work that contains vital insights on the emergence of the Ottoman state amid the political chaos in Anatolia.

Chapter 12: Contact, Commerce, and Colonization, 1450–1600

Axtell, James, *Beyond 1492: Encounters in Colonial North America* (1992). A wonderfully informed speculation about Indian reactions to Europeans.

Brady, Thomas A., Heiko A. Oberman, and James D. Tracy (eds.), *Handbook of European History 1400–1600: Late Middle Ages, Renaissance, and Reformation*, vol. 1, *Structures and Assertions* (1996). A good synthetic survey of recent literature and historiographical debates.

Brook, Timothy, *Vermeer's Hat: The Seventeenth Century and the Dawn of the Global World* (2008). An interesting look at the connections forged across the globe through the works of a well-known European artist.

Casale, Giancarlo, *The Ottoman Age of Exploration* (2010). The author places Ottoman exploration in a comparative context alongside European overseas expansion.

Cass, Victoria, *Dangerous Women: Warriors, Grannies, and Geishas of the Ming* (1999). An original study of Chinese female archetypes in memoirs, miscellanies, short stories, and novels.

Chaudhuri, K. N., *Trade and Civilisation in the Indian Ocean: An Economic History from the Rise of Islam to 1750* (1985). An excellent, comprehensive work that deals with the Indian Ocean economy and the appearance of European merchants there from the sixteenth century onward.

Clendinnen, Inga, *Aztecs: An Interpretation* (1991). Brilliantly reconstructs the culture of Tenochtitlán in the years before its conquest.

Crosby, Alfred W., *The Columbian Exchange: Biological and Cultural Consequences of 1492* (1972). A provocative discussion of the ecological consequences that followed the European "discovery" of the Americas.

———, *Ecological Imperialism: The Biological Expansion of Europe, 900–1900* (1986). Another important work on the ecological consequences of European expansion.

Curtin, Philip, *Cross-Cultural Trade in World History* (1984). A work stressing the role of trade and commerce in establishing cross-cultural contacts.

Faroqhi, Suraiya N. (ed.), *The Cambridge History of Turkey*, vol. 3, *The Later Ottoman Empire, 1603–1839* (2008). Definitive articles on this important period in Ottoman history.

Faroqhi, Suraiya N., and Kate Fleet (eds.), *The Cambridge History of Turkey*, vol. 2, *The Ottoman Empire as a World Power, 1453–1603* (2013). A collection of articles written by leading scholars of this crucial period in Ottoman history.

Febvre, Lucien, *The Problem of Unbelief in the Sixteenth Century: The Religion of Rabelais* (1982). A tour de force of intellectual history by the man who moved the study of the Reformation away from great men to the broader question of religious revival and mentalities.

Flynn, Dennis, and Arturo Giráldez (eds.), *Metals and Monies in an Emerging Global Economy* (1997). Contains several articles relating to silver and the Asian trade.

Frank, Andre Gunder, *ReOrient: Global Economy in the Asian Age* (1998). A reassessment of the role of Asia in the economic development of the world from around 1400 onward.

Glahn, Richard von, *The Economic History of China: From Antiquity to the Nineteenth Century* (2016). A masterful new survey of Chinese economic history.

———, *Fountain of Fortune: Money and Monetary Policy in China, 1000–1700* (1996). Includes an excellent analysis of the history of silver in Ming China.

Gruzinski, Serge, *The Conquest of Mexico* (1993). An important work on the conquest of Mexico.

Habib, Irfan, *The Agrarian System of Mughal India* (1963). One of the best studies on the subject.

Hall, Richard Seymour, *Empires of the Monsoon: A History of the Indian Ocean and Its Invaders* (1996). A very engaging journalistic account with fabulous details.

Hodgson, Marshall, *The Venture of Islam*, vols. 2 and 3 (1974). A magisterial work that includes the Indian subcontinent in its careful study of the political and cultural history of the whole Islamic world.

Hulme, Peter, *Colonial Encounters: Europe and the Native Caribbean, 1492–1797* (1986). Presents an interesting interpretation of the encounters of Europeans and Native Americans.

Lach, Donald F., *Asia in the Making of Europe*, 5 books in 3 vols. (1965–). Perhaps the single most comprehensive and innovative guide to the European voyages of discovery.

Lockhart, James, and Stuart Schwartz, *Early Latin America* (1983). One of the finest studies of European expansion in the late fifteenth century.

McCann, James, *Maize and Grace: Africa's Encounter with a New World Crop, 1500–2000* (2005).

Melville, Elinor G. K., *A Plague of Sheep: Environmental Consequences of the Conquest of Mexico* (1994). A history of the transformation of a valley in Mexico from the Aztec period to the era of Spanish rule.

Mignolo, Walter D., *The Darker Side of the Renaissance: Literacy, Territoriality, and Colonization* (1995). Uses literary theory and literary images to present provocative interpretations of the encounter of Europeans and Native Americans.

Ozbaran, Salih, *Ottoman Expansion toward the Indian Ocean in the 16th Century* (2009). An important treatment of the Ottoman entry into the Indian Ocean at a time when the Portuguese were also expanding there.

Pagden, Anthony, *European Encounters with the New World* (1993). A complex look at the deep and lasting imprint of the New World on its conquerors.

Parker, Geoffrey, *The Military Revolution: Military Innovation and the Rise of the West, 1500–1800* (1996). Traces the changes in technology and tactics in the early modern period and discusses the political significance of this "revolution."

Pelikan, Jaroslav, *Reformation of Church and Dogma (1300–1700)* (1988). An important overview of major religious controversies.

Phillips, William D., and Carla Rahn Phillips, *The World of Christopher Columbus* (1992). One of the finest studies of European expansion in the late fifteenth century.

Roper, Lyndal, *Martin Luther: Renegade and Prophet* (2016). A magisterial biography that demonstrates the ways in which Luther was a rebel but also a man of his time.

Russell-Wood, A. J. R., *The Portuguese Empire, 1415–1808* (1992). An important survey of early Portuguese exploration.

Chapter 13: Worlds Entangled, 1600–1750

Alam, Muzaffar, *The Crisis of Empire in Mughal North India* (1993). Represents the best of the new scholarly interpretations of the subject.

Bay, Edna, *Wives of the Leopard: Gender, Politics, and Culture in the Kingdom of Dahomey* (1998). A useful treatment of gender issues in Dahomey.

Blackburn, Robin, *The Making of New World Slavery: From the Baroque to the Modern, 1492–1800* (1997). A good place to begin when studying African slavery and the Atlantic slave trade, this book compares the early expansion of the plantation systems across the Atlantic and throughout the Americas.

Bushkovitch, Paul, *Peter the Great* (2016). An updated version of a standard work, offering a concise overview of one of Russia's most celebrated and energetic rulers.

Calloway, Colin G., *One Vast Winter Count: The Native American West before Lewis and Clark* (2003). A sweeping survey of North American Indian histories prior to the nineteenth century.

Crossley, Pamela, *A Translucent Mirror: History and Identity in Qing Imperial Ideology* (1999). The author deals with the formation of identities such as "Manchu" and "Chinese" during the Qing period.

Dale, Stephen F., *The Muslim Empires of the Ottomans, Safavids, and Mughals* (2010). A comparative overview of Islam's three most powerful empires of the sixteenth and seventeenth centuries.

Eltis, David, and David Richardson, *Atlas of the Transatlantic Slave Trade* (2010). This work contains the most up-to-date data on the Atlantic slave trade, including the numbers transported, where the captives came from, and where they landed.

Flynn, Dennis O., and Arturo Giráldez (eds.), *Metals and Money in an Emerging World Economy* (1997). A collection of articles about the place of silver in the world economy.

Forsyth, James, *A History of the Peoples of Siberia: Russia's North Asian*

Colony 1581–1990 (1992). A narrative overview of a violent history reminiscent of the western expansion of the United States.

Glahn, Richard von, *Fountains of Fortune: Money and Monetary Policy in China, 1000–1700* (1996). A discussion of the place of silver in the Chinese economy.

Halperin, Charles J., *Russia and the Golden Horde: The Mongol Impact on Medieval Russian History* (1985). A book on the rise of Muscovy, forebear of the Russian Empire, from within the Mongol realm.

Hämäläinen, Pekka, *The Comanche Empire* (2008). A book that inverts the conventional history of empires in North America by arguing that the Comanches were the most successful expansionist power in the middle of the continent during the eighteenth century.

Hartley, Janet, *Siberia: A History of the People* (2014). A vivid portrait of the diverse conquerors—fur traders, Cossack adventurers, political criminals—of a region larger than almost all continents.

Hattox, Ralph S., *Coffee and Coffeehouses: The Origins of a Social Beverage in the Medieval Near East* (1985). This work shows how widespread and popular coffee consumption and coffeehouses were around the world.

Herzog, Tamar, *Frontiers of Possession: Spain and Portugal in Europe and the Americas* (2015). An exploration of how Spanish and Portuguese rulers carved up the New World, less by military action and diplomatic treaties than by quarrels over land settlement and rights to trade and travel.

Huang, Ray, *1587, A Year of No Significance: The Ming Dynasty in Decline* (1981). An insightful analysis of the problems confronting the late Ming.

Lensen, George, *The Russian Push toward Japan: Russo-Japanese Relations 1697–1875* (1959). A discussion of why and how Japan established its first border with another state and how Russia pursued its ambitions in the Pacific.

Lockhart, James, *The Nahuas after the Conquest* (1992). A landmark study of the social reorganization of Mesoamerican societies under Spanish rule.

Lovejoy, Paul, *Transformations in Slavery: A History of Slavery in Africa* (1983). An excellent discussion of African slavery.

Mathee, Rudi, *Persia in Crisis, Safavid Decline, and the Fall of Isfahan* (2012). A study of the disintegration of the Safavid state.

Mikhail, Alan, *Nature and Empire in Ottoman Egypt: An Environmental History* (2011). An important study of the impact of the environment on Egypt in the eighteenth century.

Monahan, Erika, *The Merchants of Siberia: Trade in Early Modern Eurasia* (2016). A stirring account of entrepreneurs battling the harshest imaginable conditions to establish trading networks connecting the far-flung territories north of the ancient Silk Road.

Moon, David, *The Plough That Broke the Steppes: Agriculture and Environment in Russia's Grasslands, 1700–1913* (2013). A bold incorporation of environmental aspects to retell the epic story of Russia's most numerous social group.

Nakane, Chie, and Shinzaburo Oishi (eds.), *Tokugawa Japan: The Social and Economic Antecedents of Modern Japan* (1990). First-rate essays on Japanese village society, urban life, literacy, and culture.

Nwokeji, G. Uko, *The Slave Trade and Culture in the Bight of Biafra: An African Society in the Atlantic World* (2010). A study of the Aro peoples of southeastern Nigeria and their use of their commercial powers to promote a vigorous trade with European slavers on the coast.

Pamuk, Sevket, *A Monetary History of the Ottoman Empire* (2000). A discussion of the place of silver in the Ottoman Empire.

Parker, Geoffrey, Global Crisis: *War, Climate Change, and Catastrophe in the Seventeenth Century* (2013). A comprehensive and exhaustively researched study of the effects of the Little Ice Age on the governments and societies of the entire world in the seventeenth century.

——— (ed.), *The Thirty Years' War* (1997). The standard account of the conflict and its outcomes.

Perdue, Peter C., *China Marches West: The Qing Conquest of Central Asia* (2005). This volume chronicles the expansion of the Qing Empire to its northwest, drawing comparisons to other colonial empires and their legacies.

Platonov, S. F., *Ivan the Terrible* (1986). Covers the controversies over Russia's infamous tsar.

Rawski, Evelyn, *The Last Emperors: A Social History of Qing Imperial Institutions* (1998). This volume explores the mechanisms and processes through which the Qing court negotiated its Manchu identity.

Reid, Anthony, *Charting the Shape of Early Modern Southeast Asia* (1999). A collection of articles by a leading historian of Southeast Asia.

Spence, Jonathan, and John Wills (eds.), *From Ming to Ch'ing: Conquest, Region, and Continuity in Seventeenth-Century China* (1979). Covers the various aspects of a tumultuous period of dynastic transition.

Subramanyam, Sanjay, *From the Tigris to the Ganges: Explorations in Connected History* (2012). A study that demonstrates that Afro-Eurasia in the seventeenth and eighteenth centuries contained a porous network of empires, cultures, and economies.

Subramanyam, Sanjay, and Muzaffar Alam, *Indo-Persian Travels in the Age of Discoveries, 1400–1800* (2012). A lively portrait of cultural exchanges between Persia, central Asia, and India as seen in travel literature.

Taylor, Alan, *American Colonies: The Settling of North America* (2001). Brings together British, French, and Spanish colonial histories and shows how the fortunes of each were entangled with one another and with those of diverse Native American peoples.

Thornton, John K., *Africa and Africans in the Making of the Atlantic World, 1400–1800* (1998). A wonderful discussion of the large role African slaves played in the formation of the Atlantic world.

———, *The Kongolese Saint Anthony: Dona Beatriz Kimpa Vita and the Antonian Movement, 1684–1706* (1998). An excellent monograph on religious movements in the Kongo.

Toby, Ronald P., *State and Diplomacy in Early Modern Japan: Asia in the Development of the Tokugawa Bakufu* (1984). The author shows that the Japanese, far from being isolated from the outside world, engaged in vigorous and successful diplomacy.

Van Dusen, Nancy E., *Global Indios: The Indigenous Struggle for Justice in Sixteenth-Century Spain* (2015). A remarkable study of the ways that Spanish rulers enslaved Amerindians in the Americas and even exported them back to Europe.

Vilar, Pierre, *A History of Gold and Money* (1991). An excellent study of the development of the early silver and gold economies.

Chapter 14: Cultures of Splendor and Power, 1500–1780

Axtell, James, *The Invasion of America: The Contest of Cultures in Colonial North America* (1985). Discusses the strategies of Christian missionaries in converting the Indians, as well as the success of Indians in converting Europeans.

Babaie, Sussan, *Isfahan and Its Palaces: Statecraft, Shi'ism and the Architecture of Conviviality in Early Modern Iran* (2008). An overview of the city of Isfahan as the capital of the Safavid state.

Barmé, Geremie R., *The Forbidden City* (2008). A concise introduction to the history of one of the most important physical emblems of Chinese imperial power.

Berlin, Ira, *Many Thousands Gone: The First Two Centuries of Slavery in North America* (1998). Surveys the development of African-American culture in colonial North America.

Bleichmar, Daniela, *Visible Empire: Botanical Expeditions and Visual Culture in the Hispanic Enlightenment* (2012). A fascinating and beautifully illustrated history of creole botanical expeditions in the eighteenth century.

Brook, Timothy, *The Confusions of Pleasure: Commerce and Culture in Ming China* (1999). An insightful survey of Ming society.

Clunas, Craig, *Superfluous Things: Material Culture and Social Status in Early Modern China* (1991). A good account of the late Ming elite's growing passion for material things.

Collcutt, Martin, Marius Jansen, and Isao Kumakura, *A Cultural Atlas of Japan* (1988). A sweeping look at the many different forms of Japanese cultural expression over the centuries, including the flourishing urban culture of Edo.

Darnton, Robert, *The Business of the Enlightenment: A Publishing History of the Encyclopédie, 1775–1800* (1979). The classic study of Europe's first great compendium of knowledge.

Dash, Mike, *Tulipomania: The Story of the World's Most Coveted Flower and the Extraordinary Passions It Aroused* (1999). A global perspective on and lively account of the spread of the tulip around the world as a flower signifying both beauty and status.

Doniger, Wendy, *The Hindus: An Alternative History* (2009). A deeply scholarly yet accessibly written history of Hinduism that takes into account both texts and popular practices and contains a lively account of dissenting traditions.

Elman, Benjamin A., *On Their Own Terms: Science in China, 1550–1900* (2005). A study of the development of "native" Chinese science and how the process interacted with the introduction of western science to China over the course of three and a half centuries.

Eze, Emmanuel Chukwudi (ed.), *Race and the Enlightenment: A Reader* (1997). Readings examining the idea of race in the context of the Enlightenment.

Fleischer, Cornell, *Bureaucrat and Intellectual in the Ottoman Empire: The Historian Mustafa Ali (1540–1600)* (1986). Offers good insight into the world of culture and intellectual vitality in the Ottoman Empire.

Grafton, Anthony, April Shelford, and Nancy Siraisi, *New Worlds,*

Ancient Texts: The Power of Tradition and the Shock of Discovery (1995). A concise discussion of the impact of the New World on European thought.

Gutiérrez, Ramón, When Jesus Came, the Corn Mothers Went Away: Marriage, Sexuality, and Power in New Mexico, 1500–1846 (1991). A provocative dissection of the spiritual dimensions of European colonialism in the Americas.

Harley, J. B., and David Woodward (eds.), The History of Cartography, vol. 2, book 2, Cartography in the Traditional East and Southeast Asian Societies (1994). An authoritative treatment of the subject.

Hart, Roger, Imagined Civilizations: China, the West, and Their First Encounter (2013). A treatment of the Jesuit mission to China as the first contact between Chinese and European cultures.

Horton, Robin, Patterns of Thought in Africa and the West: Essays on Magic, Religion, and Science (1993). Reflections on African patterns of thought and attitudes toward nature, which can help us understand African-American religious beliefs and resistance movements.

Huff, Toby, Intellectual Curiosity and the Scientific Revolution: A Comparative Perspective (2011). This book deals with Europe's scientific revolution comparatively, asking why it occurred Europe and not in China or the Islamic world.

Kai, Ho Yi (ed.), Science in China, 1600–1900: Essays by Benjamin Elman (2015). Elman, an expert on Chinese science, offers his latest word on China's scientific achievements in a context of Europe's transmission of science through the Jesuit mission.

Keene, Donald, The Japanese Discovery of Europe: Honda Toshiaki and Other Discoverers, 1720–1798 (1952). A study of the ways Japan managed to incorporate knowledge from the outside world with the development of national traditions.

Ko, Dorothy, Teachers of the Inner Chambers: Women and Culture in Seventeenth-Century China (1994). Explores the lives of elite women in late Ming and early Qing China.

Lewis, Bernard, Race and Color in Islam (1979). Examines the Islamic attitude toward race and color.

Morgan, Philip D., Slave Counterpoint: Black Culture in the Eighteenth-Century Chesapeake and Lowcountry (1998). Describes the development of African-American culture in colonial North America.

Munck, Thomas, The Enlightenment: A Comparative Social History, 1721–1794 (2000). A wonderful survey, with unusual examples from the periphery, especially from Scandinavia and the Habsburg Empire.

Necipoğlu, Gülru, Architecture, Ceremonial, and Power: The Topkapi Palace in the Fifteenth and Sixteenth Centuries (1991). A magnificently illustrated book that shows the enormous artistic talent that the Ottoman rulers poured into their imperial structure.

"Publishing and the Print Culture in Late Imperial China," special issue, Late Imperial China 17, no. 1 (June 1996). Contains a collection of important articles with a foreword by the French cultural historian Roger Chartier.

Qaisar, Ahsan Jan, The Indian Response to European Technology, AD 1498–1707 (1998). A meticulous, scholarly work on this little-studied subject.

Rizvi, Athar Abbas, The Wonder That Was India, vol. 2, A Survey of the History and Culture of the Indian Sub-continent from the Coming of the Muslims to the British Conquest, 1200–1700 (1987). A deeply learned work in intellectual history.

Safier, Neil, Measuring the New World: Enlightenment Science and South America (2008). Examines the ways in which European, and especially Parisian, surveyors set about gauging the curvature of the earth, starting in Quito, Ecuador. Along the way, they learned much more about local natural history, which flowed back to Paris to inform the Enlightenment.

Smith, Bernard, European Vision and the South Pacific (1985). An excellent cultural history of Cook's voyages.

Smith, Richard J., Chinese Maps: Images of "All under Heaven" (1996). Provides a good introduction to the history of cartography in China.

Sorkin, David, The Religious Enlightenment: Protestants, Jews, and Catholics from London to Vienna (2008). Discusses a wide range of thinkers who were able to reconcile Enlightenment thought with religious belief.

Welch, Anthony, Shah Abbas and the Arts of Isfahan (1973). Describes the astonishing architectural and artistic renaissance of the city of Isfahan under the Safavid ruler Shah Abbas.

Whitfield, Peter, The Image of the World: Twenty Centuries of World Maps (1994). A good introduction to the history of cartography in different parts of the world.

Wilks, Ivor, Forests of Gold: Essays on the Akan and the Kingdom of Asante (1993). A study that focuses on the Asante's drive for wealth.

Zilfi, Madeline C., *The Politics of Piety: The Ottoman Ulema in the Post-Classical Age (1600–1800)* (1988). Explores the cultural flourishing that took place within the Islamic world in this period.

Chapter 15: Reordering the World, 1750–1850

Allen, Robert C., *The British Industrial Revolution in Global Perspective* (2009). The most recent and authoritative study of the industrial revolution in Britain and its implications around the world.

Anderson, Fred, *Crucible of War: The Seven Years' War and the Fate of Empire in British North America, 1754–1766* (2000). The best synthesis of the "great war for empire" that set the stage for the American Revolution.

Bayly, C. A., *Indian Society and the Making of the British Empire* (1998). A useful work on the early history of the British conquest of India.

Blackburn, Robin, *The Overthrow of Colonial Slavery, 1776–1848* (1988). Places the abolition of the Atlantic slave trade and colonial slavery in a large historical context.

Cassel, Par Kristoffer, *Grounds of Judgement: Extraterritoriality and Imperial Powers in Nineteenth-Century China and Japan* (2012). A study of the idea and practice of extraterritoriality within the context of the triangular relationship between China, Japan, and the west.

Chaudhuri, K. N., *The Trading World of Asia and the East India Company, 1660–1760* (1978). An authoritative economic history of the East India Company's operations.

Crafts, N. F. R., *British Economic Growth during the Industrial Revolution* (1985). A pioneering study that emphasizes a long-term, more gradual process of adaptation to new institutional and social circumstances.

Daly, M. W. (ed.), *Cambridge History of Egypt, vol. 2, Modern Egypt, from 1517 to the End of the Twentieth Century* (1998). Contains authoritative essays on all aspects of modern Egyptian history, including the impact of the French invasion and the rule of Muhammad Ali.

de Vries, Jan, *Industrious Revolution: Consumer Behavior and the Household Economy, 1650 to the Present* (2008). A book on the lead-up to the industrial revolution, written by the leading economic historian who coined the term "industrious revolution."

Diamond, Jared, and James A. Robinson (eds.), *Natural Experiments of History* (2010). This book consists of eight comparative studies drawn from history, archaeology, economics, economic history, geography, and political science, covering a spectrum of approaches, ranging from a nonquantitative narrative style to quantitative statistical analyses.

Drescher, Seymour, *Abolition: A History of Slavery and Anti-Slavery* (2009). A recent and authoritative overview of slavery and its opponents.

Dubois, Laurent, *Avengers of the New World: The Story of the Haitian Revolution* (2004). The most up-to-date synthesis on the Haitian Revolution.

Elvin, Mark, *The Retreat of the Elephants: An Environmental History of China* (2004). A study of the different ways in which China's natural environment was shaped.

Findley, Carter, *Bureaucratic Reform in the Ottoman Empire: The Sublime Porte, 1789–1922* (1980). A useful guide to Ottoman reform efforts in the nineteenth century.

Geggus, David (ed.), *The Impact of the Haitian Revolution in the Atlantic World* (2001). A lively effort to disentangle the effects of the Haitian Revolution from those of the French Revolution.

Hevia, James, *Cherishing Men from Afar: Qing Guest Ritual and the Macartney Embassy of 1793* (1995). Offers a definitive interpretation of the nature of Sino-British conflict in the Qing period.

Hobsbawm, Eric, *Nations and Nationalism since 1780* (1990). An important overview of the rise of the nation-state and nationalism around the world.

Howe, Daniel Walker, *What Hath God Wrought: The Transformation of America, 1815–1848* (2007). A Pulitzer Prize–winning interpretation of how new technologies and new ideas reshaped the economy, society, culture, and politics of the United States in the first half of the nineteenth century.

Hunt, Lynn, *Politics, Culture and Class in the French Revolution* (1984). Examines the influence of sociocultural shifts as causes and consequences of the French Revolution, emphasizing the symbols and practice of politics invented during the revolution.

Inikori, Joseph, *Africans and the Industrial Revolution in England* (2002). Demonstrates the important role that Africa and Africans played in facilitating the industrial revolution.

Isset, Christopher Mills, *State, Peasant, and Merchant in Qing Manchuria, 1644–1862* (2007). A study of the relationships between sociopolitical structures and peasant lives in a key region during the Qing.

James, C. L. R., *The Black Jacobins: Toussaint L'Ouverture and the San Domingo Revolution* (1938). A classic chronicle of the only successful slave revolt in history, it provides a critical portrait of their leader, Toussaint L'Ouverture.

Jones, E. L., *Growth Recurring* (1988). Discusses the controversy over why the industrial revolution took place in Europe, stressing the unique ecological setting that encouraged long-term investment.

Kinsbruner, Jay, *Independence in Spanish America* (1994). A fine study of the Latin American revolutions that argues that the struggle was as much a civil war as a fight for national independence.

Landers, Jane, *Atlantic Creoles in the Age of Revolutions* (2011). A collection of fascinating and unique portraits of Atlantic world creoles who managed to move freely and purposefully through French, Spanish, and English colonies, and through Indian territory, in the unstable century between 1750 and 1850.

Lieven, Dominic, *Russia Against Napoleon* (2010). Explains how outnumbered Russian forces were able to defeat the massive army that Napoleon assembled for his conquest of Russia.

Mokyr, Joel, *Enlightened Economy: An Economic History of Britain, 1700–1850* (2009). Perspectives on the evolution of the British economy in the era that produced the industrial revolution.

———, *The Lever of Riches* (1990). An important study of the causes of the industrial revolution that emphasizes the role of small technological and organizational breakthroughs.

Naquin, Susan, and Evelyn Rawski, *Chinese Society in the Eighteenth Century* (1987). A survey of mid-Qing society.

Neal, Larry, *The Rise of Financial Capitalism* (1990). An important study of the making of financial markets.

Nikitenko, Aleksandr, *Up from Serfdom: My Childhood and Youth in Russia, 1804–1824* (2001). One of the very few recorded life stories of a Russian serf.

Parthasarathi, Prasannan, *Why Europe Grew Rich and Asia Did Not: Global Economic Divergence, 1600–1800* (2011). A work that places the British industrial revolution in a global context, with much emphasis on India's textile industry before it was superseded by British manufacturers.

Pomeranz, Kenneth, *The Great Divergence: Europe, China, and the Making of the Modern World Economy* (2000). Offers explanations of why Europe and not some other place in the world, like parts of China or India, forged ahead economically in the nineteenth century.

Popkin, Jeremy D., *You Are All Free: The Haitian Revolution and the Abolition of Slavery* (2010). A revisionist account that calls attention to the role of local factors in the emancipation of Haiti's slaves.

Tackett, Timothy, *The Coming of the Terror in the French Revolution* (2017). An authoritative account of the most controversial phase of the French Revolution.

Taylor, Alan, *American Revolutions: A Continental History, 1750–1804* (2016). A sweeping interpretation of the founding of the United States that places the War of Independence in a North American perspective, bringing together the diverse revolutions that transformed societies and borders across the continent.

Wakeman, Frederic, Jr., "The Canton Trade and the Opium War," in John K. Fairbank (ed.), *The Cambridge History of China*, vol. 10 (1978), pp. 163–212. The standard account of the episode.

Wong, R. Bin, *China Transformed: Historical Change and the Limits of European Experience* (2000). Draws attention to the relative autonomy of merchant capitalists in relation to dynastic states in Europe as compared with China.

Wood, Gordon S., *Empire of Liberty: A History of the Early Republic, 1789–1815* (2009). An excellent synthesis of the history of the United States in the tumultuous years between the ratification of the Constitution and the War of 1812.

Wortman, Richard, *Scenarios of Power: Myth and Ceremony in Russian Monarchy*, 2 vols. (1995–2000). Examines how dynastic Russia confronted the challenges of the revolutionary epoch.

Chapter 16: Alternative Visions of the Nineteenth Century

Anderson, David M., *Revealing Prophets: Prophets in Eastern African History* (1995). Good discussion of the prophets in eastern Africa.

Beecher, Jonathan, *The Utopian Vision of Charles Fourier* (1983). A fine biography of this important thinker.

Boyd, Jean, *The Caliph's Sister: Nana Asma'u, 1793–1865, Teacher, Poet, and Islamic Leader* (1988). A study of the most powerful female Muslim leader in the Fulani religious revolt.

Brower, Benjamin Claude, *A Desert Named Peace: The Violence of France's Empire in the Algerian Sahara, 1844–1902* (2009).

Examines colonial violence across a few fields of research and through multiple stories to reveal some unexpected causes—for instance, France's difficult revolutionary past and its sway on the military's institutional culture.

Clancy-Smith, Julia, *Rebel and Saint: Muslim Notables, Populist Protest, Colonial Encounter (Algeria and Tunisia, 1800–1904)* (1994). Examines Islamic protest movements against western encroachments in North Africa.

Clogg, Richard, *A Concise History of Greece* (1997). A good introduction to the history of Greece in its European context.

Dalrymple, William, *The Last Mughal: The Fall of a Dynasty: Delhi, 1857* (2007). A deeply researched and riveting account of Delhi during the 1857 revolt.

Danziger, Raphael, *Abd al-Qadir: Resistance to the French and Internal Consolidation* (1977). Still the indispensable work on this important Algerian Muslim leader.

Dowd, Gregory E., *A Spirited Resistance: The North American Indian Struggle for Unity, 1745–1815* (1992). Emphasizes the importance of prophets like Tenskwatawa in the building of pan-Indian confederations in the era between the Seven Years' War and the War of 1812.

Guha, Ranajit, *Elementary Aspects of Peasant Insurgency in Colonial India* (1983). Not specifically on the Indian Rebellion of 1857, but includes it in its pioneering "subalternist" interpretation of South Asian history.

Hamilton, Carolyn (ed.), *The Mfecane Aftermath: Reconstructive Debates in Southern African History* (1995). Debates on Shaka's *Mfecane* movement and its impact on southern Africa.

Hiskett, Mervyn, *The Sword of Truth: The Life and Times of the Shehu Usman dan Fodio* (1994). An authoritative study of the Fulani revolt in northern Nigeria.

Johnson, Douglas H., *Nuer Prophets: A History of Prophecy from the Upper Nile in the Nineteenth and Twentieth Centuries* (1994). Deals with African prophetic and charismatic movements in eastern Africa.

Keddie, Nikki, *An Islamic Response to Imperialism: Political and Religious Writings of Sayyid Jamal ad-Din "al-Afghani"* (1968). Definitive information on the Afghani's life and influence, coupled with a translation of one of his most important essays.

Michael, Franz, and Chung-li Chang, *The Taiping Rebellion: History and Documents,* 3 vols. (1966–1971). The basic source for the history of the Taiping.

Mukherjee, Rudrangshu, *Awadh in Revolt 1857–58* (1984). A careful case study of the Indian Rebellion.

Omer-Cooper, J. D., *The Zulu Aftermath: A Nineteenth-Century Revolution in Bantu Africa* (1966). A good place to start in studying Shaka's *Mfecane* movement, which greatly rearranged the political and ethnic makeup of southern Africa.

Ostler, Jeffrey, *The Plains Sioux and U.S. Colonialism from Lewis and Clark to Wounded Knee* (2004). Uses the lens of colonial theory to track relations between the Sioux and the United States, offering fresh insights about the Ghost Dance movement.

Peires, J. B. (ed.), *Before and After Shaka* (1981). Discusses elements in the debate over Shaka's *Mfecane* movement.

Pilbeam, Pamela, *French Socialists before Marx: Workers, Women and the Social Question in France* (2001). Describes the development

of a variety of socialist ideas in early nineteenth-century France.

Platt, Stephen R., *Autumn in the Heavenly Kingdom: China, the West, and the Epic Story of the Taiping Civil War* (2012). A study of the Taiping Rebellion from a global perspective.

Reed, Nelson, *The Caste War of Yucatan* (1964). A classic narrative of the Caste War of the Yucatán.

Restall, Matthew, *The Maya World* (1997). Describes in economic and social terms the origins of the Yucatán upheaval in southern Mexico.

Rugeley, Terry, *Rebellion Now and Forever: Mayans, Hispanics, and Caste War Violence in Yucatán, 1800–1880* (2009). Explains the combination of economic and cultural pressures that drove the Maya in the Yucatán to revolt in the Caste War.

Spence, Jonathan, *God's Chinese Son: The Taiping Heavenly Kingdom of Hong Xiuquan* (1996). A fascinating portrayal of the Taiping through the prism of its founder.

Sperber, Jonathan, *Karl Marx: A Nineteenth-Century Life* (2013). An engaging and authoritative biography of Marx that emphasizes his role as a radical journalist.

Stedman Jones, Gareth, *Karl Marx: Greatness and Illusion* (2016). Now the authoritative biography of the founder of communism, showing Marx's own ambivalence about what he had created.

Wagner, Rudolf, *Reenacting the Heavenly Vision: The Role of Religion in the Taiping Rebellion* (1982). A brief but insightful analysis of the religious elements in the Taiping's doctrines.

White, Richard, *The Middle Ground: Indians, Empires, and Republics in the Great Lakes Region, 1650–1815* (1991). A pathbreaking exploration of intercultural relations in North America that offers a provocative interpretation of the visions of Tenskwatawa and the efforts of Tecumseh to resist the expansion of the United States.

Chapter 17: Nations and Empires, 1850–1914

Berry, Sara, *Cocoa, Custom and Socio-Economic Change in Western Nigeria* (1975). Innovative study based on interviews with local farmers that suggests that farmer enterprise and microeconomic theory better explain the spectacular growth in cocoa production than grand economic theory.

Cain, P. A., and A. G. Hopkins, *British Imperialism: Innovation and Expansion, 1688–1914* (1993). An excellent discussion of British imperialism, especially British expansion into Africa.

Clark, Christopher, *Iron Kingdom: The Rise and Downfall of Prussia, 1600–1947* (2009). Includes an excellent discussion of the rise of German nationalism and Prussian power.

Cooper, Frederick, *Colonialism in Question: Theory, Knowledge, History* (2005). A collection of essays by one of the leading scholars of colonial studies.

Cronon, William, *Nature's Metropolis: Chicago and the Great West* (1991). Makes connections among territorial expansion, industrialization, and urban development.

Davis, John, *Conflict and Control: Law and Order in Nineteenth-Century Italy* (1988). A superb study of the north-south and other rifts after Italian political unification.

Frankel, S. Herbert, *Capital Investment in Africa: Its Course and Effects* (1938). A careful study based on a mass of detailed figures and statistics on the general economic development of states in sub-Saharan Africa.

Friesen, Gerald, *The Canadian Prairies* (1984). The most comprehensive account of Canadian westward expansion.

Gluck, Carol, *Japan's Modern Myths: Ideology in the Late Meiji Period* (1985). A study of how states fashion useful historical traditions to consolidate and legitimize their rule.

Headrick, Daniel R., *The Tools of Empire: Technology and European Imperialism in the Nineteenth Century* (1981). A useful general study of the relationship between imperialism and technology.

Herbst, Jeffrey, *States and Power in Africa: Comparative Lessons in Authority and Control* (2000). An overview of the impact of colonial rule on contemporary African states.

Hill, Polly, *The Gold Coast Cocoa Farmer: A Preliminary Survey* (1965). A socioeconomic report detailing three issues facing the cocoa farmer: labor; indebtedness and pledging; and income and expenditure.

Hine, Robert V., and John Mack Faragher, *The American West: A New Interpretive History* (2000). Presents an excellent synthesis of the conquests by which the United States expanded from the Atlantic to the Pacific.

Hobsbawm, Eric J., *Nations and Nationalism since 1780: Programme, Myth, Reality* (1993). An insightful survey of the origins and development of nationalist thought throughout Europe.

Hochschild, Adam, *King Leopold's Ghost* (1998). A full-scale, eminently readable study of Europe's most egregiously destructive colonial regime in Africa.

Judson, Peter, *The Habsburg Empire: A New History* (2016). An innovative history of the relationship between "the people" and the state in a multiethnic empire.

Lee, Leo Ou-fan, and Andrew Nathan, "The Beginnings of Mass Culture: Journalism and Fiction in the Late Ch'ing and Beyond," in David Johnson, Andrew Nathan, and Evelyn Rawski (eds.), *Popular Culture in Late Imperial China* (1985), pp. 360–95. An important article on the emergence of a mass-media market in late nineteenth- and early twentieth-century China.

Lieven, Dominic, *Empire: The Russian Empire and Its Rivals* (2000). A comparison of the British, Ottoman, Habsburg, and Russian empires.

Mackenzie, John M., *Propaganda and Empire* (1984). Contains a series of useful chapters showing the importance of the empire to Britain.

Mamdani, Mahmood, *Citizen and State: Contemporary Africa and the Legacy of Late Colonialism* (1996). A survey of the impact of European colonial powers on African political systems.

McClintock, Anne, *Imperial Leather: Race, Gender and Sexuality in the Colonial Contest* (1995). A study of the imperial relationship between Victorian Britain and South Africa from the point of view of cultural studies.

McNeil, William, *Europe's Steppe Frontier: 1500–1800* (1964). An excellent study of the definitive victory of Russia's agricultural empire over grazing nomads and independent frontier people.

Mitchell, B. R., *International Historical Statistics: Africa, Asia, and Oceania, 1750–2005* (2007). This comparative volume provides data from over two centuries for all principal areas of economic and social activity in both eastern and western Europe.

Montgomery, David, *The Fall of the House of Labor: The Workplace, the State, and American Labor Activism, 1865–1925* (1987). An excellent discussion of changes in work in the late nineteenth century.

Myers, Ramon, and Mark Peattie (eds.), *The Japanese Colonial Empire, 1895–1945* (1984). A collection of essays exploring different aspects of Japanese colonialism.

Needell, Jeffrey, *A Tropical Belle Epoque: Elite Culture and Society in Turn-of-the-Century Rio de Janeiro* (1987). Shows the strength of the Brazilian elites at the turn of the century.

Pan, Lynn (ed.), *The Encyclopedia of Chinese Overseas* (1999). A comprehensive coverage of the history of the Chinese diaspora.

Porter, Bernard, *The Absent-Minded Imperialists: What the British Really Thought about Empire* (2004). A careful dissection of the ways in which empire changed the British—and did not.

Prasad, Ritika, *Tracks of Change: Railways and Everyday Life in Colonial India* (2016). A detailed analysis of how railways transformed the everyday experience of Indians under colonial rule.

Stengers, Jean, *Combien le Congo a-t-il coûté à la Belgique* (1957). A detailed financial accounting of how much Leopold put into the Congo and how much he took out, underscoring just how ruthlessly he exploited this possession.

Topik, Steven, *The Political Economy of the Brazilian State, 1889–1930* (1987). An excellent discussion of the Brazilian state, and especially of its elites.

Walker, Mack, *German Home Towns: Community, State, and the General State, 1648–1871* (1971; reprint, 1998). A brilliant, street-level analysis of the Holy Roman Empire (the First Reich) and the run-up to the German unification of 1871 (the Second Reich).

Wasserman, Mark, *Everyday Life and Politics in Nineteenth-Century Mexico* (2000). Wonderfully captures the way in which people coped with social and economic dislocation in late nineteenth-century Mexico.

Weeks, Theodore R., *Nation and State in Late Imperial Russia: Nationalism and Russification on the Western Frontier, 1863–1914* (1996). A good discussion of the Russian Empire's responses to the concept of the nation-state.

White, Richard, *Railroaded: The Transcontinentals and the Making of Modern America* (2011). A searing exposé of the corruptions and a startling critique of the economic and environmental costs associated with the expansion of railroad lines across Canada, the United States, and Mexico.

Yung, Wing, *My Life in China and America* (1909). The autobiography of the first Chinese graduate of an American university.

Zarrow, Peter, *After Empire: The Conceptual Transformation of the Chinese State, 1885–1924* (2012). A history of the changing ideas regarding the Chinese state that eventually led to the abandonment of monarchical rule by the Chinese people.

Chapter 18: An Unsettled World, 1890–1914

Bayly, C. A., *The Birth of the Modern World, 1780–1914: Global Connections and Comparisons* (2004). A general study of the key political, economic, social, and cultural features of the modern era in world history.

Bergère, Marie-Claire, *Sun Yat-sen* (1998). Originally published in French in 1994, this is a judicious biography of the man generally known as the father of the modern Chinese nation.

Brinkley, Douglas, *Wilderness Warrior: Theodore Roosevelt and the Crusade to Save America* (2010). An important account of Roosevelt's environmental policies, based on new research.

Chatterjee, Partha, *The Nation and Its Fragments* (1993). One of the most important works on Indian nationalism by a leading scholar of "subaltern studies."

Conrad, Joseph, *Heart of Darkness* (1899). First published in a magazine in 1899, this novella contained a searing critique of King Leopold's oppressive and exploitative policies in the Congo and was part of a growing concern for the effects that European empires were having around the world, especially in Africa.

Esherick, Joseph, "How the Qing Became China," in Joseph W. Esherick, Hasan Kayali, and Eric Van Young (eds.), *Empire to Nation: Historical Perspectives on the Making of the Modern World* (2006). A study of the processes through which the Qing Empire became the nation-state of China.

———, *The Origins of the Boxer Uprising* (1987). The definitive account of the episode.

Everdell, William R., *The First Moderns: Profiles in the Origins of Twentieth-Century Thought* (1997). A rich account of the many faces of modernism, focusing particularly on science and art.

Finnane, Antonia, *Changing Clothes in China: Fashion, History, Nation* (2008). An exploration of changing Chinese identities from the perspective of clothing.

Gay, Peter, *The Cultivation of Hatred* (1994). A provocative discussion of the violent passions of the immediate pre–Great War era.

Gilmartin, Christina, et al. (eds.), *Engendering China: Women, Culture, and the State* (1994). Analyzes politics and society in modern China from the perspective of gender.

Hochschild, Adam, *King Leopold's Ghost: A Story of Greed, Terror, and Heroism in Colonial Africa* (1998). A well-written account of the violent colonial history of the Belgian Congo under King Leopold in the late nineteenth century.

Judge, Joan, *The Precious Raft of History: The Past, the West, and the Woman Question in China* (2008). An insightful exploration of the "woman question" in China at the turn of the twentieth century.

Katz, Friedrich, *The Life and Times of Pancho Villa* (1998). An exploration of the Mexican Revolution that shows how Villa's armies destroyed the forces of Díaz and his followers.

Keddie, Nikki, *An Islamic Response to Imperialism: Political and Religious Writings of Sayyid Jamal ad-Din "al-Afghani"* (1968). Definitive information on the Afghani's life and influence, coupled with a translation of one of his most important essays.

Kern, Stephen, *The Culture of Time and Space 1880–1918* (1986). A useful study of the enormous changes in the experience of time and space in the age of late industrialism in Europe and America.

Kuhn, Philip, *Chinese among Others: Emigration in Modern Times* (2008). An overview of the history of Chinese migration.

McKeown, Adam, *Melancholy Order: Asian Migration and the Globalization of Borders* (2008). An examination of global migration patterns since the mid-nineteenth century and how regulations designed to restrict Asian migration to other parts of the world led to the modern regime of migration control.

Meade, Teresa, *"Civilizing" Rio: Reform and Resistance in a Brazilian City, 1889–1930* (1997). A wonderful study of cultural and class conflict in Brazil.

Moon, David, *The Plough That Broke the Steppes: Agriculture and Environment on Russia's Grasslands, 1700–1914* (2013). A pathbreaking study of Russian environmental history before the twentieth century.

Morris, Edmund, *Theodore Rex* (2002). A thorough biography of Theodore Roosevelt.

Pick, Daniel, *Faces of Degeneration: A European Disorder, c. 1848–c. 1918* (1993). A study of Europe's fear of social and biological decline, particularly focusing on France and Italy.

Pretorius, Fransjohn (ed.), *Scorched Earth* (2001). A study of the Anglo-Boer War in terms of its environmental impacts.

Saler, Michael (ed.), *The Fin de Siècle World* (2014). A comprehensive anthology of essays on turn-of-the-century politics and culture across the world.

Sarkar, Sumit, *The Swadeshi Movement in Bengal* (1973). A comprehensive study of an early militant movement against British rule.

Schorske, Carl E., *Fin-de-Siècle Vienna: Politics and Culture* (1980). The classic treatment of the birth of modern ideas and political movements in turn-of-the-century Austria.

Trachtenberg, Alan, *The Incorporation of America: Culture and Society in the Gilded Age* (1982). A provocative synthesis of changes in the American economy, society, and culture in the last decades of the nineteenth century.

Wang, David Der-wei, *Fin-de-Siècle Splendor: Repressed Modernities of Late Qing Fiction, 1849–1911* (1997). A fine work that attempts to locate the "modern" within the writings of the late Qing period.

Warren, Louis, *Buffalo Bill's America: William Cody and the Wild West Show* (2005). A superb portrait of William F. Cody, the person; of Buffalo Bill, the persona Cody (and others) created; and of the popular culture his Wild West shows brought to audiences in Europe and North America.

Warwick, Peter, *Black People and the South African War, 1899–1902* (1983). An important study that reminds readers of the crucial involvement of black South Africans in this bloody conflict.

Womack, John, Jr., *Zapata and the Mexican Revolution* (1968). A major work on the Mexican Revolution that discusses peasant struggles in the state of Morelos in great detail.

Chapter 19: Of Masses and Visions of the Modern, 1910–1939

Akcam, Taner, *The Young Turks' Crime against Humanity: The Armenian Genocide and Ethnic Cleansing in the Ottoman Empire* (2012). An exhaustive examination of the factors that impelled the Turkish authorities to carry out ethnic cleansing against the Armenians during World War I.

Aksakal, Mustafa, *The Ottoman Road to War in 1914: The Ottoman Empire and the First World War* (2008). An important study of the personalities and factors that led the Ottomans to join with Germany and Austria-Hungary during World War I, a fateful decision that ultimately spelled the end of the Ottoman Empire.

Anderson, Scott, *Lawrence in Arabia: War, Deceit, Imperial Folly, and the Making of the Middle East* (2013). A new and authoritative biography of T. E. Lawrence, with significant new material on British policies in the Middle East as seen through the eyes of a strong pro-Arab figure.

Bloxham, Donald, *The Great Game of Genocide: Imperialism, Nationalism, and the Destruction of the Ottoman Armenians* (2005). The definitive work on the Armenian genocide, set in a wide historical context.

Brown, Judith, *Gandhi: Prisoner of Hope* (1990). A biography of Gandhi as a political activist.

Clark, Christopher, *Sleepwalkers: How Europe Went to War* (2012). A reexamination of the crucial role of Austria-Hungary in triggering the world war.

De Grazia, Victoria, and Ellen Furlough (eds.), *The Sex of Things: Gender and Consumption in Historical Perspective* (1996). Pathbreaking essays on how gender affects consumption.

Dumenil, Lynn, *The Modern Temper: America in the 1920s* (1995). A general discussion of American culture in the decade after World War I.

Fainsod, Merle, *Smolensk under Soviet Rule* (1989). The most accessible and sophisticated interpretation of the Stalin revolution in the village.

Friedman, Edward, *Backward toward Revolution: The Chinese Revolutionary Party* (1974). An insightful look at the failure of liberalism in early republican China through the prism of the short-lived Chinese Revolutionary Party.

Gelvin, James, *Divided Loyalties: Nationalism and Mass Politics in Syria at the Close of Empire* (1998). Offers important insights into the development of nationalism in the Arab world.

Horne, John (ed.), *A Companion to World War I* (2010). A collection of articles written by leading scholars of World War I; the most comprehensive and up-to-date work on this war.

———, *State, Society, and Mobilization during the First World War* (1997). Essays on what it took to wage total war among all the belligerents.

Johnson, G. Wesley, *The Emergence of Black Politics in Senegal* (1971). A useful examination of the stirrings of African nationalism in Senegal.

Kennedy, David M., *Freedom from Fear: The American People in Depression and War, 1929–1945* (1999). A wonderful narrative of turbulent years.

Kershaw, Ian, *Hitler*, 2 vols. (1998–2000). A masterpiece combining biography and context.

Kimble, David, *A Political History of Ghana* (1963). An excellent discussion of the beginnings of African nationalism in Ghana.

Kotkin, Stephen, *Magnetic Mountain: Stalinism as a Civilization* (1995). Recaptures the atmosphere of a time when everything seemed possible, even creating a new world.

———, *Stalin*, vol. 1, *Paradoxes of Power* (2014). A sweeping history of the tsarist regime, world war, Russian Revolution, civil war, and rise of Stalin.

Lambert, Nicholas A., *Planning Armageddon: British Economic Warfare and the First World War* (2012). Mines new archives to show that the British had an aggressive plan before the war to destroy Germany financially, which the British government approved and began to enact until the United States forced them to back off.

LeMahieu, D. L., *A Culture for Democracy: Mass Communication and the Cultivated Mind in Britain between the Wars* (1988). One of the great works on mass culture.

Lyttelton, Adrian, *The Seizure of Power: Fascism in Italy, 1919–1929* (1961). Still the classic account.

Marchand, Roland, *Advertising the American Dream: Making Way for Modernity, 1920–1945* (1985). An excellent discussion of the force of mass production and mass consumption.

Mazower, Mark, *Dark Continent: Europe's Twentieth Century* (1999). A wide-ranging overview of Europe's tempestuous twentieth century.

McGirr, Lisa, *The War on Alcohol: Prohibition and the Rise of the American State* (2016). Emphasizes the power of cultural reaction against modernity that brought about Prohibition and the irony that its enforcement helped to expand the power of the modern state.

McKeown, Adam, *Melancholy Order: Asian Migration and the Globalization of Border* (2008). A major study of the vast movement of peoples around the globe between the middle of the nineteenth and the twentieth centuries.

Morrow, John H., Jr., *The Great War: An Imperial History* (2004). Places World War I in the context of European imperialism.

Musgrove, Charles D., *China's Contested Capital: Architecture, Ritual, and Response in Nanjing* (2013). An exploration of how the Chinese Nationalist capital of Nanjing served as a focal point for the making of a nation and a new form of mass politics.

Nottingham, John, and Carl Rosberg, *The Myth of "Mau Mau": Nationalism in Kenya* (1966). Dispels the myths in describing the roots of nationalism in Kenya.

Pedersen, Susan, *The Guardians: the League of Nations and the Crisis of Empire* (2015). Skillfully reexamines the neglected effort to regulate the colonial world under a so-called mandate system.

Rosenberg, Clifford, *Policing Paris: The Origins of Modern Immigration Control between the Wars* (2006). Explores the first systematic efforts to enforce distinctions of nationality and citizenship status in a major urban setting.

Rutledge, Ian, *Enemy on the Euphrates: The British Occupation of Iraq and the Great Arab Revolt, 1914–1921* (2014). An impassioned investigation of Britain's effort to take control of the oil-rich territory of Iraq and the determined resistance of the Iraqi peoples.

Strand, David, *An Unfinished Republic: Leading by Word and Deed in Modern China* (2011). A study of how the need for popular support led to a new political culture characterized by public speaking and performance in early twentieth-century China.

Suny, Ronald Gregor, *"They Can Live in the Desert but Nowhere Else": A History of the Armenian Genocide* (2015). A careful, document-based analysis of the Armenian genocide.

Taylor, Jay, *The Generalissimo: Chiang Kai-shek and the Struggle for Modern China* (2009). The first serious biographical study of Chiang Kai-shek in English, although its reliance on Chiang's own diary as a source does raise some questions of historical interpretation.

Thorp, Rosemary (ed.), *Latin America in the 1930s* (1984). An important collection of essays on Latin America's response to the shakeup of the interwar years.

Tsin, Michael, *Nation, Governance, and Modernity in China: Canton, 1900–1927* (1999). An analysis of the vision and social dynamics behind the Guomindang-led revolution of the 1920s.

Vianna, Hermano, *The Mystery of Samba* (1999). Discusses the history of samba, emphasizing its African heritage as well as its persistent popular content.

Wakeman, Frederic, Jr., *Policing Shanghai, 1927–1937* (1995). An excellent account of Guomindang rule in China's largest city during the Nanjing decade.

Winter, J. M., *The Experience of World War* (1988). A comprehensive presentation of the many sides of the twentieth century.

Young, Louise, *Japan's Total Empire: Manchuria and the Culture of Wartime Imperialism* (1998). An innovative case study of Japanese imperialism and mass culture with broad implications.

Chapter 20: The Three-World Order, 1940–1975

Aburish, Said K., *Nasser: The Last Arab* (2004). An impressive look at Egypt's most powerful political leader in the 1950s and 1960s.

Anderson, Jon Lee, *Che Guevara: A Revolutionary Life* (1997). A sweeping study of the radicalization of Latin American nationalism.

Bayly, Christopher, and Tim Harper, *Forgotten Armies: Britain's Asian Empire and the War with Japan* (2004). A brilliant social and military history of the Second World War as fought and lived in South and Southeast Asia.

Chatterjee, Partha, *Nationalist Thought and the Colonial World: A Derivative Discourse?* (1986). An influential interpretation of the ideological and political nature of Indian nationalism and the struggle for a postcolonial nation-state.

Cook, Alexander C. (ed.), *Mao's Little Red Book: A Global History* (2014). A look at the global impact of the Chinese Cultural Revolution through the lens of the iconic "little red book" of quotations from Mao.

Crampton, R. J., *Eastern Europe in the Twentieth Century and After,* 2nd ed. (1997). Comprehensive overview covering all Soviet-bloc countries.

Dikötter, Frank, *Mao's Great Famine: The History of China's Most Devastating Catastrophe, 1958–1962* (2010). A recent detailed account of one of the greatest man-made disasters in twentieth-century history.

Dower, John W., *Embracing Defeat: Japan in the Wake of World War II* (1999). A prize-winning study of the transformation of one of the war's vanquished.

Elkins, Caroline, *Imperial Reckoning: The Untold Story of Britain's Gulag in Kenya* (2005). Pulitzer Prize–winning study of the brutal war to suppress the nationalist uprising in Kenya in the 1950s that ultimately led to independence for that country.

Evans, Martin, *Algeria: France's Undeclared War* (2011). Gives the history of the Algerian nationalist movements and provides an overview of the Algerian war for independence.

Feshbach, Murray, and Alfred Friendly, Jr., *Ecocide in the USSR: Health and Nation under Siege* (1992). A crucial study of ecological disasters in the Soviet Union.

Gao, Yuan, *Born Red: A Chronicle of the Cultural Revolution* (1987). A gripping personal account of the Cultural Revolution by a former Red Guard.

Gordon, Andrew (ed.), *Postwar Japan as History* (1993). Essays covering a wide range of topics on postwar Japan.

Hargreaves, John D., *Decolonization in Africa* (1996). A good place to start when exploring the history of African decolonization.

Hasan, Mushirul (ed.), *India's Partition: Process, Strategy and Mobilization* (1993). A useful anthology of scholarly articles, short stories, and primary documents on the partition of India.

Iriye, Akira, *Power and Culture: The Japanese-American War, 1941–1945* (1981). A discussion that goes beyond the military confrontation in Asia.

Jackson, Kenneth T., *Crabgrass Frontier: The Suburbanization of the United States* (1985). An insightful and influential consideration of the movement of the American population from cities to suburbs.

Jalal, Ayesha, *The Sole Spokesman: Jinnah, the Muslim League and the Demand for Pakistan* (1985). A study of the high politics leading to the violent partition of British India.

Keep, John L. H., *Last of the Empires: A History of the Soviet Union 1945–1991* (1995). A detailed overview of the core of the "Second World."

Morris, Benny, *Righteous Victims: A History of the Zionist-Arab Conflict, 1881–1999* (2000). On the Arab-Israeli War of 1948.

Pantsov, Alexander V., *Mao: The Real Story*, trans. Steven I. Levine (2012). A well-researched biography of Mao Zedong.

Patterson, James T., *Grand Expectations: The United States, 1945–1974* (1996). Synthesizes the American experience in the postwar decades.

Patterson, Thomas, *Contesting Castro* (1994). The best study of the tension between the United States and Cuba. Culminating in the Cuban Revolution, it explores the deep American misunderstanding of Cuban national aspirations.

Roberts, Geoffrey, *Stalin's Wars: From World War to Cold War, 1939–1953* (2007). A reassessment of Stalin's wartime leadership that conveys the vast scale of what took place.

Saich, Tony, and Hans van de Ven (eds.), *New Perspectives on the Chinese Communist Revolution* (1995). A collection of essays reexamining different aspects of the Chinese communist movement.

Schram, Stuart, *The Thought of Mao Tse-tung* (1989). Standard work on the subject.

Tignor, Robert L., *W. Arthur Lewis and the Birth of Development Economics* (2006). An intellectual biography of the Nobel Prize–winning, West Indian–born economist, who proposed formulas to promote the economic development of less developed societies and then sought to implement them in Africa and the West Indies.

Wiener, Douglas R., *A Little Corner of Freedom: Russian Nature Protection from Stalin to Gorbachev* (2002). A groundbreaking book about Russian environmentalism.

Zubkova, Elena, *Russia after the War: Hopes, Illusions, and Disappointments, 1945–1957* (1998). Uses formerly secret archives to catalogue the devastation and difficult reconstruction of one of the war's victors.

Chapter 21: Globalization, 1970–2000

Collier, Paul, *The Bottom Billion: Why the Poorest Countries Fail and What Can Be Done about It* (2007). Shows that despite the world's advancing prosperity, more than a billion people have been left behind in abject poverty.

Davis, Deborah (ed.), *The Consumer Revolution in Urban China* (2000). A look at the different aspects of the recent, profound social transformation of urban China.

Davis, Mike, *City of Quartz: Excavating the Future in Los Angeles* (1990). Offers provocative reflections on the recent history, current condition, and possible future of Los Angeles.

Dutton, Michael, *Streetlife China* (1999). A fascinating portrayal of the survival tactics of those inhabiting the margins of society in modern China.

Eichengreen, Barry, *Globalizing Capital: A History of the International Monetary System* (1996). An insightful analysis of how international capital markets changed in the period from 1945 to 1980.

Ferguson, Niall, and Moritz Schularick, "'Chimerica' and the Global Asset Market Boom," *International Finance* 10, no. 3 (Winter 2007): 215–39. Coined the term "Chimerica" to designate a single, intertwined economic entity made up of a productive partner, China, and a consuming partner, the United States.

Gourevitch, Philip, *We Wish to Inform You That Tomorrow We Will Be Killed with Our Families: Stories from Rwanda* (1999). A volume that reveals the hatreds that culminated in the Rwanda genocide.

Guillermoprieto, Alma, *Looking for History: Dispatches from Latin America* (2001). A collection of articles by the most important journalist reporting on Latin American affairs.

Han Minzhu (ed.), *Cries for Democracy: Writings and Speeches from the*

1989 Chinese Democracy Movement (1990). A collection of documents from the events leading up to the incident in Tiananmen Square on June 4, 1989.

Herbst, Jeffrey, *States and Power in Africa: Comparative Lessons in Authority and Control* (2000). Explores the political dilemmas facing modern African polities.

Honig, Emily, and Gail Hershatter, *Personal Voices: Chinese Women in the 1980's* (1988). A record of Chinese women during a period of rapid social change.

Huang, Yasheng, *Capitalism with Chinese Characteristics: Entrepreneurship and the State* (2008). A sharp, unsentimental inside look at China's market economy and its future prospects.

Kavoori, Anandam P., and Aswin Punathambekar (eds.), *Global Bollywood* (2008). A collection of essays by leading scholars of Indian cinema on different aspects of the processes by which the Hindi film industry became Bollywood.

Klitgaard, Robert, *Tropical Gangsters* (1990). On the intimate connections between corrupt native elites and international aid agencies.

Kotkin, Stephen, *Armageddon Averted: The Soviet Collapse, 1970–2000* (2001). Places the surprise fall of the Soviet Union in the context of the great shifts in the post–World War II order.

Macekura, Stephen, *Of Limits and Growth: The Rise of Global Sustainable Development in the Twentieth Century* (2016). Explores the rise of global environmental politics in the 1970s and 1980s and the debate about resources and climate change.

Mamdani, Mahmood, *When Victims Become Killers: Colonialism, Nativism, and the Genocide in Rwanda* (2001). Discusses the genocide in Rwanda in light of the legacy of colonialism.

Mehta, Suketu, *Maximum City: Bombay Lost and Found* (2005). Examines one of the great, and contradictory, cities in the era of globalization.

Miller, Chris, *The Struggle to Save the Soviet Economy: Mikhail Gorbachev and the Collapse of the USSR* (2016). An insightful analysis of internal debates in Moscow over rival directions for the Soviet economy and the response to Chinese reforms after 1978.

Mottahedeh, Roy, *The Mantle of the Prophet: Religion and Politics in Iran*, 2nd ed. (2008). Perhaps the best book on the 1979 Iranian Revolution and its aftermath.

Nathan, Andrew, and Perry Link, *The Tiananmen Papers* (2002). An inside look at the divisions within the Chinese elite in connection with the 1989 crackdown.

Portes, Alejandro, and Rubén G. Rumbaut, *Immigrant America*, 2nd ed. (1996). A good comparative study of how immigration has transformed the United States.

Prakash, Gyan, *Mumbai Fables* (2010). A spirited account of the rise of India's most modern city, a center of intellectual, commercial, and political vitality.

Prunier, Gerald, *Africa's World War: Congo, the Rwandan Genocide, and the Making of a Continental Catastrophe* (2009). A chilling discussion of the spillover effects of the Rwandan genocide on central, eastern, and southern Africa.

Punathambekar, Aswin, *From Bombay to Bollywood: The Making of a Global Media Industry* (2013). A study of the transformation of the Indian film industry that globalizes its content and reach.

Reinhart, Carmen, and Kenneth Rogoff, *This Time Is Different: Eight Centuries of Financial Folly* (2009). Explains the latest financial crash using historical perspective.

Ruggie, John Gerard, *Just Business: Multinational Corporations and Human Rights* (2013). Shows how even big businesses became involved in human rights advocacy.

Sen, Amartya, *Poverty and Famines: An Essay on Entitlement and Deprivation* (1982). A major study that reoriented the study of famines from a narrow concentration on food supply to broader questions of ownership, exchange, and democracy.

Sikkink, Kathryn, *The Justice Cascade: How Human Rights Prosecutions Are Changing World Politics* (2011). Shows how new forms of global organizing and new social norms are changing the political rules across borders.

Stein, Judith, *Pivotal Decade: How the United States Traded Factories for Finance in the Seventies* (2010). A comprehensive study of the rise of American banking and the decline of heartland industries.

Ther, Philipp, *Europe since 1989: A History* (2016). A concise account of European integration and neoliberalism since the fall of the Berlin Wall.

Van Der Wee, Hermann, *Prosperity and Upheaval: The World Economy, 1945–1980* (1986). Describes very well the transformation and problems of the world economy, particularly from the 1960s onward.

Westad, Odd Arne, *The Global Cold War: Third World Interventions and the Making of Our Times* (2007). A genuinely global perspective on the Cold War and its consequences.

Winn, Peter, *Americas: The Changing Face of Latin America and the Caribbean* (1992). A useful portrayal of Latin America since the 1970s.

Epilogue: 2001–The Present

Achcar, Gilbert, *Morbid Symptoms: Relapse in the Arab Uprising* (2016). An up-to-date overview of the difficulties that the proponents of the Arab Spring encountered, with long and detailed treatments of Syria and Egypt.

Blinder, Alan S., *After the Music Stopped: The Financial Crisis, the Response, and the Work Ahead* (2013). A definitive and detailed treatment of the Great Contraction.

Christensen, Thomas J., *The China Challenges: Shaping the Choices of a Rising Power* (2015). A survey of "China's Rise" and the challenges and choices the country faces in the contemporary world.

Cleveland, William L., and Martin Bunton, *A History of the Modern Middle East*, 6th ed. (2016). The sixth edition of an important textbook that covers the whole of the Middle East from 1800 to the present.

Cooper, Frederick, *Africa in the World: Capitalism, Empire, Nation-State* (2014). An overview of Africa's place in global history, based on the most recent scholarship.

Crutzer, Paul J., and Eugene F. Stoemer, "The Anthropocene," IGBP Newsletter, no. 41 (May 2000): 17–18. The first coining of the term Anthropocene and the argument for a new geologic epoch.

Darwall, Rupert, *The Age of Global Warming: A History* (2013). An accessible narrative describing how scientists became increasingly aware of the threat of climate change and the multinational effort to reduce carbon emissions.

Deaton, Angus, *The Great Escape: Health, Wealth, and the Origins of Inequality* (2013). An examination of rising inequality by a Nobel Prize–winning authority who emphasizes that contemporary well-to-do individuals have largely failed to help those not so fortunate to achieve their potential.

Eichengreen, Barry J., *Hall of Mirrors: The Great Depression and the Great Recession, and the Uses—and Misuses—of History* (2015). The expert on the Great Depression now writes about the Great Contraction.

Esposito, John L., Tamara Sonn, and John O. Voll, *Islam and Democracy after the Arab Spring* (2016). An analysis of the prospects of democracy in Muslim countries, with case studies of Tunisia, Egypt, and Turkey, among others.

Ferguson, James, *Give a Man a Fish: Reflections on the New Politics of Distribution* (2015). An analysis of social welfare programs in southern Africa, which involve cash payments to the poorest members of societies, and their implications for neoliberal capitalism.

Franco, Jean, *Cruel Modernity* (2013). An examination of the cultural dimensions of Latin America's experience with recent neoliberal policies and the tensions and violence of relatively stateless societies.

Friedman, Milton, and Anne Jacobson Schwartz, *A Monetary History of the United States, 1867–1960* (1963). A classic account of monetary policy. Still essential reading even though it leaves off in 1960.

Gerges, Fawaz A., *ISIS: A History* (2016). One of a series of books that explores the rise of ISIS and stresses the place of violence in building a new Islamic state.

Guillen, Mauro F., *The Architecture of Collapse: The Global System in the 21st Century* (2015). A work that stresses the interconnectedness and complexity of the global capitalist system and argues that global financial systems have an "intrinsic propensity to instability, disruption, and crisis."

Jaffrelot, Christophe, *Saffron Modernity in India: Narendra Modi and His Experiment with Gujarat* (2014). A political history of how Narendra Modi emerged dominant in Gujarat using anti-Muslim nationalist ideology, captured the leadership of the BJP, and built a personality cult that catapulted him to national leadership.

Judis, John, *The Populist Explosion: How the Great Recession Transformed American and European Politics* (2016). A book by a journalist and political analyst that argues that the contemporary populist upsurges on both the right and the left are responses to neoliberal globalization.

Kindleberger, Charles P., and Robert Aliber, *Manias, Panics, and Crashes: A History of Financial Crises*, 5th edition (2005). A brilliant overview of the financial crises that have beset the global economy prior to the Great Contraction of 2008.

Lepore, Jill, *The Whites of Their Eyes: The Tea Party's Revolution and the Battle over American History* (2011). A history of the American far right and the Tea Party and their imagination of a nostalgic American past.

Lynch, Marc, *The New Arab Wars: Uprisings and Anarchy in the Middle East* (2016). Brings the narrative of the Arab Spring and the ambitions of its diverse proponents up to the present.

McCants, William, *The ISIS Apocalypse: The History, Strategy, and Doomsday Vision of the Islamic State* (2015). An important study of ISIS based on a wide reading of its own publications.

McNeill, J. R., *Something New under the Sun: An Environmental History of the Twentieth Century* (2000).

An important overview of the environmental history of the twentieth century, with considerable statistical data that underscore the impact of humans on the environment and the atmosphere.

McNeill, J. R., and Peter Engelkes, "Into the Anthropocene: People and Their Planet," in Akira Iriye (ed.), *Global Interdependence: The World after 1945* (2014). Two environmental historians embrace the concept of the Anthropocene Epoch.

Milankovic, Brian, *Global Inequality: A New Approach for the Age of Globalization* (2016). Using the most up-to-date data on worldwide incomes, the author shows how the last quarter century has yielded a convergence in global income distribution across societies and the widening of a gap within societies.

Moubayed, Sami, *Under the Black Flag: At the Frontier of the New Jihad* (2015). A study of the rise of jihadism within the Arab world, with a concentration on Syria.

Muller, Jan-Werner, *What Is Populism?* (2016). The sharpest analysis yet of the nature and prospects of populism, especially its relations to political establishments, which it condemns but on which it depends.

Owen, Roger, *The Rise and Fall of Arab Presidents for Life, with a New Afterword* (2014). A study that examines the emergence of Arab leaders who endeavored to hold on to power for as long as they lived, with insights into the actions of those who brought many of those leaders down during the Arab Spring.

Pietz, David A., *The Yellow River: The Problem of Water in Modern China* (2015). A critical look at health and environmental issues in China today, from a historical perspective through the lens of one of its major rivers.

Radelet, Steven, *Emerging Africa: How Seventeen Countries Are Leading the Way* (2010). An Afro-optimist sees many African countries enjoying economic growth and political stability, proving that Africa can join much of the rest of the world in achieving economic and political progress.

———, *The Great Surge: The Ascent of the Developing World* (2015). An overview of the extraordinary progress that many of the countries in what once was called the Third World have achieved in the economic and political realms.

Reid, Michael, *Forgotten Continent: The Battle for Latin America's Soul* (2009). A journalistic account of how Latin America grappled with market openings, new democratic forces, and the search for policies to close the gap between the haves and have-nots.

Shambaugh, David, *China Goes Global: The Partial Power* (2013). An analysis of China's role in the global arena and its impact, from economics to culture.

Trenin, Dmitri, *Should We Fear Russia?* (2016). A clear-eyed view of what contemporary Russia is and is not.

Warwick, John, *Black Flags Flying: The Rise of ISIS* (2015). A detailed account of the leadership groups within ISIS and its relationship to al-Qaeda.

Weiss, Michael, and Hassan Hassan, *ISIS: Inside the Army of Terror* (2015). An account based on interviews and wide reading of western and Arabic sources on the rise of ISIS.

Wright, Lawrence, *The Looming Tower: Al-Qaeda and the Road to 9/11* (2006). A Pulitzer Prize–winning study of the origins and evolution of al-Qaeda.

———, *The Terror Years: From al-Qaeda to ISIS* (2016). Primarily a study of the decline of the power of al-Qaeda, which created an opening for the more territorially based ISIS.

Glossary

Abd al-Rahman III Islamic ruler in Spain who held a countercaliphate and reigned from 912 to 961 CE.

aborigines Original, native inhabitants of a region, as opposed to invaders, colonizers, or later peoples of mixed ancestry.

absolute monarchy Form of government in which one body, usually the monarch, controls the right to tax, judge, make war, and coin money. The term *enlightened absolutist* was often used to refer to state monarchies in seventeenth- and eighteenth-century Europe.

acid rain Precipitation containing large amounts of sulfur, which comes mainly from coal-fired power plants.

adaptation Ability to alter behavior and to innovate, finding new ways of doing things.

African National Congress (ANC) Multiracial organization founded in 1912 in an effort to end racial discrimination in South Africa.

Afrikaners Descendants of the original Dutch settlers of South Africa; formerly referred to as Boers.

Agones Athletic contests in ancient Greece.

Ahmosis Egyptian ruler in the southern part of the country who ruled from 1550 to 1525 BCE; Ahmosis used Hyksos weaponry—chariots in particular—to defeat the Hyksos themselves.

Ahura Mazda Supreme God of the Persians, believed to have created the world and all that is good and to have appointed earthly kings.

AIDS See HIV/AIDS.

Akbarnamah Mughal intellectual Abulfazl's *Book of Akbar*, which attempted to reconcile the traditional Sufi interest in the inner life within the worldly context of a great empire.

Alaric II Visigothic king who issued a simplified code of innovative imperial law.

Alexander the Great (356–323 BCE) Leader who used novel tactics and new kinds of armed forces to conquer the Persian Empire, which extended from Egypt and the Mediterranean Sea to the interior of what is now Afghanistan and as far as the Indus River valley. Alexander's conquests broke down barriers between the Mediterranean world and Southwest Asia and transferred massive amounts of wealth and power to the Mediterranean, transforming it into a more unified world of economic and cultural exchange.

Alexandria Port city in Egypt named after Alexander the Great. Alexandria was a model city in the Hellenistic world. It was built up by a multiethnic population from around the Mediterranean world.

Al-Khwarizmi Scientist and mathematician who lived from 780 to 850 CE and is known for having modified Indian digits into Arabic numerals.

Allied Powers Name given to the alliance between Britain, France, Russia, and Italy, all of which fought against Germany and Austria-Hungary (the Central Powers) in World War I. In World War II, the name was used for the alliance between Britain, France, and the United States, all of which fought against the Axis powers (Germany, Italy, and Japan).

allomothering System in which mothers relied on other women, including their own mothers, daughters, sisters, and friends, to help in the nurturing and protecting of their children.

alluvium Area of land created by river deposits.

alphabet A mid-second-millennium BCE Phoenician system of writing based on relatively few letters (twenty-two) that combined to make sounds and words. Adaptable to many languages, the alphabet was simpler and more flexible than writing based on symbols for syllables and ideas.

American Railway Union Workers' union that initiated the Pullman strike of 1894, which led to violence and ended in the leaders' arrest.

Amnesty International Nongovernmental organization formed to defend "prisoners of conscience"—those detained for their beliefs, race, sex, ethnic origin, language, or religion.

Amorites Name, which means "westerners," used by Mesopotamian urbanites to describe the transhumant herders who began to migrate into their cities in the late third millennium BCE.

Amun Once-insignificant Egyptian god elevated to higher status by Amenemhet (1991–1962 BCE).

Amun means "hidden" in Ancient Egyptian; the name was meant to convey the god's omnipresence.

Analects Texts that included the teachings and cultural ideals of Confucius.

anarchists Advocates of anarchism, the belief that society should be a free association of its members, not subject to government, laws, or police.

Anatolia The area now mainly known as modern Turkey. In the sixth millennium BCE, people from Anatolia, Greece, and the Levant took to boats and populated the Aegean. Their small villages endured almost unchanged for two millennia.

Angkor Wat Magnificent temple complex that crowned the royal palace of the Khmer Empire in Angkor, adorned with statues representing the Hindu pantheon of gods.

Anglo-Boer War (1899–1902) Anti-colonial struggle in South Africa between the British and the Afrikaners over the gold-rich Transvaal. In response to the Afrikaners' guerrilla tactics and in order to contain the local population, the British instituted the first concentration camps. Ultimately, Britain won the conflict.

animal domestication Gradual process that occurred simultaneously with or just before the domestication of plants, depending on the region.

annals Historical records. Notable annals are the cuneiform inscriptions that record successful Assyrian military campaigns.

Anti-Federalists Critics of the U.S. Constitution who sought to defend the people against the power of the federal government and insisted on a Bill of Rights to protect individual liberties from government intrusion.

apartheid Racial segregation policy of the Afrikaner-dominated South African government. Legislated in 1948 by the Afrikaner National Party, it had existed in South Africa for many years.

Arab-Israeli War of 1948–1949 Conflict between Israeli and Arab armies that arose in the wake of a U.N. vote to partition Palestine into Arab and Jewish territories. The war shattered the legitimacy of Arab ruling elites.

Aramaic Dialect of a Semitic language spoken in Southwest Asia; it became the lingua franca of the Persian Empire.

Aristotle (384–322 BCE) Philosopher who studied under Plato but came to different conclusions about nature and politics. Aristotle believed in collecting observations about nature and discerning patterns to ascertain how things worked.

Aryans Nomadic charioteers who spoke Indo-European languages and entered South Asia in 1500 BCE. The early Aryan settlers were herders.

Asante state State located in present-day Ghana, founded by the Asantes at the end of the seventeenth century. It grew in power in the next century because of its access to gold and its involvement in the slave trade.

ascetic One who rejects material possessions and physical pleasures.

Asiatic Society Cultural organization founded by British Orientalists who supported native culture but still believed in colonial rule.

Aśoka Emperor of the Mauryan dynasty from 268 to 231 BCE; he was a great conqueror and unifier of India. He is said to have embraced Buddhism toward the end of his life.

Assur One of two cities on the upper reaches of the Tigris River that were the heart of Assyria proper (the other was Nineveh).

Aśvaghosa First known Sanskrit writer. He may have lived from 80 to 150 CE and may have composed a biography of the Buddha.

Ataturk, Mustafa Kemal (1881–1938) Ottoman army officer and military hero who helped forge the modern Turkish nation-state. He and his followers deposed the sultan, declared Turkey a republic, and constructed a European-like secular state, eliminating Islam's hold over civil and political affairs.

Atlantic system New system of trade and expansion that linked Europe, Africa, and the Americas. It emerged in the wake of European voyages across the Atlantic Ocean.

Atma Vedic term signifying the eternal self, represented by the trinity of deities.

Atman In the Upanishads, an eternal being who exists everywhere. The atman never perishes, but is reborn or transmigrates into another life.

Attila Sole ruler of all Hunnish tribes from 433 to 453 CE. Harsh and much feared, he formed the first empire to oppose Rome in northern Europe.

Augustus Latin term meaning "the Revered One"; title granted by the Senate to the Roman ruler Octavian in 27 BCE to signify his unique political position. Along with his adopted family name, *Caesar*, the military honorific *imperator*, and the senatorial term *princeps*, *Augustus* became a generic term for a leader of the Roman Empire.

australopithecines Hominid species, including *anamensis*, *afarensis* (Lucy), and *africanus*, that appeared in Africa beginning around 4 million years ago and, unlike other animals, sometimes walked on two legs. Their brain capacity was a little less than one-third of a modern human's. Although not humans, they carried the genetic and biological material out of which modern humans would later emerge.

Austro-Hungarian Empire Dual monarchy established by the Habsburg family in 1867; it collapsed at the end of World War I.

authoritarianism Centralized and dictatorial form of government, proclaimed by its adherents to be superior to parliamentary democracy and especially effective at mobilizing the masses. This idea was widely accepted in parts of the world during the 1930s.

Avesta Compilation of Zoroastrian holy works transmitted orally by priests for millennia and eventually recorded in the sixth century BCE.

Awadh Kingdom in northern India; one of the first successor states to have gained a measure of independence from the Mughal ruler in Delhi, and the most prized object for annexation by the East India Company.

Axial Age Pivotal period in the mid-first millennium BCE when radical thinkers, such as Zoroaster in Persia, Confucius and Master Lao in East Asia, Siddhartha Gautama (the Buddha) in South Asia, and Socrates in the Mediterranean, offered dramatically new ideas that challenged their times.

Axis powers The three aggressor states in World War II: Germany, Japan, and Italy.

Aztec Empire Mesoamerican empire that originated with a league of three Mexica cities in 1430 and gradually expanded through the Central Valley of Mexico, uniting numerous small, independent states under a single monarch who ruled with the help of counselors, military leaders, and priests. By the late fifteenth century, the Aztec realm may have embraced 25 million people. In 1521, the Aztecs were defeated by the conquistador Hernán Cortés.

baby boom Post–World War II upswing in U.S. birth rates, which reversed a century of decline.

Bactria (c. 200–50 BCE) Hellenistic kingdom in Gandhara region (modern Pakistan), with a major city at Aï Khanoum. Its people and culture are sometimes called "Indo-Greek" because of the blending of Indian and Greek populations and ideas.

Bactrian camel Two-humped animal domesticated in central Asia around 2500 BCE. The Bactrian camel was heartier than the one-humped dromedary and became the animal of choice for the harsh and varied climates typical of Silk Road trade.

Baghdad Capital of the Islamic empire under the Abbasid dynasty, founded in 762 CE (located in modern-day Iraq). In the medieval period, it was a center of administration, scholarship, and cultural growth for what came to be known as the Golden Age of Islamic science.

Baghdad Pact (1955) Middle Eastern military alliance between countries friendly with America that were also willing to align themselves with the western countries against the Soviet Union.

Balam Na Stone temple and place of pilgrimage for the Maya people of Mexico's Yucatán Peninsula.

Balfour Declaration Letter (November 2, 1917) written by Lord Arthur J. Balfour, British foreign secretary, that promised a homeland for the Jews in Palestine.

Bamboo Annals Shang stories and foundation myths that were written on bamboo strips and later collected.

Bantu Language first spoken by people who lived in the southeastern region of modern Nigeria around 1000 CE.

Bantu migrations Waves of population movement from West Africa into eastern and southern Africa during the first millennium CE, bringing new agricultural practices to these regions and absorbing much of the hunting and gathering population.

barbarian Derogatory term used to describe pastoral nomads, painting them as enemies of civilization; the term *barbarian* used to have a more neutral meaning than it does today.

barbarian invasions Violent migration of people in the late fourth and fifth centuries from the frontiers of the Roman Empire into its western provinces. These migrants had long been used as non-Roman soldiers.

basilicas Early Christian churches modeled on Roman law-court buildings that could accommodate over a thousand worshippers.

Battle of Adwa (1896) Battle in which the Ethiopians defeated Italian colonial forces; it inspired many of Africa's later national leaders.

Battle of Wounded Knee (1890) Bloody massacre of Sioux Ghost Dancers by U.S. armed forces.

Bay of Pigs (1961) Unsuccessful invasion of Cuba by Cuban exiles supported by the U.S. government. The invaders intended to incite an insurrection in Cuba and overthrow the communist regime of Fidel Castro.

Bedouins Nomadic pastoralists in the deserts of Southwest Asia.

Beer Hall Putsch (1923) Nazi intrusion into a meeting of Bavarian leaders in a Munich beer hall in an attempt to force support for their cause; Adolf Hitler was imprisoned for a year after the incident.

Beghards (1500s) Eccentric European group whose members claimed to be in a state of grace that allowed them to do what they pleased—ranging from adultery, free love, and nudity to murder; also called Brethren of Free Speech.

bell beaker Ancient drinking vessel, an artifact from Europe, so named because its shape resembles an inverted bell.

Berenice of Egypt Egyptian queen who helped rule over the kingdom of the Nile from 320 to 280 BCE.

Beringia Prehistoric thousand-mile-long land bridge that linked Siberia and North America (which had not been populated by hominids). About 18,000 years ago, *Homo sapiens* edged into this landmass.

Berlin Airlift (1948) Supply of vital necessities to West Berlin by air transport, primarily under U.S. auspices, initiated in response to a land and water blockade of the city instituted by the Soviet Union in the hope that the Allies would be forced to abandon West Berlin.

Berlin Wall Wall dividing the city of Berlin, built in 1961 by communist East Germany to prevent its citizens from fleeing to West Germany; torn down in 1989.

Bhakti Religious practice that grew out of Hinduism and emphasizes personal devotion to gods.

big men Leaders of the extended household communities that formed village settlements in African rain forests.

big whites French plantation owners in Saint-Domingue (present-day Haiti) who created one of the wealthiest slave societies.

Bilad al-Sudan Arabic for "the land of the blacks"; it consisted of the land lying south of the Sahara.

bilharzia Debilitating waterborne illness that was widespread in Egypt, where it infected peasants who worked in the irrigation canals.

Bill of Rights First ten amendments to the U.S. Constitution; ratified in 1791.

bipedalism Walking on two legs, thereby freeing hands and arms to carry objects such as weapons and tools; one of several traits that distinguished hominids.

Black Death Great epidemic of the bubonic plague that ravaged Europe, East Asia, and North Africa in the fourteenth century, killing large numbers of people, including perhaps as much as one-third of the European population.

Black Jacobins Nickname for the rebels in Saint-Domingue, including Toussaint L'Ouverture, a former slave who led the slaves of this French colony in the world's largest and most successful slave insurrection.

Black Panthers Radical African American group in the 1960s and 1970s that advocated black separatism and pan-Africanism.

black shirts Fascist troops of Mussolini's regime; these squads received money from Italian landowners to attack socialist leaders.

Black Tuesday (October 29, 1929) Historic day when the U.S. stock market crashed, plunging the United States and international trading systems into crisis and leading the world into the Great Depression.

blitzkrieg "Lightning war"; type of warfare waged by the Germans during World War II, using coordinated aerial bombing campaigns along with tanks and infantry in motorized vehicles.

bodhisattvas In Mahayana Buddhism, enlightened beings who have earned nirvana but remain in this world to help others reach it.

Bolívar, Simón (1783–1830) Venezuelan leader who urged his followers to overcome their local identities and become "American." He wanted the liberated South American countries to form a Latin American confederation, urging Peru and Bolivia to join Venezuela, Ecuador, and Colombia in the "Gran Colombia."

Bolsheviks Former members of the Russian Social Democratic Party who advocated the destruction of capitalist political and economic institutions and seized power in Russia in 1917 when the Russian Empire collapsed. In 1918, the Bolsheviks changed their name to the Russian Communist Party.

Book of the Dead Ancient Egyptian funerary text that contains drawings and paintings as well as spells describing how to prepare the jewelry and amulets that were buried with a person in preparation for the afterlife.

bourgeoisie A French term originally designating non-noble city dwellers (*Bürger* in German). They sought to be recognized not by birth or aristocratic title but by property and ability. In the nineteenth century, *bourgeois* came to refer to non-noble property owners, especially those who controlled modern industry. A bourgeois was an individual. We can refer to "bourgeois values." *Bourgeoisie* refers to the entire class, as in the French bourgeoisie as a whole.

Boxer Protocol Written agreement between the victors of the Boxer Uprising and the Qing Empire in 1901 that placed western troops in Beijing and required the regime to pay exorbitant damages for foreign life and property.

Boxer Uprising (1899–1900) Chinese peasant movement that opposed foreign influence, especially that of Christian missionaries; it was put down after the Boxers were defeated by an army composed mostly of Japanese, Russians, British, French, and Americans.

Brahma One of three major deities that form a trinity in Vedic religion. Brahma signifies birth. *See also* Vishnu *and* Siva.

Brahmans Vedic priests who performed rituals and communicated with the gods. Brahmans provided guidance on how to live in balance with the forces of nature as represented by the various deities. Brahmanism was reborn as Hinduism sometime during the first half of the first millennium CE.

British Commonwealth of Nations Union formed in 1926 that conferred "dominion status" on Britain's white settler colonies in Canada, Australia, and New Zealand.

British East India Company *See* East India Company.

bronze Alloy of copper and tin brought into Europe from Anatolia; used to make hard-edged weapons.

brown shirts Troops of German men who advanced the Nazi cause by holding street marches, mass rallies, and confrontations and by beating Jews and anyone who opposed the Nazis.

Buddha "Enlightened One." The term was applied to Kshatriya-born Siddhartha Gautama (c. 563–483 BCE), whose ideas—about the relationship between desire and suffering and how to eliminate both through wisdom, ethical behavior, and mental discipline in order to achieve contentment (*nirvana*)—offered a radical challenge to Brahmanism.

Buddhism Major South Asian religion that aims to end human suffering through the renunciation of desire. Buddhists believe that removing the illusion of a separate identity would lead to a state of contentment (*nirvana*). These beliefs challenged the traditional Brahmanic teachings of the time and provided the peoples of South Asia with an alternative to established traditions.

bullion Uncoined gold or silver.

Byzantium Modern term for the Eastern Roman Empire (which would last until 1453), centered at its "New Rome," Constantinople, which was founded in 324 CE by Constantine on the site of the Greek city Byzantium.

Cahokia Commercial city on the Mississippi for regional and long-distance trade of commodities such as salt, shells, and skins and of manufactured goods such as pottery, textiles, and jewelry; marked by massive artificial hills, akin to earthen pyramids, used to honor spiritual forces.

calaveras Allegorical skeleton drawings by the Mexican printmaker and artist José Guadalupe Posada. The works drew on popular themes of betrayal, death, and festivity.

caliphate Islamic state, headed by a caliph—chosen either by election from the community (Sunni) or from the lineage of Muhammad (Shia)—with political authority over the Muslim community.

Calvin, Jean (1509–1564) A French theologian during the Protestant Reformation. Calvin developed a Christianity that emphasized moral regeneration through church teachings and laid out a doctrine of predestination.

candomblé Yoruba-based religion in northern Brazil; it interwove African practices and beliefs with Christianity.

Canton system System officially established by imperial decree in 1759 that required European traders to have Chinese guild merchants act as guarantors for their good behavior and payment of fees.

caravan cities Cities (like Petra and Palmyra) that were located along land routes of the Silk Roads and served as hubs of commerce and cultural exchange between travelers and merchants participating in long-distance trade.

caravans Companies of men who transported and traded goods along overland routes in North Africa and central Asia; large caravans consisted of 600–1,000 camels and as many as 400 men.

caravanserais Inns along major trade routes that accommodated large numbers of traders, their animals, and their wares.

caravel Sailing vessel suited for nosing in and out of estuaries and navigating in waters with unpredictable currents and winds.

carrack Ship used on open bodies of water, such as the Mediterranean.

Carthage City in what is modern-day Tunisia; emblematic of the trading aspirations and activities of merchants in the Mediterranean. Pottery and other archaeological remains demonstrate that trading contacts with Carthage were as far-flung as Italy, Greece, France, Iberia, and West Africa.

cartography Mapmaking.

caste system Hierarchical system of organizing people and distributing labor.

Caste War of the Yucatán (1847–1901) Conflict between Maya Indians and the Mexican state over Indian autonomy and legal equality, which resulted in the Mexican takeover of the Yucatán Peninsula.

Castro, Fidel (1926–2016) Cuban communist leader who seized power in January 1959. Castro became increasingly radical as he consolidated power, announcing a massive redistribution of land and the nationalization of foreign oil refineries; he declared himself a socialist and aligned himself with the Soviet Union in the wake of the 1961 CIA-backed Bay of Pigs invasion.

Çatal Hüyük Site in Anatolia discovered in 1958. It was a dense honeycomb of settlements filled with rooms whose walls were covered with paintings of wild bulls, hunters, and pregnant women. Çatal Hüyük symbolizes an early transition to urban dwelling and dates to the eighth millennium BCE.

cathedra Bishop's seat, or throne, in a church.

Catholic Church *See* Roman Catholic Church.

Cato the Elder (234–149 BCE) Roman statesman, often seen as emblematic of the transition from a Greek to a Roman world. He wrote a manual for the new economy of slave plantation agriculture, invested in shipping and trading, learned Greek rhetoric, and added the genre of history to Latin literature.

caudillos South American local military chieftains.

cave drawings Images on cave walls. The subjects are most often large game, although a few are images of humans. Other elements are impressions made by hands dipped in paint and pressed on a wall as well as abstract symbols and shapes.

Celali revolts (1595–1610) Peasant and artisan uprisings against the Ottoman state.

Central Powers Alliance of Germany and Austria-Hungary in World War I.

Chan Chan City founded between 850 and 900 CE by the Moche people in what is now modern-day Peru. It became the largest city of the Chimú Empire with a core population of 30,000 inhabitants.

Chan Santa Cruz Separate Maya community formed as part of a crusade for spiritual salvation and the complete cultural separation of the Maya Indians; means "little holy cross."

Chandra Gupta II King who reigned in South Asia from 320 to 335 CE. He shared his name with Chandragupta, the founder of the Mauryan Empire.

Chandravamsha One of two main lineages (the lunar one) of Vedic society, each with its own creation myth, ancestors, language, and rituals. Each lineage included many clans. *See also* Suryavamsha.

chapatis Flat, unleavened Indian bread.

chariot Horse-drawn vehicle with two spoked and metal-rimmed wheels that revolutionized warfare in the second millennium BCE and was made possible through the interaction of pastoralists and settled communities.

charismatic Person who uses personal strengths or virtues, often laced with a divine aura, to command followers.

Charlemagne Emperor of the west and heir to Rome from 764 to 814 CE.

chartered companies Firms that were awarded monopoly trading rights over vast areas by European monarchs (for example, the Virginia Company and the Dutch East India Company).

Chartism (1834–1848) Mass democratic movement to pass the Peoples' Charter in Britain, granting male suffrage, secret ballot, equal electoral districts, and annual parliaments and absolving the requirement of property ownership for members of the parliament.

chattel slavery Form of slavery that sold people as property, the rise of which coincided with the expansion of city-states. Chattel slavery was eschewed by the Spartans, who also rejected the innovation of coin money.

Chavín Agrarian people living from 1400 to 200 BCE in complex societies in what is now Peru. They manufactured goods (ceramics, textiles, and precious metals), conducted limited long-distance trade, and shared an artistic and religious tradition, most notably at Chavín de Huántar.

Chernobyl (1986) Site in the Soviet Union (in present-day Ukraine) of the meltdown of a nuclear reactor.

Chiang Kai-shek (1887–1975) Leader of the Guomindang following Sun Yat-sen's death who mobilized the Chinese masses through the New Life movement. In 1949, he lost the Chinese Revolution to the Communists and moved his regime to Taiwan.

Chimú Empire South America's first empire, centered at Chan Chan, in the Moche Valley on the Pacific coast from 1000 through 1470 CE, whose development was fueled by agriculture and commercial exchange.

chinampas Floating gardens used by Aztecs in the 1300s and 1400s to grow crops.

China's Sorrow Name for the Yellow River, which, when it changed course or flooded, could cause mass death and waves of migration.

chinoiserie Chinese silks, teas, tableware, jewelry, and paper; popular among Europeans in the seventeenth and eighteenth centuries.

Christendom Entire portion of the world in which Christianity prevailed.

Christianity New religious movement originating in the Eastern Roman Empire in the first century CE, with roots in Judaism and resonance with various Greco-Roman religious traditions. The central figure, Jesus, was tried and executed by Roman authorities, and his followers believed he rose from the dead. The tradition was spread across the Mediterranean by his followers, and Christians were initially persecuted—to varying degrees—by Roman authorities. The religion was eventually legalized in 312 CE, and by the late fourth century CE it became the official state religion of the Roman Empire.

Church of England Established form of Christianity in England dating from the sixteenth century.

city Highly populated concentration of economic, religious, and political power. The first cities appeared in river basins, which could produce a surplus of agriculture. The abundance of food freed most city inhabitants from the need to produce their own food, which allowed them to work in specialized professions.

city-state Political organization based on the authority of a single, large city that controls outlying territories.

Civil Rights Act (1964) U.S. legislation that banned racial segregation in public facilities, outlawed racial discrimination in employment, and marked an important step in correcting legal inequality.

civil rights movement Powerful movement for equal rights and the end of racial segregation in the United States that began in the 1950s with court victories against school segregation and nonviolent boycotts.

civil service examinations Set of challenging exams instituted by the Tang to help assess potential bureaucrats' literary skill and knowledge of the Confucian classics.

Civil War, American (1861–1865) Conflict between the northern and southern states of America that led to the abolition of slavery in the United States.

clan A social group comprising many households, claiming descent from a common ancestor.

clandestine presses Small printing operations that published banned texts in the early modern era, especially in Switzerland and the Netherlands.

climate change A wide range of phenomena caused by global warming. These changes encompass not only rising temperatures, but also changes in precipitation patterns; ice mass loss on mountain glaciers around the world; shifts in the life cycles and migration patterns of flora and fauna; extreme weather events; and sea level rise.

Clovis people Early humans in America who used basic chipped blades and pointed spears in pursuing prey. They extended the hunting traditions they had learned in Afro-Eurasia, such as establishing campsites and moving with the herds. They were known as "Clovis people" because the type of arrowhead point that they used was first found by archaeologists at a site near Clovis, New Mexico.

Code of Manu Brahmanic code of law that took shape in the third to fifth centuries CE and expressed ideas going back to Vedic times. Framed as a conversation between Manu (the first human and an ancient lawgiver) and a group of wise men, it articulated the rules of the hierarchical *varna* system.

codex Early form of book, with separate pages bound together; it replaced the scroll as the main medium for written texts. The codex emerged around 300 CE.

cognitive skills Skills such as thought, memory, problem solving, and—ultimately—language. Hominids were able to use these skills and their hands to create new adaptations, like tools, which helped them obtain food and avoid predators.

Cohong Chinese merchant guild that traded with Europeans under the Qing dynasty.

coins Form of money that replaced goods, which previously had been bartered for services and other products. Originally used mainly to hire mercenary soldiers, coins became the commonplace method of payment linking buyers and producers throughout the Mediterranean.

Cold War (1945–1990) Ideological rivalry in which the Soviet Union and eastern Europe opposed the United States and western Europe, but no direct military conflict occurred between the two rival blocs.

colonies Regions under the political control of another country.

colons French settlers in Algeria.

colosseum Huge amphitheater in Rome completed by Titus and dedicated in 80 CE. Originally begun by Flavian, the structure is named after a colossal statue of Nero that formerly stood beside it.

Columbian exchange Movements between Afro-Eurasia and the Americas of previously unknown plants, animals, people, diseases, and products that followed in the wake of Columbus's voyages.

commanderies The thirty-six provinces (*jun*) into which Shi Huangdi divided territories. Each commandery had a civil governor, a military governor, and an imperial inspector.

Communist Manifesto Pamphlet published by Karl Marx and Friedrich Engels in 1848 at a time when political revolutions were sweeping Europe. It called on the workers of all nations to unite in overthrowing capitalism.

Compromise of 1867 Agreement between the Habsburg state and the peoples living in Hungarian parts of the empire that the state would be officially known as the Austro-Hungarian Empire.

concession areas Territories, usually ports, where Chinese emperors allowed European merchants to trade and European people to settle.

Confucian ideals The ideals of honoring tradition, emphasizing the responsibility of the emperor, and respect for the lessons of history, promoted by Confucius, which the Han dynasty made the official doctrine of the empire by 50 BCE.

Confucianism Ethics, beliefs, and practices stipulated by the Chinese philosopher Kong Qiu, or Confucius, which served as a guide for Chinese society up to modern times.

Confucius (551–479 BCE) Radical thinker whose ideas—especially about how ethical living that was centered on *ren* (benevolence), *li* (proper ritual), and *xiao* (filial piety toward ancestors living and dead) shaped the politically engaged superior gentleman—transformed society and government in East Asia.

cong tube Ritual object crafted by the Liangzhu, made of jade and used in divination practices.

Congo Free State Large colonial state in Africa created by Leopold II, king of Belgium, during the 1880s and ruled by him alone. After rumors of mass slaughter and enslavement, the Belgian parliament took possession of the colony.

Congress of Vienna (1814–1815) International conference to reorganize Europe after the downfall of Napoleon. European monarchies agreed to respect one another's borders and to cooperate in guarding against future revolutions and war.

conquistadors Spanish military leaders who led the conquest of the New World in the sixteenth century.

Constantine Roman emperor who converted to Christianity in 312 CE. In 313, he issued a proclamation that gave Christians new freedoms in the empire. He also founded Constantinople (at first called "New Rome").

Constantinople Capital city of Byzantium, which was founded as the New Rome by the emperor Constantine.

Constitutional Convention (1787) Meeting to formulate the Constitution of the United States of America.

Contra rebels Opponents of the Sandinistas in Nicaragua; they were armed and financed by the United States and other anticommunist countries (1980).

conversos Jewish and Muslim converts to Christianity in the Iberian Peninsula and the New World.

Coptic Form of Christianity practiced in Egypt. It was doctrinally different from Christianity elsewhere, and Coptic Christians had their own views of the nature of Christ.

Corn Laws Laws that imposed tariffs on grain imported to Great Britain, intended to protect British farming interests. The Corn Laws were abolished in 1846 as part of a British movement in favor of free trade.

cosmology Branch of metaphysics devoted to understanding the order of the universe.

cosmopolitans Meaning "citizens of the world," as opposed to a city-state, this term refers particularly to inhabitants of the large, multiethnic cities that were nodes of exchange in the Hellenistic world.

Council of Nicaea Church council convened in 325 CE by Constantine and presided over by him as well. At this council, a Christian creed was articulated and made into a formula that expressed the philosophical and technical elements of Christian belief.

Counter-Reformation Movement to counter the spread of the Reformation; initiated by the Catholic Church at the Council of Trent in 1545. The Catholic Church enacted reforms to attack clerical corruption and placed a greater emphasis on individual spirituality. During this time, the Jesuits were founded to help revive the Catholic Church.

coup d'état Overthrow of an established state by a group of conspirators, usually from the military.

creation narratives Narratives constructed by different cultures that draw on their belief systems and available evidence to explain the origins of the world and humanity.

creed From the Latin *credo* meaning "I believe," an authoritative statement of belief. The Nicene Creed, formulated by Christian bishops at the Council of Nicaea in 325 CE, is an example of one such formal belief statement.

creoles Persons of full-blooded European descent who were born in the Spanish American colonies.

Crimean War (1853–1856) War waged by Russia against Great

Britain and France. Spurred by Russia's encroachment on Ottoman territories, the conflict revealed Russia's military weakness when Russian forces fell to British and French troops.

crossbow Innovative weapon used at the end of China's Warring States period that allowed archers to shoot their enemies with accuracy, even from a distance.

Crusades Wave of attacks launched in the late eleventh century by western European Christians against Muslims. The First Crusade began in 1095, when Pope Urban II appealed to the warrior nobility of France to free Jerusalem from Muslim rule. Four subsequent Crusades were fought over the next two centuries.

Cuban Missile Crisis (1962) Diplomatic standoff between the United States and the Soviet Union that was provoked by the Soviet Union's attempt to base nuclear missiles in Cuba; it brought the world close to a nuclear war.

cult Religious movement, often based on the worship of a particular god or goddess.

cultigen Organism that has diverged from its ancestors through domestication or cultivation.

cuneiform Wedge-shaped form of writing. As people combined rebus symbols with other visual marks that contained meaning, they became able to record and transmit messages over long distances by using abstract symbols or signs to denote concepts; such signs later came to represent syllables, which could be joined into words. By impressing these signs into wet clay with the cut end of a reed, scribes engaged in cuneiform.

Cyrus the Great Founder of the Persian Empire. This sixth-century ruler (559–529 BCE) conquered the Medes and unified the Iranian kingdoms.

czar *See* tsar.

Daimyo Ruling lords who commanded private armies in pre-Meiji Japan.

dan Fodio, Usman (1754–1817) Fulani Muslim cleric whose visions led him to challenge the Hausa ruling classes, whom he believed were insufficiently faithful to Islamic beliefs and practices. His ideas gained support among those who had suffered under the Hausa landlords. In 1804, his supporters and allies overthrew the Hausa in what is today northern Nigeria.

Daoism East Asian philosophy of the Axial Age introduced by Master Lao and expanded by his student Zhuangzi. It was remarkable for its emphasis on following the *dao* (the natural way of the cosmos) and that the best way to do that was through *wuwei* (doing nothing).

dar al-Islam Arabic for "the House of Islam"; describes a sense of common identity.

Darius I (521–486 BCE) Leader who put the emerging unified Persian Empire onto solid footing after Cyrus the Great's death.

Darwin, Charles (1809–1882) British scientist who became convinced that the species of organic life had evolved under the uniform pressure of natural laws, not by means of a special, one-time creation as described in the Bible.

D-Day (June 6, 1944) Day of the Allied invasion of Normandy under General Dwight Eisenhower to liberate western Europe from German occupation.

Dear Boy Nickname of an early human skull discovered in 1931 by a team of archaeologists named the Leakeys. Other objects discovered with Dear Boy demonstrated that by his time, early humans had begun to fashion tools and to use them for butchering animals and possibly for hunting and killing smaller animals.

Decembrists Russian army officers who were influenced by events in revolutionary France and formed secret societies that espoused liberal governance. They launched a revolt that was put down by Nicholas I in December 1825.

Declaration of Independence U.S. document stating the theory of government on which America was founded.

Declaration of the Rights of Man and Citizen (1789) French charter of liberties formulated by the National Assembly that marked the end of dynastic and aristocratic rule. The seventeen articles later became the preamble to the new constitution, which the assembly finished in 1791.

decolonization End of empire and emergence of new independent nation-states in Asia and Africa as a result of the defeat of Japan in World War II and weakened European influence after the war.

Delhi Sultanate (1206–1526) A Turkish Muslim regime in northern India that, through its tolerance for cultural diversity, brought political integration without enforcing cultural homogeneity.

democracy The idea that people, through membership in a nation, should choose their own representatives and be governed by them.

Democritus Thinker in ancient Greece who lived from 470 to 360 BCE; he deduced the existence of the atom and postulated that there was such a thing as an indivisible particle.

demotic writing The second of two basic forms of ancient Egyptian writing. Demotic was a cursive script written with ink on papyrus, on pottery, or on other absorbent objects. It was the most common and practical form of writing in Egypt and was used for administrative record keeping and in private or pseudo-private forms like letters and works of literature. *See also* hieroglyphs.

developing world Term applied to poor countries of the Third World and the former eastern communist bloc seeking to develop viable nation-states and prosperous economies. The term has come under sustained criticism for suggesting that there is a single path of economic growth that countries everywhere follow. It has been replaced by equally problematic terms like "advanced economy" and "emerging markets."

devshirme The Ottoman system of taking non-Muslim children in place of taxes in order to educate them in Muslim ways and prepare them for service in the sultan's bureaucracy.

dhamma Moral code espoused by Aśoka in the Kalinga edict, which was meant to apply to all—Buddhists, Brahmans, and Greeks alike.

dhimma system Ottoman law that permitted followers of religions other than Islam, such as Armenian Christians, Greek Orthodox Christians, and Jews, to choose their own religious leaders and to settle internal disputes within their religious communities as long as they accepted Islam's political dominion.

dhows Ships used by Arab seafarers whose large sails were rigged to maximize the capture of wind.

Dien Bien Phu (1954) Site of a defining battle in the war between French colonialists and the Viet Minh that secured North Vietnam for Ho Chi Minh and his army and left the south to form its own

government with French and American support.

Din-I-Ilahi "House of worship" in which the Mughal emperor Akbar engaged in religious debate with Hindu, Muslim, Jain, Parsi, and Christian theologians.

Diogenes Greek philosopher who lived from 412 to 323 BCE and who espoused a doctrine of self-sufficiency and freedom from social laws and customs. He rejected cultural norms as out of tune with nature and therefore false.

Directory Temporary military committee in France that took over affairs of the state from the radicals in 1795 and held control until the coup of Napoleon Bonaparte.

divination Rituals used to communicate with gods or royal ancestors and to foretell future events. Divination was used to legitimize royal authority and demand tribute.

Djoser Ancient Egyptian king who reigned from 2630 to 2611 BCE. He was the second king of the Third Dynasty and celebrated the Sed festival in his tomb complex at Saqqara.

domestication Bringing a wild animal or plant under human control.

Dominion in the British Commonwealth Canadian promise to keep up the country's fealty to the British crown, even after its independence in 1867. Later applied to Australia and New Zealand.

Dong Zhongshu Emperor Wu's chief minister, who advocated a more powerful view of Confucius by promoting texts that focused on Confucius as a man who possessed aspects of divinity.

double-outrigger canoes Vessels used by early Austronesians to cross the Taiwan Straits and colonize islands in the Pacific. These sturdy canoes could cover over 120 miles per day.

Duma Russian parliament.

Dutch learning Broad term for European teachings that were strictly regulated by the shoguns inside Japan.

dynastic cycle Political narrative in which influential families vied for supremacy. Upon gaining power, they legitimated their authority by claiming to be the heirs of previous grand dynasts and by preserving or revitalizing the ancestors' virtuous governing ways. This continuity conferred divine support.

Earth Summit (1992) Meeting in Rio de Janeiro between many of the world's governments in an effort to address international environmental problems.

East India Company (1600–1858) British charter company created to outperform Portuguese and Spanish traders in the Far East; in the eighteenth century the company became, in effect, the ruler of a large part of India.

Eastern Front Battlefront between Berlin and Moscow during World War I and World War II.

Edict of Nantes (1598) Edict issued by Henry IV to end the French Wars of Religion. The edict declared France a Catholic country but tolerated some Protestant worship.

Eiffel Tower Steel monument completed in 1889 for the Paris Exposition. It was twice the height of any other building at the time.

eight-legged essay Highly structured essay form with eight parts, required on Chinese civil service examinations.

Ekklesia Church or early gathering committed to leaders chosen by God and fellow believers.

Ekpe Powerful slave trade institution that organized the supply and purchase of slaves inland from the Gulf of Guinea in West Africa.

Elamites A people with their capital in the upland valley of modern Fars who became a cohesive polity that incorporated transhumant people of the Zagros Mountains. A group of Elamites who migrated south and west into Mesopotamia helped conquer the Third Dynasty of Ur in 2400 BCE.

empire Group of states or ethnic groups governed, through a range of methods and with varying degrees of centralization, by a single sovereign power.

Enabling Act (1933) Emergency act passed by the Reichstag (German parliament) that helped transform Hitler from Germany's chancellor, or prime minister, into a dictator following the suspicious burning of the Reichstag building and a suspension of civil liberties.

enclosure A movement in which landowners took control of lands that traditionally had been common property serving local needs.

encomenderos Commanders of the labor services of the colonized peoples in Spanish America.

encomiendas Grants from European Spanish governors to control the labor services of colonized peoples.

Endeavor Ship of Captain James Cook, whose celebrated voyages to the South Pacific in the late eighteenth century supplied Europe with information about the plants, birds, landscapes, and people of this uncharted territory.

Engels, Friedrich (1820–1895) German social and political philosopher who collaborated with Karl Marx on many publications, including the *Communist Manifesto*.

English Navigation Act of 1651 Act stipulating that only English ships could carry goods between the mother country and its colonies.

English Peasants' Revolt (1381) Uprising of serfs and free farm workers that began as a protest against a tax levied to raise money for a war on France. The revolt was suppressed, but led to the gradual emergence of a free peasantry as labor shortages made it impossible to keep peasants bound to the soil.

enlightened absolutists Seventeenth- and eighteenth-century monarchs who claimed to rule rationally and in the best interests of their subjects and who hired loyal bureaucrats to implement the knowledge of the new age.

Enlightenment Intellectual movement in eighteenth-century Europe, which extended the methods of the natural sciences, especially physics, to society, stressing natural laws and reason as the basis of authority.

entrepôts Multiethnic trading stations, often supported and protected by regional leaders, where traders exchanged commodities and replenished supplies in order to facilitate long-distance trade.

Epicurus Greek philosopher who espoused emphasis on the self. He lived from 341 to 279 BCE and founded a school in Athens called The Garden. He stressed the importance of sensation, teaching that pleasurable sensations were good and painful sensations bad. Members of his school sought to find peace and relaxation by avoiding unpleasantness or suffering.

Estates-General French quasi-parliamentary body called in 1789 to deal with the financial problems that afflicted France. It had not met since 1614.

Etruscans A dominant people on the Italian Peninsula until the fourth century BCE. The Etruscan states were part of the foundation of the Roman Empire.

eunuchs Surgically castrated men who rose to high levels of military, political, and personal power in several empires (for instance, the Tang and the Ming Empires in China; the Abbasid and Ottoman Empires; and the Byzantine Empire).

Eurasia The combined area of Europe and Asia.

European Union (EU) International body organized after World War II as an attempt at reconciliation between Germany and the rest of Europe. It initially aimed to forge closer industrial cooperation. Eventually, through various treaties, many European states relinquished some of their sovereignty, and the cooperation became a full-fledged union with a common parliament. Some EU members adopted a single currency, the euro.

evolution Process by which species of plants and animals change over time, through the favoring, through reproduction, of certain traits that are useful in that species' environment.

Exclusion Act of 1882 U.S. congressional act prohibiting nearly all immigration from China to the United States; fueled by animosity toward Chinese workers in the American West.

Ezo Present-day Hokkaido, Japan's fourth main island.

fascism Form of hypernationalism that emerged in Europe after World War I, in which a charismatic leader was followed by a mass party and supported by established elites and churches and existing government institutions. Fascist movements were widespread but came to power only in Italy and Germany.

Fatehpur Sikri Mughal emperor Akbar's temporary capital near Agra.

Fatimids Shiite dynasty that ruled parts of the Islamic empire beginning in the tenth century CE. They were based in Egypt and founded the city of Cairo.

February Revolution (1917) The first of two uprisings of the Russian Revolution, which led to the end of the Romanov dynasty.

Federal Deposit Insurance Corporation (FDIC) Organization created in 1933 to guarantee all bank deposits up to $5,000 as part of the New Deal in the United States.

Federal Republic of Germany (1949–1990) Country formed from the areas of Germany occupied by the Allies after World War II. Also known as West Germany, this country experienced rapid demilitarization, democratization, and integration into the world economy.

Federal Reserve Act (1913) U.S. legislation that created a series of boards to monitor the supply and demand of the nation's money.

Federalists Supporters of the ratification of the U.S. Constitution, which was written to replace the Articles of Confederation.

feminist movements Movements that call for equal treatment for men and women—equal pay and equal opportunities for obtaining jobs and advancement. Feminism arose mainly in Europe and in North America in the 1960s and then became global in the 1970s.

Ferangi Arabic word meaning "Frank," which was used to describe Crusaders.

Fertile Crescent An area in Southwest Asia, bounded by the Mediterranean Sea in the west and the Zagros Mountains in the east;

site of the world's first agricultural revolution.

feudalism System instituted in medieval Europe after the collapse of the Carolingian Empire (814 CE) whereby each peasant was under the authority of a lord.

fiefdoms Medieval economic and political units.

First World Term invented during the Cold War to refer to western Europe and North America (also known as the "free world" or the west); Japan later joined this group. Following the principles of liberal modernism, First World states sought to organize the world on the basis of capitalism and democracy.

five pillars of Islam Five practices that unite all Muslims: (1) proclaiming that "there is no God but God and Muhammad is His Prophet"; (2) praying five times a day; (3) fasting during the daylight hours of the holy month of Ramadan; (4) traveling on pilgrimage to Mecca; and (5) paying alms to support the poor.

Five-Year Plan Soviet effort launched under Stalin in 1928 to replace the market with a state-owned and state-managed economy in order to promote rapid economic development over a five-year period and thereby "catch and overtake" the leading capitalist countries. The First Five-Year Plan was followed by the Second Five-Year Plan (1933–1937), and so on, until the collapse of the Soviet Union in 1991.

Flagellants European social group that came into existence during the Black Death in the fourteenth century; they believed that the plague was the wrath of God.

floating population Poor migrant workers in China who supplied labor under Emperor Wu.

Fluitschips Dutch shipping vessels that could carry heavy, bulky cargo with relatively small crews.

flying cash Letters of exchange—early predecessors of paper money—first developed by guilds in the northern Song province Shanxi that eclipsed coins by the thirteenth century.

fondûqs Complexes in caravan cities that included hostels, storage houses, offices, and temples.

Forbidden City of Beijing Palace city of the Ming and Qing dynasties.

Force Publique Colonial army used to maintain order in the Belgian Congo; during the early stages of King Leopold's rule, it was responsible for bullying local communities.

Fourierism Form of utopian socialism based on the ideas of Charles Fourier (1772–1837), who envisioned communes where work was made enjoyable and systems of production and distribution were run without merchants. His ideas appealed to the middle class, especially women, as a higher form of Christian communalism.

free labor Wage-paying rather than slave labor.

free markets Unregulated markets.

Free Officers Movement Secret organization of Egyptian junior military officers who came to power in a coup d'état in 1952, forced King Faruq to abdicate, and consolidated their own control through dissolving the parliament, banning opposing parties, and rewriting the constitution.

free trade (laissez-faire) Domestic and international trade unencumbered by tariff barriers, quotas, and fees.

Front de Libération Nationale (FLN) Algerian anticolonial, nationalist party that waged an eight-year war against French troops, beginning in 1954, that forced nearly all of the 1 million European colonists to leave.

Fulani Muslim group in West Africa that carried out religious revolts at the end of the eighteenth and the beginning of the nineteenth centuries in an effort to return to the pure Islam of the past.

fur trade Trading of animal pelts (especially beaver skins) by Indians for European goods in North America.

Gandharan style Style of artwork, especially statuary, originating in the Gandharan region of modern Pakistan, that blends Hellenistic artistic influences with Buddhist stylistic features and subjects.

Gandhi, Mohandas Karamchand (Mahatma) (1869–1948) Indian leader who led a nonviolent struggle for India's independence from Britain.

garrison towns Stations for soldiers originally established in strategic locations to protect territorial acquisitions. Eventually, they became towns. Alexander the Great's garrison towns evolved into cities that served as centers from which Hellenistic culture was spread to his easternmost territories.

garrisons Military bases inside cities; often used for political purposes, such as protecting rulers, putting down domestic revolts, or enforcing colonial rule.

gauchos Argentine, Brazilian, and Uruguayan cowboys who wanted a decentralized federation, with autonomy for their provinces and respect for their way of life.

Gdansk shipyard Site of mass strikes in Poland that led in 1980 to the formation of the first independent trade union, Solidarity, in the Soviet bloc.

gender relations A relatively recent development that implies roles emerged only with the appearance of modern humans and perhaps Neanderthals. When humans began to think imaginatively and in complex symbolic ways and give voice to their insights, perhaps around 150,000 years ago, gender categories began to crystallize.

genealogy History of the descent of a person or family from a distant ancestor.

Geneva Peace Conference (1954) International conference to restore peace in Korea and Indochina. The chief participants were the United States, the Soviet Union, Great Britain, France, the People's Republic of China, North Korea, South Korea, Vietnam, the Viet Minh party, Laos, and Cambodia. The conference resulted in the division of North and South Vietnam.

Genoa One of two Italian cities (the other was Venice) that linked Europe, Africa, and Asia as nodes of commerce in 1300. Genoese ships linked the Mediterranean to the coast of Flanders through consistent routes along the Atlantic coasts of Spain, Portugal, and France.

German Democratic Republic (1949–1990) Country formed from the areas of Germany occupied by the Soviet Union after World War II. Also known as East Germany.

German Social Democratic Party Founded in 1875, the most powerful socialist party in Europe before 1917.

Ghana The most celebrated medieval political kingdom in West Africa.

Ghost Dance American Indian ritual performed in the nineteenth century in the hope of restoring the world to precolonial conditions.

Gilgamesh Heroic narrative written in the Babylonian dialect of Semitic Akkadian. This story and others like it were meant to circulate and unify the kingdom.

Girondins Liberal revolutionary group that supported the creation of a constitutional monarchy during the early stages of the French Revolution.

global warming Upward temperature trends worldwide due to the release of carbon into the air, mainly by the burning of fossil fuels and other human activities.

globalization Development of integrated worldwide cultural and economic structures.

globalizing empires Empires that cover immense territory, exert significant influence beyond their borders, include large, diverse populations, and work to integrate conquered peoples.

Gold Coast Name that European mariners and merchants gave to that part of West Africa from which gold was exported. This area was conquered by the British in the nineteenth century and became a British colony; upon independence, it became Ghana.

Goths One of the groups of "barbarian" migrants into Roman territory in the fourth century CE.

government schools Schools founded by the Han dynasty to provide an adequate number of officials to fill positions in the administrative bureaucracy. The Imperial University had 30,000 members by the second century BCE.

Gracchus brothers Two tribunes, the brothers Tiberius and Gaius Gracchus, who in 133 and 123–121 BCE attempted to institute land reforms that would guarantee all of Rome's poor citizens a basic amount of land that would qualify them for army service. Both men were assassinated.

Grand Canal A thousand-mile-long connector between the Yellow and Yangzi Rivers created in 486 BCE to link the north and south of China.

grand unity Guiding political idea embraced by Qin rulers and ministers with an eye toward joining the states of the Central Plains into one empire and centralizing administration.

"greased cartridge" controversy Controversy spawned by the rumor that cow and pig fat had been used to grease the shotguns of the sepoys in the British army in India. Believing that this was a British attempt to defile their religions and speed their conversion to Christianity, the sepoys mutinied against the British officers.

Great Depression Worldwide depression following the U.S. stock market crash on October 29, 1929.

great divide The division between economically developed nations and less developed nations.

Great East Asia Co-Prosperity Sphere Term used by the Japanese during the 1930s and 1940s to refer to Hong Kong, Singapore, Malaya, Burma, and other states that they seized during their attempt to dominate Asia.

Great Flood One of many traditional Mesopotamian stories that were transmitted orally from one generation to another before being recorded. The Sumerian King List refers to this crucial event in Sumerian memory and identity. The Great Flood narrative assigned responsibility for Uruk's demise to the gods.

Great Game Competition over areas such as Turkistan, Persia (present-day Iran), and Afghanistan. The British (in India) and the Russians believed that controlling these areas was crucial to preventing their enemies' expansion.

Great League of Peace and Power Iroquois Indian alliance that united previously warring communities.

Great Leap Forward (1958–1961) Plan devised by Mao Zedong to achieve rapid agricultural and industrial growth in China. The plan, which failed miserably, may have led to the deaths of as many as 45 million people from famine and malnutrition.

great plaza at Isfahan The center of Safavid power in the seventeenth century created by Shah Abbas (r. 1587–1629) to represent the unification of trade, government, and religion under one supreme political authority.

Great Proletarian Cultural Revolution (1966–1976) Mass mobilization of urban Chinese youth inaugurated by Mao Zedong in an attempt to reinvigorate the Chinese Revolution and to prevent the development of a bureaucratized Soviet style of communism; with this movement, Mao turned against his longtime associates in the Communist Party.

Great Trek Afrikaner migration to the interior of Africa after the British Empire abolished slavery in 1833.

Great War (World War I) (August 1914–November 1918) A total war involving the armies of Britain, France, and Russia (the Allies) against those of Germany, Austria-Hungary, and the Ottoman Empire (the Central Powers). Italy joined the Allies in 1915, and the United States joined them in 1917, helping tip the balance in favor of

the Allies, who also drew upon the populations and material of their colonial possessions.

Greek Orthodoxy Branch of eastern Christianity, originally centered in Constantinople, that emphasizes the role of Jesus in helping humans achieve union with God.

Greek philosophers "Wisdom lovers" of the ancient Greek city-states, including Socrates, Plato, Aristotle, and others, who pondered such issues as self-knowledge, political engagement and withdrawal, and evidence-based inquiry to understand the order of the cosmos.

Greenbacks An American political party of the late nineteenth century that worked to advance the interests of farmers by promoting cheap money.

griots Counselors and other officials serving the royal family in African kingships. They were also responsible for the preservation and transmission of oral histories and repositories of knowledge.

Group Areas Act (1950) Act that divided South Africa into separate racial and tribal areas and required Africans to live in their own separate communities, including the "homelands."

guerrillas Portuguese and Spanish peasant bands who resisted the revolutionary and expansionist efforts of Napoleon; after the French word *guerre*.

guest workers Migrants seeking temporary employment abroad.

Gulag Administrative name for the vast system of forced labor camps under the Soviet regime; it originated in a small monastery near the Arctic Circle and spread throughout the Soviet Union and to other Soviet-style socialist countries. Penal labor was required of both ordinary criminals (rapists, murderers, thieves) and those accused of political crimes (counterrevolution, anti-Soviet agitation).

Gulf War (1991) Armed conflict between Iraq and a coalition of thirty-two nations, including the United States, Britain, Egypt, France, and Saudi Arabia. It was started by Iraq's invasion of Kuwait, which it had long claimed, on August 2, 1990.

gunpowder Explosive powder. By 1040, the first gunpowder recipes were being written down. Over the next 200 years, Song entrepreneurs invented several incendiary devices and techniques for controlling explosions.

gunpowder empires Muslim empires of the Ottomans, Safavids, and Mughals that used cannonry and gunpowder to advance their military causes.

Guomindang Nationalist Party of China, founded just before World War I by Sun Yat-sen and later led by Chiang Kai-shek.

Habsburg Empire Ruling house of Austria, which once ruled both Spain and central Europe but came to settle in lands along the Danube River; it played a prominent role in European affairs for many centuries. In 1867, the Habsburg Empire was reorganized into the Austro-Hungarian Empire, and in 1918 it collapsed.

hadith Sayings, attributed to the Prophet Muhammad and his early converts, used to guide the behavior of Muslim peoples.

Hagia Sophia Enormous and impressive church sponsored by Justinian and built starting in 532 CE. At the time, it was the largest church in the world.

hajj Pilgrimage to Mecca; an obligation for Muslims.

Hammurapi's Code Legal code created by Hammurapi (r. 1792–1750 BCE). The code divided society into three classes—free, dependent, and slave—each with distinct rights and responsibilities.

Han agrarian ideal Guiding principle for the free peasantry that made up the base of Han society. In this system, peasants were honored for their labors, while merchants were subjected to a range of controls, including regulations on luxury consumption, and were belittled for not engaging in physical labor.

Han Chinese Inhabitants of China proper who considered others to be outsiders and felt that they were the only authentic Chinese.

Han Fei Chinese state minister who lived from 280 to 223 BCE; a proponent and follower of Xunzi.

Han military Like its Roman counterpart, a ruthless military machine that expanded the Han Empire and created stable conditions that permitted the safe transit of goods by caravans. Emperor Wu heavily influenced the transformation of the military forces and reinstituted a policy that made military service compulsory.

Hangzhou City and former provincial seaport that became the political center of the Chinese people in their ongoing struggles with northern steppe nomads. It was also one of China's gateways to the rest of the world by way of the South China Sea.

Hannibal Great general from Carthage whose campaigns in the third century BCE swept from Spain toward the Italian peninsula. He crossed the Pyrenees and the Alps with war elephants. He was unable, however, to defeat the Romans in 217 BCE.

Harappa One of the two largest of the cities that, by 2500 BCE, began to take the place of villages throughout the Indus River valley (the other was Mohenjo Daro). Each covered an area of about 250 acres and probably housed 35,000 residents.

harem Secluded women's quarters in a Muslim household.

Harlem Renaissance Cultural movement in the 1920s that was based in Harlem, a part of New York City with a large African American population. The movement gave voice to black novelists, poets, painters, and musicians, many of whom used their art to protest racism; also referred to as the "New Negro movement."

harnesses Tools made from wood, bone, bronze, and iron for steering and controlling chariot horses. Harnesses discovered by archaeologists reveal the evolution of headgear from simple mouth bits to full bridles with headpiece, mouthpiece, and reins.

Hatshepsut Leader known as ancient Egypt's most powerful woman ruler. Hatshepsut served as regent for her young son, Thutmosis III, whose reign began in 1479 BCE. She remained co-regent until her death.

Haussmannization Redevelopment and beautification of urban centers; named after the city planner who "modernized" mid-nineteenth century Paris.

Heian period Period from 794 to 1185 CE during which the pattern of regents ruling Japan in the name of the sacred emperor began.

Hellenism Process by which the individuality of the cultures of the earlier Greek city-states gave way to a uniform culture that stressed the common identity of all who embraced

Greek ways. This culture emphasized the common denominators of language, style, and politics to which anyone, anywhere in the Afro-Eurasian world, could have access.

hieroglyphs One of two basic forms of Egyptian writing that were used in conjunction throughout antiquity. Hieroglyphs are pictorial symbols; the term derives from a Greek word meaning "sacred carving." They were employed exclusively in temple, royal, and divine contexts. *See also* demotic writing.

hijra Tradition of Islam whereby one withdraws from one's community to create another, holier, one. The practice is based on the Prophet Muhammad's withdrawal from the city of Mecca to Medina in 622 CE.

Hinayana Buddhism (termed "Lesser Vehicle" Buddhism by the Mahayana/"Greater Vehicle" school; also called Theraveda Buddhism) A more traditional, conservative branch of Buddhism that accepted the divinity of the Buddha but not of bodhisattvas.

Hindu revivalism Movement to reconfigure traditional Hinduism to be less diverse and more amenable to producing a narrowed version of Indian tradition.

Hinduism Ancient Brahmanic Vedic religion that emerged as the dominant faith in India in the third century CE. It reflected rural and agrarian values and focused on the trinity of Brahma (birth), Vishnu (existence), and Shiva (destruction).

Hiroshima Japanese port devastated by an atomic bomb on August 6, 1945.

Hitler, Adolf (1889–1945) German dictator and leader of the Nazi Party who seized power in Germany after its economic collapse in the Great Depression. Hitler and his Nazi regime started World War II in Europe and systematically murdered Jews and other non-Aryan groups in the name of racial purity.

Hittites An Anatolian chariot warrior group that spread east to northern Syria, though they eventually faced weaknesses in their own homeland. Rooted in their capital at Hattusa, they interacted with contemporary states both violently (as at the Battle of Qadesh against Egypt) and peacefully (as in the correspondence of the Amarna letters).

HIV/AIDS An epidemic of acquired immunodeficiency syndrome (AIDS) caused by the human immunodeficiency virus (HIV), which compromises the ability of the infected person's immune system to ward off other diseases. First detected in 1981, AIDS killed 12 million people in the two decades that followed.

Holocaust Deliberate racial extermination by the Nazis of Jews, along with some other groups the Nazis considered "inferior" (including Sinta and Roma [gypsies], Jehovah's Witnesses, homosexuals, and people with mental illness) that claimed the lives of around 6 million European Jews.

Holy Roman Empire Enormous realm that encompassed much of Europe and aspired to be the Christian successor state to the Roman Empire. In the time of the Habsburg dynasts, the empire was a loose confederation of principalities that obeyed an emperor elected by elite lower-level sovereigns. Despite its size, the empire never effectively centralized power; it was split into Austrian and Spanish factions when Charles V abdicated to his sons in 1556.

Holy Russia Name applied to Muscovy and then to the Russian Empire by Slavic Eastern Orthodox clerics who were appalled by the Muslim conquest in 1453 of Constantinople (the capital of Byzantium and of eastern Christianity) and who were hopeful that Russia would become the new protector of the faith.

home charges Fees India was forced to pay to Britain as its colonial master; these fees included interest on railroad loans, salaries to colonial officers, and the maintenance of imperial troops outside India.

hominids The family, in scientific classification, that includes gorillas, chimpanzees, and humans (that is, *Homo sapiens*, in addition to our now-extinct hominid ancestors such as the various australopithecines as well as *Homo habilis*, *Homo erectus*, and *Homo neanderthalis*).

Homo The genus, in scientific classification, that contains only "true human" species.

Homo caudatus "Tailed man," believed by some European Enlightenment thinkers to be an early human species.

Homo erectus Species that emerged about 1.8 million years ago, had a large brain, walked truly upright, migrated out of Africa, and likely mastered fire. *Homo erectus* means "standing man."

Homo habilis Species, confined to Africa, that emerged about 2.5 million years ago and whose toolmaking ability truly made *it* the forerunner, though a very distant one, of modern humans. *Homo habilis* means "skillful man."

Homo sapiens The first humans; emerged in Africa as early as 300,000 years ago and migrated out of Africa beginning about 180,000 years ago. They had bigger brains and greater dexterity than previous hominid species, whom they eventually eclipsed.

homogeneity Uniformity of the languages, customs, and religion of a particular people or place. It can also be demonstrated by a consistent calendar, set of laws, administrative practices, and rituals.

horses Animals used by full-scale nomadic communities to dominate the steppe lands in western Afro-Eurasia by the second millennium BCE. Horse-riding nomads moved their large herds across immense tracts of land within zones defined by rivers, mountains, and other natural geographic features. In the arid zones of central Eurasia, the nomadic economies made horses a crucial component of survival.

Huguenots French Protestants who endured severe persecution in the sixteenth and seventeenth centuries.

humanism The Renaissance aspiration to develop a greater understanding of the human experience than the Christian scriptures offered by reaching back into ancient Greek and Roman texts.

Hundred Days' Reform (1898) Abortive modernizing reform program of the Qing government of China.

hunting and gathering Lifestyle in which food is acquired through hunting animals, fishing, and foraging for wild berries, nuts, fruit, and grains, rather than planting crops, vines, or trees. As late as 1500 CE, as much as 15 percent of the world's population still lived by this method.

Hyksos Chariot-driving, axe- and composite-bow-wielding, Semitic-speaking people (their name means "rulers of foreign lands") who invaded Egypt, overthrew the Thirteenth Dynasty, set up their own rule over Egypt, and were expelled by Ahmosis to begin the period known as New Kingdom Egypt.

Ibn Sina Philosopher and physician who lived from 980 to 1037 CE. He was also schooled in the Quran, geometry, literature, and Indian and Euclidian mathematics.

ideology Dominant set of ideas of a widespread culture or movement.

Il Duce (leader) Name used by the fascist Italian leader Benito Mussolini.

Iliad Epic Greek poem about the Trojan War, composed several centuries after the events it describes. It was based on oral tales passed down for generations.

Il-Khanate Mongol-founded dynasty in thirteenth-century Persia.

imam Muslim religious leader and politico-religious descendant of Ali; believed by some to have a special relationship with Allah.

Imperial University Founded in 136 BCE by Emperor Wu (Han Wudi) not only to train future bureaucrats in the Confucian classics but also to foster scientific advances in other fields.

imperialism Acquisition of new territories by a state and the incorporation of these territories into a political system as subordinate colonies.

Imperium Latin word used to express Romans' power and command over their subjects. It is the basis of the English words *empire* and *imperialism.*

Inca Empire Empire of Quechua-speaking rulers in the Andean valley of Cuzco that encompassed a population of 4 to 6 million. The Incas lacked a clear inheritance system, causing an internal split that Pizarro's forces exploited in 1533.

Indian Institutes of Technology (IIT) Institutions originally designed as engineering schools to expand knowledge and to modernize India, which produced a generation of pioneering computer engineers, many of whom moved to the United States.

Indian National Congress Formed in 1885, a political party deeply committed to constitutional methods, industrialization, and cultural nationalism.

Indian National Muslim League Founded in 1906, an organization dedicated to advancing the political interests of Muslims in India.

Indo-European migrations The migrations, tracked linguistically and culturally, of the peoples of a distinct language group (including Sanskrit, Persian, Greek, Latin, and German) from central Eurasian steppe lands into Europe, Southwest Asia, and South Asia.

Indo-Greek Of or relating to the fusion of Indian and Greek culture in the area under the control of the Bactrians, in the northwestern region of India, around 200 BCE.

Indu Name used for what we would today call India by Xuanzang, a Chinese Buddhist pilgrim who visited the area in the 630s and 640s CE.

indulgences Church-sponsored fund-raising mechanism that gave certification that one's sins had been forgiven in return for money.

industrial revolution Gradual accumulation and diffusion of old and new technical knowledge that led to major economic changes in Britain, northwestern Europe, and North America. It resulted in large-scale industry and the harnessing of fossil fuels, which allowed economic growth to outpace the rate of population increase.

industrious revolution Dramatic economic change in which households that had traditionally produced for themselves decided to work harder and longer hours in order to produce more for the market, which enabled them to increase their income and standard of living. Areas that underwent the industrious revolution shifted from peasant farming to specialized production for the market.

innovation Creation of new methods that allowed humans to make better adaptations to their environment, such as the making of new tools.

Inquisition General term for a tribunal of the Roman Catholic Church that enforced religious orthodoxy. Several inquisitions took place over centuries, seeking to punish heretics, witches, Jews, and those whose conversion to Christianity was called into doubt.

internal and external alchemy In Daoist ritual, use of trance and meditation or chemicals and drugs, respectively, to cause transformations in the self.

International Monetary Fund (IMF) Agency founded in 1944 to help restore financial order in Europe and the rest of the world, to revive international trade, and to offer financial support to Third World governments.

invisible hand As described in Adam Smith's *The Wealth of Nations*, the idea that the operations of a free market produce economic efficiency and economic benefits for all.

iron Malleable metal found in combined forms almost everywhere in the world; it became the most important and widely used metal in world history after the Bronze Age.

Iron Curtain Term popularized by Winston Churchill after World War II to refer to a rift that divided western Europe, under American influence, from eastern Europe, under the domination of the Soviet Union.

irrigation Technological advance whereby water delivery systems and water sluices in floodplains or riverine areas were channeled or redirected and used to nourish soil.

Islam A religion that dates to 610 CE, when the Prophet Muhammad believed God came to him in a vision. Islam (which means submission—in this case, to the will of God) requires its followers to act righteously, to submit themselves to the one and only true God, and to care for the less fortunate. Muhammad's most insistent message was the oneness of God, a belief that has remained central to the Islamic faith ever since.

Jacobins Radical French political group that came into existence during the French Revolution; executed the French king and sought to remake French culture.

Jacquerie (1358) French peasant revolt in defiance of feudal restrictions.

jade The most important precious substance in East Asia; associated with goodness, purity, luck, and virtue. Jade was carved into such items as ceremonial knives, blade handles, religious objects, and elaborate jewelry.

Jagat Seths Enormous trading and banking empire in eastern India during the first half of the eighteenth century.

Jainism System of thought, originating in the seventh century BCE, that challenged Brahmanism. Spread by Vardhamana Mahavira, Jainism encouraged purifying the soul through self-denial and nonviolence.

Jaja (1821–1891) A merchant prince who founded the Opobo city-state, in what is known in modern times as the Rivers state of Nigeria.

janissaries Corps of infantry soldiers conscripted as children under the *devshirme* system of the Ottoman Empire and brought up with intense loyalty to the Ottoman state and its sultan. The sultan used these forces to clip local autonomy and to serve as his personal bodyguards.

jatis Social groups as defined by Hinduism's caste system.

Jesuits Religious order founded by Ignatius Loyola to counter the inroads of the Protestant Reformation; the Jesuits, or the Society of Jesus, were active in politics, education, and missionary work.

jihad Literally, "striving" or "struggle." This word also connotes military efforts, or "striving in the way of God." In addition, it came to mean spiritual struggles against temptation or inner demons, especially in Sufi, or mystical, usage.

Jih-pen Chinese for "Japan."

Jim Crow laws Laws that codified racial segregation and inequality in the southern part of the United States after the Civil War.

jizya Special tax that non-Muslims were forced to pay to their Islamic rulers in return for which they were given security and property and granted cultural autonomy.

jong Large oceangoing vessels built by Southeast Asians that plied the regional trade routes from the fifteenth century to the early sixteenth century.

Judah The southern kingdom of David, which had been an Assyrian vassal until 612 BCE, when it became a vassal of Assyria's successor, Babylon, against whom the people of Judah rebelled, resulting in the destruction of Jerusalem in the sixth century BCE.

Julius Caesar Formidable Roman general who lived from 100 to 44 BCE. He was also a man of letters, a great orator, and a ruthless military man who boasted that his campaigns had led to the deaths of over a million people.

junks Large seafaring vessels used in the South China seas after 1000 CE, which helped make shipping by sea less dangerous.

Justinian Roman or Byzantine emperor who ascended to the throne in 527 CE. In addition to his many building projects and military expeditions, he issued a new law code.

Kabuki Theater performance that combined song, dance, and skillful staging to dramatize conflicts between duty and passion in Tokogawa, Japan.

kamikaze Japanese for "divine winds," or typhoons; such a storm saved Japan from a Mongol attack.

kanun Highly detailed system of Ottoman administrative law that jurists developed to deal with matters not treated in the religious law of Islam.

Karim Loose confederation of shippers banding together to protect convoys.

karma Literally, "fate" or "action"; in Confucian thought, a universal principle of cause and effect.

Kassites Nomads who entered Mesopotamia from the eastern Zagros Mountains and the Iranian plateau as early as 2000 BCE. They gradually integrated into Babylonian society by officiating at temples. By 1745 BCE, they had asserted order over the region, and they controlled southern Mesopotamia for the next 350 years, creating one of the territorial states.

Keynesian Revolution Post-Depression economic ideas developed by the British economist John Maynard Keynes, wherein the state took a greater role in managing the economy, stimulating it by increasing the money supply and creating jobs.

KGB Soviet political police and spy agency, formed as the Cheka not long after the Bolshevik coup in October 1917. Grew to more than 750,000 operatives with military rank by the 1980s.

Khan Mongol ruler acclaimed at an assembly of elites, who was supposedly descended from Chinggis Khan on the male line; those not descended from Chinggis continually faced challenges to their legitimacy.

Khanate Major political unit of the vast Mongol Empire. There were four Khanates, including the Yuan Empire in China, forged by Chinggis Khan's grandson Kublai.

Kharijites Radical sect from the early days of Islam. The Kharijites seceded from the "party of Ali" (who themselves came to be known as the Shiites) because of disagreements over succession to the role of the caliph. They were known for their strict militant piety.

Khmer A people who created the most powerful empire in Southwest Asia between the tenth and thirteenth centuries in what is modern-day Cambodia.

Khomeini, Ayatollah Ruhollah (1902–1989) Iranian religious leader who used his traditional Islamic education and his training in Muslim ethics to accuse Shah Reza Pahlavi's government of gross violations of Islamic norms. He also identified the shah's ally, America, as the great Satan. The shah fled the country in 1979; in his wake, Khomeini established a theocratic state ruled by a council of Islamic clerics.

Khufu A pyramid, among those put up in the Fourth Dynasty in ancient Egypt (2575–2465 BCE), which is the largest stone structure in the world. It is in an area called Giza, just outside modern-day Cairo.

Khusro I Anoshirwan Sasanian emperor who reigned from 530 to 579 CE. He was a model ruler and was seen as the personification of justice.

Kiev City that became one of the greatest cities of Europe after the eleventh century. It was built to be a small-scale Constantinople on the Dnieper.

Kikuyu Kenya's largest ethnic group; organizers of a revolt against the British in the 1950s.

King, Martin Luther, Jr. (1929–1968) Civil rights leader who borrowed his most effective weapon—the commitment to nonviolent protest and the appeal to conscience—from Gandhi.

Kingdom of Jerusalem What Crusaders set out to liberate from Muslim rule when they launched their attacks.

Kizilbash Mystical, Turkish-speaking tribesmen who facilitated the Safavid rise to power.

Knossos Area in Crete where, during the second millennium BCE, a primary palace town existed.

Koine Greek Simpler than regional versions of Greek such as Attic or Ionic, this "common Greek" dialect became an international language across the regions influenced by Hellenism and facilitated trade of goods and ideas.

Koprulu reforms Reforms named after two grand viziers who revitalized the Ottoman Empire in the seventeenth century through administrative and budget trimming as well as by rebuilding the military.

Korean War (1950–1953) Cold War conflict between Soviet-backed North Korea and U.S.- and U.N.-backed South Korea. The two sides seesawed back and forth over the same boundaries until 1953, when an armistice divided the country at roughly the same spot as at the start of the war. Casualties included 33,000 Americans, at least 250,000 Chinese, and up to 3 million Koreans.

Koryo dynasty Leading dynasty of the northern-based Koryo kingdom in Korea. It is from this dynasty that the name "Korea" derives.

Kremlin Moscow's walled city center, whose name was once synonymous with the Soviet government.

Kshatriyas Originally the warrior caste in Vedic society, the dominant clan members and ruling caste who controlled the land.

Ku Klux Klan Racist organization that first emerged in the U.S. South after the Civil War and then gained national strength as a radically traditionalist movement during the 1920s.

Kublai Khan (1215–1294) Mongol leader who seized southern China after 1260 and founded the Yuan dynasty.

kulak Originally a pejorative word used to designate better-off peasants, a term used in the late 1920s and early 1930s to refer to any peasant, rich or poor, perceived as an opponent of the Soviet regime. Russian for "fist."

Kumarajiva Renowned Buddhist scholar and missionary who lived from 344 to 413 CE. He was brought to China by Chinese regional forces from Kucha, modern-day Xinjiang.

Kushans Northern nomadic group that migrated into South Asia in

50 CE. They unified the tribes of the region and set up the Kushan Empire, which embraced a large and diverse territory and played a critical role in the formation of the Silk Roads.

Labour Party Political party founded in Britain in 1900 that represented workers and was based on socialist principles.

laissez-faire The concept that the economy works best when it is left alone—that is, when the state does not regulate or interfere with the workings of the market.

"Land under the Yoke of Ashur" Lands not in Neo-Assyria proper, but under its authority, which had to pay the Neo-Assyrian Empire exorbitant amounts of tribute.

language System of communication reflecting cognitive abilities. Natural language is generally defined as words arranged in particular sequences to convey meaning and is unique to modern humans.

language families Related tongues with a common ancestral origin; language families contain languages that diverged from one another but share grammatical features and root vocabularies. More than a hundred language families exist.

Laozi Also known as Master Lao; perhaps a contemporary of Confucius, and the person after whom Daoism is named. His thought was elaborated upon by generations of thinkers.

latifundia Broad estates that produced goods for big urban markets, including wheat, grapes, olives, cattle, and sheep.

League of Nations Organization founded after World War I to solve international disputes through arbitration; it was dissolved in 1946

and its assets were transferred to the United Nations.

Legalism Also called Statism, a system of thought about how to live an ordered life. Developed by Master Xun, or Xunzi (310–237 BCE), it is based on the principle that people, being inherently inclined toward evil, require authoritarian control to regulate their behavior.

Lenin, Nikolai (1870–1924) Leader of the Bolshevik Revolution in Russia and the first leader of the Soviet Union.

Liangzhu Culture spanning centuries from the fourth to the third millennium BCE that represented the last new Stone Age culture in the Yangzi River delta. One of the Ten Thousand States, it was highly stratified and is known for its jade objects.

liberalism Political and social theory that advocates representative government, free trade, and freedom of speech and religion.

limited-liability joint-stock company Company that mobilized capital from a large number of investors, called shareholders, who were not to be held personally liable for financial losses incurred by the company.

Linear A and B Two linear scripts first discovered on Crete in 1900. On the island of Crete and on the mainland areas of Greece, documents of the palace-centered societies were written on clay tablets in these two scripts. Linear A script, apparently written in Minoan, has not yet been deciphered. Linear B was first deciphered in the early 1950s.

"Little Europes" Urban landscapes between 1100 and 1200 composed of castles, churches, and towns in what are today Poland, the Czech Republic, Hungary, and the Baltic States.

Little Ice Age A period of global cooling—not a true ice age—that extended roughly from the sixteenth to the nineteenth century. The dates, especially for the start of the period, remain the subject of scientific controversy.

Liu Bang Chinese emperor from 206 to 195 BCE; after declaring himself the prince of his home area of Han, in 202 BCE, Liu declared himself the first Han emperor.

llamas Animals domesticated in the Americas that are similar in utility and function to camels in Afro-Eurasia. Llamas can carry heavy loads for long distances.

Long March (1934–1935) Trek of over 10,000 kilometers by Mao Zedong and his communist followers to establish a new base of operations in northwestern China.

Longshan peoples Peoples who lived in small agricultural and riverine villages in East Asia at the end of the third millennium BCE. They set the stage for the Shang dynasty in terms of a centralized state, urban life, and a cohesive culture.

lord Privileged landowner who exercised authority over the people who lived on his land.

lost generation The 17 million former members of the Red Guard and other Chinese youth who were denied education from the late 1960s to the mid-1970s as part of the Chinese government's attempt to prevent political disruptions.

Louisiana Purchase (1803) American purchase of French territory from Napoleon that included much of the present-day United States between the Mississippi River and the Rocky Mountains.

Lucy Relatively intact skeleton of a young adult female australopithecine unearthed in the valley of the Awash River in 1974 by an archaeological team working at a site in present-day Hadar, Ethiopia. The researchers nicknamed the skeleton Lucy. She stood just over 3 feet tall and walked upright at least some of the time. Her skull contained a brain within the ape size range, but her jaw and teeth were humanlike. Lucy's skeleton was relatively complete and at the time was the oldest hominid skeleton ever discovered.

Luftwaffe German air force.

Luther, Martin (1483–1546) A German monk and theologian who sought to reform the Catholic Church; he believed in salvation through faith alone, the importance of reading scripture, and the priesthood of all believers. His Ninety-Five Theses, which enumerated the abuses by the Catholic Church as well as his reforms, started the Protestant Reformation.

Maastricht Treaty (1991) Treaty that formed the European Union, a fully integrated trading and financial bloc with its own bureaucracy and elected representatives.

Ma'at Term used in ancient Egypt to refer to stability or order, the achievement of which was the primary task of Egypt's ruling kings, the pharaohs.

Maccabees Leaders of a riot in Jerusalem in 166 BCE that was a response to a Roman edict outlawing the practice of Judaism.

madrassas Higher schools of Muslim education that taught law, the Quran, religious sciences, and the regular sciences.

magnetic needle compass A navigational instrument invented by the Chinese that helped guide sailors on the high seas after 1000 CE.

Mahayana Buddhism "Great Vehicle" Buddhism; an accessible form of Buddhism that spread along the Silk Roads and included in its theology a divine Buddha as well as bodhisattvas.

Mahdi The "chosen one" in Islam whose appearance was believed to foretell the end of the world and the final day of reckoning for all people.

maize Grains, the crops that the settled agrarian communities across the Americas cultivated, along with legumes (beans) and tubers (potatoes).

Maji-Maji Revolt (early 1900s) Swahili insurrection against German colonialists; inspired by the belief that those who were anointed with specially blessed water (*maji*) would be immune to bullets. It resulted in 200,000–300,000 African deaths.

Mali Empire West African empire, founded by the legendary king Sundiata in the early thirteenth century. It facilitated thriving commerce along routes linking the Atlantic Ocean, the Sahara, and beyond.

Mamluks (Arabic for "owned" or "possessed") Military men who ruled Egypt as an independent regime from 1250 until the Ottoman conquest in 1517.

Manaus Opera House Opera house built in the interior of Brazil in a lucrative rubber-growing area at the turn of the twentieth century.

Manchukuo Japanese puppet state in Manchuria in the 1930s.

Manchus Descendants of the Jurchens who helped the Ming army recapture Beijing in 1644 after its seizure by the outlaw Li Zicheng. The Manchus numbered around 1 million but controlled a domain that included perhaps 250 million people. Their rule lasted more than 250 years and became known as the Qing dynasty.

mandate of heaven Religious ideology established by Zhou leaders to communicate legitimate transfer and retention of royal power as the will of their supreme god. The mandate later became Chinese political doctrine.

Mande A people who lived in the area between the bend in the Senegal River to the west and the bend in the Niger River to the east and between the Senegal River to the north and the Bandama River to the south. Also known as the Mandinka. Their civilization emerged around 1100.

Mandela, Nelson (1918–2013) Leader of the African National Congress (ANC) who was imprisoned for more than two decades by the apartheid regime in South Africa for his political activities, until worldwide protests led to his release in 1990. In 1994, Mandela won the presidency in South Africa's first free mass elections.

Manifest Destiny Belief that it was God's will for the American people to expand their territory and political processes across the North American continent.

manorialism System in which the manor (a lord's home, its associated industry, and surrounding fields) served as the basic unit of economic power; an alternative to the concept of feudalism (the hierarchical relationships of king, lords, and peasantry) for thinking about the nature of power in western Europe from 1000 to 1300 CE.

Mao Zedong (1893–1976) Chinese communist leader who rose to power during the Long March (1934). In 1949, he defeated the nationalists and established a communist regime in China.

maroon community Sanctuary for runaway slaves in the Americas.

Marshall Plan Economic aid package given by the United States to Europe after World War II in hopes of a rapid period of reconstruction and economic gain that would secure the countries that received the aid from a communist takeover.

martyr Literally meaning "witness," a person executed by Roman authorities for maintaining his or her Christian beliefs rather than worshipping the emperor.

Marx, Karl (1818–1883) German philosopher and economist who created Marxism and believed that a revolution of the working classes would overthrow the capitalist order and create a classless society.

Marxism A current of socialism created by Karl Marx and Friedrich Engels. It stressed the primacy of economics and technology—and, above all, class conflict—in shaping human history. Economic production provided the foundation, the "base" for society, which shaped politics, values, art, and culture (the superstructure). In the modern, industrial era, they believed class conflict boiled down to a two-way struggle between the bourgeoisie (who controlled the means of industrial production) and the proletariat (workers who had only their labor power to sell).

mass consumption Increased purchasing power and appetite for goods in the prosperous and mainly middle-class societies of the early twentieth-century, stemming from mass production.

mass culture Distinctive form of popular culture that arose in the wake of World War I. It reflected the tastes of the working and middle classes, who now had more time and money to spend on entertainment, and relied on new technologies, especially film and radio, that could

reach an entire nation's population and consolidate their sense of being a single state.

mass production System in which factories were set up to produce huge quantities of identical products, reflecting the early twentieth-century world's demands for greater volume, faster speed, reduced cost, and standardized output.

Mastaba Word meaning "bench" in Arabic; it refers to a huge flat structure identical to earlier royal tombs of ancient Egypt.

Mau-Mau Revolt (1952–1957) Uprising orchestrated by a Kenyan guerrilla movement; this conflict forced the British to grant independence to the black majority in Kenya.

Mauryan Empire (321–184 BCE) The first large-scale empire in South Asia, stretching from the Indus in the west to the mouth of the Ganges in the east and nearly to the southern tip of the Indian subcontinent; begun by Chandragupta Maurya, in the aftermath of Alexander's time in India, and expanded to its greatest extent by his grandson Aśoka.

Mawali Non-Arab "clients" to Arab tribes in the early Islamic empire. Because tribal patronage was so much a part of the Arabian cultural system, non-Arabs who converted to Islam affiliated themselves with a tribe and became clients of that tribe.

Maxim gun European weapon that was capable of firing many bullets per second; it was used against Africans in the conquest of the continent.

Mayas Civilization that ruled over large stretches of Mesoamerica; it was composed of a series of kingdoms, each built around ritual centers rather than cities. The Mayas engaged neighboring peoples in warfare and trade and expanded borders through tributary relationships. They were not defined by a great ruler or one capital city, but by their shared religious beliefs.

McCarthyism Campaign by U.S. Republican senator Joseph McCarthy in the late 1940s and early 1950s to uncover closet communists, particularly in the State Department and in Hollywood.

Meat Inspection Act (1906) Legislation that provided for government supervision of meatpacking operations; it was part of a broader progressive reform movement dedicated to correcting the negative consequences of urbanization and industrialization in the United States.

Mecca Arabian city in which the Prophet Muhammad was born. Mecca was a trading center and pilgrimage destination in the pre-Islamic and Islamic periods. Exiled in 622 CE because of resistance to his message, Muhammad returned to Mecca in 630 CE and claimed the city for Islam.

Medes Rivals of the Assyrians and the Persians. The Medes inhabited the area from the Zagros Mountains to the modern city of Tehran; known as expert horsemen and archers, they were eventually defeated by the Persians.

megalith Literally, "great stone"; the word *megalith* is used when describing structures such as Stonehenge. These massive structures are the result of cooperative planning and work.

megarons Large buildings found in Troy (level II) that are the predecessors of the classic Greek temple.

Meiji Empire Empire created under the leadership of Mutsuhito, emperor of Japan from 1868 until 1912. During the Meiji period Japan became a world industrial and naval power.

Meiji Restoration (1868–1912) Reign of the Meiji Emperor, which was characterized by a new nationalist identity, economic advances, and political transformation.

Mencius Disciple of Confucius who lived from 372 to 289 BCE.

mercantilism Economic theory that drove European empire builders. In this economic system, the world had a fixed amount of wealth, which meant one country's wealth came at the expense of another's. Mercantilism assumed that colonies existed for the sole purpose of enriching the country that controlled the colony.

Mercosur Free-trade pact between the governments of Argentina, Brazil, Paraguay, and Uruguay.

meritocracy Rule by persons of talent.

Meroitic kingdom Thriving kingdom from the fourth century BCE to 300 CE. A successor to Kush, it was influenced by both Egyptian and Sudanic cultures.

mestizos Mixed-blood offspring of Spanish settlers and Amerindians.

métis Mixed-blood offspring of French settlers and Amerindians.

Mexican Revolution (1910–1920) Conflict fueled by the unequal distribution of land and by disgruntled workers; it erupted when political elites split over the succession of General Porfirio Díaz after decades of his rule. The fight lasted over ten years and cost 1 million lives, but it resulted in widespread reform and a new constitution.

Mfecane movement African political revolts in the first half of the nineteenth century that were caused by the expansionist methods of King Shaka of the Zulu people.

microsocieties Small-scale, fragmented communities that had little interaction with others. These communities were the norm for peoples living in the Americas and islanders in the Pacific and Aegean from 2000 to 1200 BCE.

Middle Kingdom Period of Egyptian history lasting from about 2040 to 1640 BCE, characterized by a consolidation of power and building activity in Upper Egypt.

migration Long-distance travel for the purpose of resettlement. In the case of early humans, the need to move was usually a response to an environmental shift, such as climate change during the Ice Age.

millenarian Believer in the imminent coming of a just and ideal society.

millenarian movement Believer (usually religious) in the cataclysmic destruction of a corrupt, fallen society and its replacement by an ideal, utopian future.

Millets Minority religious communities of the Ottoman Empire.

minaret Slender tower within a mosque from which Muslims are called to prayer.

minbar Pulpit inside a mosque from which Muslim religious speakers broadcast their message to the faithful.

Ming dynasty Successor to the Mongol Yuan dynasty that reinstituted and reinforced Han Chinese ceremonies and ideals, including rule by an ethnically Han bureaucracy.

Minoans A people who built a large number of elaborate, independent palace centers on Crete, at Knossos, and elsewhere around 2000 BCE. Named after the legendary King Minos, said to have ruled Crete at the time, they sailed throughout the Mediterranean and by 1600 BCE had planted colonies on many Aegean islands, which in turn became trading and mining centers.

mission civilisatrice Term French colonizers used to refer to France's form of "rationalized" colonial rule, which attempted to bring "civilization" to the "uncivilized."

mitochondrial DNA Form of DNA found in mitochondria, structures located outside the nuclei of cells. Examining mitochondrial DNA enables researchers to measure the genetic variation among living organisms, including human beings. Only females pass mitochondrial DNA to their offspring.

Moche A people who extended their power and increased their wealth at the height of the Chimú Empire over several valleys in what is now Peru.

Model T Automobile manufactured by the Ford Motor Company, which was the first to be priced reasonably enough to be sold to the masses.

modernism In the arts, modernism refers to the effort to break with older conventions and seek new ways of seeing and describing the world.

Mohism School of thought in ancient China, named after Mo Di, or Mozi, who lived from 479 to 438 BCE. It emphasized one's obligation to society as a whole, not just to one's immediate family or social circle.

monarchy Political system in which one individual holds supreme power and passes that power on to his or her next of kin.

monasticism From the Greek word *monos* (meaning "alone"), the practice of living without the ties of marriage or family, forsaking earthly luxuries for a life of prayer and study. While Christian monasticism originated in Egypt, a variant of

ascetic life had long been practiced in Buddhism.

monetization An economic shift from a barter-based economy to one dependent on currency.

Mongols Combination of nomadic forest and steppe peoples who lived by hunting and livestock herding and were expert horsemen. Beginning in 1206, the Mongols launched a series of conquests that brought far-flung parts of the world together under their rule. By incorporating conquered peoples and adapting some of their customs, the Mongols created a unified empire that stretched from the Pacific Ocean to the shores of the eastern Mediterranean and the southern steppes of Eurasia.

monotheism The belief in only one god; to be distinguished from polytheism (the belief in many gods) and henotheism (the belief that there may be many gods but one is superior to the others).

Moors Term employed by Europeans in the medieval period to refer to Muslim occupants of North Africa, the western Sahara, and the Iberian Peninsula.

mosque Place of worship for the people of Islam.

mound people Name for the people of Cahokia, since its landscape was dominated by earthen monuments in the shapes of mounds. The mounds were carefully maintained and were the loci from which Cahokians paid respect to spiritual forces. *See also* Cahokia.

Mu Chinese ruler (956–918 BCE) who put forth a formal bureaucratic system of governance, appointing officials, supervisors, and military captains to whom he was not related. He also instituted a formal legal code.

muckrakers Journalists who aimed to expose political and commercial corruption in late nineteenth- and early twentieth-century America.

Muftis Experts on Muslim religious law.

Mughal Empire One of Islam's greatest regimes. Established in 1526, it was a vigorous, centralized state whose political authority encompassed most of modern-day India. During the sixteenth century, it had a population of between 100 and 150 million.

Muhammad (570–632 CE) Prophet and founder of the Islamic faith. Born in Mecca in Saudi Arabia and orphaned when young, Muhammad lived under the protection of his uncle. His career as a prophet began around 610 CE, with his first experience of spiritual revelation.

Muhammad Ali (r. 1805–1848) Ruler of Egypt who initiated a set of modernizing reforms that sought to make it competitive with the great powers.

mullahs Religious leaders in Iran who in the 1970s led a movement opposing Shah Reza Pahlavi and denounced American materialism and secularism.

multinational corporations Corporations based in many different countries that have global investment, trading, and distribution goals.

Muscovy The principality of Moscow. Originally a mixture of Slavs, Finnish tribes, Turkic speakers, and many others, Muscovy used territorial expansion and commercial networks to consolidate a powerful state and expanded to become the Russian Empire, a huge realm that spanned parts of Europe, much of northern Asia, numerous North Pacific islands, and even—for a time—a corner of North America (Alaska).

Muslim Brotherhood Egyptian organization founded in 1938 by Hassan al-Banna. It attacked liberal democracy as a cover for middle-class, business, and landowning interests and fought for a return to a purified Islam.

Muslim League National Muslim party of India.

Mussolini, Benito (1883–1945) Italian dictator and founder of the fascist movement in Italy. During World War II, he allied Italy with Germany and Japan.

Muwahhidin Literally, "unitarians"; followers of the Wahhabi movement that emerged in the Arabian Peninsula in the eighteenth century.

Mycenaeans Mainland competitors of the Minoans who took over Crete around 1400 BCE. Migrating to Greece from central Europe, they brought their Indo-European language, chariots, and metalworking skills, which they used to dominate until 1200 BCE.

Nagasaki Second Japanese city to be hit by an atomic bomb near the end of World War II.

Napoleon Bonaparte (1769– 1821) General who rose to power in a postrevolutionary coup d'état, eventually proclaiming himself emperor of France. He placed security and order ahead of social reform and created a civil legal code. Napoleon expanded his empire through military action, but after his disastrous Russian campaign, the united European powers defeated Napoleon and forced him into exile. He escaped and reassumed command of his army but was later defeated at the Battle of Waterloo.

Napoleonic Code Legal code drafted by Napoleon in 1804; it distilled different legal traditions to create one uniform law. The code confirmed the abolition of feudal privileges of all kinds and set the conditions for exercising property rights.

National Assembly of France Governing body of France that succeeded the Estates-General in 1789 during the French Revolution. It was composed of, and defined by, the delegates of the Third Estate.

National Association for the Advancement of Colored People (NAACP) A U.S. civil rights organization, founded in 1910, dedicated to ending inequality and segregation for black Americans.

National Recovery Administration (NRA) U.S. New Deal agency created in 1933 to prepare codes of fair administration and to plan for public works. It was later declared unconstitutional.

nationalism The idea that members of a shared community called a nation should have sovereignty within the borders of their state.

nation-state Form of political organization that derived legitimacy from its inhabitants, often referred to as citizens, who in theory, if not always in practice, shared a common language, common culture, and common history.

native learning Japanese movement to promote nativist intellectual traditions and the celebration of Japanese texts.

native paramountcy British form of "rationalized" colonial rule, which attempted to bring "civilization" to the "uncivilized" by proclaiming that when the interests of European settlers in Africa clashed with those of the African population, the latter should take precedence.

natural rights Belief that emerged in eighteenth-century western Europe and North America that rights fundamental to human nature were discernible to reason and should be affirmed in human-made law.

natural selection Charles Darwin's theory that populations grew faster than the food supply, creating a "struggle for existence" among species. In later work he showed how the passing on of individual traits was also determined by what he called sexual selection—according to which the "best" mates are chosen for their strength, beauty, or talents. The outcome: the "fittest" survived to reproduce, while the less adaptable did not.

Nazis (National Socialist German Workers' Party) German organization dedicated to winning workers over from socialism to nationalism; the first Nazi Party platform combined nationalism with anticapitalism and anti-Semitism.

Neanderthals Members of an early wave of hominids from Africa who settled in western Afro-Eurasia, in an area reaching from present-day Uzbekistan and Iraq to Spain, approximately 150,000 years ago.

negritos Hunter-gatherer inhabitants of the East Asian coastal islands who migrated there around 28,000 BCE but by 2000 BCE had been replaced by new migrants.

Negritude The idea of a black identity and culture different from, but not inferior to, European cultural forms; shaped by African and African American intellectuals like Senegal's first president, Léopold Sédar Senghor.

Nehemiah Jewish eunuch of the Persian court who was given permission to rebuild the fortification walls around the city of Jerusalem from 440 to 437 BCE.

Neo-Assyrian Empire Afro-Eurasian empire that dominated around

950 BCE. The Neo-Assyrians extended their control over resources and people beyond their own borders, and their empire lasted for three centuries.

Nestorian Christians Denomination of Christians whose beliefs about Christ differed from those of the official Byzantine church. Named after Nestorius, former bishop of Constantinople, they emphasized the human aspects of Jesus.

New Deal President Franklin Delano Roosevelt's package of government reforms that were enacted during the 1930s to provide jobs for the unemployed, social welfare programs for the poor, and security to the financial markets.

New Economic Policy Enacted decrees of the Bolsheviks between 1921 and 1927 that grudgingly sanctioned private trade and private property.

New Negro movement *See* Harlem Renaissance.

New World Term applied to the Americas that reflected the Europeans' view that anything previously unknown to them was "new," even if it had existed and supported societies long before European explorers arrived on its shores.

nirvana Literally, "nonexistence"; *nirvana* is the state of complete liberation from the concerns of worldly life, as in Buddhist thought.

Nō drama Masked theater favored by Japanese bureaucrats and regional lords during the Tokugawa period.

Noble Eightfold Path Buddhist concept of a way of life by which people may rid themselves of individual desire to achieve *nirvana*. The path consists of wisdom, ethical behavior, and mental discipline.

Nok culture Spectacular culture that arose in present-day Nigeria in the sixth century BCE. Iron smelting occurred there around 600 BCE. Thus the Nok people made the transition from stone to iron materials.

nomads People who move across vast distances without settling permanently in a particular place. Often pastoralists, nomads and transhumant herders introduced new forms of chariot-based warfare that transformed the Afro-Eurasian world.

nongovernmental organizations (NGOs) Term used to refer to private organizations like the Red Cross that play a large role in international affairs. See *supranational organizations*.

nonviolent resistance Moral and political philosophy of resistance developed by Indian National Congress leader Mohandas Gandhi. Gandhi believed that if Indians pursued self-reliance and self-control in a nonviolent way, the British would eventually have to leave.

North American Free Trade Agreement (NAFTA) Treaty negotiated in the early 1990s to promote free trade between Canada, the United States, and Mexico.

North Atlantic Treaty Organization (NATO) International organization set up in 1949 to provide for the defense of western European countries and the United States from the perceived Soviet threat.

Northern Wei dynasty Regime founded in 386 CE by the Tuoba, a people originally from Inner Mongolia, that lasted one and a half centuries. The rulers of this dynasty adopted many practices of the earlier Chinese Han regime. At the same time, they struggled to consolidate authority over their own nomadic people. Ultimately, several decades of intense internal conflict led to the dynasty's downfall.

Northwest Passage Long-sought marine passageway between the Atlantic and Pacific Oceans along the northern coast of North America.

Oceania Collective name for the lands of Australia and New Zealand and the islands of the southwest Pacific Ocean.

Odyssey An epic tale, composed in the eighth century BCE, of the journey of Odysseus, who traveled the Mediterranean back to his home in Ithaca after the siege of Troy.

oikos The word for "small family unit" in ancient Greece, similar to the *familia* in Rome. Its structure, with men as heads of household over women and children, embodied the fundamental power structure in Greek city-states.

oligarchy Clique of privileged rulers.

Olmecs Mesoamerican people, emerging around 1500 BCE, whose name means "inhabitants of the land of rubber," one of their major trade goods. Living in decentralized agrarian villages, this complex, stratified society shared language and religious ideas that were practiced at sacred ritual centers.

open door policy Policy proposed by U.S. Secretary of State John Hay that would give all foreign nations equal access to trade with China. As European imperial powers carved out spheres of influence in late nineteenth-century China, American leaders worried that the United States would be excluded from trade with China.

Opium Wars (1839–1842, 1856–1860) Wars fought between the British and Qing China over British trade in opium; the result was that China granted to the British the right to trade in five different ports and ceded Hong Kong to the British.

oracle bones Animal bones inscribed, heated, and interpreted by Shang ritual specialists to determine the will of the ancestors.

Organization of Petroleum Exporting Countries (OPEC) International association established in 1960 to coordinate price and supply policies of oil-producing states.

orientalism Genre of literature and painting that portrayed the non-western peoples of North Africa and Asia as exotic, sensuous, and economically backward with respect to Europeans.

orientalists Western scholars who specialized in the study of the East.

Orrorin tugenensis Predecessor to hominids that first appeared 6 million years ago.

Ottoman Empire A Turkish warrior band that transformed itself into a vast, multicultural, bureaucratic empire that lasted from the early fourteenth century through the early twentieth century and encompassed Anatolia, the Arab world, and large swaths of southern and eastern Europe.

Pacific War (1879–1883) War between Chile and the alliance of Bolivia and Peru.

pagani Pejorative word used by Christians to designate pagans.

palace Official residence of the ruler, his family, and his entourage. The palace was both a social institution and a set of buildings. It first appeared around 2500 BCE, about a millennium later than the Mesopotamian temple, and quickly joined the temple as a defining landmark of city life. Eventually, it became a source of power rivaling the temple, and palace and temple life often blurred, as did the boundary between the sacred and the secular.

Palace of Versailles The palace complex, 11 miles away from the French capital of Paris, built by Louis XIV in the 1670s and 1680s to house and entertain his leading clergymen and nobles, with the hopes of diverting them from plotting against him.

Palmyra Roman trading depot in located modern-day Syria; part of a network of trading cities that connected various regions of Afro-Eurasia.

pan movements Groups that sought to link people across state boundaries in new communities based on ethnicity or, in some cases, religion (e.g., pan-Germanism, pan-Islamism, pan-Slavism).

Pansophia Ideal republic of inquisitive Christians united in the search for knowledge of nature as a means of loving God.

papacy The institution of the pope, the Catholic spiritual leader in Rome.

papal Of, relating to, or issued by a pope.

Parthians Horse-riding people who pushed southward around the middle of the second century BCE and wiped out the Greek kingdoms in Iran. They then extended their power all the way to the Mediterranean, where they ran up against the Roman Empire in Anatolia and Mesopotamia.

pastoral nomads Peoples who move with their herds in perpetual motion across large areas, like the steppe lands of Inner Eurasia, and facilitate long-distance trade.

pastoralism A way of life in which humans herd domesticated animals and exploit their products (hides/fur, meat, and milk). Pastoralists include nomadic groups that range across vast distances, as well as transhumant herders who migrate seasonally in a more limited range.

paterfamilias Latin for "father of the family," the foundation of the Roman social order.

patria Latin, meaning "fatherland."

patrons In the Roman system of patronage, men and women of wealth and high social status who protected dependents or "clients" of a lower class.

Pax Mongolica The political and especially the commercial stability that the vast Mongol Empire provided for the travelers and merchants of Eurasia during the thirteenth and fourteenth centuries.

Pax Romana Latin term for "Roman Peace," referring to The period from 25 BCE to 235 CE, when conditions in the Roman Empire were relatively settled and peaceful, allowing trade and the economy to thrive.

Pax Sinica Modern term (paralleling the term Pax Romana) for the "Chinese Peace" that lasted from 149 to 87 BCE, a period when agriculture and commerce flourished, fueling the expansion of cities and the growth of the population of Han China.

Peace Preservation Act (1925) Act instituted in Japan that specified up to ten years' hard labor for any member of an organization advocating a basic change in the political system or the abolition of private property.

Pearl Harbor American naval base in Hawaii on which the Japanese launched a surprise attack on December 7, 1941, bringing the United States into World War II.

Peloponnesian War War fought between 431 and 404 BCE between two of Greece's most powerful city-states, Athens and Sparta.

Peninsular War (1808–1814) Conflict in which the Portuguese and

Spanish populations, supported by the British, resisted an invasion of the Iberian Peninsula by the French under Napoleon.

peninsulares Spaniards who, although born in Spain, resided in the Spanish colonial territories. They regarded themselves as superior to Spaniards born in the colonies (creoles).

Peoples' Charter Document calling for universal suffrage for adult males, the secret ballot, electoral districts, and annual parliamentary elections. It was signed by over 3 million British between 1839 and 1842.

periplus "Sailing around" manual that preserved firsthand knowledge of navigation strategies and trading advice.

Persepolis Darius I's capital city in the highlands of Fars; a ceremonial center and expression of imperial identity as well as an important administrative hub of the Persian Empire.

Peterloo Massacre (1819) The killing of 11 and wounding of 460 following a peaceful demonstration for political reform by workers in Manchester, England.

Petra Literally, "rock"; city in modern-day Jordan that was the Nabataean capital. It profited greatly by supplying provisions and water to travelers and traders. Many of its houses and shrines were cut into the rocky mountains.

phalanx Military formation used by Philip II of Macedonia, whereby heavily armored infantry were closely arrayed in battle.

Philip II of Macedonia Father of Alexander the Great, under whose rule Macedonia developed into a large ethnic and territorial state. After unifying Macedonia, Philip went on to conquer neighboring states.

philosophes Enlightenment thinkers who applied scientific reasoning to human interaction and society as opposed to nature.

philosophia Literally, "love of wisdom"; a system of thought that originally included speculation on the nature of the cosmos, the environment, and human existence. It eventually came to include thought about the nature of humans and life in society.

Phoenicians An ethnic group in the Levant known for their ships, trading, and alphabet, and referred to in Hebrew scripture as the Canaanites. The term *Phoenician* (Greek for "Purple People") derives from the major trade good they manufactured, a rare and expensive purple dye.

phonemes Primary and distinctive sounds that are characteristic of human language.

piety Strong sense of religious duty and devoutness, often inspiring extraordinary actions.

plant domestication The practice of growing plants, harvesting their seeds, and saving some of the seeds for planting in subsequent growing cycles, resulting in a steady food supply. Plant domestication was practiced as far back as 5000 BCE in the southern Levant and spread from there into the rest of Southwest Asia.

plantation slavery System whereby labor was used for the cultivation of crops wholly for the sake of producing surplus that was then used for profit; slave plantations were a crucial part of the growth of the Mediterranean economy.

Plato (427–347 BCE) Disciple of the great philosopher Socrates; his works are the only record we have of Socrates's teaching. He was also the author of formative philosophical works on ethics and politics.

plebs The "common people" of Rome, whose interests were protected by officials called tribunes.

Pochteca Archaic term for merchants of the Mexicos.

polities Politically organized communities or states.

polyglot communities Societies composed of diverse linguistic and ethnic groups.

popular culture Affordable and accessible forms of art and entertainment available to people at all levels of society.

popular sovereignty The idea that the power of the state resides in the people.

populists Members of a political movement that supported U.S. farmers in late nineteenth-century America. The term is often used generically to refer to political groups who appeal to the majority of the population.

potassium-argon dating Major dating technique based on the decay of potassium into argon over time. This method makes possible the dating of objects up to a million years old.

potato famine (1840s) Severe famine in Ireland that led to the rise of radical political movements and the migration of large numbers of Irish to the United States.

potter's wheel Fast wheel that enabled people to mass-produce vessels in many different shapes. This advance, invented at the city of Uruk, enabled potters to make significant technical breakthroughs.

pottery Vessels made of mud and, later, clay used for storing and transporting food.

Prague Spring (1968) Program of liberalization by which communist authorities in Czechoslovakia strove to create a democratic and pluralist socialism; crushed by the Soviets, who branded it a "counterrevolutionary" movement.

predestination Belief of many sixteenth- and seventeenth-century Protestant groups that God had foreordained the lives of individuals, including their bad and good deeds.

primitivism Western art movement of the late nineteenth and early twentieth centuries that drew upon the so-called primitive art forms of Africa, Oceania, and pre-Columbian America.

progressive reformers Members of the U.S. reform movement in the early twentieth century that aimed to eliminate political corruption, improve working conditions, and regulate the power of large industrial and financial enterprises.

proletarians Industrial wage workers.

prophets Charismatic freelance religious men of power who found themselves in opposition to the formal power of kings, bureaucrats, and priests.

Prophet's Town Indian village in present-day Indiana that was burned down by American forces in the early nineteenth century.

Protestant Reformation Religious movement initiated by sixteenth-century monk Martin Luther, who openly criticized the corruption in the Catholic Church and voiced his belief that Christians could speak directly to God. His doctrines gained wide support, and those who followed this new view of Christianity rejected the authority of the papacy and the Catholic clergy, broke away from the Catholic Church, and called themselves "Protestants."

Protestantism Division of Christianity that emerged in western Europe from the Protestant Reformation.

Proto-Indo-European The parent of all the languages in the Indo-European family, which includes, among many others, English, German, Norwegian, Portuguese, French, Russian, Persian, Hindi, and Bengali.

Pullman Strike (1894) American Railway Union strike in response to wage cuts and firings.

Punic Wars Series of three wars fought between Rome and Carthage from 264 to 146 BCE that resulted in the end of Carthaginian hegemony in the western Mediterranean, the growth of Roman military might (army and navy), and the beginning of Rome's aggressive foreign imperialism.

puppet states Governments with little power in the international arena that follow the dictates of their more powerful neighbors or patrons.

Puritans Seventeenth-century reform group of the Church of England; also known as dissenters or nonconformists.

Qadiriyya Sufi order that facilitated the spread of Islam into West Africa.

Qadis Judges in the Ottoman Empire.

qanats Underground water channels, vital for irrigation, that were used in Persia. Little evaporation occurred when water was being moved through qanats.

Qing dynasty (1644–1911) Minority Manchu rule over China that incorporated new territories, experienced substantial population growth, and sustained significant economic growth.

Questions of King Milinda (Milindapunha) Name of a second-century BCE text espousing the teachings of Buddhism as set forth by Menander, a Yavana king. It featured a discussion between the king and a sophisticated Buddhist sage named Nagasena.

Quetzalcoatl Ancient deity and legendary ruler of Native American peoples living in Mexico.

Quran The scripture of the Islamic faith. Originally a verbal recitation, the Quran was eventually compiled into a book with its verses in the order in which we have them today. According to traditional Islamic interpretation, the Quran was revealed to Muhammad by the angel Gabriel over a period of twenty-three years.

radicals Widely used term in nineteenth-century Europe that referred to those individuals and political organizations that favored the total reconfiguration of Europe's old state system.

radiocarbon dating Dating technique using the isotope C^{14}, contained by all living organisms, which plants acquire directly from the atmosphere and animals acquire indirectly when they consume plants or other animals. When organisms die, the C^{14} they contain begins to decay into a stable nonradioactive isotope, C^{12}. The rate of decay is regular and measurable, making it possible to ascertain the ages of fossils that leave organic remains up to 40,000 years.

raj British crown's administration of India following the end of the East India Company's rule after the Rebellion of 1857.

raja "King" in the Kshatriya period in South Asia; could also refer to the head of a family, but indicated the person who had control of land and resources in South Asian city-states.

Ramadan Ninth month of the Muslim year, during which all Muslims must fast during daylight hours.

rape of Nanjing Attack against the Chinese in which the Japanese slaughtered at least 100,000 civilians and raped thousands of women between December 1937 and February 1938.

Rashtriya Swayamsevak Sangh (RSS) (1925) Campaign to organize Hindus as a militant, modern community in India; translated in English as "National Volunteer Organization."

Rebellion of 1857 Indian uprising against the East India Company whose aims were religious purification, an egalitarian society, and local and communal solidarity without the interference of British rule.

rebus Probably originating in Uruk, a representation that transfers meaning from the name of a thing to the sound of that name. For example, a picture of a bee can represent the sound "b." Such pictures opened the door to writing: a technology of symbols that uses marks to represent specific discrete sounds.

Reconquista Spanish reconquest of territories lost to the Islamic empire, beginning with Toledo in 1061.

Red Guards Chinese students who were the shock troopers in the early phases of Mao Zedong's Great Proletarian Cultural Revolution in 1966–1968.

Red Lanterns Female supporters of the Chinese Boxers who dressed in red garments. Most were teenage girls and unmarried women.

Red Turban movement Diverse religious movement in China during the fourteenth century that spread the belief that the world was drawing to an end as Mongol rule was collapsing.

Reds Bolsheviks.

Reich German empire composed of Denmark, Austria, and parts of western France (1933–1945).

Reichstag The German parliament.

Reign of Terror Campaign at the height of the French Revolution in the early 1790s that used violence, including systematic execution of opponents of the revolution, to purge France of its enemies and to extend the revolution beyond its borders; radicals executed as many as 40,000 persons who were judged enemies of the state.

Renaissance Term meaning "rebirth" used by historians to characterize the cultural flourishing of European nations between 1430 and 1550, which emphasized a break from the church-centered medieval world and a new concept of humankind as the center of the world.

republican government Government in which power and rulership rest with representatives of the people, not with a king.

res publica Term (meaning "the public thing") used by Romans to describe their Republic, which was advised by a Senate and was governed by popular assemblies of free adult males, who were arranged into voting units, based on wealth and social status, to elect officers and legislate.

Restoration (1815–1848) European movement after the defeat of Napoleon to restore Europe to its pre-French-revolutionary status and to quash radical movements.

Rift Valley Area of northeastern Africa where some of the most important early human archaeological discoveries of fossils were made, especially one of an intact skull that is 1.8 million years old.

river basin Area drained by a river, including all its tributaries. River basins were rich in fertile soil, water for irrigation, and plant and animal life, which made them attractive for human habitation. Cultivators were able to produce surplus agriculture to support the first cities.

riverine Of or relating to an area whose inhabitants depend on irrigation for their well-being and whose populations are settled near great rivers. Egypt was, in a sense, the most riverine of all these cultures, in that it had no hinterland of plains, as did Mesopotamia and the Indus Valley. Away from the banks of the Nile, there is only largely uninhabitable desert.

Roman army Military force of the Roman Empire. The Romans devised a military draft that could draw from a huge population. In their encounter with Hannibal, they lost up to 80,000 men in three separate encounters and still won the war.

Roman Catholic Church Western European Christianity, centered on the papacy at Rome, that emphasizes the atoning power of Jesus's death and aims to expand as far as possible.

Roman law The legal system of Rome, under which disputes were brought to public courts and decisions were made by judges and sometimes by large juries. Rome's legal system featured written law and institutions for settling legal disputes.

roving bandits Large bands of dispossessed and marginalized peasants who vented their anger at tax collectors in the waning years of the Ming dynasty.

Royal Road A 1,600-mile road from Sardis in Anatolia to Susa in Iran; used by messengers, traders, the army, and those taking tribute to the king in the fifth century BCE.

Russification Programs to assimilate people of over 146 dialects into the Russian Empire.

Sack of Constantinople Rampage in 1204 by the Frankish armies on the capital city of Constantinople.

sacred kingships Institutions that marked the centralized politics of West Africa. The inhabitants of these kingships believed that their kings were descendants of the gods.

Sahel The area of sub-Saharan Africa spanning the continent just south of the Sahara Desert.

St. Bartholomew's Day Massacre (1572) Roman Catholic massacre of French Protestants in Paris.

St. Patrick Former slave brought to Ireland from Britain who later became a missionary, also called the "Apostle of Ireland." He died in 470 CE.

Salt March (1930) A 240-mile trek to the sea in India, led by Mohandas Gandhi, to gather salt for free, thus breaking the British colonial monopoly on salt.

Samurai Japanese warriors who made up the private armies of Japanese daimyos.

Sandinista coalition Left-leaning Nicaraguan coalition of the 1970s and 1980s.

Sanskrit cosmopolis Cultural synthesis based on Hindu spiritual beliefs expressed in the Sanskrit language that unified South Asia in place of a centralized empire.

Santería African-based religion, blended with Christian influences, that was first practiced by slaves in Cuba.

Sargon the Great King of Akkad, a city-state located near present-day Baghdad. Reigning from 2334 to 2279 BCE, Sargon helped bring the competitive era of city-states to an end and sponsored monumental works of architecture, art, and literature.

Sasanian Empire Empire that succeeded the Parthians in the mid-220s CE in Inner Eurasia. The Sasanian Empire controlled the trade crossroads of Afro-Eurasia and possessed a strong armored cavalry, which made it a powerful rival to Rome. The Sasanians were also tolerant of Judaism and Christianity, which allowed Christians to flourish.

sati Hindu practice whereby a widow was burned to death on the pyre of her dead husband.

satrap Governor of a province in the Persian Empire. Each satrap was a relative or intimate associate of the king.

satrapy Province in the Persian empire, ruled over by a governor, called a satrap, who was usually a relative or associate of the king.

satyagraha *See* nonviolent resistance.

scientific method Method of inquiry based on experimentation in nature. Many of its principles were first laid out by the philosopher Sir Francis Bacon (1561–1626), who claimed that real science entailed the formulation of hypotheses that could be tested in carefully controlled experiments.

Scramble for Africa European rush to colonize parts of Africa at the end of the nineteenth century.

scribes Those who wield writing tools; from the very beginning they were at the top of the social ladder, under the major power brokers.

Scythian ethos Warrior ethos that embodied the extremes of aggressive horse-mounted culture. In part, the Scythian ethos was the result of the constant struggle between settlers, hunter-gatherers, and nomads on the northern frontier of Europe around 1000 BCE.

Sea Peoples Migrants from north of the Mediterranean who invaded cities of Egypt, Asia Minor, and the Levant in the second millennium BCE.

SEATO (Southeast Asia Treaty Organization) Military alliance of pro-American, anticommunist states in Southeast Asia from 1954 to 1977.

Second World Term invented during the Cold War to refer to the communist countries, as opposed to the west (or First World) and the former colonies (or Third World).

second-generation societies First-millennium BCE societies that innovated on their older political, religious, and cultural ideas by incorporating new aspects of cultures they encountered to reshape their way of life.

Seleucus Nikator Successor of Alexander the Great who lived from 358 to 281 BCE. He controlled Mesopotamia, Syria, Persia, and parts of the Punjab.

Self-Strengthening movement A movement of reformist Chinese bureaucrats in the latter half of the nineteenth century that attempted to adopt western elements of learning and technological skill while retaining their core Chinese culture.

Semu Term meaning "outsiders," or non-Chinese people—Mongols, Tanguts, Khitan, Jurchen, Muslims, Tibetans, Persians, Turks, Nestorians, Jews, and Armenians—who became a new ruling elite over a Han majority population in the late thirteenth century.

sepoys Hindu and Muslim recruits of the East India Company's military force.

serfs Peasants who farmed the land and paid fees to be protected and governed by lords under a system of rule called feudalism.

settled agriculture Humans' use of tools, animals, and their own labor to work the same plot of land for more than one growing cycle.

It involves switching from a hunting and gathering lifestyle to one based on farming.

Seven Years' War (1756–1763) Worldwide war that ended when Prussia defeated Austria, establishing itself as a European power, and when Britain gained control of India and many of France's colonies through the Treaty of Paris.

sexual revolution Increased freedom in sexual behavior, resulting in part from advances in contraception, notably the introduction of oral contraception in 1960, that allowed men and women to limit childbearing and to have sex with less fear of pregnancy.

shah Traditional title of Persian rulers.

shamans Certain humans whose powers supposedly enabled them to commune with the supernatural and to transform themselves wholly or partly into beasts.

shamisen Three-stringed instrument, often played by Japanese geisha.

Shandingdong Man A *Homo sapiens* whose fossil remains and relics can be dated to about 18,000 years ago. His physical characteristics were close to those of modern humans, and he had a similar brain size.

Shang state Dynasty in northeastern China that ruled from 1600 to 1045 BCE. Though not as well defined by borders as the territorial states in the southwest of Asia, it did have a ruling lineage. Four fundamental elements of the Shang state were a metal industry based on copper, pottery making, standardized architectural forms and walled towns, and divination using animal bones.

Shanghai School Late nineteenth-century style of painting characterized by an emphasis on spontaneous brushwork, feeling, and the incorporation of western influences into classical Chinese pieces.

sharecropping System of farming in which tenant farmers rented land and gave over a share of their crops to the land's owners. Sometimes seen as a cheap way for the state to conduct agricultural affairs, sharecropping often resulted in the impoverishment and marginalization of the underclass.

sharia Body of Islamic law that has developed over centuries, based on the Quran, the sayings of Muhammad (*hadith*), and the legal opinions of Muslim scholars (*ulama*).

Sharpeville Massacre (1960) Massacre of sixty-nine black Africans when police fired upon a rally against the recently passed laws requiring nonwhite South Africans to carry identity papers.

Shawnees Native American tribe that inhabited the Ohio Valley during the eighteenth century.

Shays's Rebellion (1786) Uprising of armed farmers that broke out when the Massachusetts state government refused to offer them economic relief.

Shi Huangdi Title taken by King Zheng in 221 BCE when he claimed the mandate of heaven and consolidated the Qin dynasty. He is known for his tight centralization of power, including standardizing weights, measures, and writing; constructing roads, canals, and the beginnings of the Great Wall; and preparing a massive tomb for himself filled with an army of terra-cotta warriors.

Shiism One of the two main branches of Islam, practiced in the Safavid Empire. Although always a minority sect in the Islamic world, Shiism contains several subsects, each of which has slightly different interpretations of theology and politics.

Shiites Minority tradition within modern Islam that traces political succession through the lineage of Muhammad and breaks with Sunni understandings of succession at the death of Ali (cousin and son-in-law of Muhammad and fourth caliph) in 661 CE.

Shinto Literally, "the way of the gods"; Japan's official religion, which promoted the state and the emperor's divinity.

shoguns Japanese military commanders. From 1192 to 1333, the Kamakura shoguns served as military "protectors" of the ruler in the city of Heian.

Shotoku Prince in the early Japanese Yamoto state (574–622 CE) who is credited with having introduced Buddhism to Japan.

shudras Literally, "small ones"; workers and slaves from outside the Vedic lineage.

Siddhartha Gautama *See* Buddha.

Sikhism Islamic-inspired religion that calls on its followers to renounce the caste system and to treat all believers as equal before God.

Silicon Valley Valley between the California cities of San Francisco and San Jose, known for its innovative computer and high-technology industries.

silk Luxury textile that became a vastly popular export from China (via the Silk Roads) to the cities of the Roman world.

Silk Roads More than 5,000 miles of trade routes linking China, central Asia, and the Mediterranean. They were named for the silk famously traded along their land and sea routes, although ideas, people, and many other high-value commodities also moved along their lengths.

Silla One of three independent Korean states that may have emerged as early as the third century BCE. These states lasted until 668 CE, when Silla took control over the entire peninsula.

Silver Islands Term used by European merchants in the sixteenth century to refer to Japan because of its substantial trade in silver with China.

Sino-Japanese War (1894–1895) Conflict over the control of Korea in which China was forced to cede the province of Taiwan to Japan.

Sipahi Urdu for "soldier."

Siva The third of three Vedic deities, signifying destruction. *See also* Brahma *and* Vishnu.

small seal script Unified script that was used to the exclusion of other scripts under the Qin with the aim of centralizing administration; its use led to a less complicated style of clerical writing than had been in use under the Han.

social contract The idea, drawn from the writings of British philosopher John Locke, that the law should bind both ruler and people.

Social Darwinism Belief that Charles Darwin's theory of evolution was applicable to humans and justified the right of the ruling classes or countries to dominate the weak.

social hierarchies Distinctions between the privileged and the less privileged.

Social Security Act (1935) New Deal act that instituted old-age pensions and insurance for the unemployed.

socialism Political ideology that calls for a classless society with collective ownership of all property.

Socrates (469–399 BCE) Philosopher of Athens who encouraged people to reflect on ethics and morality. He stressed the importance of honor and integrity as opposed to wealth and power. Plato was his student.

Sogdians A people who lived in central Asia's commercial centers and maintained the stability and accessibility of the Silk Roads. They were crucial to the interconnectedness of the Afro-Eurasian landmass.

Solidarity The Soviet bloc's first independent trade union, established in Poland at the Gdansk shipyard.

Song dynasty Chinese dynasty that took over the mandate of heaven for three centuries starting in 976 CE. It ruled in an era of many economic and political successes, but it eventually lost northern China to nomadic tribes.

Song porcelain Type of porcelain perfected during the Song dynasty that was light, durable, and quite beautiful.

South African War (1899–1902) *See* Anglo-Boer War.

Soviet bloc International alliance that included the eastern European countries of the Warsaw Pact as well as the Soviet Union, but also came to include Cuba.

Spanish-American War (1898) War between the United States and Spain in Cuba, Puerto Rico, and the Philippines. It ended with a treaty in which the United States took over the Philippines, Guam, and Puerto Rico; Cuba won partial independence.

speciation The formation of species.

specie Money in coin.

species A group of animals or plants sharing one or more distinctive characteristics.

spiritual ferment Process that occurred after 300 CE in which religion touched more areas of society and culture than before and in different, more demanding ways.

Spring and Autumn period Period between the eighth and fifth centuries BCE during which China was ruled by the feudal system. In this anarchic and turbulent time, there were 148 different tributary states.

S.S. (*Schutzstaffel*) Hitler's security police force.

Stalin, Joseph (1879–1953) Leader of the Communist Party and the Soviet Union; sought to create "socialism in one country."

steel A metal more malleable and stronger than iron that became essential for industries like shipbuilding and railways.

stoicism Widespread philosophical movement initiated by Zeno (334–262 BCE). Zeno and his followers sought to understand the role of people in relation to the cosmos. For the Stoics, everything was grounded in nature. Being in love with nature and living a good life required being in control of one's passions and thus indifferent to pleasure or pain.

Strait of Malacca Seagoing gateway to Southeast and East Asia.

Strategic Defense Initiative Master plan, championed by U.S. president Ronald Reagan in the 1980s, that envisioned the deployment of satellites and space missiles to protect the United States from incoming nuclear bombs; nicknamed "Star Wars."

stupa Dome monument marking the burial site of relics of the Buddha.

Suez Canal Channel built in 1869 across the Isthmus of Suez to connect the Mediterranean Sea with the

Red Sea in order to lower the costs of international trade.

Sufi brotherhoods Sufi religious orders that were responsible for the expansion of Islam into many regions of the world.

Sufism Emotional and mystical form of Islam that appealed to the common people.

sultan Islamic political leader. In the Ottoman Empire, the sultan combined a warrior ethos with an unwavering devotion to Islam.

Sumerian King List Text that recounts the making of political dynasties. Recorded around 2000 BCE, it organizes the reigns of kings by dynasty, one city at a time.

Sumerian pantheon The Sumerian gods, each of whom had a home in a particular floodplain city. In the Sumerian belief system, both gods and the natural forces they controlled had to be revered.

Sumerian temples Homes of the gods and symbols of Sumerian imperial identity. Sumerian temples also represented the gods' ability to hoard wealth at sites where people exchanged goods and services. In addition, temples distinguished the urban from the rural world.

Sun Yat-sen (1866–1925) Chinese revolutionary and first provisional president of the Republic of China. Sun played an important role in the overthrow of the Qing dynasty and later founded the Guomindang, the Nationalist Party of China.

Sunnis Majority sect within modern Islam that follows a line of political succession from Muhammad, through the first four caliphs (Abu Bakr, Umar, Uthman, and Ali), to the Umayyads and beyond, with caliphs chosen by election from the *umma* (not from Muhammad's direct lineage).

superior man In the Confucian view, a person of perfected moral character, fit to be a leader.

superpowers Label applied to the United States and the Soviet Union after World War II because of their size, their possession of the atomic bomb, and the fact that each embodied a model of civilization (capitalism and communism, respectively) applicable to the whole world.

supranational organizations Organizations that transcend national boundaries, such as nongovernmental organizations (NGOs), the World Bank, and the International Monetary Fund (IMF).

survival of the fittest Charles Darwin's belief that as animal populations grew and resources became scarce, a struggle for existence arose, the outcome of which was that only the "fittest" survived to reproduce.

Suryavamsha The second lineage of two (the solar) in Vedic society. *See also* Chandravamsha.

Swadeshi movement Voluntary organizations in India that championed the creation of indigenous manufacturing enterprises and schools of nationalist thought in order to gain autonomy from Britain.

syndicalists Advocates of syndicalism, a movement of workplace associations that included unskilled labor and sought a replacement for capitalism led by workers.

tabula rasa Term used by John Locke to describe the human mind before it begins to acquire ideas from experience; Latin for "clean slate."

Taiping Heavenly Kingdom (Heavenly Kingdom of Great Peace) Religious sect established by the Chinese prophet Hong Xiuquan

in the mid-nineteenth century. Hong Xiuquan believed that he was Jesus's younger brother. The group struggled to rid the world of evil and "restore" the heavenly kingdom, imagined as a just and egalitarian order.

Taiping Rebellion (1850–1864) Rebellion by followers of Hong Xiuquan and the Taiping Heavenly Kingdom against the Qing government over the economic and social turmoil caused by the Opium War. Despite raising an army of 100,000 rebels, the rebellion was crushed.

Taj Mahal Royal palace of the Mughal Empire, built by Shah Jahan in the seventeenth century in homage to his wife, Mumtaz.

Tale of Genji Japanese work written in the early eleventh century by Lady Murasaki that gives vivid accounts of Heian court life; Japan's first novel.

talking cure Psychological practice developed by Sigmund Freud whereby the symptoms of neurotic and traumatized patients would decrease after regular periods of thoughtful discussion.

Talmud Huge volumes of oral commentary on Jewish law eventually compiled in two versions, the Palestinian and the Babylonian, in the fifth and sixth centuries BCE.

Talmud of Jerusalem Codified written volumes of the traditions of Judaism; produced by the rabbis of Galilee around 400 CE.

Tang dynasty (608–907 CE) Regime that promoted a cosmopolitan culture, turning China into the hub of East Asian cultural integration, while expanding the borders of its empire. In order to govern such a diverse empire, the Tang established a political culture and civil service based on Confucian teachings. Candidates for the civil service were required to take examinations, the first of their kind in the world.

Tanzimat Reorganization period of the Ottoman Empire in the mid-nineteenth century; its modernizing reforms affected the military, trade, foreign relations, and civilian life.

tappers Rubber harvesters in Brazil, most of whom were either Indian or mixed-blood people.

Tarascans Mesoamerican society of the 1400s; rivals to and sometimes subjects of the Aztecs.

Tatish Ruler of Chan Santa Cruz during the Caste War of the Yucatán. The name means "father."

Tecumseh (1768–1813) Shawnee who circulated Tenskwatawa's message of Indian renaissance among Indian villages from the Great Lakes to the Gulf Coast. He preached the need for Indian unity, insisting that Indians resist any American attempts to get them to sell more land. In response, thousands of followers renounced their ties to colonial ways and prepared to combat the expansion of the United States.

Tekkes Schools that taught the devotional strategies and religious knowledge needed for students to enter Sufi orders and become masters of the brotherhood.

temple Building where believers worshipped their gods and goddesses and where some peoples believed the deities had their earthly residence.

Tenskwatawa (1775–1836) Shawnee prophet who urged disciples to abstain from alcohol and return to traditional customs, reducing dependence on European trade goods and severing connections to Christian missionaries. His message spread to other tribes, raising the specter of a pan-Indian confederacy.

Teotihuacán City-state in a large, mountainous valley in present-day Mexico; the first major community to emerge after the Olmecs.

territorial state A kingdom made up of city-states and hinterlands joined together by a shared identity, controlled through the centralized rule of a charismatic leader, and supported by a large bureaucracy, legal codes, and military expansion.

Third Estate The French people minus the clergy and the aristocracy; this term was popularized in the late eighteenth century and used to exalt the power of the bourgeoisie during the French Revolution.

Third Reich The German state from 1933 to 1945 under Adolf Hitler.

Third World A collective term used for nations of the world, mostly in Asia, Latin America, and Africa, that were not highly industrialized like First World nations or tied to the Soviet bloc (the Second World). It implies a revolutionary challenge to the existing (liberal, capitalist) order.

Thirty Years' War (1618–1648) Conflict begun between Protestants and Catholics in Germany that escalated into a general European war fought against the unity and power of the Holy Roman Empire.

Tiananmen Square Largest public square in the world and site of the pro-democracy demonstrations in 1989 that ended with the killing of as many as a thousand protesters by the Chinese army.

Tiers monde Term meaning "Third World," coined by French intellectuals to describe countries seeking a "third way" between Soviet communism and western capitalism.

Tiglath Pileser III Assyrian ruler from 745 to 728 BCE who instituted reforms that changed the administrative and social structure of the empire to make it more efficient, and who introduced a standing army.

Tiwanaku Another name for Tihuanaco, the first great Andean polity, on the shores of Lake Titicaca.

Tlaxcalans Mesoamerican society of the 1400s; these people were enemies of the powerful Aztec Empire.

Tokugawa shogunate Hereditary military administration founded in 1603 that ruled Japan while keeping the emperor as a figurehead; it was toppled in 1868 by reformers who felt that Japan should adopt, not reject, western influences.

Toltecs Mesoamerican peoples who filled the political vacuum left by Teotihuacán's decline; established a temple-filled capital and commercial hub at Tula.

Tomb Culture Warlike group from Northeast Asia who arrived by sea in the middle of the third century CE and imposed their military and social power on southern Japan. These conquerors are known today as the tomb culture because of their elevated necropolises near present-day Osaka.

Topkapi Palace Palace complex located in Istanbul that served as both the residence of the sultan, along with his harem and larger household, and the political headquarters of the Ottoman Empire.

total war All-out war involving civilian populations as well as military forces, often used in reference to World War II.

transhumant herders Pastoral peoples who move seasonally from lowlands to highlands in proximity to city-states, with which they trade the products of their flocks (milk, fur, hides) for urban products (manufactured goods, such as metals).

Trans-Siberian Railroad Railroad built over very difficult terrain between 1891 and 1903 and subsequently expanded; it created an overland bridge for troops, peasant settlers, and commodities to move between Europe and the Pacific.

Treaty of Brest-Litovsk (1918) Separate peace between imperial Germany and the new Bolshevik regime in Russia. The treaty acknowledged the German victory on the Eastern Front and withdrew Russia from the war.

Treaty of Nanjing (1842) Treaty between China and Britain following the Opium War; it called for indemnities, the opening of new ports, and the cession of Hong Kong to the British.

Treaty of Tordesillas (1494) Treaty in which the pope decreed that the non-European world would be divided into spheres of trade and missionary responsibility between Spain and Portugal.

trickle trade Method by which a good is passed from one village to another, as in the case of obsidian among farming villages; the practice began around 7000 BCE. Also called "down-the-line trade."

Tripartite Pact (1940) Pact that stated that Germany, Italy, and Japan would act together in all future military ventures.

Triple Entente Alliance developed before World War I that included Britain, France, and Russia.

Troy City founded around 3000 BCE in the far west of Anatolia. Troy is legendary as the site of the war that was launched by the Greeks (the Achaeans) and that was recounted by Homer in the *Iliad*.

Truman Doctrine (1947) Declaration promising U.S. economic and military intervention, whenever and wherever needed, for the sake of preventing communist expansion.

Truth and Reconciliation Commission Quasi-judicial body established after the overthrow of the apartheid system in South Africa and the election of Nelson Mandela as the country's first black president in 1994. The commission was to gather evidence about crimes committed during the apartheid years. Those who showed remorse for their actions could appeal for clemency. The South African leaders believed that an airing of the grievances from this period would promote racial harmony and reconciliation.

truth commissions Commissions established to inquire into human rights abuses by previous regimes. In Argentina, El Salvador, Guatemala, and South Africa, these commissions were vital for creating a new aura of legitimacy for democracies and for promising to uphold the rights of individuals.

tsar Russian word derived from the Latin *Caesar* to refer to the Russian ruler of Kiev, and eventually to all rulers in Russia. Also given as czar.

Tula Toltec capital city; a commercial hub and political and ceremonial center.

Uitlanders Literally, "outsiders"; British populations living in Afrikaner republics, who were denied voting rights and subjected to other forms of discrimination in the late nineteenth century.

ulama Arabic word that means "learned ones" or "scholars"; used for those who devoted themselves to knowledge of Islamic sciences.

Umayyads Family who founded the first dynasty in Islam. They established family rule and dynastic succession to the role of caliph. The first Umayyad caliph established Damascus as his capital and was named Mu'awiya ibn Abi Sufyan.

umma Arabic word for "community"; used to refer to the Islamic polity or Islamic community.

Universal Declaration of Human Rights (1948) U.N. declaration that laid out the rights to which all human beings are entitled.

universalizing religions Religions that appeal to diverse populations; are adaptable to new cultures and places; promote universal rules and principles; proselytize new believers, often through missionaries; foster community; and, in some cases, do all of this through the support of an empire.

universitas Term used from the end of the twelfth century to denote scholars who came together, first in Paris. The term is borrowed from the merchant communities, where it denoted the equivalent of the modern union.

untouchables Caste in the Indian system whose jobs, usually in the more unsanitary aspects of urban life, rendered them "ritually and spiritually" impure.

Upanishads First-millennium BCE Vedic wisdom literature, in the form of a dialogue between students and teacher; together with the Vedas, they brought a cultural and spiritual unity to much of South Asia.

urban-rural divide Division between those living in cities and those living in rural areas. One of history's most durable worldwide distinctions, the urban-rural divide eventually encompassed the globe. Where cities arose, communities adopted lifestyles based on the mass production of goods and on specialized labor. Those living in the countryside remained close to nature, cultivating the land or tending livestock. They diversified their labor and exchanged their grains and animal products for necessities available in urban centers.

utopian socialism The most visionary of all Restoration-era movements. Utopian socialists like Charles Fourier dreamed of transforming states, workplaces, and human relations and proposed plans to do so.

Vaishyas Householders or lesser clan members in Vedic society who worked the land and tended livestock.

Vardhamana Mahavira Advocate of Jainism who lived from 540 to 468 BCE; he emphasized interpretation of the Upanishads to govern and guide daily life.

varna Sanskrit for "color"; refers to the four ranked social groups within early Vedic society (priests, warriors, commoners, and laborers). The term *caste*, which derives from the term *casta* ("race/breed" in Spanish and Portuguese) is a later, anachronistic term often used for these divisions.

vassal states Subordinate states that had to pay tribute in luxury goods, raw materials, and manpower as part of a broad confederation of polities under a king's protection.

Vedas Rhymes, hymns, and explanatory texts composed and orally transmitted in Sanskrit by Brahman priests. They shaped the society and religious rituals of Vedic peoples and became central texts in Hinduism.

Vedic people People who came from the steppes of Inner Asia around 1500 BCE and entered the fertile lowlands of the Indus River basin, gradually moving as far south as the Deccan plateau. They called themselves Aryan, which means

"respected ones," and spoke Sanskrit, an Indo-European language.

veiling Practice of modest dress required of respectable women in the Assyrian Empire, introduced by Assyrian authorities in the thirteenth century BCE.

Venus figures Representations of the goddess of fertility drawn on the Chauvet Cave in southeastern France. Discovered in 1994, they are probably about 35,000 years old.

Versailles Conference (1919) Peace conference among the victors of World War I; resulted in the Treaty of Versailles, which forced Germany to pay reparations and to give up its colonies to the victors.

Viet Cong Vietnamese communist group committed to overthrowing the government of South Vietnam and reunifying North and South Vietnam.

Viet Minh (League for the Independence of Vietnam) Group founded in 1941 by Ho Chi Minh to oppose the Japanese occupation of Indochina; it later fought the French colonial forces for independence.

Vietnam War (1965–1975) Conflict that resulted from U.S. concern over the spread of communism in Southeast Asia. The United States intervened on the side of South Vietnam in its struggle against peasant-supported Viet Cong guerrilla forces, who wanted to reunite Vietnam under a communist regime. Faced with antiwar opposition at home and ferocious resistance from the Vietnamese, American troops withdrew in 1973; the puppet South Vietnamese government collapsed two years later.

Vikings Warrior group from Scandinavia that used its fighting skills and sophisticated ships to raid and trade deep into eastern Europe, southward

into the Mediterranean, and westward to Iceland, Greenland, and North America.

Vishnu The second of three Vedic deities, signifying existence. *See also* Brahma *and* Siva.

viziers Bureaucrats of the Ottoman Empire.

vodun Mixed religion of African and Christian customs practiced by slaves and free blacks in the colony of Saint-Domingue.

Voting Rights Act (1965) Law that granted universal suffrage in the United States.

Wafd Nationalist party that came into existence during a rebellion in Egypt in 1919 and held power sporadically after Egypt was granted limited independence from Britain in 1922.

Wahhabism Early eighteenth-century reform movement organized by Muhammad Ibn Abd al-Wahhab, who preached the absolute oneness of Allah and a return to the pure Islam of Muhammad.

Wang Mang Han minister who usurped the throne in 9 CE because he believed that the Han had lost the mandate of heaven. He ruled until 23 CE.

war ethos Strong social commitment to a continuous state of war. The Roman army constantly drafted men and engaged in annual spring military campaigns. Soldiers were taught to embrace a sense of honor that did not allow them to accept defeat, and those who repeatedly threw themselves into battle were commended.

War of 1812 Conflict between Britain and the United States arising from U.S. grievances over oppressive British maritime practices in the Napoleonic Wars.

War on Poverty U.S. president Lyndon Johnson's push for an increased range of social programs and increased spending on social security, health, education, and assistance for the disabled.

Warring States period Period extending from the fifth century to 221 BCE, when China's regional warring states were unified by the Qin dynasty.

Warsaw Pact (1955–1991) Military alliance between the Soviet Union and other communist states that was established in response to the creation of the North American Treaty Organization (NATO).

Weimar Republic (1919–1933) Constitutional republic of Germany that was subverted by Hitler soon after he became chancellor.

Western Front Battlefront that stretched from the English Channel through Belgium and France to the Alps during World War I.

White and Blue Niles The two main branches of the Nile, rising out of central Africa and Ethiopia, respectively. They come together at the present-day capital city of Sudan, Khartoum.

White Lotus Rebellion Series of uprisings in northern China (1790–1800s) inspired by mystical beliefs in folk Buddhism and, at times, the idea of restoring the Ming dynasty.

White Wolf Mysterious militia leader, depicted in popular myth as a Chinese Robin Hood whose mission was to rid the country of the injustices of Yuan Shikai's government in the early years of the Chinese Republic (1910s).

Whites "Counterrevolutionaries" of the Bolshevik Revolution (1918–1921) who fought the Bolsheviks (the Reds); included former supporters of the tsar, Social Democrats, and large independent peasant armies.

witnessing Dying for one's faith, or becoming a martyr.

Wokou Supposedly Japanese pirates, many of whom were actually Chinese subjects of the Ming dynasty.

Works Progress Administration (WPA) New Deal program instituted in 1935 that put nearly 3 million people to work building roads, bridges, airports, and post offices.

World Bank International agency established in 1944 to provide economic assistance to war-torn and poor countries. Its formal title is the International Bank for Reconstruction and Development.

World War I *See* Great War.

World War II (1939–1945) Worldwide war that began in September 1939 in Europe, and even earlier in Asia, and pitted Britain, the United States, and the Soviet Union (the Allies) against Nazi Germany, Japan, and Italy (the Axis).

Wu (r. 140–87 BCE) Also known as Han Wudi, or the "Martial Emperor"; the ruler of the Han dynasty for more than fifty years, during which he expanded the empire through his extensive military campaigns.

Wu Zhao Chinese empress who lived from 626 to 706 CE. She began as a concubine in the court of Li Shimin and became the mother of his son's child. She eventually gained power equal to that of the emperor, and she named herself regent when she finagled a place for one of her own sons after their father's death.

Xiongnu The most powerful and intrusive of the nomadic peoples of Inner Asia; originally pastoralists from the eastern part of the Asian steppe in what is modern-day Mongolia. They appeared along the frontier with China in the late Zhou dynasty and by the third century BCE had become the most powerful of all the pastoral communities in that area.

Xunzi (310–237 BCE) Confucian moralist whose ideas were influential to Qin rulers. He believed that rational statecraft was more reliable than fickle human nature and that strict laws and severe punishments could create stability in society.

Yalta Accords Results of a meeting between President Roosevelt, Prime Minister Churchill, and Premier Stalin held in the Crimea in 1945 to plan for the post–World War II order.

Yavana kings Sanskrit name for Greek rulers, derived from the Greek name for the area of western Asia Minor called Ionia, a term that was then extended to anyone who spoke Greek or came from the Mediterranean.

yellow press Newspapers that sought mass circulation by featuring sensationalist reporting.

Yellow Turbans One of several local Chinese religious movements that emerged across the empire, especially under Wang Mang's officials, who considered him a usurper. The Yellow Turbans, so called because of the yellow scarves they wore around their heads, were Daoist millenarians.

Yin City that became the capital of the Shang dynasty in 1350 BCE, ushering in a golden age.

Young Egypt Antiliberal, fascist group that gained a large following in Egypt during the 1930s.

Young Italy Nationalist organization founded in 1832, made up of young students and intellectuals devoted to the unification and renewal of the Italian state.

Yuan dynasty Dynasty established by the Mongols after the defeat of the Song. The Yuan dynasty was strong from 1280 to 1368; its capital was at Dadu, or modern-day Beijing.

Yuan Mongols Mongol rulers of China who were overthrown by the Ming dynasty in 1368.

Yuezhi A Turkic nomadic people who roamed pastoral lands to the west of the Xiongnu territory of central Mongolia. They had friendly relationships with the farming societies in China, but detested the Xiongnu and had frequent armed clashes with them.

Zaibatsu Large-scale, family-owned corporations in Japan, consisting of factories, import-export businesses, and banks, that dominated the Japanese economy until 1945.

Zamindars Archaic tax system of the Mughal Empire in which decentralized lords collected tribute for the emperor.

Zapatistas Group of indigenous rebels that rose up against the Mexican government in 1994 and drew inspiration from an earlier Mexican rebel, Emiliano Zapata.

Zheng *See* Shi Huangdi.

Zheng He Ming naval commander who, from 1405 to 1433, led seven massive naval expeditions to impress other peoples with Ming might and to establish tributary relations with Southeast Asia, Indian Ocean ports, the Persian Gulf, and the east coast of Africa.

Zhong Shang Administrative central complex of the Shang.

Zhongguo Term originating in the ancient period and subsequently used to emphasize the central cultural and geographic location of China in the world; means "Middle Kingdom."

ziggurat Stepped platform that served as the base of a Sumerian temple, which had evolved from the earlier elevated platform base by the end of the third millennium BCE.

Zionism Political movement advocating the reestablishment of a Jewish homeland in Palestine.

Zoroaster Sometimes known as Zarathustra, thought to have been a teacher around 1000 BCE in eastern Iran and credited with having solidified the region's religious beliefs into a unified system that moved away from animistic nomadic beliefs. The main source for his teachings is a compilation called the Avesta.

Zoroastrianism Dualistic Persian religion, based on the teaching of Zoroaster, in which forces of light and truth battle with those of darkness and falsehood.

Zulus African tribe that, under Shaka, created a ruthless warrior state in southern Africa in the early 1800s.

Credits

Front Matter

Photos World Map: National Geographic; King of Mali: HIP/Art Resource, NY; p. viii: HIP/Art Resource, NY; p. ix: Snark/Art Resource; p. x: Fine Art Images/Heritage Images/Getty Images; p. xi (top): Reunion de Musees Nationaux/Art Resource; p. xi (bottom): Scala/Art Resource, NY; p. xii: Christophel Fine Art/UIG via Getty Images; p. xiii: Pictures from History/Bridgeman Images; p. xiv: Granger Collection; p. xv: SuperStock; p. xvi: The Illustrated London News Picture Library/The Bridgeman Images; p. xvii: © Hulton-Deutsch Collection/CORBIS/Corbis via Getty Images; p. xviii (top): AP Photo/Anat Givon; p. xviii (bottom): Jeff Swensen/Getty Images.

Chapter 10

Photos Pages 442–443: HIP/Art Resource, NY; p. 446: Granger Collection; p. 447: Nik Wheeler/Getty Images; p. 449: Alamy Stock Photo; p. 455: De Agostini Picture Library/Getty Images; p. 460: Granger Collection, NY; p. 461 (bottom): Hemis/Alamy Stock Photo; p. 466: British Library, London, UK/© British Library Board. All Rights Reserved/Bridgeman Images; p. 470: HIP/Art Resource, NY; p. 473 (top): Thomas Cockrem/Alamy Stock Photo; p. 475 (bottom): INTERFOTO/Alamy Stock Photo; p. 482: akg-images; p. 494: Giraudo/Art Resource, NY; p. 495 (bottom): Pictorial Press Ltd/Alamy Stock Photo; p. 495 (top): Art Resource, NY.

Text Primary Source 10.1: Rabban Bar Sāwmā, from *The Monks of Kublai Khan,*

Emperor of China: Medieval Travels from China through Central Asia to Persia and Beyond, translated by Sir E.A. Wallis Budge. Originally published by Harrison & Sons, Ltd. in 1928 for the Religious Tract Society. Reprinted by permission of Lutterworth Press. Primary Source 10.3: From *Ibn Battuta: Travels in Asia & Africa, 1325–1354* translated by H. A. R. Gibb, pp. 55–57. Copyright © 1929 George Routledge & Sons. Reprinted by permission of Taylor & Francis Books (UK). Primary Source 10.4: Al-'Umarī, from *Corpus of Early Arabic Sources for West African History*, translated by J.F.P. Hopkins, edited and annotated by N. Levtzion and J.F.P. Hopkins (Cambridge: Cambridge University Press, 1981). © University of Ghana, International Academic Union, Cambridge University Press 1991. Reprinted with the permission of Cambridge University Press.

Chapter 11

Photos Photos 496–497: Snark/Art Resource; p. 500: The Granger Collection, New York; p. 504: Emo Bardazzi/Electa/Mondadori Portfolio via Getty Images; p. 508: Album/Art Resource; p. 509: Muhammed Enes Yldrm/Anadolu Agency/Getty Images; p. 510: Stapleton Collection, UK/Bridgeman Art Library; p. 517: The Granger Collection; p. 519 (left): Scala/Art Resource; p. 519 (right): Scala/Art Resource; p. 522: Réunion des Musées Nationaux/Art Resource, NY; p. 523 (China): Detail from the painting 'Beauties in History', attributed to the Ming Dynasty artist Qiu Ying (c. 1492–1552)/Pictures from History/

Bridgeman Images; p. 524: The Granger Collection, New York; p. 525: © RMN-Grand Palais/Art Resource, NY; p. 528 (left): The Picture Art Collection/Alamy Stock Photo; p. 528 (right): A. HARLIN/National Geographic Creative; p. 542 (right): Opkapi Palace Museum, Istanbul, Turkey/Bridgeman Images; p. 542 (left): Bridgeman Images; p. 543: The Granger Collection, New York.

Text Primary Source 11.1: Michael Dols, "Ibn al-Wardi's Risalah al-Naba' 'an al-Waba', a Translation of a Major Source for the History of the Black Death in the Middle East" in *Near Eastern Numismatics, Iconography, Epigraphy and History: Studies in Honor of George C. Miles*, ed. Dickran K. Kouymjian (Beirut: American University of Beirut, 1974), 447–454. Reprinted by permission of the American University of Beirut Press. Primary Source 11.2: Marchione di Coppo Stefani, Cronaca Fiorentina, edited by Niccolo Rodolico, Vol. 30 of Rerum Italicarum Scriptores (Citta di Castello: S. Lapi, 1903–1913), as translated by Duane Osheim at http://www2.iath.virginia.edu/osheim/marchione.html. Reprinted by permission of Duane Osheim. Primary Source 11.3: Ibn Khaldûn, excerpts from *The Muqaddimah: An Introduction to History Vol. 1*, translated by Franz Rosenthal (New York: Pantheon Books, 1958). © 1958 by Bollingen Foundation, Inc. Reprinted by permission of Princeton University Press. Primary Source 11.4: al-Maqrizi, "The Guide to the Knowledge of Dynasties and Kings," translated by Hamid Irbouh and excerpted in *The Middle East* and *Islamic World Reader*, copyright © 2003, Revised edition copyright © 2012 by Marvin Gettleman and Stuart Schaar. Used by permission of Grove/Atlantic, Inc. Any third party use of this material, outside of this publication, is prohibited.

Chapter 12

Photos Pages 544–545: Fine Art Images/Heritage Images/Getty Images; p. 548: Reunion des Musees; Nationaux/Art Resource, NY; p. 549: akg-images/Cameraphoto; p. 554: Christophel Fine Art/UIG via Getty Images; p. 555: Bildarchiv Preussischer Kulturbesitz/Art Resource, NY; p. 558 (left): The Granger Collection, New York; p. 559: The Granger Collection, New York; p. 559 (right): HIP/Art Resource, NY; p. 565 (top): Francois Guenet/Art Resource; p. 567 (bottom): The Granger Collection; p. 578: Bridgeman Images; p. 588 (left): Scala/Art Resource, NY; p. 588 (right): The Granger Collection; p. 589: Reunion des Musees Nationaux/Art Resource.

Text Primary Source 12.1: Book Twelve of the Florentine Codex, translated by James Lockhart in *We People Here: Nahuatl accounts of the conquest of Mexico* (Berkeley: University of California Press, 1993), pp. 56–86. Reprinted by permission of the University of California Press. Primary Source 12.4: T'ien-Tsê Chang, from *Sino-Portuguese Trade From 1514 to 1644: A Synthesis of Portuguese and Chinese Sources* (Leyden: E.J. Brill, 1934), pp. 51–52. Reprinted by permission of Brill Academic Publishers.

Chapter 13

Photos Pages 590–591: Reunion de Musees Nationaux/Art Resource; p. 595 right: British Museum, London/E.T. Archives, London/SuperStock; p. 595 left: Chester Beatty Library and Gallery of Oriental Art, Dublin/Bridgeman Images; p. 598: Rijksmuseum, Amsterdam, The Netherlands/Bridgeman Images; p. 602: MPI/Getty Images; p. 605: MPI/Getty Images; p. 608 (left): North Wind Picture Archives; p. 608 (right): Private Collection/Bridgeman

Images; p. 609: Sarin Images / GRANGER , All rights reserved; p. 613: DEA/G. DAGLI ORTI/Getty Images; p. 622: Gianni Dagli Orti/Shutterstock; p. 627: Musee Bargoin, Clermont-Ferrand, France/Bridgeman Images; p. 630: Chateau de Versailles, France/Bridgeman Images; p. 642 (left): Image copyright © The Metropolitan Museum of Art. Image source: Art Resource, NY; p. 642 (right): Bridgeman Images; p. 643 (top): Museum of Fine Arts, Boston, Massachusetts, USA/William Sturgis Bigelow Collection/Bridgeman Images; p. 643 (bottom): Image Copyright © Metropolitan Museum of Art Image source: Art Resource, NY.

Text Primary Source 13.1: Olaudah Equiano, from *Interesting Narrative of the Life of Olaudiah Equiano, or Gustavus Vassa, The African, Written by Himself: A Norton Critical Edition*, edited by Werner Sollors. Copyright © 2001 by W. W. Norton & Company, Inc. Used by permission of W. W. Norton & Company, Inc. Primary Source 13.4: Katherine Holt, "Population by Racial Classification, Santiago de Iguape 1835," "Free and Freed Population by Racial Classification, Iguape 1835," and "Enslaved Population by Place of Birth, Santiago do Iguape, 1835." From The Bahian History Project, www.mappingbahia.org. Reproduced with permission from Katherine Holt.

Chapter 14

Photos Pages 644–645: Scala/Art Resource, NY; p. 649 (left): ART Collection/Alamy Stock Photo; p. 649 (right): Victoria & Albert Museum, London/Art Resource, NY; p. 651: Dea Picture Library/Getty Images; p. 655 (left): George Rinhart/Corbis via Getty Images; p. 655 (right): Underwood & Underwood/Library of Congress/Corbis/VCG via Getty Images; p. 656: Werner Forman/Art Resource, NY; p. 658: British Library, London, UK © British Library Board. All Rights Reserved/Bridgeman Images; p. 661: Image copyright © The Metropolitan Museum of Art/Art Resource, NY;

p. 667 (top): Private Collection/Bridgeman Images; p. 667 (bottom): Private Collection/Bridgeman Images; p. 670 Alamy Stock Photo; p. 673 (left): Album/Art Resource, NY; p. 673 (right): Museo de America, Madrid/The Bridgeman Images; p. 677 (left): HIP/Art Resource NY; p. 677 (right): The Granger Collection, New York; p. 690 (bottom left): Art Collection 3/Alamy Stock Photo; p. 690 (top right): Fine Art Images/Heritage Images/Getty Images; p. 690 (top left) Library of Congress, Geography and Map Division; p. 690 (bottom right) Private Collection/Photo © Christie's Images/Bridgeman Images; p. 691 (bottom right): Library of Congress, Geography and Map Division; p. 691 (bottom left): Art Collection 4/Alamy Stock Photo; p. 691 (top): Private Collection/Bridgeman Images.

Text Primary Source 14.1: Excerpts from *Montesquieu: The Spirit of the Laws*. Cambridge Texts in the History of Political Thought, translated and edited by Anne M. Cohler, Basia Carolyn Miller and Harold Samuel Stone (Cambridge: Cambridge University Press, 1989), pp. 338–339. Reprinted by permission of Cambridge University Press. Primary Source 14.3: Jean-Jacques Rousseau, from *Rousseau's Political Writings: A Norton Critical Edition*, edited by Alan Ritter and Julia Conaway Bondanella, translated by Julia Conaway Bondanella. Copyright © 1988 by W.W. Norton & Company, Inc. Used by permission of W.W. Norton & Company, Inc. Primary Source 14.4: "The Testament of Shimai Soshitsu," from *Sources of Japanese Tradition, 2nd. Ed. Vol. 2: 1600 to 2000*, compiled by Wm. Theodore de Bary, Carol Gluck, and Arthur E. Tiedemann, pp. 310–313. Copyright © 2005 Columbia University Press. Reprinted with permission of the publisher. Primary Source 14.5: Excerpts from "Two Edicts from the Ch'ien-Lung Emperor to King George III of England," in J. Mason Gentzler (ed.), *Changing China: readings in the history of China from the Opium War to the present*. Copyright © 1977 Praeger Publishers. Reprinted by permission of Cengage Learning.

Index

Italic page references indicate maps, illustrations, or chronology entries.

aristocracy. *see* elites

Aristotle, 452

Armenia, Armenians, 479, 889

arms race, 943–46, 960, 987

army. *see* military

artists, artisans

between 1600–1750, 594, 642–43

between 1750–1850, 714, *715,* 724

between 1890–1914, 853–58, 855, *880,* 880–81, *881*

and Africa, 660, *661*

and alternative visions of nineteenth century, 756, 759, 769

and coffeehouses, 594

and commerce and colonization between 1450–1600, 547

and culture, 645, 646–47, 649–50, 650–51, 651–52, 653, 658–59, *659,* 853–58, 855, 856

in East Asia, 653

and economic reordering, 714, *715*

and Enlightenment, 736–37

and insurgencies against colonizing and centralizing states, 769

and Islam, 647–48

material objects created by, *642,* 642–43, *643*

of Renaissance, 517–19

see also arts; paintings; *specific nations and empires*

arts, 653, 837, 853–58, 856, 866, 885–86

modernism in, *880,* 880–81, *881*

realism in, *736,* 736–37, *737,* 880–81

see also architecture; artists, artisans; culture; paintings

Asante state, *470,* 564–65, 610, *635,* 660–62, *680*

Asia

between 1600–1750, 594, 610–23, 631

between 1750–1850, 694, 715–17, 727

between 1850–1914, 774, 802, 803, 810, 812, 835, 841, 851, 854, 866

between 1910–1939, 883, 912–13

and alternative visions of nineteenth century, 774, 779–81

and anti-colonialism, 774, 777–79, 912–13, 934

and climate change, 612

and colonization between 1450–1600, 547–48, 550–51, 555, 562, 573–79

commerce and trade with, 547–48, 550–51, 562, 573–79

consolidation of empires in, 588

culture in, 669, 854

and economy, 1053

economy of, 715–17

European relations with, 576–78

and expansion and nation-building, 787

and globalization, 994–95, 998, 1006–7, 1009–10

health care in, 1007

and imperialism, 803, 810, 812, 841

and mercantilism, 631

and Mughal Empire, 588, 615

and pan movements, 866

and politics, 912–13

population changes in 14th century, 501, 504

population of, 1005

Portuguese in, 551, 576

and Russia, 624

in seventeenth and eighteenth centuries, 610–23

and spread of capitalism through migration, 912

and three-world order, 934, 954–55, 960–61

and transformation of Europe, 624

and worldwide insecurities, 851

see also specific countries and regions

Asma'u, Nana, 746, 774, 776–77

assembly lines, 899, 930, *931*

Atahualpa, 561

Ataturk, Mustafa Kemal, 918–19, *922*

Atlantes, *475*

Atlantic world

between 1600–1750, 591–92, *604,* 605–8, *606–7,* 609–10, 628, 631, 632–33

between 1750–1850, 636–37, 693–94, 695–98

and colonization between 1450–1600, 554–56, 579

and commerce and trade, 554–56, 579

and culture between 1600–1780, 646–47, 655

and economy, 628, 714

and mercantilism, 631

and new colonies in Americas, 605

revolutions of national independence in, *696–97*

and slave trade, 608, 637–41, 711

transformations in, 693–94, 695–98

atomic warfare, 940–41, *941,* 943–46, *946,* 955, 960

Aurangzeb (Mughal ruler), 573, *634*

Auschwitz-Birkenau concentration camp, 938

Australia, 675, *677,* 677–78, 850, 889, 1009

Austria

between 1750–1850, 702, 704

between 1850–1914, 799, 860, 866, 868

and alternative visions of nineteenth century, 754, 758

anti-immigrant sentiments, 1050

Mahmud II (Ottoman ruler), 720
Mahmud of Ghazna, 454
maize, 473, 562, 610
Maji-Maji Revolt, 835, 843, 846–47, *871*
Majorica, Spain, 494
Malabar Coast, 454
Malacca. *see* Melaka
Malay Archipelago, 445, 446
Malay Peninsula, 460, 548, 675, 840, 940
Malcolm X, 964–65
males. *see* gender
Mali, 582, 1062
Mali, Empire of, 468–70, *470, 484*
Maluku Islands, 611
Mamluks, 482, 550, 613–14
Manaus, Brazil, 795, *795*
Manchu, 617, 619
    and invasions, 599
    and Japan, 940
    and Little Ice Age, 599
    and trade, 687–88
Manchukuo, 908, 940
Manchuria, 817, 840, 908, *909, 923,* 940, *947*
Manchus, 617–20, *618,* 749–52, 840, 861, 864
    see also Qing dynasty
"mandate of heaven"
    of Ming, 505
Mande, 468–69, *469*
Mandela, Nelson, 953, 992, *992,* 1017, 1020, *1023*
Manet, Édouard, 736
Manifest Destiny, 790, 810
Manila, Philippines, 576, 611
manorialism, 463, 465
Mansa Musa, king of Mali, 469–70, *470, 484,* 494
manufacturing, 714–15, 904, 908, 958, 994, 995
Mao Zedong, 946–47, 954, 961–62, 972–75, 1019, *1019*
mapmaking, 445, *494,* 494–95, *495,* 654–57, *690,* 690–91, *691*
Mappa Mundi, 494, *495*
Marathas, 1003

Marey, Étienne-Jules, 930, *930*
Marie Antoinette, queen of France, 664, 703
Markos, 443
Marley, Bob, 1001, 1002, *1004*
Marne, Battles of the, 892
marriage
    between 1600–1750, 601, 619
    between 1910–1939, 907
    in Americas, 601, 672–73, *673*
    among Aztecs, 558
    in China, 619, 947
    and culture, 672–73, *673*
    and German Nazism, 907
    and globalization, 1006
    interracial, 672–73, *673*
    and mass politics, 907
    in Mughal Empire, 573
    see also gender
Marshall, George C., 943
Marshall Plan, 943
Martí, José, 787
Marx, Karl, 684–85, 758–59, 771, *773, 774,* 781–83, *864,* 930, 972
Marxism, 758–59, 817
Mary of Orange, queen of England, 631
Massachusetts, 699
mass production, *930,* 930–31, *931*
Maulavi Ahmadullah Shah, 770
Mauritius, 802
Mayans, 764–67, *766,* 771, 852
McCarthy, Joseph, 955
McNeil, J. R., 1042
Meat Inspection Act (U.S., 1906), 853
Mecca, 469, 691
media, 854–55, 883, 897–98, 1000–1001
    see also radio
Medici family, 518
medicine, 619–20, 623
    see also health care
Mediterranean region
    and commerce and colonization between 1450–1600, 548, 551, 567, 579

    and expansion of Ottoman Empire, 548, 550–51
    and overland commerce, 548
    and revival of trade, 548, 551
    see also Greece, Greeks; Roman Empire
Mehmed II "the Conqueror," Ottoman emperor, 508–9, 510, 649, *649,* 649–50, 656
Mehmed the Conqueror, 545
Meiji Restoration, 814–17, *816,* 820, *822–23*
Melaka (Malacca), 446, 611
men. *see* gender
Menelik II (Ethiopian ruler), 808–9
mercantilism, 593–94, 628, 631–32, 664–65, 665–66
Mercator projection, 691, *691*
merchants
    between 1600–1750, 593–94, 594–95, 603, 605, 609–10, 615–16, 616–17, 620, 628, 631
    between 1750–1850, 636, 698, 707, 711–12, 714, 718, 720, 721, 722–23, 725–27
    between 1850–1914, 794, 796, 862–64
    and African trade, 568, 603, 605, 609–10, 711–12
    and alternative visions of nineteenth century, 756
    and American Revolution, 698
    in Americas, 593–94
    and Asia in seventeenth and eighteenth centuries, 610–11, 612
    in China, 547, 575, 616–17, 620, 725–27, 862–64
    and coffeehouses, 594, 796
    and commerce and colonization between 1450–1600, 547, 548, 551, 563, 575, 579
    and dynastic monarchies, 631
    and economy, 593–94, 594–95, 628, 714, 718
    in Egypt, 720